Great
Animal Stories

Great
Animal Stories

If Only They Could Talk
JAMES HERRIOT

Ring of Bright Water
GAVIN MAXWELL

A Cat in the Window
DERÉK TANGYE

Elephant Bill
J.H. WILLIAMS

Encounters with Animals
GERALD DURRELL

Sundial

Encounters with Animals
first published in Great Britain in 1958 by Rupert Hart-Davis Ltd

Ring of Bright Water
first published in Great Britain in 1960 by Longmans, Green

A Cat in the Window
first published in Great Britain in 1962 by Michael Joseph Ltd

Elephant Bill
first published in Great Britain in 1950 by Rupert Hart-Davis Ltd

If Only They Could Talk
first published in Great Britain 1970 by Michael Joseph Ltd

This edition first published in Great Britain in 1979 by:

Octopus Books Limited
59 Grosvenor Street
London W. 1.
in collaboration with:
William Heinemann Limited
10 Upper Grosvenor Street
London W. 1.
and
Martin Secker & Warburg Limited
54 Poland Street
London W.1.

ISBN 0 904230 96 1

Third Impression *1981*

Printed in the United States of America

Contents

If Only
They Could Talk

James Herriot

CHAPTER 1

They didn't say anything about this in the books, I thought, as the snow blew in through the gaping doorway and settled on my naked back.

I lay face down on the cobbled floor in a pool of nameless muck, my arm deep inside the straining cow, my feet scrabbling for a toe-hold between the stones. I was stripped to the waist and the snow mingled with the dirt and the dried blood on my body. I could see nothing outside the circle of flickering light thrown by the smoky oil lamp which the farmer held over me.

No, there wasn't a word in the books about searching for your ropes and instruments in the shadows; about trying to keep clean in a half bucket of tepid water; about the cobbles digging into your chest. Nor about the slow numbing of the arms, the creeping paralysis of the muscles as the fingers tried to work against the cow's powerful expulsive efforts.

There was no mention anywhere of the gradual exhaustion, the feeling of futility and the little far-off voice of panic.

My mind went back to that picture in the obstetrics book. A cow standing in the middle of a gleaming floor while a sleek veterinary surgeon in a spotless parturition overall inserted his arm to a polite distance. He was relaxed and smiling, the farmer and his helpers were smiling, even the cow was smiling. There was no dirt or blood or sweat anywhere.

That man in the picture had just finished an excellent lunch and had moved next door to do a bit of calving just for the sheer pleasure of it, as a kind of dessert. He hadn't crawled shivering from his bed at two o'clock in the morning and bumped over twelve miles of frozen snow, staring sleepily ahead till the lonely farm showed in the headlights. He hadn't climbed half a mile of white fellside to the doorless barn where his patient lay.

I tried to wriggle my way an extra inch inside the cow. The calf's head was back and I was painfully pushing a thin, looped rope towards its lower jaw with my finger tips. All the time my arm was being squeezed between the calf and the bony pelvis. With every straining effort from the cow the pressure became almost unbearable, then she would relax and I would push the rope another inch. I wondered how long I would be able to keep this up. If I didn't snare that jaw soon I would never get the calf away. I groaned, set my teeth and reached forward again.

Another little flurry of snow blew in and I could almost hear the flakes sizzling on my sweating back. There was sweat on my forehead too, and it trickled into my eyes as I pushed.

There is always a time at a bad calving when you begin to wonder if you will ever win the battle. I had reached this stage.

Little speeches began to flit through my brain. 'Perhaps it would be better to slaughter this cow. Her pelvis is so small and narrow that I can't see a calf coming through,' or 'She's a good fat animal and really of the beef type, so don't you think it would pay you better to get the butcher?' or perhaps 'This is a very bad presentation. In a roomy cow it would be simple enough to bring the head round but in this case it is just about impossible.'

Of course, I could have delivered the calf by embryotomy – by passing a wire over the neck and sawing off the head. So many of these occasions ended with the floor strewn with heads, legs, heaps of intestines. There were thick textbooks devoted to the countless ways you could cut up a calf.

But none of it was any good here, because this calf was alive. At my furthest stretch I had got my finger as far as the commissure of the mouth and had been startled by a twitch of the little creature's tongue. It was unexpected because calves in this position are usually dead, asphyxiated by the acute flexion of the neck and the pressure of the dam's powerful contractions. But this one had a spark of life in it and if it came out it would have to be in one piece.

I went over to my bucket of water, cold now and bloody, and silently soaped my arms. Then I lay down again, feeling the cobbles harder than ever against my chest. I worked my toes between the stones, shook the sweat from my eyes and for the hundredth time thrust an arm that felt like spaghetti into the cow; alongside the little dry legs of the calf, like sandpaper tearing against my flesh, then to the bend in the neck and so to the ear and then, agonizingly, along the side of the face towards the lower jaw which had become my major goal in life.

It was incredible that I had been doing this for nearly two hours; fighting as my strength ebbed to push a little noose round that jaw. I had tried everything else – repelling a leg, gentle traction with a blunt hook in the eye socket, but I was back to the noose.

It had been a miserable session all through. The farmer, Mr Dinsdale, was a long, sad, silent man of few words who always seemed to be expecting the worst to happen. He had a long, sad, silent son with him and the two of them had watched my efforts with deepening gloom.

But worst of all had been Uncle. When I had first entered the hillside barn I had been surprised to see a little bright-eyed old man in a pork-pie hat settling down comfortably on a bale of straw. He was filling his pipe and clearly looking forward to the entertainment.

'Now then, young man,' he cried in the nasal twang of the West Riding. 'I'm Mr Dinsdale's brother. I farm over in Listondale.'

I put down my equipment and nodded. 'How do you do? My name is Herriot.'

The old man looked me over, piercingly. 'My vet is Mr Broomfield. Expect you'll have heard of him – everybody knows him, I reckon. Wonderful man, Mr Broomfield, especially at calving. Do you know, I've never seen 'im beat yet.'

I managed a wan smile. Any other time I would have been delighted to hear how good my colleague was, but somehow not now, not now. In fact, the words set a mournful little bell tolling inside me.

'No, I'm afraid I don't know Mr Broomfield,' I said, taking off my jacket and, more reluctantly, peeling my shirt over my head. 'But I haven't been around these parts very long.'

Uncle was aghast. 'You don't know him! Well you're the only one as doesn't. They think the world of him in Listondale, I can tell you.' He lapsed into a shocked silence and applied a match to his pipe. Then he shot a glance at my goose-pimpled torso. 'Strips like a boxer does Mr Broomfield. Never seen such muscles on a man.'

A wave of weakness coursed sluggishly over me. I felt suddenly leaden-footed and inadequate. As I began to lay out my ropes and instruments on a clean towel the old man spoke again.

'And how long have you been qualified, may I ask?'

'Oh, about seven months.'

'Seven months!' Uncle smiled indulgently, tamped down his tobacco and blew out a cloud of rank, blue smoke. 'Well, there's nowt like a bit of experience. I always says. Mr Broomfield's been doing my work now for over ten years and he really knows what he's about. No, you can 'ave your book learning. Give me experience every time.'

I tipped some antiseptic into the bucket and lathered my arms carefully. I knelt behind the cow.

'Mr Broomfield always puts some special lubricating oils on his arms first,' Uncle said, pulling contentedly on his pipe. 'He says you get infection of the womb if you just use soap and water.'

I made my first exploration. It was the burdened moment all vets go through when they first put their hand into a cow. Within seconds I would know whether I would be putting on my jacket in fifteen minutes or whether I had hours of hard labour ahead of me.

I was going to be unlucky this time; it was a nasty presentation. Head back and no room at all; more like being inside an undeveloped heifer than a second calver. And she was bone dry – the 'waters' must have come away from her hours ago. She had been running out on the high fields and had started to calve a week before her time; that was why they had had to bring her into this half-ruined barn. Anyway, it would be a long time before I saw my bed again.

'Well now, what have you found, young man?' Uncle's penetrating voice cut through the silence. 'Head back, eh? You won't have much trouble, then. I've seen Mr Broomfield do 'em like that – he turns calf right round and brings it out back legs first.'

I had heard this sort of nonsense before. A short time in practice had taught me that all farmers were experts with other farmers' livestock. When their own animals were in trouble they tended to rush to the phone for the vet, but with their neighbours' they were confident, knowledgeable and full of helpful advice. And another phenomenon I had observed was that their advice was usually regarded as more valuable than the vet's. Like now, for instance; Uncle was obviously an accepted sage and the Dinsdales listened with deference to everything he said.

'Another way with a job like this,' continued Uncle, 'is to get a few strong chaps with ropes and pull the thing out, head back and all.'

I gasped as I felt my way around. 'I'm afraid it's impossible to turn a calf completely round in this small space. And to pull it out without bringing the head round would certainly break the mother's pelvis.'

The Dinsdales narrowed their eyes. Clearly they thought I was hedging in the face of Uncle's superior knowledge.

And now, two hours later, defeat was just round the corner. I was just about whacked. I had rolled and grovelled on the filthy cobbles while the Dinsdales watched me in morose silence and Uncle kept up a non-stop stream of comment. Uncle, his ruddy face glowing with delight, his little eyes sparkling, hadn't had such a happy night for years. His long trek up the hillside had been repaid a hundredfold. His vitality was undiminished; he had enjoyed every minute.

As I lay there, eyes closed, face stiff with dirt, mouth hanging open, Uncle took his pipe in his hand and leaned forward on his straw bale. 'You're about beat, young man,' he said with deep satisfaction. 'Well, I've never seen Mr Broomfield beat but he's had a lot of experience. And what's more, he's strong, really strong. That's one man you couldn't tire.'

Rage flooded through me like a draught of strong spirit. The right thing to do, of course, would be to get up, tip the bucket of bloody water over Uncle's head, run down the hill and drive away; away from Yorkshire, from Uncle, from the Dinsdales, from this cow.

Instead, I clenched my teeth, braced my legs and pushed with everything I had; and with a sensation of disbelief I felt my noose slide over the sharp little incisor teeth and into the calf's mouth. Gingerly, muttering a prayer, I pulled on the thin rope with my left hand and felt the slipknot tighten. I had hold of that lower jaw.

At last I could start doing something. 'Now hold this rope, Mr Dinsdale, and just keep a gentle tension on it. I'm going to repel the calf and if you pull steadily at the same time, the head ought to come round.'

'What if the rope comes off?' asked Uncle hopefully.

I didn't answer. I put my hand in against the calf's shoulder and began to push against the cow's contractions. I felt the small body moving away from me. 'Now a steady pull, Mr Dinsdale, without jerking.' And to myself, 'Oh God, don't let it slip off.'

The head was coming round. I could feel the neck straightening against my arm, then the ear touched my elbow. I let go the shoulder and grabbed the little muzzle. Keeping the teeth away from the vaginal wall with my hand, I guided the head till it was resting where it should be, on the fore limbs.

Quickly I extended the noose till it reached behind the ears. 'Now pull on the head as she strains.'

'Nay, you should pull on the legs now,' cried Uncle.

'Pull on the bloody head rope, I tell you!' I bellowed at the top of my voice and felt immediately better as Uncle retired, offended, to his bale.

With traction the head was brought out and the rest of the body followed easily. The little animal lay motionless on the cobbles, eyes glassy and unseeing, tongue blue and grossly swollen.

'It'll be dead. Bound to be,' grunted Uncle, returning to the attack.

I cleared the mucus from the mouth, blew hard down the throat and began artificial respiration. After a few pressures on the ribs, the calf gave a gasp and the eyelids flickered. Then it started to inhale and one leg jerked.

Uncle took off his hat and scratched his head in disbelief. 'By gaw, it's alive. I'd have thowt it'd sure to be dead after you'd messed about all that time.' A lot of the fire had gone out of him and his pipe hung down empty from his lips.

'I know what this little fellow wants,' I said. I grasped the calf by its fore legs and pulled it up to its mother's head. The cow was stretched out on her side, her head extended wearily along the rough floor. Her ribs heaved, her eyes were almost closed; she looked past caring about anything. Then she felt the calf's body against her face and there was a transformation; her eyes opened wide and her muzzle began a snuffling exploration of the new object. Her interest grew with every sniff and she struggled onto her chest, nosing and probing all over the calf, rumbling deep in her chest. Then she began to lick him methodically. Nature provides the perfect stimulant massage for a time like this and the little creature arched his back as the coarse papillae on the tongue dragged along his skin. Within a minute he was shaking his head and trying to sit up.

I grinned. This was the bit I liked. The little miracle. I felt it was something that would never grow stale no matter how often I saw it. I cleaned as much of the dried blood and filth from my body as I could, but most of it had caked on my skin and not even my finger nails would move it. It would have to wait for the hot bath at home. Pulling my shirt over my head, I felt as though I had been beaten for a long time with a thick stick. Every muscle ached. My mouth was dried out, my lips almost sticking together.

A long, sad figure hovered near. 'How about a drink?' asked Mr Dinsdale.

I could feel my grimy face cracking into an incredulous smile. A vision of hot tea well laced with whisky swam before me. 'That's very kind of you, Mr Dinsdale, I'd love a drink. It's been a hard two hours.'

'Nay,' said Mr Dinsdale looking at me steadily, 'I meant for the cow.'

I began to babble. 'Oh yes, of course, certainly, by all means give her a drink. She must be very thirsty. It'll do her good. Certainly, certainly, give her a drink.'

I gathered up my tackle and stumbled out of the barn. On the moor it was still dark and a bitter wind whipped over the snow, stinging my eyes. As I plodded down the slope, Uncle's voice, strident and undefeated, reached me for the last time.

'Mr Broomfield doesn't believe in giving a drink after calving. Says it chills the stomach.'

CHAPTER 2

It was hot in the rickety little bus and I was on the wrong side where the July sun beat on the windows. I shifted uncomfortably inside my best suit and eased a finger inside the constricting white collar. It was a foolish outfit for this weather but a few miles ahead, my prospective employer was waiting for me and I had to make a good impression.

There was a lot hanging on this interview; being a newly qualified veterinary surgeon in this year of 1937 was like taking out a ticket for the dole queue. Agriculture was depressed by a decade of government neglect, the draught horse which had been the mainstay of the profession was fast disappearing. It was easy to be a prophet of doom when the young men emerging from the colleges after a hard five years' slog were faced by a world indifferent to their enthusiasm and bursting knowledge. There were usually two or three situations vacant in the *Record* each week and an average of eighty applicants for each one.

It hadn't seemed true when the letter came from Darrowby in the Yorkshire Dales. Mr Siegfried Farnon MRCVS would like to see me on the Friday afternoon; I was to come to tea and if we were mutually suited I could stay on as assistant. I had grabbed at the lifeline unbelievingly; so many friends who had qualified with me were unemployed or working in shops or as labourers in the shipyards that I had given up hope of any other future for myself.

The driver crashed his gears again as he went into another steep bend. We had been climbing steadily now for the last fifteen miles or so, moving closer to the distant blue swell of the Pennines. I had never been in Yorkshire before but the name had always raised a picture of a county as stodgy and unromantic as its pudding; I was prepared for solid worth, dullness and a total lack of charm. But as the bus groaned its way higher I began to wonder. The formless heights were resolving into high, grassy hills and wide valleys. In the valley bottoms, rivers twisted among the trees and solid grey-stone farmhouses lay among islands of cultivated land which pushed bright green promontories up the hillsides into the dark tide of heather which lapped from the summits.

I had seen the fences and hedges give way to dry stone walls which bordered the roads, enclosed the fields and climbed endlessly over the surrounding fells. The walls were everywhere, countless miles of them, tracing their patterns high on the green uplands.

But as I neared my destination the horror stories kept forcing their way into my mind; the tales brought back to college by veterans hardened and embittered by a few months of practice. Assistants were just little bits of dirt to be starved and worked into the ground by the principals who were heartless and vicious to a man. Dave Stevens, lighting a cigarette with trembling hand: 'Never a night off or a half day. He made me wash the car, dig the garden, mow the lawn, do the family shopping. But when he told me to sweep the chimney I left.' Or Willie Johnstone: 'First job I had to do was pass the stomach tube on a horse. Got it into the trachea instead of the oesophagus. Couple of quick pumps and down went the horse with a hell of a crash – dead as a hammer. That's when I started these grey hairs.' Or that dreadful one they passed around about Fred Pringle. Fred had trocharized a bloated cow and the farmer had been so impressed by the pent-up gas hissing from the abdomen that Fred had got carried away and applied his cigarette lighter to the canula. A roaring sheet of flame had swept onto some straw bales and burned the byre to the ground. Fred had taken up a colonial appointment immediately afterwards – Leeward Islands wasn't it?

Oh hell, that one couldn't be true. I cursed my fevered imagination and tried to shut out the crackling of the inferno, the terrified bellowing of the cattle as they were led to safety. No, it couldn't be as bad as that; I rubbed my sweating palms on my knees and tried to concentrate on the man I was going to meet.

Siegfried Farnon. Strange name for a vet in the Yorkshire Dales. Probably a German who had done his training in this country and decided to set up in practice. And it wouldn't have been Farnon in the beginning; probably Farrenen. Yes, Siegfried Farrenen. He was beginning to take shape; short, fat, roly poly type with merry eyes and a bubbling laugh. But at the same time I had trouble with the obtruding image of a hulking, cold-eyed, bristle-skulled Teuton more in keeping with the popular idea of the practice boss.

I realized the bus was clattering along a narrow street which opened onto a square where we stopped. Above the window of an unpretentious grocershop I read 'Darrowby Co-operative Society'. We had arrived.

I got out and stood beside my battered suitcase, looking about me. There was something unusual and I couldn't put my finger on it at first. Then I realized what it was – the silence. The other passengers had dispersed, the driver had switched off his engine and there was not a sound or a movement anywhere. The only visible sign of life was a group of old men sitting round the clock tower in the centre of the square but they might have been carved from stone.

Darrowby didn't get much space in the guide-books but when it was mentioned it was described as a grey little town on the river Darrow with a cobbled market place and little of interest except its two ancient bridges. But when you looked at it, its setting was beautiful on the pebbly river where the houses clustered thickly and straggled unevenly along the lower slopes of Herne Fell. Everywhere in Darrowby, in the streets, through the windows of the houses you could see the Fell rearing its calm, green bulk more than two thousand feet above the huddled roofs.

There was a clarity in the air, a sense of space and airiness that made me feel I had shed something on the plain, twenty miles behind. The confinement of the city, the grime, the smoke – already they seemed to be falling away from me.

Trengate was a quiet street leading off the square and I had my first sight of Skeldale House. I knew it was the right place before I was near enough to read 'S. Farnon MRCVS' on the old-fashioned brass plate hanging slightly askew on the iron railings. I knew by the ivy which climbed untidily over the mellow brick to the topmost windows. It was what the letter had said – the only house with ivy; and this could be where I would work for the first time as a veterinary surgeon.

Now that I was here, right on the doorstep, I felt breathless, as though I had been running. If I got the job, this was where I would find out about myself. There were many things to prove.

But I liked the look of the old house. It was Georgian with a fine, white-painted doorway. The windows, too, were white – wide and graceful on the ground floor and first storey but small and square where they peeped out from under the overhanging tiles far above. The paint was flaking and the mortar looked crumbly between the bricks, but there was a changeless elegance about the place. There was no front garden and only the railings separated the house from the street a few feet away.

I rang the doorbell and instantly the afternoon peace was shattered by a distant baying like a wolf pack in full cry. The upper half of the door was of glass and, as I peered through, a river of dogs poured round the corner of a long passage and dashed itself with frenzied yells against the door. If I hadn't been used to animals I would have turned and run for my life. As it was I stepped back warily and watched the dogs as they appeared, sometimes two at a time, at the top of their leap, eyes glaring, jaws slavering. After a minute or two of this I was able to sort them out and I realized that my first rough count of about fourteen was exaggerated. There were, in fact, five; a huge fawn greyhound who appeared most often as he hadn't so far to jump as the others, a cocker spaniel, a Scottie, a whippet and a tiny, short-legged hunt terrier. This terrier was seldom seen since the glass was rather high for him, but when he did make it he managed to get an even more frantic note into his bark before he disappeared.

I was thinking of ringing the bell again when I saw a large woman in the passage. She rapped out a single word and the noise stopped as if by magic. When she opened the door the ravening pack was slinking round her feet ingratiatingly, showing the whites of their eyes and wagging their tucked-in tails. I had never seen such a servile crew.

'Good afternoon,' I said with my best smile. 'My name is Herriot.'

The woman looked bigger than ever with the door open. She was about sixty but her hair, tightly pulled back from her forehead, was jet black and hardly streaked with grey. She nodded and looked at me with grim benevolence, but she seemed to be waiting for further information. Evidently, the name struck no answering spark.

'Mr Farnon is expecting me. He wrote asking me to come today.'

'Mr Herriot?' she said thoughtfully. 'Surgery is from six to seven o'clock. If you wanted to bring a dog in, that would be your best time.'

'No, no,' I said, hanging onto my smile. 'I'm applying for the position of assistant. Mr Farnon said to come in time for tea.'

'Assistant? Well, now, that's nice.' The lines in her face softened a little. 'I'm Mrs Hall. I keep house for Mr Farnon. He's a bachelor, you know. He never said anything to me about you, but never mind, come in and have a cup of tea. He shouldn't be long before he's back.'

I followed her between whitewashed walls, my feet clattering on the tiles. We turned right at the end into another passage and I was beginning to wonder just how far back the house extended when I was shown into a sunlit room.

It had been built in the grand manner, high-ceilinged and airy with a massive fireplace flanked by arched alcoves. One end was taken up by a french window which gave on a long, high-walled garden. I could see unkempt lawns, a rockery and many fruit trees. A great bank of peonies blazed in the hot sunshine and at the far end, rooks cawed in the branches of a group of tall elms. Above and beyond were the green hills with their climbing walls.

Ordinary-looking furniture stood around on a very worn carpet. Hunting prints hung on the walls and books were scattered everywhere, some on shelves in the alcoves but others piled on the floor in the corners. A pewter pint pot occupied a prominent place at one end of the mantelpiece. It was an interesting pot. Cheques and bank-notes had been stuffed into it till they bulged out of the top and overflowed onto the hearth beneath. I was studying this with astonishment when Mrs Hall came in with a tea tray.

'I suppose Mr Farnon is out on a case.' I said.

'No, he's gone through to Brawton to visit his mother. I can't really say when he'll be back.' She left me with my tea.

The dogs arranged themselves peacefully around the room and, except for a brief dispute between the Scottie and the cocker spaniel about the occupancy of a deep chair, there was no sign of their previous violent behaviour. They lay regarding me with friendly boredom and, at the same time, fighting a losing battle against sleep. Soon the last nodding head had fallen back and a chorus of heavy breathing filled the room.

But I was unable to relax with them. A feeling of let-down gripped me; I had screwed myself up for an interview and I was left dangling. This was all very odd. Why should anyone write for an assistant, arrange a time to meet him and then go to visit his mother? Another thing – if I was engaged, I would be living in this house, yet the housekeeper had no instructions to prepare a room for me. In fact, she had never even heard of me.

My musings were interrupted by the door bell ringing and the dogs, as if touched by a live wire, leapt screaming into the air and launched themselves in a solid mass through the door. I wished they didn't take their duties so seriously. There was no sign of Mrs Hall so I went out to the front door where the dogs were putting everything into their fierce act.

'Shut up!' I shouted and the din switched itself off. The five dogs cringed abjectly round my ankles, almost walking on their knees. The big greyhound got the best effect by drawing his lips back from his teeth in an apologetic grin.

I opened the door and looked into a round, eager face. Its owner, a plump man in wellington boots leant confidently against the railings.

'Hello, 'ello, Mr Farnon in?'

'Not at the moment. Can I help you?'

'Aye, give 'im a message when he comes in. Tell 'im Bert Sharpe of Barrow Hills has a cow wot wants borin' out?'

'Boring out?'

'That's right, she's nobbut going on three cylinders.'

'Three cylinders?'

'Aye and if we don't do summat she'll go wrang in 'er ewer, won't she?'

'Very probably.'

'Don't want felon, do we?'

'Certainly not.'

'O.K., you'll tell 'im, then. Ta-ta.'

I returned thoughtfully to the sitting-room. It was disconcerting but I had listened to my first case history without understanding a word of it.

I had hardly sat down when the bell rang again. This time I unleashed a frightening yell which froze the dogs when they were still in mid-air; they took the point and returned, abashed, to their chairs.

This time it was a solemn gentleman with a straightly adjusted cloth cap resting on his ears, a muffler knotted precisely over his adam's apple and a clay pipe growing from the exact centre of his mouth. He removed the pipe and spoke with a rich, unexpected accent.

'Me name's Mulligan and I want Misther Farnon to make up some
midicine for me dog.'

'Oh, what's the trouble with your dog, Mr Mulligan?'

He raised a questioning eyebrow and put a hand to his ear. I tried
again with a full-blooded shout.

'What's the trouble?'

He looked at me doubtfully for a moment. 'He's womitin', sorr.
Womitin' bad.'

I immediately felt on secure ground now and my brain began to
seethe with diagnostic procedures. 'How long after eating does he
vomit?'

The hand went to the ear again. 'Phwhat's that?'

I leant close to the side of his head, inflated my lungs and bawled:
'When does he womit − I mean vomit?'

Comprehension spread slowly across Mr Mulligan's face. He gave a
gentle smile. 'Oh aye, he's womitin'. Womitin' bad, sorr.'

I didn't feel up to another effort so I told him I would see to it and
asked him to call later. He must have been able to lip-read me because
he seemed satisfied and walked away.

Back in the sitting-room, I sank into a chair and poured a cup of tea. I
had taken one sip when the bell rang again. This time, a wild glare from
me was enough to make the dogs cower back in their chairs; I was
relieved they had caught on so quickly.

Outside the front door a lovely, red-haired girl was standing. She
smiled, showing a lot of very white teeth.

'Good afternoon,' she said in a loud, well-bred voice. 'I am Diana
Brompton. Mr Farnon is expecting me for tea.'

I gulped and clung to the door handle. 'He's asked YOU to tea?'

The smile became fixed. 'Yes, that is correct,' she said, spelling the
words out carefully. 'He asked me to tea.'

'I'm afraid Mr Farnon isn't at home. I can't say when he'll be
back.'

The smile was plucked away. 'Oh,' she said, and she got a lot into the
word. 'At any rate, perhaps I could come in.'

'Oh, certainly, do come in. I'm sorry.' I babbled, suddenly conscious
that I had been staring open-mouthed at her.

I held open the door and she brushed past me without a word. She
knew her way about because, when I got to the first corner, she had
disappeared into the room. I tiptoed past the door and broke into a
gallop which took me along another thirty yards or so of twisting passage
to a huge, stone-flagged kitchen. Mrs Hall was pottering about there
and I rushed at her.

'There's a young lady here, a Miss Brompton. She's come to tea, too.'
I had to fight an impulse to pluck at her sleeve.

Mrs Hall's face was expressionless. I thought she might have started to
wave her arms about, but she didn't even seem surprised.

'You go through and talk to her and I'll bring a few more cakes,' she
said.

'But what the heck am I going to talk to her about? How long is Mr
Farnon going to be?'

'Oh, just chat to her for a bit. I shouldn't think he'll be very long,' she
said calmly.

Slowly, I made my way back to the sitting-room and when I opened
the door the girl turned quickly with the makings of another big smile.
She made no attempt to hide her disgust when she saw it was only me.

'Mrs Hall thinks he should be back fairly soon. Perhaps you would
join me in a cup of tea while you're waiting.'

She gave me a quick glance which raked me from my rumpled hair to
my scuffed old shoes. I realized suddenly how grimy and sweaty I was
after the long journey. Then she shrugged her shoulders and turned
away. The dogs regarded her apathetically. A heavy silence blanketed
the room.

I poured a cup of tea and held it out to her. She ignored me and lit a
cigarette. This was going to be tough, but I could only try.

I cleared my throat and spoke lightly. 'I've only just arrived myself. I
hope to be the new assistant.'

This time she didn't trouble to look round. She just said 'Oh' and
again the monosyllable carried a tremendous punch.

'Lovely part of the world, this,' I said, returning to the attack.

'Yes.'

'I've never been in Yorkshire before, but I like what I've seen.'

'Oh.'

'Have you known Mr Farnon very long?'

'Yes.'

'I believe he's quite young – about thirty?'

'Yes.'

'Wonderful weather.'

'Yes.'

I kept at it with courage and tenacity for about five minutes, hunting
for something original or witty, but finally, Miss Brompton, instead of
answering, took the cigarette from her mouth, turned towards me and
gave me a long, blank stare. I knew that was the end and shrank into
silence.

After that, she sat staring out of the french window, pulling deeply at her cigarette, narrowing her eyes as the smoke trickled from her lips. As far as she was concerned, I just wasn't there.

I was able to observe her at will and she was interesting. I had never met a living piece of a society magazine before. Cool, linen, dress, expensive-looking cardigan, elegant legs and the glorious red hair falling on her shoulders.

And yet here was a fascinating thought. She was sitting there positively hungering for a little fat German vet. This Farnon must have something.

The tableau was finally broken up when Miss Brompton jumped to her feet. She hurled her cigarette savagely into the fireplace and marched from the room.

Wearily, I got out of my chair. My head began to ache as I shuffled through the french window into the garden. I flopped down among the knee-deep grass on the lawn and rested my back against a towering acacia tree. Where the devil was Farnon? Was he really expecting me or had somebody played a horrible practical joke on me? I felt suddenly cold. I had spent my last few pounds getting here and if there was some mistake I was in trouble.

But, looking around me, I began to feel better. The sunshine beat back from the high old walls, bees droned among the bright masses of flowers. A gentle breeze stirred the withered blooms of a magnificent wistaria which almost covered the back of the house. There was peace here.

I leant my head against the bark and closed my eyes. I could see Herr Farrenen, looking just as I had imagined him, standing over me. He wore a shocked expression.

'Wass is dis you haff done?' he spluttered, his fat jowls quivering with rage. 'You kom to my house under false pretences, you insult Fräulein Brompton, you trink my tea, you eat my food. Vat else you do, hein? Maybe you steal my spoons. You talk about assistant but I vant no assistant. Is best I telephone the police.'

Herr Farrenen seized the phone in a pudgy hand. Even in my dream, I wondered how the man could use such a completely corny accent. I heard the thick voice saying 'Hello, hello.'

And I opened my eyes. Somebody was saying 'Hello', but it wasn't Herr Farrenen. A tall, thin man was leaning against the wall, his hands in his pockets. Something seemed to be amusing him. As I struggled to my feet, he heaved himself away from the wall and held out his hand. 'Sorry you've had to wait. I'm Siegfried Farnon.'

He was just about the most English looking man I had ever seen. Long, humorous, strong-jawed face. Small, clipped moustache, untidy, sandy hair. He was wearing an old tweed jacket and shapeless flannel trousers. The collar of his check shirt was frayed and the tie carelessly knotted. He looked as though he didn't spend much time in front of a mirror.

Studying him, I began to feel better despite the ache in my neck where it had rested against the tree. I shook my head to get my eyes fully open and tufts of grass fell from my hair. 'There was a Miss Brompton here,' I blurted out. 'She came to tea. I explained you had been called away.'

Farnon looked thoughtful, but not put out. He rubbed his chin slowly. 'Mm, yes – well, never mind. But I do apologize for being out when you arrived. I have a shocking memory and I just forgot.'

It was the most English voice, too.

Farnon gave me a long, searching look, then he grinned. 'Let's go inside. I want to show you round the place.'

CHAPTER 3

The long offshoot behind the house had been the servants' quarters in grander days. Here, everything was dark and narrow and poky as if in deliberate contrast with the front.

Farnon led me to the first of several doors which opened off a passage where the smell of ether and carbolic hung on the air. 'This,' he said, with a secret gleam in his eye as though he were about to unveil the mysteries of Aladdin's cave, 'is the dispensary.'

The dispensary was an important place in the days before penicillin and the sulphonamides. Rows of gleaming Winchester bottles lined the white walls from floor to ceiling. I savoured the familiar names: Sweet Spirits of Nitre, Tincture of Camphor, Chlorodyne, Formalin, Salammoniac, Hexamine, Sugar of Lead, Linimentum Album, Perchloride of Mercury, Red Blister. The lines of labels were comforting.

I was an initiate among old friends. I had painfully accumulated their lore, ferreting out their secrets over the years. I knew their origins, actions and uses, and their maddeningly varied dosage. The examiner's voice—— 'And what is the dose for the horse? – and the cow? – and the sheep? – and the pig? – and the dog? – and the cat?'

These shelves held the vets' entire armoury against disease and, on a bench under the window, I could see the instruments for compounding them; the graduated vessels and beakers, the mortars and pestles. And underneath, in an open cupboard, the medicine bottles, piles of corks of all sizes, pill boxes, powder papers.

As we moved around, Farnon's manner became more and more animated. His eyes glittered and he talked rapidly. Often, he reached up and caressed a Winchester on its shelf; or he would lift out a horse ball or an electuary from its box, give it a friendly pat and replace it with tenderness.

'Look at this stuff, Herriot,' he shouted without warning. 'Adrevan! This is the remedy, *par excellence*, for red worms in horses. A bit expensive, mind you – ten bob a packet. And these gentian violet pessaries. If you shove one of these into a cow's uterus after a dirty cleansing, it turns the discharges a very pretty colour. Really looks as though it's doing something. And have you seen this trick?'

He placed a few crystals of resublimated iodine on a glass dish and added a drop of turpentine. Nothing happened for a second then a dense cloud of purple smoke rolled heavily to the ceiling. He gave a great bellow of laughter at my startled face.

'Like witchcraft, isn't it? I use it for wounds in horses' feet. The chemical reaction drives the iodine deep into the tissues.'

'It does?'

'Well, I don't know, but that's the theory, and anyway, you must admit it looks wonderful. Impresses the toughest client.'

Some of the bottles on the shelves fell short of the ethical standards I had learned in college. Like the one labelled 'Colic Drench' and featuring a floridly drawn picture of a horse rolling in agony. The animal's face was turned outwards and wore an expression of very human anguish. Another bore the legend 'Universal Cattle Medicine' in ornate script – 'A Sovereign Remedy for coughs, chills, scours, pneumonia, milk fever, gargett and all forms of indigestion.' At the bottom of the label, in flaring black capitals was the assurance, 'Never Fails to Give Relief'.

Farnon had something to say about most of the drugs. Each one had its place in his five years' experience of practice; they all had their fascination, their individual mystique. Many of the bottles were beautifully shaped, with heavy glass stoppers and their Latin names cut deeply into their sides; names familiar to physicians for centuries, gathering fables through the years.

The two of us stood gazing at the gleaming rows without any idea that it was nearly all useless and that the days of the old medicines were nearly over. Soon they would be hustled into oblivion by the headlong rush of the new discoveries and they would never return.

'This is where we keep the instruments.' Farnon showed me into another little room. The small animal equipment lay on green baize shelves, very neat and impressively clean. Hypodermic syringes, whelping forceps, tooth scalers, probes, searchers, and, in a place of prominence, an ophthalmoscope.

Farnon lifted it lovingly from its black box. 'My latest purchase,' he murmured, stroking its smooth shaft. 'Wonderful thing. Here, have a peep at my retina.'

I switched on the bulb and gazed with interest at the glistening, coloured tapestry in the depths of his eye. 'Very pretty. I could write you a certificate of soundness.'

He laughed and thumped my shoulder. 'Good, I'm glad to hear it. I always fancied I had a touch of cataract in that one.'

He began to show me the large animal instruments which hung from hooks on the walls. Docking and firing irons, bloodless castrators, emasculators, casting ropes and hobbles, calving ropes and hooks. A new, silvery embryotome hung in the place of honour, but many of the instruments, like the drugs, were museum pieces. Particularly the blood stick and fleam, a relic of medieval times, but still used to bring the rich blood spouting into a bucket.

'You still can't beat it for laminitis,' Farnon declared seriously.

We finished up in the operating room with its bare white walls, high table, oxygen and ether anaesthetic outfit and a small sterilizer.

'Not much small animal work in this district.' Farnon smoothed the table with his palm. 'But I'm trying to encourage it. It makes a pleasant change from lying on your belly in a cow house. The thing is, we've got to do the job right. The old castor oil and prussic acid doctrine is no good at all. You probably know that a lot of the old hands won't look at a dog or a cat, but the profession has got to change its ideas.'

He went over to a cupboard in the corner and opened the door. I could see glass shelves with a few scalpels, artery forceps, suture needles and bottles of catgut in spirit. He took out his handkerchief and flicked at an auroscope before closing the doors carefully.

'Well, what do you think of it all?' he asked as he went out into the passage.

'Great,' I replied. 'You've got just about everything you need here. I'm really impressed.'

He seemed to swell visibly. The thin cheeks flushed and he hummed softly to himself. Then he burst loudly into song in a shaky baritone, keeping time with our steps as we marched along.

Back in the sitting-room, I told him about Bert Sharpe. 'Something about boring out a cow which was going on three cylinders. He talked about her ewer and felon – I didn't quite get it.'

Farnon laughed. 'I think I can translate. He wants a Hudson's operation doing on a blocked teat. Ewer is the udder and felon the local term for mastitis.'

'Well, thanks. And there was a deaf Irishman, a Mr Mulligan ...'

'Wait a minute.' Farnon held up a hand. 'Let me guess womitin'?'

'Aye, womitin' bad, sorr.'

'Right, I'll put up another pint of bismuth carb for him. I'm in favour of long-range treatment for this dog. He looks like an airedale but he's as big as a donkey and has a moody disposition. He's had Joe Mulligan on the floor a few times – just gets him down and worries him when he's got nothing better to do. But Joe loves him.'

'How about the womitin'?'

'Doesn't mean a thing. Natural reaction from eating every bit of rubbish he finds. Well, we'd better get out to Sharpe's. And there are one or two other visits – how about coming with me and I'll show you a bit of the district.'

Outside the house, Farnon motioned me towards a battered Hillman and, as I moved round to the passenger's side, I shot a startled glance at the treadless tyres, the rusty bodywork, the almost opaque windscreen with its network of fine cracks. What I didn't notice was that the passenger seat was not fixed to the floor but stood freely on its sledge-like runners. I dropped into it and went over backwards, finishing with my head on the rear seat and my feet against the roof. Farnon helped me up, apologizing with great charm, and we set off.

Once clear of the market place, the road dipped quite suddenly and we could see all of the Dale stretching away from us in the evening sunshine. The outlines of the great hills were softened in the gentle light and a broken streak of silver showed where the Darrow wandered on the valley floor.

Farnon was an unorthodox driver. Apparently captivated by the scene, he drove slowly down the hill, elbows resting on the wheel, his chin cupped in his hands. At the bottom of the hill he came out of his reverie and spurted to seventy miles an hour. The old car rocked crazily along the narrow road and my movable seat slewed from side to side as I jammed my feet against the floorboards.

Then he slammed on the brakes, pointed out some pedigree Shorthorns in a field and jolted away again. He never looked at the road in front; all his attention was on the countryside around and behind him. It was that last bit that worried me, because he spent a lot of time driving fast and looking over his shoulder at the same time.

We left the road at last and made our way up a gated lane. My years of seeing practice had taught me to hop in and out very smartly as students were regarded primarily as gate-opening machines. Farnon, however, thanked me gravely every time and once I got over my surprise I found it refreshing.

We drew up in a farmyard. 'Lame horse here,' Farnon said. A strapping Clydesdale gelding was brought out and we watched attentively as the farmer trotted him up and down.

'Which leg do you make it?' my colleague asked. 'Near fore? Yes, I think so, too. Like to examine it?'

I put my hand on the foot, feeling how much hotter it was than the other. I called for a hammer and tapped the wall of the hoof. The horse flinched, raised the foot and held it trembling for a few seconds before replacing it carefully on the ground. 'Looks like pus in the foot to me.'

'I'll bet you're right,' Farnon said. 'They call it gravel around here, by the way. What do you suggest we do about it?'

'Open up the sole and evacuate the pus.'

'Right.' He held out a hoof knife. 'I'll watch your technique.'

With the uncomfortable feeling that I was on trial, I took the knife, lifted the foot and tucked it between my knees. I knew what I had to do – find the dark mark on the sole where the infection had entered and follow it down till I reached the pus. I scraped away the caked dirt and found not one, but several marks. After more tapping to find the painful area I selected a likely spot and started to cut.

The horn seemed as hard as marble and only the thinnest little shaving came away with each twist of the knife. The horse, too, appeared to appreciate having his sore foot lifted off the ground and gratefully leaned his full weight on my back. He hadn't been so comfortable all day. I groaned and dug him in the ribs with my elbow and, though it made him change his position for a second, he was soon leaning on again.

The mark was growing fainter and, after a final gouge with the knife, it disappeared altogether. I swore quietly and started on another mark. With my back at breaking point and the sweat trickling into my eyes, I knew that if this one petered out, too, I would have to let the foot go and take a rest. And with Farnon's eye on me I didn't want to do that.

Agonizingly, I hacked away and, as the hole deepened, my knees began an uncontrollable trembling. The horse rested happily, his fifteen hundredweight cradled by this thoughtful human. I was wondering how it would look when I finally fell flat on my face when, under the knife blade, I saw a thin spurt of pus followed by a steady trickle.

'There it goes,' the farmer grunted. 'He'll get relief now.'

I enlarged the drainage hole and dropped the foot. It took me a long time to straighten up and when I stepped back, my shirt clung to my back.

'Well done, Herriot.' Farnon took the knife from me and slipped it into his pocket. 'It just isn't funny when the horn is as hard as that.'

He gave the horse a shot of tetanus antitoxin then turned to the farmer. 'I wonder if you'd hold up the foot for a second while I disinfect the cavity.' The stocky little man gripped the foot between his knees and looked down with interest as Farnon filled the hole with iodine crystals and added some turpentine. Then he disappeared behind a billowing purple curtain.

I watched, fascinated, as the thick pall mounted and spread. I could locate the little man only by the spluttering noises from somewhere in the middle.

As the smoke began to clear, a pair of round, startled eyes came into view. 'By Gaw, Mr Farnon, I wondered what the 'ell had happened for a minute,' the farmer said between coughs. He looked down again at the blackened hole in the hoof and spoke reverently: 'It's wonderful what science can do nowadays.'

We did two more visits, one to a calf with a cut leg which I stitched, dressed and bandaged, then to the cow with the blocked teat.

Mr Sharpe was waiting, still looking eager. He led us into the byre and Farnon gestured towards the cow. 'See what you can make of it.'

I squatted down and palpated the teat, feeling the mass of thickened tissue half-way up. It would have to be broken down by a Hudson's instrument and I began to work the thin metal spiral up the teat. One second later, I was sitting gasping in the dung channel with the neat imprint of a cloven hoof on my shirt front, just over the solar plexus.

It was embarrassing, but there was nothing I could do but sit there fighting for breath, my mouth opening and shutting like a stranded fish.

Mr Sharpe held his hand over his mouth, his innate politeness at war with his natural amusement at seeing the vet come to grief. 'I'm sorry, young man, but I owt to 'ave told you that this is a very friendly cow. She allus likes to shake hands.' Then, overcome by his own wit, he rested his forehead on the cow's back and went into a long paroxysm of silent mirth.

I took my time to recover, then rose with dignity from the channel. With Mr Sharpe holding the nose and Farnon lifting up the tail, I managed to get the instrument past the fibrous mass and by a few downward tugs I cleared the obstruction; but, though the precautions cramped the cow's style a little, she still got in several telling blows on my arms and legs.

When it was over, the farmer grasped the teat and sent a long white jet frothing on the floor. 'Capital! She's going on four cylinders now!'

CHAPTER 4

'We'll go home a different way.' Farnon leant over the driving wheel and wiped the cracked windscreen with his sleeve. 'Over the Brenkstone Pass and down Sildale. It's not much further and I'd like you to see it.'

We took a steep, winding road, climbing higher and still higher with the hillside falling away sheer to a dark ravine where a rocky stream rushed headlong to the gentler country below. On the top, we got out of the car. In the summer dusk, a wild panorama of tumbling fells and peaks rolled away and lost itself in the crimson and gold ribbons of the western sky. To the east, a black mountain overhung us, menacing in its naked black bulk. Huge, square-cut boulders littered the lower slopes.

I whistled softly as I looked around. This was different from the friendly hill country I had seen on the approach to Darrowby.

Farnon turned towards me. 'Yes, one of the wildest spots in England. A fearsome place in winter. I've known this pass to be blocked for weeks on end.'

I pulled the clean air deeply into my lungs. Nothing stirred in the vastness, but a curlew cried faintly and I could just hear the distant roar of the torrent a thousand feet below.

It was dark when we got into the car and started the long descent into Sildale. The valley was a shapeless blur but points of light showed where the lonely farms clung to the hillsides.

We came to a silent village and Farnon applied his brakes violently. I tobogganed effortlessly across the floor on my mobile seat and collided with the windscreen. My head made a ringing sound against the glass but Farnon didn't seem to notice. 'There's a grand little pub here. Let's go in and have a beer.'

The pub was something new to me. It was, simply, a large kitchen, square and stone-flagged. An enormous fireplace and an old black cooking range took up one end. A kettle stood on the hearth and a single large log hissed and crackled, filling the room with its resinous scent.

About a dozen men sat on the high-backed settles which lined the walls. In front of them, rows of pint mugs rested on oak tables which were fissured and twisted with age.

There was a silence as we went in. Then somebody said 'Now then, Mr Farnon,' not enthusiastically, but politely, and this brought some friendly grunts and nods from the company. They were mostly farmers or farm workers taking their pleasure without fuss or excitement. Most were burnt red by the sun and some of the younger ones were tieless, muscular necks and chests showing through the open shirt fronts. Soft murmurs and clicks rose from a peaceful domino game in the corner.

Farnon guided me to a seat, ordered two beers and turned to face me. 'Well, you can have this job if you want it. Four quid a week and full board. O.K.?'

The suddenness struck me silent. I was in. And four pounds a week! I remembered the pathetic entries in the *Record*. 'Veterinary surgeon, fully experienced, will work for keep.' The BVMA had had to put pressure on the editor to stop him printing these cries from the heart. It hadn't looked so good to see members of the profession offering their services free. Four pounds a week was affluence.

'Thank you,' I said, trying hard not to look triumphant. 'I accept.'

'Good.' Farnon took a hasty gulp at his beer. 'Let me tell you about the practice. I bought it a year ago from an old man of eighty. Still practising, mind you, a real tough old character. But he'd got past getting up in the middle of the night, which isn't surprising. And, of course, in lots of other ways he had let things slide – hanging onto all the old ideas. Some of those ancient instruments in the surgery were his. One way and another, there was hardly any practice left and I'm trying to work it up again now. There's very little profit in it so far, but if we stick in for a few years, I'm confident we'll have a good business. The farmers are pleased to see a younger man taking over and they welcome new treatments and operations. But I'm having to educate them out of the three and sixpenny consulting fee the old chap used to charge and it's been a hard slog. These Dalesmen are wonderful people and you'll like them, but they don't like parting with their brass unless you can prove they are getting something in return.'

He talked on enthusiastically of his plans for the future, the drinks kept coming and the atmosphere in the pub thawed steadily. The place filled up as the regulars from the village streamed in, the noise and heat increased and by near closing time I had got separated from my colleague and was in the middle of a laughing group I seemed to have known for years.

But there was one odd character who swam repeatedly into my field of vision. An elderly little man with a soiled white panama perched above a smooth, brown, time-worn face like an old boot. He was dodging round the edge of the group, beckoning and winking.

I could see there was something on his mind, so I broke away and allowed myself to be led to a seat in the corner. The old man sat opposite me, rested his hands and chin on the handle of his walking stick and regarded me from under drooping eyelids.

'Now then, young man, ah've summat to tell thee. Ah've been among beasts all me life and I'm going to tell tha summat.'

My toes began to curl. I had been caught this way before. Early in my college career I had discovered that all the older inhabitants of the agricultural world seemed to have the idea that they had something priceless to impart. And it usually took a long time. I looked around me in alarm but I was trapped. The old man shuffled his chair closer and began to talk in a conspiratorial whisper. Gusts of beery breath hit my face from six inches range.

There was nothing new about the old man's tale – just the usual recital of miraculous cures he had wrought, infallible remedies known only to himself and many little side-tracks about how unscrupulous people had tried in vain to worm his secrets from him. He paused only to take expert pulls at his pint pot; his tiny frame seemed to be able to accommodate a surprising amount of beer.

But he was enjoying himself and I let him ramble on. In fact I encouraged him by expressing amazement and admiration at his feats.

The little man had never had such an audience. He was a retired smallholder and it had been years since anybody had shown him the appreciation he deserved. His face wore a lopsided leer and his swimmy eyes were alight with friendship. But suddenly he became serious and sat up straight.

'Now, afore ye go, young man, I'm going to tell thee summat nobody knows but me. Ah could've made a lot o' money out o' this. Folks 'ave been after me for years to tell 'em but I never 'ave.'

He lowered the level in his glass by several inches then narrowed his eyes to slits. 'It's the cure for mallenders and sallenders in 'osses.'

I started up in my chair as though the roof had begun to fall in. 'You can't mean it,' I gasped. 'Not mallenders and sallenders.'

The old man looked smug. 'Ah, but ah do mean it. All you have to do is rub on this salve of mine and the 'oss walks away sound. He's better by that!' His voice rose to a thin shout and he made a violent gesture with his arm which swept his nearly empty glass to the floor.

I gave a low, incredulous whistle and ordered another pint. 'And you're really going to tell me the name of this salve?' I whispered.

'I am, young man, but only on one condition. Tha must tell no one. Tha must keep it to thaself, than nobody'll know but thee and me.' He effortlessly tipped half of his fresh pint down his throat. 'Just thee and me, lad.'

'All right, I promise you. I'll not tell a soul. Now what is this wonderful stuff?'

The old man looked furtively round the crowded room. Then he took a deep breath, laid his hand on my shoulder and put his lips close to my ear. He hiccuped once, solemnly, and spoke in a hoarse whisper. 'Marshmallow ointment.'

I grasped his hand and wrung it silently. The old man, deeply moved, spilled most of his final half pint down his chin.

But Farnon was making signals from the door. It was time to go. We surged out with our new friends, making a little island of noise and light in the quiet village street. A tow-haired young fellow in shirt sleeves opened the car door with natural courtesy and, waving a final goodnight, I plunged in. This time, the seat went over quicker than usual and I hurtled backwards, coming to rest with my head among some wellingtons and my knees tucked underneath my chin.

A row of surprised faces peered in at me through the back window, but soon, willing hands were helping me up and the trick seat was placed upright on its rockers again. I wondered how long it had been like that and if my employer had ever thought of having it fixed.

We roared off into the darkness and I looked back at the waving group. I could see the little man, his panama gleaming like new in the light from the doorway. He was holding his finger to his lips.

CHAPTER 5

The past five years had been leading up to óne moment and it hadn't arrived yet. I had been in Darrowby for twenty-four hours now and I still hadn't been to a visit on my own.

Another day had passed in going around with Farnon. It was a funny thing, but, for a man who seemed careless, forgetful and a few other things, Farnon was frustratingly cautious about launching his new assistant.

We had been over into Lidderdale today and I had met more of the clients – friendly, polite farmers who received me pleasantly and wished me success. But working under Farnon's supervision was like being back at college with the professor's eye on me. I felt strongly that my professional career would not start until I, James Herriot, went out and attended a sick animal, unaided and unobserved.

However, the time couldn't be very far away now. Farnon had gone off to Brawton to see his mother again. A devoted son, I thought wonderingly. And he had said he would be back late, so the old lady must keep unusual hours. But never mind about that – what mattered was that I was in charge.

I sat in an armchair with a frayed loose cover and looked out through the french windows at the shadows thrown by the evening sun across the shaggy lawn. I had the feeling that I would be doing a lot of this.

I wondered idly what my first call would be. Probably an anticlimax after the years of waiting. Something like a coughing calf or a pig with constipation. And maybe that would be no bad thing – to start with something I could easily put right. I was in the middle of these comfortable musings when the telephone exploded out in the passage. The insistent clamour sounded abnormally loud in the empty house. I lifted the receiver.

'Is that Mr Farnon?' It was a deep voice with a harsh edge to it. Not a local accent; possibly a trace of the South West.

'No, I'm sorry, he's out. This is his assistant.'

'When will he be back?'

'Not till late, I'm afraid. Can I do anything for you?'

'I don't know whether you can do anything for me or not.' The voice took on a hectoring tone. 'I am Mr Soames, Lord Hulton's farm manager. I have a valuable hunting horse with colic. Do you know anything about colic?'

I felt my hackles rising. 'I am a veterinary surgeon, so I think I should know something about it.'

There was a long pause, and the voice barked again. 'Well, I reckon you'll have to do. In any case, I know the injection the horse wants. Bring some arecoline with you. Mr Farnon uses it. And for God's sake, don't be all night getting here. How long will you be?'

'I'm leaving now.'

'Right.'

I heard the receiver bang down onto its rest. My face felt hot as I walked away from the phone. So my first case wasn't going to be a formality. Colics were tricky things and I had an aggressive know-all called Soames thrown in for good measure.

On the eight-mile journey to the case, I re-read from memory the great classic, Caulton Reeks' *Common Colics of the Horse*. I had gone through it so often in my final year that I could recite stretches of it like poetry. The well-thumbed pages hovered in front of me, phantom-like, as I drove.

This would probably be a mild impaction or a bit of spasm. Might have had a change of food or too much rich grass. Yes, that would be it; most colics were like that. A quick shot of arecoline and maybe some chlorodyne to relieve the discomfort and all would be well. My mind went back to the cases I had met while seeing practice. The horse standing quietly except that it occasionally eased a hind leg or looked round at its side. There was nothing to it, really.

I was elaborating this happy picture when I arrived. I drove into a spotless, gravelled yard surrounded on three sides by substantial loose boxes. A man was standing there, a broad-shouldered, thick-set figure, very trim in check cap and jacket, well-cut breeches and shiny leggings.

The car drew up about thirty yards away and, as I got out, the man slowly and deliberately turned his back on me. I walked across the yard, taking my time, waiting for the other to turn round, but he stood motionless, hands in pockets, looking in the other direction.

I stopped a few feet away but still the man did not turn. After a long time, and when I had got tired of looking at the back, I spoke.

'Mr Soames?'

At first the man did not move, then he turned very slowly. He had a thick, red neck, a ruddy face and small, fiery eyes. He made no answer but looked me over carefully from head to foot, taking in the worn raincoat, my youth, my air of inexperience. When he had completed his examination he looked away again.

'Yes, I am Mr Soames.' He stressed the 'Mr' as though it meant a lot to him. 'I am a very great friend of Mr Farnon.'

'My name is Herriot.'

Soames didn't appear to have heard. 'Yes, a clever man is Mr Farnon. We are great friends.'

'I understand you have a horse with colic.' I wished my voice didn't sound so high and unsteady.

Soames's gaze was still directed somewhere into the sky. He whistled a little tune softly to himself before replying. 'In there,' he said, jerking his head in the direction of one of the boxes. 'One of his lordship's best hunters. In need of expert assistance, I think.' He put a bit of emphasis on the 'expert'.

I opened the door and went inside. And I stopped as though I had walked into a wall. It was a very large box, deeply bedded with peat moss. A bay horse was staggering round and round the perimeter where he had worn a deep path in the peat. He was lathered in sweat from nose to tail, his nostrils were dilated and his eyes stared blankly in front of him. His head rolled about at every step and, through his clenched teeth, gobbets of foam dripped to the floor. A rank steam rose from his body as though he had been galloping.

My mouth had gone dry. I found it difficult to speak and when I did, it was almost in a whisper. 'How long has he been like this?'

'Oh, he started with a bit of belly ache this morning. I've been giving him black draughts all day, or at least this fellow has. I wouldn't be surprised if he's made a bloody mess of it like he does everything.'

I saw that there was somebody standing in the shadows in the corner; a large, fat man with a head collar in his hand.

'Oh, I got the draughts down him, right enough, Mr Soames, but they haven't done 'im no good.' The big man looked scared.

'You call yourself a horseman,' Soames said, 'but I should have done the damn job myself. I reckon he'd have been better by now.'

'It would take more than a black draught to help him,' I said. 'This is no ordinary colic.'

'What the hell is it, then?'

'Well, I can't say till I've examined him, but severe, continuous pain like that could mean a torsion – a twisted bowel.'

'Twisted bowel, my foot! He's got a bit of belly ache, that's all. He hasn't passed anything all day and he wants something to shift him. Have you got the arecoline with you?'

'If this is a torsion, arecoline would be the worst thing you could give him. He's in agony now, but that would drive him mad. It acts by contracting the muscles of the intestines.'

'God dammit,' snarled Soames. 'Don't start giving me a bloody lecture. Are you going to start doing something for the horse or aren't you?'

I turned to the big man in the corner. 'Slip on that head collar and I'll examine him.'

With the collar on, the horse was brought to a halt. He stood there, trembling and groaning as I passed a hand between ribs and elbows, feeling for the pulse. It was as bad as it could be – a racing, thready beat. I everted an eyelid with my fingers; the mucous membrane was a dark, brick red. The thermometer showed a temperature of a hundred and three.

I looked across the box at Soames. 'Could I have a bucket of hot water, soap and a towel, please?'

'What the devil for? You've done nothing yet and you want to have a wash?'

'I want to make a rectal examination. Will you please bring me the water?'

'God help us, I've never seen anything like this.' Soames passed a hand wearily over his eyes then swung round on the big. 'Well, come on, don't stand around there. Get him his water and we'll maybe get something done.'

When the water came, I soaped my arm and gently inserted it into the animal's rectum. I could feel plainly the displacement of the small intestine on the left side and a tense, tympanitic mass which should not have been there. As I touched it, the horse shuddered and groaned again.

As I washed and dried my arms, my heart pounded. What was I to do? What could I say?

Soames was stamping in and out of the box, muttering to himself as the pain-maddened animal writhed and twisted. 'Hold the bloody thing,' he bellowed at the horseman who was gripping the head collar. 'What the bloody hell are you playing at?'

The big man said nothing. He was in no way to blame but he just stared back stolidly at Soames.

I took a deep breath. 'Everything points to the one thing. I'm convinced this horse has a torsion.'

'All right then, have it your own way. He's got a torsion. Only for God's sake do something, will you? Are we going to stand in here all night?'

'There's nothing anybody can do. There is no cure for this. The important thing is to put him out of his pain as quickly as possible.'

Soames screwed up his face. 'No cure? Put him out of his pain? What rubbish is this you're talking? Just what are you getting at?'

I took a hold on myself. 'I suggest you let me put him down immediately.'

'What do you mean?' Soames's mouth fell open.

'I mean that I should shoot him now, straight away. I have a humane killer in the car.'

Soames looked as if he was going to explode. 'Shoot him! Are you stark raving mad? Do you know how much that horse is worth?'

'It makes no difference what he's worth, Mr Soames. He has been going through hell all day and he's dying now. You should have called me out long ago. He might live a few hours more but the end would be the same. And he's in dreadful pain, continuous pain.'

Soames sunk his head in his hands. 'Oh God, why did this have to happen to me? His lordship is on holiday or I'd call him out to try to make you see some sense. I tell you, if your boss had been here he'd have given that horse an injection and put him right in half an hour. Look here, can't we wait till Mr Farnon gets back tonight and let him have a look at him?'

Something in me leapt gladly at the idea. Give a shot of morphine and get away out of it. Leave the responsibility to somebody else. It would be easy. I looked again at the horse. He had recommenced his blind circling of the box, stumbling round and round in a despairing attempt to leave his agony behind. As I watched, he raised his lolling head and gave a little whinny. It was a desolate, uncomprehending, frantic sound and it was enough for me.

I strode quickly out and got the killer from the car. 'Steady his head,' I said to the big man and placed the muzzle between the glazing eyes. There was a sharp crack and the horse's legs buckled. He thudded down on the peat and lay still.

I turned to Soames who was staring at the body in disbelief. 'Mr Farnon will come round in the morning and carry out a post-mortem. I'd like Lord Hulton to have my diagnosis confirmed.'

I put on my jacket and went out to the car. As I started the engine, Soames opened the door and pushed his head in. He spoke quietly but his voice was furious. 'I'm going to inform his lordship about this night's work. And Mr Farnon too. I'll let him know what kind of an assistant he's landed himself with. And let me tell you this. You'll be proved wrong at that post-mortem tomorrow and then I'm going to sue you.' He banged the door shut and walked away.

Back at the surgery, I decided to wait up for my boss and I sat there trying to rid myself of the feeling that I had blasted my career before it had got started. Yet, looking back, I knew I couldn't have done anything else. No matter how many times I went over the ground, the conclusion was always the same.

It was 1 a.m. before Farnon got back. His evening with his mother had stimulated him. His thin cheeks were flushed and he smelt pleasantly of gin. I was surprised to see that he was wearing evening dress and though the dinner jacket was of old-fashioned cut and hung in loose folds on his bony frame, he still managed to look like an ambassador.

He listened in silence as I told him about the horse. He was about to comment when the phone rang. 'A late one,' he whispered, then 'Oh, it's you, Mr Soames.' He nodded at me and settled down in his chair. He was a long time saying 'Yes' and 'No' and 'I see', then he sat up decisively and began to speak.

'Thank you for ringing, Mr Soames, and it seems as though Mr Herriot did the only possible thing in the circumstances. No, I cannot agree. It would have been cruel to leave him. One of our duties is to prevent suffering. Well, I'm sorry you feel like that, but I consider Mr Herriot to be a highly capable veterinary surgeon. If I had been there I have no doubt I'd have done the same thing. Goodnight, Mr Soames, I'll see you in the morning.'

I felt so much better that I almost launched into a speech of gratitude, but in the end, all I said was 'Thanks'.

Farnon reached up into the glass-fronted cupboard above the mantelpiece and pulled out a bottle of whisky. He carelessly slopped out half a tumblerful and pushed it at me. He gave himself a similar measure and fell back into the armchair.

He took a deep swallow, stared for a few seconds at the amber fluid in the glass then looked up with a smile. 'Well, you certainly got chucked in at the deep end tonight, my boy. Your first case! And it had to be Soames, too.'

'Do you know him very well?'

'Oh, I know all about him. A nasty piece of work and enough to put anybody off their stroke. Believe me, he's no friend of mine. In fact, rumour has it that he's a bit of a crook. They say he's been feathering his nest for a long time at his lordship's expense. He'll slip up one day, I expect.'

The neat whisky burned a fiery path down to my stomach but I felt I needed it. 'I wouldn't like too many sessions like tonight's, but I don't suppose veterinary practice is like that all the time.'

'Well, not quite,' Farnon replied, 'but you never know what's in store for you. It's a funny profession, ours, you know. It offers unparalleled opportunities for making a chump of yourself.'

'But I expect a lot depends on your ability.'

'To a certain extent. It helps to be good at the job, of course, but even if you're a positive genius humiliation and ridicule are lurking just round the corner. I once got an eminent horse specialist along here to do a rig operation and the horse stopped breathing half-way through. The sight of that man dancing frantically on his patient's ribs taught me a great truth – that I was going to look just as big a fool at fairly regular intervals throughout my career.'

I laughed. 'Then I might as well resign myself to it right at the beginning.'

'That's the idea. Animals are unpredictable things so our whole life is unpredictable. It's a long tale of little triumphs and disasters and you've got to really like it to stick it. Tonight it was Soames, but another night it'll be something else. One thing, you never get bored. Here, have some more whisky.'

I drank the whisky and then some more and we talked. It seemed no time at all before the dark bulk of the acacia tree began to emerge from the grey light beyond the french window, a blackbird tried a few tentative pipes and Farnon was regretfully shaking the last drops from the bottle into his glass.

He yawned, jerked the knot out of his black tie and looked at his watch. 'Well, five o'clock. Who would have thought it? But I'm glad we had a drink together – only right to celebrate your first case. It was a right one, wasn't it?'

CHAPTER 6

Two and a half hours sleep was a meagre ration but I made a point of being up by seven thirty and downstairs, shaved and scrubbed, by eight.

But I breakfasted alone. Mrs Hall, impassively placing scrambled eggs before me, told me that my employer had left some time ago to do the P.M. on Lord Hulton's horse. I wondered if he had bothered to go to bed at all.

I was busy with the last of the toast when Farnon burst into the room. I was getting used to his entrances and hardly jumped at all as he wrenched at the door handle and almost leapt into the middle of the carpet. He looked rosy and in excellent spirits.

'Anything left in that coffee pot? I'll join you for a cup.' He crashed down on a protesting chair. 'Well, you've nothing to worry about. The P.M. showed a classical torsion. Several loops of bowel involved – black and tympanitic. I'm glad you put the poor beggar down straight away.'

'Did you see my friend Soames?'

'Oh, he was there, of course. He tried to get in a few digs about you but I quietened him. I just pointed out that he had delayed far too long in sending for us and that Lord Hulton wasn't going to be too pleased when he heard how his horse had suffered. I left him chewing over that.'

The news did a lot to lighten my outlook. I went over to the desk and got the day book. 'Here are this morning's calls. What would you like me to do?'

Farnon picked out a round of visits, scribbled the list on a scrap of paper and handed it over. 'Here you are,' he said. 'A few nice, trouble-free cases to get yourself worked in.'

I was turning to leave when he called me back. 'Oh, there's one other thing I'd like you to do. My young brother is hitching from Edinburgh today. He's at the Veterinary College there and the term finished yesterday. When he gets within striking distance he'll probably give us a ring. I wonder if you'd slip out and pick him up?'

'Certainly. Glad to.'

'His name is Tristan, by the way.'

'Tristan?'

'Yes. Oh, I should have told you. You must have wondered about my own queer name. It was my father. Great Wagnerian. It nearly ruled his life. It was music all the time – mainly Wagner.'

'I'm a bit partial myself.'

'Ah well, yes, but you didn't get it morning noon and night like we did. And then to be stuck with a name like Siegfried. Anyway, it could have been worse – Wotan, for instance.'

'Or Pogner.'

Farnon looked startled. 'By golly, you're right. I'd forgotten about old Pogner. I suppose I've a lot to be thankful for.'

It was late afternoon before the expected call came. The voice at the other end was uncannily familiar.

'This is Tristan Farnon.'

'Gosh, you sound just like your brother.'

A pleasant laugh answered me. 'Everybody says that – oh, that's very good of you. I'd be glad of a lift. I'm at the Holly Tree Café on the Great North Road.'

After the voice I had been expecting to find a younger edition of my employer but the small, boyish-faced figure sitting on a rucksack could hardly have been less like him. He got up, pushed back the dark hair from his forehead and held out his hand. The smile was charming.

'Had much walking to do?' I asked.

'Oh, a fair bit, but I needed the exercise. We had a roughish end of term party last night.' He opened the car door and threw the rucksack into the back. As I started the engine he settled himself in the passenger seat as though it were a luxurious armchair, pulled out a paper packet of Woodbines, lit one with tender concentration and gulped the smoke down blissfully. He produced the *Daily Mirror* from a side pocket and shook it open with a sigh of utter content. The smoke, which had been gone a long time, began to wisp from his nose and mouth.

I turned west off the great highway and the rumble of traffic faded rapidly behind us. I glanced round at Tristan. 'You'll have just finished exams?' I said.

'Yes, pathology and parasitology.'

I almost broke one of my steadfast rules by asking him if he had passed, but stopped myself in time. It is a chancy business. But in any case, there was no shortage of conversation. Tristan had something to say about most of the news items and now and then he read out an extract and discussed it with me. I felt a growing conviction that I was in the presence of a quicker and livelier mind than my own. It seemed no time at all before we pulled up outside Skeldale House.

Siegfried was out when we arrived and it was early evening when he returned. He came in through the french window, gave me a friendly greeting and threw himself into an armchair. He had begun to talk about one of his cases when Tristan walked in.

The atmosphere in the room changed as though somebody had clicked a switch. Siegfried's smile became sardonic and he gave his brother a long, appraising look. He grunted a 'hello', then reached up and began to run his finger along the titles of the books in the alcove. He seemed absorbed in this for a few minutes and I could feel the tension building up. Tristan's expression had changed remarkably; his face had gone completely deadpan but his eyes were wary.

Siegfried finally located the book he was looking for, took it down from the shelf and began to leaf through it unhurriedly. Then, without looking up, he said quietly: 'Well, how did the exams go?'

Tristan swallowed carefully and took a deep breath. 'Did all right in parasitology,' he replied in a flat monotone.

Siegfried didn't appear to have heard. He had found something interesting in his book and settled back to read. He took his time over it, then put the book back on the shelf. He began again the business of going along the titles; still with his back to his brother, he spoke again in the same soft voice.

'How about pathology?'

Tristan was on the edge of his chair now, as if ready to make a run for it. His eyes darted from his brother to the book shelves and back again. 'Didn't get it,' he said tonelessly.

There was no reaction from Siegfried. He kept up his patient search for his book, occasionally pulling a volume out, glancing at it and replacing it carefully. Then he gave up the hunt, lay back in the chair with his arms dangling almost to the floor and looked at Tristan. 'So you failed pathology,' he said conversationally.

I was surprised to hear myself babbling with an edge of hysteria in my voice. 'Well now that's pretty good you know. It puts him in the final year and he'll be able to sit path. at Christmas. He won't lose any time that way and, after all, it's a tough subject.'

Siegfried turned a cold eye on me. 'So you think it's pretty good, do you?' There was a pause and a long silence which was broken by a totally unexpected bellow as he rounded on his brother. 'Well, I don't! I think it is bloody awful! It's a damned disgrace, that's what it is. What the hell have you been doing all this term, anyway? Boozing, I should think, chasing women, spending my money, anything but working. And now you've got the bloody nerve to walk in here and tell me you've failed pathology. You're lazy, that's your trouble, isn't it? You're bloody bone idle!'

He was almost unrecognizable. His face was darkly flushed and his eyes glared. He yelled wildly again at his brother. 'But I've had enough this time. I'm sick of you. I'm not going to work my fingers to the bloody bone to keep you up there idling your time away. This is the end. You're sacked, do you hear me. Sacked once and for all. So get out of here – I don't want to see you around any more. Go on, get out!'

Tristan, who had preserved an air of injured dignity throughout, withdrew quietly.

Writhing with embarrassment, I looked at Siegfried. He was showing the strain of the interview. His complexion had gone blotchy; he muttered to himself and drummed his fingers on the arm of the chair.

I was aghast at having to witness this break-up and I was grateful when Siegfried sent me on a call and I was able to get out of the room.

It was nearly dark when I got back and I drove round to the back lane and into the yard at the foot of the garden. The creaking of the garage doors disturbed the rooks in the great elms which overhung the buildings. Far up in the darkness there was a faint fluttering, a muffled cawing then silence. As I stood listening, I became aware of a figure in the gloom, standing by the yard door, looking down the garden. As the face turned towards me I saw it was Tristan.

Again, I felt embarrassed. It was an unfortunate intrusion when the poor fellow had come up here to brood alone. 'Sorry about the way things turned out,' I said awkwardly.

The tip of the cigarette glowed brightly as Tristan took a long pull. 'No, no, that's all right. Could have been a lot worse, you know.'

'Worse? Well, it's bad enough, isn't it? What are you going to do?'

'Do? What do you mean?'

'Well, you've been kicked out, haven't you? Where are you going to sleep tonight?'

'I can see you don't understand,' Tristan said. He took his cigarette from his mouth and I saw the gleam of very white teeth as he smiled. 'You needn't worry. I'm sleeping here and I'll be down to breakfast in the morning.'

'But how about your brother?'

'Siegfried? Oh, he'll have forgotten all about it by then.'

'Are you sure?'

'Dead sure. He's always sacking me and he always forgets. Anyway, things turned out very well. The only tricky bit back there was getting him to swallow that bit about the parasitology.'

I stared at the shadowy form by my side. Again, there was a rustling as the rooks stirred in the tall trees then settled into silence.

'The parasitology?'

'Yes. If you think back, all I said was that I had done all right. I wasn't any more specific than that.'

'Then you mean ...?'

Tristan laughed softly and thumped my shoulder.

'That's right, I didn't get parasitology. I failed in both. But don't worry. I'll pass them at Christmas.'

CHAPTER 7

I huddled deeper in the blankets as the strident brreeng-brreeng, brreeng-brreeng of the telephone echoed through the old house.

It was three weeks since Tristan's arrival and life at Skeldale House had settled into a fairly regular pattern. Every day began much the same with the phone ringing between seven and eight o'clock after the farmers had had the first look at their stock.

There was only one phone in the house. It rested on a ledge in the tiled passage downstairs. Siegfried had impressed on me that I shouldn't get out of bed for these early calls. He had delegated the job to Tristan; the responsibility would be good for him. Siegfried had been emphatic about it.

I listened to the ringing. It went on and on – it seemed to get louder. There was neither sound nor movement from Tristan's room and I waited for the next move in the daily drama. It came, as always, with a door crashing back on its hinges, then Siegfried rushed out onto the landing and bounded down the stairs three at a time.

A long silence followed and I could picture him shivering in the draughty passage, his bare feet freezing on the tiles as he listened to the farmer's leisurely account of the animal's symptoms. Then the ting of the phone in its rest and the mad pounding of feet on the stairs as Siegfried made a dash for his brother's room.

Next a wrenching sound as the door was flung open, then a yell of rage. I detected a note of triumph; it meant Tristan had been caught in bed – a definite victory for Siegfried and he didn't have many victories. Usually, Tristan exploited his quick-dressing technique and confronted his brother fully dressed. It gave him a psychological advantage to be knotting his tie when Siegfried was still in pyjamas.

But this morning Tristan had overplayed his hand; trying to snatch the extra few seconds he was caught between the sheets. I listened to the shouts. 'Why didn't you answer the bloody phone like I told you? Don't tell me you're deaf as well as idle! Come on, out of it, out, out!'

But I knew Tristan would make a quick comeback. When he was caught in bed he usually scored a few points by being half-way through his breakfast before his brother came in.

Later, I watched Siegfried's face as he entered the dining-room and saw Tristan munching his toast happily, his *Daily Mirror* balanced against the coffee pot. It was as if he had felt a sudden twinge of toothache.

It all made for a strained atmosphere and I was relieved when I was able to escape to collect my things for the morning round. Down the narrow passage with its familiar, exciting smell of ether and carbolic and out into the high-walled garden which led to the yard where the cars were kept.

It was the same every morning but, to me, there was always the feeling of surprise. When I stepped out into the sunshine and the scent of flowers it was as though I was doing it for the first time. The clear air held a breath of the nearby moorland; after being buried in a city for five years it was difficult to take it all in.

I never hurried over this part. There could be an urgent case waiting but I still took my time. Along the narrow part between the ivy-covered wall and the long offshoot of the house where the wistaria climbed, pushing its tendrils and its withered blooms into the very rooms. Then past the rockery where the garden widened to the lawn, unkempt and lost-looking but lending coolness and softness to the weathered brick. Around its borders flowers blazed in untidy profusion, battling with a jungle of weeds.

And so to the rose garden, then an asparagus bed whose fleshy fingers had grown into tall fronds. Further on were strawberries and raspberries. Fruit trees were everywhere, their branches dangling low over the path. Peaches, pears, cherries and plums were trained against the south wall where they fought for a place with wild-growing rambler roses.

Bees were at work among the flowers and the song of blackbirds and thrushes competed with the cawing of the rooks high up in the elms.

Life was full for me. There were so many things to find out and a lot I had to prove to myself. The days were quick and challenging and they pressed on me with their very newness. But it all stopped here in the garden. Everything seemed to have stopped here a long time ago. I looked back before going through the door into the yard and it was like suddenly coming across a picture in an old book; the empty, wild garden and the tall, silent house beyond. I could never quite believe it was there and that I was a part of it.

And the feeling was heightened when I went into the yard. It was square and cobbled and the grass grew in thick tufts beween the stones. Buildings took up two sides; the two garages, once coach houses, a stable and saddle room, a loose box and a pig sty. Against the free wall a rusty iron pump hung over a stone water trough.

Above the stable was a hay loft and over one of the garages a dovecot. And there was old Boardman. He, too, seemed to have been left behind from grander days, hobbling round on his lame leg, doing nothing in particular.

He grunted good morning from his cubby hole where he kept a few tools and garden implements. Above his head his reminders of the war looked down; a row of coloured prints of Bruce Bairnsfather cartoons. He had stuck them up when he came home in 1918 and there they were still, dusty and curled at the edges but still speaking to him of Kaiser Bill and the shell holes and muddy trenches.

Boardman washed a car sometimes or did a little work in the garden, but he was content to earn a pound or two and get back to his yard. He spent a lot of time in the saddle room, just sitting. Sometimes he looked round the empty hooks where the harness used to hang and then he would make a rubbing movement with his fist against his palm.

He often talked to me of the great days. 'I can see t'owd doctor now, standing on top step waiting for his carriage to come round. Big, smart-looking feller he was. Allus wore a top hat and frock coat, and I can remember him when I was a lad, standing there, pulling on 'is gloves and giving his hat a tilt while he waited.'

Boardman's features seemed to soften and a light came into his eyes as though he was taking more to himself than to me. 'The old house was different then. A housekeeper and six servants there were and everything just so. And a full time gardener. There weren't a blade of grass out of place in them days and the flowers all in rows and the trees pruned, tidy-like. And this yard – it were t'owd doctor's favourite spot. He'd come and look over t' door at me sitting here polishing the harness and pass time o' day, quiet like. He were a real gentleman but you couldn't cross 'im. A few specks o' dust anywhere down here and he'd go nearly mad.

'But the war finished it all. Everybody's rushing about now. They don't care about them things now. They've no time, no time at all.'

He would look round in disbelief at the overgrown cobbles, the

peeling garage doors hanging crazily on their hinges. At the empty
stable and the pump from which no water flowed.

He was always friendly with me in an absent way, but with Siegfried
he seemed to step back into his former character, holding himself up
smartly and saying 'Very good, sir,' and saluting repeatedly with one
finger. It was as though he recognized something there – something of
the strength and authority of t'owd doctor – and reached out eagerly
towards the lost days.

'Morning, Boardman,' I said, as I opened the garage door. 'How are
you today?'

'Oh, middlin', lad, just middlin'.' He limped across and watched me
get the starting handle and begin the next part of the daily routine. The
car allotted to me was a tiny Austin of an almost forgotten vintage and
one of Boardman's voluntary duties was towing it off when it wouldn't
start. But this morning, surprisingly, the engine coughed into life after
six turns.

As I drove round the corner of the back lane, I had the feeling, as I did
every morning, that this was where things really got started. The
problems and pressures of my job were waiting for me out there and at
the moment I seemed to have plenty.

I had arrived in the Dales, I felt, at a bad time. The farmers, after a
generation of neglect, had seen the coming of a prophet, the wonderful
new vet, Mr Farnon. He appeared like a comet, trailing his new ideas in
his wake. He was able, energetic and charming and they received him as
a maiden would a lover. And now, at the height of the honeymoon, I had
to push my way into the act, and I just wasn't wanted.

I was beginning to get used to the questions. 'Where's Mr Farnon?' –
'Is he ill or something?' – 'I expected Mr Farnon.' It was a bit daunting
to watch their faces fall when they saw me walking onto their farms.
Usually they looked past me hopefully and some even went and peered
into the car to see if the man they really wanted was hiding in there.

And it was uphill work examining an animal when its owner was
chafing in the background, wishing with all his heart that I was
somebody else.

But I had to admit they were fair. I got no effusive welcomes and when
I started to tell them what I thought about the case they listened with
open scepticism, but I found that if I got my jacket off and really worked
at the job they began to thaw a little. And they were hospitable. Even
though they were disappointed at having me they asked me into their
homes. 'Come in and have a bit o' dinner,' was a phrase I heard nearly
every day. Sometimes I was glad to accept and I ate some memorable
meals with them.

Often, too, they would slip half a dozen eggs or a pound of butter into the car as I was leaving. This hospitality was traditional in the Dales and I knew they would probably do the same for any visitor, but it showed the core of friendliness which lay under the often unsmiling surface of these people and it helped.

I was beginning to learn about the farmers and what I found I liked. They had a toughness and a philosophical attitude which was new to me. Misfortunes which would make the city dweller want to bang his head against a wall were shrugged off with 'Aye, well, these things happen.'

It looked like being another hot day and I wound down the car windows as far as they would go. I was on my way to do a tuberculin test; the national scheme was beginning to make its first impact in the Dales and the more progressive farmers were asking for survey tests.

And this was no ordinary herd. Mr Copfield's Galloway cattle were famous in their way. Siegfried had told me about them. 'The toughest lot in this practice. There's eighty-five of them and none has ever been tied up. In fact, they've scarcely been touched by hand. They live out on the fells, they calve and rear their calves outside. It isn't often anybody goes near them so they're practically wild animals.'

'What do you do when there's anything wrong with them?' I had asked.

'Well, you have to depend on Frank and George – they're the two Copfield sons. They've been reared with those cattle since they were babies – started tackling the little calves as soon as they could walk, then worked up to the big ones. They're about as tough as the Galloways.'

Copfield's place was one of the bleak ones. Looking across the sparse pastures to the bald heights with their spreading smudges of heather it was easy to see why the farmer had chosen a breed hardier than the local shorthorns. But this morning the grim outlines were softened by the sunshine and there was a desert peace in the endless greens and browns.

Frank and George were not as I expected. The durable men who helped me in my daily jobs tended to be dark and lean with stringy muscles but the Copfields were golden-haired and smooth-skinned. They were good-looking young men about my own age and their massive necks and wide spread of shoulder made their heads look small. Neither of them was tall but they looked formidable with their shirt sleeves rolled high to reveal wrestlers' arms and their thick legs encased in cloth gaiters. Both wore clogs.

The cattle had been herded into the buildings and they just about filled all the available accommodation. There were about twenty-five in a long passage down the side of the fold yard; I could see the ragged line of heads above the rails, the steam rising from their bodies. Twenty more occupied an old stable and two lots of twenty milled about in large loose boxes.

I looked at the black, untamed animals and they looked back at me, their reddish eyes glinting through the rough fringe of hair which fell over their faces. They kept up a menacing, bad-tempered swishing with their tails.

It wasn't going to be easy to get an intradermal injection into every one of them. I turned to Frank.

'Can you catch these beggars?' I asked.

'We'll 'ave a bloody good try,' he replied calmly, throwing a halter over his shoulder. He and his brother lit cigarettes before climbing into the passage where the biggest beasts were packed. I followed them and soon found that the tales I had heard about the Galloways hadn't been exaggerated. If I approached them from the front they came at me with their great hairy heads and if I went behind them they kicked me as a matter of course.

But the brothers amazed me. One of them would drop a halter on a beast, get his fingers into its nose and then be carried away as the animal took off like a rocket. They were thrown about like dolls but they never let go; their fair heads bobbed about incongruously among the black backs; and the thing that fascinated me was that through all the contortions the cigarettes dangled undisturbed.

The heat increased till it was like an oven in the buildings and the animals, their bowels highly fluid with their grass diet, ejected greenish-brown muck like non-stop geysers.

The affair was conducted in the spirit of a game with encouragement shouted to the man in action: 'Thou 'as 'im, Frank.' 'Sniggle 'im, George.' In moments of stress the brothers cursed softly and without heat: 'Get off ma bloody foot, thou awd bitch.' They both stopped work and laughed with sincere appreciation when a cow slashed me across the face with her sodden tail; and another little turn which was well received was when I was filling my syringe with both arms raised and a bullock, backing in alarm from the halter, crashed its craggy behind into my midriff. The wind shot out of me in a sharp hiccup, then the animal decided to turn round in the narrow passage, squashing me like a fly against the railings. I was pop-eyed as it scrambled round; I wondered whether the creaking was coming from my ribs or the wood behind me.

We finished up with the smallest calves and they were just about the most difficult to handle. The shaggy little creatures kicked, bucked, sprang into the air, ran through our legs and even hurtled straight up the walls. Often the brothers had to throw themselves on top of them and bear them to the ground before I could inject them and when the calves felt the needle they stuck out their tongues and bawled deafeningly; outside, the anxious mothers bellowed back in chorus.

It was midday when I reeled out of the buildings. I seemed to have been a month in there, in the suffocating heat, the continuous din, the fusillade of muck.

Frank and George produced a bucket of water and a scrubbing brush and gave me a rough clean-up before I left. A mile from the farm I drove off the unfenced road, got out of the car and dropped down on the cool fellside. Throwing wide my arms I wriggled my shoulders and my sweat-soaked shirt into the tough grass and let the sweet breeze play over me. With the sun on my face I looked through half-closed eyes at the hazy-blue sky.

My ribs ached and I could feel the bruises of a dozen kicks on my legs. I knew I didn't smell so good either. I closed my eyes and grinned at the ridiculous thought that I had been conducting a diagnostic in-vestigation for tuberculosis back there. A strange way to carry out a scientific procedure; a strange way, in fact, to earn a living.

But then I might have been in an office with the windows tight shut against the petrol fumes and the traffic noise, the desk light shining on the columns of figures, my bowler hat hanging on the wall.

Lazily I opened my eyes again and watched a cloud shadow riding over the face of the green hill across the valley. No, no ... I wasn't complaining.

CHAPTER 8

I hardly noticed the passage of the weeks as I rattled along the moorland roads on my daily rounds; but the district was beginning to take shape, the people to emerge as separate personalities. Most days I had a puncture. The tyres were through to the canvas on all wheels; it surprised me that they took me anywhere at all.

One of the few refinements on the car was a rusty 'sunshine roof'. It grated dismally when I slid it back, but most of the time I kept it open and the windows too, and I drove in my shirt sleeves with the delicious air swirling about me. On wet days it didn't help much to close the roof because the rain dripped through the joints and formed pools on my lap and the passenger seat.

I developed great skill in zig-zagging round puddles. To drive through was a mistake as the muddy water fountained up through the gaps in the floorboards.

But it was a fine summer and long days in the open gave me a tan which rivalled the farmers'. Even mending a puncture was no penance on the high, unfenced roads with the wheeling curlews for company and the wind bringing the scents of flowers and trees up from the valleys. And I could find other excuses to get out and sit on the crisp grass and look out over the airy roof of Yorkshire. It was like taking time out of life. Time to get things into perspective and assess my progress. Everything was so different that it confused me. This countryside after years of city streets, the sense of release from exams and study, the job with its daily challenge. And then there was my boss.

Siegfried Farnon charged round the practice with fierce energy from dawn till dark and I often wondered what drove him on. It wasn't money because he treated it with scant respect. When the bills were paid, the cash went into the pint pot on the mantelpiece and he grabbed handfuls when he wanted it. I never saw him take out a wallet, but his pockets bulged with loose silver and balled-up notes. When he pulled out a thermometer they flew around him in a cloud.

After a week or two of headlong rush he would disappear; maybe for the evening, maybe overnight and often without saying where he was going. Mrs Hall would serve a meal for two, but when she saw I was eating alone she would remove the food without comment.

He dashed off the list of calls each morning with such speed that I was quite often sent hurrying off to the wrong farm or to do the wrong thing. When I told him later of my embarrassment he would laugh heartily.

There was one time when he got involved himself. I had just taken a call from a Mr Heaton of Bronsett about doing a P.M. on a dead sheep.

'I'd like you to come with me, James,' Siegfried said. 'Things are quiet this morning and I believe they teach you blokes a pretty hot post-mortem procedure. I want to see you in action.'

We drove into the village of Bronsett and Siegfried swung the car left into a gated lane.

'Where are you going?' I said. 'Heaton's is at the other end of the village.'

'But you said Seaton's.'

'No, I assure you ...'

'Look, James, I was right by you when you were talking to the man. I distinctly heard you say the name.'

I opened my mouth to argue further but the car was hurtling down the lane and Siegfried's jaw was jutting. I decided to let him find out for himself.

We arrived outside the farmhouse with a screaming of brakes. Siegfried had left his seat and was rummaging in the boot before the car had stopped shuddering. 'Hell!' he shouted. 'No post-mortem knife. Never mind, I'll borrow something from the house.' He slammed down the lid and bustled over to the door.

The farmer's wife answered and Siegfried beamed on her. 'Good morning to you, Mrs Seaton, have you a carving knife?'

The good lady raised her eyebrows. 'What was that you said?'

'A carving knife, Mrs Seaton, a carving knife, and a good sharp one, please.'

'You want a carving knife?'

'Yes, that's right, a carving knife!' Siegfried cried, his scanty store of patience beginning to run out. 'And I wonder if you'd mind hurrying. I haven't much time.'

The bewildered woman withdrew to the kitchen and I could hear whispering and muttering. Children's heads peeped out at intervals to get a quick look at Siegfried stamping irritably on the step. After some delay, one of the daughters advanced timidly, holding out a long, dangerous-looking knife.

Siegfried snatched it from her hand and ran his thumb up and down the edge. 'This is no damn good!' he shouted in exasperation. 'Don't you understand I want something really sharp. Fetch me a steel.'

The girl fled back into the kitchen and there was a low rumble of voices. It was some minutes before another young girl was pushed round the door. She inched her way up to Siegfried, gave him the steel at arm's length and dashed back to safety.

Siegfried prided himself on his skill at sharpening a knife. It was something he enjoyed doing. As he stropped the knife on the steel, he warmed to his work and finally burst into song. There was no sound from the kitchen, only the ring of steel on steel backed by the tuneless singing; there were silent intervals when he carefully tested the edge, then the noise would start again.

When he had completed the job to his satisfaction he peered inside the door. 'Where is your husband?' he called.

There was no reply so he strode into the kitchen, waving the gleaming blade in front of him. I followed him and saw Mrs Seaton and her daughters cowering in the far corner, staring at Siegfried with large, frightened eyes.

He made a sweeping gesture at them with the knife. 'Well, come on, I can get started now!'

'Started what?' the mother whispered, holding her family close to her. 'I want to P.M. this sheep. You have a dead sheep, haven't you?' Explanations and apologies followed.

Later, Siegfried remonstrated gravely with me for sending him to the wrong farm.

'You'll have to be a bit more careful in future, James,' he said seriously. 'Creates a very bad impression, that sort of thing.'

. . .

Another thing about my new life which interested me was the regular traffic of women through Skeldale House. They were all upper-class, mostly beautiful and they had one thing in common – eagerness. They came for drinks, for tea, to dinner, but the real reason was to gaze at Siegfried like parched travellers in the desert sighting an oasis.

I found it damaging to my own ego when their eyes passed over me without recognition or interest and fastened themselves hungrily on my colleague. I wasn't envious, but I was puzzled. I used to study him furtively, trying to fathom the secret of his appeal. Looking at the worn jacket hanging from the thin shoulders, the frayed shirt collar and anonymous tie, I had to conclude that clothes had nothing to do with it.

There was something attractive in the long, bony face and humorous blue eyes, but a lot of the time he was so haggard and sunken-cheeked that I wondered if he was ill.

I often spotted Diana Brompton in the queue and at these times I had to fight down an impulse to dive under the sofa. She was difficult to recognize as the brassy beauty of that afternoon as she looked up meltingly at Siegfried, hanging on his words, giggling like a schoolgirl.

I used to grow cold at the thought that Siegfried might pick her out of the mob and marry her. It worried me a lot because I knew I would have to leave just when I was beginning to enjoy everything about Darrowby.

But Siegfried showed no sign of marrying any of them and the procession continued hopefully. I finally got used to it and stopped worrying.

. . .

I got used, too, to my employer's violent changes of front. There was one morning when Siegfried came down to breakfast, rubbing a hand wearily over red-rimmed eyes.

'Out at 4 a.m., he groaned, buttering his toast listlessly. 'And I don't like to have to say this, James, but it's all your fault.'

'My fault?' I said, startled.

'Yes, lad, your fault. This was a cow with a mild impaction of the rumen. The farmer had been mucking about with it himself for days; a pint of linseed oil one day, a bit of bicarb and ginger the next, and at four o'clock in the morning he decides it is time to call the vet. When I pointed out it could have waited a few hours more he said Mr Herriot told him never to hesitate to ring – he'd come out any hour of the day or night.'

He tapped the top of his egg as though the effort was almost too much for him. 'Well, it's all very well being conscientious and all that, but if a thing has waited several days it can wait till morning. You're spoiling these chaps, James, and I'm getting the backwash of it. I'm sick and tired of being dragged out of my bed for trifles.'

'I'm truly sorry, Siegfried. I honestly had no wish to do that to you. Maybe it's just my inexperience. If I didn't go out, I'd be worried the animal might die. If I left it till morning and it died, how would I feel?'

'That's all right,' snapped Siegfried. 'There's nothing like a dead animal to bring them to their senses. They'll call us out a bit earlier next time.'

I absorbed this bit of advice and tried to act on it. A week later, Siegfried said he wanted a word with me.

'James, I know you won't mind my saying this, but old Sumner was complaining to me today. He says he rang you the other night and you refused to come out to his cow. He's a good client, you know, and a very nice fellow, but he was quite shirty about it. We don't want to lose a chap like that.'

'But it was just a chronic mastitis,' I said. 'A bit of thickening in the milk, that's all. He'd been dosing it himself for nearly a week with some quack remedy. The cow was eating all right, so I thought it would be quite safe to leave it till next day.'

Siegfried put a hand on my shoulder and an excessively patient look spread over his face. I steeled myself. I didn't mind his impatience; I was used to it and could stand it. But the patience was hard to take.

'James,' he said in a gentle voice, 'there is one fundamental rule in our job which transcends all others, and I'll tell you what it is. YOU MUST ATTEND. That is it and it ought to be written on your soul in letters of fire.' He raised a portentous forefinger. 'YOU MUST ATTEND. Always remember that, James: it is the basis of everything. No matter what the circumstances, whether it be wet or fine, night or day, if a client calls you out, you must go; and go cheerfully. You say this didn't sound like an urgent case. Well, after all, you have only the owner's description to guide you and he is not equipped with the knowledge to decide whether it is urgent or not. No, lad, you have to go. Even if they have been treating the animal themselves, it may have taken a turn for the worse. And don't forget,' wagging the finger solemnly, 'the animal may die.'

'But I thought you said there was nothing like a dead animal to bring them to their senses,' I said querulously.

'What's that?' barked Siegfried, utterly astonished. 'Never heard such rubbish. Let's have no more of it. Just remember – YOU MUST ATTEND.'

. . .

Sometimes he would give me advice on how to live. As when he found me hunched over the phone which I had just crashed down; I was staring at the wall, swearing softly to myself.

Siegfried smiled whimsically. 'Now what is it, James?'

'I've just had a torrid ten minutes with Rolston. You remember that outbreak of calf pneumonia? Well, I spent hours with those calves, poured expensive drugs into them. There wasn't a single death. And now he's complaining about his bill. Not a word of thanks. Hell, there's no justice.'

Siegfried walked over and put his arm round my shoulders. He was wearing his patient look again. 'My dear chap,' he coo'd. 'Just look at you. Red in the face, all tensed up. You mustn't let yourself get upset like this; you must try to relax. Why do you think professional men are cracking up all over the country with coronaries and ulcers? Just because they allow themselves to get all steamed up over piffling little things like you are doing now. Yes, yes, I know these things are annoying, but you've got to take them in your stride. Keep calm, James, calm. It just isn't worth it – I mean, it will all be the same in a hundred years.'

He delivered the sermon with a serene smile, patting my shoulder reassuringly like a psychiatrist soothing a violent patient.

I was writing a label on a jar of red blister a few days later when Siegfried catapulted into the room. He must have kicked the door open because it flew back viciously against the rubber stop and rebounded almost into his face. He rushed over to the desk where I was sitting and began to pound on it with the flat of his hand. His eyes glared wildly from a flushed face.

'I've just come from that bloody swine Holt!' he shouted.

'Ned Holt, you mean?'

'Yes, that's who I mean, damn him!'

I was surprised. Mr Holt was a little man who worked on the roads for the county council. He kept four cows as a sideline and had never been known to pay a veterinary bill; but he was a cheerful character and Siegfried had rendered his unpaid services over the years without objection.

'One of your favourites, isn't he?' I said.

'Was, by God, was,' Siegfried snarled. 'I've been treating Muriel for him. You know, the big red cow second from the far end of his byre. She's had recurrent tympany – coming in from the field every night badly blown – and I'd tried about everything. Nothing did any good. Then it struck me that it might be actinobacillosis of the reticulum. I shot some sodium iodide into the vein and when I saw her today the difference was incredible – she was standing there, chewing her cud, right as rain. I was just patting myself on the back for a smart piece of diagnosis, and do you know what Holt said? He said he knew she'd be better today because last night he gave her half a pound of epsom salts in a bran mash. That was what had cured her.'

Siegfried took some empty cartons and bottles from his pockets and hurled them savagely into the wastepaper basket. He began to shout again.

'Do you know, for the past fortnight I've puzzled and worried and damn nearly dreamt about that cow. Now I've found the cause of the trouble, applied the most modern treatment and the animal has recovered. And what happens? Does the owner express his grateful thanks for my skill? Does he hell – the entire credit goes to the half pound of epsom salts. What I did was a pure waste of time.'

He dealt the desk another sickening blow.

'But I frightened him, James,' he said, his eyes staring. 'By God, I frightened him. When he made that crack about the salts, I yelled out "You bugger!" and made a grab for him. I think I would have strangled him, but he shot into the house and stayed there. I didn't see him again.'

Siegfried threw himself into a chair and began to churn his hair about. 'Epsom salts!' he groaned. 'Oh God, it makes you despair.'

I thought of telling him to relax and pointing out that it would all be the same in a hundred years, but my employer still had an empty serum bottle dangling from one hand. I discarded the idea.

· · ·

Then there came the day when Siegfried decided to have my car rebored. It had been using a steady two pints of oil a day and he hadn't thought this excessive, but when it got to half a gallon a day he felt something ought to be done. What probably decided him was a farmer on market day saying he always knew when the young vet was coming because he could see the cloud of blue smoke miles away.

When the tiny Austin came back from the garage, Siegfried fussed round it like an old hen. 'Come over here, James,' he called. 'I want to talk to you.'

I saw he was looking patient again and braced myself.

'James,' he said, pacing round the battered vehicle, whisking specks from the paintwork. 'You see this car?'

I nodded.

'Well, it has been rebored, James, rebored at great expense, and that's what I want to talk to you about. You now have in your possession what amounts to a new car.' With an effort he unfastened the catch and the bonnet creaked open in a shower of rust and dirt. He pointed down at the engine, black and oily, with unrelated pieces of flex and rubber tubing hanging around it like garlands. 'You have a piece of fine mechanism here and I want you to treat it with respect. I've seen you belting along like a maniac and it won't do. You've got to nurse this machine for the next two or three thousand miles; thirty miles an hour is quite fast enough. I think it's a crime the way some people abuse a new engine – they should be locked up – so remember, lad, no flogging or I'll be down on you.'

He closed the bonnet with care, gave the cracked windscreen a polish with the cuff of his coat and left.

These strong words made such an impression on me that I crawled round the visits all day almost at walking pace.

The same night, I was getting ready for bed when Siegfried came in. He had two farm lads with him and they both wore silly grins. A powerful smell of beer filled the room.

Siegfried spoke with dignity, slurring his words only slightly. 'James, I met these gentlemen in the Black Bull this evening. We have had several excellent games of dominoes but unfortunately they have missed the last bus. Will you kindly bring the Austin round and I will run them home.'

I drove the car to the front of the house and the farm lads piled in, one in the front, the other in the back. I looked at Siegfried lowering himself unsteadily into the driving seat and decided to go along. I got into the back.

The two young men lived in a farm far up on the North Moors and, three miles out of the town, we left the main road and our headlights picked out a strip of track twisting along the dark hillside.

Siegfried was in a hurry. He kept his foot on the boards, the note of the engine rose to a tortured scream and the little car hurtled on into the blackness. Hanging on grimly, I leant forward so that I could shout into my employer's ear. 'Remember this is the car which has just been rebored,' I bellowed above the din.

Siegfried looked round with an indulgent smile. 'Yes, yes, I remember, James. What are you fussing about?' As he spoke, the car shot off the road and bounded over the grass at sixty miles an hour. We all bounced around like corks till he found his way back. Unperturbed, he carried on at the same speed. The silly grins had left the lads' faces and they sat rigid in their seats. Nobody said anything.

The passengers were unloaded at a silent farmhouse and the return journey began. Since it was downhill all the way, Siegfried found he could go even faster. The car leapt and bumped over the uneven surface with its engine whining. We made several brief but tense visits to the surrounding moors, but we got home.

It was a month later that Siegfried had occasion to take his assistant to task once more. 'James, my boy,' he said sorrowfully, 'you are a grand chap, but by God, you're hard on cars. Look at this Austin. Newly rebored a short time ago, in tip-top condition, and look at it now – drinking oil. I don't know how you did it in the time. You're a real terror.'

CHAPTER 9

'First, please,' I called as I looked into the waiting-room. There was an old lady with a cat in a cardboard box, two small boys trying to keep hold of a rabbit, and somebody I didn't recognize at first. Then I remembered – it was Soames.

When it was his turn, he came into the surgery but he was a vastly different character from the one I knew. He wore an ingratiating smile. His head bobbed up and down as he spoke. He radiated anxiety to please. And the most interesting thing was that his right eye was puffed and closed and surrounded by an extensive area of bluish-black flesh.

'I hope you don't mind my coming to see you, Mr Herriot,' he said. 'The fact is I have resigned my position with his lordship and am looking for another post. I was wondering if you and Mr Farnon would put in a word for me if you heard of anything.'

I was too astonished at the transformation to say much. I replied that we would do what we could and Soames thanked me effusively and bowed himself out.

I turned to Siegfried after he had gone. 'Well, what do you make of that?'

'Oh, I know all about it.' Siegfried looked at me with a wry smile. 'Remember I told you he was working one or two shady sidelines up there – selling a few bags of corn or a hundredweight of fertilizer here and there. It all mounted up. But it didn't last; he got a bit careless and he was out on his ear before he knew what had happened.'

'And how about the lovely black eye?'

'Oh, he got that from Tommy. You must have seen Tommy when you were there. He's the horseman.'

My mind went back to that uncomfortable night and to the quiet man holding the horse's head. 'I remember him – big fat chap.'

'Yes, he's a big lad and I'd hate to have him punch me in the eye. Soames gave him a hell of a life and as soon as Tommy heard about the sacking he paid a visit just to settle the score.'

.   .   .

I was now comfortably settled into the way of life in Skeldale House. At first I wondered where Tristan fitted into the set-up. Was he supposed to be seeing practice, having a holiday, working or what? But it soon became clear that he was a factotum who dispensed and delivered medicines, washed the cars, answered the phone and even, in an emergency, went to a case.

At least, that was how Siegfried saw him and he had a repertoire of tricks aimed at keeping him on his toes. Like returning unexpectedly or bursting into a room in the hope of catching him doing nothing. He never seemed to notice the obvious fact that the college vacation was over and Tristan should have been back there. I came to the conclusion over the next few months that Tristan must have had some flexible arrangement with the college authorities because, for a student, he seemed to spend a surprising amount of time at home.

He interpreted his role rather differently from his brother and, while resident in Darrowby, he devoted a considerable amount of his acute intelligence to the cause of doing as little as possible. Tristan did, in fact, spend much of his time sleeping in a chair. When he was left behind to dispense when we went out on our rounds he followed an unvarying procedure. He half-filled a sixteen-ounce bottle with water, added a few drachms of chlorodyne and a little epicacuanha, pushed the cork in and took it through to the sitting-room to stand by his favourite chair. It was a wonderful chair for his purpose; old-fashioned and high-backed with wings to support the head.

He would get out his *Daily Mirror*, light a Woodbine and settle down till sleep overcame him. If Siegfried rushed in on him he grabbed the bottle and started to shake it madly, inspecting the contents at intervals. Then he went through to the dispensary, filled up the bottle and labelled it.

It was a sound, workable system but it had one big snag. He never knew whether it was Siegfried or not when the door opened and often I walked in and found him half lying in his chair, staring up with startled, sleep-blurred eyes while he agitated his bottle.

Most evenings found him sitting on a high stool at the bar counter of the Drovers' Arms, conversing effortlessly with the barmaid. At other times he would be out with one of the young nurses from the local hospital which he seemed to regard as an agency to provide him with female company. All in all, he managed to lead a fairly full life.

· · ·

Saturday night, 10.30 p.m. and I was writing up my visits when the phone rang. I swore, crossed my fingers and lifted the receiver.

'Hello, Herriot speaking.'

'Oh, it's you is it,' growled a dour voice in broadest Yorkshire. 'Well, ah want Mr Farnon.'

'I'm sorry, Mr Farnon is out. Can I help you?'

'Well, I 'ope so, but I'd far raither 'ave your boss. This is Sims of Beal Close.

(Oh no, please no, not Beal Close on a Saturday night. Miles up in the hills at the end of a rough lane with about eight gates.)

'Yes, Mr Sims, and what is the trouble?'

'Ah'll tell you, there is some trouble an' all. I 'ave a grand big show 'oss here. All of seventeen hands. He's cut 'isself badly on the hind leg, just above the hock. I want him stitched immediately.'

(Glory be! Above the hock! What a charming place to have to stitch a horse. Unless he's very quiet, this is going to be a real picnic.)

'How big is the wound, Mr Sims?'

'Big? It's a gurt big thing about a foot long and bleedin' like 'ell. And this 'oss is as wick as an eel. Could kick a fly's eye out. Ah can't get near 'im nohow. Goes straight up wall when he sees anybody. By gaw, I tell you I had 'im to t'blacksmith t'other day and feller was dead scared of 'im. Twiltin' gurt 'oss 'e is.'

(Damn you, Mr Sims, damn Beal Close and damn your twiltin' gurt 'oss.)

'Well, I'll be along straight away. Try to have some men handy just in case we have to throw him.'

'Throw 'im? Throw 'im? You'd never throw this 'oss. He'd kill yer first. Anyways, I 'ave no men here so you'll have to manage on your own. Ah know Mr Farnon wouldn't want a lot of men to help 'im.'

(Oh lovely, lovely. This is going to be one for the diary.)

'Very well, I'm leaving now, Mr Sims.'

'Oh, ah nearly forgot. My road got washed away in the floods yesterday. You'll 'ave to walk the last mile and a half. So get a move on and don't keep me waiting all night.'

(This is just a bit much.)

'Look here, Mr Sims, I don't like your tone. I said I would leave now and I will get there just as soon as I can.'

'You don't like ma tone, eh? Well, ah don't like useless young apprentices practising on my good stock, so ah don't want no cheek from you. You know nowt about t'damn job, any road.'

(That finally does it.)

'Now just listen to me, Sims. If it wasn't for the sake of the horse I'd refuse to come out at all. Who do you think you are, anyway? If you ever try to speak to me like that again . . .'

'Now, now, Jim, get a grip on yourself. Take it easy old boy. You'll burst a blood vessel if you go on like this.'

'Who the devil . . . ?'

'Ah, ah, Jim, calm yourself now. That temper of yours, you know. You'll really have to watch it.'

'Tristan! Where the hell are you speaking from?'

'The kiosk outside the Drovers. Five pints inside me and feeling a bit puckish. Thought I'd give you a ring.'

'By God, I'll murder you one of these days if you don't stop this game. It's putting years on me. Now and again isn't so bad, but this is the third time this week.'

'Ah, but this was by far the best, Jim. It was really wonderful. When you started drawing yourself up to your full height – it nearly killed me. Oh God, I wish you could have heard yourself.' He trailed off into helpless laughter.

And then my feeble attempts at retaliation; creeping, trembling, into some lonely phone box.

'Is that young Mr Farnon?' in a guttural croak. 'Well, this is Tilson of High Woods. Ah want you to come out here immediately I 'ave a terrible case of . . .'

'Excuse me for interrupting, Jim, but is there something the matter with your tonsils? Oh, good. Well, go on with what you were saying, old lad. Sounds very interesting.'

.   .   .

There was only one time when I was not on the receiving end. It was Tuesday – my half day – and at 11.30 a.m. a call came in. An eversion of the uterus in a cow. This is the tough job in country practice and I felt the usual chill.

It happens when the cow, after calving, continues to strain until it pushes the entire uterus out and it hangs down as far as the animal's hocks. It is a vast organ and desperately difficult to replace, mainly because the cow, having once got rid of it, doesn't want it back. And in a straightforward contest between man and beast the odds were very much on the cow.

The old practitioners, in an effort to even things up a bit, used to sling the cow up by its hind limbs and the more inventive among them came up with all sorts of contraptions like the uterine valise which was supposed to squeeze the organ into smaller bulk. But the result was usually the same – hours of backbreaking work.

The introduction of the epidural anaesthetic made everything easier by removing sensation from the uterus and preventing the cow from straining but, for all that, the words 'calf bed out' coming over the line were guaranteed to wipe the smile off any vet's face.

I decided to take Tristan in case I needed a few pounds of extra push. He came along but showed little enthusiasm for the idea. He showed still less when he saw the patient, a very fat shorthorn lying, quite unconcerned, in her stall, Behind her, a bloody mass of uterus, afterbirth, muck and straw spilled over into the channel.

She wasn't at all keen to get up, but after we had done a bit of shouting and pushing at her shoulder she rose to her feet, looking bored.

The epidural space was difficult to find among the rolls of fat and I wasn't sure if I had injected all the anaesthetic into the right place. I removed the afterbirth, cleaned the uterus and placed it on a clean sheet held by the farmer and his brother. They were frail men and it was all they could do to keep the sheet level. I wouldn't be able to count on them to help me much.

I nodded to Tristan; we stripped off our shirts, tied clean sacks round our waists and gathered the uterus in our arms.

It was badly engorged and swollen and it took us just an hour to get it back. There was a long spell at the beginning when we made no progress at all and the whole idea of pushing the enormous organ through a small hole seemed ludicrous, like trying to thread a needle with a sausage. Then there was a few minutes when we thought we were doing famously only to find we were feeding the thing down through a tear in the sheet, (Siegfried once told me he had spent half a morning trying to stuff a uterus up a cow's rectum. What really worried him, he said, was that he nearly succeeded) and at the end when hope was fading, there was the blissful moment when the whole thing began to slip inside and incredibly disappeared from sight.

Somewhere half-way through we both took a breather at the same time and stood panting, our faces almost touching. Tristan's cheeks were prettily patterned where a spouting artery had sprayed him; I was able to look deep into his eyes and I read there a deep distaste for the whole business.

Lathering myself in the bucket and feeling the ache in my shoulders and back, I looked over at Tristan. He was pulling his shirt over his head as though it cost him the last of his strength. The cow, chewing contentedly at a mouthful of hay, had come best out of the affair.

Out in the car, Tristan groaned. 'I'm sure that sort of thing isn't good for me. I feel as though I've been run over by a steam-roller. Hell, what a life this is at times.'

After lunch I rose from the table. 'I'm off to Brawton now, Triss, and I think I'd better mention that you may not have seen the last of that cow. These bad cases sometimes recur and there's a chance that little lot may come out again. If it does, it's all yours because Siegfried won't be back for hours and nothing is going to stop me having my half-day.'

For once Tristan's sense of humour failed him. He became haggard, he seemed to age suddenly. 'Oh God,' he moaned, 'don't even talk about it. I'm all in – another session like that would kill me. And on my own! It would be the end of me, I tell you.'

'Ah well,' I said sadistically, 'try not to worry. It may never happen.'

It was when I saw the phone box about ten miles along the Brawton road that the thought struck me. I slowed down and got out of the car. 'I wonder,' I muttered, 'I wonder if I could do it just once.'

Inside the box, inspiration was strong in me. I wrapped my handkerchief over the mouthpiece, dialled the practice number and when I heard Tristan on the line I shouted at the top of my voice. 'Are you t'young feller that put our cow's calf bed back this morning?'

'Yes, I'm one of them.' Tension sprang into Tristan's voice. 'Why, is there something wrong?'

'Aye, there is summat wrong,' I bawled. 'She's putten it out again.'

'Out again? Out again? All of it?' He was almost screaming.

'Aye, it's a terrible mess. Pourin' blood and about twice size it was this morning. You'll 'ave some job with 'er.'

Ther was a long silence and I wondered if he had fainted. Then I heard him again, hoarse but resolute. 'Very well, I'll come straight away.'

There was another pause, then he spoke again almost in a whisper. 'Is it out completely?'

I broke down then. There was a wistful quality about the words which defeated me; a hint of a wild hope that the farmer may have been exaggerating and that there might be only a tiny piece peeping out. I began to laugh. I would have liked to toy with my victim a little longer but it was impossible. I laughed louder and took my handkerchief from the mouthpiece so that Tristan could hear me.

I listened for a few seconds to the frenzied swearing at the other end then gently replaced the receiver. It would probably never happen again but it was sweet, very sweet.

CHAPTER 10

'You want Mr Herriot? Certainly, I'll get him for you.' Siegfried cupped the phone with his hand. 'Come on, James, here's another one prefers you to me.' I glanced at him quickly, but he was smiling. He was pleased.

I thought, as I took the phone, of the tales I had heard of the other kind of boss; the man who couldn't bear to be knocked off his little pedestal. And I thought, too, of the difference a few weeks had made in the farmers' attitude; they didn't look past me now, hoping that Mr Farnon had come with me. They were beginning to accept me, and I liked to think that it wasn't only their hospitable traditions that made them ask me in for a 'bit o' dinner'.

This really meant something, because, with the passage of time, an appreciation of the Dales people had grown in me; a sense of the value of their carefully given friendship. The higher up the country, the more I liked them. At the bottom of the valley, where it widened into the plain, the farmers were like farmers everywhere, but the people grew more interesting as the land heightened, and in the scattered hamlets and isolated farms near the bleak tops I found their characteristics most marked; their simplicity and dignity, their rugged independence and their hospitality.

This Sunday morning it was the Bellerbys and they lived at the top of Halden, a little valley branching off the main Dale. My car bumped and rattled over the last rough mile of an earth road with the tops of boulders sticking up every few yards.

I got out and from where I stood, high at the head, I could see all of the strangely formed cleft in the hills, its steep sides grooved and furrowed by countless streams feeding the boisterous Halden Beck which tumbled over its rocky bed far below. Down there, were trees and some cultivated fields, but immediately behind me the wild country came crowding in on the bowl where the farmhouse lay. Halsten Pike, Alstang, Birnside – the huge fells with their barbarous names were very near.

Up here the trappings of civilization seemed far away. The farm buildings had been built massively of stone hundreds of years ago with the simple object of sheltering the animals. Those ancient masons were untroubled by regulations about the light and ventilation and the cow byre was gloomy, thick walled, almost windowless. The floor was broken and pitted, and rotting wooden partitions separated the cows from each other.

I went in, groping my way until my eyes grew accustomed to the dim light. There was nobody there but a roan cow had a label tied to its tail. Since this was a common way of communicating with the vet I lifted the tail and read 'Felon, back quarters'.

I pushed the cow over and began to examine the back teats. I was drawing out the stringy, discoloured milk when a voice addressed me from the doorway: 'Oh, it's you, Mr Herriot. I'm right glad you've come to see us this morning. You could do us such a great favour if you would.'

I looked up and saw Ruth Bellerby, a fine-looking woman in her late thirties. She was the go-ahead member of the family and had an intelligent, questing mind. She was a great believer in self-improvement for the Dales people.

'I'll be glad to help you if I can, Miss Bellerby. What is it you'd like me to do?'

'Well, Mr Herriot, you know they are putting on the Messiah at Darrowby church this afternoon and we did badly want to go, but it's such a job getting the pony and trap ready and it's so slow. If you could give us a lift down in your car, I know we'd be able to get a ride back. It would be such a help.'

'Of course I'll run you down,' I replied. 'I'll be delighted to do it. I'm going myself as a matter of fact. You don't get many chances to hear good music in Darrowby.'

It was good to have a chance to help these kindly people. I had always marvelled at the Bellerbys. They seemed to me to be survivors from another age and their world had a timeless quality. They were never in a hurry; they rose when it was light, went to bed when they were tired, ate when they were hungry and seldom looked at a clock.

Ruth led the way over to the house. 'There's just mother and dad and me going. Bob's not interested, I'm afraid.'

I was slightly taken aback when I entered the house. The family were just sitting down to Sunday dinner and were still in their working clothes. I stole a look at my watch; a quarter to twelve and the performance started at 2 p.m. Oh well, I probably had plenty of time.

'Come on, young man,' said little Mr Bellerby. 'Sit down and have a bit o' dinner.'

It was always a bit tricky refusing these invitations without causing offence, but I pointed out that my own meal would be ready when I got back and it would be hard on Mrs Hall if it were wasted.

They were quick to appreciate this argument and settled down round the scrubbed kitchen table. Mrs Bellerby served a large, round Yorkshire pudding to each of them and poured a pool of gravy into it from a quart size enamel jug. I had had a hard morning and the delicious scent that rose from the gravy as it ran over the golden slabs was a sweet torture. But I consoled myself with the thought that the fact of my sitting there would make them hurry.

The pudding was consumed in leisurely silence, then Bob, an amiable, thick-set youth in his twenties, pushed out his empty plate. He did not say anything, but his mother planked down another pudding on the plate and plied the gravy jug again. His parents and sister watched him benevolently as he methodically demolished the thick, doughy mass.

Next, a tremendous roast appeared from the oven and Mr Bellerby hacked and sawed at it till they all had a heap of thick slices on their plates. Then mountains of mashed potatoes were served from something that looked like a washing-up bowl. Chopped turnip followed and the family went into action again.

There was no sign of haste. They ate calmly and quietly without any small talk. Bob had an extra helping of mashed potatoes.

The Bellerbys were relaxed and happy, but I couldn't say the same about myself. Hunger was tearing fiercely at me and the minutes on my watch were ticking away relentlessly.

There was a decent interval before Mrs Bellerby went over to the old fire oven in the corner, opened the door and pulled forth a great flat baking tin of steaming apple pie. She then proceeded to carve off about a square foot for each of them and deluged it with something like a pint of custard from another towering enamel jug.

The family set to as though they were just beginning the meal and once more a busy silence fell on the group. Bob cleared his plate in effortless style and pushed it wordlessly into the middle of the table. His mother was ready with another great rectangle of pie and another copious libation of custard.

It was going to be a close thing, I thought, but this surely must be the end. They would realize time was getting short and start to change. But, to my consternation, Mrs Bellerby moved slowly over to the fire and put the kettle on, while her husband and Bob pushed their chairs back and stretched out their legs. They both wore corduroy breeches with the lacing undone and on their feet were enormous hobnailed boots. Bob, after a search through his pockets, brought out a battered packet of cigarettes and lay back in a happy coma as his mother put a cup of tea in front of him. Mr Bellerby produced a clasp knife and began to cut up some plug tobacco for his pipe.

As they rearranged themselves round the table and began to slowly sip the hot tea, I found I had started to exhibit all the classical symptoms of tension. Pounding pulse, tightly clenched jaws and the beginnings of a headache.

After a second cup of tea, there were signs of activity. Mr Bellerby rose with a groan, scratched his shirt front and stretched luxuriously. 'Well, young man, we'll just have a bit of a wash and get changed. Bob'll stay and talk to you – he's not coming with us.'

There was a lot of splashing and spluttering in the big stone sink at the far end of the kitchen as they made their ablutions, then they disappeared upstairs. I was greatly relieved to find that it didn't take them long to change. Mr Bellerby was down very soon, transformed in appearance by a stiff and shiny suit of navy blue serge with a faint greenish tinge. His wife and daughter followed soon in a blaze of flowered cotton.

'Ah well, now, here we are. All ready, eh?' There was a note of hysteria in my heartiness. 'Right, then, off we go. After you, ladies.'

But Ruth did not move. She was pulling on a pair of white gloves and looking at her brother sprawled in his chair. 'You know, Bob, you're nowt but a disgrace!' she burst out. 'Here we are going off to hear this lovely music and you're lying there in your muck, not caring. You've no interest in culture at all. You care no more about bettering yourself than one of them bullocks out there.'

Bob stirred uneasily under this sudden attack, but there was more to come.

Ruth stamped her foot. 'Really, it makes my blood boil to look at you. And I know we won't be right out of t'door before you're asleep. Aye, snoring there all afternoon like a pig.' She swung round to Mrs Bellerby. 'Mother! I've made up my mind. I'm not going to leave him snoring here. He's got to come with us!'

I felt the sweat start out on my brow. I began to babble. 'But don't you think, perhaps ... might be just a little late ... starts at two o'clock ... my lunch ...'

But my words were utterly lost. Ruth had the bit properly between her teeth. 'Get up out of there, Bob! Get up this minute and get dressed!' She shut her mouth tightly and thrust out her lower jaw.

She was too much for Bob. Although an impressive eater, he didn't seem to have much mind of his own. He mumbled sulkily and shuffled over to the sink. He took off his shirt and they all sat down and watched as he lathered his torso with a large block of White Windsor and sluiced his head and neck by working the pump handle by the side of the sink.

The family regarded him happily, pleased that he was coming with them and content in the knowledge that it would be good for him. Ruth watched his splashings with the light of love in her eyes. She kept looking over at me as if to say 'Isn't this grand'.

For my part, I was only just stopping myself from tearing out my hair in great handfuls. A compulsion to leap up and pace the floor, to scream at the top of my voice showed that I was nearing the end of my tether. I fought this feeling by closing my eyes and I must have kept them closed for a long time because, when I opened them, Bob was standing by my side in a suit exactly like his father's.

I could never remember much about that ride to Darrowby. I had only a vague recollection of the car hurtling down the stony track at forty miles an hour. Of myself staring straight ahead with protruding eyes and the family, tightly packed but cheerful, thoroughly enjoying the ride.

Even the imperturbable Mrs Hall was a little tight lipped as I shot into the house at ten to two and out again at two after bolting her good food.

I was late for the Messiah. The music had started as I crept into the church and I ran a gauntlet of disapproving stares. Out of the corner of my eye I saw the Bellerbys sitting very upright, all in a row. It seemed to me that they looked disapproving, too.

CHAPTER 11

I looked again at the slip of paper where I had written my visits. 'Dean, 3, Thompson's Yard. Old dog ill.'

There were a lot of these 'yards' in Darrowby. They were, in fact, tiny streets, like pictures from a Dickens novel. Some of them opened off the market place and many more were scattered behind the main thorough-fares in the old part of the town. From the outside you could see only an archway and it was always a surprise to me to go down a narrow passage and come suddenly upon the uneven rows of little houses with no two alike, looking into each other's windows across eight feet of cobbles.

In front of some of the houses a strip of garden had been dug out and marigolds and nasturtiums straggled over the rough stones; but at the far end the houses were in a tumbledown condition and some were abandoned with their windows boarded up.

Number three was down at this end and looked as though it wouldn't be able to hold out much longer.

The flakes of paint quivered on the rotten wood of the door as I knocked; above, the outer wall bulged dangerously on either side of a long crack in the masonry.

A small, white-haired man answered. His face, pinched and lined, was enlivened by a pair of cheerful eyes; he wore a much-darned woollen cardigan, patched trousers and slippers.

'I've come to see your dog,' I said, and the old man smiled.

'Oh, I'm glad you've come, sir,' he said. 'I'm getting a bit worried about the old chap. Come inside, please.'

He led me into the tiny living-room. 'I'm alone now, sir. Lost my missus over a year ago. She used to think the world of the old dog.'

The grim evidence of poverty was everywhere. In the worn out lino, the fireless hearth, the dank, musty smell of the place. The wall-paper hung away from the damp patches and on the table the old man's solitary dinner was laid; a fragment of bacon, a few fried potatoes and a cup of tea. This was life on the old-age pension.

In the corner, on a blanket, lay my patient, a cross-bred labrador. He must have been a big, powerful dog in his time, but the signs of age showed in the white hairs round his muzzle and the pale opacity in the depth of his eyes. He lay quietly and looked at me without hostility.

'Getting on a bit, isn't he, Mr Dean?'

'Aye he is that. Nearly fourteen, but he's been like a pup galloping about until these last few weeks. Wonderful dog for his age, is old Bob and he's never offered to bite anybody in his life. Children can do anything with him. He's my only friend now – I hope you'll soon be able to put him right.'

'Is he off his food, Mr Dean?'

'Yes, clean off, and that's a strange thing because by gum, he could eat. He always sat by me and put his head on my knee at meal times, but he hasn't been doing it lately.'

I looked at the dog with growing uneasiness. The abdomen was grossly distended and I could read the tell-tale symptoms of pain; the catch in the respirations, the retracted commissures of the lips, the anxious, preoccupied expression in the eyes.

When his master spoke, the tail thumped twice on the blankets and a momentary interest showed in the white old eyes; but it quickly disappeared and the blank, inward look returned.

I passed my hand carefully over the dog's abdomen. Ascites was pronounced and the dropsical fluid had gathered till the pressure was intense. 'Come on, old chap,' I said. 'Let's see if we can roll you over.'

The dog made no resistance as I eased him slowly onto his other side, but, just as the movement was completed, he whimpered and looked round. The cause of the trouble was now only too easy to find.

I palpated gently. Through the thin muscle of the flank I could feel a hard, corrugated mass; certainly a splenic or hepatic carcinoma, enormous and completely inoperable. I stroked the old dog's head as I tried to collect my thoughts. This wasn't going to be easy.

'Is he going to be ill for long?' the old man asked, and again came the thump, thump of the tail at the sound of the loved voice. 'It's miserable when Bob isn't following me round the house when I'm doing my little jobs.'

'I'm sorry, Mr Dean, but I'm afraid this is something very serious. You see this large swelling. It is caused by an internal growth.'

'You mean ... cancer?' the little man said faintly.

'I'm afraid so, and it has progressed too far for anything to be done. I wish there was something I could do to help him, but there isn't.'

The old man looked bewildered and his lips trembled. 'Then he's going to die?'

I swallowed hard. 'We really can't just leave him to die, can we? He's in some distress now, but it will soon be an awful lot worse. Don't you think it would be kindest to put him to sleep? After all, he's had a good, long innings.' I always aimed at a brisk, matter-of-fact approach, but the old clichés had an empty ring.

The old man was silent, then he said, 'Just a minute,' and slowly and painfully knelt down by the side of the dog. He did not speak, but ran his hand again and again over the grey old muzzle and the ears, while the tail thump, thump, thumped on the floor.

He knelt there a long time while I stood in the cheerless room, my eyes taking in the faded pictures on the walls, the frayed, grimy curtains, the broken-springed armchair.

At length the old man struggled to his feet and gulped once or twice. Without looking at me, he said huskily, 'All right, will you do it now?'

I filled the syringe and said the things I always said. 'You needn't worry, this is absolutely painless. Just an overdose of an anaesthetic. It is really an easy way out for the old fellow.'

The dog did not move as the needle was inserted, and, as the barbiturate began to flow into the vein, the anxious expression left his face and the muscles began to relax. By the time the injection was finished, the breathing had stopped.

'Is that it?' the old man whispered.

'Yes, that's it,' I said. 'He is out of his pain now.'

The old man stood motionless except for the clasping and unclasping of his hands. When he turned to face me his eyes were bright. 'That's right, we couldn't let him suffer, and I'm grateful for what you've done. And now, what do I owe you for your services, sir?'

'Oh, that's all right, Mr Dean,' I said quickly. 'It's nothing – nothing at all. I was passing right by here – it was no trouble.'

The old man was astonished. 'But you can't do that for nothing.'

'Now please say no more about it, Mr Dean. As I told you, I was passing right by your door.' I said goodbye and went out of the house, through the passage and into the street. In the bustle of people and the bright sunshine, I could still see only the stark, little room, the old man and his dead dog.

As I walked towards my car, I heard a shout behind me. The old man was shuffling excitedly towards me in his slippers. His cheeks were streaked and wet, but he was smiling. In his hand he held a small, brown object.

'You've been very kind, sir. I've got something for you.' He held out the object and I looked at it. It was tattered but just recognizable as a precious relic of a bygone celebration.

'Go on, it's for you,' said the old man. 'Have a cigar.'

CHAPTER 12

It was unfortunate that Siegfried ever had the idea of delegating the book-keeping to his brother, because Skeldale House had been passing through a period of peace and I found it soothing.

For nearly a fortnight there had been hardly a raised voice or an angry word except for one unpleasant interlude when Siegfried had come in and found his brother cycling along the passage. Tristan found all the rage and shouting quite incomprehensible – he had been given the job of setting the table and it was a long way from kitchen to dining-room; it seemed the most natural thing in the world to bring his bike in.

Autumn had come with a sharpness in the air and at nights the log fire burned bright in the big room, sending shadows flickering over the graceful alcoves and up to the high, carved ceiling. It was always a good time when the work of the day was through and the three of us lay back in the shabby armchairs and stretched our feet out to the blaze.

Tristan was occupied with the *Daily Telegraph* crossword which he did every night. Siegfried was reading and I was dozing. It embarrassed me to be drawn into the crossword; Siegfried could usually make a contribution after a minute's thought but Tristan could have the whole thing worked out while I wrestled with the first clue.

The carpet round our feet was hidden by the dogs, all five of them, draped over each other in heavy-breathing layers and adding to the atmosphere of camaraderie and content.

It seemed to me that a chill breath struck through the comfort of the room as Siegfried spoke. 'Market day tomorrow and the bills have just gone out. They'll be queueing up to give us their money so I want you, Tristan, to devote the entire day to taking it from them. James and I are going to busy, so you'll be in sole charge. All you have to do is take their cheques, give them a receipt and enter their names in the receipt book. Now do you think you can manage that without making a bloody hash of it?'

I winced. It was the first discordant note for a long time and it struck deep.

'I think I might just about cope with that,' Tristan replied haughtily.

'Good. Let's get to bed then.'

But, next day, it was easy to see that the assignment was right up Tristan's street. Stationed behind the desk, he took in the money in handfuls; and all the time he talked. But he did not talk at random; each character got a personal approach.

With the upright methodist, it was the weather, the price of cows and the activities of the village institute. The raffish type with his cap on one side, exhaling fumes of market ale, got the latest stories which Tristan kept on the backs of envelopes. But with the ladies he rose to his greatest heights. They were on his side from the first because of his innocent, boyish face, and when he turned the full blast of his charm on them their surrender was complete.

I was amazed at the giggles which came from behind the door. I was pleased the lad was doing well. Nothing was going wrong this time.

Tristan was smug at lunch-time and cock-a-hoop at tea. Siegfried, too, was satisfied with the day's takings which his brother presented in the form of a column of neat figures accurately totalled at the bottom. 'Thank you, Tristan, very efficient.' All was sweetness.

At the end of the day I was in the yard, throwing the used bottles from the boot of my car into a bin. It had been a busy day and I had accumulated a bigger than usual load of empties.

Tristan came panting in from the garden. 'Jim, I've lost the receipt book!'

'Always trying to pull my leg, always joking,' I said. 'Why don't you give your sense of humour a rest some time?' I laughed heartily and sent a liniment bottle crashing among the others.

He plucked at my sleeve. 'I'm not joking, Jim, believe me. I really have lost the bloody thing.' For once, his sang-froid had deserted him. His eyes were wide, his face pale.

'But it can't just have disappeared,' I said. 'It's bound to turn up.'

'It'll never turn up.' Tristan wrung his hands and did a bit of pacing on the cobbles. 'Do you know I've spent about two hours searching for it. I've ransacked the house. It's gone, I tell you.'

'But it doesn't matter, does it? You'll have transferred all the names into the ledger.'

'That's just it. I haven't. I was going to do it tonight.'

'So that means that all the farmers who have been handing you money today are going to get the same bill next month?'

'Looks like it. I can't remember the names of more than two or three of them.'

I sat down heavily on the stone trough. 'Then God help us all, especially you. These Yorkshire lads don't like parting with their brass once, but when you ask them to do it twice – oh, brother!'

Another thought struck me and I said with a touch of cruelty. 'And how about Siegfried. Have you told him yet?'

A spasm crossed Tristan's face. 'No, he's just come in. I'm going to do it now.' He squared his shoulders and strode from the yard.

I decided not to follow him to the house. I didn't feel strong enough for the scene which was bound to follow. Instead, I went out into the back lane and round behind the house to the market place where the lighted entrance of the Drovers' Arms beckoned in the dusk.

I was sitting behind a pint when Tristan came in looking as though somebody had just drained half a gallon of blood from him.

'How did it go?' I asked.

'Oh, the usual, you know. Bit worse this time, maybe. But I can tell you this, Jim. I'm not looking forward to a month from today.'

· · ·

The receipt book was never found and, a month later, all the bills were sent out again, timed, as usual, to arrive on market day morning.

The practice was quiet that particular day and I had finished my round by mid-morning. I didn't go into the house, because through the waiting-room window I could see rows of farmers sitting round the walls; they all wore the same offended, self-righteous expression.

I stole away to the market place. When I had time, I enjoyed moving among the stalls which crowded the ancient square. You could buy fruit, fish, second-hand books, cheeses, clothes, in fact nearly everything; but the china stall was my favourite.

It was run by a Jewish gentleman from Leeds – fat, confident,

sweating, and with a hypnotic selling-technique. I never got tired of
watching him. He fascinated me. He was in his best form today, standing
in a little clearing surrounded on all sides by heaps of crockery, while
beyond, the farmers' wives listened open-mouthed to his oratory.

'Ah'm not good lookin',' he was saying. 'Ah'm not clever, but by God
ah can talk. Ah can talk the hind leg off a donkey. Now look 'ere.' He
lifted a cheap cup and held it aloft, but tenderly, gripping it between his
thick thumb and forefinger, his little finger daintily outspread.
'Beautiful, isn't it? Now isn't that lovely?' Then he placed it reverently
on the palm of his hand and displayed it to the audience. 'Now I tell you
ladies, you can buy this selfsame tea-set in Conners in Bradford for three
pounds fifteen. I'm not jokin' nor jestin', it's there and that's the price.
But my price, ladies?' and here he fished out an old walking-stick with a
splintered handle. 'My price for this beautiful tea-set?' He held the stick
by its end and brought it crashing down on an empty tea-chest. 'Never
mind three pound fifteen.' Crash! 'Never mind three pound.' Crash!
'Never mind two pound.' Crash! 'Never mind thirty bob.' Crash! ''Ere,
'ere, come on, who'll give me a quid?' Not a soul moved. 'All right, all
right, I can see ah've met me match today. Go on, seventeen and a
tanner the lot.' A final devastating crash and the ladies began to make
signals and fumble in their handbags. A little man emerged from the
back of the stall and started to hand out the tea-sets. The ritual had been
observed and everybody was happy.

I was waiting, deeply content, for the next item from the virtuoso
when I saw a burly figure in a check cap waving wildly at me from the
edge of the crowd. He had his hand inside his jacket and I knew what he
was feeling for. I didn't hesitate but dodged quickly behind a stall laden
with pig troughs and wire netting. I had gone only a few steps before
another farmer hailed me purposefully. He was brandishing an
envelope.

I felt trapped, then I saw a way of escape. Rapidly skirting a counter
displaying cheap jewellery, I plunged into the doorway of the Drovers'
Arms and, avoiding the bar which was full of farmers, slipped into the
manager's office. I was safe; this was one place where I was always
welcome.

The manager looked up from his desk, but he did not smile. 'Look
here,' he said sharply, 'I brought my dog in to see you some time ago and
in due course I received an account from you.' I cringed inwardly. 'I
paid by return and was extremely surprised this morning to find that
another account had been rendered. I have here a receipt signed by . . .'

I couldn't stand any more. 'I'm very sorry, Mr Brooke, but there's
been a mistake. I'll put it right. Please accept our apologies.'

This became a familiar refrain over the next few days, but it was Siegfried who had the most unfortunate experience. It was in the bar of his favourite pub, the Black Swan. He was approached by Billy Breckenridge, a friendly, jocular little character, one of Darrowby's worthies. 'Hey, remember that three and six I paid at your surgery? I've had another bill for it.'

Siegfried made a polished apology – he'd had a lot of practice – and bought the man a drink. They parted on good terms.

The pity of it was that Siegfried, who seldom remembered anything, didn't remember this. A month later, also in the Swan, he ran into Billy Breckenridge again. This time, Billy wasn't so jocular. 'Hey, remember that bill you sent me twice? Well, I've had it again.'

Siegfried did his best, but his charm bounced off the little man. He was offended. 'Right, I can see you don't believe I paid your bill. I had a receipt from your brother, but I've lost it.' He brushed aside Siegfried's protestations. 'No, no, there's only one way to settle this. I say I've paid the three and six, you say I haven't. All right, I'll toss you for it.'

Miserably, Siegfried demurred, but Billy was adamant. He produced a penny and, with great dignity, balanced it on his thumbnail. 'O.K. you call.'

'Heads,' muttered Siegfried and heads it was. The little man did not change expression. Still dignified, he handed the three and six to Siegfried. 'Perhaps we might be able to consider the matter closed.' He walked out of the bar.

Now there are all kinds of bad memories, but Siegfried's was of the inspired type. He somehow forgot to make a note of this last transaction and, at the end of the month, Billy Breckenridge received a fourth request for the amount which he had already paid twice. It was about then that Siegfried changed his pub and started going to the Cross Keys.

CHAPTER 13

As autumn wore into winter and the high tops were streaked with the first snows, the discomforts of practice in the Dales began to make themselves felt.

Driving for hours with frozen feet, climbing to the high barns in biting winds which seared and flattened the wiry hill-grass. The interminable stripping off in draughty buildings and the washing of hands and chest in buckets of cold water, using scrubbing soap and often a piece of sacking for a towel.

I really found out the meaning of chapped hands. When there was a rush of work, my hands were never quite dry and the little red fissures crept up almost to my elbows.

This was when some small-animal work came as a blessed relief. To step out of the rough, hard routine for a while; to walk into a warm drawing-room instead of a cow house and tackle something less formidable than a horse or a bull. And among all those comfortable drawing-rooms there was none so beguiling as Mrs Pumphrey's.

Mrs Pumphrey was an elderly widow. Her late husband, a beer baron whose breweries and pubs were scattered widely over the broad bosom of Yorkshire, had left her a vast fortune and a beautiful house on the outskirts of Darrowby. Here she lived with a large staff of servants, a gardener, a chauffeur and Tricki Woo. Tricki Woo was a Pekinese and the apple of his mistress's eye.

Standing now in the magnificent doorway, I furtively rubbed the toes of my shoes on the backs of my trousers and blew on my cold hands. I could almost see the deep armchair drawn close to the leaping flames, the tray of cocktail biscuits, the bottle of excellent sherry. Because of the sherry, I was always careful to time my visits for half an hour before lunch.

A maid answered my ring, beaming on me as an honoured guest and led me to the room, crammed with expensive furniture and littered with glossy magazines and the latest novels. Mrs Pumphrey, in the high-backed chair by the fire, put down her book with a cry of delight. 'Trick! Tricki! Here is your uncle Herriot.' I had been made an uncle very early and, sensing the advantages of the relationship, had made no objection.

Tricki, as always, bounded from his cushion, leapt onto the back of a sofa and put his paws on my shoulders. He then licked my face thoroughly before retiring, exhausted. He was soon exhausted because he was given roughly twice the amount of food needed for a dog of his size. And it was the wrong kind of food.

'Oh, Mr Herriot,' Mrs Pumphrey said, looking at her pet anxiously. 'I'm so glad you've come. Tricki has gone flop-bott again.'

This ailment, not to be found in any textbook, was her way of describing the symptoms of Tricki's impacted anal glands. When the glands filled up, he showed discomfort by sitting down suddenly in mid-walk and his mistress would rush to the phone in great agitation.

'Mr Herriot! Please come, he's going flop-bott again!'

I hoisted the little dog onto a table and, by pressure on the anus with a pad of cotton wool, I evacuated the glands.

It baffled me that the Peke was always so pleased to see me. Any dog who could still like a man who grabbed him and squeezed his bottom hard every time they met had to have an incredibly forgiving nature. But Tricki never showed any resentment; in fact he was an outstandingly equable little animal, bursting with intelligence, and I was genuinely attached to him. It was a pleasure to be his personal physician.

The squeezing over, I lifted my patient from the table, noticing the increased weight, the padding of extra flesh over the ribs. 'You know, Mrs Pumphrey, you're overfeeding him again. Didn't I tell you to cut out all those pieces of cake and give him more protein?'

'Oh yes, Mr Herriot,' Mrs Pumphrey wailed. 'But what can I do? He's so tired of chicken.'

I shrugged; it was hopeless. I allowed the maid to lead me to the palatial bathroom where I always performed a ritual handwashing after the operation. It was a huge room with a fully stocked dressing-table, massive green ware and rows of glass shelves laden with toilet preparations. My private guest towel was laid out next to the slab of expensive soap.

Then I returned to the drawing-room, my sherry glass was filled and I settled down by the fire to listen to Mrs Pumphrey. It couldn't be called a conversation because she did all the talking, but I always found it rewarding.

Mrs Pumphrey was likeable, gave widely to charities and would help anybody in trouble. She was intelligent and amusing and had a lot of waffling charm; but most people have a blind spot and hers was Tricki Woo. The tales she told about her darling ranged far into the realms of fantasy and I waited eagerly for the next instalment.

'Oh Mr Herriot, I have the most exciting news. Tricki has a pen pal! Yes, he wrote a letter to the editor of *Doggy World* enclosing a donation, and told him that even though he was descended from a long line of Chinese emperors, he had decided to come down and mingle freely with the common dogs. He asked the editor to seek out a pen pal for him among the dogs he knew so that they could correspond to their mutual benefit. And for this purpose, Tricki said he would adopt the name of Mr Utterbunkum. And, do you know, he received the most beautiful letter from the editor' (I could imagine the sensible man leaping upon this potential gold mine) 'who said he would like to introduce Bonzo Fotheringham, a lonely Dalmation who would be delighted to exchange letters with a new friend in Yorkshire.'

I sipped the sherry. Tricki snored on my lap. Mrs Pumphrey went on.

'But I'm so disappointed about the new summerhouse – you know I got it specially for Tricki so we could sit out together on warm afternoons. It's such a nice little rustic shelter, but he's taken a passionate dislike to it. Simply loathes it – absolutely refuses to go inside. You should see the dreadful expression on his face when he looks at it. And do you know what he called it yesterday? Oh, I hardly dare tell you.' She looked around the room before leaning over and whispering: 'He called it "the bloody hut"!'

The maid struck fresh life into the fire and refilled my glass. The wind hurled a handful of sleet against the window. This, I thought, was the life. I listened for more.

'And did I tell you, Mr Herriot, Tricki had another good win yesterday? You know, I'm sure he must study the racing columns, he's such a tremendous judge of form. Well, he told me to back Canny Lad in the three o'clock at Redcar yesterday and, as usual, it won. He put on a shilling each way and got back nine shillings.'

These bets were always placed in the name of Tricki Woo and I thought with compassion of the reactions of the local bookies. The Darrowby turf accountants were a harassed and fugitive body of men. A board would appear at the end of some alley urging the population to invest with Joe Downs and enjoy perfect security. Joe would live for a few months on a knife-edge while he pitted his wits against the knowledgeable citizens, but the end was always the same; a few favourites would win in a row and Joe would be gone in the night, taking his board with him. Once I had asked a local inhabitant about the sudden departure of one of these luckless nomads. He replied unemotionally: 'Oh, we brok 'im.'

Losing a regular flow of shillings to a dog must have been a heavy cross for these unfortunate men to bear.

'I had such a frightening experience last week,' Mrs Pumphrey continued. 'I was sure I would have to call you out. Poor little Tricki – he went completely crackerdog!'

I mentally lined this up with flop-bott among the new canine diseases and asked for more information.

'It was awful. I was terrified. The gardener was throwing rings for Tricki – you know he does this for half an hour every day.' I had witnessed this spectacle several times. Hodgkin, a dour, bent old Yorkshireman who looked as though he hated all dogs and Tricki in particular, had to go out on the lawn every day and throw little rubber rings over and over again. Tricki bounded after them and brought them back, barking madly till the process was repeated. The bitter lines on the old man's face deepened as the game progressed. His lips moved continually, but it was impossible to hear what he was saying.

Mrs Pumphrey went on: 'Well, he was playing his game, and he does adore it so, when suddenly, without warning, he went crackerdog. He forgot all about his rings and began to run around in circles, barking and yelping in such a strange way. Then he fell over on his side and lay like a little dead thing. Do you know, Mr Herriot, I really though he was dead, he lay so perfectly still. And what hurt me most was that Hodgkin began to laugh. He has been with me for twenty-four years and I have never even seen him smile, and yet, when he looked down at that still form, he broke into a queer, high-pitched cackle. It was horrid. I was just going to rush to the telephone when Tricki got up and walked away – he seemed perfectly normal.'

Hysteria, I thought, brought on by wrong feeding and over-excitement. I put down my glass and fixed Mrs Pumphrey with a severe glare. 'Now look, this is just what I was talking about. If you persist in feeding all that fancy rubbish to Tricki you are going to ruin his health. You really must get him onto a sensible dog diet of one or, at the most, two small meals a day of meat and brown bread or a little biscuit. And nothing in between.'

Mrs Pumphrey shrank into her chair, a picture of abject guilt. 'Oh, please don't speak to me like that. I do try to give him the right things, but it is so difficult. When he begs for his little titbits, I can't refuse him.' She dabbed her eyes with a handkerchief.

But I was unrelenting. 'All right, Mrs Pumphrey, it's up to you, but I warn you that if you go on as you are doing, Tricki will go crackerdog more and more often.'

I left the cosy haven with reluctance, pausing on the gravelled drive to look back at Mrs Pumphrey waving and Tricki, as always, standing against the window, his widemouthed face apparently in the middle of a hearty laugh.

Driving home, I mused on the many advantages of being Tricki's uncle. When he went to the seaside he sent me boxes of oak-smoked kippers; and when the tomatoes ripened in his greenhouse, he sent a pound or two every week. Tins of tobacco arrived regularly, sometimes with a photograph carrying a loving inscription.

But it was when the Christmas hamper arrived from Fortnum and Mason's that I decided that I was on a really good thing which should be helped along a bit. Hitherto, I had merely rung up and thanked Mrs Pumphrey for the gifts, and she had been rather cool, pointing out that it was Tricki who had sent the things and he was the one who should be thanked.

With the arrival of the hamper it came to me, blindingly, that I had been guilty of a grave error of tactics. I set myself to compose a letter to Tricki. Avoiding Siegfried's sardonic eye, I thanked my doggy nephew for his Christmas gifts and for all his generosity in the past. I expressed my sincere hopes that the festive fare had not upset his delicate digestion and suggested that if he did experience any discomfort he should have recourse to the black powder his uncle always prescribed. A vague feeling of professional shame was easily swamped by floating visions of kippers, tomatoes and hampers. I addressed the envelope to Master Tricki Pumphrey, Barlby Grange and slipped it into the post-box with only a slight feeling of guilt.

On my next visit, Mrs Pumphrey drew me to one side. 'Mr Herriot,' she whispered, 'Tricki adored your charming letter and he will keep it always, but he was very put out about one thing – you addressed it to Master Tricki and he does insist upon Mister. He was dreadfully affronted at first, quite beside himself, but when he saw it was from you he soon recovered his good temper. I can't think why he should have these little prejudices. Perhaps it is because he is an only dog – I do think an only dog develops more prejudices than one from a large family.'

Entering Skeldale House was like returning to a colder world. Siegfried bumped into me in the passage. 'Ah, who have we here? Why I do believe it's dear Uncle Herriot. And what have you been doing, Uncle? Slaving away at Barlby Grange, I expect. Poor fellow, you must be tired out. Do you really think it's worth it, working your fingers to the bone for another hamper?'

CHAPTER 14

Looking back, I can scarcely believe we used to spend all those hours in making up medicines. But our drugs didn't come to us in proprietary packages and before we could get out on the road we had to fill our cars with a wide variety of carefully compounded and largely useless remedies.

When Siegfried came upon me that morning I was holding a twelve-ounce bottle at eye level while I poured syrup of coccilana into it. Tristan was moodily mixing stomach powders with a mortar and pestle and he stepped up his speed of stroke when he saw his brother's eye on him. He was surrounded by packets of the powder and, further along the bench, were orderly piles of pessaries which he had made by filling cellophane cylinders with boric acid.

Tristan looked industrious; his elbow jogged furiously as he ground away at the ammon carb and nux vomica. Siegfried smiled benevolently.

I smiled too. I felt the strain badly when the brothers were at variance, but I could see that this was going to be one of the happy mornings. There had been a distinct improvement in the atmosphere since Christmas when Tristan had slipped casually back to college and, apparently without having done any work, had re-sat and passed his exams. And there was something else about my boss today; he seemed to glow with inner satisfaction as though he knew for certain that something good was on the way. He came in and closed the door.

'I've got a bit of good news.'

I screwed the cork into the bottle. 'Well, don't keep us in suspense. Let's have it.'

Siegfried looked from one of us to the other. He was almost smirking. 'You remember that bloody awful shambles when Tristan took charge of the bills?'

His brother looked away and began to grind still faster, but Siegfried laid a friendly hand on his shoulder. 'No, don't worry, I'm not going to ask you to do it again. In fact, you'll never have to do it again because, from now on, the job will be done by an expert.' He paused and cleared his throat. 'We're going to have a secretary.'

As we stared blankly at him he went on. 'Yes, I picked her myself and I consider she's perfect.'

'Well, what's she like?' I asked.

Siegfried pursed his lips. 'It's difficult to describe her. But just think – what do we want here? We don't want some flighty young thing hanging about the place. We don't want a pretty little blonde sitting behind that desk powdering her nose and making eyes at everybody.'

'We don't?' Tristan interrupted, plainly puzzled.

'No, we don't!' Siegfried rounded on him. 'She'd be daydreaming about her boy friends half the time and just when we'd got her trained to our ways she'd be running off to get married.'

Tristan still looked unconvinced and it seemed to exasperate his brother. Siegfried's face reddened. 'And there's another thing. How could we have an attractive young girl in here with somebody like you in the house. You'd never leave her alone.'

Tristan was nettled. 'How about you?'

'I'm talking about you, not me!' Siegfried roared. I closed my eyes. The peace hadn't lasted long. I decided to cut in. 'All right, tell us about the new secretary.'

With an effort, he mastered his emotion. 'Well, she's in her fifties and she has retired after thirty years with Green and Moulton in Bradford. She was company secretary there and I've had the most wonderful reference from the firm. They say she is a model of efficiency and that's what we want in this practice – efficiency. We're far too slack. It's just a stroke of luck for us that she decided to come and live in Darrowby. Anyway, you'll be able to meet her in a few minutes – she's coming at ten o'clock this morning.'

The church clock was chiming when the door bell rang. Siegfried hastened out to answer it and led his great discovery into the room in triumph. 'Gentlemen, I want you to meet Miss Harbottle.'

She was a big, high-bosomed woman with a round healthy face and gold-rimmed spectacles. A mass of curls, incongruous and very dark, peeped from under her hat; they looked as if they might be dyed and they didn't go with her severe clothes and brogue shoes.

It occurred to me that we wouldn't have to worry about her rushing off to get married. It wasn't that she was ugly, but she had a jutting chin and an air of effortless command that would send any man running for his life.

I shook hands and was astonished at the power of Miss Harbottle's grip. We looked into each other's eyes and had a friendly trial of strength for a few seconds, thcn she seemed happy to call it a draw and turned away. Tristan was entirely unprepared and a look of alarm spread over his face as his hand was engulfed; he was released only when his knees started to buckle.

She began a tour of the office while Siegfried hovered behind her, rubbing his hands and looking like a shopwalker with his favourite customer. She paused at the desk, heaped high with incoming and outgoing bills, Ministry of Agriculture forms, circulars from drug firms with here and there stray boxes of pills and tubes of udder ointment.

Stirring distastefully among the mess, she extracted the dog-eared old ledger and held it up between finger and thumb. 'What's this?'

Siegfried trotted forward. 'Oh, that's our ledger. We enter the visits into it from our day book which is here somewhere.' He scrabbled about on the desk. 'Ah, here it is. This is where we write the calls as they come in.'

She studied the two books for a few minutes with an expression of amazement which gave way to a grim humour. 'You gentlemen will have to learn to write if I am going to look after your books. There are three different hands here, but this one is by far the worst. Quite dreadful. Whose is it?'

She pointed to an entry which consisted of a long, broken line with an occasional undulation.

'That's mine, actually,' said Siegfried, shuffling his feet. 'Must have been in a hurry that day.'

'But it's all like that, Mr Farnon. Look here and here and here. It won't do, you know.'

Siegfried put his hands behind his back and hung his head.

'I expect you keep your stationery and envelopes in here.' She pulled open a drawer in the desk. It appeared to be filled entirely with old seed packets, many of which had burst open. A few peas and french beans rolled gently from the top of the heap. The next drawer was crammed tightly with soiled calving ropes which somebody had forgotten to wash. They didn't smell so good and Miss Harbottle drew back hurriedly; but she was not easily deterred and tugged hopefully at the third drawer. It came open with a musical clinking and she looked down on a dusty row of empty pale ale bottles.

She straightened up slowly and spoke patiently. 'And where, may I ask, is your cash box?'

'Well, we just stuff it in there, you know.' Siegfried pointed to the pint pot on the corner of the mantelpiece. 'Haven't got what you'd call a proper cash box, but this does the job all right.'

Miss Harbottle looked at the pot with horror. 'You just stuff ...' Crumpled cheques and notes peeped over the brim at her; many of their companions had burst out onto the hearth below. 'And you mean to say that you go out and leave that money there day after day?'

'Never seems to come to any harm,' Siegfried replied.

'And how about your petty cash?'

Siegfried gave an uneasy giggle. 'All in there, you know. All cash – petty and otherwise.'

Miss Harbottle's ruddy face had lost some of its colour.' Really, Mr Farnon, this is too bad. I don't know how you have gone on so long like this. I simply do not know. However, I'm confident I will be able to straighten things out very soon. There is obviously nothing complicated about your business – a simple card-index system would be the thing for your accounts. The other little things,' – she glanced back unbelieving at the pot – 'I will put right very quickly.'

'Fine, Miss Harbottle fine.' Siegfried was rubbing his hands harder than ever. 'We'll expect you on Monday morning.'

'Nine o'clock sharp, Mr Farnon.'

After she had gone there was a silence. Tristan had enjoyed her visit and was smiling thoughtfully, but I felt uncertain.

'You know, Siegfried,' I said, 'maybe she is a demon of efficiency but isn't she just a bit tough?'

'Tough?' Siegfried gave a loud, rather cracked laugh. 'Not a bit of it. You leave her to me. I can handle her.'

CHAPTER 15

There was little furniture in the dining-room but the noble lines and the very size of the place lent grace to the long sideboard and the modest mahogany table where Tristan and I sat at breakfast.

The single large window was patterned with frost and in the street outside, the footsteps of the passers-by crunched in the crisp snow. I looked up from my boiled egg as a car drew up. There was a stamping in the porch, the outer door banged shut and Siegfried burst into the room. Without a word he made for the fire and hung over it, leaning his elbows on the grey marble mantelpiece. He was muffled almost to the eyes in greatcoat and scarf but what you could see of his face was purplish blue.

He turned a pair of streaming eyes to the table. 'A milk fever up at old Heseltine's. One of the high buildings. God, it was cold up there. I could hardly breathe.'

As he pulled off his gloves and shook his numbed fingers in front of the flames, he darted sidelong glances at his brother. Tristan's chair was nearest the fire and he was enjoying his breakfast as he enjoyed everything, slapping the butter happily onto his toast and whistling as he applied the marmalade. His *Daily Mirror* was balanced against the coffee pot. You could almost see the waves of comfort and contentment coming from him.

Siegfried dragged himself unwillingly from the fire and dropped into the chair. 'I'll just have a cup of coffee, James. Heseltine was very kind – asked me to sit down and have breakfast with him. He gave me a lovely slice of home-fed bacon – a bit fat, maybe, but what a flavour! I can taste it now.'

He put down his cup with a clatter. 'You know, there's no reason why we should have to go to the grocer for our bacon and eggs. There's a perfectly good hen house at the bottom of the garden and a pig sty in the yard with a boiler for the swill. All our household waste could go towards feeding a pig. We'd probably do it quite cheaply.'

He rounded on Tristan who had just lit a Woodbine and was shaking out his *Mirror* with the air of ineffable pleasure which was peculiar to him. 'And it would be a useful job for you. You're not producing much sitting around here on your arse all day. A bit of stock keeping would do you good.'

Tristan put down his paper as though the charm had gone out of it. 'Stock keeping? Well, I feed your mare as it is.' He didn't enjoy looking after Siegfried's new hunter because every time he turned her out to water in the yard she would take a playful kick at him in passing.

Siegfried jumped up. 'I know you do, and it doesn't take all day, does it? It won't kill you to take on the hens and pigs.'

'Pigs?' Tristan looked startled. 'I thought you said pig?'

'Yes, pigs. I've just been thinking. If I buy a litter of weaners we can sell the others and keep one for ourselves. Won't cost a thing that way.'

'Not with free labour, certainly.'

'Labour? Labour? You don't know what it means! Look at you lying back there puffing your head off. You smoke too many of those bloody cigarettes!'

'So do you.'

'Never mind me, I'm talking about you!' Siegfried shouted.

I got up from the table with a sigh. Another day had begun.

·   ·   ·

When Siegfried got an idea he didn't muck about. Immediate action was his watchword. Within forty-eight hours a litter of ten little pigs had taken up residence in the sty and twelve Light Sussex pullets were pecking about behind the wire of the hen house. He was particularly pleased with the pullets. 'Look at them, James; just on point of lay and a very good strain, too. There'll be just a trickle of eggs at first, but once they get cracking we'll be snowed under. Nothing like a nice fresh egg warm from the nest.'

It was plain from the first that Tristan didn't share his brother's enthusiasm for the hens. I often found him hanging about outside the hen house, looking bored and occasionally throwing bread crusts over the wire. There was no evidence of the regular feeding, the balanced diet recommended by the experts. As egg producers, the hens held no appeal for him, but he did become mildly interested in them as personalities. An odd way of clucking, a peculiarity in gait – these things amused him.

But there were no eggs and as the weeks passed, Siegfried became increasingly irritable. 'Wait till I see the chap that sold me those hens. Damned scoundrel. Good laying strain my foot!' It was pathetic to see him anxiously exploring the empty nesting boxes every morning.

One afternoon, I was going down the garden when Tristan called to me. 'Come over here, Jim. This is something new. I bet you've never seen anything like it before.' He pointed upwards and I saw a group of unusually coloured large birds perched in the branches of the elms. There were more of them in the neighbour's apple trees.

I stared in astonishment. 'You're right, I've never seen anything like them. What are they?'

'Oh, come on,' said Tristan, grinning in delight, 'surely there's something familiar about them. Take another look.'

I peered upwards again. 'No, I've never seen birds as big as that and with such exotic plumage. What is it – a freak migration?'

Tristan gave a shout of laughter. 'They're our hens!'

'How the devil did they get up there?'

'They've left home. Hopped it.'

'But I can only see seven. Where are the rest of them?'

'God knows. Let's have a look over the wall.'

The crumbling mortar gave plenty of toe-holds between the bricks and we looked down into the next garden. The other five hens were there, pecking contentedly among some cabbages.

It took a long time to get them all back into the hen house and the tedious business had to be repeated several times a day thereafter. For the hens had clearly grown tired of life under Tristan and decided that they would do better living off the country. They became nomads, ranging even further afield in their search for sustenance.

At first the neighbours chuckled. They phoned to say their children were rounding up the hens and would we come and get them; but with the passage of time their jocularity wore thin. Finally Siegfried was involved in some painful interviews. His hens, he was told, were an unmitigated nuisance.

It was after one particularly unpleasant session that Siegfried decided that the hens must go. It was a bitter blow and as usual he vented his fury on Tristan. 'I must have been mad to think that any hens under your care would ever lay eggs. But really, isn't it just a bit hard? I give you this simple little job and one would have thought that even you would be hard put to it to make a mess of it. But look at the situation after only three weeks. Not one solitary egg have we seen. The bloody hens are flying about the countryside like pigeons. We are permanently estranged from our neighbours. You've done a thorough job haven't you?' All the frustrated egg producer in Siegfried welled out in his shrill tones.

Tristan's expression registered only wounded virtue, but he was rash enough to try to defend himself. 'You know, I thought there was something queer about those hens from the start,' he muttered.

Siegfried shed the last vestiges of his self-control. 'Queer!' he yelled wildly. 'You're the one that's queer, not the poor bloody hens. You're the queerest bugger there is. For God's sake get out – get out of my sight!'

Tristan withdrew with quiet dignity.

It took some time for the last echoes of the poultry venture to die away but after a fortnight, sitting again at the dining-table with Tristan, I felt sure that all was forgotten. So that it was with a strange sense of the workings of fate that I saw Siegfried stride into the room and lean menacingly over his brother. 'You remember those hens, I suppose,' he said almost in a whisper, 'you'll recall that I gave them away to Mrs Dale, that old-aged pensioner down Brown's Yard. Well, I've just been speaking to her. She's delighted with them. Gives them a hot mash night and morning and she's collecting ten eggs a day.'His voice rose almost to a scream. 'Ten eggs, do you hear, ten eggs!'

I hurriedly swallowed the last of my tea and excused myself. I trotted along the passage out the back door and up the garden to my car. On the way I passed the empty hen house. It had a forlorn look. It was a long way to the dining-room but I could still hear Siegfried.

CHAPTER 16

'Jim! Come over here and look at these little beggars.' Tristan laughed excitedly as he leaned over the door of the pig sty.

I walked across the yard. 'What is it?'

'I've just given them their swill and it's a bit hot. Just look at them!'

The little pigs were seizing the food, dropping it and walking suspiciously round it. Then they would creep up, touch the hot potatoes with their muzzles and leap back in alarm. There was none of the usual meal-time slobbering; just a puzzled grunting.

Right from the start Tristan had found the pigs more interesting than the hens which was a good thing because he had to retrieve himself after the poultry disaster. He spent a lot of time in the yard, sometimes feeding or mucking out but more often resting his elbows on the door watching his charges.

As with the hens, he was more interested in their characters than their ability to produce pork or bacon. After he poured the swill into the long trough he always watched, entranced, while the pigs made their first rush. Soon, in the desperate gobbling there would be signs of uneasiness. The tiny animals would begin to glance sideways till their urge to find out what their mates were enjoying so much became unbearable; they would start to change position frantically, climbing over each other's backs and falling into the swill.

Old Boardman was a willing collaborator, but mainly in an advisory capacity. Like all countrymen he considered he knew all about the husbandry and diseases of animals and, it turned out, pigs were his speciality. There were long conferences in the dark room under the Bairnsfather cartoons and the old man grew animated over his descriptions of the vast, beautiful animals he had reared in that very sty.

Tristan listened with respect because he had solid proof of Boardman's expertise in the way he handled the old brick boiler. Tristan could light the thing but it went out if he turned his back on it; but it was docile in Boardman's hands. I often saw Tristan listening wonderingly to the steady blub-blub while the old man rambled on and the delicious scent of cooking pig potatoes drifted over them both.

But no animal converts food more quickly into flesh than a pig and as the weeks passed the little pink creatures changed with alarming speed into ten solid, no-nonsense porkers. Their characters deteriorated, too. They lost all their charm. Meal-times stopped being fun and became a battle with the odds growing heavier against Tristan all the time.

I could see that it brought a lot of colour into old Boardman's life and he always dropped whatever he was doing when he saw Tristan scooping the swill from the boiler.

He obviously enjoyed watching the daily contest from his seat on the stone trough. Tristan bracing himself, listening to the pigs squealing at the rattle of the bucket; giving a few fearsome shouts to encourage himself then shooting the bolt and plunging among the grunting, jostling animals; broad, greedy snouts forcing into the bucket, sharp feet grinding his toes, heavy bodies thrusting against his legs.

I couldn't help smiling when I remembered the light-hearted game it used to be. There was no laughter now. Tristan finally took to brandishing a heavy stick at the pigs before he dared to go in. Once inside his only hope of staying on his feet was to clear a little space by beating on the backs.

. . .

It was on a market day when the pigs had almost reached bacon weight that I came upon Tristan sprawled in his favourite chair. But there was something unusual about him; he wasn't asleep, no medicine bottle, no Woodbines, no *Daily Mirror*. His arms hung limply over the sides of the chair, his eyes were half closed and sweat glistened on his forehead.

'Jim,' he whispered. 'I've had the most hellish afternoon I've ever had in my life.'

I was alarmed at his appearance. 'What's happened.'

'The pigs,' he croaked. 'They escaped today.'

'Escaped! How the devil could they do that?'

Tristan tugged at his hair. 'It was when I was feeding the mare. I gave

her her hay and thought I might as well feed the pigs at the same time.
You know what they've been like lately – well, today they went berserk.
Soon as I opened the door they charged out in a solid block. Sent me up
in the air, bucket and all, then ran over the top of me.' He shuddered and
looked up at me wide-eyed. 'I'll tell you this, Jim, when I was lying there
on the cobbles, covered with swill and that lot trampling on me, I
thought it was all over. But they didn't savage me. They belted out
through the yard door at full gallop.'

'The yard door was open then?'

'Too true it was. I would just choose this one day to leave it open.'

Tristan sat up and wrung his hands. 'Well, you know, I thought it was
all right at first. You see, they slowed down when they got into the lane
and trotted quietly round into the front street with Boardman and I
hard on their heels. They formed a group there. Didn't seem to know
where to go next. I was sure we were going to be able to head them off,
but just then one of them caught sight of itself in Robson's shop window.'

He gave a remarkable impression of a pig staring at its reflection for a
few moments then leaping back with a startled grunt.

'Well, that did it, Jim. The bloody animal panicked and shot off into
the market place at about fifty miles an hour with the rest after it.'

I gasped. Ten large pigs loose among the packed stalls and market-
day crowds was difficult even to imagine.

'Oh God, you should have seen it.' Tristan fell back wearily into his
chair. 'Women and kids screaming. The stall holders, police and
everybody else cursing me. There was a terrific traffic jam too – miles of
cars tooting like hell while the policeman on point duty concentrated on
browbeating me.' He wiped his brow. 'You know that fast-talking
merchant on the china stall – well, today I saw him at a loss for words.
He was balancing a cup on his palm and in full cry when one of the pigs
got its fore feet on his stall and stared him straight in the face. He stopped
as if he'd been shot. Any other time it would have been funny but I
thought the perishing animal was going to wreck the stall. The counter
was beginning to rock when the pig changed its mind and made
off.'

'What's the position now?' I asked. 'Have you got them back?'

'I've got nine of them back,' Tristan replied, leaning back and closing
his eyes. 'With the help of almost the entire male population of the
district I've got nine of them back. The tenth was last seen heading north
at a good pace. God knows where it is now. Oh, I didn't tell you – one of
them got into the post office. Spent quite some time in there.' He put his
hands over his face. 'I'm for it this time, Jim. I'll be in the hands of the
law after this lot. There's no doubt about it.'

I leant over and slapped his leg. 'Oh, I shouldn't worry. I don't suppose there's been any serious damage done.'

Tristan replied with a groan. 'But there's something else. When I finally closed the door after getting the pigs back in their sty I was on the verge of collapse. I was leaning against the wall gasping for breath when I saw the mare had gone. Yes, gone. I'd gone straight out after the pigs and forgot to close her box. I don't know where she is. Boardman said he'd look around – I haven't the strength.'

Tristan lit a trembling Woodbine. 'This is the end, Jim. Siegfried will have no mercy this time.'

As he spoke, the door flew open and his brother rushed in. 'What the hell is going on?' he roared. 'I've just been speaking to the vicar and he says my mare is in his garden eating his wallflowers. He's hopping mad and I don't blame him. Go on, you lazy scoundrel. Don't lie there, get over to the vicarage this instant and bring her back!'

Tristan did not stir. He lay inert, looking up at his brother. His lips moved feebly.

'No,' he said.

'What's that?' Siegfried shouted incredulously. 'Get out of that chair immediately. Go and get that mare!'

'No,' replied Tristan.

I felt a chill of horror. This sort of mutiny was unprecedented. Siegfried had gone very red in the face and I steeled myself for an eruption; but it was Tristan who spoke.

'If you want your mare you can get her yourself.' His voice was quiet with no note of defiance. He had the air of a man to whom the future is of no account.

Even Siegfried could see that this was one time when Tristan had had enough. After glaring down at his brother for a few seconds he turned and walked. He got the mare himself.

Nothing more was said about the incident but the pigs were moved hurriedly to the bacon factory and were never replaced. The stock-keeping project was at an end.

CHAPTER 17

When I came in, Miss Harbottle was sitting, head bowed, over the empty cash box; she looked bereaved. It was a new, shiny, black box with the words 'Petty Cash' printed on top in white letters. Inside was a red book with the incomings and outgoings recorded in neat columns. But there was no money.

Miss Harbottle's sturdy shoulders sagged. She listlessly took up the red book between finger and thumb and a lonely sixpence rolled from between its pages and tinkled into the box. 'He's been at it again,' she whispered.

A stealthy footstep sounded in the passage. 'Mr Farnon!' she called out. And to me: 'It's really absurd the way the man always tries to slink past the door.'

Siegfried shuffled in. He was carrying a stomach tube and pump, calcium bottles bulged from his jacket pockets and a bloodless castrator dangled from the other hand.

He smiled cheerfully but I could see he was uncomfortable, not only because of the load he carried, but because of his poor tactical position. Miss Harbottle had arranged her desk across the corner diagonally opposite the door and he had to walk across a long stretch of carpet to reach her. From her point of view it was strategically perfect. From her corner she could see every inch of the big room, into the passage when the door was open and out onto the front street from the window on her left. Nothing escaped her – it was a position of power.

Siegfried looked down at the square figure behind the desk. 'Good morning, Miss Harbottle, can I do anything for you?'

The grey eyes glinted behind the gold-rimmed spectacles. 'You can, indeed, Mr Farnon. You can explain why you have once more emptied my petty-cash box.'

'Oh, I'm so sorry. I had to rush through to Brawton last night and I found myself a bit short. There was really nowhere else to turn to.'

'But Mr Farnon, in the two months I have been here, we must have been over this a dozen times. What is the good of my trying to keep an accurate record of the money in the practice if you keep stealing it and spending it?'

'Well, I suppose I got into the habit in the old pint-pot days. It wasn't a bad system, really.'

'It wasn't a system at all. It was anarchy. You cannot run a business that way. But I've told you this so many times and each time you have promised to alter your ways. I feel almost at my wits' end.'

'Oh, never mind, Miss Harbottle. Get some more out of the bank and put it in your box. That'll put it right.' Siegfried gathered up the loose coils of the stomach tube from the floor and turned to go, but Miss Harbottle cleared her throat warningly.

'There are one or two other matters. Will you please try to keep your other promise to enter your visits in the book every day and to price them as you do so. Nearly a week has gone by since you wrote anything in. How can I possibly get the bills out on the first of the month? This is most important, but how do you expect me to do it when you impede me like this?'

'Yes, yes, I'm sorry, but I have a string of calls waiting. I really must go.' He was half-way across the floor and the tube was uncoiling itself again when he heard the ominous throat clearing behind him.

'And one more thing, Mr Farnon. I still can't decipher your writing. These medical terms are difficult enough, so please take a little care and don't scribble.'

'Very well, Miss Harbottle.' He quickened his pace through the door and into the passage where, it seemed, was safety and peace. He was clattering thankfully over the tiles when the familiar rumbling reached him. She could project that sound a surprising distance by giving it a bit of extra pressure, and it was a summons which had to be obeyed. I could hear him wearily putting the tube and pump on the floor; the calcium bottles must have been digging into his ribs because I heard them go down too.

He presented himself again before the desk. Miss Harbottle wagged a finger at him. 'While I have you here I'd like to mention another point which troubles me. Look at this day book. You see all these slips sticking out of the pages? They are all queries – there must be scores of them – and I am at a standstill until you clear them for me. When I ask you you never have the time. Can you go over them with me now?'

Siegfried backed away hurriedly. 'No, no, not just now. As I said, I have some urgent calls waiting. I'm very sorry but it will have to be some other time. First chance I get I'll come in and see you.' He felt the door behind him and with a last glance at the massive, disapproving figure behind the desk, he turned and fled.

CHAPTER 18

I could look back now on six months of hard practical experience. I had treated cows, horses, pigs, dogs and cats seven days a week; in the morning, afternoon, evening and through the hours when the world was asleep. I had calved cows and farrowed sows till my arms ached and the skin peeled off. I had been knocked down, trampled on and sprayed liberally with every kind of muck. I had seen a fair cross-section of the diseases of animals. And yet a little voice had begun to niggle at the back of my mind; it said I knew nothing, nothing at all.

This was strange, because those six months had been built upon five years of theory; a slow, painful assimilation of thousands of facts and a careful storage of fragments of knowledge like a squirrel with its nuts. Beginning with the study of plants and the lowest forms of life, working up to dissection in the anatomy lab and physiology and the vast, soulless territory of *materia medica*. Then pathology which tore down the curtain of ignorance and let me look for the first time into the deep secrets. And parasitology, the teeming other world of the worms and fleas and mange mites. Finally, medicine and surgery, the crystallization of my learning and its application to the everyday troubles of animals.

And there were many others, like physics, chemistry, hygiene; they didn't seem to have missed a thing. Why then should I feel I knew nothing? Why had I begun to feel like an astronomer looking through a telescope at an unknown galaxy? This sensation that I was only groping about on the fringes of limitless space was depressing. It was a funny thing, because everybody else seemed to know all about sick animals. The chap who held the cow's tail, the neighbour from the next farm, men in pubs, jobbing gardeners; they all knew and were free and confident with their advice.

I tried to think back over my life. Was there any time when I had felt this supreme faith in my own knowledge. And then I remembered.

I was back in Scotland, I was seventeen and I was walking under the arch of the Veterinary College into Montrose Street. I had been a student for three days but not until this afternoon had I felt the thrill of fulfilment. Messing about with botany and zoology was all right but this afternoon had been the real thing; I had had my first lecture in animal husbandry.

The subject had been the points of the horse. Professor Grant had hung up a life-size picture of a horse and gone over it from nose to tail, indicating the withers, the stifle, the hock, the poll and all the other rich, equine terms. And the professor had been wise; to make his lecture more interesting he kept throwing in little practical points like 'This is where we find curb,' or 'Here is the site for windgalls.' He talked of thorough-pins and sidebones, splints and quittor; things the students wouldn't learn about for another four years, but it brought it all to life.

The words were still spinning in my head as I walked slowly down the sloping street. This was what I had come for. I felt as though I had undergone an initiation and become a member of an exclusive club. I really knew about horses. And I was wearing a brand-new riding mac with all sorts of extra straps and buckles which slapped against my legs as I turned the corner of the hill into busy Newton Road.

I could hardly believe my luck when I saw the horse. It was standing

outside the library below Queen's Cross like something left over from
another age. It drooped dispiritedly between the shafts of a coal cart
which stood like an island in an eddying stream of cars and buses.
Pedestrians hurried by, uncaring, but I had the feeling that fortune was
smiling on me.

A horse. Not just a picture but a real, genuine horse. Stray words from
the lecture floated up into my mind; the pastern, cannon bone, coronet
and all those markings – snip, blaze, white sock near hind. I stood on the
pavement and examined the animal critically.

I thought it must be obvious to every passer-by that here was a true
expert. Not just an inquisitive onlooker but a man who knew and
understood all. I felt clothed in a visible aura of horsiness.

I took a few steps up and down, hands deep in the pockets of the new
riding mac, eyes probing for possible shoeing faults or curbs or bog
spavins. So thorough was my inspection that I worked round to the
offside of the horse and stood perilously among the racing traffic.

I glanced around at the people hurrying past. Nobody seemed to care,
not even the horse. He was a large one, at least seventeen hands, and he
gazed apathetically down the street, easing his hind legs alternatively in
a bored manner. I hated to leave him but I had completed my
examination and it was time I was on my way. But I felt that I ought to
make a gesture before I left; something to communicate to the horse that
I understood his problems and that we belonged to the same
brotherhood. I stepped briskly forward and patted him on the neck.

Quick as a striking snake, the horse whipped downwards and seized
my shoulder in his great strong teeth. He laid back his ears, rolled his eyes
wickedly and hoisted me up, almost off my feet. I hung there helplessly,
suspended like a lopsided puppet. I wriggled and kicked but the teeth
were clamped immovably in the material of my coat.

There was no doubt about the interest of the passers-by now. The
grotesque sight of a man hanging from a horse's mouth brought them to a
sudden halt and a crowd formed with people looking over each other's
shoulders and others fighting at the back to see what was going on.

A horrified old lady was crying: 'Oh, poor boy! Help him, somebody!'
Some of the braver characters tried pulling at me but the horse
whickered ominously and hung on tighter. Conflicting advice was
shouted from all sides. With deep shame I saw two attractive girls in the
front row giggling helplessly.

Appalled at the absurdity of my position, I began to thrash about
wildly; my shirt collar tightened round my throat; a stream of the horse's
saliva trickled down the front of my mac. I could feel myself choking and
was giving up hope when a man pushed his way through the crowd.

He was very small. Angry eyes glared from a face blackened by coal dust. Two empty sacks were draped over an arm.

'Whit the hell's this?' he shouted. A dozen replies babbled in the air.

'Can ye no leave the bloody hoarse alone?' he yelled into my face. I made no reply, being pop-eyed, half throttled and in no mood for conversation.

The coalman turned his fury on the horse. 'Drop him, ya big bastard! Go on, let go, drop him!'

Getting no response he dug the animal viciously in the belly with his thumb. The horse took the point at once and released me like an obedient dog dropping a bone. I fell on my knees and ruminated in the gutter for a while till I could breathe more easily. As from a great distance I could still hear the little man shouting at me.

After some time I stood up. The coalman was still shouting and the crowd was listening appreciatively. 'Whit d'ye think you're playing at – keep yer hands off ma bloody hoarse – get the poliss tae ye.'

I looked down at my new mac. The shoulder was chewed to a sodden mass. I felt I must escape and began to edge my way through the crowd. Some of the faces were concerned but most were grinning. Once clear I started to walk away rapidly and as I turned the corner the last faint cry from the coalman reached me.

'Dinna meddle wi' things ye ken nuthin' aboot!'

CHAPTER 19

I flipped idly through the morning mail. The usual stack of bills, circulars, brightly coloured advertisements for new drugs; after a few months the novelty had worn off and I hardly bothered to read them. I had almost reached the bottom of the pile when I came on something different; an expensive-looking envelope in heavy, deckle-edged paper addressed to me personally. I ripped it open and pulled out a gilt-coloured card which I scanned quickly. I felt my face redden as I slipped the card into an inside pocket.

Siegfried finished ticking off the visits and looked up. 'What are you looking so guilty about, James? Your past catching up with you. What is it, anyway – a letter from an outraged mother?'

'Go on then,' I said sheepishly, pulling out the card and handing it to him, 'have a good laugh. I suppose you'd find out, anyway.'

Siegfried's face was expressionless as he read the card aloud. 'Tricki requests the pleasure of Uncle Herriot's company on Friday, February

5th. Drinks and dancing.' He looked up and spoke seriously. 'Now isn't that nice. You know, that must be one of the most generous Pekineses in England. Sending you kippers and tomatoes and hampers isn't enough – he has to ask you to his home for a party.'

I grabbed the card and slipped it out of sight. 'All right, all right, I know. But what am I supposed to do?'

'Do? What you do is to sit down right away and get a letter off saying thank you very much, you'll be there on February 5th. Mrs Pumphrey's parties are famous. Mountains of exotic food, rivers of champagne. Don't miss it whatever you do.'

'Will there be a lot of people there?' I asked, shuffling my feet.

Siegfried struck himself on the forehead with his open hand. 'Of course there'll be a lot of people. What d'you think. Did you expect it would be just you and Tricki? You'd have a few beers together and then you'd dance a slow foxtrot with him? The cream of the county will be there in full regalia but my guess is that there will be no more honoured guest than Uncle Herriot. Why? Because Mrs Pumphrey invited the others but Tricki invited you.'

'O.K., O.K.,' I groaned. 'I'll be on my own and I haven't got a proper evening suit. I don't fancy it.'

Siegfried rose and put a hand on my shoulder. 'My dear chap, don't mess about. Sit down and accept the invitation and then go into Brawton and hire a suit for the night. You won't be on your own for long – the debs will be tramping over each other for a dance with you.' He gave the shoulder a final pat before walking to the door. Before leaving he turned round and his expression was grave. 'And remember for Pete's sake don't write to Mrs Pumphrey. Address your letter to Tricki himself or you're sunk.'

· · · ·

I had a lot of mixed feelings churning around in me when I presented myself at the Pumphrey home on the night of February 5th. A maid let me into the hall and I could see Mrs Pumphrey at the entrance to the ballroom receiving her guests and beyond, an elegant throng standing around with drinks. There was a well-bred clamour, a general atmosphere of wealth. I straightened the tie on my hired outfit, took a deep breath and waited.

Mrs Pumphrey was smiling sweetly as she shook hands with the couple in front of me but when she saw me her face became radiant. 'Oh Mr Herriot, how nice of you to come. Tricki was so delighted to have your letter – in fact we really must go in and see him now.' She led me across the hall.

'He's in the morning-room,' she whispered. 'Between ourselves he finds these affairs rather a bore, but he'll be simply furious if I don't take you in for a moment.'

Tricki was curled up in an armchair by the side of a bright fire. When he saw me he jumped on the back of the chair barking in delight, his huge, laughing mouth bisecting his face. I was trying to fend off his attempts to lick my face when I caught sight of two large food bowls on the carpet. One contained about a pound of chopped chicken, the other a mass of crumbled cake.

'Mrs Pumphrey!' I thundered, pointing at the bowls. The poor woman put her hand to her mouth and shrank away from me.

'Oh do forgive me,' she wailed, her face a picture of guilt. 'It's just a special treat because he's alone tonight. And the weather is so cold, too.' She clasped her hands and looked at me abjectly.

'I'll forgive you,' I said sternly, 'if you will remove half the chicken and all the cake.'

Fluttering, like a little girl caught in naughtiness, she did as I said.

I parted regretfully from the little Peke. It had been a busy day and I was sleepy from the hours in the biting cold. The room with its fire and soft lighting looked more inviting than the noisy glitter of the ballroom and I would have preferred to curl up here with Tricki on my knee for an hour or two.

Mrs Pumphrey became brisk. 'Now you must come and meet some of my friends.' We went into the ballroom where light blazed down from three cut-glass chandeliers and was reflected dazzlingly from the cream-and-gold, many-mirrored walls. We moved from group to group as Mrs Pumphrey introduced me and I squirmed in embarrassment as I heard myself described as 'Tricki's dear kind uncle'. But either they were people of superb self-control or they were familiar with their hostess's blind spot because the information was received with complete gravity.

Along one wall a five-piece orchestra was tuning up; white-jacketed waiters hurried among the guests with trays of food and drinks. Mrs Pumphrey stopped one of the waiters. 'François, some champagne for this gentleman.'

'Yes, Madame.' The waiter proffered his tray.

'No, no, no, not those. One of the big glasses.'

François hurried away and returned with something like a soup plate with a stem. It was brimming with champagne.

'François.'

'Yes, Madame?'

'This is Mr Herriot. I want you to take a good look at him.'

The waiter turned a pair of sad, spaniel eyes on me and drank me in for a few moments.

'I want you to look after him. See that his glass is full and that he has plenty to eat.'

'Certainly, Madame.' He bowed and moved away.

I buried my face in the ice cold champagne and when I looked up, there was François holding out a tray of smoked salmon sandwiches.

It was like that all the evening. François seemed always to be at my elbow, filling up the enormous glass or pushing dainties at me. I found it delightful; the salty snacks brought on a thirst which I quenched with deep draughts of champagne, then I had more snacks which made me thirsty again and François would unfailingly pop up with the magnum.

It was the first time I had had the opportunity of drinking champagne by the pint and it was a rewarding experience. I was quickly aware of a glorious lightness, a heightening of the perceptions. I stopped being overawed by this new world and began to enjoy it. I danced with everybody in sight – sleek young beauties, elderly dowagers and twice with a giggling Mrs Pumphrey.

Or I just talked. And it was witty talk; I repeatedly amazed myself by my lightning shafts. Once I caught sight of myself in the mirror – a distinguished figure, glass in hand, the hired suit hanging on me with quiet grace. It took my breath away.

Eating, drinking, talking, dancing, the evening winged past. When it was time to go and I had my coat on and was shaking hands with Mrs Pumphrey in the hall, François appeared again with a bowl of hot soup. He seemed to be worried lest I grow faint on the journey home.

After the soup, Mrs Pumphrey said: 'And now you must come and say goodnight to Tricki. He'll never forgive you if you don't.' We went into his room and the little dog yawned from the depths of the chair and wagged his tail. Mrs Pumphrey put her hand on my sleeve. 'While you're here, I wonder if you would be so kind as to examine his claws. I've been so worried in case they might be growing too long.'

I lifted up the paws one by one and scrutinized the claws while Tricki lazily licked my hands. 'No, you needn't worry, they're perfectly all right.'

'Thank you so much, I'm so grateful to you. Now you must wash your hands.'

In the familiar bathroom with the sea-green basins and the enamelled fishes on the walls and the dressing-table and the bottles on the glass shelves, I looked around as the steaming water ran from the tap. There was my own towel by the basin and the usual new slab of soap – soap that lathered in an instant and gave off an expensive scent. It was the final touch of balm on a gracious evening. It had been a few hours of luxury and light and I carried the memory back with me to Skeldale House.

I got into bed, switched off the light and lay on my back looking up into the darkness. Snatches of music still tinkled about in my head and I was beginning to swim back to the ballroom when the phone rang.

'This is Atkinson of Beck Cottage,' a far-away voice said. 'I 'ave a sow 'ere what can't get pigged. She's been on all night. Will you come?'

I looked at the clock as I put down the receiver. It was 2 a.m. I felt numbed. A farrowing right on top of the champagne and the smoked salmon and those little biscuits with the black heaps of caviare. And at Beck Cottage, one of the most primitive smallholdings in the district. It wasn't fair.

Sleepily, I took off my pyjamas and pulled on my shirt. As I reached for the stiff, worn corduroys I used for work, I tried not to look at the hired suit hanging on a corner of the wardrobe.

I groped my way down the long garden to the garage. In the darkness of the yard I closed my eyes and the great chandeliers blazed again, the mirrors flashed and the music played.

It was only two miles out to Beck Cottage. It lay in a hollow and in the winter the place was a sea of mud. I left my car and squelched through the blackness to the door of the house. My knock was unanswered and I moved across to the cluster of buildings opposite and opened the half door into the byre. The warm, sweet bovine smell met me as I peered towards a light showing dimly at the far end where a figure was standing.

I went inside past the shadowy row of cows standing side by side with broken wooden partitions between them and past the mounds of manure piled behind them. Mr Atkinson didn't believe in mucking out too often.

Stumbling over the broken floor, splashing through pools of urine, I arrived at the end where a pen had been made by closing off a corner with a gate. I could just make out the form of a pig, pale in the gloom, lying on her side. There was a scanty bed of straw under her and she lay very still except for the trembling of her flanks. As I watched, she caught her breath and strained for a few seconds; then the straining began again.

Mr Atkinson received me without enthusiasm. He was middle-aged, sported a week's growth of beard and wore an ancient hat with a brim which flopped round his ears. He stood hunched against a wall, one hand deep in a ragged pocket, the other holding a bicycle lamp with a fast-failing battery.

'Is this all the light we've got?' I asked.

'Aye, it is,' Mr Atkinson replied, obviously surprised. He looked from the lamp to me with a 'what more does he want?' expression.

'Let's have it, then.' I trained the feeble beam on my patient. 'Just a young pig, isn't she?'

'Aye, nobbut a gilt. Fust litter.'

The pig strained again, shuddered and lay still.

'Something stuck there, I reckon,' I said. 'Will you bring me a bucket of hot water, some soap and a towel, please.'

'Haven't got no 'ot water. Fire's out.'

'O.K., bring me whatever you've got.'

The farmer clattered away down the byre taking the light with him and, with the darkness, the music came back again. It was a Strauss waltz and I was dancing with Lady Frenswick; she was young and very fair and she laughed as I swung her round. I could see her white shoulders and the diamonds winking at her throat and the wheeling mirrors.

Mr Atkinson came shuffling back and dumped a bucket of water on the floor. I dipped a finger in the water; it was ice cold. And the bucket had seen many hard years – I would have to watch my arms on that jagged rim.

Quickly stripping off jacket and shirt, I sucked in my breath as a villainous draught blew through a crack onto my back.

'Soap, please,' I said through clenched teeth.

'In t'bucket.'

I plunged an arm into the water, shivered, and felt my way round till I found a roundish object about the size of a golf ball. I pulled it out and examined it; it was hard and smooth and speckled like a pebble from the seashore and, optimistically, I began to rub it between my hands and up my arms, waiting for the lather to form. But the soap was impervious; it yielded nothing.

I discarded the idea of asking for another piece in case this would be construed as another complaint. Instead, I borrowed the light and tracked down the byre into the yard, the mud sucking at my wellingtons, goose-pimples rearing on my chest. I searched around in the car boot, listening to my teeth chattering, till I came on a jar of antiseptic lubricating cream.

Back in the pen, I smeared the cream on my arm, knelt behind the pig and gently inserted my hand into the vagina. I moved my hand forward and as wrist and elbow disappeared inside the pig I was forced to roll over on my side. The stones were cold and wet but I forgot my discomfort when my fingers touched something; it was a tiny tail. Almost a transverse presentation, biggish piglet stuck like a cork in a bottle.

Using one finger, I worked the hind legs back until I was able to grasp them and draw the piglet out. 'This is the one that's been causing the trouble. He's dead, I'm afraid – been squashed in there too long. But there could be some live ones still inside. I'll have another feel.'

I greased my arm and got down again. Just inside the os uteri, almost at arm's length, I found another piglet and I was feeling at the face when a set of minute but very sharp teeth sank into my finger.

I yelped and looked up at the farmer from my stony bed. 'This one's alive, anyway. I'll soon have him out.'

But the piglet had other ideas. He showed no desire to leave his warm haven and every time I got hold of his slippery little foot between my fingers he jerked it away. After a minute or two of this game I felt a cramping in my arm. I relaxed and lay back, my head resting on the cobbles, my arm still inside the pig. I closed my eyes and immediately I was back in the ballroom, in the warmth and the brilliant light. I was holding out my immense glass while François poured from the magnum; then I was dancing, close to the orchestra this time and the leader, beating time with one hand, turned round and smiled into my face; smiled and bowed as though he had been looking for me all his life.

I smiled back but the bandleader's face dissolved and there was only Mr Atkinson looking down at me expressionlessly, his unshaven jaw and shaggy eyebrows thrown into sinister relief by the light striking up from the bicycle lamp.

I shook myself and raised my cheek from the floor. This wouldn't do. Falling asleep on the job; either I was very tired or there was still some champagne in me. I reached again and grasped the foot firmly between two fingers and this time, despite his struggles, the piglet was hauled out into the world. Once arrived, he seemed to accept the situation and tottered round philosophically to his mother's udder.

'She's not helping at all,' I said. 'Been on so long that she's exhausted. I'm going to give her an injection.'

Another numbing expedition through the mud to the car, a shot of pituitrin into the gilt's thigh and within minutes the action began with powerful contractions of the uterus. There was no obstruction now and soon a wriggling pink piglet was deposited in the straw; then quite quickly another and another.

'Coming off the assembly line now, all right,' I said. Mr Atkinson grunted.

Eight piglets had been born and the light from the lamp had almost given out when a dark mass of afterbirth welled from the gilt's vulva.

I rubbed my cold arms. 'Well, I should say that's the lot now.' I felt suddenly chilled; I couldn't say how long I had been standing there looking at the wonder that never grew stale; the little pigs struggling onto their legs and making their way unguided to the long double row of teats; the mother with her first family easing herself over to expose as much as possible of her udder to the hungry mouths.

Better get dressed quickly. I had another try at the marble-like soap but it defeated me as easily as the first time. I wondered how long it had been in the family. Down my right side my cheek and ribs were caked with dirt and mucus. I did my best to scrape some off with my finger nails then I swilled myself down with the cold water from the bucket.

'Have you a towel there?' I gasped.

Mr Atkinson wordlessly handed me a sack. Its edges were stiff with old manure and it smelled musty from the meal it had long since contained. I took it and began to rub my chest and as the sour grains of the meal powdered my skin, the last bubbles of champagne left me, drifted up through the gaps in the tiles and burst sadly in the darkness beyond.

I dragged my shirt over my gritty back, feeling a sense of coming back to my own world. I buttoned my coat, picked up the syringe and the bottle of pituitrin and climbed out of the pen. I had a last look before I left. The bicycle lamp was shedding its final faint glow and I had to lean over the gate to see the row of little pigs sucking busily, utterly absorbed. The gilt carefully shifted her position and grunted. It was a grunt of deep content.

Yes, I was back and it was all right. I drove through the mud and up the hill where I had to get out to open a gate and the wind, with the cold, clean smell of the frosty grass in it caught at my face. I stood for a while looking across the dark fields, thinking of the night which was ending now. My mind went back to my schooldays and an old gentleman talking to the class about careers. He had said: 'If you decide to become a veterinary surgeon you will never grow rich but you will have a life of endless interest and variety.'

I laughed aloud in the darkness and as I got into the car I was still chuckling. That old chap certainly wasn't kidding. Variety. That was it – variety.

CHAPTER 20

As I checked my list of calls it occurred to me that, this time, Siegfried didn't look so much like a schoolboy as he faced Miss Harbottle. For one thing, he hadn't marched straight in and stood in front of the desk; that was disastrous and he always looked beaten before he started. Instead, he had veered off over the last few yards till he stood with his back to the window. This way she had to turn her head slightly to face him and besides, he had the light at his back.

He thrust his hands into his pockets and leant back against the window-frame. He was wearing his patient look, his eyes were kind and his face was illumined by an almost saintly smile. Miss Harbottle's eyes narrowed.

'I just wanted a word with you, Miss Harbottle. One or two little points I'd like to discuss. First, about your petty-cash box. It's a nice box and I think you were quite right to institute it, but I think you would be the first to agree that the main function of a cash box is to have cash in it.' He gave a light laugh. 'Now last night I had a few dogs in the surgery and the owners wanted to pay on the spot. I had no change and went for some to your box – it was quite empty. I had to say I would send them a bill, and that isn't good business, is it Miss Harbottle? It didn't look good, so I really must ask you to keep some cash in your cash box.'

Miss Harbottle's eyes widened incredulously. 'But Mr Farnon, you removed the entire contents to go to the hunt ball at ...'

Siegfried held up a hand and his smile took on an unearthly quality. 'Please hear me out. There is another very small thing I want to bring to your attention. It is now the tenth day of the month and the accounts have not gone out. Now this is a very undesirable state of affairs and there are several points to consider here.'

'But Mr Farnon ...!'

'Just one moment, Miss Harbottle, till I explain this to you. It is a known fact that farmers pay their bills more readily if they receive them on the first of the month. And there is another, even more important factor.' The beautiful smile left his face and was replaced by an expression of sorrowing gravity. 'Have you ever stopped to work out just how much interest the practice is losing on all the money lying out there because you are late in sending out the accounts.'

'Mr Farnon ...!'

'I am almost finished, Miss Harbottle, and, believe me, it grieves me to have to speak like this. But the fact is, I can't afford to lose money in this way.' He spread out his hands in a gesture of charming frankness. 'So if you will just apply yourself to this little matter I'm sure all will be well.'

'But will you tell me how I can possibly send the accounts when you refuse to write up the ...'

'In conclusion, Miss Harbottle, let me say this. I have been very satisfied with your progress since you joined us, and I am sure that with time you will tighten up on those little points I have just mentioned.' A certain roguishness crept into his smile and he put his head on one side.

Miss Harbottle's strong fingers closed tightly round a heavy ebony ruler.

'Efficiency,' he said, crinkling his eyes. 'That's what we must have – efficiency.'

CHAPTER 21

I dropped the suture needle into the tray and stepped back to survey the finished job. 'Well though I say it myself, that looks rather nice.'

Tristan leant over the unconscious dog and examined the neat incision with its row of regular stitches. 'Very pretty indeed, my boy. Couldn't have done better myself.'

The big black labrador lay peacefully on the table, his tongue lolling, his eyes glazed and unseeing. He had been brought in with an ugly growth over his ribs and I had decided that it was a simple lipoma, quite benign and very suitable for surgery. And so it had turned out. The tumour had come away with almost ridiculous ease, round, intact and shining, like a hard-boiled egg from its shell. No haemorrhage, no fear of recurrence.

The unsightly swelling had been replaced by this tidy scar which would be invisible in a few weeks. I was pleased.

'We'd better keep him here till he comes round,' I said. 'Give me a hand to get him onto these blankets.' We made the dog comfortable in front of an electric stove and I left to start my morning round.

It was during lunch that we first heard the strange sound. It was something between a moan and a howl, starting quite softly but rising to a piercing pitch before shuddering back down the scale to silence.

Siegfried looked up, startled, from his soup. 'What in God's name is that?'

'Must be that dog I operated on this morning,' I replied. 'The odd one does that coming out of barbiturates. I expect he'll stop soon.'

Siegfried looked at me doubtfully. 'Well, I hope so – I could soon get tired of that. Gives me the creeps.'

We went through and looked at the dog. Pulse strong, respirations deep and regular, mucous membranes a good colour. He was still stretched out, immobile, and the only sign of returning consciousness was the howl which seemed to have settled down into a groove of one every ten seconds.

'Yes, he's perfectly all right,' Siegfried said. 'But what a bloody noise! Let's get out of here.'

Lunch was finished hastily and in silence except for the ceaseless background wailing. Siegfried had scarcely swallowed his last mouthful before he was on his feet. 'Well, I must fly. Got a lot on this afternoon. Tristan, I think it would be a good idea to bring that dog through to the sitting-room and put him by the fire. Then you could stay by him and keep an eye on him.'

Tristan was stunned. 'You mean I have to stay in the same room as that noise all afternoon?'

'Yes, I mean just that. We can't send him home as he is and I don't want anything to happen to him. He needs care and attention.'

'Maybe you'd like me to hold his paw or perhaps wheel him round the market place?'

'Don't give me any of your bloody cheek. You stay with the dog and that's an order!'

Tristan and I stretchered the heavy animal along the passage on the blankets, then I had to leave for the afternoon round. I paused and looked back at the big black form by the fire and Tristan crouched miserably in his chair. The noise was overpowering. I closed the door hurriedly.

It was dark when I got back and the old house hung over me, black and silent against the frosty sky. Silent, that is, except for the howling which still echoed along the passage and filtered eerily into the deserted street.

I glanced at my watch as I slammed the car door. It was six o'clock, so Tristan had had four hours of it. I ran up the steps and along the passage and when I opened the sitting-room door the noise jarred in my head. Tristan was standing with his back to me, looking through the french window into the darkness of the garden. His hands were deep in his pockets; tufts of cotton wool drooped from his ears.

'Well, how is it going?' I asked.

There was no reply so I walked over and tapped him on the shoulder. The effect was spectacular. Tristan leapt into the air and corkscrewed round. His face was ashen and he was trembling violently.

'God help us, Jim, you nearly killed me there. I can't hear a damn thing through these ear plugs – except the dog, of course. Nothing keeps that out.'

I knelt by the labrador and examined him. The dog's condition was excellent but, except for a faint eye reflex there was no sign that he was regaining consciousness. And all the time there were the piercing, evenly spaced howls.

'He's taking a hell of a time to come out of it,' I said. 'Has he been like this all afternoon?'

'Yes, just like that. Not one bit different. And don't waste any sympathy on him, the yowling devil. He's as happy as a sandboy down by the fire – doesn't know a thing about it. But how about me? My nerves are about shot to bits listening to him hour after hour. Much more of it and you'll have to give me a shot too.' He ran a shaking hand through his hair and a twitching started in his cheek.

I took his arm. 'Well, come through and eat. You'll feel better after some food.' I led him unresisting into the dining-room.

Siegfried was in excellent form over the meal. He seemed to be in a mood of exhilaration and monopolized the conversation but he did not once refer to the shrill obbligato from the other room. There was no doubt, however, that it was still getting through to Tristan.

As they were leaving the room, Siegfried put his hand on my shoulder. 'Remember we've got that meeting in Brawton tonight, James. Old Reeves on diseases of sheep – he's usually very good. Pity you can't come too, Tristan, but I'm afraid you'll have to stay with the dog till he comes round.'

Tristan flinched as if he had been struck. 'Oh not another session with that bloody animal! He's driving me mad!'

'I'm afraid there's nothing else for it. James or I could have taken over tonight but we have to show up at this meeting. It would look bad if we missed it.'

Tristan stumbled back into the room and I put on my coat. As I went out into the street I paused for a moment and listened. The dog was still howling.

The meeting was a success. It was held in one of Brawton's lush hotels and, as usual, the best part was the get-together of the vets in the bar afterwards. It was infinitely soothing to hear the other men's problems and mistakes – especially the mistakes.

It amused me to look round the crowded room and try to guess what the little knots of men were talking about. That man over there, bent double and slashing away at the air with one hand – he was castrating a colt in the standing position. And the one with his arm out at full stretch, his fingers working busily at nothing – almost certainly foaling a mare; probably correcting a carpal flexion. And doing it effortlessly too. Veterinary surgery was a childishly simple matter in a warm bar with a few drinks inside you.

It was eleven o'clock before we all got into our cars and headed for our own particular niche in Yorkshire – some to the big industrial towns of the West Riding, others to the seaside places of the East coast and Siegfried and I hurrying thankfully back on the narrow road which twisted between its stone walls into the Northern Pennines.

I thought guiltily that for the last few hours I had completely forgotten about Tristan and his vigil. Still, it must have been better tonight. The dog would surely have quietened down by now. But, jumping from the car in Darrowby, I froze in mid-stride as a thin wail came out faintly from Skeldale House. This was incredible; it was after midnight and the dog was still at it. And what of Tristan? I hated to think what kind of shape he'd be in. Almost fearfully I turned the knob on the sitting-room door.

Tristan's chair made a little island in a sea of empty beer bottles. An upturned crate lay against the wall and Tristan was sitting very upright and looking solemn. I picked my way over the debris.

'Well, has it been rough, Triss? How do you feel now?'

'Could be worse, old lad, could be worse. Soon as you'd gone I slipped over to the Drovers' for a crate of pint Magnets. Made all the difference. After three or four the dog stopped worrying me – matter of fact, I've been yowling back at him for hours now. We've had quite an interesting evening. Anyway, he's coming out now. Look at him.'

The big dog had his head up and there was recognition in his eyes. The howling had stopped. I went over and patted him and the long black tail jerked in a fair attempt at a wag.

'That's better, old boy,' I said. 'But you'd better behave yourself now. You've given your uncle Tristan one hell of a day.'

The labrador responded immediately by struggling to his feet. He took a few swaying steps and collapsed among the bottles.

Siegfried appeared in the doorway and looked distastefully at Tristan, still very upright and wearing a judicial expresssion, and at the dog scrabbling among the bottles. 'What an infernal mess! Surely you can do a little job without making an orgy out of it.'

At the sound of his voice the labrador staggered up and, in a flush of over-confidence, tried to run towards him, wagging his tail unsteadily. He didn't get very far and went down in a heap, sending an empty Magnet rolling gently up to Siegfried's feet.

Siegfried bent over and stroked the shining black head. 'Nice friendly animal that. I should think he's a grand dog when he's got his senses about him. He'll be normal in the morning, but the problem is what to do with him now. We can't leave him staggering about down here – he could break a leg.' He glanced at Tristan who had not moved a muscle. He was sitting up straighter than ever; stiff and motionless like a Prussian general. 'You know, I think the best thing would be for you to take him up to your room tonight. Now we've got him so far, we don't want him to hurt himself. Yes, that's it, he can spend the night with you.'

'Thank you, thank you very much indeed,' Tristan said in a flat voice, still looking straight to his front.

Siegfried looked at him narrowly for a moment, then turned away. 'Right then, clear away this rubbish and let's get to bed.'

My bedroom and Tristan's were connected by a door. Mine was the main room, huge, square, with a high ceiling, pillared fireplace and graceful alcoves like the ones downstairs. I always felt a little like a duke lying there.

Tristan's had been the old dressing-room and was long and narrow with his small bed crouching at one end as if trying to hide. There were no carpets on the smooth, varnished boards so I laid the dog on a heap of blankets and talked down soothingly at Tristan's wan face on the pillow.

'He's quiet now – sleeping like a baby and looks as though he's going to stay that way. You'll be able to have a well-earned rest now.'

I went back to my own room, undressed quickly and got into bed. I went to sleep immediately and I couldn't tell just when the noises started next door, but I came suddenly wide awake with an angry yell ringing in my ears. Then there was a slithering and a bump followed by another distracted cry from Tristan.

I quailed at the idea of going into the dressing-room – there was nothing I could do, anyway – so I huddled closer into the sheets and listened. I kept sliding into a half sleep then starting into wakefulness as more bumping and shouting came through the wall.

After about two hours the noises began to change. The labrador seemed to have gained mastery over his legs and was marching up and down the room, his claws making a regular tck-a-tck, tck-a-tck, tck-a-tck on the wooden floor. It went on and on, interminably. At intervals, Tristan's voice, hoarse now, burst out. 'Stop it, for Christ's sake! Sit down, you bloody dog!'

I must have fallen into a deeper sleep because when I awoke the room was grey with the cold light of morning. I rolled onto my back and listened. I could still hear the tck-a-tck of the claws but it had become irregular as though the labrador was strolling about instead of blundering blindly from one end of the room to the other. There was no sound from Tristan.

I got out of bed, shivering as the icy air of the room gripped me, and pulled on my shirt and trousers. Tiptoeing across the floor, I opened the connecting door and was almost floored as two large feet were planted on my chest. The labrador was delighted to see me and appeared to be thoroughly at home. His fine brown eyes shone with intelligence and well-being and he showed rows of glittering teeth and a flawlessly pink tongue in a wide, panting grin. Far below, the tail lashed ecstatically.

'Well, you're all right, chum,' I said. 'Let's have a look at that wound.' I removed the horny paws from my chest and explored the line of stitches over the ribs. No swelling, no pain, no reaction at all. 'Lovely!' I cried. 'Beautiful. You're as good as new again.' I gave the dog a playful slap on the rump which sent him into a transport of joy. He leapt all over me, clawing and licking.

I was fighting him off when I heard a dismal groan from the bed. In the dim light Tristan looked ghastly. He was lying on his back, both hands clutching the quilt and there was a wild look in his eyes. 'Not a wink of sleep, Jim,' he whispered. 'Not a bloody wink. He's got a wonderful sense of humour, my brother, making me spend the night with this animal. It'll really make his day when he hears what I've been through. Just watch him – I'll bet you anything you like he'll look pleased.'

Later, over breakfast, Siegfried heard the details of his brother's harrowing night and was very sympathetic. He condoled with him at length and apologized for all the trouble the dog had given him. But Tristan was right. He did look pleased.

CHAPTER 22

As I came into the operating room I saw that Siegfried had a patient on the table. He was thoughtfully stroking the head of an elderly and rather woebegone border terrier.

'James,' he said, 'I want you to take this little dog through to Grier.'

'Grier?'

'Vet at Brawton. He was treating the case before the owner moved into our district. I've seen it a couple of times – stones in the bladder. It needs an immediate operation and I think I'd better let Grier do it. He's a touchy devil and I don't want to stand on his toes.'

'Oh, I think I've heard of him,' I said.

'Probably you have. A cantankerous Aberdonian. Since he practises in a fashionable town he gets quite a few students and he gives them hell. That sort of thing gets around.' He lifted the terrier from the table and handed him to me. 'The sooner you get through there the better. You can see the op and bring the dog back here afterwards. But watch yourself – don't rub Grier the wrong way or he'll take it out of you somehow.'

. . .

At my first sight of Angus Grier I thought immediately of whisky. He was about fifty and something had to be responsible for the fleshy, mottled cheeks, the swimmy eyes and the pattern of purple veins which chased each other over his prominent nose. He wore a permanently insulted expression.

He didn't waste any charm on me; a nod and a grunt and he grabbed the dog from my arms. Then he stabbed a finger at a slight, fairish youth in a white coat. 'That's Clinton – final year student. Do ye no' think there's some pansy-lookin' buggers coming into this profession?'

During the operation he niggled constantly at the young man and, in an attempt to create a diversion, I asked when he was going back to college.

'Beginning of next week,' he replied.

'Aye, but he's awa hame tomorrow,' Grier rasped. 'Wasting his time when he could be gettin' good experience here.'

The student blushed. 'Well, I've been seeing practice for over a month and I felt I ought to spend a couple of days with my mother before the term starts.'

'Oh, I ken, I ken. You're all the same – canna stay away from the titty.'

The operation was uneventful and as Grier inserted the last stitch he looked up at me. 'You'll no' want to take the dog back till he's out of the anaesthetic. I've got a case to visit – you can come with me to pass the time.'

We didn't have what you could call a conversation in the car. It was a monologue; a long recital of wrongs suffered at the hands of wicked clients and predatory colleagues. The story I liked best was about a retired admiral who had asked Grier to examine his horse for soundness. Grier said the animal had a bad heart and was not fit to ride, whereupon the admiral flew into a fury and got another vet to examine the horse. The second vet said there was nothing the matter with the heart and passed the animal sound.

The admiral wrote Grier a letter and told him what he thought of him in fairly ripe quarter-deck language. Having got this out of his system he felt refreshed and went out for a ride during which, in the middle of a full gallop the horse fell down dead and rolled on the admiral who sustained a compound fracture of the leg and a crushed pelvis.

'Man,' said Grier with deep sincerity, 'man, I was awfu' glad.'

We drew up in a particularly dirty farmyard and Grier turned to me. 'I've got a cow tae cleanse here.'

'Right,' I said, 'fine.' I settled down in my seat and took out my pipe. Grier paused, half-way out of the car. 'Are you no' coming to give me a hand?'

I couldn't understand him. 'Cleansing' of cows is simply the removal of retained afterbirth and is a one-man job.

'Well, there isn't much I can do is there?' I said. 'And my wellingtons and coat are back in my car. I didn't realize it was a farm visit – I'd probably get messed up for nothing.'

I knew immediately that I'd said the wrong thing. The toad-skin jowls flushed darker and he gave me a malevolent glance before turning away; but half-way across the yard he stopped and stood for a few moments in thought before coming back to the car. 'I've just remembered. I've got something here you can put on. You might as well come in with me – you'll be able to pass me a pessary when I want one.'

It sounded nutty to me, but I got out of the car and went round to the back. Grier was fishing out a large wooden box from his boot.

'Here, ye can put this on. It's a calving outfit I got a bit ago. I haven't used it much because I found it a mite heavy, but it'll keep ye grand and clean.'

I looked in the box and saw a suit of thick, black, shining rubber. I lifted out the jacket; it bristled with zip fasteners and press studs and felt as heavy as lead. The trousers were even more weighty, with many clips and fasteners. The whole thing was a most imposing creation, obviously designed by somebody who had never seen a cow calved and having the disadvantage that anybody wearing it would be pretty well immobilized.

I studied Grier's face for a moment but the watery eyes told me nothing. I began to take off my jacket – it was crazy but I didn't want to offend the man.

And, in truth, Grier seemed anxious to get me into the suit because he was holding it up in a helpful manner. It was a two-man operation. First the gleaming trousers were pulled on and zipped up fore and aft, then it was the turn of the jacket, a wonderful piece of work, fitting tightly round the waist and possessing short sleeves about six inches long with powerful elastic gripping my biceps.

Before I could get it on I had to roll my shirt sleeves to the shoulder, then Grier, heaving and straining, worked me into it. I could hear the zips squeaking into place, the final one being at the back of my neck to close a high, stiff collar which held my head in an attitude of supplication, my chin pointing at the sky.

Grier's heart really seemed to be in his work and, for the final touch, he produced a black rubber skull cap. I shrank away from the thing and began to mouth such objections as the collar would allow, but Grier insisted. 'Stand still a wee minute longer. We might as well do the job right.'

When he had finished he stood back admiringly. I must have been a grotesque sight, sheathed from head to foot in gleaming black, my arms, bare to the shoulders, sticking out almost at right angles. Grier appeared well satisfied. 'Well, come on, it's time we got on wi' the job.' He turned and hurried towards the byre; I plodded ponderously after him like an automaton.

Our arrival in the byre caused a sensation. There were present the farmer, two cowmen and a little girl. The men's cheerful greeting froze on their lips as the menacing figure paced slowly, deliberately in. The little girl burst into tears and ran outside.

'Cleansing' is a dirty, smelly job for the operator and a bore for the onlooker who may have to stand around for twenty minutes without being able to see anything. But this was one time the spectators were not bored. Grier was working away inside the cow and mumbling about the weather, but the men weren't listening; they never took their eyes away from me as I stood rigid, like a suit of armour against the wall. They studied each part of the outfit in turn, wonderingly. I knew what they were thinking. Just what was going to happen when this formidable unknown finally went into action. Anybody dressed like that must have some tremendous task ahead of him.

The intense pressure of the collar against my larynx kept me entirely out of any conversation and this must have added to my air of mystery. I began to sweat inside the suit.

The little girl had plucked up courage and brought her brothers and sisters to look at me. I could see the row of little heads peeping round the door and, screwing my head round painfully, I tried to give them a reassuring smile; but the heads disappeared and I heard their feet clattering across the yard.

I couldn't say how long I stood there, but Grier at last finished his job and called out, 'All right, I'm ready for you now.' The atmosphere became suddenly electric. The men straightened up and stared at me with slightly open mouths. This was the moment they had been waiting for.

I pushed myself away from the wall and did a right turn with some difficulty before heading for the tin of pessaries. It was only a few yards away but it seemed a long way as I approached it like a robot, head in the air, arms extended stiffly on either side. When I arrived at the tin I met a fresh difficulty; I could not bend. After a few contortions I got my hand into the tin, then had to take the paper off the pessary with one hand; a new purgatory. The men watched in fascinated silence.

Having removed the paper, I did a careful about turn and paced back along the byre with measured tread. When I came level with the cow I extended my arm stiffly to Grier who took the pessary and inserted it in the uterus.

I then took up my old position against the wall while my colleague cleaned himself down. I glanced down my nose at the men; their expressions had changed to open disbelief. Surely the mystery man's assignment was tougher than that – he couldn't be wearing that outfit just to hand over a pessary. But when Grier started the complicated business of snapping open the studs and sliding the zips they realized the show was over; and fast on the feeling of let-down came amusement.

As I tried to rub some life back into my swollen arms which had been strangulated by the elastic sleeves, I was surrounded by grinning faces. They could hardly wait, I imagined, to get round to the local that night to tell the tale. Pulling together the shreds of my dignity, I put on my jacket and got into the car. Grier stayed to say a few words to the men, but he wasn't holding their attention; it was all on me, huddling in the seat. They couldn't believe I was true.

Back at the surgery the border terrier was coming out of the anaesthetic. He raised his head and tried bravely to wag his tail when he saw me. I wrapped him in a blanket, gathered him up and was preparing to leave when I saw Grier through the partly open door of a small store-room. He had the wooden box on a table and he was lifting out the rubber suit, but there was something peculiar about the way he was doing it; the man seemed to be afflicted by a kind of rigor – his body shook and jerked, the mottled face was strangely contorted and a half-stifled wailing issued from his lips.

I stared in amazement. I would have said it was impossible, yet it was happening right in front of me. There was not a shadow of a doubt about it – Angus Grier was laughing.

CHAPTER 23

Milk fever is one of the straightforward conditions, but, looking down into the beck in the dreary dawn light, I realized that this was one of its more bizarre manifestations. The illness had struck immediately after calving and the cow had slithered down the muddy bank into the water. She was unconscious when I arrived, her hindquarters completely submerged, the head resting on a shelf of rock. Her calf, sodden and pathetic in the driving rain, trembled by her side.

Dan Cooper's eyes were anxious as we made our way down. 'I doubt we're too late. She's dead, isn't she? I can't see her breathing.'

'Pretty far gone, I'm afraid,' I replied, 'but I think there's still life

there. If I can get some calcium into her vein she might still come round.'
'Damn, I 'ope so,' Dan grunted. 'She's one of my best milkers. It allus
happens to the good 'uns.'
'It does with milk fever, anyway. Here, hold these bottles for me.' I
pulled out the syringe box and selected a wide-bored needle. My
fingers, numb with the special kind of cold you felt in the early morning
with your circulation sluggish and your stomach empty, could hardly
hold it. The water was deeper than I thought and it was over my
wellington tops at the first stride. Gasping, I bent down and dug my
thumb into the jugular furrow at the base of the neck. The vein came up
and as I pushed the needle in, the blood ran warm and dark over my
hand. I fumbled the flutter valve from my pocket, pushed a bottle into
the cup end and inserted the other end into the needle. The calcium
began to flow into the vein.

Standing there in the icy beck, holding the bottle aloft with bloody
fingers and feeling the rain working its way inside my collar, I tried to
keep out the black thoughts; about all those people I knew who were still
in bed and would only leave it when their alarm clocks rang; and they
would read their papers over breakfast and drive out to their cosy banks
or insurance offices. Maybe I should have been a doctor – they treated
their patients in nice, warm bedrooms.

I pulled the needle from the vein and threw the empty bottle onto the
bank. There was no response to the injection. I took the other bottle and
began to run more calcium under the skin. Might as well go through the
motions, futile though it seemed now. It was when I was rubbing away
the subcutaneous injection that I noticed the eyelids quiver.

A quick ripple of relief and excitement went through me. I looked up
at the farmer and laughed. 'She's still with us, Dan.' I flicked her ear and
her eyes opened wide. 'We'll wait a few minutes and then try to roll her
onto her chest.'

Within a quarter of an hour she was beginning to toss her head about
and I knew it was time. I caught hold of her horns and pulled while Dan
and his tall son pushed at her shoulder. We made slow progress but after
several concerted heaves the cow took over herself and settled on her
chest. Immediately everything looked rosier; when a cow is lying on her
side she always has the look of death on her.

I was pretty sure then that she would recover, but I couldn't go away
and leave her lying in the beck. Milk fever cows can stay down for days
on end but I had the feeling this one would be up soon. I decided to stick
it out a bit longer.

She didn't seem to relish her situation in the peaty water and began to
make determined efforts to rise, but it was another half-hour and my

teeth were chattering uncontrollably before she finally staggered to her feet.

'Well, that's a licker!' Dan said. 'Ah never thought she'd stand again. Must be good stuff you gave her.'

'It's a bit quicker than the old bicycle pump,' I laughed. The spectacular effects of intravenous calcium were still enough of a novelty to intrigue me. For generations, cows with milk fever had just died. Then inflation of the udder had saved many; but the calcium was the thing – when they got up within an hour like this one, I always felt like a successful conjurer.

We guided the cow up the bank and at the top, the full force of the wind and rain struck us. The house was only a hundred yards away and we battled towards it, Dan and his son leading, holding the calf in a sack slung between them. The tiny animal swung to and fro, screwing up its eyes against the hard world it had entered. Close behind followed the anxious mother, still rocky on her legs but doing her best to poke her muzzle into the sack. I squelched along in the rear.

We left the cow knee deep in straw in a warm shed, licking her calf vigorously. In the porch of the house, the others dutifully pulled off their wellingtons; I did the same, pouring about a pint of beck water from each boot. Mrs Cooper had the reputation of being a firebrand who exercised an iron rule over Dan and her family, but from my previous contacts with her I had the feeling that Dan didn't do so badly.

I thought so again as I saw her, square-built but comely, plaiting a little girl's pigtails in readiness for school. A crackling fire was mirrored in the gleaming brass of the hearth and above the clean farmhouse smell there was a hint of home-cured bacon just beginning to fry.

Mrs Cooper sent Dan and the boy scurrying upstairs to change their socks then she turned a calm gaze on me as I dripped on her linoleum. She shook her head as though I were a naughty child.

'All right, off with the socks,' she rapped out. 'And your coat, and roll up your trousers, and sit down here, and dry your hair with this.' A clean towel landed on my lap and Mrs Cooper bent over me. 'Don't you ever think of wearing a hat?'

'Not keen on them, I'm afraid,' I mumbled, and she shook her head again.

She poured hot water from a kettle into a large bowl and added mustard from a pound tin. 'Here, stick your feet in this.'

I had obeyed all her commands with alacrity and I gave an involuntary yelp as I made contact with the bubbling mixture. At this, she shot a fierce glance at me and I took care to keep my feet in the bowl.

I was sitting, teeth clenched, enveloped in steam, when she pushed a pint pot of tea into my hand.

It was old-fashioned treatment but effective. By the time I was half-way down the pint pot I felt as though I were being consumed by fire. The river-bed chill was a dream which vanished completely as Mrs Cooper topped up my bowl with another scalding quart from the kettle.

Next, she grabbed chair and bowl and swivelled me round till I was sitting at the table, still with my feet in the water. Dan and the children were already at their breakfast and in front of me was a plate with two eggs, a rough-cut piece of bacon and several sausages. I had learned enough of Dales ways to keep quiet at meals; when I first came to the district I had thought it incumbent on me to provide light conversation in return for their hospitality but the questioning glances they exchanged with each other silenced me effectively.

So this morning, I attacked the food without preamble, but the first mouthful almost made me break my new-found rule. It was the first time I had tasted a home-made Yorkshire sausage and it was an effort to restrain the cries of congratulation which would have been natural in other circles. But Mrs Cooper had been watching me out of the corner of her eye and she must have noticed my rapt expression. Casually, she rose, brought over the frying pan and rolled a few more links onto my plate.

'Killed a pig last week,' she said, pulling open the pantry door. I could see the dishes heaped with chopped meat, spare rib, liver, the rows of pies with the jelly gleaming on their pale gold crusts.

I finished my meal, pulled on a thick pair of socks borrowed from Dan and my dry shoes. I was about to leave when Mrs Cooper tucked a parcel under my arm. I knew it contained further samples from the pantry but her eyes dared me to say much about it. I muttered a few words of thanks and went out to the car.

The church clock was chiming a quarter past nine when I pulled up outside Skeldale House. I felt good – warm, full of superb food and with the satisfying memory of the cow's quick recovery. And there was my parcel on the back seat; it was always a stroke of luck to land on a farm after a pig killing and there was usually a gift from the hospitable farmers, but these sausages were something I would never forget.

I took the surgery steps at a jump and trotted along the passage, but as I rounded the corner my progress was halted. Siegfried was standing there, rigid, his back pressed against the wall. Over his shoulder dangled a long, flexible, leather probang. Between us was the half-open door of the office with Miss Harbottle clearly visible at her desk.

I waved cheerfully. 'Hello, hello, off to a choke?'

Siegfried's face twisted in anguish and he held up a warning hand. Then he began to creep past the door, balancing on the balls of his feet like a tightrope walker. He was beyond the door and the tense lines of his body had begun to relax when the brass end of the swinging probang clattered against the wall and, as if in reply came the familiar rumble from Miss Harbottle's corner. Siegfried gave me a single despairing glance then, shoulders drooping, he went slowly into the room.

Watching him go, I thought wonderingly of how things had built up since the secretary's arrival. It was naked war now and it gave life an added interest to observe the tactics of the two sides.

At the beginning it seemed that Siegfried must run out an easy winner. He was the employer; he held the reins and it appeared that Miss Harbottle would be helpless in the face of his obstructive strategy. But Miss Harbottle was a fighter and a resourceful one and it was impossible not to admire the way she made use of the weapons at her command.

In fact, over the past week the tide had been running in her favour. She had been playing Siegfried like an expert fisherman with a salmon; bringing him repeatedly back to her desk to answer footling questions. Her throat clearing had developed into an angry bark which could penetrate the full extent of the house. And she had a new weapon; she had taken to writing Siegfried's clerical idiocies on slips of paper; mis-spellings, errors in addition, wrong entries – they were all faithfully copied down.

Miss Harbottle used these slips as ammunition. She never brought one out when things were slack and her employer was hanging about the surgery. She saved them until he was under pressure, then she would push a slip under his nose and say 'How about this?'

She always kept an expressionless face at these times and it was impossible to say how much pleasure it gave her to see him cower back like a whipped animal. But the end was unvarying – mumbled explanations and apologies from Siegfried and Miss Harbottle, radiating self-righteousness, correcting the entry.

As Siegfried went into the room I watched through the partly open door. I knew my morning round was waiting but I was impelled by morbid curiosity. Miss Harbottle, looking brisk and businesslike, was tapping an entry in the book with her pen while Siegfried shuffled his feet and muttered replies. He made several vain attempts to escape and, as the time passed, I could see he was nearing breaking-point. His teeth were clenched and his eyes had started to bulge.

The phone rang and the secretary answered it. Her employer was making again for the door when she called happily, 'Colonel Brent for you.' Like a man in a dream he turned back. The Colonel, a racehorse owner, had been a thorn in our flesh for a long time with his complaints and his continual questioning and probing; a call from him was always liable to send up the blood-pressure.

I could see it was that way this morning. The minutes ticked away and Siegfried's face got redder. He made his replies in a choked voice which finally rose almost to a shout. At the end he crashed the receiver down and leaned on the desk, breathing heavily.

Then, as I watched, unbelieving, Miss Harbottle began to open the drawer where she kept her slips. She fished one out, coughed and held it in Siegfried's face.

'How about this?' she asked.

I resisted the impulse to close my eyes and stared in horror. For a few seconds nothing happened and there was a tense interval while Siegfried stood quite motionless. Then his face seemed to break up and with a scything sweep of his arm he snatched the slip from the secretary's hand and began to tear at it with fierce intensity. He didn't say a word but as he tore, he leaned forward over the desk and his glaring eyes approached ever nearer to Miss Harbottle who slowly edged her chair back till it was jammed against the wall.

It was a weird picture. Miss Harbottle straining back, her mouth slightly open, her tinted curls bobbing in alarm, and Siegfried, his ravaged features close to hers, still tearing with insane vigour at the piece of paper. The scene ended when Siegfried, putting every ounce of his strength into an action like a javelin thrower, hurled the torn-up slip at the wastepaper basket. It fell in a gentle shower, like confetti, in and around the basket and Siegfried, still without speaking, wrapped his probang around him and strode from the room.

In the kitchen, Mrs Hall opened the parcel and extracted a pie, a chunk of liver and a cluster of the exquisite sausages. She turned a quizzical eye on me. 'You look kind of pleased with yourself this morning, Mr Herriot.'

I leaned back against the oak dresser. 'Yes, Mrs Hall, I've just been thinking. It must be very nice to be the principal of a practice but, you know, it's not such a bad life being an assistant.'

CHAPTER 24

The day had stared badly. Tristan had been trapped by his brother at 4 a.m. returning from the Bellringers' Outing.

This function took place annually when a bus load of the bellringers of all the local churches made a trip to Morecambe. They spent very little time on the beach, however, and when they weren't working their way from one pub to another, they were attacking the crates of beer they had brought with them.

When they rolled into Darrowby in the small hours most of the occupants of the bus were unconscious. Tristan, an honoured guest of the party, had been tipped out in the back lane behind Skeldale House. He waved weakly as the bus moved away, but drew no response from the unseeing faces at the windows. Lurching down the garden path, he was horrified to see a light in Siegfried's room. Escape was impossible and, when asked to explain where he had been, he made a series of attempts to articulate 'Bellringers' Outing' without success.

Siegfried, seeing he was wasting his time, had saved his wrath till breakfast-time. That was when Tristan told me the story – just before his brother came into the dining-room and started on him.

But, as usual, it seemed to take more out of Siegfried who went off on his rounds glowering and hoarse from shouting. Ten minutes after he had gone I found Tristan closeted cheerfully in Boardman's cubby hole, Boardman listening to some fresh material from the backs of the envelopes and sniggering appreciatively.

The old man had cheered up greatly since Tristan came home and the two of them spent a lot of time in the gloom where the light from the tiny window picked out the rows of rusting tools, the Bairnsfather cartoons looking down from the wall. The place was usually kept locked and visitors were not encouraged; but Tristan was always welcome.

Often, when I was passing by, I would peep in and see Tristan patiently pulling at a Woodbine while Boardman rambled on. 'We was six weeks up the line. The French was on our right and the Jocks on our left ...' or 'Poor old Fred – one minute 'e was standing by me and next 'e was gone. Never found as much as a trouser button ...'

This morning, Tristan hailed me boisterously and I marvelled again at his resilience and his power to bend like a willow before the winds of misfortune and spring back unscathed. He held up two tickets.

'Village dance tonight, Jim, and I can guarantee it. Some of my harem from the hospital are going, so I'll see you're all right. And that's not all – look here.' He went into the saddle room, lifted out a loose board and produced a bottle of sherry. 'We'll be able to have a toothful between dances.'

I didn't ask where the tickets or the sherry had come from. I liked the village dances. The packed hall with the three-piece band at one end – piano, scraping fiddle and drums – and at the other end, the older ladies looking after the refreshments. Glasses of milk, mounds of sandwiches, ham, home-made brawn, trifles heaped high with cream.

That evening, Tristan came out with me on my last visit and in the car the talk was all about the dance. The case was simple enough – a cow with an infected eye – but the farm was in a village high up the dale, and when we finished, it was dusk. I felt good, and everything seemed to stand out, clear and meaningful. The single, empty, grey-stone street, the last red streaks in the sky, the dark purple of the enclosing fells. There was no wind, but a soft breath came from the quiet moors, sweet and fresh and full of promise. Among the houses, the thrilling smell of wood smoke was everywhere.

When we got back to the surgery, Siegfried was out but there was a note for Tristan propped up on the mantelpiece. It said simply: 'Tristan. Go home. Siegfried.'

This had happened before, everything in Skeldale House being in short supply, especially beds and blankets. When unexpected visitors arrived, Tristan was packed off to stay with his mother in Brawton. Normally he would board a train without comment, but tonight was different.

'Good God,' he said. 'Somebody must be coming for the night and, of course, I'm the one who's just expected to disappear. It's a nice bloody carry-on, I must say! And isn't that a charming letter! It doesn't matter if I've made any private arrangements. Oh no! There's no question of asking me if it's convenient to leave. It's just "Tristan, go home", Polite, and thoughtful, isn't it?'

It was unusual for him to get worked up like this. I spoke soothingly. 'Look, Triss. Maybe we'd better just skip this dance. There'll be others.'

Tristan clenched his fists. 'Why should I let him push me around like this?' he fumed. 'I'm a person, am I not? I have my own life to lead and I tell you I am not going to Brawton tonight. I've arranged to go to a dance and I am damn well going to a dance.'

This was fighting talk but I felt a twinge of alarm. 'Wait a minute. What about Siegfried? What's he going to say when he comes in and finds you still here?'

'To hell with Siegfried!' said Tristan. So I left it at that.

Siegfried came home when we were upstairs, changing. I was first down and found him sitting by the fire, reading. I said nothing but sat down and waited for the explosion.

After a few minutes, Tristan came in. He had chosen with care among his limited wardrobe and was resplendent in a dark grey suit; a scrubbed face shone under carefully combed hair; he was wearing a clean collar.

Siegfried flushed as he looked up from his book. 'What the bloody hell are you doing here? I told you to go to Brawton. Joe Ramage is coming tonight.'

'Couldn't go.'

'Why not?'

'No trains.'

'What the hell do you mean, no trains?'

'Just that – no trains.'

The cross-talk was bringing on the usual sense of strain in me. The interview was falling into the habitual pattern; Siegfried red-faced, exasperated; his brother expressionless, answering in a flat monotone, fighting a defensive battle with the skill of long practice.

Siegfried sank back in his chair, baffled for the moment, but he kept a slit-eyed gaze on his brother. The smart suit, the slicked hair and polished shoes all seemed to irritate him further.

'All right,' he said suddenly, 'it's maybe just as well you are staying. I want you to do a job for me. You can open that haematoma on Charlie Dent's pig's ear.'

This was a bombshell. Charlie Dent's pig's ear was something we didn't talk about.

A few weeks earlier, Siegfried himself had gone to the smallholding half-way along a street on the outskirts of the town to see a pig with a swollen ear. It was an aural haematoma and the only treatment was to lance it, but for some reason, Siegfried had not done the job but had sent me the following day.

I had wondered about it, but not for long. When I climbed into the sty, the biggest sow I had ever seen rose from the straw, gave an explosive bark and rushed at me with its huge mouth gaping. I didn't stop to argue. I made the wall about six inches ahead of the pig and vaulted over into the passage. I stood there, considering the position, looking thoughtfully at the mean little red eyes, the slavering mouth with its long, yellow teeth.

Usually, I paid no attention when pigs barked and grumbled at me but this one really seemed to mean it. As I wondered what the next step would be, the pig gave an angry roar, reared up on its hind legs and tried to get over the wall at me. I made up my mind quickly.

'I'm afraid I haven't got the right instrument with me, Mr Dent. I'll pop back another day and open the ear for you. It's nothing serious – only a small job. Goodbye.'

There the matter had rested, with nobody caring to mention it till now.

Tristan was aghast. 'You mean you want me to go along there tonight. Saturday night? Surely some other time would do? I'm going to a dance.'

Siegfried smiled bitterly from the depths of his chair. 'It has to be done now. That's an order. You can go to your dance afterwards.'

Tristan started to say something, but he knew he had pushed his luck far enough. 'Right,' he said, 'I'll go and do it.'

He left the room with dignity, Siegfried resumed his book, and I stared into the fire, wondering how Tristan was going to handle this one. He was a lad of infinite resource, but he was going to be tested this time.

Within ten minutes he was back. Siegfried looked at him suspiciously. 'Have you opened that ear?'

'No.'

'Why not?'

'Couldn't find the place. You must have given me the wrong address. Number 98, you said.'

'It's number 89 and you know damn well it is. Now get back there and do your job.'

The door closed behind Tristan and again, I waited. Fifteen minutes later it opened again and Tristan reappeared looking faintly triumphant. His brother looked up from his book.

'Done it?'

'No.'

'Why not?'

'The family are all out at the pictures. Saturday night, you know.'

'I don't care a damn where the family are. Just get into that sty and lance that ear. Now get out, and this time I want the job done.'

Again Tristan retreated and a new vigil began. Siegfried did not say a word, but I could feel the tension building up. Twenty minutes passed and Tristan was with us again.

'Have you opened that ear?'

'No.'

'Why not?'

'It's pitch dark in there. How do you expect me to work? I've only got two hands – one for the knife and one for the torch. How can I hold the ear?'

Siegfried had been keeping a tight hold on himself, but now his control snapped. 'Don't give me any more of your bloody excuses,' he shouted, leaping from his chair. 'I don't care how you do it, but, by God, you are going to open that pig's ear tonight or I've finished with you. Now get the hell out of here and don't come back till it's done!'

My heart bled for Tristan. He had been dealt a poor hand and had played his cards with rare skill, but he had nothing left now. He stood silent in the doorway for a few moments, then he turned and walked out.

The next hour was a long one. Siegfried seemed to be enjoying his book and I even tried to read myself; but I got no meaning out of the words and it made my head ache to sit staring at them. It would have helped if I could have paced up and down the carpet but that was pretty well impossible in Siegfried's presence. I had just decided to excuse myself and go out for a walk when I heard the outer door open, then Tristan's footsteps in the passage.

A moment later, the man of destiny entered but the penetrating smell of pig got into the room just ahead of him, and as he walked over to the fire, pungent waves seemed to billow round him. Pig muck was spattered freely over his nice suit, and on his clean collar, his face and hair. There was a great smear of the stuff on the seat of his trousers but despite his ravaged appearance he still maintained his poise.

Siegfried pushed his chair back hurriedly but did not change expression.

'Have you got that ear opened?' he asked quietly.

'Yes.'

Siegfried returned to his book without comment. It seemed that the matter was closed and Tristan, after staring briefly at his brother's bent head, turned and marched from the room. But even after he had gone, the odour of the pig sty hung in the room like a cloud.

Later, in the Drovers', I watched Tristan draining his third pint. He had changed, and if he didn't look as impressive as when he started the evening, at least he was clean and hardly smelt at all. I had said nothing yet, but the old light was returning to his eye. I went over to the bar and ordered my second half and Tristan's fourth pint and, as I set the glasses on the table, I thought that perhaps it was time.

'Well, what happened?'

Tristan took a long, contented pull at his glass and lit a Woodbine. 'Well now, all in all, Jim, it was rather a smooth operation, but I'll start at the beginning. You can imagine me standing all alone outside the sty in the pitch darkness with that bloody great pig grunting and growling on the other side of the wall. I didn't feel so good, I can tell you.

'I shone my torch on the thing's face and it jumped up and ran at me, making a noise like a lion and showing all those dirty yellow teeth. I nearly wrapped it up and came home there and then, but I got to thinking about the dance and all and, on the spur of the moment, I hopped over the wall.

'Two seconds later, I was on my back. It must have charged me but couldn't see enough to get a bite in. I just heard a bark, then a terrific weight against my legs and I was down.

'Well, it's a funny thing, Jim. You know I'm not a violent chap, but as I lay there, all my fears vanished and all I felt was a cold hatred of that bloody animal. I saw it as the cause of all my troubles and before I knew what I was doing I was up on my feet and booting its arse round and round the sty. And, do you know, it showed no fight at all. That pig was a coward at heart.'

I was still puzzled. 'But the ear – how did you manage to open the haematoma?'

'No problem, Jim. That was done for me.'

'You don't mean to say ...'

'Yes,' Tristan said, holding his pint up to the light and studying a small foreign body floating in the depths. 'Yes, it was really very fortunate. In the scuffle in the dark, the pig ran up against the wall and burst the thing itself. Made a beautiful job.'

CHAPTER 25

I realized, quite suddenly, that spring had come. It was late March and I had been examining some sheep in a hillside fold. On my way down, in the lee of a small pine wood I leaned my back against a tree and was aware, all at once, of the sunshine, warm on my closed eyelids, the clamour of the larks, the muted sea-sound of the wind in the high branches. And though the snow still lay in long runnels behind the walls and the grass was lifeless and winter-yellowed, there was the feeling of change; almost of liberation, because, unknowing, I had surrounded myself with a carapace against the iron months, the relentless cold.

It wasn't a warm spring but it was dry with sharp winds which fluttered the white heads of the snowdrops and bent the clumps of daffodils on the village greens. In April the roadside banks were bright with the fresh yellow of the primroses.

And in April, too, came the lambing. It came in a great tidal wave, the most vivid and interesting part of the veterinary surgeon's year, the zenith of the annual cycle, and it came as it always does when we were busiest with our other work.

In the spring the livestock were feeling the effects of the long winter. Cows had stood for months in the same few feet of byre and were in dire need of the green grass and the sun on their backs, while their calves had very little resistance to disease. And just when we were wondering how we could cope with the coughs and colds and pneumonias and acetonaemias the wave struck us.

The odd thing is that for about ten months of the year, sheep hardly entered into the scheme of our lives. They were just woolly things on the hills. But for the other two months they almost blotted out everything else.

First came the early troubles, the pregnancy toxaemias, the prolapses. Then the lambings in a concentrated rush followed by the calcium deficiencies, the horrible gangrenous mastitis when the udder turns black and sloughs away; and the diseases which beset the lambs themselves – swayback, pulpy kidney, dysentery. Then the flood slackened, became a trickle and by the end of May had almost dried up. Sheep became woolly things on the hills again.

But in this first year I found a fascination in the work which has remained with me. Lambing, it seemed to me, had all the thrill and interest of calving without the hard labour. It was usually uncomfortable in that it was performed in the open; either in draughty pens improvised from straw bales and gates or more often out in the fields. It didn't seem to occur to the farmers that the ewe might prefer to produce her family in a warm place or that the vet may not enjoy kneeling for an hour in his shirt sleeves in the rain.

But the actual job was as easy as a song. After my experiences in correcting the malpresentations of calves it was delightful to manipulate these tiny creatures. Lambs are usually born in twos or threes and some wonderful mix-ups occur; tangles of heads and legs all trying to be first out and it is the vet's job to sort them around and decide which leg belongs to which head. I revelled in this. It was a pleasant change to be for once stronger and bigger than my patient, but I didn't over-stress this advantage; I have not changed the opinion I formed then that there are just two things to remember in lambing – cleanliness and gentleness.

And the lambs. All young animals are appealing but the lamb has been given an unfair share of charm. The moments come back; of a bitterly cold evening when I had delivered twins on a wind-scoured hillside; the lambs shaking their heads convulsively and within minutes one of them struggling upright and making its way, unsteady, knock-kneed, towards the udder while the other followed resolutely on its knees.

The shepherd, his purpled, weather-roughened face almost hidden by the heavy coat which muffled him to his ears, gave a slow chuckle. 'How the 'ell do they know?'

He had seen it happen thousands of times and he still wondered. So do I.

And another memory of two hundred lambs in a barn on a warm afternoon. We were inoculating them against pulpy kidney and there was no conversation because of the high-pitched protests of the lambs and the unremitting deep baa-ing from nearly a hundred ewes milling anxiously around outside. I couldn't conceive how these ewes could ever get their own families sorted out from that mass of almost identical little creatures. It would take hours.

It took about twenty-five seconds. When we had finished injecting we opened the barn doors and the outpouring lambs were met by a concerted rush of distraught mothers. At first the noise was deafening but it died away rapidly to an occasional bleat as the last stray was rounded up. Then, neatly paired off, the flock headed calmly for the field.

Through May and early June my world became softer and warmer. The cold wind dropped and the air, fresh as the sea, carried a faint breath of the thousands of wild flowers which speckled the pastures. At times it seemed unfair that I should be paid for my work; for driving out in the early morning with the fields glittering under the first pale sunshine and the wisps of mist hanging on the high tops.

At Skeldale House the wistaria exploded into a riot of mauve blooms which thrust themselves through the open windows and each morning as I shaved I breathed in the heady fragrance from the long clusters drooping by the side of the mirror. Life was idyllic.

There was only one jarring note; it was the time of the horse. In the thirties there were still quite a lot of horses on the farms though the tractors had already sounded their warning knell. In the farms near the foot of the Dale where there was a fair amount of arable land the rows of stables were half empty but there were still enough horses to make May and June uncomfortable. This was when the castrations were done.

Before that came the foaling and it was a common enough thing to see a mare with her foal either trotting beside her or stretched flat on the ground as its mother nibbled at the grass. Nowadays the sight of a cart mare and foal in a field would make me pull up my car to have another look.

There was all the work connected with the foalings: cleansing the mares, docking the foals' tails, treating the illnesses of the newborn – joint ill, retained meconium. It was hard and interesting but as the weather grew warmer the farmers began to think of having the year-old colts castrated.

I didn't like the job and since there might be up to a hundred to be done, it cast a shadow over this and many subsequent springs. For generations the operation had been done by casting the colt and tying him up very like a trussed chicken. It was a bit laborious but the animal was under complete restraint and it was possible to concentrate entirely on the job; but at about the time I qualified, standing castration was coming very much to the fore. It consisted simply of applying a twitch to the colt's upper lip, injecting a shot of local anaesthetic into each testicle and going straight ahead. There was no doubt it was a lot quicker.

The obvious disadvantage was that the danger of injury to the operator and his helpers was increased tenfold, but for all that the method rapidly became more popular. A local farmer called Kenny Bright who considered himself an advanced thinker took the step of introducing it to the district. He engaged Major Farley, the horse specialist, to give a demonstration on one of his colts, and a large gathering of farmers came to spectate. Kenny, smug and full of self-importance was holding the twitch and beaming round the company as his protégé prepared to disinfect the operation site, but as soon as the Major touched the scrotum with his antiseptic the colt reared and brought a fore foot crashing down on Kenny's head. He was carried away on a gate with his skull fractured and spent a long time in hospital. The other farmers didn't stop laughing for weeks but the example failed to deter them. Standing castration was in.

I said it was quicker. It was when everything went smoothly, but there were other times when the colt kicked or threw himself on top of us or just went generally mad. Out of ten jobs nine would be easy and the tenth would be a rodeo. I don't know how much apprehension this state of affairs built up in other vets but I was undeniably tense on castration mornings.

Of course, one of the reasons was that I was not, am not and never will be a horseman. It is difficult to define the term but I am convinced that horsemen are either born or acquire the talent in early childhood. I knew it was no good my trying to start in my mid-twenties. I had the knowledge of equine diseases, I believed I had the ability to treat sick horses efficiently but that power the real horseman had to soothe and quieten and mentally dominate an animal was beyond my reach. I didn't even try to kid myself.

It was unfortunate because there is no doubt horses know. It is quite different with cows; they don't care either way; if a cow feels like kicking you she will kick you; she doesn't give a damn whether you are an expert or not. But horses know.

So on those mornings my morale was never very high as I drove out with my instruments rattling and rolling about on an enamel tray on the back seat. Would he be wild or quiet? How big would he be? I had heard my colleagues airily stating their preference for big horses – the two-year-olds were far easier, they said, you could get a better grip on the testicles. But there was never any doubt in my own mind. I liked them small; the smaller the better.

One morning when the season was at its height and I had had about enough of the equine race, Siegfried called to me as he was going out. 'James, there's a horse with a tumour on its belly at Wilkinson's of White Cross. Get along and take it off – today if possible but otherwise fix your own time; I'll leave it with you.'

Feeling a little disgruntled at fate having handed me something on top of the seasonal tasks, I boiled up a scalpel, tumour spoons and syringe and put them on my tray with local anaesthetic, iodine and tetanus antitoxin.

I drove to the farm with the tray rattling ominously behind me. That sound always had a connotation of doom for me. I wondered about the horse – maybe it was just a yearling; they did get those little dangling growths sometimes – nanberries, the farmers called them. Over the six miles I managed to build up a comfortable picture of a soft-eyed little colt with pendulous abdomen and over-long hair; it hadn't done well over the winter and was probably full of worms – shaky on its legs with weakness, in fact.

At Wilkinson's all was quiet. The yard was empty except for a lad of about ten who didn't know where the boss was.

'Well, where is the horse?' I asked.

The lad pointed to the stable. 'He's in there.'

I went inside. At one end stood a high, open-topped loose box with a metal grille topping the wooden walls and from within I heard a deep-throated whinnying and snorting followed by a series of tremendous thuds against the sides of the box. A chill crept through me. That was no little colt in there.

I opened the top half door and there, looking down at me was an enormous animal; I hadn't realized horses ever came quite as big as this; a chestnut stallion with a proud arch to his neck and feet like manhole covers. Surging swathes of muscle shone on his shoulders and quarters and when he saw me he laid back his ears, showed the whites of his eyes and lashed out viciously against the wall. A foot-long splinter flew high in the air as the great hoof crashed against the boards.

'God almighty,' I breathed and closed the half door hurriedly. I leaned my back against the door and listened to my heart thumping.

I turned to the lad. 'How old is that horse?'

'Over six years, sir.'

I tried a little calm thinking. How did you go about tackling a man-eater like this. I had never seen such a horse – he must weigh over a ton. I shook myself; I hadn't even had a look at the tumour I was supposed to remove. I lifted the latch, opened the door about two inches and peeped inside. I could see it plainly dangling from the belly; probably a papilloma, about the size of a cricket ball, with a lobulated surface which made it look like a little cauliflower. It swung gently from side to side as the horse moved about.

No trouble to take it off. Nice narrow neck to it; a few cc's of local in there and I could twist it off easily with the spoons.

But the snag was obvious. I would have to go under that shining barrel of an abdomen within easy reach of the great feet and stick a needle into those few inches of skin. Not a happy thought.

But I pulled my mind back to practical things; like a bucket of hot water, soap and a towel. And I'd need a good man on the twitch. I began to walk towards the house.

There was no answer to my knock. I tried again; still nothing – there was nobody at home. It seemed the most natural thing in the world to leave everything till another day; the idea of going round the buildings and fields till I found somebody never entered my head.

I almost broke into a gallop on my way to the car, backed it round with the tyres squealing and roared out of the yard.

Siegfried was surprised. 'Nobody there? Well that's a damn funny thing. I'm nearly sure they were expecting you today. But never mind, it's in your hands, James. Give them a ring and fix it up again as soon as possible.'

.   .   .

I found it wonderfully easy to forget about the stallion over the days and weeks that followed; except when my defences were down. At least once a night it thundered through my dreams with gaping nostrils and flying mane and I developed an uncomfortable habit of coming bolt awake at five o'clock in the morning and starting immediately to operate on the horse. On an average, I took that tumour off twenty times before breakfast each morning.

I told myself it would be a lot easier to fix the job up and get it over. What was I waiting for, anyway? Was there a subconscious hope that if I put it off long enough something would happen to get me off the hook? The tumour might fall off or shrink away and disappear, or the horse might drop down dead.

I could have passed the whole thing onto Siegfried – he was good with horses – but my confidence was low enough without that.

All my doubts were resolved one morning when Mr Wilkinson came on the phone. He wasn't in the least upset at the long delay but he made it quite clear that he could wait no longer. 'You see, I want to sell this 'oss, young man, but I can't let him go with that thing on him, can I?'

My journey to Wilkinson's wasn't enlivened by the familiar clatter of the tray on the back seat; it reminded me of the last time when I was wondering what was ahead of me. This time I knew.

Stepping out of the car, I felt almost disembodied. It was like walking a few inches above the ground. I was greeted by a reverberating din from the loose box; the same angry whinnies and splintering crashes I had heard before. I tried to twist my stiff face into a smile as the farmer came over.

'My chaps are getting a halter on him,' he said, but his words were cut short by an enraged squealing from the box and two tremendous blows against the wooden sides. I felt my mouth going dry.

The noise was coming nearer; then the stable doors flew open and the great horse catapulted out into the yard, dragging two big fellows along on the end of the halter shank. The cobbles struck sparks from the men's boots as they slithered about but they were unable to stop the stallion backing and plunging. I imagined I could feel the ground shudder under my feet as the hooves crashed down.

At length, after much manoeuvring, the men got the horse standing with his offside against the wall of the barn. One of them looped the twitch onto the upper lip and tightened it expertly, the other took a firm grip on the halter and turned towards me. 'Ready for you now, sir.'

I pierced the rubber cap on the bottle of cocaine, withdrew the plunger of the syringe and watched the clear fluid flow into the glass barrel. Seven, eight, ten cc's. If I could get that in, the rest would be easy; but my hands were trembling.

Walking up to the horse was like watching an action from a film. It wasn't really me doing this – the whole thing was unreal. The nearside eye flickered dangerously at me as I raised my left hand and passed it over the muscles of the neck, down the smooth, quivering flank and along the abdomen till I was able to grasp the tumour. I had the thing in my hand now, the lobulations firm and lumpy under my fingers. I pulled gently downwards, stretching the brown skin joining the growth to the body. I would put the local in there – a few good weals. It wasn't going to be so bad. The stallion laid back his ears and gave a warning whicker.

I took a long, careful breath, brought up the syringe with my right hand, placed the needle against the skin, then thrust it in.

The kick was so explosively quick that at first I felt only surprise that such a huge animal could move so swiftly. It was a lightning outward slash that I never even saw and the hoof struck the inside of my right thigh, spinning me round helplessly. When I hit the ground I lay still, feeling only a curious numbness. Then I tried to move and a stab of pain went through my leg.

When I opened my eyes Mr Wilkinson was bending over me. 'Are you all right, Mr Herriot?' The voice was anxious.

'I don't think so.' I was astonished at the matter-of-fact sound of my own words; but stranger still was the feeling of being at peace with myself for the first time for weeks. I was calm and completely in charge of the situation.

'I'm afraid not, Mr Wilkinson. You'd better put the horse back in his box for now – we'll have a go at him another day – and I wonder if you'd ring Mr Farnon to come and pick me up. I don't think I'll be able to drive.'

. . .

My leg wasn't broken but it developed a massive haematoma at the point of impact and then the whole limb blossomed into an unbelievable range of colours from delicate orange to deepest black. I was still hobbling like a Crimean veteran when, a fortnight later, Siegfried and I with a small army of helpers went back and roped the stallion, chloroformed him and removed that little growth.

I have a cavity in the muscle of my thigh to remind me of that day, but some good came out of the incident. I found that the fear is worse than the reality and horse work has never worried me as much since then.

CHAPTER 26

The first time I saw Phin Calvert was in the street outside the surgery when I was talking to Brigadier Julian Coutts-Browne about his shooting dogs. The Brigadier was almost a stage version of an English aristocrat; immensely tall with a pronounced stoop, hawk features and a high drawling voice. As he spoke, smoke from a narrow cigar trickled from his lips.

I turned my head at the clatter of heavy boots on the pavement. A thick-set figure was stumping rapidly towards us, hands tucked behind his braces, ragged jacket pulled wide to display a curving expanse of collarless shirt, wisps of grizzled hair hanging in a fringe beneath a greasy cap. He was smiling widely at nobody in particular and he hummed busily to himself.

The Brigadier glanced at him. 'Morning, Calvert,' he grunted coldly.

Phineas threw up his head in pleased recognition. 'Now then, Charlie, 'ow is ta?' he shouted.

The Brigadier looked as though he had swallowed a swift pint of vinegar. He removed his cigar with a shaking hand and stared after the retreating back. 'Impudent devil,' he muttered.

Looking at Phin, you would never have thought he was a prosperous farmer. I was called to his place a week later and was surprised to find a substantial house and buildings and a fine dairy herd grazing in the fields.

I could hear him even before I got out of the car.

'Hello, 'ello, 'ello! Who's this we've got then? New chap eh? Now we're going to learn summat!' He still had his hands inside his braces and was grinning wider than ever.

'My name is Herriot,' I said.

'Is it now?' Phin cocked his head and and surveyed me, then he turned to three young men standing by. 'Hasn't he a nice smile, lads. He's a real Happy Harry!'

He turned and began to lead the way across the yard. 'Come on, then and we'll see what you're made of. I 'ope you know a bit about calves because I've got some here that are right dowly.'

As he went into the calf house I was hoping I would be able to do something impressive – perhaps use some of the new drugs and sera I had in my car; it was going to take something special to make an impact here.

There were six well-grown young animals, almost stirk size, and three of them were behaving very strangely; grinding their teeth, frothing at the mouth and blundering about the pen as though they couldn't see. As I watched, one of them walked straight into the wall and stood with its nose pressed against the stone.

Phin, apparently unconcerned, was humming to himself in a corner. When I started to take my thermometer from its case he burst into a noisy commentary. 'Now what's he doing? Ah, we're off now, get up there!'

The half-minute which my thermometer spends in an animal's rectum is usually devoted to hectic thought. But this time I didn't need the time to work out my diagnosis; the blindness made it easy. I began to look round the walls of the calf house; it was dark and I had to get my face close to the stone.

Phin gave tongue again. 'Hey, what's going on? You're as bad as t' calves, nosing about there, dozy like. What d'you think you're lookin' for?'

'Paint, Mr Calvert. I'm nearly sure your calves have got lead poisoning.'

Phin said what all farmers say at this juncture. 'They can't have. I've had calves in here for thirty years and they've never taken any harm before. There's no paint in here, anyway.'

'How about this, then?' I peered into the darkest corner and pulled at a piece of loose board.

'Oh, that's nobbut a bit of wood I nailed down there last week to block up a hole. Came off an old hen house.'

I looked at the twenty-year-old paint hanging off in the loose flakes which calves find so irresistible. 'This is what's done the damage,' I said. 'Look, you can see the tooth marks where they've been at it.'

Phin studied the board at close quarters and grunted doubtfully. 'All right, what do we do now?'

'First thing is to get this painted board out of here and then give all the calves epsom salts. Have you got any?'

Phin gave a bark of laughter. 'Aye, I've got a bloody great sack full, but can't you do owt better than that? Aren't you going to inject them?'

It was a little embarrassing. The specific antidotes to metal poisoning had not been discovered and the only thing which sometimes did a bit of good was magnesium sulphate which caused the precipitation of insoluble lead sulphate. The homely term for magnesium sulphate is of course, epsom salts.

'No,' I said. 'There's nothing I can inject that will help at all and I can't even guarantee the salts will. But I'd like you to give the calves two heaped tablespoonfuls three times a day.'

'Oh 'ell, you'll skitter the poor buggers to death!'

'Maybe so, but there's nothing else for it,' I said.

Phin took a step towards me so that his face, dark-skinned and deeply wrinkled, was close to mine. The suddenly shrewd, mottled brown eyes regarded me steadily for a few seconds, then he turned away quickly. 'Right,' he said. 'Come in and have a drink.'

Phin stumped into the farm kitchen ahead of me, threw back his head and let loose a bellow that shook the windows. 'Mother! Feller 'ere wants a glass o' beer. Come and meet Happy Harry!'

Mrs Calvert appeared with magical speed and put down glasses and bottles. I glanced at the labels – 'Smith's Nutty Brown Ale', and filled my glass. It was a historic moment though I didn't know it then; it was

IF ONLY THEY COULD TALK

the first of an incredible series of Nutty Browns I was to drink at that table.

Mrs Calvert sat down for a moment, crossed her hands on her lap and smiled encouragingly. 'Can you do anything for the calves, then?' she asked.

Phin butted in before I could reply. 'Oh aye, he can an' all. He's put them onto epsom salts.'

'Epsom salts?'

'That's it, Missis. I said when he came that we'd get summat real smart and scientific like. You can't beat new blood and modern ideas.' Phin sipped his beer gravely.

Over the following days the calves gradually improved and at the end of a fortnight they were all eating normally. The worst one still showed a trace of blindness, but I was confident this too would clear up.

It wasn't long before I saw Phin again. It was early afternoon and I was in the office with Siegfried when the outer door banged and the passage echoed to the clumping of hob nails. I heard a voice raised in song – hi-ti-tiddly-rum-te-tum. Phineas was in our midst once more.

'Well, well, well!' he bawled heartily at Miss Harbottle. 'It's Flossie! And what's my little darlin' doing this fine day?'

There was not a flicker from Miss Harbottle's granite features. She directed an icy stare at the intruder but Phin swung round on Siegfried with a yellow-toothed grin. 'Now, gaffer, 'ow's tricks?'

'Everything's fine, Mr Calvert,' Siegfried replied. 'What can we do for you?'

Phin stabbed a finger at me. 'There's my man. I want him out to my place right sharpish.'

'What's the trouble?' I asked. 'Is it the calves again?'

'Damn, no! Wish it was. It's me good bull. He's puffin' like a bellows – bit like pneumonia but worse than I've known. He's in a 'ell of a state. Looks like he's peggin' out.' For an instant Phin lost his jocularity.

I had heard of this bull; pedigree shorthorn, show winner, the foundation of his herd. 'I'll be right after you, Mr Calvert. I'll follow you along.'

'Good lad. I'm off, then.' Phin paused at the door, a wild figure, tireless, tattered; baggy trousers ballooning from his ample middle. He turned again to Miss Harbottle and contorted his leathery features into a preposterous leer. 'Ta-ra, Floss!' he cried and was gone.

For a moment the room seemed very empty and quiet except for Miss Harbottle's acid 'Oh, that man! Dreadful! Dreadful!'

I made good time to the farm and found Phin waiting with his three sons. The young men looked gloomy but Phin was still indomitable.

'Here 'e is!' he shouted. 'Happy Harry again. Now we'll be all right.' He even managed a little tune as we crossed to the bull pen but when he looked over the door his head sank on his chest and his hands worked deeper behind his braces.

The bull was standing as though rooted to the middle of the pen. His great rib cage rose and fell with the most laboured respirations I had ever seen. His mouth gaped wide, a bubbling foam hung round his lips and his flaring nostrils; his eyes, almost starting from his head in terror, stared at the wall in front of him. This wasn't pneumonia, it was a frantic battle for breath; and it looked like a losing one.

He didn't move when I inserted my thermometer and though my mind was racing I suspected the half-minute wasn't going to be long enough this time. I had expected accelerated breathing, but nothing like this.

'Poor aud beggar,' Phin muttered. 'He's bred me the finest calves I've ever had and he's quiet as as a sheep, too. I've seen me little grandchildren walk under 'is belly and he's took no notice. I hate to see him sufferin' like this. If you can't do no good, just tell me and I'll get the gun out.'

I took the thermometer out and read it. One hundred and ten degrees fahrenheit. This was ridiculous; I shook it vigorously and pushed it back into the rectum.

I gave it nearly a minute this time so that I could get in some extra thinking. The second reading said a hundred and ten again and I had an unpleasant conviction that if the thermometer had been a foot long the mercury would still have been jammed against the top.

What in the name of God was this? Could be anthrax . . . must be . . . and yet . . . I looked over at the row of heads above the half door; they were waiting for me to say something and their silence accentuated the agonized groaning and panting. I looked above the heads to the square of deep blue and a tufted cloud moving across the sun. As it passed, a single dazzling ray made me close my eyes and a faint bell rang in my mind.

'Has he been out today?' I asked.

'Aye, he's been out on the grass on his tether all morning. It was that grand and warm.'

The bell became a triumphant gong. 'Get a hosepipe in here quick. You can rig it to that tap in the yard.'

'A hosepipe? What the 'ell . . . ?'

'Yes, quick as you can – he's got sunstroke.'

They had the hose fixed in less than a minute. I turned it full on and began to play the jet of cold water all over the huge form – his face and neck, along the ribs, up and down the legs. I kept this up for about five minutes but it seemed a lot longer as I waited for some sign of improvement. I was beginning to think I was on the wrong track when the bull gulped just once.

It was something – he had been unable to swallow his saliva before in his desperate efforts to get the air into his lungs; and I really began to notice a change in the big animal. Surely he was looking just a little less distressed and wasn't the breathing slowing down a bit?

Then the bull shook himself, turned his head and looked at us. There was an awed whisper from one of the young men: 'By gaw, it's working!'

I enjoyed myself after that. I can't thing of anything in my working life that has given me more pleasure than standing in that pen directing the life-saving jet and watching the bull savouring it. He liked it on his face best and as I worked my way up from the tail and along the steaming back he would turn his nose full into the water, rocking his head from side to side and blinking blissfully.

Within half an hour he looked almost normal. His chest was still heaving a little but he was in no discomfort. I tried the temperature again. Down to a hundred and five.

'He'll be all right now,' I said, 'but I think one of the lads should keep the water on him for another twenty minutes or so. I'll have to go now.'

'You've time for a drink,' Phin grunted.

In the farm kitchen his bellow of 'Mother' lacked some of its usual timbre. He dropped into a chair and stared into his glass of Nutty Brown. 'Harry,' he said, 'I'll tell you, you've flummoxed me this time.' He sighed and rubbed his chin in apparent disbelief. 'I don't know what the 'ell to say to you.'

.   .   .

It wasn't often that Phin lost his voice, but he found it again very soon at the next meeting of the farmers' discussion group.

A learned and earnest gentleman had been expounding on the advances in veterinary medicine and how the farmers could now expect their stock to be treated as the doctors treated their human patients, with the newest drugs and procedures.

It was too much for Phin. He jumped to his feet and cried: 'Ah think you're talking a lot of rubbish. There's a young feller in Darrowby not long out of college and it doesn't matter what you call 'im out for he uses nowt but epsom salts and cold water.'

CHAPTER 27

It was during one of Siegfried's efficiency drives that Colonel Merrick's cow picked up a wire. The colonel was a personal friend, which made things even more uncomfortable.

Everybody suffered when Siegfried had these spells. They usually came on after he had been reading a technical work or when he had seen a film of some new technical procedure. He would rampage around, calling on the cowering household to stir themselves and be better men. He would be obsessed, for a time, with the craving for perfection.

'We must put on a better show at these operations on the farms. It just isn't good enough to fish out a few old instruments from a bag and start hacking at the animal. We must have cleanliness, asepsis if possible, and an orderly technique.'

So he was jubilant when he diagnosed traumatic reticulitis (foreign body in the second stomach) in the colonel's cow. 'We'll really show old Hubert something. We'll give him a picture of veterinary surgery he'll never forget.'

Tristan and I were pressed into service as assistants, and our arrival at the farm was really impressive. Siegfried led the procession, looking unusually smart in a brand-new tweed jacket of which he was very proud. He was a debonair figure as he shook hands with his friend.

The colonel was jovial. 'Hear you're going to operate on my cow. Take out a wire, eh? Like to watch you do it, if it's all right with you.'

'By all means, Hubert, please do. You'll find it very interesting.'

In the byre, Tristan and I had to bustle about. We arranged tables alongside the cow and on these we placed new metal trays with rows of shining, sterilized instruments. Scalpels, directors, probes, artery forceps, hypodermic syringes, suture needles, gut and silk in glass phials, rolls of cotton wool and various bottles of spirit and other antiseptics.

Siegfried fussed around, happy as a schoolboy. He had clever hands and, as a surgeon, he was worth watching. I could read his mind without much trouble. This, he was thinking, was going to be good.

When all was to his liking, he took off his jacket and donned a brilliantly white smock. He handed the jacket to Tristan and almost instantly gave a roar of anger. 'Hey, don't just throw it down on that meal bin! Here, give it to me. I'll find a safe place for it.' He dusted the new garment down tenderly and hung it on a nail on the wall.

Meanwhile, I had shaved and disinfected the operation site on the flank and everything was ready for the local anaesthetic. Siegfried took the syringe and quickly infiltrated the area. 'This is where we go inside, Hubert. I hope you aren't squeamish.'

The colonel beamed. 'Oh, I've seen blood before. You needn't worry, I shan't faint.'

With a bold sweep of the scalpel, Siegfried incised the skin, then the muscles and finally, with delicate care, the glistening peritoneum. The smooth wall of the rumen (the large first stomach) lay exposed.

Siegfried reached for a fresh scalpel and looked for the best place to cut in. But as he poised his knife, the wall of the rumen suddenly bulged out through the skin incision. 'Unusual,' he muttered. 'Probably a bit of rumenal gas.' Unflurried, he gently thrust back the protrusion and prepared again to make his cut; but as he withdrew his hand, the rumen welled out after it, a pinkish mass bigger than a football. Siegfried pushed it back and it shot out again immediately, ballooning to a startling size. This time, he took two hands to the job, pushing and pressing till he forced the thing once more out of sight. He stood for a moment with his hands inside the cow, breathing heavily. Two beads of sweat trickled down his forehead.

Carefully, he withdrew his hands. Nothing happened. It must have settled down. He was reaching back for his knife when, like a live thing, the rumen again came leaping and surging out. It seemed almost as though the entire organ had escaped through the incision – a slippery, gleaming mass rising and swelling till it was level with his eyes.

Siegfried had dropped all pretence of calm and was fighting desperately, both arms round the thing, pressing downwards with all his strength. I hastened forward to help and, as I drew near, he whispered hoarsely: 'What the hell is it?' Clearly, he was wondering if this pulsating heap of tissue was some part of the bovine anatomy he had never even heard of.

Silently, we fought the mass down till it was level with the skin. The colonel was watching intently. He hadn't expected the operation to be so interesting. His eyebrows were slightly raised.

'It must be gas that's doing this,' panted Siegfried. 'Pass me the knife and stand back.'

He inserted the knife into the rumen and cut sharply downwards. I was glad I had moved away because, through the incision shot a high-pressure jet of semi-liquid stomach contents – a greenish-brown, foul-smelling cascade which erupted from the depths of the cow as from an invisible pump.

The first direct hit was on Siegfried's face. He couldn't release his hold of the rumen or it would have slipped back into the abdomen and contaminated the peritoneum. So he hung onto each side of the opening while the evil torrent poured onto his hair, down his neck and all over his lovely white smock.

Now and then, the steady stream would be varied by a sudden explosion which sent the fermenting broth spouting viciously over everything in the immediate vicinity. Within a minute, the trays with their gleaming instruments were thoroughly covered. The tidy rows of swabs, the snowy tufts of cotton wool disappeared without trace, but it was the unkindest cut of all when a particular powerful jet sent a liberal spray over the new jacket hanging on the wall. Siegfried's face was too obscured for me to detect any change of expression but at this disaster, I saw real anguish in his eyes.

The colonel's eyebrows were now raised to the maximum and his mouth hung open as he gazed in disbelief at the chaotic scene. Siegfried, still hanging grimly on, was the centre of it all, paddling about in a reeking swamp which came half-way up his wellington boots. He looked like a Fiji Islander with his hair stiffened and frizzled and his eyes rolling whitely in the brown face.

Eventually, the flood slowed to a trickle and stopped. I was able to hold the lips of the wound while Siegfried inserted his arm and felt his way to the reticulum. I watched him as he groped inside the honey-combed organ far out of sight against the diaphragm. A satisfied grunt told me he had located the piercing wire and within seconds he had removed it.

Tristan had been frantically salvaging and washing suture materials and soon the incision in the rumen was stitched. Siegfried's heroic stand had not been in vain; there was no contamination of the peritoneum.

Silently and neatly, he secured the skin and muscles with retention sutures and swabbed round the wound. Everything looked fine. The cow seemed unperturbed; under the anaesthetic she had known nothing of the titanic struggle with her insides. In fact, freed from the discomfort of the transfixing wire, she appeared already to be feeling better.

It took quite a time to tidy up the mess and the most difficult job was to make Siegfried presentable. We did our best by swilling him down with buckets of water while, all the time, he scraped sadly at his new jacket with a flat stick. It didn't make much difference.

The colonel was hearty and full of congratulations. 'Come in, my dear chap. Come in and have a drink.' But the invitation had a hollow ring and he took care to stand at least ten feet away from his friend. Siegfried threw his bedraggled jacket over his shoulder. 'No thank you, Hubert. It's most kind of you, but we must be off.' He went out of the byre. 'I think you'll find the cow will be eating in a day or two. I'll be back in a fortnight to take out the stitches.'

In the confined space of the car, Tristan and I were unable to get as far away from him as we could have liked. Even with our heads stuck out of the windows it was still pretty bad.

Siegfried drove for a mile or two in silence, then he turned to me and his streaked features broke into a grin. There was something indomitable about him. 'You never know what's round the corner in this game, my boys, but just think of this – that operation was a success.'

CHAPTER 28

There were three of us in the cheerless yard, Isaac Cranford, Jeff Mallock and myself. The only one who looked at ease was Mallock and it was fitting that it should be so, since he was, in a manner of speaking, the host. He owned the knacker's yard and he looked on benignly as we peered into the carcass of the cow he had just opened.

In Darrowby the name Mallock had a ring of doom. It was the graveyard of livestock, of farmers' ambitions, of veterinary surgeons' hopes. If ever an animal was very ill somebody was boud to say: 'I reckon she'll be off to Mallock's afore long,' or 'Jeff Mallock'll have 'er in t' finish.' And the premises fitted perfectly into the picture; a group of drab, red-brick buildings standing a few fields back from the road with a stumpy chimney from which rolled endlessly a dolorous black smoke.

It didn't pay to approach Mallock's too closely unless you had a strong stomach, so the place was avoided by the townspeople, but if you ventured up the lane and peeped through the sliding metal doors you could look in on a nightmare world. Dead animals lay everywhere. Most of them were dismembered and great chunks of meat hung on hooks, but here and there you could see a bloated sheep or a greenish, swollen pig which not even Jeff could bring himself to open.

Skulls and dry bones were piled to the roof in places and brown mounds of meat stood in the corners. The smell was bad at any time but when Jeff was boiling up the carcasses it was indescribable. The Mallock family bungalow stood in the middle of the buildings and strangers could be pardoned if they expected a collection of wizened gnomes to dwell there. But Jeff was a pink-faced, cherubic man in his forties, his wife plump, smiling and comely. Their family ranged from a positively beautiful girl of nineteen down to a robust five-year-old boy. There were eight young Mallocks and they had spent their lifetimes playing among tuberculous lungs and a vast spectrum of bacteria from salmonella to anthrax. They were the healthiest children in the district.

It was said in the pubs that Jeff was one of the richest men in the town but the locals, as they supped their beer, had to admit that he earned his money. At any hour of the day or night he would rattle out into the country in his ramshackle lorry, winch on a carcass, bring it back to the yard and cut it up. A dog-food dealer came twice a week from Brawton with a van and bought the fresh meat. The rest of the stuff Jeff shovelled into his boiler to make the meat meal which was in great demand for mixing in pig and poultry rations. The bones went for making fertilizer, the hides to the tanner and the nameless odds and ends were collected by a wild-eyed individual known only as the 'ket feller'. Sometimes, for a bit of variety, Jeff would make long slabs of strange-smelling soap which found a brisk sale for scrubbing shop floors. Yes, people said, there was no doubt Jeff did all right. But, by gaw, he earned it.

My contacts with Mallock were fairly frequent. A knacker's yard had a useful function for a vet. It served as a crude post-mortem room, a place where he could check on his diagnosis in fatal cases; and on occasions where he had been completely baffled, the mysteries would be revealed under Jeff's knife.

Often, of course, farmers would send in an animal which I had been treating and ask Jeff to tell them 'what had been wrong wi' t' and this was where a certain amount of friction arose. Because Jeff was placed in a position of power and seldom resisted the temptation to wield it. Although he could neither read nor write, he was a man of great professional pride; he didn't like to be called a knacker man but preferred 'fell-monger'. He considered in his heart that, after twenty-odd years of cutting up diseased animals he knew more than any vet alive, and it made things rather awkward that the farming community unhesitatingly agreed with him.

It never failed to spoil my day if a farmer called in at the surgery and told me that, once more, Jeff Mallock had confounded my diagnosis. 'Hey, remember that cow you were treating for magnesium deficiency? She never did no good and ah sent 'er into Mallock's. Well, you know what was really the matter wi' 'er? Worm i' the tail. Jeff said if you'd nobbut cut tail off, that cow would have gotten up and walked away.' It was no good arguing or saying there was no such thing as worm in the tail. Jeff knew – that was all about it.

If only Jeff had taken his priceless opportunities to acquire a common-sense knowledge it wouldn't have been so bad. But instead, he had built up a weird pathology of his own and backed it up by black magic remedies gleaned from his contacts with the more primitive members of the farming community. His four stock diseases were Stagnation of t'lungs, Black Rot, Gastric Ulsters and Golf Stones. It was a quartet which made the vets tremble for miles around.

Another cross which the vets had to bear was his unique gift of being able to take one look at a dead animal on a farm and pronounce immediately on the cause of death. The farmers, awe-struck by his powers, were always asking me why I couldn't do it. But I was unable to dislike the man. He would have had to be more than human to resist the chance to be important and there was no malice in his actions. Still, it made things uncomfortable at times and I liked to be on the spot myself whenever possible. Especially when Isaac Cranford was involved.

Cranford was a hard man, a man who had cast his life in a mould of iron austerity. A sharp bargainer, a win-at-all-cost character and, in a region where thrift was general, he was noted for meanness. He farmed some of the best land in the lower Dale, his shorthorns won prizes regularly at the shows but he was nobody's friend. Mr Bateson, his neighbour to the north, summed it up: 'That feller 'ud skin a flca for its hide.' Mr Dickon, his neighbour to the south, put it differently: 'If he gets haud on a pound note, by gaw it's a prisoner.'

This morning's meeting had had its origin the previous day. A phone call mid-afternoon from Mr Cranford. 'I've had a cow struck by lightning. She's laid dead in the field.'

I was surprised. 'Lightning? Are you sure? We haven't had a storm today.'

'Maybe you haven't, but we have 'ere.'

'Mmm, all right, I'll come and have a look at her.'

Driving to the farm, I couldn't work up much enthusiasm for the impending interview. This lightning business could be a bit of a headache. All farmers were insured against lightning stroke – it was usually part of their fire policy – and after a severe thunderstorm it was common enough for the vets' phones to start ringing with requests to examine dead beasts.

The insurance companies were reasonable about it. If they received a certificate from the vet that he believed lightning to be the cause of death they would usually pay up without fuss. In cases of doubt they would ask for a post-mortem or a second opinion from another practitioner. The difficulty was that there are no diagnostic post-mortem features to go on; occasionally a bruising of the tissues under the skin, but very little else. The happiest situation was when the beast was found with the tell-tale scorch marks running from an ear down the leg to earth into the ground. Often the animal would be found under a tree which itself had obviously been blasted and torn by lightning. Diagnosis was easy then.

Ninety-nine per cent of the farmers were looking only for a square deal and if their vet found some other clear cause of death they would accept his verdict philosophically. But the odd one could be very difficult.

I had heard Siegfried tell of one old chap who had called him out to verify a lightning death. The long scorch marks on the carcass were absolutely classical and Siegfried, viewing them, had been almost lyrical. 'Beautiful, Charlie, beautiful, I've never seen more typical marks. But there's just one thing.' He put an arm round the old man's shoulder. 'What a great pity you let the candle grease fall on the skin.'

The old man looked closer and thumped a fist into his palm. 'Dang it, you're right, maister! Ah've mucked t'job up. And ah took pains ower it an' all – been on for dang near an hour.' He walked away muttering. He showed no embarrassment, only disgust at his own technological shortcomings.

But this, I thought, as the stone walls flipped past the car windows, would be very different. Cranford was in the habit of getting his own way, right or wrong, and if he didn't get it today there would be trouble.

I drove through the farm gate and along a neat tarmac road across the single field. Mr Cranford was standing motionless in the middle of the yard and I was struck, not for the first time, by the man's resemblance to a big, hungry bird. The hunched narrow shoulders, the forward-thrust, sharp-beaked face, the dark overcoat hanging loosely on the bony frame. I wouldn't have been surprised if he had spread his wings and flapped his way onto the byre roof. Instead, he nodded impatiently at me and began to hasten with short, tripping steps to a field at the back of the house.

It was a large field and the dead cow lay almost in the centre. There were no trees, no hedges, not even a small bush. My hopeful picture of the body under a stricken tree melted immediately, leaving an anxious void.

We stopped beside the cow and Mr Cranford was the first to speak. 'Bound to be lightning. Can't be owt else. Nasty storm, then this good beast dropping down dead.'

I looked at the grass around the big Shorthorn. It had been churned and torn out, leaving patches of bare earth. 'But it hasn't exactly dropped down, has it? It died in convulsions – you can see where its feet have kicked out the grass.'

'All right then, it 'ad a convulsion, but it was lightning that caused it.' Mr Cranford had fierce little eyes and they darted flitting glances at my shirt collar, mackintosh belt, wellingtons. He never could quite bring himself to look anybody in the eye.

'I doubt it, Mr Cranford. One of the signs of lightning stroke is that the beast has fallen without a struggle. Some of them even have grass in their mouths.'

'Oh, I know all about that,' Cranford snapped, his thin face flushing. 'I've been among livestock for half a century and this isn't the first beast I've seen that's been struck. They're not all t'same, you know.'

'Oh, I realize that, but, you see, this death could have been caused by so many things.'

'What sort o' things?'

'Well, anthrax for a start, magnesium deficiency, heart trouble – there's quite a list. I really think we ought to do a post-mortem to make sure.'

'Now see here, are you saying I'm trying to do summat I shouldn't?'

'Not at all. I'm only saying we should make sure before I write a certificate. We can go and see her opened at Mallock's and, believe me, if there's no other obvious cause of death you'll get the benefit of the doubt. The insurance people are pretty good about it.'

Mr Cranford's predatory features sank lower into his coat collar. He dug his hands viciously into his pockets. 'I've had vitneries at these jobs afore. Proper, experienced vitneries, too.' The little eyes flashed in the direction of my left ear. 'They've never messed about like this. What's the use of going to all that trouble? Why do you have to be so damn particular?'

Why indeed, I thought. Why make an enemy of this man? He wielded a lot of power in the district. Prominent in the local Farmers' Union, a member of every agricultural committee for miles around. He was a wealthy, successful man and, if people didn't like him they respected his knowledge and listened to him. He could do a young vet a lot of harm. Why not write the certificate and go home? This is to certify that I have examined that above-mentioned animal and, in my opinion, lightning stroke was the cause of death. It would be easy and Cranford would be mollified. It would be the end of the whole thing. Why antagonize this dangerous character for nothing? Maybe it really was lightning, anyway.

I turned to face Mr Cranford, trying in vain to look into his eyes that always veered away at the last moment. 'I'm sorry, but I feel we ought to have a look inside this cow. I'll ring Mallock and ask him to pick her up and we can see her in the morning. I'll meet you there at ten o'clock. Will that be all right?'

'Reckon it'll have to be,' Cranford spat out. 'It's a piece o' nonsense, but I suppose I've got to humour you. But just let me remind you – this was a good cow, worth all of eighty pounds. I can't afford to lose that amount of money. I want my rights.'

'I'm sure you'll get them, Mr Cranford. And before I have her moved I'd better take a blood film to eliminate anthrax.'

The farmer had been under a mounting load of pressure. As a pillar of the methodist chapel his range of language was restricted, so he vented his pent-up feelings by kicking out savagely at the carcass. His toe made contact with the unyielding backbone and he hopped around on one leg for a few seconds. Then he limped off towards the house.

I was alone as I nicked the dead ear with my knife and drew a film of blood across a couple of glass slides. It hadn't been a happy session and the one tomorrow didn't hold out much more promise. I enclosed the blood films carefully in a cardboard box and set off for Skeldale House to examine them under the microscope.

. . .

So it wasn't a particularly cheerful group which assembled at the knacker's yard the following morning. Even Jeff, though he preserved his usual Buddha-like expression, was, in fact, deeply offended. The account he had given me when I first arrived at the yard was fragmentary, but I could piece the scene together. Jeff, leaping from his lorry at Cranford's sweeping the carcass with a piercing glance and making his brilliant spot diagnosis. 'Stagnation o' t'lungs. I can allus tell by the look in their eyes and the way their hair lies along t'back.' Waiting confidently for the wondering gasps, the congratulatory speeches which always followed his *tour de force*.

Then Mr Cranford, almost dancing with rage. 'Shut your big, stupid mouth, Mallock, tha knows nowt about it. This cow was struck by lightning and you'd better remember that.'

And now, bending my head over the carcass, I couldn't find a clue anyway. No sign of bruising when the skin was removed. The internal organs clean and normal.

I straightened up and pushed my fingers through my hair. The boiler bubbled softly, puffing out odoriferous wisps into the already highly charged atmosphere. Two dogs licked busily at a pile of meat meal.

Then a chill of horror struck through me. The dogs had competition. A little boy with golden curls was pushing a forefinger into the heap, inserting it in his mouth and sucking with rapt enjoyment.

'Look at that!' I quavered.

The knacker man's face lit up with paternal pride. 'Aye,' he said happily. 'It isn't only the four-legged 'uns wot likes my meal. Wonderful stuff – full of nourishment!'

His good humour completely restored, he struck a match and began to puff appreciatively at a short pipe which was thickly encrusted with evidence of his grisly trade.

I dragged my attention back to the job in hand. 'Cut into the heart, will you, Jeff,' I said.

Jeff deftly sliced the big organ from top to bottom and I knew immediately that my search was over. The auricles and ventricles were almost completely occluded by a cauliflowerlike mass growing from the valves. Verrucose endocarditis, common in pigs but seldom seen in cattle.

'There's what killed your cow, Mr Cranford,' I said.

Cranford aimed his nose at the heart. 'Fiddlesticks! You're not telling me them little things could kill a beast like that.'

'They're not so little. Big enough to stop the flow of blood. I'm sorry, but there's no doubt about it – your cow died of heart failure.'

'And how about lightning?'

'No sign of it, I'm afraid. You can see for yourself.'

'And what about my eighty pounds?'

'I'm truly sorry about that, but it doesn't alter the facts.'

'Facts! What facts? I've come along this morning and you've shown me nowt to make me change my opinion.'

'Well, there's nothing more I can say. It's a clear-cut case.'

Mr Cranford stiffened in his perching stance. He held his hands against the front of his coat and the fingers and thumbs rubbed together unceasingly as though fondling the beloved bank-notes which were slipping away from him. His face, sunk deeper in his collar, appeared still sharper in outline.

Then he turned to me and made a ghastly attempt to smile. And his eyes, trained on my lapels, tried valiantly to inch their way upwards. There was a fleeting instance when they met my gaze before flickering away in alarm.

He drew me to one side and addressed himself to my larynx. There was a wheedling note in the hoarse whisper.

'Now look here, Mr Herriot, we're both men of the world. You know as well as I do that the insurance company can afford this loss a lot better nor me. So why can't you just say it is lightning?'

'Even though I think it isn't?'

'Well, what the hangment does it matter? You can say it is, can't you? Nobody's going to know.'

I scratched my head. 'But what would bother me, Mr Cranford, is that I would know.'

'You would know?' The farmer was mystified.

'That's right. And it's no good – I can't give you a certificate for this cow and that's the end of it.'

Dismay, disbelief, frustration chased across Mr Cranford's features. 'Well, I'll tell you this. I'm not leaving the matter here. I'm going to see your boss about you.' He swung round and pointed at the cow. 'There's no sign of disease there. Trying to tell me it's all due to little things in the heart. You don't know your job – you don't even know what them things are!'

Jeff Mallock removed his unspeakable pipe from his mouth. 'But ah know. It's what ah said. Stagnation o' t'lungs is caused by milk from milk vein getting back into the body. Finally it gets to t'heart and then it's over wi't. Them's milk clots you're looking at.'

Cranford rounded on him. 'Shut up, you great gumph! You're as bad as this feller here. It was lightning killed my good cow. Lightning!' He was almost screaming. Then he controlled himself and spoke quietly to me. 'You'll hear more of this, Mr Knowledge, and I'll just tell you one thing. You'll never walk on my farm again.' He turned and hurried away with his quick-stepping gait.

I said good morning to Jeff and climbed wearily into my car. Well, everything had worked out just great. If only vetting just consisted of treating sick animals. But it didn't. There were so many other things. I started the engine and drove away.

CHAPTER 29

It didn't take Mr Cranford long to make good his threat. He called at the surgery shortly after lunch the following day and Siegfried and I, enjoying a post-prandial cigarette in the sitting-room, heard the jangle of the door bell. We didn't get up, because most of the farmers walked in after ringing.

The dogs, however, went into their usual routine. They had had a long run on the high moor that morning and had just finished licking out their dinner bowls. Tired and distended, they had collapsed in a snoring heap around Siegfried's feet. There was nothing they wanted more than ten minutes' peace but, dedicated as they were to their self-appointed role of fierce guardians of the house, they did not hesitate. They leapt, baying, from the rug and hurled themselves into the passage.

People often wondered why Siegfried kept five dogs. Not only kept them but took them everywhere with him. Driving on his rounds it was difficult to see him at all among the shaggy heads and waving tails; and anybody approaching the car would recoil in terror from the savage barking and the bared fangs and glaring eyes framed in the windows.

'I cannot for the life of me understand,' Siegfried would declare, thumping his fist on his knee, 'why people keep dogs as pets. A dog should have a useful function. Let it be used for farm work, for shooting, for guiding; but why anybody should keep the things just hanging around the place beats me.'

It was a pronouncement he was continually making, often through a screen of flapping ears and lolling tongues as he sat in his car. His listener would look wonderingly from the huge greyhound to the tiny terrier, from the spaniel to the whippet to the Scottie; but nobody ever asked Siegfried why he kept his own dogs.

I judged that the pack fell upon Mr Cranford about the bend of the passage and many a lesser man would have fled; but I could hear him fighting his way doggedly forward. When he came through the sitting-room door he had removed his hat and was beating the dogs off with it. It wasn't a wise move and the barking rose to a higher pitch. The man's eyes stared and his lips moved continuously, but nothing came through.

Siegfried, courteous as ever, rose and indicated a chair. His lips, too, were moving, no doubt in a few gracious words of welcome. Mr Cranford flapped his black coat, swooped across the carpet and perched. The dogs sat in a ring round him and yelled up into his face. Usually they collapsed after their exhausting performance but there was something in the look or smell of Mr Cranford that they didn't like.

Siegfried leant back in his chair, put his fingers together and assumed a judicial expression. Now and again he nodded understandingly or narrowed his eyes as if taking an interesting point. Practically nothing could be heard from Mr Cranford but occasionally a word or phrase penetrated.

'... have a serious complaint to make ...'
'... doesn't know his job ...'
'... can't afford ... not a rich man ...'
'... these danged dogs ...'
'... won't have 'im again ...'
'... down dog, get by ...'
'... nowt but robbery ...'

Siegfried, completely relaxed and apparently oblivious of the din, listened attentively but as the minutes passed I could see the strain beginning to tell on Mr Cranford. His eyes began to start from their sockets and the veins corded on his scrawny neck as he tried to get his

message across. Finally it was too much for him; he jumped up and a
leaping brown tide bore him to the door. He gave a last defiant cry,
lashed out again with his hat and was gone.

. . .

Pushing open the dispensary door a few weeks later, I found my boss
mixing an ointment. He was working with great care, turning and
returning the glutinous mass on a marble slab.

'What's this you're doing?' I asked.

Siegfried threw down his spatula and straightened his back.
'Ointment for a boar.' He looked past me at Tristan who had just come
in. 'And I don't know why the hell I'm doing it when some people are
sitting around on their backsides.' He indicated the spatula. 'Right,
Tristan, you can have a go. When you've finished your cigarette, that is.'

His expression softened as Tristan hastily nipped out his Woodbine
and began to work away on the slab. 'Pretty stiff concoction, that. Takes
a bit of mixing,' Siegfried said with satisfaction, looking at his brother's
bent head. 'The back of my neck was beginning to ache with it.'

He turned to me. 'By the way, you'll be interested to hear it's for your
old friend Cranford. For that prize boar of his. It's got a nasty sore across
its back and he's worried to death about it. Wins him a lot of money at
the shows and a blemish there would be disastrous.'

'Cranford's still with us, then.'

'Yes, it's a funny thing, but we can't get rid of him. I don't like losing
clients but I'd gladly make an exception of this chap. He won't have you
near the place after that lightning job and he makes it very clear he
doesn't think much of me either. Tells me I never do his beasts any good
– says it would have been a lot better if he'd never called me. And moans
like hell when he gets his bill. He's more bother than he's worth and on
top of everything he gives me the creeps. But he won't leave – he damn
well won't leave.'

'He knows which side his bread's buttered,' I said. 'He gets first-rate
service and the moaning is part of the system to keep the bills down.'

'Maybe you're right, but I wish there was a simple way to get rid of
him.' He tapped Tristan on the shoulder. 'All right, don't strain
yourself. That'll do. Put it into this ointment box and label it: "Apply
liberally to the boar's back three times daily, working it well in with the
fingers". And post it to Mr Cranford. And while you're on, will you post
this faeces sample to the laboratory at Leeds to test for Johne's disease.'
He held out a treacle tin brimming with foul-smelling, liquid diarrhoea.

It was a common thing to collect such samples and send them away
for Johne's tests, worm counts, etc., and there was always one thing all
the samples had in common – they were very large. All that was needed

for the tests was a couple of teaspoonfuls but the farmers were lavish in their quantities. They seemed pleasantly surprised that all the vet wanted was a bit of muck from the dung channel; they threw aside their natural caution and shovelled the stuff up cheerfully into the biggest container they could find. They brushed aside all protests; 'take plenty, we've lots of it' was there attitude.

Tristan took hold of the tin gingerly and began to look along the shelves. 'We don't seem to have any of those little glass sample jars.'

'That's right, we're out of them,' said Siegfried. 'I meant to order some more. But never mind – shove the lid on that tin and press it down tight, then parcel it up well in brown paper. It'll travel to the lab all right.'

It took only three days for Mr Cranford's name to come up again. Siegfried was opening the morning mail, throwing the circulars to one side and making a pile of the bills and receipts when he became suddenly very still. He had frozen over a letter on blue notepaper and he sat like a statue till he read it through. At length he raised his head; his face was expressionless. 'James, this is just about the most vitriolic letter I have ever read. It's from Cranford. He's finished with us for good and all and is considering taking legal action against us.'

'What have we done this time?' I asked.

'He accuses us of grossly insulting him and endangering the health of his boar. He says we sent him a treacle tin full of cow shit with instructions to rub it on the boar's back three times daily.'

Tristan, who had been sitting with his eyes half closed, became fully awake. He rose unhurriedly and began to make his way towards the door. His hand was on the knob when his brother's voice thundered out.

'Tristan! Come back here! Sit down – I think we have something to talk about.'

Tristan looked up resolutely, waiting for the storm to break, but Siegfried was unexpectedly calm. His voice was gentle.

'So you've done it again. When will I ever learn that I can't trust you to carry out the simplest task. It wasn't much to ask, was it? Two little parcels to post – hardly a tough assignment. But you managed to botch it. You got the labels wrong, didn't you?'

Tristan wriggled in his chair. 'I'm sorry, I can't think how ...'

Siegfried held up his hand. 'Oh, don't worry. Your usual luck has come to your aid. With anybody else this bloomer would be catastrophic but with Cranford – it's like divine providence.' He paused for a moment and a dreamy expression crept into his eyes. 'The label said to work it well in with the fingers, I seem to recall. And Mr Cranford says he

opened the package at the breakfast table ... Yes, Tristan, I think you
have found the way. This, I do believe, has done it.'

I said, 'But how about the legal action?'

'Oh, I think we can forget about that. Mr Cranford has a great sense
of his own dignity. Just think how it would sound in court.' He crumpled
the letter and dropped it into the wastepaper basket. 'Well, let's get on
with some work.'

He led the way out and stopped abruptly in the passage. He turned to
face us. 'There's another thing, of course. I wonder how the lab is
making out, testing that ointment for Johne's disease?'

CHAPTER 30

I was really worried about Tricki this time. I had pulled up my car when
I saw him in the street with his mistress and I was shocked at his
appearance. He had become hugely fat, like a bloated sausage with a leg
at each corner. His eyes, bloodshot and rheumy, stared straight ahead
and his tongue lolled from his jaws.

Mrs Pumphrey hastened to explain. 'He was so listless, Mr Herriot.
He seemed to have no energy. I thought he must be suffering from
malnutrition, so I have been giving him some little extras between meals
to build him up. Some calf's foot jelly and malt and cod-liver oil and a
bowl of Horlick's at night to make him sleep – nothing much really.'

'And did you cut down on the sweet things as I told you?'

'Oh, I did for a bit, but he seemed to be so weak. I had to relent. He
does love cream cakes and chocolates so. I can't bear to refuse him.'

I looked down again at the little dog. That was the trouble. Tricki's
only fault was greed. He had never been known to refuse food; he would
tackle a meal at any hour of the day or night. And I wondered about all
the things Mrs Pumphrey hadn't mentioned; the pâté on thin biscuits,
the fudge, the rich trifles – Tricki loved them all.

'Are you giving him plenty of exercise?'

'Well, he has his little walks with me as you can see, but Hodgkin has
been down with lumbago, so there has been no ring-throwing lately.'

I tried to sound severe. 'Now I really mean this. If you don't cut his
food right down and give him more exercise he is going to be really ill.
You must harden your heart and keep him on a very strict diet.'

Mrs Pumphrey wrung her hands. 'Oh I will, Mr Herriot. I'm sure you
are right, but it is so difficult, so very difficult.' She set off, head down,

along the road, as if determined to put the new regime into practice immediately.

I watched their progress with growing concern. Tricki was tottering along in his little tweed coat; he had a whole wardrobe of these coats – warm tweed or tartan ones for the cold weather and mackintoshes for the wet days. He struggled on, drooping in his harness. I thought it wouldn't be long before I heard from Mrs Pumphrey.

The expected call came within a few days. Mrs Pumphrey was distraught. Tricki would eat nothing. Refused even his favourite dishes; and besides, he had bouts of vomiting. He spent all his time lying on a rug, panting. Didn't go for walks, didn't want to do anything.

I had made my plans in advance. The only way was to get Tricki out of the house for a period. I suggested that he be hospitalized for about a fortnight to be kept under observation.

The poor lady almost swooned. She had never been separated from her darling before; she was sure he would pine and die if he did not see her every day.

But I took a firm line. Tricki was very ill and this was the only way to save him; in fact, I thought it best to take him without delay and, followed by Mrs Pumphrey's wailings, I marched out to the car carrying the little dog wrapped in a blanket.

The entire staff was roused and maids rushed in and out bringing his day bed, his night bed, favourite cushions, toys and rubber rings, breakfast bowl, lunch bowl, supper bowl. Realizing that my car would never hold all the stuff, I started to drive away. As I moved off, Mrs Pumphrey, with a despairing cry, threw an armful of the little coats through the window. I looked in the mirror before I turned the corner of the drive; everybody was in tears.

Out on the road, I glanced down at the pathetic little animal gasping on the seat by my side. I patted the head and Tricki made a brave effort to wag his tail. 'Poor old lad,' I said, 'You haven't a kick in you but I think I know a cure for you.'

At the surgery, the household dogs surged round me. Tricki looked down at the noisy pack with dull eyes and, when put down, lay motionless on the carpet. The other dogs, after sniffing round him for a few seconds, decided he was an uninteresting object and ignored him.

I made up a bed for him in a warm loose box next to the one where the other dogs slept. For two days I kept an eye on him, giving him no food but plenty of water. At the end of the second day he started to show some interest in his surroundings and on the third he began to whimper when he heard the dogs in the yard.

When I opened the door, Tricki trotted out and was immediately engulfed by Joe the greyhound and his friends. After rolling him over and thoroughly inspecting him, the dogs moved off down the garden. Tricki followed them, rolling slightly with his surplus fat but obviously intrigued.

Later that day, I was present at feeding-time. I watched while Tristan slopped the food into the bowls. There was the usual headlong rush followed by the sounds of high-speed eating; every dog knew that if he fell behind the others he was liable to have some competition for the last part of his meal.

When they had finished, Tricki took a walk round the shining bowls, licking casually inside one or two of them. Next day, an extra bowl was put out for him and I was pleased to see him jostling his way towards it.

From then on, his progress was rapid. He had no medicinal treatment of any kind but all day he ran about with the dogs, joining in their friendly scrimmages. He discovered the joys of being bowled over, trampled on and squashed every few minutes. He became an accepted member of the gang, an unlikely, silky little object among the shaggy crew, fighting like a tiger for his share at meal-times and hunting rats in the old hen house at night. He had never had such a time in his life.

All the while, Mrs Pumphrey hovered anxiously in the background, ringing a dozen times a day for the latest bulletins. I dodged the questions about whether his cushions were being turned regularly or his correct coat worn according to the weather; but I was able to tell her that the little fellow was out of danger and convalescing rapidly.

The word 'convalescing' seemed to do something to Mrs Pumphrey. She started to bring round fresh eggs, two dozen at a time, to build up Tricki's strength. For a happy period there were two eggs each for breakfast, but when the bottles of sherry began to arrive, the real possibilities of the situation began to dawn on the household.

It was the same delicious vintage that I knew so well and it was to enrich Tricki's blood. Lunch became a ceremonial occasion with two glasses before and several during the meal. Siegfried and Tristan took turns at proposing Tricki's health and the standard of speechmaking improved daily. As the sponsor, I was always called upon to reply.

We could hardly believe it when the brandy came. Two bottles of Cordon Bleu, intended to put a final edge on Tricki's constitution. Siegfried dug out some balloon glasses belonging to his mother. I had never seen them before, but for a few nights they saw constant service as the fine spirit was rolled around, inhaled and reverently drunk.

They were days of deep content, starting well with the extra egg in the morning, bolstered up and sustained by the midday sherry and finishing luxuriously round the fire with the brandy.

It was a temptation to keep Tricki on as a permanent guest, but I knew Mrs Pumphrey was suffering and after a fortnight, felt compelled to phone and tell her that the little dog had recovered and was awaiting collection.

Within minutes, about thirty feet of gleaming black metal drew up outside the surgery. The chauffeur opened the door and I could just make out the figure of Mrs Pumphrey almost lost in the interior. Her hands were tightly clasped in front of her; her lips trembled. 'Oh, Mr Herriot, do tell me the truth. Is he really better?'

'Yes, he's fine. There's no need for you to get out of the car – I'll go and fetch him.'

I walked through the house into the garden. A mass of dogs was hurtling round and round the lawn and in their midst, ears flapping, tail waving, was the little golden figure of Tricki. In two weeks he had been transformed into a lithe, hard-muscled animal; he was keeping up well with the pack, stretching out in great bounds, his chest almost brushing the ground.

I carried him back along the passage to the front of the house. The chauffeur was still holding the car door open and when Tricki saw his mistress he took off from my arms in a tremendous leap and sailed into Mrs Pumphrey's lap. She gave a startled 'Ooh!' and then had to defend herself as he swarmed over her, licking her face and barking.

During the excitement, I helped the chauffeur to bring out the beds, toys, cushions, coats and bowls, none of which had been used. As the car moved away, Mrs Pumphrey leaned out of the window. Tears shone in her eyes. Her lips trembled.

'Oh, Mr Herriot,' she cried. 'How can I ever thank you? This is a triumph of surgery!'

CHAPTER 31

I came suddenly and violently awake, my heart thudding and pounding in time with the insistent summons of the telephone. These bedside phones were undoubtedly an improvement on the old system when you had to gallop downstairs and stand shivering with your bare feet on the tiles of the passage; but this explosion a few inches from your ear in the small hours when the body was weak and the resistance low was shattering. I felt sure it couldn't be good for me.

The voice at the other end was offensively cheerful. 'I have a mare on foaling. She doesn't seem to be getting on wi' t'job. Reckon foal must be laid wrong – can you come and give me a hand?'

My stomach contracted to a tight ball. This was just a little bit too much; once out of bed in the middle of the night was bad enough, but twice was unfair, in fact it was sheer cruelty. I had had a hard day and had been glad to crawl between the sheets at midnight. I had been hauled out at one o'clock to a damned awkward calving and hadn't got back till nearly three. What was the time now? Three fifteen. Good God, I had only had a few minutes' sleep. And a foaling! Twice as difficult as a calving as a rule. What a life! What a bloody awful life!

I muttered into the receiver, 'Right, Mr Dixon, I'll come straight away' and shuffled across the room, yawning and stretching, feeling the ache in my shoulders and arms. I looked down at the pile of clothing in the chair; I had taken them off, put them on again, taken them off already tonight and something in me rebelled at the thought of putting them on yet again. With a weary grunt I took my mackintosh from the back of the door and donned it over my pyjamas, went downstairs to where my wellingtons stood outside the dispensary door and stuck my feet into them. It was a warm night, what was the point of getting dressed up; I'd only have to strip off again at the farm.

I opened the back door and trailed slowly down the long garden, my tired mind only faintly aware of the fragrance that came from the darkness. I reached the yard at the bottom, opened the double doors into the lane and got the car out of the garage. In the silent town the buildings glowed whitely as the headlights swept across the shuttered shop fronts, the tight-drawn curtains. Everybody was asleep. Everybody except me, James Herriot, creeping sore and exhausted towards another spell of hard labour. Why the hell had I ever decided to become a country vet? I must have been crazy to pick a job where you worked seven days a week and through the night as well. Sometimes I felt as though the practice was a malignant, living entity; testing me, trying me out; putting the pressure on more and more to see just when at what point I would drop down dead.

It was a completely unconscious reaction which hoisted me from my bath of self-pity and left me dripping on the brink, regarding the immediate future with a return of some of my natural optimism. For one thing. Dixon's place was down at the foot of the Dale just off the main road and they had that unusual luxury, electric light in the buildings. And I couldn't be all that tired; not at the age of twenty-four with all my faculties unimpaired. I'd take a bit of killing yet.

I smiled to myself and relapsed into the state of half-suspended animation which was normal to me at these times; a sleepy blanketing of all the senses except those required for the job in hand. Many times over the past months I had got out of bed, driven far into the country, done my job efficiently and returned to bed without ever having been fully awake.

I was right about Dixon's. The graceful Clydesdale mare was in a well-lit loose box and I laid out my ropes and instruments with a feeling of deep thankfulness. As I tipped antiseptic into the steaming bucket I watched the mare straining and paddling her limbs. The effort produced nothing; there were no feet protruding from the vulva. There was almost certainly a malpresentation.

Still thinking hard, I removed my mackintosh and was jerked out of my reverie by a shout of laughter from the farmer. 'God 'elp us, what's this, the Fol-de-rols?'

I looked down at my pyjamas which were pale blue with an arresting broad stripe. 'This, Mr Dixon,' I replied with dignity, 'is my night attire. I didn't bother to dress.'

'Oh, I see now.' The farmer's eyes glinted impishly. 'I'm sorry, but I thought I'd got the wrong chap for a second. I saw a feller just like you at Blackpool last year – same suit exactly, but he 'ad a stripy top hat too and a stick. Did a champion little dance.'

'Can't oblige you, I'm afraid,' I said with a wan smile. 'I'm just not in the mood right now.'

I stripped off, noting with interest the deep red grooves caused by the calf's teeth a couple of hours ago. Those teeth had been like razors, peeling off neat little rolls of skin every time I pushed my arm past them.

The mare trembled as I felt my way inside her. Nothing, nothing, then just a tail and the pelvic bones and the body and hind legs disappearing away beyond my reach. Breech presentation; easy in the cow for a man who knew his job but tricky in the mare because of the tremendous length of the foal's legs.

It took me a sweating, panting half-hour with ropes and a blunt hook on the end of a flexible cane to bring the first leg round. The second leg came more easily and the mare seemed to know there was no obstruction now. She gave a great heave and the foal shot out onto the straw with myself, arms around its body, sprawling on top of it. To my delight I felt the small form jerking convulsively; I had felt no movement while I was working and had decided that it was dead, but the foal was very much alive, shaking its head and snorting out the placental fluid it had inhaled during its delayed entry.

When I had finished towelling myself I turned to see the farmer with an abnormally straight face, holding out my colourful jacket like a valet. 'Allow me, sir,' he said gravely.

'O.K., O.K.,' I laughed, 'I'll get properly dressed next time.' As I was putting my things in the car boot the farmer carelessly threw a parcel onto the back seat.

'Bit o' butter for you,' he muttered. When I started the engine he bent level with the window. 'I think a bit about that mare and I've been badly wanting a foal out of her. Thank ye lad, thank ye very much.'

He waved as I moved away and I heard his parting cry. 'You did all right for a Kentucky Minstrel!'

I leant back in my seat and peered through heavy lids at the empty road unwinding in the pale morning light. The sun had come up – a dark crimson ball hanging low over the misted fields. I felt utterly content, warm with the memory of the foal trying to struggle onto its knees, its absurdly long legs still out of control. Grand that the little beggar had been alive after all – there was something desolate about delivering a lifeless creature.

The Dixon farm was in the low country where the Dale widened out and gave onto the great plain of York. I had to cross a loop on the busy road which connected the West Riding with the industrial North East. A thin tendril of smoke rose from the chimney of the all-night transport café which stood there and as I slowed down to take the corner a faint but piercing smell of cooking found its way into the car; the merest breath but rich in the imagery of fried sausages and beans and tomatoes and chips.

God, I was starving. I looked at my watch; five fifteen, I wouldn't be eating for a long time yet. I turned in among the lorries on the broad strip of tarmac.

Hastening towards the still lighted building I decided that I wouldn't be greedy. Nothing spectacular, just a nice sandwich. I had been here a few times before and the sandwiches were very good; and I deserved some nourishment after my hard night.

I stepped into the warm interior where groups of lorry drivers sat behind mounded plates, but as I crossed the floor the busy clatter died and was replaced by a tense silence. A fat man in a leather jacket sat transfixed, a loaded fork half-way to his mouth, while his neighbour, gripping a huge mug of tea in an oily hand stared with bulging eyes at my ensemble.

It occurred to me then that bright red striped pyjamas and wellingtons might seem a little unusual in those surroundings and I hastily buttoned my mackintosh which had been billowing behind me. Even closed, it was on the short side and at least a foot of pyjama leg showed above my boots.

Resolutely I strode over to the counter. An expressionless blonde bulging out of a dirty white overall on the breast pocket of which was inscribed 'Dora' regarded me blankly.

'A ham sandwich and a cup of Bovril, please,' I said huskily. As the blonde put a teaspoonful of Bovril into a cup and filled it with a hissing jet of hot water I was uncomfortably aware of the silence behind me and of the battery of eyes focused on my legs. On my right I could just see the leather-jacketed man. He filled his mouth and chewed reflectively for a few moments.

'Takes all kinds, don't it, Ernest,' he said in a judicial tone.

'Does indeed, Kenneth, does indeed,' replied his companion.

'Would you say, Ernest, that this is what the Yorkshire country gentleman is wearing this spring?'

'Could be, Kenneth, could be.'

Listening to the titters from the rear, I concluded that these two were the accepted café wags. Best to eat up quickly and get out. Dora pushed the thickly meated sandwich across the counter and spoke with all the animation of a sleep-walker. 'That'll be a shillin'.'

I slipped my hand inside my coat and encountered the pocketless flannelette beneath. God almighty, my money was in my trousers back in Darrowby! A wave of sickly horror flooded me as I began a frantic, meaningless search through my mackintosh.

I looked wildly at the blonde and saw her slip the sandwich under the counter. 'Look, I've come out without any money. I've been in here before – do you know who I am?'

Dora gave a single bored shake of her head.

'Well, never mind,' I babbled, 'I'll pop in with the money next time I'm passing.'

Dora's expression did not alter but she raised one eyebrow fractionally; she made no effort to retrieve the sandwich from its hiding place.

Escape was the only thing in my mind now. Desperately I sipped at the scalding fluid.

Kenneth pushed back his plate and began to pick his teeth with a match. 'Ernest,' he said as though coming to a weighty conclusion. 'It's my opinion that this 'ere gentleman is eccentric.'

'Eccentric?' Ernest sniggered into his tea. 'Bloody daft, more like.'

'Ah, but not so daft, Ernest. Not daft enough to pay for 'is grub.'

'You 'ave a point there, Kenneth, a definite point.'

'You bet I have. He's enjoying a nice cup of Bovril on the house and if 'e hadn't mistimed his fumble he'd be at the sandwich too. Dora moved a bit sharpish for 'im there – another five seconds and he'd have had 'is choppers in the ham.'

'True, true,' muttered Ernest, seemingly content with his role of straight man.

Kenneth put away his match, sucked his teeth noisily and leant back. 'There's another possibility we 'aven't considered. He could be on the run.'

'Escaped convict, you mean, Kenneth.'

'I do, Ernest, I do indeed.'

'But them fellers allus have arrows on their uniforms.'

'Ah, some of 'em do. But I 'eard somewhere that some of the prisons is going in for stripes now.'

I had had enough. Tipping the last searing drops of Bovril down my throat I made headlong for the door. As I stepped out into the early sunshine Kenneth's final pronouncement reached me.

'Prob'ly got away from a working party. Look at them wellingtons ...'

POSTSCRIPT

I remember it was an afternoon when the sun blazed. I filled my car with Siegfried's dogs and drove to where an old mine track climbed green and inviting on the side of a steep gill. We walked a mile or two on the smooth turf then turned off and headed straight up the hillside through the hot bracken scent and the hum of flies to the very top where the wind was sweet and welcome and you could see nearly all of the Dale laid out there beneath; nearly all of it from the head where the great bare hills stood on the edge of the wild right down to the rich plain, chequered and hazy, at the foot.

I was sitting in the heather with the dogs in an expectant ring when the Dales smell came up on the breeze, the fragrance which the wind stole from the miles of warm grass and the shy flowers of the moorland. It had met me when I first stepped off the bus at Darrowby a year ago. And I realized that I had worked my way through the full cycle: I had travelled that magical first time round.

And it had all happened down there. Many of the farms in the practice were visible from where I sat; splashes of grey stone with their livestock, motionless dots from this distance, scattered in the fields around them. They were unrecognizable as the battlegrounds of the past year, the scenes of my first struggles where everything had happened from heady success to abject failure.

There were people down there who thought I was a pretty fair vet, some who regarded me as an amiable idiot, a few who were convinced I was a genius and one or two who would set their dogs on me if I put a foot inside their gates.

All this in a year. What would be the position in thirty years? Well, as it turned out, very much the same.

And what of the animals around whom the whole little drama revolves? It is a pity they cannot talk because it would be charming to have their views. There are a few things I would like to know. What do they think of their widely varying lives? What do they think of us? And do they manage to get a laugh out of it all?

THE END

Ring of
Bright Water

Gavin Maxwell

For John Donald
and Mary MacLeod of Tormor

THE RING

He has married me with a ring, a ring of bright water
Whose ripples travel from the heart of the sea,
He has married me with a ring of light, the glitter
Broadcast on the swift river.
He has married me with the sun's circle
Too dazzling to see, traced in summer sky.
He has crowned me with the wreath of white cloud
That gathers on the snowy summit of the mountain,
Ringed me round with the world-circling wind,
Bound me to the whirlwind's centre.
He has married me with the orbit of the moon
And with the boundless circle of the stars
With the orbits that measure years, months, days, and nights.
Set the tides flowing,
Command the winds to travel or be at rest.

At the ring's centre,
Spirit, or angel troubling the still pool,
Causality not in nature,
Finger's touch that summons at a point, a moment
Stars and planets, life and light
Or gathers cloud about an apex of cold,
Transcendent touch of love summons my world to being.

FOREWORD

In writing this book about my home I have not given to the house
its true name. This is from no desire to create mystery – indeed it will
be easy enough for the curious to discover where I live – but because
identification in print would seem in some sense a sacrifice, a betrayal
of its remoteness and isolation, as if by doing so I were to bring nearer
its enemies of industry and urban life. Camusfeàrna, I have called it,
the Bay of the Alders, from the trees that grow along the burn side;
but the name is of little consequence, for such bays and houses, empty
and long disused, are scattered throughout the wild sea lochs of the
Western Highlands and the Hebrides, and in the description of one
the reader may perhaps find the likeness of others of which he has himself
been fond, for these places are symbols. Symbols, for me and for many,
of freedom, whether it be from the prison of over-dense communities
and the close confines of human relationships, from the less complex
incarceration of office walls and hours, or simply freedom from the
prison of adult life and an escape into the forgotten world of childhood,
of the individual or the race. For I am convinced that man has suffered
in his separation from the soil and from the other living creatures of
the world; the evolution of his intellect has outrun his needs as an
animal, and as yet he must still, for security, look long at some portion
of the earth as it was before he tampered with it.

This book, then, is about my life in a lonely cottage on the north-west
coast of Scotland, about animals that have shared it with me, and about
others who are my only immediate neighbours in a landscape of rock
and sea.

Camusfeàrna   GAVIN MAXWELL
October 1959

ACKNOWLEDGEMENTS

We are indebted to the following for permission to quote copyright material:

Messrs Faber and Faber Ltd for 'Thank You' from *The Earth Compels* by Louis MacNeice; Miss Kathleen Raine and Messrs Hamish Hamilton Ltd for 'The Ring' from *Year One* from which the title of this book is taken; and the literary agents of the late Mr Ernest Thompson Seton for an extract from *Life Histories of Northern Animals*, published by Messrs Constable and Co. Ltd.

PART ONE

THE BAY OF THE ALDERS

CHAPTER I

I sit in a pitch-pine panelled kitchen-living-room, with an otter asleep upon its back among the cushions on the sofa, forepaws in the air, and with the expression of tightly shut concentration that very small babies wear in sleep. On the stone slab beneath the chimney-piece are inscribed the words '*Non fatuum huc persecutus ignem*' – 'It is no will-o'-the-wisp that I have followed here'. Beyond the door is the sea, whose waves break on the beach no more than a stone's throw distant, and encircling, mist-hung mountains. A little group of greylag geese sweep past the window and alight upon the small carpet of green turf; but for the soft, contented murmur of their voices and the sounds of the sea and the waterfall there is utter silence. This place has been my home now for ten years and more, and wherever the changes of my life may lead me in the future it will remain my spiritual home until I die, a house to which one returns not with the certainty of welcoming fellow human beings, nor with the expectation of comfort and ease, but to a long familiarity in which every lichen-covered rock and rowan tree show known and reassuring faces.

I had not thought that I should ever come back to live in the West Highlands; when my earlier sojourn in the Hebrides had come to an end it had in retrospect seemed episodic, and its finish uncompromisingly final. The thought of return had savoured of a jilted lover pleading with an indifferent mistress upon whom he had no further claim; it seemed to me then that it was indeed a will-o'-the-wisp that I had followed, for I had yet to learn that happiness can neither be achieved nor held by endeavour.

. . .

Looking back with distaste to the brashness of my late adolescence I perceive that I was an earnest member of the Celtic fringe, avid for tartan and twilight. This was no by-product of a Nationalistic outlook, nor could my yearnings have found outlet in that direction, for I was at that time also an arrant snob, and the movement seemed to me essentially plebeian; supported, moreover, by youths whose title to a foothold in the West Highlands was as controversial as my own. It was not to the company of such as these that I aspired; the healthier and more robust enthusiasm of tartaned hikers from the industrial cities inspired in me a nausea akin to that of Compton Mackenzie's Macdonald of Ben Nevis. It was not with the awe due to surviving dinosaurs that I viewed certain backwoods Highland chieftains with moustaches as long as their lineage, but with the enthusiastic reverence that the vintage-car cult accords to Bentleys of the 1920s. Nothing in my early life had led me to question the prescriptive rightness of the established order as it had been in the days of my grandparents; to me the West Highlands were composed of deer forests and hereditary chieftains, and the sheep, the hikers and the Forestry Commission were regrettable interlopers upon the romantic life of the indigenous aristocracy.

I was no whit abashed by the fact that I came of a lowland family who had been established in one spot for more than five hundred years, and that it was there and as a Galloway Scot that I had been born and brought up. It was a handicap, certainly, as was also my inability to perform Highland dances or to speak Gaelic; to learn would have been to acknowledge that I had not known before, and so would have been unthinkable. I did learn, however, to play a few tunes, very badly, on the bagpipes; I had had a Gaelic-speaking nurse; I had been brought up to wear a kilt – though of shepherd's plaid; and, strongest card of all and probably what started the rot, my maternal grandmother had been a daughter of the Duke of Argyll, of MacCallum Mor himself. At Inveraray Castle and at Strachur on the opposite side of Loch Fyne I passed most of my long vacs from Oxford. Inveraray under the reign of the late Duke was a temple of twilight both Celtic and other, and its atmosphere was hardly calculated to cure my disease. The melancholy beauty of Strachur and Inveraray was for me still further complicated by the agonies of first love; I was well and truly pixillated, and I soaked myself in the works of Neil Munro and Maurice Walsh when I should have been laying the foundations of a literary education. All this was basically the outcome of an inherently romantic nature tinged with melancholy, for which a special home and uniform had clearly been prepared among the precipitous hills and sea lochs of the West Highlands.

There existed during my time at Oxford a curious clique of landed gentry so assertively un-urban that we affected a way of dressing quite unsuited to University life; at all times, for example, we wore tweed shooting suits and heavy shooting shoes studded with nails and dull with dubbin, and at our heels trotted spaniels or Labrador retrievers. Some of us were Englishmen, but the majority were Scots or those whose parents were in the habit of renting Highland shootings, and I have no doubt that the cult was akin to my own, for I remember that in the autumn term the rooms of its members were hung with the heads of stags killed during the vac. and there was endless talk of the Highlands. Most of us were, in fact, a species of privileged hiker, and we were also a striking example of the fact that aristocracy and education were no longer synonymous.

My own yearning for the Highlands was in those days as tormenting as an unconsummated love affair, for no matter how many stags I might kill or feudal castles inhabit I lacked an essential involvement; I was further from them than any immigrated Englishman who planted one potato or raised one stone upon another. It is often those who dream of a *grande passion* who find it and suffer and are the sadder for it, and so it was with me, for when at last I came to the West Highlands by right of ownership and of effort they brought me to my knees and sent me away defeated and almost bankrupt. But during that five years' struggle the false image for which I had yearned had faded, and a truer one, less bedizened with tartan but no whit less beautiful, had taken its place.

Immediately after the war's end I bought the Island of Soay, some four thousand acres of relatively low-lying 'black' land cowering below the bare pinnacles and glacial corries of the Cuillins of Skye. There, seventeen miles by sea from the railway, I tried to found a new industry for the tiny and discontented population of the island, by catching and processing for oil the great basking sharks that appear in Hebridean waters during the summer months. I built a factory, bought boats and equipped them with harpoon guns, and became a harpoon gunner myself. For five years I worked in that landscape that before had been, for me, of a nebulous and cobwebby romance, and by the time it was all over and I was beaten I had in some way come to terms with the Highlands – or with myself, for perhaps in my own eyes I had earned the right to live among them, and the patent unauthenticity of the Maxwell tartan no longer disturbed me.

When the Soay venture was finished, the island and the boats sold, the factory demolished, and the population evacuated, I went to London and tried to earn my living as a portrait painter. One autumn I was staying with an Oxford contemporary who had bought an estate in the West Highlands, and in an idle moment after breakfast on a Sunday morning he said to me:

'Do you want a foothold on the west coast, now that you've lost Soay? If you're not too proud to live in a cottage, we've got an empty one, miles from anywhere. It's right on the sea and there's no road to it – Camusfeàrna, it's called. There's some islands, and an automatic lighthouse. There's been no one there for a long time, and I'd never get any of the estate people to live in it now. If you'll keep it up you're welcome to it.'

It was thus casually, ten years ago, that I was handed the keys of my home, and nowhere in all the West Highlands and islands have I seen any place of so intense or varied a beauty in so small a compass.

The road, single-tracked for the past forty miles, and reaching in the high passes a gradient of one in three, runs southwards a mile or so inland of Camusfeàrna and some four hundred feet above it. At the point on the road which is directly above the house there is a single cottage at the roadside, Druimfiaclach, the home of my friends and nearest neighbours, the MacKinnons. Inland from Druimfiaclach the hills rise steeply but in rolling masses to a dominating peak of more than three thousand feet, snow-covered or snow-dusted for the greater part of the year. On the other side, to the westward, the Isle of Skye towers across a three-mile-wide sound, and farther to the south the stark bastions of Rhum and the couchant lion of Eigg block the sea horizon. The descent to Camusfeàrna is so steep that neither the house nor its islands and lighthouse are visible from the road above, and that paradise within a paradise remains, to the casual road-user, unguessed. Beyond Druim- fiaclach the road seems, as it were, to become dispirited, as though already conscious of its dead end at sea-level six miles farther on, caught between the terrifying massif of mountain scree overhanging it and the dark gulf of sea loch below.

Druimfiaclach is a tiny oasis in a wilderness of mountain and peat bog, and it is a full four miles from the nearest roadside dwelling. An oasis, an eyrie; the windows of the house look westward over the Hebrides and over the tyrian sunsets that flare and fade behind their peaks, and when the sun has gone and the stars are bright the many lighthouses of the reefs and islands gleam and wink above the surf. In the westerly gales of winter the walls of Druimfiaclach rock and shudder, and heavy stones are roped to the corrugated iron roof to prevent it blowing away as other roofs here have gone before. The winds rage in from the Atlantic and the hail roars and batters on the windows and the iron roof, all hell let loose, but the house stands and the MacKinnons remain here, as, nearby, the forefathers of them both remained for many generations.

It seems strange to me now that there was a time when I did not know the MacKinnons, strange that the first time I came to live at Camusfeàrna I should have passed their house by a hundred yards and left my car by the roadside without greeting or acknowledgement of a dependence now long established. I remember seeing some small children staring from the house door; I cannot now recall my first meeting with their parents.

I left my car at a fank, a dry-stone enclosure for dipping sheep, close to the burn side, and because I was unfamiliar with the ill-defined footpath that is the more usual route from the road to Camusfeàrna, I began to follow the course of the burn downward. The burn has its source far back in the hills, near to the very summit of the dominant peak; it has worn a fissure in the scarcely sloping mountain wall, and for the first thousand feet of its course it part flows, part falls, chill as snow-water even in summer, between tumbled boulders and small multicoloured lichens. Up there, where it seems the only moving thing besides the eagles, the deer and the ptarmigan, it is called the Blue Burn, but at the foot of the outcrop, where it passes through a reedy lochan and enters a wide glacial glen it takes the name of its destination – Allt na Feàrna, the Alder Burn. Here in the glen the clear topaz-coloured water rushes and twitters between low oaks, birches and alders, at whose feet the deep-cushioned green moss is stippled with bright toadstools of scarlet and purple and yellow, and in summer swarms of electric-blue dragonflies flicker and hover in the glades.

After some four miles the burn passes under the road at Druimfiaclach, a stone's throw from the fank where I had left my car. It was early spring when I came to live at Camusfeàrna for the first time, and the grass at the burn side was gay with thick-clustering primroses and violets, though the snow was still heavy on the high peaks and lay like lace over the lower hills of Skye across the Sound. The air was fresh and sharp, and from east to west and north to south there was not a single cloud upon the cold clear blue; against it, the still-bare birch branches were purple in the sun and the dark-banded stems were as white as the distant snows. On the sunny slopes grazing Highland cattle made a foreground to a landscape whose vivid colours had found no place on Landseer's palette. The rucksack bounced and jingled on my shoulders; I was coming to my new home like one of the hikers whom long ago I had so much despised.

I was not quite alone, for in front of me trotted my dog Jonnie, a huge black-and-white springer spaniel whose father and grandfather before him had been my constant companions during an adolescence devoted largely to sport. We were brought up to shoot, and by the curious paradox that those who are fondest of animals become, in such an environment, most bloodthirsty at a certain stage of their development, shooting occupied much of my time and thoughts during my school and university years. Many people find an especial attachment for a dog whose companionship has bridged widely different phases in their lives, and so it was with Jonnie; he and his forebears had spanned my boyhood, maturity, and the war years, and though since then I had found little leisure nor much inclination for shooting, Jonnie adapted himself placidly to a new role, and I remember how during the shark fishery years he would, unprotesting, arrange himself to form a pillow for my head in the well of an open boat as it tossed and pitched in the waves.

Now Jonnie's plump white rump bounced and perked through the heather and bracken in front of me, as times without number at night I was in the future to follow its pale just-discernible beacon through the darkness from Druimfiaclach to Camusfeàrna.

Presently the burn became narrower, and afforded no foothold at its steep banks, then it tilted sharply seaward between rock walls, and below me I could hear the roar of a high waterfall. I climbed out from the ravine and found myself on a bluff of heather and red bracken, looking down upon the sea and upon Camusfeàrna.

The landscape and seascape that lay spread below me was of such beauty that I had no room for it all at once; my eye flickered from the house to the islands, from the white sands to the flat green pasture round the croft, from the wheeling gulls to the pale satin sea and on to the snow-topped Cuillins of Skye in the distance.

Immediately below me the steep hillside of heather and ochre mountain grasses fell to a broad green field, almost an island, for the burn flanked it at the right and then curved round seaward in a glittering horseshoe. The sea took up where the burn left off, and its foreshore formed the whole frontage of the field, running up nearest to me into a bay of rocks and sand. At the edge of this bay, a stone's throw from the sea on one side and the burn on the other, the house of Camusfeàrna stood unfenced in green grass among grazing black-faced sheep. The field, except immediately opposite to the house, sloped gently upwards from the sea, and was divided from it by a ridge of sand dunes grown over with pale marram grass and tussocky sea-bents. There were rabbits scampering on the short turf round the house, and out over the dunes the bullet heads of two seals were black in the tide.

Beyond the green field and the wide shingly outflow of the burn were the islands, the nearer ones no more than a couple of acres each, rough and rocky, with here and there a few stunted rowan trees and the sun red on patches of dead bracken. The islands formed a chain of perhaps half a mile in length, and ended in one as big as the rest put together, on whose seaward shore showed the turret of a lighthouse. Splashed among the chain of islands were small beaches of sand so white as to dazzle the eye. Beyond the islands was the shining enamelled sea, and beyond it again the rearing bulk of Skye, plum-coloured distances embroidered with threads and scrolls of snow.

Even at a distance Camusfeàrna house wore that strange look that comes to dwellings after long disuse. It is indefinable, and it is not produced by obvious signs of neglect; Camusfeàrna had few slates missing from the roof and the windows were all intact, but the house wore that secretive expression that is in some way akin to a young girl's face during her first pregnancy.

As I went on down the steep slope two other buildings came into view tucked close under the skirt of the hill, a byre facing Camusfeàrna across the green turf, and an older, windowless, croft at the very sea's edge, so close to the waves that I wondered how the house had survived. Later, I learned that the last occupants had been driven from it by a great storm which had brought the sea right into the house, so that they had been forced to make their escape by a window at the back.

At the foot of the hill the burn flowed calmly between an avenue of single alders, though the sound of unseen waterfalls was loud in the rock ravine behind me. I crossed a solid wooden bridge with stone piers, and a moment later I turned the key in Camusfeàrna door for the first time.

CHAPTER 2

There was not one stick of furniture in the house; there was no water and no lighting, and the air inside struck chill as a mortuary, but to me it was Xanadu. There was much more space in the house than I had expected. There were two rooms on the ground floor, a parlour and a living-kitchen, besides a little 'back kitchen' or scullery, and two rooms and a landing upstairs. The house was entirely lined with varnished pitch pine, in the manner of the turn of the century.

I had brought with me on my back the essentials of living for a day or two while I prospected – a bedding roll, a Primus stove with a little fuel, candles, and some tinned food. I knew that something to sit upon would present no problems, for my five years' shark hunting round these coasts had taught me that every west-facing beach is littered with fish-boxes. Stacks of fish-boxes arranged to form seats and tables were the mainstay of Camusfeàrna in those early days, and even now, despite the present comfort of the house, they form the basis of much of its furniture, though artifice and padding have done much to disguise their origin.

Ten years of going into retreat at Camusfeàrna have taught me, too, that if one waits long enough practically every imaginable household object will sooner or later turn up on the beaches within a mile of the house, and beachcombing retains for me now the same fascination and eager expectancy that it held then. After a westerly or south-westerly gale one may find almost anything. Fish-boxes – mostly stamped with the names of Mallaig, Buckie, or Lossiemouth firms, but sometimes from France or Scandinavia – are too common to count, though they are still gathered, more from habit than from need. Fish baskets, big open two-handled baskets of withy, make firewood baskets and wastepaper baskets. Intact wooden tubs are a rarity, and I have found only three in my years here; it has amused me wryly to see cocktail bars in England whose proprietors have through whimsy put them to use as stools as I have by necessity.

A Robinson Crusoe or Swiss Family Robinson instinct is latent in most of us, perhaps from our childhood games of house-building, and since I came to Camusfeàrna ten years ago I find myself scanning every weird piece of flotsam or jetsam and considering what useful purpose it might be made to serve. As a beachcomber of long standing now I have been amazed to find that one of the commonest of all things among jetsam is the rubber hot-water bottle. They compete successfully – in the long straggling line of brown sea-wrack dizzy with jumping sand-hoppers – with odd shoes and empty boot-polish and talcum-powder tins, with the round corks that buoy lobster-pots and nets, even with the ubiquitous skulls of sheep and deer. A surprising number of the hot-water bottles are undamaged, and Camusfeàrna is by now overstocked with them, but from the damaged ones one may cut useful and highly functional table mats.

At the beginning, however, there was no table to protect, and after my first days at Camusfeàrna it seemed clear that I should have to import at least one small load of essential furniture. This was not an easy matter, for there was no road approach, and I was some fifteen miles by sea from the nearest village to which I could have furniture sent. (Because of the long sea lochs that, like Norwegian fiords, cut deep into the west coast, that same village is one hundred and twenty miles by road.) At length I motored to Lochailort Inn – a hundred miles – whose highly individual proprietor, Uilleamena Macrae, I had come to know well during my shark-fishing years. Uilleamena was a very beautiful Lewis woman of humble origin, but she had been to Hollywood as an actress in the early days of silent films; she had been a medium for Conan Doyle's spiritualistic experiments; she had been taught logic – rather unsuccessfully – by an uncle who had become a professor in America; she had friends, real ones, in many high places. During the war, when she was already in late middle age, she married, very briefly, the contractor who was repairing the road outside her door; in a few months he was called up and killed, and Uilleamena reverted to her maiden name and never again mentioned her *mésalliance*. She was, I think, one of the warmest, most human, most delightful, and, perhaps, most domineering people I have ever known, and her faults were all on the surface. As an innkeeper she was unorthodox and capricious; lunch might cost anything between two shillings and a pound, according to her mood (or sometimes there would be no lunch at all, if she did not feel like cooking or did not care for the look of the visitors); the bar would remain closed for days or even weeks because she had forgotten to order new stock, and the same applied to the petrol pump; she was more concerned with the welfare of a host of animals ranging from a parrot (I can still hear those two screeching 'hullo' to each other in demoniac crescendo) to geese and Shetland ponies than with that of stranger tourists (she told me that she had once given chicken-food to some American visitors, telling them it was porridge, and that they had asked for more); yet with all that, her personality was so spontaneous and vital and endearing that her death a few years ago made a hole in more hearts than she would have known. She left a truly phenomenal amount of debts behind her, but it was perhaps a measure of her personality that she was able to owe her grocer £3,000.

Uilleamena sold me some really frightful furniture for Camusfeàrna – two small chests whose drawers open and close only under the most careful coaxing, two kitchen tables, a bed, three hard kitchen chairs, and a threadbare Brussels carpet. I prefer not to think what these outrages had finally cost me by the time they had travelled by rail and then fifteen miles in a hired launch by sea. They were the last bulk of furniture that ever came into Camusfeàrna; the rest had just grown, found on the beach or constructed by ingenious friends who have stayed here, and importations have been confined to what can be carried down the hill. Into this category fall a surprising number of objects that may be used to convert fish-boxes into apparent furniture. Half of one of the kitchen walls, for example, is now occupied by a very large sofa; that is to say it appears to be a sofa, but in fact it is all fish-boxes, covered with sheet foam rubber under a corduroy cover and many cushions. Next to it is a tall rectangle, draped over with a piece of material that was once the seat-cover of my cabin in the *Sea Leopard*, my chief shark-hunting boat; lift aside this relic and you are looking into a range of shelves filled with shoes – the whole structure is made of five fish-boxes with their sides knocked out. The same system, this time of orange-boxes from the shore and fronted by some very tasteful material from Primavera, holds shirts and sweaters in my bedroom, and looks entirely respectable. The art of fish-box furniture should be more widely cultivated; in common with certain widely advertised makes of contemporary furniture it has the peculiar advantage that one may add unit to unit indefinitely.

There came a time, in my second or third year at the house, when I said, 'There's only one thing we really lack now – a clothes-basket,' and a few weeks later a clothes-basket came up on the beach, a large stately clothes-basket, completely undamaged.

Whether it is because the furnishings of these rooms have grown around me year by year since that first afternoon when I entered the chill and empty house, each room as bare as a weathered bone, or because of my deep love for Camusfeàrna and all that surrounds it, it is to me now the most relaxing house that I know, and guests, too, feel it a place in which they are instantly at ease. Even in this small matter of furniture there is also a continuous sense of anticipation; it is as though a collector of period furniture might on any morning find some rare and important piece lying waiting to be picked up on the street before his door.

There is much pathos in the small jetsam that lies among the sea-wrack and drifted timber of the long tide-lines; the fire-blackened transom of a small boat; the broken and wave-battered children's toys; a hard-carved wooden egg-cup with the name 'John' carefully incised upon it; the scattered skeleton of a small dog, the collar with an illegible nameplate lying among the whitened bones, long since picked clean by the ravens and the hooded crows. To me the most personal poignancy was in my search one morning that first year for a suitable piece of wood from which to fashion a bread-board. A barrel top would be ideal, I thought, if I could find one intact, and very soon I did, but when I had it in my hands I turned it over to read the letters I.S.S.F., Island of Soay Shark Fisheries – the only thing the sea has ever given me back for all that I poured into it during those five years of Soay.

Some pieces of jetsam are wholly enigmatic, encouraging the most extravagant exercise of fantasy to account for their existence. A ten-foot-long bamboo pole, to which have been affixed by a combination of careful, seaman-like knots and the lavish use of insulating tape three blue pennants bearing the words 'Shell' and 'B.P.'; this has exercised my imagination since first I found it. A prayer flag made by a Lascar seaman? – a distress signal, pitifully inadequate, constructed over many hours adrift in an open boat surrounded by cruising sharks or tossed high on the crests of Atlantic rollers a thousand miles from land? I have found no satisfactory solution. Two broom-handles, firmly tied into the form of a cross by the belt from a woman's plastic macintosh; a scrap of sailcloth with the words 'not yet' scrawled across it in blue paint; a felt Homburg hat so small that it appeared to have been made for a diminutive monkey – round these and many others one may weave idle tapestries of mystery.

But it is not only on such man-made objects as these that the imagination builds to evoke drama, pathos, or remembered splendour. When one is much alone one's vision becomes more extensive; from the tide-wrack rubbish-heap of small bones and dry, crumpled wings, relics of lesser lives, rise images the brighter for being unconfined by the physical eye. From some feathered mummy, stained and thin, soars the spinning lapwing in the white March morning; in the surface crust of rotting weed, where the foot explodes a whirring puff of flies, the withered fins and scales hold still, intrinsically, the sway and dart of glittering shoals among the tide-swung sea-tangle; smothered by the mad parabolic energy of leaping sand-hoppers the broken antlers of a stag re-form and move again high in the bare, stony corries and the October moonlight.

Comparatively little that is thrown up by the waves comes ashore at Camusfeàrna itself, for the house stands on a south-facing bay in a west-facing coastline, and it gains, too, a little shelter from the string of islands that lead out from it to the lighthouse. To the north and south the coast is rock for the most part, but opening here and there to long gravel beaches which the prevailing westerly gales pile high with the sea's litter. It is a fierce shoreline, perilous with reef and rock, and Camusfeàrna with its snow-white sand beaches, green close-cropped turf, and low white lighthouse has a welcoming quality enhanced by the dark, rugged coastline on either side.

It is a coast of cliffs and of caves, deep commodious caves that have their entrances, for the most part, well above the tides' level, for over the centuries the sea has receded, and between the cliffs the shingle of its old beaches lies bare. Until recently many of these caves were regularly inhabited by travelling pedlars, of whom there were many, for shops were far distant and communications virtually non-existent. They were welcoming among the local people, these pedlars, for besides what they could sell they brought news from far-away villages and of other districts in which they travelled; they fulfilled the function of provincial newspapers, and the inhabitants of wild and lonely places awaited their coming with keen anticipation.

One of these men made his home and headquarters in a cave close to Camusfeàrna, a man who had been, of all improbable professions, a jockey. Andrew Tait was his real name, but as a deserter from the army he had changed it to Joe Wilson, and Joe's Cave his erstwhile home remains, even on the maps, though it is many years past since an angry people lit fires to crack the rock roof and banish him from that shore.

Joe was popular at first, for he was a likeable enough man, and if he and his cave consort Jeannie had never heard the wedding service a cave was perhaps safer than a glasshouse if there were any stones to be thrown. Such pebbles that came his way seem mainly to have been on the question of his desertion. Jeannie was no slut nor Joe a slum-maker, and their troglodyte life was a neat and orderly affair, with a clean white tablecloth laid over the fish-box table for meals, meals that were of fish and crustaceans and every manner of edible shell. They walled in the front of their cave and built steps from it down to the sea, and even now the little runway where they drew up their boat is still free from boulders.

Only one thing marred their littoral idyll; both Jeannie and Joe were over-fond of the bottle. Jeannie held the purse-strings, and despite her own indulgence she was the wiser of the two. She would spend so much on drink and no more, but every time the two drank they quarrelled, and when Joe got past a certain point he would fight her for the money.

One night they had, as was their custom, rowed the four miles to the village pub, and there they began to drink in company with another pedlar, a simpleton, named John MacQueen, whom people called The Pelican. The Pelican was a player of the fiddle, and together they stayed late at the inn, bickering and drinking to the music of his strings.

What followed no one knows truly to this day, but it was the end of their Eden, the end of Jeannie and of Joe's Cave. Joe returned to the village in the morning proclaiming over and over again that Jeannie was 'Killt and droont, killt and droont'. Their boat was washed up ten miles to the south, half full of water, and in it was the dead body of Jeannie; the pocket of her skirt had been torn off, and there was no money about her. Police came from the nearest township, but though local feeling ran high against Joe and The Pelican the details of Jeannie's death remained unsolved, and no charge of murder was brought against them. It seemed clear that Jeannie had been knocked out before she drowned; some, those who stood by Joe, said that she had fallen into the sea after a blow and then drowned; others that Joe and The Pelican had beaten her senseless in a drunken rage, had half-filled the boat with water, and then set Jeannie adrift to drown.

Whatever the truth, the people of the neighbourhood – if such it could be called, for Joe had no neighbours – believed that they had a monster in their midst; they came and built great fires in his cave, and set ablaze the heather of the hillside above it, so that the heat split the rock and the outer part of the cave fell, and Joe was left a homeless wanderer. He died years ago, but on the floor beneath the fire-blackened rock still lie small relics of his life with Jeannie, mouldering shoes, scraps of metal, a filigree tracery of rusted iron that was once a kettle. Above, on the ledges that formed the cornice of his dwelling, the rock-doves have made their homes, and their feathers float down upon the ruined hearth.

. . .

Pedlars of the traditional type were rare by the time I began to live at Camusfeàrna; their place had been taken by Indians, often importunate, who from time to time toured the roadside dwellings with small vans full of cheap materials. The local inhabitants, unused to high-pressure doorstep salesmanship, mistook these methods for effrontery; not all of the vendors were of savoury nature, but even the most innocuous were regarded with a wary suspicion. I met only one of Joe's lost tribe, and he has died since, hastened to the churchyard by a lifelong predilection for drinking methylated spirits. He was, I think, in his early sixties when I first encountered him; he told me then that the perils of his preferred liquor were greatly exaggerated, for he had been indulging for forty years and only now was his eyesight beginning to suffer. He confided, however, that it was an inconvenient craving, for most ironmongers throughout the length and breadth of the West Highlands had been warned against supplying him, and he had been driven to the most elaborate of subterfuges to keep his cellar stocked. It was, perhaps, as well for him that he died before electricity came to the remote and outlying areas, for then, as I discovered to my cost, methylated spirits became virtually unobtainable.

The cave-dwelling pedlars had not always been the only inhabitants of the Camusfeàrna coastline, for before the Clearances in the early nineteenth century – whose cruelty and injustice are still a living ancestral memory in a great part of the West Highlands and Hebrides – there had been a thriving community of some two hundred people not far from where Camusfeàrna house now stands. The descendants of one of these families still live in California, where their forebears settled when driven from their homes, and of them is told one of the few local tales of 'second sight' that I have come across in the district.

The children of the old settlement at Camusfeàrna used to walk the five miles to the village school every morning and five miles home again at night; each child, too, had in winter to provide his contribution to the school fire, and they would set off before dawn for the long trudge with a creel of peats on their backs. One night this family had given shelter to an old pedlar, and as he watched the two sons of the house making ready their load in the morning he turned to their parents and said, 'Many a green sea they will go over, but many a green sea will go over them.' The boys came of a seafaring line, and when they grew up they too followed the sea; one became a captain and the other a first mate, but both were drowned.

The tumbled briar-grown ruins of the old village are scattered round the bay and down the shore, but the people are gone and the pedlars are gone and the house at Camusfeàrna stands alone.

Whereas the stories of 'second sight' are comparatively few, and refer most commonly to past generations, it should be realized that this bears no relation at all either to current credence in the faculty or to the number of people who are still believed to possess it. Quite contrary to general opinion, a person having or believing him or herself to have this occult power is extremely reticent about it, usually afraid of it, and conceals it from all but his most intimate friends. This is not because he is afraid of mockery or disbelief in the sense that his neighbour will say 'Behold this dreamer', but because men fear proof of a power beyond their own, and are uncomfortable in the company of one who claims or admits to it. These people who are convinced of being endowed with what is now more usually called extrasensory perception are also frightened of what their own clairvoyance may show them, and it seems that they would willingly exchange their lot for that of the common man. Only when they are convinced that their gift can at that moment be turned to benign use are they prepared to call it voluntarily into play. My impression is that a deep, fundamental belief in the existence of 'second sight' is practically universal throughout the Western Highlands and the Hebrides, even among intelligent and well-read people, and that the few scoffers are paying lip-service to a sceptical sophistication they do not share. Circumstantial tales of other less controversial matters survive in the oral tradition with but little change in these districts to which literacy came late in history, and there is no reason to assume that those concerning 'second sight' should have suffered disproportionate distortion.

My nearest neighbour at Camusfeàrna, Calum Murdo MacKinnon, of whom I shall have more to say presently, comes of Skye stock, and tells a tale of his forebears which by its very simplicity is hard to ascribe to past invention. In the days of his great-grandfather a boy was drowned at sea, fishing in the bay before the village, and his mother became distraught with the desire to recover her son's body and give it Christian burial. Some half-dozen boats with grappling irons cruised to and fro all day over the spot where he had been lost, but found nothing. The talk of all the village was naturally centred on the subject, and in the late evening Calum Murdo's great-grandfather, over eighty years of age, infirm and totally blind, learned for the first time of all that had taken place. At length he said, 'If they will take me to the knoll overlooking the bay in the morning I will tell them where the body lies. They will need just the one boat.' The searchers obeyed him, and in the morning he was carried to the summit of the knoll by his grandson, who brought with him a plaid with which to signal at command. For more than half an hour the boat rowed to and fro in the bay below them with grapples hanging ready, but the old man sat with his blind head in his hands and said never a word. Suddenly he cried in a strong voice, ' *Tog an tonnag! –* Hoist the plaid!' His grandson did so, and the grapples sank and returned to the surface with the body of the drowned boy.

It is easier to be sceptical when one is not in the Hebrides; easier when one's vision is not clarified – or obscured – by the common sense of one's fellow men.

.   .   .

Very little survives in legend from the early inhabitants of Camusfeàrna; surprisingly little when one comes to consider that in all likelihood the community existed for thousands of years. The earliest stories date, probably, from the Middle Ages, and one of these tells of a wild sea reiver, born in the bay, who harried the coast to the southward – notably the Island of Mull, with its many secret harbours and well-hid anchorages – in a galley, one of whose sides was painted black and the other white; an attempt, presumably, to refute description or to undermine morale by reports that in aggregate might give the impression of a pirate fleet. Whatever his tactics, they seem to have been successful, for he is said to have returned to Camusfeàrna and to have died, in old age, a natural death.

In the British Isles it is a strange sensation to lie down to sleep knowing that there is no human being within a mile and a half in any direction, that apart from one family there is none for three times that distance. Indeed few people ever have the experience, for the earth's surface is so overrun with mankind that where land is habitable it is inhabited; and whereas it is not difficult to pitch a camp in those circumstances it is very rare to be between four permanent walls that one may call one's home. It brings a sense of isolation that is the very opposite of the loneliness a stranger finds in a city, for that loneliness is due to the proximity of other humans and the barriers between him and them, to the knowledge of being alone among them, with every inch of the walls wounding and every incommunicable stranger planting a separate bandillo. But to be quite alone where there are no other human beings is sharply exhilarating; it is as though some pressure had suddenly been lifted, allowing an intense awareness of one's surroundings, a sharpening of the senses, and an intimate recognition of the teeming sub-human life around one. I experienced it first as a very young man, travelling alone, on the tundra three hundred miles north of the Arctic Circle, and there was the added strangeness of nights as light as noon, so that only the personal fact of sleep divided night from day; paradoxically, for the external circumstances were the very opposite, I had the same or an allied sensation during the heavy air-raids in 1940, as though life were suddenly stripped of inessentials such as worries about money and small egotistical ambitions and one was left facing an ultimate essential.

That first night as I lay down to sleep in the bare kitchen of Camusfeàrna I was aware of the soft thump of rabbits' feet about the sand-dune warren at the back of the house, the thin squeak of hawking bats, woken early by the warm weather from their winter hibernation, and the restless piping of oyster-catchers waiting for the turn of the tide; these were middle-distance sounds against the muffled roar of the waterfall that in still weather is the undertone to all other sound at Camusfeàrna.

I slept that night with my head pillowed upon Jonnie's soft fleece-like flank, as years before I had been wont to in open boats.

The first thing that I saw in the morning, as I went down to the burn for water, was a group of five stags, alert but unconcerned, staring from the primrose bank just beyond the croft wall. Two of them had cast both horns, for it was the end of the first week in April, two had cast one, but the fifth stag still carried both, wide, long and strong, with seven points one side and six on the other, a far nobler head than ever I had seen during my years of bloodthirstiness. I came to know these stags year by year, for they were a part of a group that passed every winter low in the Camusfeàrna burn, and Morag MacKinnon used to feed them at Druimfiaclach – a little surreptitiously, for they were outside the forest fence and on the sheep ground. Monarch, she called the thirteen-pointer, and though he never seemed to break out to the rut in autumn I think he must have sired at least one stag-calf, for in the dark last year the headlights of my car lit up a partially stunned stag that had leapt at the concrete posts of the new forestry plantation fence, trying to get down to Camusfeàrna, and the head, though no more than a royal, was the very double of Monarch's wide sweep. I came near to killing him, for I thought that he was a stag wounded and lost by a stalking party from the lodge that day, but dazed as he was he managed to stagger out of the headlights' beam before I could get the rifle from its case.

·   ·   ·

I miss the stags that used to winter close to the house, for now there are young trees planted over the hill face between Camusfeàrna and Druimfiaclach, and the deer have been forced back behind the forest fence, so that there is none, save an occasional interloper, within a mile of the bay. In the first winter that I was at Camusfeàrna I would wake to see from the window a frieze of their antlers etching the near skyline, and they were in some way important to me, as were the big footprints of the wildcats in the soft sand at the burn's edge, the harsh cry of the ravens, and the round shiny seals' heads in the bay below the house. These creatures were my neighbours.

English visitors who have come to Camusfeàrna are usually struck inarticulate by the desolate grandeur of the landscape and the splendour of pale blue and gold spring mornings, but they are entirely articulate in their amazement at the variety of wild life by which I am surrounded. Many Englishmen are, for example, quite unaware that wildcats are common animals in the West Highlands, and assume, when one refers to them, that one is speaking of domestic cats run wild, not of the tawny lynx-like ferals that had their den, that and every other year, within two hundred yards of my door. They bear as much relation to the domestic cat as does a wolf to a terrier; they were here before our first uncouth ancestors came to live in the caves below the cliffs, and they are reputedly untameable. When I first came here the estate on whose land the house stood had long waged war upon the wildcats, and a tree by the deer-larder of the lodge, four miles away, was decorated with their banded tails hanging like monstrous willow catkins from its boughs. Now, since the estate has turned from general agriculture to forestry, the wildcats are protected, for they are the worst enemy of the voles, who are in turn the greatest destroyers of the newly planted trees. Under this benign regime the number of wildcats has marvellously increased. The males sometimes mate with domestic females, but the offspring rarely survives, either because the sire returns to kill the kittens as soon as they are born, and so expunge the evidence of his peasant wenching, or because of the distrust in which so many humans hold the taint of the untameable. It is the wild strain that is dominant, in the lynx-like appearance, the extra claw, and the feral instinct; and the few half-breeds that escape destruction usually take to the hills and the den life of their male ancestors. An old river-watcher at Lochailort, who for some reason that now eludes me was known as Tipperary, told me that one night, awoken by the caterwauling outside, he had gone to the door with a torch and in its beam had seen his own black-and-white she-cat in the fierce embrace of a huge wild tom. Thereafter he had waited eagerly for the birth of the kittens. When the time came she made her nest in the byre, and all that day he waited for the first birth, but at nightfall she had not yet brought forth. In the small hours of the morning he became conscious of piteous mewing at his door, and opened it to find his cat carrying in her mouth one wounded and dying kitten. In the dark background he heard a savage sound of worrying and snarling, and flashing his torch towards the byre he saw the wild tom in the act of killing a kitten. There was a green ember-glow of eyes, the flash of a big bottlebrush tail, and then the torch lit up nothing more but a pathetic trail of mangled newborn kittens. The single survivor, whom the mother had tried to carry to the house for sanctuary, died a few minutes later.

Wildcats grow to an enormous size, at least double that of the very largest domestic cat; this year there is one who leaves close to the house Homeric droppings of dimensions that would make an Alsatian wolfhound appear almost constipated. It is comparatively rarely that one sees the animals themselves in the daytime, for they are creatures of the dark and the starlight. Once I caught one accidentally in a rabbit snare, a vast tom with ten rings to his tail, and that first year at Camusfeàrna I twice saw the kittens at play in the dawn, frolicking among the primroses and budding birch on the bank beyond the croft wall. They looked beautiful, very soft and fluffy, and almost gentle; there was no hint of the ferocity that takes a heavy annual toll of lambs and red-deer calves. Before man exterminated the rabbits they were the staple food both of the big leggy hill foxes and of these low-ground wildcats, and every morning I would see the heavily indented pad-marks in the sand at the burrow mouths. But now the rabbits have gone and the lambs are still here in their season, and where there has been a strong lamb at dusk, at dawn there are raw bones and a fleece like a bloodstained swab in a surgery. Then come the ravens from the sea cliffs, and the hooded crows, the ubiquitous grey-mantled scavengers, and by nightfall there is nothing to show for those slow months in the womb but white skeleton and a scrap of soft, soiled fleece that seems no bigger than a handkerchief.

Among the mammals it is, next to the wildcats, the seals that surprise my southern visitors most. Right through the summer months they are rarely out of sight, and, being unmolested at Camusfeàrna, they become very tame. In the evenings they will follow a dinghy through the smooth sunset-coloured water, their heads emerging ever nearer and nearer until they are no more than a boat's length away. It is only a change in rhythm that frightens them; one must row steadily onwards as if intent on one's own business and unconcerned with theirs. The brown seals, with their big round skulls and short, dog-like noses, are everywhere, and I have counted more than a hundred in an hour's run down the shore in the dinghy; besides these, which breed locally, the Atlantic seals stay round the islands from May till early autumn, when they return to their scattered and comparatively few breeding rocks. The Atlantic seals that spend the summer at Camusfeàrna probably breed on the rocks west of Canna, by a long way the nearest to me of their colonies. They are never in large parties away from the breeding grounds; through the long still days of summer when the sea is smooth as silk and the sun is hot on the lichened rocks above the tide they loaf about the Camusfeàrna islands in twos and threes, usually bulls, eating largely of the rock fish and storing up energy to be used recklessly on their harems in the autumn, for during the rut the bulls may not feed for many weeks. To one who sees them for the first time the Atlantic seals seem vast; a big bull is some nine feet long and weighs nearly half a ton. They are splendid beasts, but to me they lack the charm of the little brown seal with its less dignified habits, inquisitive and dog-like. Once, on the rocks off Rhu Arisaig, I picked up a brown seal pup no more than a day or so old – he had the soft white baby coat that is more often shed in the womb, and he seemed for all the world like a toy designated to please a child. He was warm and tubby and not only unafraid but squirmingly affectionate, and I set him down again with some reluctance. But he was not to be so easily left, for as I moved off he came shuffling and humping along at my heels. After a few minutes of trying to shake him off I tried dodging and hiding behind rocks, but he discovered me with amazing agility. Finally I scrambled down to the boat and rowed quickly away, but after twenty yards he was there beside me muzzling an oar. I was in desperation to know what to do with this unexpected foundling whose frantic mother was now snorting twenty yards away, when suddenly he responded to one of her calls and the two went off together, the pup no doubt to receive the lecture of his life.

The red-deer calves, too, have no natural fear of man during their first days of life, and if in June one stumbles upon a calf lying dappled and sleek among the long green bracken stems one must avoid handling him if one wants to make a clean get-away. I used to pet them and fondle them before I knew better, and my efforts to leave led to more frenzied games of hide-and-seek than with the seal pup, while a distracted hind stamped and barked unavailingly. But while the calves during those first uninstructed days display no instinctive fear of humans, they are from the first terrified of their natural enemies, the eagles, the wildcats and the foxes. I have seen a hind trying to defend her calf from an eagle, rearing up with her ears back and slashing wickedly with her fore-hooves each time he stooped with an audible rush of wind through his great upswept pinions; if one hoof had struck home she would have brought him down disembowelled, but though she never touched more than a wingtip the eagle grew wary and finally sailed off down the glen, the sun gleaming whitely on the burnish of his mantle.

It is the helpless red-deer calves that are the staple food of the hill foxes in June, and the young lambs in April and May, but what they live on for the rest of the year now that the rabbits have gone and the blue mountain hares become so scarce, remains a mystery to me. Possibly they eat more seldom than we imagine, and certainly mice form a large part of their diet. Some years ago I went out with a stalker to kill hill foxes after lambing time. The foxes' cairn was some two thousand feet up the hill, and we left at dawn, before the sun was up over hills that were still all snow at their summits, silhouetted against a sky that was apple-green with tenuous scarlet streamers. The cairn, a big tumble of granite boulders in a fissure of the hillside, was just below the snowline, and by the time we reached it the sun had lifted in a golden glare over the high tops. The terriers went into the cairn and we shot the vixen as she bolted, and the dogs killed and brought out the five cubs; but of the dog fox there was no sign at all. We found his footprints in a peat hag a few hundred yards below, going downhill, and he had not been galloping but quietly trotting, so we concluded that he had left the cairn some time before we had reached it and was probably unaware of anything amiss. We sat down under cover to wait for his return.

We waited all day. The spring breeze blew fresh in our faces from where the sea and the islands lay spread out far below us, and we could see the ring-net boats putting out for the first of the summer herring. All day there was very little movement on the hill; once a party of stags in early velvet crossed the lip of the corrie on our right, and once an eagle sailed by within a stone's throw, to bank sharply and veer off with a harsh rasp of air between the quills as his searching eye found us. In the evening it became chilly, and when the sun was dipping over the Outer Hebrides and the snow-shadows had turned to a deep blue, we began to think of moving. We were starting to gather up our things when my eye caught a movement in the peat hags below us. The dog fox was trotting up hill to the cairn, quite unsuspicious, and carrying something in his jaws. The rifle killed him stone dead at fifty yards, and we went down to see what he had been carrying; it was a nest of pink new-born mice – all he had found to bring home in a long day's hunting for his vixen and five cubs.

At first sight it is one of the enigmas of the country around Camusfeàrna, this great number of predators surviving with so little to prey upon; in the air the eagles, buzzards, falcons, ravens and hooded crows, and on the ground the wildcats, foxes, badgers and pine martens. There is no doubt that a surprising number of the animal species spend much time during the off seasons – when there are no young creatures to feed on – in my own hobby of beachcombing. In the soft sand around the tide-wrack I come constantly upon the footprints of wildcats, badgers and foxes. Sometimes, they find oiled seabirds, sometimes the carcass of a sheep, fallen from one of the green cliff ledges that throughout the West Highlands form such well-baited and often fatal traps, or of a stag that has tottered down from the March snowdrifts to seek seaweed as the only uncovered food, or they may creep up upon sleeping oyster-catchers and curlews as they wait in the dark for the turn of the tide. But whatever they find it is to the shore that the fanged creatures come at night, and at times, perhaps, they find little, for I have seen undigested sand-hoppers in the droppings of both wildcats and foxes.

The ravens and hooded crows, though they will peck out the eyes of a living lamb or deer calf if he is weak, are in fact offal feeders for the greater part of the time. The hoodies spend much of their time about the shore in the late summer and midwinter, opening mussels by carrying them up to house-height and dropping them to smash on the rocks, but at most other seasons of the year there are routine harvests for them to gather elsewhere. In the back end of winter, when the ground is as yet unstirred by spring, the old stags that have wintered poorly grow feeble and die in the snowdrifts and the grey scavengers squawk and squabble over the carcasses; a little later, when the first warmth comes, and the hinds interrupt their grazing to turn their heads and nibble irritably at their spines, the hoodies strut and pick around them, gobbling the fat warble-grubs that emerge from under the deer-hides and fall to the ground. When the lambing season comes they quarter the ground for the afterbirths, and from then on there are the eggs and young of every bird lesser than themselves.

· · ·

Of my human neighbours, the MacKinnons, I have so far said little. Calum Murdo MacKinnon is always given both his Christian names, for there are so many Calum MacKinnons in the district that Calum alone would be ambiguous; there are so many Murdos as to make that name by itself ineffective too; and there are so many Murdo Calums, which is the true sequence of his names, that to retain his identity he has had to invert them. This was a common practice under the clan system, and is still the general rule in many parts of the West Highlands, where the clan names still inhabit their old territory. Sometimes he was abbreviated to 'Calum the Road' (in the same way I have known elsewhere a 'John the Hearse', a 'Duncan the Lorry', a 'Ronald the Shooter' and a 'Ronald Donald the Dummy' – the last not in any aspersion upon his human reality but because he was dumb). But the necessity for this strict taxonomy is a strange situation for one whose nearest neighbour other than myself is four miles distant.

Calum Murdo, then, is a small wiry man in middle age, who, when I first came to Camusfeàrna, had for long been the roadmender responsible for several miles of the single-track road on either side of Druimfiaclach. It might be expected that a Highlander living in this remarkable isolation would have few topics of conversation beyond the small routine of his own existence; one would not, for example, expect him to be able to quote the greater part of the *Golden Treasury*, to have read most of the classics, to have voluble and well-informed views on politics national and international, or to be a subscriber to the *New Statesman*. Yet these were the facts, and I fear it must have been a sad disappointment to Calum Murdo to find his new neighbour, of a supposedly higher educational level, to be on many subjects less well informed than himself. He would impart to me much fascinating and anecdotal information on a host of subjects, and would close every session with a rounded formula: 'And now, Major, an educated man like yourself will be fair sick of listening to the haverings of an old prole.' Over a period of ten years he has contributed much to my education.

With Calum Murdo's wife Morag, a woman of fine-drawn iron beauty softened by humour, I found an immediate common ground in a love of living creatures. One reads and hears much at second hand of the spiritual descendants of St Francis and of St Cuthbert, those who experience an immediate intimate communication with bird and beast, and of whom wild things feel no fear, but I had never encountered one of them in the flesh until I met Morag, and I had become a little sceptical of their existence. What little success I myself have with animals is due, I think, solely to patience, experience, and a conscious effort to put myself in the animal's position, but I do not think that any of these things have been necessary to Morag. She frankly finds more to like and to love in animals than in human beings, and they respond to her immediately as if she were one of themselves, with a trust and respect that few of us receive from our own kind. I am convinced that there exists between her and them some rapport that is not for the achievement, even by long perseverance, of the bulk of those humans who would wish it. It would not, perhaps, be difficult to find more understandable explanations for individual cases in which, with her, this rapport seems apparent, but it is the number of these cases, and the consistency with which the animal's behaviour departs from its established pattern towards mankind, that convinces me of something not yet explainable in existing terms.

A single instance will be enough for illustration. Across the road from the MacKinnons' door is a reedy hillside lochan some hundred yards long by fifty wide, and every winter the wild swans, the whoopers, would come to it as they were driven south by Arctic weather, to stay often for days and sometimes for weeks. Morag loved the swans, and from the green door of her house she would call a greeting to them several times a day, so that they came to know her voice, and never edged away from her to the other side of the lochan as they did when other human figures appeared on the road. One night she heard them restless and calling, the clear bugle voices muffled and buffeted by the wind, and when she opened the door in the morning she saw that there was something very much amiss. The two parent birds were at the near edge of the loch, fussing, if anything so graceful and dignified as a wild swan can be said to fuss, round a cygnet that seemed in some way to be captive at the margin of the reeds. Morag began to walk towards the loch, calling to them all the while as she was wont. The cygnet flapped and struggled and beat the water piteously with his wings, but he was held fast below the peaty surface, and all the while the parents, instead of retreating before Morag, remained calling at his side. Morag waded out, but the loch bottom is soft and black, and she was sinking thigh deep before she realized that she could not reach the cygnet. Then suddenly he turned and struggled towards her, stopped the thrashing of his wings, and was still. Groping in the water beneath him, Morag's hand came upon a wire, on which she pulled until she was able to feel a rusty steel trap clamped to the cygnet's leg, a trap set for a fox, and fastened to a long wire so that he might drown himself and die the more quickly. Morag lifted the cygnet from the water; he lay passive in her arms while she eased the jaws open, and as she did this the two parents swam right in and remained one on either side of her, as tame, as she put it, as domestic ducks; neither did they swim away when she put the cygnet undamaged onto the water and began to retrace her steps.

The swans stayed for a week or more after that, and now they would not wait for her to call to them before greeting her; every time she opened her door their silver-sweet bell-like voices chimed to her from the lochan across the road. If Yeats had possessed the same strange powers as Morag, his nine and fifty swans would perhaps not have suddenly mounted, and his poem would not have been written.

. . .

It was not through childlessness that Morag had turned to animals, as do so many spinters, for she had three sons. The eldest, Lachlan, was thirteen when I came to Camusfeàrna, and he had twin brothers of eleven, Ewan and Donald. The twins were eager, voluble, and helpful, by intention if not in every case in result, and after the first weeks, when the family had become my friends, it was they who would carry my mail down from Druimfiaclach in the evenings after school, and at week-ends do various odd jobs for me about the house. They painted the outside

walls of the house with Snowcem for me – or as much of the walls as their
diminutive statures and a broken ladder could compass. They carried
the heavy white powder down from Druimfiaclach in paper bags, and
one day I suggested that they would find it easier to use my rucksack.
They were delighted with the suggestion, and returned the following
day with the whole rucksack full to the lip with loose Snowcem powder,
and not only the main well of the rucksack but every zip-fastening
pocket that the makers had designed for such personal possessions as
toothbrushes and tobacco. That was nine years ago, and the twins are
grown-up and out in the world, but in wet weather that rucksack still
exudes a detectable whitish paste at the seams.

Gradually the MacKinnon household became my lifeline, my only
link with the remote world of shops and post offices, of telegrams and
anger, that I would so much have wished to dispense with altogether. It
is not easy at any time to victual a house that has no road to it, and it
becomes the more difficult when the nearest village with more than one
shop is between thirty and forty miles distant by road. The mails
themselves arrive at Druimfiaclach, once a day, by a complicated
mixture of sea and road transport from the railhead at the shopping
village. From it they are carried by motor launch to a tiny village five
miles from Druimfiaclach, where originally a vast old Humber and now
a Land Rover takes over and distributes them among the scattered
dwellings of the neighbourhood. I am, therefore, reasonably certain of
receiving one post a day if I plod up the hill to Druimfiaclach to fetch it
(though occasionally it is too rough for the launch to put out, and it is not
unknown, this being the West Highlands, for the whole mailbag to be
sent to Skye through oversight or petulance), but I can only leave a reply
to that post at Druimfiaclach the following night, for collection by the
Land Rover on the morning after that; so that if I receive a letter on, for
example, a Tuesday evening, it will be Friday before the sender gets my
reply. Newspapers reach me on the evening of the day after they are
published, if I go to Druimfiaclach to fetch them. Because of the height
of the surrounding mountain massifs no radio will emit more than a
furtive whisper; by pressing one's ear to the set one may catch
tantalizingly fragmentary snatches of news, too often of wars and
rumours of wars, or of equally intrusive and unwelcome strains of rock
'n' roll, mouse-squeak reminders of far-off human frenzy, whose
faintness underlines the isolation of Camusfeàrna more effectively than
could utter silence.

In practice, the exchange of letters often takes a full week, and the
frustrations inherent in this situation have led the more impatient of my
friends to the copious use of telegrams. The only way in which a telegram

can be delivered, other than by the Land Rover carrying the mail to Druimfiaclach in the evenings, is by five steep and weary miles' bicycling from the Post Office to Druimfiaclach, followed by a mile and a half of hill-track on foot. In all, ten miles' bicycling and three miles' walking. The village postmaster is a man of extreme rectitude and sense of duty; the first telegram I ever received at Camusfeàrna was when on a sweltering summer's day, the hills shimmering in the heat haze and the fly-tormented cattle knee-deep in the motionless sea, he stood exhausted before my door bearing a message which read 'Many happy returns of the day'. The mountains had travailed and brought forth a mouse; after that I persuaded him, with great difficulty, to exercise his own judgement as to whether or not a telegram was urgent, and to consign those that were not to the Land Rover for delivery to Druimfiaclach in the evening.

Telegrams between the West Highlands and England are often liable to a little confusion in transit, to the production of what the services call 'corrupt groups'. During my first stay at Camusfeàrna I realized that though the house had, as it were, dropped into my lap from heaven, I had no subsidiary rights; a diet composed largely of shellfish might, I thought, be suitably varied by rabbits, and I telegraphed to the owner of the estate to ask his permission. The telegram he received from me read: 'May I please shoot at Robert and if so where?'

The reply to this sadistic request being in the affirmative, I shot at Robert morning and evening, with a silenced .22 from the kitchen window, and he went far to solve the supply problem both for myself and for my dog Jonnie. Alas, Robert and all his brothers have now gone from Camusfeàrna, and except by living entirely from the sea it is difficult to approach self-subsistence.

· · ·

For a year or two there was goats' milk, for Morag had, characteristically, given asylum to four goats left homeless by their owner's demise; one of these, a dainty, frolicsome white sprite called Mairi Bhan, she presented to Camusfeàrna. It was but a token gesture, for the little nanny was unaware of any change in ownership, preferring the company of her co-concubines and her rancid, lecherous overlord. The herd, however, took to spending much of their time at Camusfeàrna, where they would pick their way delicately along the top of the croft wall to plunder and maim the old apple and plum trees by the bridge, necessitating strange high barriers that seem cryptic now, for the goats are long gone. Their cynical, predatory yellow eyes, bright with an ancient, egotistical wisdom, were ever alert for an open door, and more than once I came back to the house from an afternoon's fishing to find the kitchen in chaos, my last loaves disappearing between agile rubbery lips, and Mairi Bhan posturing impudently on the table.

In the end their predilection for Camusfeàrna was their undoing, for where a past occupier of the house had once grown a kitchen garden sprung rhubarb leaves in profusion; of these, one spring, they ate copiously, and all but the billy died. Never sweet to the nostrils or continent of habit, he became, deprived of his harem, so gross both in odour and in behaviour, that only the undeniable splendour of his appearance prevented my joining the ranks of his numerous enemies. He survived, a lonely satyr, a sad solitary symbol of thwarted virility, until the burden of his chastity became too great for him, and he wandered and perished.

. . .

The goats were not the only invaders of the house, for in those days there was no fence surrounding it, and a door left ajar was taken as tacit invitation to the most improbable and unwelcome of visitors. Once, on my return to the house after a few hours' absence, I was warned of some crisis while as yet a quarter of a mile distant; a succession of mighty, hollow groans, interspersed with a sound as of one striking wooden boarding with a heavy mallet, conjured an image worse, if possible, than the bizarre reality. Half-way up the wooden stairway, where it turns at right angles to reach the small landing, an enormous, black, and strikingly pregnant cow was wedged fast between the two walls, unable to progress forward and fearful of the gradient in reverse. Her rear aspect, whose copious activity – whether under the stress of anxiety or from an intelligent desire to reduce her dimensions – covered the stairs below her with a positively Augean litter of dung, blocked both view and passage to any would-be rescuer; moreover she proved, despite her precarious foothold and elephantine fecundity, to be capable of kicking with a veritably faun-like flourish. It was, however, one of these moments of petulant aggression that brought, literally, her downfall; an attempt with both heels simultaneously collapsed her with a ponderous and pathetic rumble, and she lay on her great gravid belly with her legs trailing, mire-covered, down the stairs. When at the end of nearly an hour's haulage I had restored her to the outside world I feared for her calf, but I need not have worried. Not long afterwards I assisted at her delivery, not with forceps but with ropes attached to protruding hooves; the calf fell with a terrifying crash to a stone floor, and half an hour later was on his feet and suckling.

. . .

With the goats cut short, as I have said, in their connubial prime, Camusfeàrna has ever since been dependent upon tinned milk. General supplies reach me by the same three-stage route as the mail, with the assistance of the friendly, haphazard co-operation to be found in remote places. I leave my order for the grocer, the ironmonger, or the chemist at Druimfiaclach in the evening; the Land Rover collects it in the morning and hands it to the skipper of the mail launch, who delivers it to the shops and brings the goods back – if, that is, they are to be obtained at the 'shopping centre'. For though there are a surprising number of shops for what is really no more than a hamlet, there is also surprisingly little in them – the nearest place where such commonplace objects as, for example, a coat-hanger or a pair of blue jeans may be bought, is Inverness, nearly a hundred miles away on the opposite coast of Scotland, or Fort William, the same distance to the south. This is not due entirely to a somewhat characteristic lack of enterprise, but also to a Foolish Virgin attitude to the necessities of life that I had seen exemplified again and again during my ownership of the Island of Soay. It is only during my own time at Camusfeàrna that electricity has come to the district – though not to me – through the West of Scotland Hydro-Electric Board; before that all the houses were lit by paraffin lamps, and many of the people cooked by Primus stove. Yet, despite the notoriously capricious quality of the electric light in the north-west Highlands, every single shop in every single village immediately stopped stocking paraffin, methylated spirits, and candles. Last year, there was to my certain knowledge, no drop of methylated spirits for sale within a hundred miles. The friendly spirit of co-operation is, however, equal even to this situation: once I sent an S.O.S. for methylated spirits to a distant village and received an odd-looking package in return. It did not look like methylated spirits, and I unwrapped it in puzzlement. Inside was a pencil note which I deciphered with difficulty: 'Sorry no methylated spirits but am sending you two pounds of sausages instead'.

. . .

With a view to avoiding the monotony of tinned food I began early to experiment with edible fungi, but the results were not encouraging, and I have never succeeded in making them a substantial item of Camusfeàrna diet. I possessed two books, representing respectively and most decoratively the edible and harmful species; thus armed I set off one August day, the sun as hot as it can be upon rock lichen and bell heather, to collect and identify all I could. At evening I returned laden with, it appeared, considerably more varieties than existed in both books put together. With these arranged like a palette of pastel shades upon the kitchen table, and both slim volumes at hand for consultation,

I began eagerly to separate the sheep from the goats. Almost at once, however, I discovered that every edible species had a poisonous counterpart whose uniform was so exactly similar as to defy detection. At the end of half an hour I gathered friend and masquerading enemy indiscriminately together and bundled them into the refuse pit. Now there is only one fungus that I find worth the trouble of search, the *Boletus edulis*, that has a glazed brown top like a bun, and tastes strongly of mushroom. The *chanterelles*, delicate orange creatures shaped like toy trumpets, grow in enormous profusion under the trees about the hillside burns, but though an eighteenth-century writer said of them that dead men would come to life at the taste, I have found them flavourless and insipid, their beauty but skin-deep, more appropriate to the magic of moss and fern and rushing water than to the table.

As children the members of my family were brought up to regard fungi with a conservative eye, and though we gathered and consumed vast quantities of horse-mushrooms, we were taught to believe that puffballs were poisonous. More recently I have learned that they are not, but how they have won the gourmet's esteem remains to me a marvel; they are the most non-committal, self-effacing food I have ever eaten, tasting of nothing and being of no definable consistency, gastronomic nonentities *par excellence*. Sometimes I wonder whether their adulators have ever tasted them; Miss Rowena Farre ate them in *Seal Morning*, if one may put it that way, and found them delicious.

So the fungi at Camusfeàrna remain, for the most part, unmolested, and flourish among the ferns and dappled sunlight of the birches by the burns and the hidden waterfalls, their many hues of violet and green, red and orange, nibbled at by discerning and appreciative rodents whose perceptions are undimmed by attempted identification of their diet.

CHAPTER 3

I had been at Camusfeàrna for eight years before I piped water to the house; before that it came from the burn in buckets. During the first years there was a stout stone-pierced bridge across the burn, and under it one could draw water that had not been fouled by the cattle at their ford a little lower; then, in 1953, the bridge was swept away by a winter spate, and there was none built again for five years. In the summer there is no more than a foot or so of water among the stones, deepening to three or four feet when it runs amber-coloured and seemingly motionless between the alder banks, but wedged high among the branches are wads of debris that show the level of its torrential winter spates. When the gales blow in from the south-west and the burn comes roaring down in a foaming peaty cataract to meet the invading sea, the alders stand under water for half their height, and in the summer blackened trailers of dry seaweed dangle from branches ten feet and more above the stream.

After the bridge had gone, the winter crossing of the burn to climb the hill to Druimfiaclach was always perilous, sometimes impossible. I stretched a rope between the alders from bank to bank, but it was slender support, for even when the water was no more than thigh deep the pure battering weight of it as it surged down from the waterfall would sweep one's legs from the bottom and leave one clinging to the rope without foothold, feet trailing seaward.

The purely natural changes that have taken place during my ten years at Camusfeàrna are astonishing. One is inclined to think of such a landscape as immutable without the intervention of man, yet in these few years the small alterations to the scene have been continuous and progressive. The burn has swept the soil from under its banks so that the alder roots show white and bare, and some of the trees have fallen; where there are none at the burn side the short green turf has been tunnelled under by the water so that it falls in and the stream's bed becomes even wider and shallower. Farther down towards the sea, where the burn bends round to encircle Camusfeàrna, the burrowing of a colony of sand martins in the sand cliff that is its landward bank has had the same effect, undermining the turf above so that it gives beneath the sheep's feet and rolls down to the water's edge. Below the sand martins' burrows is now a steep slope of loose sand where ten years ago it was vertical. The sand-dunes between the house and the sea form and re-form, so that their contour is never the same for two years, though the glaucous, rasping marram grass that grows on them imparts an air of static permanency. The whole structure of these dunes that now effectively block much of the beach from the house, and incidentally afford to it some shelter from the southerly gales, is in any case a thing of recent times, for I am told that when the present house was built fifty-odd years ago the field stretched flat to the sea, and the seaward-facing wall of the house was left windowless for that reason.

The beach itself, wherever the rock does not shelve straight into the sea, is in constant change too; broad belts of shingle appear in the sand where there was no shingle before; soft stretches of quicksand come and go in a few weeks; sand bars as white as snowdrifts and jewelled with bright shells rise between the islands and vanish as though they had melted under the summer suns.

Even the waterfall, to me perhaps the most enduring symbol of

Camusfeàrna, has changed and gone on changing. When I am away from the place and think of it, it is of the waterfall that I think first. Its voice is in one's ears day and night; one falls asleep to it, dreams with it and wakens to it; the note changes with the season, from the dull menacing roar of winter nights to the low crooning of the summer, and if I hold a shell to my ear it is not the sea's murmur that comes to me but the sound of the Camusfeàrna waterfall. Above the bridge where I used to draw my water the burn rushes over stones and between boulders with the alders at its banks, and a wealth of primroses and wild hyacinths among the fern and mosses. In spring it is loud with bird song from the chaffinches that build their lichen nests in the forks of the alders, and abob with wagtails among the stones. This part of the burn is 'pretty' rather than beautiful, and it seems to come from nowhere, for the waterfall is hidden round a corner and the stream seems to emerge from a thirty-foot wall of rock hung with honeysuckle and with rowan trees jutting from cracks and fissures. But looking up the burn from the foot of that rock the word 'pretty' becomes wholly inapplicable; the waterfall is of a beauty it would be hard to devise. It is not high, for the tall cataracts of eighty feet are some two hundred yards higher up its course; it emerges between boulders and sheer rock walls to drop some fifteen feet, over about the same breadth, from the twilight world of the deep narrow gorge it has carved through the hill face over thousands, perhaps millions, of years. It emerges frothing from that unseen darkness to fall like a tumbling cascade of brilliants into a deep rounded cauldron enclosed by rock walls on three sides, black water in whorled black rock, with the fleecy white spume ringing the blackness of the pool. Up above the black sides of the pot there are dark-green watery mosses growing deep and cushioned wherever there is a fingerhold for soil; the domed nest that the dippers build here every year is distinguishable from the other moss cushions by nothing but its symmetry. The sun reaches the waterfall for only a short time in the afternoon; it forms a rainbow over the leaping spray, and at the top of the fall between the boulders it gives to the smooth-flowing, unbroken water the look of spun green glass.

For most of the year the waterfall has volume enough for a man to stand on a ledge between it and the rock and remain almost dry; between oneself and the sky it forms a rushing, defeaning curtain of milky brilliance through which nothing but light is discernible. If one steps forward so that the weight of water batters full on head and shoulders it is of the massiveness only that one is conscious, and it would be impossible to say whether the water were cold or hot. Only when one steps from it again, and the flying icy drops tingle on the skin, does the sensation become one of snow water.

It would seem that the waterfall could never change, yet year by year its form differs as a new boulder is swept down by the spates to lodge above its lip; or a tree falls from its precarious grip on the cliff face above it and jams the doorway of its emergence; or a massive section of rock breaks away, split by the prising leverage of slow-growing tree roots.

In spring and autumn the natural decoration surrounding the waterfall surpasses anything that artifice could achieve; in spring the green banks above the rock are set so thickly with primroses that blossom almost touches blossom, and the wild blue hyacinths spring from among them seemingly without leaf; in late summer and autumn the scarlet rowanberries flare from the ferned rock walls, bright against the falling white water and the darkness of the rock.

It is the waterfall, rather than the house, that has always seemed to me the soul of Camusfeàrna, and if there is anywhere in the world to which some part of me may return when I am dead it will be there.

If it is the waterfall that seems the soul of Camusfeàrna, it is the burn and the sea that give its essential character, that sparkling silver that rings the green field and makes it almost an island. Below the house the beach is long and shelving, the tide running back at low springs for more than two hundred yards over alternate stone and sand. There is only one thing lacking at Camusfeàrna; within its narrow compass it contains every attraction but an anchorage. To look down from the hill above upon the bay and the scattered, intricate network of islands and skerries it would appear incredible that no one of those bights or niches should afford shelter, yet because of the long ebb of the tide each one of these seemingly tranquil miniature harbours rides out at low water. For years I had no boat at Camusfeàrna, and when at last I did buy a dinghy I was intimidated by the thought of those interminable hauls to and from the water's edge, and I bought a little nine-foot flat-bottomed pram that one could almost pick up. But to have a boat again at all, even that toy, brought a hankering to extend one's range up and down the coast and over to Skye, and now I have two dinghies with outboard motors, one of them a sturdy lifeboat's dinghy of fifteen feet, with decked-in bows. There are moorings laid in the bay where the burn flows out to the sea, and the pram is kept drawn up on the beach as ferry to and from the larger boat, but when the wind blows strong from the south it is always an anxious business. The suddenness and intensity of West Highland squalls, even in summer, has to be experienced to be understood; pale-blue satin water can become in a matter of minutes an iron-grey menace raging in white at the crests of massive waves. But the compensations outweigh the anxiety, for it was frustrating to live at the sea's edge and be unable to voyage upon it, to be unable to visit the distant islands, to fish in summer, to reach the nearest shop without the long climb to Druimfiaclach. The possession of the boats opened a whole new world around Camusfeàrna, a wide extension of its small enclosed paradise, and in summer the hours afloat drift by with work unheeded and the business of life seeming far off and worthless.

There is a perpetual mystery and excitement in living on the seashore, which is in part a return to childhood and in part because for all of us the sea's edge remains the edge of the unknown; the child sees the bright shells, the vivid weeds and red sea-anemones of the rock pools with wonder and with the child's eye for minutiae; the adult who retains wonder brings to his gaze some partial knowledge which can but increase it, and he brings, too, the eye of association and of symbolism, so that at the edge of the ocean he stands at the brink of his own unconscious.

The beaches of Camusfeàrna are a treasure house for any man whose eye finds wealth at the sea's edge. There are more shells than I have seen on any other littoral; a great host of painted bivalves of bewildering variety and hue, from coral pinks and primrose yellows to blues and purples and mother-of-pearl, from jewel-like fan shells no bigger than a little fingernail to the great scallops as big as a side plate; nutshells and Hebridean ark shells and pearly top-shells and delicate blush-pink cowries. The sand bars and beaches between the islands are formed of the disintegration of these myriad calceous houses, true shell sand that is blindingly white under the sun and crusted in deep layers at the tide's edge with tiny intact empty shells gaudy as multicoloured china beads. A little above the shells, because they are heavier, lies a filigree of white and purple coral, loose pieces each of which would lie in the palm of a hand, but there are so many of them that they form a dense, brittle layer over the sand. On still summer days when the tide wells up the beaches without so much as a wrinkle or ripple of wavelet at its edge, the coral floats off on the meniscus of the water, so that the sea seems to be growing flowers as an ornamental pond grows water lilies, delicately branched white and purple flowers on the aquamarine of the clear water.

Where shells lie thick it is often those that are broken that have the greatest beauty of form; a whelk is dull until one may see the sculptural perfection of the revealed spiral, the skeletal intricacy of the whorled mantle. Many of the shells at Camusfeàrna, and the stones, too, have been embroidered with the white limy tunnels of the Serpulid tube-worm, strange hieroglyphics that even in their simplest forms may appear urgently significant, the symbols of some forgotten alphabet, and when a surface is thickly encrusted it assumes the appearance of Hindoo temple carving, or of Rodin's 'Gates of Hell', precise in every riotous ramification. Parts of the sculpture appear almost representational; a terrified beast flees before a pursuing predator; a well-meaning saint impales a dragon; the fingers of a hand are raised, like those of a Byzantine Christ, in a gesture that seems one of negation rather than benediction.

But above all it is the fantastic colouring of the beaches that as an image overpowers the minutiae. Above the tideline the grey rocks are splashed gorse-yellow with close-growing lichen, and with others of blue-green and salmon pink. Beneath them are the vivid orange-browns and siennas of wrack-weeds, the violet of mussel beds, dead-white sand, and water through which one sees down to the bottom, as through pale green bottle-glass, to where starfish and big spiny sea urchins of pink and purple rest upon the broad leaves of the sea-tangle.

.   .   .

The beaches are rich, too, in edible shellfish. Besides the ubiquitous mussels, limpets and periwinkles, there are cockle beds, razor-shell beds, and even an oyster bed, though this last remains one of the mysteries of Camusfeàrna. The oysters were introduced many years ago by a former owner of the estate, in a little circular bay almost closed from the sea and no more than twenty yards across, where a trickle of fresh water comes down over the sand from an island spring. At the tideline above this bay arrives a constant litter of tantalizingly freshly emptied oyster shells that would not disgrace Wheeler's, and, very occasionally, a live oyster, but for all my searching year by year I have never discovered where the bed lies. This is as well, perhaps, for I suspect that by now the colony would have succumbed to my gluttony.

Below the tide around the islands the white sand alternates with a heavy rubbery jungle of sea-tangle or umbrella weed. The lobsters lurk in this dimness by day, and lobster-pots set in the sand patches between the weed are rarely unsuccessful. A variety of other life besides lobsters enters the pots, creatures couth and uncouth; sometimes the bait is covered with gigantic whelks, and almost always there are big edible crabs. Often there is a curious beast called the velvet swimming crab, with a shield of brown velvet and reproachful red eyes, and once I caught one of the most repulsive creatures I have ever come across, a spider crab. It was not only the enormously long legs and absence of pincers that were nauseating; he was grown over from head to foot, as it were, with a crinkly, purplish-red seaweed, lending him the same air of doubtful reality as a shroud traditionally imparts to a ghost. The weed is, in fact, grafted into position by the crab itself, for camouflage, and this implication of furtive cunning coming on top of the outrageous personal appearance is not reassuring.

I must confess to a slight but perceptible revulsion to all crabs before they are prepared for eating, greatest in the case of the spider crab and in *diminuendo* down to the hermit crabs that inhabit empty shells, for their unattractive nakedness is decently covered in someone else's discarded finery. Hermit crabs have given rise to some of the few occasions in my adult life on which I have laughed out loud when quite alone. Sometimes when gathering periwinkles to eat, bucket in hand and scooping them several dozen to a swipe, my attention has been caught by some monster winkle at the floor of a pool, one that would at least provide a mouthful for a marmoset rather than a mouse. Even as my fingers have broken the surface of the water, shaping themselves avidly for capture, the shell, its bluff so accidentally called, has suddenly scuttled away with an air of chagrin and embarrassment, as though two of the Marx brothers, detected in the front and rear halves of a stage cow, still made a last hopeless effort to maintain the deception.

CHAPTER 4

Spring comes late to Camusfeàrna. More than one year I have motored up from the south early in April to become immobilized in snowdrifts on the passes twenty miles from it, and by then the stags are still at the roadside down the long glen that leads to the sea. By mid-April there is still no tinge of green bud on the bare birches and rowans nor green underfoot, though there is often, as when I first came to Camusfeàrna, a spell of soft still weather and clear skies. The colours then are predominantly pale blues, russet browns, and purples, each with the clarity of fine enamel; pale blue of sea and sky, the russet of dead bracken and fern, deep purple-brown of unbudded birch, and the paler violets of the Skye hills and the peaks of Rhum. The landscape is lit by three whites – the pearl white of the birch trunks, the dazzle of the shell-sand beaches, and the soft filtered white of the high snows. The primroses are beginning to flower about the burn and among the island banks, though all the high hills are snow-covered and the lambs are as yet unborn. It is a time that has brought me, in all too few years, the deep contentment of knowing that the true spring and summer are still before me at Camusfeàrna, that I shall see the leaf break and the ground become green, and all the snow melt from the hills but for a few drifts that will lie summer through.

It has its own orchestration, this little prelude to the northern spring; every year there is the sound of the wild geese calling far overhead as they travel north to their thawing breeding grounds, and sometimes the wild unearthly beauty of whooper swans' voices, silver trumpets high in the clear blue air. The eider ducks have arrived to breed about the shore and the islands; they bring with them that most evocative and haunting of all sounds of the Hebridean spring and summer, the deep, echoing, woodwind crooning of the courting drakes.

One by one the breeding bird species return to the beaches and the islands where they were hatched; the sand martins to the sand cliff at the burn foot, the wheatears to the rabbit burrows in the close-bitten turf, the black guillemots and the gulls to the Camusfeàrna islands. The herring gulls come first, to the biggest island, where the lighthouse stands, some two hundred and fifty pairs of them, and the air above the white-splashed rocks and sea pinks scattered with broken shellfish is vibrant with the clang of their calling and their wheeling white wings. Among them are two or three pairs of great black-backed gulls, massive, hoarse-voiced and vulturine. Then come the common gulls, delicate, graceful, segregated shrilly onto a neighbouring promontory, beadily mistrustful of the coarse language and predatory predilections of their neighbours; and, lastly, not until well into May, come the terns, the sea swallows, to their own outlying skerry. They arrive in the same week as the swallows come up from Africa to nest in the old ruined croft across the field, and with the thin steel oar-beat of their wings spring has almost given place to summer.

By then the colour everywhere is green. The purple birch twigs are hidden in a soft cloud of new leaf; the curled, almond-bitter rods of young bracken have in those short weeks pushed up three feet from the earth, and unfurled a canopy of green frond over the rust of last year's growth; the leaves of the yellow flag iris that margin the burn and the shore form a forest of broad bayonets, and the islands, that but for rank rooty patches of heather growing knee-deep seemed so bare in April, are smothered with a jungle-growth of goose-grass and briar. To me there is always something a little stifling in this enveloping green stain, this redundant, almost Victorian, drapery over bones that need no blanketing, and were it not for the astringent presence of the sea I should find all that verdure as enervating as an Oxford water-meadow in the depths of summer. Perhaps 'depraved' is the right word after all.

Early in May comes the recurrent miracle of the elvers' migration from the sea. There is something deeply awe-inspiring about the sight of any living creatures in incomputable numbers; it stirs, perhaps, some atavistic chord whose note belongs more properly to the distant days when we were a true part of the animal ecology; when the sight of another species in unthinkable hosts brought fears or hopes no longer applicable. When the young eels reach the Camusfeàrna burn – no more than a uniform three inches long nor thicker than a meat-skewer, steel-blue when seen from above, but against the light transparent except for a red blob at the gills – they have been journeying in larval form for two whole years from their breeding grounds south-west of Bermuda, through two thousand miles of ocean and enemies. During that long, blind voyage of instinct their numbers must have been reduced not to a millionth but a billionth of those who set forth, yet it is difficult to imagine that there can have been vaster hoards than reach the Camusfeàrna burn; still more difficult to realize that these are but a tiny fraction of the hosts that are simultaneously ascending a myriad other burns.

Where the burn flows calm through the level ground their armies undulate slowly and purposefully forward towards the seemingly insurmountable barrier of the falls; on, above the bridge, into the stretch where the water rushes and stumbles over uneven stones; round the rock-twist to the foot of the falls. Here, temporarily daunted or resting before their assault upon the vertical, spray-wet rock face, they congregate almost motionless in the rock pools, forming a steel-blue carpet inches deep; dip a bucket here, and it comes up with a greater volume of elvers than of water. Some mistake the true course of the burn, and follow steep trickles leading to cul-de-sac pools of spray water; to and from these (for the miraculous powers of their multitudes do not appear to include communication or deduction), there are simultaneous streams of ascending and descending elvers, while the spray-pool itself is filled to the brim with an aimlessly writhing swarm.

It is here, during the wait at the foot of the falls, that the last heavy toll is taken of their numbers; for a week or two the rocks below the waterfall are splashed white with the droppings of herons who stand there scooping them up by the bill-full, decimating yet again, on the verge of their destination, the remnants of the great concourse that has been travelling thus perilously for two years.

But one has not been witness to the long core, as it were, of that mighty migration, and so it is in the elvers' final ascent of the falls that the colossal driving power of their instinct becomes most apparent to the onlooker. At first, where at the edges of the falls the water splashes into shallow stone troughs among the horizontal ledges, the way is easy – a few inches of horizontal climb and the elver has reached the next trough. But after a foot or two of this ladder-like progression they are faced either with the battering fall of white water at their left or with a smooth black stretch of rock wall in front, hit every few seconds by heavy splashes of spray. For a few feet at the bottom of this wall grows a close slimy fur of waterweed, and among its infinitesimal tendrils the elvers twine themselves and begin, very slowly, to squirm their way upwards, forming a vertical, close-packed queue perhaps two feet wide. Sometimes a big gob of spray lands right amid their ranks and knocks a hundred of them back into the trough below, but slowly, patiently, they climb back again. I have never marked an elver so that it is recognizable, and for all I know this may happen to the same elver many, many times in a day or even in an hour. Perhaps it is something to do with the transparency of the creatures, besides their diminutive size and bewildering numbers, that makes the mind rebel both at the blind strength of their instinct and their inherent power to implement it, as though the secret power-house should be visible.

Once above the water-draggled weed there is no further incidental support for the climbing elvers; there is just sheer wet rock, with whatever microscopic roughness their transparent bellies may apprehend. They hang there, apparently without gravity, with an occasional convulsive movement that seems born of despair. They climb perhaps six inches in an hour, sometimes slithering backward the same distance in a second, and there are a further twelve feet of rock above them.

It is not possible for more than a moment or two to identify oneself with any single one of this mass, but there is a sense of relief, of emotional satisfaction, in looking upward to the lip of the falls where they spill over from the hidden pool above, and seeing the broad band of glistening elvers that have accomplished the apparently impossible and are within an inch of safety.

Perhaps a few million out of billions top the Camusfeàrna falls; some, certainly, surmount the second and third falls too, and I have seen elvers of that size more than two thousand feet up the peak where the burn has its source. In perspective, the survival rate must be high when compared with that of spermatozoa.

Only once at Camusfeàrna have I seen any other living creatures in numbers to compare with those elvers, but I remember the occasion vividly. In the warm evenings of later summer, when the sun still flared a finger's breadth above the saw-tooth peaks of the Cuillin and glowed on the dense red berries of the rowans, the MacKinnon children would come down the hill from Druimfiaclach to bathe at the white sand beaches of the islands. Long before I could hear them my dog Jonnie, growing a little corpulent and stiff now, would prick his ears and whine, and the feathery white stub of his tail would scuff softly on the stone floor. I would go to the open door and listen and Jonnie would sit very upright on the stone flags outside, staring up at the high skyline with his nose twitching and questing, and I would hear nothing but the sounds of ever-moving water and the faint, familiar bird-cries of the wilderness, the piping of shore birds and perhaps the mew of a buzzard wheeling overhead. There was the murmur of the dwindled waterfall and the trill of the burn among the boulders, and at the other side the muted sound of wavelets breaking in a small tumble of foam along the shore; there was the twitter of sand martins hawking flies in the still golden air, the croak of a raven, and gull voices from the sea that stretched away as smooth as white silk to the distant island of Eigg lying across the sea horizon. Sometimes there was the warning thump of a rabbit from the warren among the dunes behind the house.

But Jonnie always knew when the children were coming, and when at last I could hear them too, treble voices faint and far off and high above us, he would assume a sudden unconcern, walking with stiff indifference to lift his leg in a flourish over a nearby tuft of rushes or a post that guarded the small flower-bed. From the time that the boys' heads were bobbing small on the hill horizon it would be some five minutes before they had descended the last and steepest part of the track, crossed the bridge, and come up over the green grass to the door, and all the time I would be wondering what they had brought – longed-for or unwelcome letters, some supplies that I urgently needed, a bottle of goat's milk from their mother, or just nothing at all. When it was nothing I was at once relieved and bitterly disappointed, for at Camusfeàrna I both resent the intrusion of the outside world and crave reassurance of its continued existence.

One evening when the twins had brought me a bulky packet of letters I had been sitting reading them in the twilight kitchen for some time when I was roused by the urgent excitement of their cries from the beach. I went out to a scene that is as fresh in my mind now as though it were hours rather than years that lay between.

The sun was very low; the shadow of the house lay long and dark across the grass and the rushes, while the hillside above glowed golden as though seen through orange lenses. The bracken no longer looked green nor the heather purple; all that gave back their own colour to the sun were the scarlet rowanberries, as vivid as venous blood. When I turned to the sea it was so pale and polished that the figures of the twins thigh-deep in the shallows showed in almost pure silhouette against it, bronze-coloured limbs and torsos edged with yellow light. They were shouting and laughing and dancing and scooping up the water with their hands, and all the time as they moved there shot up from the surface where they broke it a glittering spray of small gold and silver fish, so dense and brilliant as to blur the outline of the childish figures. It was as though the boys were the central décor of a strangely lit Baroque fountain, and when they bent to the surface with cupped hands a new jet of sparks flew upward where their arms submerged, and fell back in brittle, dazzling cascade.

When I reached the water myself it was like wading in silver treacle; our bare legs pushed against the packed mass of little fish as against a solid and reluctantly yielding obstacle. To scoop and to scatter them, to shout and to laugh, were as irresistible as though we were treasure hunters of old who had stumbled upon a fabled emperor's jewel vaults and threw diamonds about us like chaff. We were fish-drunk, fish-crazy, fish-happy in that shining orange bubble of air and water; the twins were about thirteen years old and I was about thirty-eight, but the miracle of the fishes drew from each of us the same response.

We were so absorbed in making the thronged millions of tiny fish into leaping fireworks for our delight that it was not for some minutes that I began to wonder what had driven this titanic shoal of herring fry – or soil, as they are called in this part of the world – into the bay, and why, instead of dispersing outwards to sea, they became moment by moment ever thicker in the shallows. Then I saw that a hundred yards out the surface was ruffled by flurries of mackerel whose darting shoals made a sputter of spray on the smooth swell of the incoming tide. The mackerel had driven the fry headlong before them into the narrow bay and held them there, but now the pursuers too were unable to go back. They were in turn harried from seaward by a school of porpoises who cruised the outermost limit of their shoals, driving them farther and farther towards the shore. Hunter and hunted pushed the herring soil ever inward to the sand, and at length every wavelet broke on the beach with a tumble of silver sprats. I wondered that the porpoises had not long since glutted and gone; then I saw that, like the fry and the mackerel that had pursued them into the bay, the porpoises' return to the open waters of the sound was cut off. Beyond them, black against the blanched sunset water, rose the towering sabre fin of a bull killer whale, the ultimate enemy of sea creatures great and small, the unattackable; his single terrible form controlling by its mere presence the billions of lives between himself and the shore.

The sun went down behind the Cuillin and the water grew cold and the tide crawled grey up the beach, clogged with its helpless burden of fish, and long after the distance had become too dim to see the killer's fin we could hear the putter of the rushing mackerel as they moved in with the tide. When it was nearly dark we fetched buckets and dipped them in the sea's edge; they came up heavy in our hands, full not of water but of thumb-length fish.

In the morning it was dead low tide, and the sea, as still as a mountain tarn as far as the eye could reach, had gone back some two hundred yards. The tide-wrack of high-water mark lay right along the slope of white sand under the dunes, but that morning it was not dark like a tarry rope ringing the bay; it gleamed blue-grey and white with the bodies of millions upon millions of motionless minnow-sized fish. The gulls had gorged themselves when the sun rose; they sat silent, hunched and distended, in long rows on the wet sand a little to seaward, their shadows still long and formal under the low sun that glared over the hill.

I gathered a few more buckets of the fry, and kept them as cool as I could in the heat of that sunny September. But manna, like everything else, should be of at least fifty-seven varieties; when heaven sends bounty it too often sends monotony. The first meal of fried whitebait had the delight of novelty and of windfall, akin to the pleasure that for the first few days I take in some humble but new treasure harvested from the shore after gales; the second had lost little, but the sixth and seventh were cloying, while there were still three buckets full. Jonnie, who entertained an unnatural passion for fish of all kinds, ate more than I did, but the level in the buckets seemed never to diminish; a guest came to stay, and we made them into fish-cakes and fish-pies, into kedgerees and fish-soups, into curries and savouries, until at last one merciful morning they began to smell. Then we used them to bait the lobster-pots, but after a while even the lobsters seemed to grow weary of them.

It so happened that about that time I made one of my rare shopping journeys to Inverness. The second item on the hotel luncheon menu was fried whitebait, and the dining-room was rich with the once-appetizing aroma. I left that hotel as might one who had perceived a corpse beneath his table, and it was some two years before I could eat whitebait again.

CHAPTER 5

The smaller members of the whale tribe are a feature of every summer at Camusfeàrna. Sometimes the great whales, the Blue and the Rorquals, pass majestically through the Sound beyond the lighthouse, but they never come into the bay, for only at the highest of tides would there be water enough to float their fantastic bulk.

Of all sea creatures whales hold for me a particular fascination, stemming, perhaps, from the knowledge of their enormously developed brains coupled with the unguessable, pressing, muffled world in which they pass their lives. So highly convoluted are those brains that it has been suggested that were it not for their frustrating limblessness they might well have outstripped man in domination of the earth's surface. Yet there are an incredible number of people who, because of the superficial similarities of bulk and habitat, confuse them with the great sharks whose brains are minute and rudimentary. Although from early times whaling men have had strange tales to tell of their quarry's extraordinary mental powers it is only comparatively recently that these things have become accepted fact. The American 'oceanariums' have allowed their porpoise and dolphin inmates to reveal themselves as highly intelligent, amiable, and playful personalities who evince an unexpected desire to please and co-operate with human beings. They will play ball games with their attendants, come up out of the water to greet them, and retrieve with obvious pleasure ladies' handbags and kindred objects that have accidentally fallen into their tank. They are also capable of unquestionable altruism to one another; like many animals, but perhaps even more than most, their behaviour compares very favourably with that of the human species. Yet for the oil in the blubber that insulates them from the cold of polar seas man has from the earliest days reserved for the whales the most brutal and agonizing death in his armoury, the harpoon buried deep in living flesh.

Until very lately zoologists held that whales were dumb, and both the system of communication that made possible concerted action by widely separated individuals, and the 'sixth sense' by which they could detect the presence of objects in water too murky for vision, remained undiscovered. We have long laboured under an obtuse presupposition that the senses by which other living creatures perceive their world must to a great extent resemble our own; but in fact we are, by scientific invention, only now beginning to approach methods of perception that the whales have always owned as their birthright. Not only can they hear sounds four times higher than the upper limit of the human ear can detect, but they possess a highly-developed system closely akin to our own recently discovered radar, sending out a constant stream of supersonic notes whose returning 'echoes' inform them of the where-abouts, size, and possibly much more as yet unguessed information, of all objects within their range. Underwater recording devices have now also established that members of the whale tribe keep up an almost continual conversational chatter among themselves, sounds that are seldom if ever uttered by a single whale with no other near him.

Because man could not hear them, man assumed that they were dumb. If a whale's cry of pain when struck with a harpoon had been audible it is just possible, but only just, that man would have felt more self-hatred in their slaughter; though the sight of two adult whales trying to keep the blow-hole of a wounded calf above water has failed to change the attitude of whaler to whale.

It is not, of course, easy for the casual shore visitor or boat passenger to deduce from the discreet, momentarily glimpsed fin of a porpoise all these complex and stimulating attributes of its owner; surprisingly few people, in fact, appear even to know that a porpoise is a whale.

The porpoises, six-foot lengths of sturdy grace, are the commonest of all the whale visitors to the Camusfeàrna bay. Unlike the rumbustious dolphins they are shy, retiring creatures, and one requires leisure and patience to see more of them than that little hooked fin that looks as if it were set on the circumference of a slowly-revolving wheel; leisure to ship the oars and remain motionless, and patience to allow curiosity to overcome timidity. Then the porpoises will blow right alongside the boat, with a little gasp that seems of shocked surprise, and at these close quarters the wondering inquisitiveness of their eyes shows as plainly as it can in a human face, a child's face as yet uninhibited against the display of emotion. The face, like the faces of all whales but the Killer, appears good-humoured, even bonhomous. But they will not stay to be stared at, and after that quick gasp they dive steeply down into the twilight; they go on about their own business, and will not linger to play as do the dolphins.

One summer a school of seventeen Bottle-nosed dolphins spent a whole week in the Camusfeàrna bay, and they would seem almost to hang about waiting for the boat to come out and play with them. They never leapt and sported unless the human audience was close at hand, but when we were out among them with the outboard motor they would play their own rollicking and hilarious games of hide-and-seek with us, and a sort of aquatic blind-man's-buff, in which we in the boat were all too literally blind to them, and a target for whatever surprises they could devise. The beginning followed an invariable routine; they would lead, close-packed, their fins thrusting from the water with a long powerful forward surge every five or ten seconds; and we would follow to see how close we could get to them. When we were within fifty feet or so there would be a sudden silence while, unseen, they swooped back under the boat to reappear dead astern of us. Sometimes they would remain submerged for many minutes, and we would cut the engine and wait. This was the dolphins' moment. As long as I live, and whatever splendid sights I have yet to see I shall remember the pure glory of the dolphins' leap as they shot up a clear ten feet out of the sea, one after the other, in high parabolas of flashing silver at the very boat's side. At the time it gave me a *déjà-vu* sensation that I could not place; afterwards I realized that it recalled irresistibly the firing in quick succession of pyrotechnic rockets, the tearing sound of the rockets' discharge duplicated by the harsh exhalation of air as each dolphin fired itself almost vertically from the waves.

In this school of dolphins there were some half a dozen calves, not more than four or five feet long as against their parents' twelve. The calves would keep close alongside their mothers' flanks – the right-hand side always – and I noticed that when the mothers leapt they kept their acrobatics strictly within the capabilities of their offspring, rising no more than half the height of those unencumbered by children.

The members of this school of dolphins spoke with voices perfectly audible to human ears; rarely when they were very close to the boat, but usually when they were heading straight away at a distance of a hundred yards or two. As they broke the surface with that strong forward-thrusting movement, one or more of their number would produce something between a shrill whistle and a squeak, on a single note held for perhaps two seconds. It seems strange that I can find no written record of any whale-sound as plainly and even obtrusively audible above water as this.

The Risso's Grampus, or more properly Risso's Dolphin, a few feet larger than the Bottle-nose, visits Camusfeàrna bay in the summer too, but whereas in the shark-fishery days I used to regard them as the sea's clowns, perpetually at play in uncouth and incongruous attitudes, the parties that come to Camusfeàrna have by comparison with the Bottle-nosed been sedate and decorous, almost always cows with small tubby calves, intent on the serious business of feeding and avoiding danger. They would not allow the boat nearly as close to them as would the other dolphins, unlike whom they seemed to resent human presence, and would soon leave the bay altogether if frequently followed.

Contrary to information contained in the majority of textbooks, in which Risso's dolphin is described as a rarity, it is in fact the commonest of all the lesser whales to visit the Hebrides in summer. During my years in the shark fishery, when our chief catcher the *Sea Leopard* would cruise day-long in search of a different shape of fin, it was a rare week in which we had not met with half a dozen schools of them. As with most other species of whale, the fishermen have their own names for them, names that they sometimes, to the confusion of an enquiring scientist, use to describe several separate species, so that it is only by the comparatively very rare strandings of individual whales that the presence of a species becomes established. The ring-net men call Risso's dolphin 'lowpers' or 'dunters', words deriving from the habit of seemingly aimless and random leaping. Neither Risso's nor the Bottle-nosed dolphins travel, as do the white-sided and common dolphins, by a series of long leaps low over the waves; both seem to jump only when they are at leisure and frolicking.

In fact it is not easy for an eye with any practice to confuse the fin of Risso's dolphin with any other than that of a cow Killer whale. 'Cow' is a strange feminine noun to give to the most terrible animal in the sea; 'bull' is little better for her butcher mate, but the forms are fixed by long usage and must stand. Imaginations have strained to find a simile from land animals; the Killer has been called the wolf of the sea, the tiger of the sea, the hyena of the sea, but none of these is really apt, and probably there is no other mammal of comparably indiscriminate ferocity.

Anyone writing of Killer whales finds it necessary to quote the discovered contents of one Killer's stomach, and indeed those contents produce so immediate an image that they will, perhaps, bear one more repetition. That particular Killer was found to contain no fewer than thirteen porpoises and fourteen seals. A gargantuan meal, one would say, for a leviathan, yet by comparison with the great whales the Killer is a small beast, the bull no more than twenty-five feet overall and the cow a mere fifteen, while an adult porpoise is six feet long and the average among the seal species little less. Killers hunt in packs, and not even the great whales themselves are safe from them; the pack goes for the mighty tongue which in itself may weigh a ton, and when it is torn out the giant bleeds to death while the Killers feed.

As I write there lies a few hundred yards down the shore the newly-dead body of a brown seal. The forepart of the head has gone, where something has crunched through the skull in front of the eyes, and from one flank there has been ripped away a foot length of flesh and blubber, exposing the entrails. There are other possible solutions, though none of them likely; it is the typical work of a Killer in killing mood. On Hyskeir the lighthouse men have told me how they have seen the Killers slash seals for sport and not for food, and leave them maimed and dying among the skerries.

A Killer or two comes every year to Camusfeàrna, but they do not linger, and if they did I would compass their deaths by any means that I could, for they banish the other sea life from my surroundings; also, I do not care to be among them in a small boat. There are many tales, but few, if any, authenticated records, of their attacking human beings; however, I do not want to be the first. Last year a single bull terrorized the tiny harbour of the Isle of Canna the summer through; John Lorne-Campbell shared my aversion to being a guinea pig for dietary research among Killers, and wrote asking my advice about its destruction. I smugly advised him to shoot it, and gave reasoned instructions as to the precise moment and bull's-eye, but I was thirty miles away, and I daresay my advice did not seem as sound and constructive on Canna as it did to me at Camusfeàrna.

No strange sea monster has ever come my way since I have been here, though in the summer of 1959 there was something not easily explicable close by. It was seen by Tex Geddes, once a harpoon gunner in the Island of Soay Shark Fisheries, and now the owner of the island, and by an English visitor whom he had taken out fishing in his boat.

On Sunday 13th September, he took this visitor, a Mr Gavin, an engineer from Hertfordshire, to fish for mackerel off the southern tip of Soay. It was a hot, flat-calm day, with every object at the sea's surface visible for miles. At about four o'clock in the afternoon Mr Gavin drew Tex's attention to a large black object about a mile away in the direction of Loch Slapin. The mackerel were playing on the surface and making the sea boil all round the boat, so Tex did not at first take any notice, and went on fishing, facing in the opposite direction. The object, however, drew steadily nearer, and at length both men stopped fishing in order to watch it. When it was some two hundred yards away Tex noticed a party of five Killer whales not far off in the direction of the Island of Rhum. Tex trusts Killers no more than I do; in the words of his letter to me the next day: 'I was not sure what kind of a thing this was that was slowly making up on us – it certainly did not look like a Killer, but nevertheless I was not over thrilled'.

As it drew near, he first thought that it was a tortoise or a turtle, but as it came abreast of the boat he changed his mind. The head of the creature was about two and a half feet out of the water, a head that had 'two huge round eyes like apples', and what Mr Gavin described as the head of a tortoise magnified to the size of a donkey's. There was a gash-like mouth, with pronounced lips, occupying about half of the head's circumference. The mouth opened and shut rhythmically, showing a red interior and emitting a wheezing sound that reminded Tex of a cow with pleurisy. He could see neither nostrils nor ears. Some two feet behind the head the back showed, higher than the head, and eight feet or more long; it rose steeply to a gradual fall aft, dark brown, but not as dark as the head. This back was not smooth but 'rose out of the water like the Cuillin hills', as Tex wrote in his letter to me the next day. The impression, he said, was of an animal weighing some five tons.

At its nearest point the creature was no more than fifteen or twenty yards from Tex's boat; it passed travelling at five knots or so, heading S.S.W. towards Barra.

Every detail of this story is corroborated by Tex's companion, and in such ideal conditions of visibility and proximity it would be difficult for either or both men to have been victims of optical illusion. It is not, incidentally, the first tale, or even the second, of monsters in the vicinity of Soay.

My old quarry the Basking Sharks I have seen but seldom since they ceased to be my bread and butter, or rather my quest for bread and butter. The first Basking Shark with which I ever came to grips, sixteen crowded years ago was, by a strange coincidence, just out to sea from Camusfeàrna lighthouse, but in the ten years on and off that I have lived here since, I have only seen sharks on a bare half-dozen occasions, and most of them a long way off. No doubt they have often been showing at times when I was not there to see them. Only once have I seen them right close inshore, and then they were being hunted by my successors: I had been sitting up all night with my dog Jonnie, who was at the very edge of death, and I was too crushed with sadness and weariness to identify myself with that strange vignette of my past life.

The stages of Jonnie's illness have become blurred in my mind; the two crises from which he made miraculous but ephemeral recoveries seem no longer related in sequence. I had been in London, and travelled to Camusfeàrna in the last week of April. Morag had telephoned to me to tell me that Jonnie was not well, and by the time I arrived he had developed pneumonia; he was a dog of enormous strength, but he was growing old, and his heart was not a young dog's heart.

At the end of one despairing night sitting with him at Druimfiaclach, Morag relieved me after she had seen to her family's wants, and I set off down the hill for Camusfeàrna, dazed and unhappy and longing desperately to get into bed and sleep. When I came to the part of the track that looks down over the house and the sea I was startled by the unmistakable boom of a harpoon gun, and woke, as it were, to find myself staring straight into the past. Below me in the calm bay was a ring-net boat from Mallaig; there was a storm of thrashing spray about her bows, and from the gun in her stem drifted a thin haze of cordite smoke. A little farther out to sea were showing the vast dorsal fins of two more sharks. I saw the white water at the boat's bows subside as the harpooned shark sounded, and I sat and watched the whole familiar procedure as they got the winches started and hauled for half an hour before they had him back at the surface; I saw that great six-foot tail break water and lash and slam the boat's sides while they struggled, as I had struggled so often before, to lasso the wildly lunging target; I saw it captured and made fast – yet because of my own state of exhaustion and preoccupation the whole scene was utterly without meaning to me, and I had no moment of mental participation while the small figures of the crew scurried about the deck in pursuance of a routine that had once been my daily life. Yet at other times, when I have watched through the field-glasses the cruising fins of sharks far down the Sound, I have been possessed by a wild and entirely illogical unrest; the same sort of unrest, I imagine, that migratory creatures feel in captivity when the season for their movement is at hand.

Though Jonnie survived pneumonia to become seemingly as strong as before, the writing was on the wall. A few months later he developed cancer of the rectum, and while it was, I think, painless, he had always been a dog of great dignity and cleanliness, and he felt acutely the concomitant humiliation of an evil-smelling discharge over the white silk-and-wool of his coat. When I was away from Camusfeàrna he lived with Morag MacKinnon, to whom he accorded a devotion no less than to myself, but when I came back after months of absence he would go mad with joy like a puppy and lead the way down the path to Camusfeàrna as if I had never left it. But it was with Morag that he died at last, for I was too cowardly to travel north and watch my old friend killed, as in all humanity he had to be.

Camusfeàrna is a very long way from a vet; the nearest, in fact, is on the Island of Skye, nearly fifty miles away by road and ferry-boat. When he visited Jonnie that winter of 1954 he said that the disease was progressing very rapidly, and that pain when it came would be sudden and acute, with a complete blockage of the rectum. He thought there was a fifty-fifty chance of Jonnie surviving what would now be a major operation, but he was insistent that action must be taken at once either to end Jonnie's life or to prolong it.

I had no car with me that year, so I hired one for the whole journey, to wait during the operation and to bring me back at night, either alone or with what I was warned would in any event be an unconscious dog. Jonnie loved car journeys, and he was enthusiastic to start on this one; as we bumped over the precipitous road to the ferry he stuck his head out of the window and quested the breeze with all the zest of his puppyhood long ago, and I was miserable to see in some sense his trust betrayed and to know that in the evening I might come back alone and leave him dead in Skye. All I could think of then and during the long long wait while he was on the operating table was of past days spent with Jonnie, many of them seeming so long ago as to span a man's rather than a dog's lifetime. I stayed to help to give the anaesthetic; Jonnie was trusting but puzzled by the curious preparations, hating the stinking rubber mask that I had to hold over his face, but giving only one pathetic whimper of despair before he lost consciousness. Then for more than an hour I wandered aimlessly up and down the shore below that Skye village. The day was grey and heavy with coming snow, and a bitter little wind blew in from the sea and rustled the dead seaweed on the tideline. I thought of how I had nursed Jonnie through distemper twelve years before; of teaching that strangely woolly spaniel puppy to retrieve and to quarter the ground for game; of how once in his early prime he had, after an evening duck flight, swum out forty-one times through forming ice that skinned over behind him as he swam and returned forty-one times with a wigeon in his mouth; of how often his fleecy flank had formed a pillow for me in open boats; of the many times I had come back to Camusfeàrna knowing that his welcome was awaiting me.

I have more than once tried to analyse this apparently deliberate form of self-torture that seems common to so many people in face of the extinction of a valued life, human or animal, and it springs, I think, from a negation of death, as if by summoning and arranging these subjective images one were in some way cheating the objective fact. It is, I believe, an entirely instinctive process, and the distress it brings with it is an incidental, a by-product, rather than a masochistic end.

But Jonnie did not die then. When I was allowed to go into the surgery he was conscious but too weak to move; only his bloodstained tail fluttered faintly, and all through the cruelly long and jolting journey home he lay utterly motionless, so that again and again I felt for his heart to make sure that he was still living. It was night before we reached Druimfiaclach, and the snow had begun, piling in thick before an icy north wind. Morag, whose whole heart had gone out to Jonnie from the first day he had come to Druimfiaclach, had endured a longer suspense than I, but though Jonnie was living he yet seemed very near to death. For many days there was little change; either Morag or I would sit up with him all through the night and tend his helplessness. His very cleanliness provided the worst problem of all; while he was too weak to move he would yet endure agonies rather than relieve himself indoors, so that he had to be carried outside in that bitter weather and supported to keep him upright while one or other of us screened him with a blanket from the wind and the snow.

.   .   .

Jonnie recovered from the operation as only a dog of his tremendous physique could do, and for six months his prime was miraculously restored, but in the autumn the cancer came back, and this time it was inoperable. Morag wrote to tell me of this, and to ask my assent to his death before the pain should start and while he was as yet happy and active. I agreed with a heavy heart, not least because I knew that to make the arrangements for his death while he felt himself sound in wind and limb would be a torture to Morag; but, weighed down at the time by a bitter human loss, I lacked the courage to go north and take an active hand in things myself. Jonnie received the vet with enthusiasm, and

Morag cuddled Jonnie while he received a lethal injection. He gave no sign of feeling the needle, and she only knew that he was dead by the increasing heaviness of his head in her hand. Morag had given her heart to Jonnie as she had to no other animal in her life, and for her that moment of betrayal must have been like death itself.

I have never had another dog since Jonnie; I have not wanted one, and shall not, perhaps, until I am of an age that would not be congenial to an active dog.

CHAPTER 6

While I was quite clear that I did not want to own another dog, and that Jonnie's death had in some sense ended an overlong chapter of nostalgia in my life, it was, I think, autumn and winter's days at Camusfeàrna that with their long hours of darkness made me crave for some animal life about the house.

Autumn begins for me with the first day on which the stags roar. Because the wind is nearly always in the west, and because the fences keep the bulk of the stags to the higher ground above Camusfeàrna, behind the low mass of the littoral hills, I hear them first on the steep slopes of Skye across the Sound, a wild, haunting primordial sound that belongs so utterly to the north that I find it difficult to realize that stags must roar, too, in European woodlands where forests are composed of trees instead of windswept mountain slopes. It is the first of the cold weather that leads in the rut, and the milder the season the later the stags break out, but it is usually during the last ten days of September. Often the first of the approaching fall comes with a night frost and clear, sharp, blue days, with the bracken turning red, the rowanberries already scarlet, and the ground hardening underfoot; so garish are the berries and the turning leaves in sunshine that in Glengarry a post-office-red pillar-box standing alone by the roadside merges, for a few weeks, anonymously into its background.

When the full moon comes at this season I have sat on the hillside at night and listened to the stags answering one another from hill to hill all round the horizon, a horizon of steel-grey peaks among moving silver clouds and the sea gleaming white at their feet, and high under the stars the drifting chorus of the wild geese flying southward out of the night and north.

On such a night, before I ever came to Camusfeàrna, I slept beside a lochan on the Island of Soay, and it was the wild swans that called overhead and came spiralling down, ghostly in the moonlight, to alight with a long rush of planing feet on the lochan's surface. All through the night I heard their restless murmur as they floated light as spume upon the peat-dark waves, and their soft voices became blended with my dreams, so that the cool convex of their breasts became my pillow. At dawn their calling awoke me as they gathered to take flight, and as they flew southward I watched the white pulse of their wings until I could see them no longer. To me they were a symbol, for I was saying goodbye to Soay, that had been my island.

Winters at Camusfeàrna vary as they do elsewhere, but at their worst they are very bad indeed. When one gets up in darkness to the lashing of rain on the window-panes and the roar of the waterfall rising even above the howl of wind and tide; when the green field is scattered with wide pools that are in part floodwater but in part the overspill of waves whose spray batters the house itself; when day by day the brief hours of light are filled with dark scudding clouds and blown spindrift from the crashing shore, one begins to know the meaning of an isolation that in summer seemed no more than an empty word.

The burn fills and runs ramping high through the trunks and limbs of the alders, carrying racing masses of debris that lodge among their branches, and through the roaring of its passage comes the hollow undertone of rolling, bumping boulders swept along its bed by the weight of white water pouring from the rock ravine. It was in such a spate as this that the bridge was washed away in 1953, and then for five years the only alternative, when the burn was full, to braving that crazy crossing clinging to a stretched rope was the long route to Druimfiaclach by the near side of its course, more than two miles of steep ground and sodden peat bog. Since the gales tear in from the south-west, funnelling themselves between the Hebridean islands into demoniac fury, the wind is usually at one's back on the upward journey, but it is in one's face coming down, and there have been nights returning from Druimfiaclach, torchless and in utter darkness, when I have taken to my hands and knees to avoid being swept away like a leaf.

There is, of course, another side to the picture, the bright log fire whose flames are reflected on the pine-panelled walls, the warmth and nursery security of that kitchen-sitting-room with the steady reassuring hiss of its Tilley lamps as a foreground sound to the tumult of sea and sky without; and, in the old days, Jonnie asleep conventionally on the hearth rug. But Jonnie was gone, and all too often the other pigments, as it were, for this picture were lacking too. The supply of paraffin would run out during the short dark days; candles became unobtainable within a hundred road miles; there was not space to store enough dry wood to keep the house heated. Until this year, when I installed a Calor gas stove, I cooked entirely by Primus, requiring both methylated spirits and paraffin, and when the house was without either and it would require an hour to coax a kettle to the boil over a fire of wet wood, there have been days when a kind of apathy would settle down upon me, days when I would rather creep back to bed than face the physical difficulties of life awake. When stores do arrive they have still to be lugged down the hill from Druimfiaclach, a long stumbling journey with an unbalancing load upon one's back and sleet slashing at one's face and eyes; and above all I remember in the past the chill, inhospitable familiarity of wet clothes, wet clothes hanging in rows above a barely-smouldering fire and with as much hope of drying as the sea itself.

Sometimes there is snow, though it rarely lies deep at Camusfeàrna itself, as the house can be no more than six feet above sea-level. But I remember one winter when it did, and it lay thick round the house and came swirling in gustily from the sea on the morning that I had to depart for the south. I left the house before dawn to catch the mail Land Rover at Druimfiaclach, the darkness only just relieved by the white wastes that ran right down to the waves. I remember that morning particularly because it was the worst, the most nightmarish, climb that I have ever made to Druimfiaclach. The weather had been so bitter that the burn was low, frozen far up its course on the snow peak, and I had thought that with the aid of the rope I should be able to ford it in long seamen's thigh-boots. I saw my mistake when I reached it, but with a hundred-weight or so of luggage on my back I preferred to try rather than to take the long route round through the bogs. Both my boots filled in the first couple of yards, but the house was locked and time was short, and I struggled across, soaked at last to the waist, hanging onto the rope with my legs swept downstream by the piling weight of snow water. At the far side of the burn I sat down and emptied my boots of a full two gallons apiece. I tried to wring out my trousers, but when, my teeth chattering like castanets, I got the boots back on again, the feet filled slowly with an icy trickle of water that still coursed down my legs. When I began the steep climb from the burn the burden on my shoulders seemed to have doubled its weight. I slipped and stumbled and panted up dim glaucous slopes that had lost all landmarks, and at the top of the first steep I was caught in a swirling, flurrying blizzard of wind and snowflakes, that spun me round in unsteady pirouettes and left me dizzy and directionless.

For all the hundreds of times that I had travelled this path in daylight and in darkness, I could recognize no curve nor contour in the merging grey pillows about me, and the snow was coming down so thick that it blanketed even the sound of the eighty-foot falls in the gorge. I had always been frightened of a stranger slipping down that precipice in the dark; now I was so hopelessly lost that I began to be afraid of it myself, and to avoid the ravine I began to climb upward over the steepest ground I could find. I reeled into snowdrifts and fell flat on my face, my feet slipped on boulders hidden by the snow and the weight on my shoulders threw me over backwards, and all the time the blizzard beat at me, slapping the wet snow into my eyes and ears, down my neck, and into every crevice of my clothing. Once I stumbled on a stag, snow-blanketed in the shelter of a rock; he was up and away and gone into snowflakes that were driving horizontally across the hillside, and for some minutes I took his place under the rock, the stag smell pungent in my nostrils, wondering how I had ever thought Camusfeàrna a paradise. It took me an hour and a half to reach Druimfiaclach that morning, and when I got there it was more by accident than judgement. This was the prelude to an hour's travel by launch and four hours in the train to Inverness before starting the true journey south.

Yet it is the best and the worst that one remembers, seldom the mediocrities that lie between and demand no attention. At the end of struggles such as those there has always been the warmth and hospitality of the long-suffering MacKinnon household, Morag's scones and ginger-bread, and cups of tea that have tasted like nectar; and there have been fair winter days at Camusfeàrna, when the sea lay calm as summer and the sun shone on the snow-covered hills of Skye, and I would not change my home for any in the world.

But after Jonnie's death it seemed, as I have said, a little lifeless, and I began in a desultory way to review in my mind various animals, other than dogs, that might keep me company. Having been encouraged in my childhood to keep pets ranging from hedgehogs to herons, I had a considerable list available for screening, but after a while I realized reluctantly that none of these creatures with which I was familiar would meet my present requirements. I put the idea aside, and for a year I thought no more of it.

Early in the New Year of 1956 I travelled with Wilfred Thesiger to spend two months or so among the little known Marsh Arabs, or Ma'dan, of Southern Iraq. By then it had crossed my mind, though with no great emphasis, that I should like to keep an otter instead of a dog, and that Camusfeàrna, ringed by water a stone's throw from its door, would be an eminently suitable spot for this experiment. I had mentioned this casually to Wilfred soon after the outset of our journey, and he, as casually, had replied that I had better get one in the Tigris marshes before I came home, for there they were as common as mosquitoes, and were often tamed by the Arabs.

We spent the better part of those two months squatting cross-legged in
the bottom of a *tarada* or war canoe, travelling in a leisurely, timeless
way between the scattered reed-built villages of the great delta marsh
both west of the Tigris and between the river and the Persian frontier;
and towards the end of our journey I did acquire an otter cub.

It is difficult to find new words in which to tell of happenings that one
has already described; if one has done one's best the first time one can
only do worse on the second attempt, when the freshness of the image has
faded; and that must be my excuse and apology for quoting here part of
what I wrote of that otter cub, Chahala, soon afterwards; that and the
fact that she is an integral and indispensable part of my narrative.

We were sitting after dark in a *mudhif*, or sheikh's guest house, on a
mud island in the marshes, and I was brooding over the delinquency of
the chatelaine, a bossy old harridan of a woman who had angered me.

'I felt an unreasonable hatred for that witless woman with her show of
bustle and competence, and contempt that not even her avarice had
mastered her stupidity. Thinking of these things, I was not trying to
understand the conversation around me when the words "celb mai"
caught my ear. "What was that about otters?" I asked Thesiger.

"I think we've got you that otter cub you said you wanted. This
fellow comes from that village half a mile away; he says he's had one for
about ten days. Very small and sucks milk from a bottle. Do you want
it?"

'The otter's owner said he would fetch it and be back in half an hour
or so. He got up and went out; through the entrance of the *mudhif* I
could see his canoe glide away silently over the star-reflecting water.

'Presently he returned carrying the cub, came across into the firelight
and put it down on my knee as I sat cross-legged. It looked up and
chittered at me gently. It was the size of a kitten or a squirrel, still a little
unsteady on its legs, with a stiff-looking tapering tail the length of a
pencil, and it exhaled a wholly delightful malty smell. It rolled over on
its back, displaying a round furry stomach and the soles of four webbed
feet.

'"Well," said Thesiger, "do you want her?" I nodded. "How much
are you prepared to pay for her?"

'"Certainly more than they would ask."

'"I'm not going to pay some ridiculous price – it's bad for prestige.
We'll take her if they'll sell her for a reasonable price; if not, we'll get one
somewhere else."

'I said, "Let's make certain of getting this one; we're near the end of
the time now, and we may not get another chance. And after all the
prestige doesn't matter so much, as this is your last visit to the marshes."

I saw this fascinating little creature eluding me for the sake of a few shillings' worth of prestige, and the negotiations seemed to me interminable.

'In the end we bought the cub for five dinar, the price to include the rubber teat and the filthy but precious bottle from which she was accustomed to drink. Bottles are a rarity in the marshes.

'Most infant animals are engaging, but this club had more charm per cubic inch of her tiny body than all the young animals I had ever seen. Even now I cannot write about her without a pang.

'I cut a collar for her from the strap of my field-glasses – a difficult thing, for her head was no wider than her neck – and tied six foot of string to this so as to retain some permanent contact with her if at any time she wandered away from me. Then I slipped her inside my shirt, and she snuggled down at once in a security of warmth and darkness that she had not known since she was reft from her mother. I carried her like that through her short life; when she was awake her head would peer wonderingly out from the top of the pullover, like a kangaroo from its mother's pouch, and when she was asleep she slept as otters like to, on her back with her webbed feet in the air. When she was awake her voice was a bird-like chirp, but in her dreams she would give a wild little cry on three falling notes, poignant and desolate. I called her Chahala, after the river we had left the day before, and because those syllables were the nearest one could write to the sound of her sleeping cry.

'I slept fitfully that night; all the pi-dogs of Dibin seemed to bark at my ears, and I dared not in any case let myself fall into too sound a sleep lest I should crush Chahala, who now snuggled in my armpit. Like all otters, she was "house-trained" from the beginning, and I had made things easy for her by laying my sleeping bag against the wall of the *mudhif*, so that she could step straight out on the patch of bare earth between the reed columns. This she did at intervals during the night, backing into the very farthest corner to produce, with an expression of infinite concentration, a tiny yellow caterpillar of excrement. Having inspected this, with evident satisfaction of a job well done, she would clamber up my shoulder and chitter gently for her bottle. This she preferred to drink lying on her back and holding the bottle between her paws as do bear cubs, and when she had finished sucking she would fall sound asleep with the teat still in her mouth and a beatific expression on her baby face.

'She accepted me as her parent from the moment that she first fell asleep in my pullover, and never once did she show fear of anything or anyone, but it was as a parent that I failed her, for I had neither the knowledge nor the instinct of her mother, and when she died it was because of my ignorance. Meanwhile this tragedy, so small but so complete, threw no shadow on her brief life, and as the days went by she learned to know her name and to play a little as a kitten does, and to come scuttling along at my heels if I could find dry land to walk on, for she hated to get her feet wet. When she had had enough of walking she would chirp and paw at my legs until I squatted down so that she could dive head first into the friendly darkness inside my pullover; sometimes she would at once fall asleep in that position, head downward with the tip of her pointed tail sticking out at the top. The Arabs called her my daughter, and used to ask me when I had last given her suck.

'I soon found that she was restrictive of movement and activity. Carried habitually inside my pullover, she made an enceinte-looking bulge which collected a whole village round me as soon as I set foot outside the door; furthermore I could no longer carry my camera round my neck as I did normally, for it bumped against her body as I walked.

'One evening Thesiger and I discussed the prospect of weaning Chahala. We both felt she should be old enough to eat solid food, and I felt that her rather skinny little body would benefit by something stronger than buffalo milk. However, I underestimated the power of instinct, for I thought that she would not connect flesh or blood with edibility and would need to be introduced to the idea very gradually. The best way to do this, I decided, was to introduce a few drops of blood into her milk to get her used to the taste. This proved to be extraordinary naïve, for while I was holding the bodies of two decapitated sparrows and trying to drip a little blood from them into her feeding bottle she suddenly caught the scent of the red meat and made a savage grab for the carcasses. I think that if I had not stopped her she would have crunched up bone and all with those tiny needle-like teeth, and we took this as evidence that she had already been introduced by her mother to adult food. I took the carcasses from her, much to her evident fury; and when I gave her the flesh from the breasts cut up small she wolfed it down savagely and went questing round for more.

'"Finish with milk," said Amara, our chief canoe-boy, with a gesture of finality, "finish, finish; she is grown up now." And it seemed so, but, alas, she was not.

'A week later we shot a Buff-backed Heron for her, and she wolfed the shredded flesh avidly. It was the last food that she ate.

'It was very cold that night. Over my head was a gap in the reed matting of the roof through which the stars showed bright and unobscured, but a thin wind that seemed as chill as the tinkle of icicles rustled the dry reeds at the foot of the wall, and I slept fitfully. Chahala was restless and would not stay still in my sleeping bag; I did not know that she was dying, and I was impatient with her. In the morning I took her to a spit of dry land beyond the edge of the village to let her walk, and only then I realized that she was very ill. She would not move, but lay looking up at me pathetically, and when I picked her up again she instantly sought the warm darkness inside my pullover.

'We made an hour's journey through flower-choked waterways in low green marsh, and stopped at another big island village. It was plain to me when we landed that Chahala was dying. She was weak but restless, and inside the house she sought the dark corners between the reed columns and the matting walls. She lay belly downward, breathing fast and in obvious distress. Perhaps something in our huge medicine chest could have saved her, but we thought only of castor oil, for everything she had eaten the night before was still inside her. The oil had little effect, and though she sucked almost automatically from her bottle there was little life in her. I sat hopelessly beside her for a couple of hours when Thesiger came in from doctoring. "Better get out for a bit," he said. "I'll keep an eye on her. It's hell for you sitting in here all the time, and you can't do her any good. This is your last marsh village, and you may never see another."

'I went out, and remembered things that I had wanted to photograph and always postponed. Then I found that the shutter of my camera was broken, and I went back into the house.

'We left an hour later. When I felt the warmth of Chahala next to my shirt again I felt a moment's spurious comfort that she would live; but she would not stay there. She climbed out with a strength that surprised me, and stretched herself restlessly on the floor of the canoe, and I spread a handkerchief over my knees to make an awning of shade for her small fevered body. Once she called faintly, the little wild lonely cry that would come from her as she slept, and a few seconds after that I saw a shiver run through her body. I put my hand on her and felt the strange rigidity that comes in the instant following death; then she became limp under my touch.

' "She's dead," I said. I said it in Arabic, so that the boys would stop paddling.

'Thesiger said, "Are you sure?" and the boys stared unbelievingly. "Quite dead?" they asked it again and again. I handed her to Thesiger; the body drooped from his hands like a miniature fur stole. "Yes," he said, "she's dead." He threw the body into the water, and it landed in the brilliant carpet of white and golden flowers and floated on its back with the webbed paws at its sides, as she had been used to sleep when she was alive.

' "Come on," said Thesiger. "Ru-hu-Ru-hu!" but the boys sat motionless, staring at the small corpse and at me, and Thesiger grew angry with them before they would move. Amara kept on looking back from the bows until at last we rounded the corner of a green reed-bed and she was out of sight.

'The sun shone on the white flowers, the blue kingfishers glinted low over them and the eagles wheeled overhead on the blue sky, but all of these seemed less living for me than Chahala was dead. I told myself that she was only one of thousands like her in these marshes, that are speared with the five-pointed trident, or shot, or taken as cubs to die slowly in more callous captivity, but she was dead and I was desolate. The fault lay with whoever, perhaps more than a million years ago, had first taken up the wild dog cub that clung to the body of its dead dam, and I wondered whether he too had in that half-animal brain been driven by the motives that in me were conscious.'

. . .

I fretted miserably over the death of Chahala, for she had convinced me utterly that it was an otter that I wanted as an animal companion at Camusfeàrna, and I felt that I had had my chance and wasted it. It was not until long afterwards that the probable cause of her death struck me. The Marsh Arabs drug fish with digitalis concealed in shrimp bait, and whereas the human system, or that of an adult Buff-backed Heron, might find the minute dose innocuous, the same quantity might be fatal to as young a creature as Chahala.

I had no more time in the marshes; Wilfred and I were to spend a few days in Basra before going on to pass the early summer among the pastoral tribes. But Chahala's death, which seemed to me like an end, was in fact a beginning.

PART TWO

LIVING WITH OTTERS

CHAPTER 7

The night that Chahala died we reached Al Azair, Ezra's tomb, on the Tigris. From there Wilfred Thesiger and I were both going to Basra to collect and answer our mail from Europe before setting off together again. At the Consulate-General at Basra we found that Wilfred's mail had arrived but that mine had not.

'I cabled to England, and when, three days later, nothing had happened, I tried to telephone. The call had to be booked twenty-four hours in advance, and could be arranged only for a single hour in the day, an hour during which, owing to the difference in time, no one in London was likely to be available. On the first day the line was out of order; on the second the exchange was closed for a religious holiday. On the third day there was another breakdown. I arranged to join Thesiger at Abd el Nebi's *mudhif* in a week's time, and he left.

'Two days before the date of our rendezvous I returned to the Consulate-General late in the afternoon, after several hours' absence, to find that my mail had arrived. I carried it to my bedroom to read, and there squatting on the floor were two Marsh Arabs; beside them lay a sack that squirmed from time to time.

'They handed me a note from Thesiger. "Here is your otter, a male and weaned. I feel you may want to take it to London – it would be a handful in the *tarada*. It is the one I originally heard of, but the sheikhs were after it, so they said it was dead. Give Ajram a letter to me saying it has arrived safely – he had taken Kathia's place..."'

With the opening of that sack began a phase of my life that in the essential sense has not yet ended, and may, for all I know, not end before I do. It is, in effect, a thraldom to otters, an otter fixation, that I have since found to be shared by most other people who have ever owned one.

The creature that emerged, not greatly disconcerted, from this sack onto the spacious tiled floor of the Consulate bedroom did not at that moment resemble anything so much as a very small medievally-conceived dragon. From the head to the tip of the tail he was coated with symmetrical pointed scales of mud armour, between whose tips was visible a soft velvet fur like that of a chocolate-brown mole. He shook himself, and I half expected this aggressive camouflage to disintegrate into a cloud of dust, but it remained unaffected by his manoeuvre, and in fact it was not for another month that I contrived to remove the last of it and see him, as it were, in his true colours.

Yet even on that first day I recognized that he was an otter of a species that I had never seen in the flesh, resembling only a curious otter skin that I had bought from the Arabs in one of the marsh villages. Mijbil, as I called the new otter, after a sheikh with whom we had recently been staying and whose name had intrigued me with a conjured picture of a platypus-like creature, was, in fact, of a race previously unknown to science, and was at length christened by zoologists, from examination of the skin and of himself, *Lutrogale perspicillata maxwelli*, or Maxwell's otter. This circumstance, perhaps, influenced on my side the intensity of the emotional relationship between us, for I became, during a year of his constant and violently affectionate companionship, fonder of him than of almost any human being, and to write of him in the past tense makes me feel as desolate as one who has lost an only child. For a year and five days he was about my bed and my bath spying out all my ways, and though I now have another otter no whit less friendly and fascinating, there will never be another Mijbil.

For the first twenty-four hours Mijbil was neither hostile nor friendly; he was simply aloof and indifferent, choosing to sleep on the floor as far from my bed as possible, and to accept food and water as though they were things that had appeared before him without human assistance. The food presented a problem, for it did not immediately occur to me that the Marsh Arabs had almost certainly fed him on rice scraps only supplemented by such portions of fish as are inedible to humans. The Consul-General sent out a servant to buy fish, but the servant's return coincided with a visit from Robert Angorly, a British-educated Christian Iraqi who was the Crown Prince's game warden and entertained a passionate interest in natural history. Angorly told me that none of the fishes that had been bought was safe for an animal, for they had been poisoned with digitalis, which, though harmless to a human in this quantity, he felt certain would be dangerous to a young otter. He offered to obtain me a daily supply of fish that had been taken with nets, and thereafter he brought every day half a dozen or so small reddish fish from the Tigris. These Mijbil consumed with gusto, holding them upright between his forepaws, tail end uppermost, and eating them like a stick of Edinburgh rock, always with five crunches of the lefthand side of the jaw alternating with five crunches on the right.

It was fortunate that I had recently met Angorly, for otherwise Mijbil might at once have gone the way of Chahala and for the same reason.

Angorly had called at the Consulate-General during the time that I had been waiting for my mail from Europe, and had invited me to a day's duck shooting on the Crown Prince's fabulous marshes, an experience that nobody can ever have again, for now the hated Crown Prince is as dead as only a mob gone berserk could make him, and of my friend Angorly, whom I cannot believe ever to have taken much interest in anything political, there has been no word since the revolution.

Of the duck shoot my most enduring memory is of a great cloud of pink flamingos flying at head height to my butt, and of the rank upon rank of crimson and white wings rustling low over my head. Duck there were in thousands, but if the Crown Prince ever killed many from that butt he was a better man than I. It stood quite alone in a great waste of unbroken water that stretched away for a mile or more in all directions; its sides were no more than waist high, and in the centre of it was a wooden seat, at the right of which pretension stood an object like a bird-table, whose tray was designed to hold eight unopened boxes of twenty-five cartridges. It held them, and the broad scarlet patch that they formed flared a warning to every duck that came within two hundred yards. I was the cynosure of every bird's eye in the place. The floor of the butt was six inches under water, so the cartridges remained where they were, and the duck did not. After some five hours I was rescued from my indignity, and Angorly and I between us took home some hundred and fifty duck, of which I had contributed a meagre third. But the flamingos were magnificent.

.   .   .

The otter and I enjoyed the Consul-General's long-suffering hospitality for a fortnight. The second night Mijbil came onto my bed in the small hours and remained asleep in the crook of my knees until the servant brought tea in the morning, and during that day he began to lose his apathy and take a keen, much too keen, interest in his surroundings. I fashioned a collar, or rather a body-belt, for him, and took him on a lead to the bathroom, where for half an hour he went wild with joy in the water, plunging and rolling in it, shooting up and down the length of the bath underwater, and making enough slosh and splash for a hippo. This, I was to learn, is a characteristic of otters; every drop of water must be, so to speak, extended and spread about the place; a bowl must at once be overturned, or, if it will not overturn, be sat in and sploshed in until it overflows. Water must be kept on the move and made to do things; when static it is as wasted and provoking as a buried talent.

It was only two days later that he escaped from my bedroom as I entered it, and I turned to see his tail disappearing round the bend of the corridor that led to the bathroom. By the time I had caught up with him he was up on the end of the bath and fumbling at the chromium taps with his paws. I watched, amazed by this early exhibition of an intelligence I had not yet guessed; in less than a minute he had turned the tap far enough to produce a dribble of water, and, after a moment or two of distraction at his success, achieved the full flow. (He had, in fact, been fortunate to turn the tap the right way; on subsequent occasions he would as often as not try with great violence to screw it up still tighter, chittering with irritation and disappointment at its failure to co-operate.)

The Consulate had a big walled garden in which I exercised him, and, within it, a high-netted tennis court. In this enclosure I established after a few days that he would follow me without a lead and come to me when I called his name. By the end of a week he had accepted me in a relationship of dependence, and with this security established he began to display the principal otter characteristic of perpetual play. Very few species of animal habitually play after they are adult; they are concerned with eating, sleeping, or procreating, or with the means to one or other of these ends. But otters are one of the few exceptions to this rule; right through their lives they spend much of their time in play that does not even require a partner. In the wild state they will play alone for hours with any convenient floating object in the water, pulling it down to let it bob up again, or throwing it with a jerk of the head so that it lands with a splash and becomes a quarry to be pursued. No doubt in their holts they lie on their backs and play, too, as my otters have, with small objects that they can roll between their paws and pass from palm to palm, for at Camusfeàrna all the sea holts contain a profusion of small shells and round stones that can only have been carried in for toys.

Mij would spend hours shuffling a rubber ball round the room like a four-footed soccer player using all four feet to dribble the ball, and he could also throw it, with a powerful flick of the neck, to a surprising height and distance. These games he would play either by himself or with me, but the really steady play of an otter, the time-filling play born of a sense of well-being and a full stomach, seems to me to be when the otter lies on its back and juggles with small objects between its paws. This they do with an extraordinarily concentrated absorption and dexterity, as though a conjurer were trying to perfect some trick, as though in this play there were some goal that the human observer could not guess. Later, marbles became Mij's favourite toys for this pastime – for pastime it is, without any anthropomorphizing – and he would lie on his back rolling two or more of them up and down his wide, flat belly without ever dropping one to the floor, or, with forepaws upstretched, rolling them between his palms for minutes on end.

Even during that first fortnight in Basra I learnt a lot of Mij's language, a language largely shared, I have discovered, by many other races of otter, though with curious variations in usage. The sounds are widely different in range. The simplest is the call note, which has been much the same in all the otters I have come across; it is a short anxious, penetrating, though not loud, mixture between a whistle and a chirp. There is also a query, used at closer quarters; Mij would enter a room, for instance, and ask whether there was anyone in it by the word 'Ha!', uttered in a loud, harsh whisper. If he saw preparations being made to take him out or to the bath, he would stand at the door making a musical bubbling sound interspersed with chirps; but it was the chirp, in all its permutations and combinations of high and low, from the single querulous note to a continuous flow of chitter, that was Mij's main means of vocal communication. He had one other note unlike any of these, a high, snarling caterwaul, a sort of screaming wail, that meant unequivocally that he was very angry, and if provoked further would bite. He bit, in anger as opposed to nips in excitable play, four times during the year that I had him. Each of these occasions was memorable in the highest degree, though I was only once at the receiving end.

An otter's jaws are, of course, enormously powerful – indeed the whole animal is of strength almost unbelievable in a creature of its size – and those jaws are equipped with teeth to crunch into instant pulp fish heads that seem as hard as stone. Like a puppy that nibbles and gnaws one's hands because he has so few other outlets for his feelings, otters seem to find the use of their mouths the most natural outlet for expression; knowing as I do their enormous crushing power I can appreciate what efforts my otters have made to be gentle in play, but their playful nips are gauged, perhaps, to the sensitivity of an otter's, rather than a human, skin. Mij used to look hurt and surprised when scolded for what must have seemed to him the most meticulous gentleness, and though after a time he learned to be as soft mouthed as a sucking dove with me he remained all his life somewhat over-excitably good-humoured and hail-fellow-well-bit with strangers.

The days passed peacefully at Basra, but I dreaded dismally the unpostponable prospect of transporting Mij to England, and to his ultimate destination, Camusfeàrna. B.O.A.C. would not fly livestock at all, and there was then no other line to London. Finally I booked a Trans-World flight to Paris, with a doubtful Air France booking on the same evening to London. Trans-World insisted that Mij should be packed into a box of not more than eighteen inches square, and that this box must be personal luggage, to be carried on the floor at my feet.

Mij's body was at that time perhaps a little over a foot long and his tail another foot; the designing of this box employed many anxious hours for myself and the ever-helpful Robert Angorly, and finally he had the container constructed by craftsmen of his acquaintance. The box was delivered on the afternoon before my departure on a 9.15 p.m. flight. It was zinc-lined, and divided into two compartments, one for sleeping and one for the relief of nature, and it appeared to my inexperienced eye as nearly ideal as could be contrived.

Dinner was at eight, and I thought that it would be as well to put Mij into the box an hour before we left, so that he would become accustomed to it before the jolting of the journey began to upset him. I manoeuvred him into it, not without difficulty, and he seemed peaceful when I left him in the dark for a hurried meal.

But when I returned, with only barely time for the Consulate car to reach the airport for the flight, I was confronted with an appalling spectacle. There was complete silence from inside the box, but from its airholes and the chinks around the hinged lid, blood had trickled and dried on the white wood. I whipped off the padlock and tore open the lid, and Mij, exhausted and blood-spattered, whimpered and tried to climb up my leg. He had torn the zinc lining to shreds, scratching his mouth, his nose and his paws, and had left it jutting in spiky ribbons all around the walls and the floor of the box. When I had removed the last of it, so that there were no cutting edges left, it was just ten minutes until the time of the flight, and the airport was five miles distant. It was hard to bring myself to put the miserable Mij back into that box, that now represented to him a torture chamber, but I forced myself to do it, slamming the lid down on my fingers as I closed it before he could make his escape. Then began a journey the like of which I hope I shall never know again.

I sat in the back of the car with the box beside me as the Arab driver tore through the streets of Basra like a ricocheting bullet. Donkeys reared, bicycles swerved wildly, out in the suburbs goats stampeded and poultry found unguessed powers of flight. Mij cried unceasingly in the box, and both of us were hurled to and fro and up and down like drinks in a cocktail shaker. Exactly as we drew to a screeching stop before the airport entrance I heard a splintering sound from the box beside me, and saw Mij's nose force up the lid. He had summoned all the strength in his small body and torn one of the hinges clean out of the wood.

The aircraft was waiting to take off; as I was rushed through the customs by infuriated officials I was trying all the time to hold down the lid of the box with one hand, and with the other, using a screwdriver purloined from the driver, to force back the screws into the splintered wood. But I knew that it could be no more than a temporary measure at best, and my imagination boggled at the thought of the next twenty-four hours.

It was perhaps my only stroke of fortune that the seat booked for me was at the extreme front of the aircraft, so that I had a bulkhead before me instead of another seat. The other passengers, a remarkable cross-section of the orient and occident, stared curiously as the dishevelled late arrival struggled up the gangway with a horrifyingly vocal Charles Addams-like box, and knowing for just what a short time it could remain closed I was on tenterhooks to see what manner of passenger would be my immediate neighbour. I had a moment of real dismay when I saw her to be an elegantly dressed and *soignée* American woman in early middle age. Such a one, I thought, would have little sympathy or tolerance for the draggled and dirty otter cub that would so soon and so inevitably be in her midst. For the moment the lid held, and as I sat down and fastened my safety belt there seemed to be a temporary silence from within.

The port engines roared, and then the starboard and the aircraft trembled and teetered against the tug of her propellers, and then we were taxiing out to take off, and I reflected that whatever was to happen now there could be no escape from it, for the next stop was Cairo. Ten minutes later we were flying westwards over the great marshes that had been Mij's home, and peering downward into the dark I could see the glint of their waters beneath the moon.

I had brought a brief-case full of old newspapers and a parcel of fish, and with these scant resources I prepared myself to withstand a siege. I arranged newspapers to cover all the floor around my feet, rang for the air hostess, and asked her to keep the fish in a cool place. I have retained the most profound admiration for that air hostess, and in subsequent sieges and skirmishes with otters in public places I have found my thoughts turning towards her as a man's mind turns to water in desert wastes. She was the very queen of her kind. I took her into my confidence; the events of the last half hour together with the prospect of the next twenty-four had shaken my equilibrium a little, and I daresay I was not too coherent, but she took it all in her graceful sheer nylon stride, and she received the ill-wrapped fish into her shapely hands as though I were travelling royalty depositing a jewel case with her for safe keeping. Then she turned and spoke with her countrywoman on my left. Would I not prefer, she then enquired, to have my pet on my knee? The animal would surely feel happier there, and my neighbour had no objection. I could have kissed her hand in the depth of my gratitude. But, not knowing otters, I was quite unprepared for what followed.

I unlocked the padlock and opened the lid, and Mij was out like a flash. He dodged my fumbling hands with an eel-like wriggle and disappeared at high speed down the fuselage of the aircraft. As I tried to get into the gangway I could follow his progress among the passengers by a wave of disturbance amongst them not unlike that caused by the passage of a stoat through a hen run. There were squawks and shrieks and a flapping of travelling-coats, and half-way down the fuselage a woman stood up on her seat screaming out, 'A rat! A rat!' Then the air hostess reached her, and within a matter of seconds she was seated again and smiling benignly. That goddess, I believe, could have controlled a panic-stricken crowd single-handed.

By now I was in the gangway myself, and, catching sight of Mij's tail disappearing beneath the legs of a portly white-turbaned Indian, I tried a flying tackle, landing flat on my face. I missed Mij's tail, but found myself grasping the sandalled foot of the Indian's female companion; furthermore my face was inexplicably covered in curry. I staggered up babbling inarticulate apology, and the Indian gave me a long silent stare, so utterly expressionless that even in my hypersensitive mood I could deduce from it no meaning whatsoever. I was, however, glad to observe that something, possibly the curry, had won over the bulk of my fellow passengers, and that they were regarding me now as a harmless clown rather than as a dangerous lunatic. The air hostess stepped into the breach once more.

'Perhaps,' she said with the most charming smile, 'it would be better if you resumed your seat, and I will find the animal and bring it to you.' She would probably have said the same had Mij been an escaped rogue elephant. I explained that Mij, being lost and frightened, might bite a stranger, but she did not think so. I returned to my seat.

I heard the ripple of flight and pursuit passing up and down the body of the aircraft behind me, but I could see little. I was craning my neck back over the seat trying to follow the hunt when suddenly I heard from my feet a distressed chitter of recognition and welcome, and Mij bounded onto my knee and began to nuzzle my face and neck. In all the strange world of the aircraft I was the only familiar thing to be found, and in that first spontaneous return was sown the seed of the absolute trust that he accorded me for the rest of his life.

For the next hour or two he slept in my lap, descending from time to time for copious evacuations upon the newspaper at my feet, and each time I had, with an unrehearsed legerdemain, to spirit this out of sight and replace it with fresh newspaper. Whenever he appeared restless I rang for fish and water, for I had a feeling that, like the story-teller of the Arabian Nights, if I failed to keep him entertained retribution would fall upon me.

Otters are extremely bad at doing nothing. That is to say that they cannot, as a dog does, lie still and awake; they are either asleep or entirely absorbed in play or other activity. If there is no acceptable toy, or if they are in a mood of frustration, they will, apparently with the utmost good humour, set about laying the land waste. There is, I am convinced, something positively provoking to an otter about order and tidiness in any form, and the greater the state of confusion that they can create about them the more contented they feel. A room is not properly habitable to them until they have turned everything upside down; cushions must be thrown to the floor from sofas and armchairs, books pulled out of bookcases, wastepaper baskets overturned and the rubbish spread as widely as possible, drawers opened and contents shovelled out and scattered. The appearance of such a room where an otter has been given free rein resembles nothing so much as the aftermath of a burglar's hurried search for some minute and valuable object that he has believed to be hidden. I had never really appreciated the meaning of the word ransacked until I saw what an otter could do in this way.

This aspect of an otter's behaviour is certainly due in part to an intense inquisitiveness that belongs traditionally to a mongoose, but which would put any mongoose to shame. An otter must find out everything and have a hand in everything; but most of all he must know what lies inside any man-made container or beyond any man-made obstruction. This, combined with an uncanny mechanical sense of how to get things open – a sense, indeed, of statics and dynamics in general – makes it much safer to remove valuables altogether rather than to challenge the otter's ingenuity by inventive obstructions. But in those days I had all this to learn.

We had been flying for perhaps five hours, and must, I thought, be nearing Cairo, when one of these moods descended upon Mijbil. It opened comparatively innocuously, with an assault upon the newspapers spread carefully round my feet, and in a minute or two the place looked like a street upon which royalty has been given a ticker-tape welcome. Then he turned his attentions to the box, where his sleeping compartment was filled with fine wood-shavings. First he put his head and shoulders in and began to throw these out backwards at enormous speed; then he got in bodily and lay on his back, using all four feet in a pedalling motion to hoist out the remainder. I was doing my best to cope with the litter, but it was like a ship's pumps working against a leak too great for them, and I was hopelessly behind in the race when he turned his attention to my neighbour's canvas Trans-World travel bag on the floor beside him. The zipper gave him pause for no more than seconds; by chance, in all likelihood, he yanked it back and was in head first, throwing out magazines, handkerchiefs, gloves, bottles of pills, tins of ear-plugs and all the personal paraphernalia of long-distance air travel. By the grace of God my neighbour was sleeping profoundly; I managed, unobserved, to haul Mij out by the tail and cram the things back somehow. I hoped that she might leave the aircraft at Cairo, before the outrage was discovered, and to my infinite relief she did so. I was still grappling with Mij when the instruction lights came on as we circled the city, and then we were down on the tarmac with forty minutes to wait.

I think it was at Cairo that I realized what a complex and – to me at that time – unpredictable creature I had acquired. I left the aircraft last, and during all the time that we were grounded he was no more trouble than a well-behaved Pekinese dog. I put the lead on him and exercised him round the edge of the airfield; there were jet aircraft landing and taking off with an appalling din all around us, but he gave no sign of noticing them at all. He trotted along at my side, stopping as a dog does to investigate small smells in the grass, and when I went into the refreshment room for a drink he sat down at my feet as if this were the only life to which he was accustomed.

On our way back to the aircraft an Egyptian official hazarded the first of the many guesses as to his identity that I was to hear during the subsequent months. 'What you got there?' he asked. 'An ermine?'

. . .

My troubles really began at Paris, an interminable time later. Mij had slept from time to time, but I had not closed an eye, and it was by now more than thirty-six hours since I had even dozed. I had to change airports, and, since I knew that Mij could slip his body strap with the least struggle, there was no alternative to putting him back into his box. In its present form, however, the box was useless, for one hinge was dangling unattached from the lid.

Half an hour out from Paris I rang for the last time for fish and water, and explained my predicament to the air hostess. She went forward to the crew's quarters, and returned after a few minutes saying that one of the crew would come and nail down the box and rope it for me. She warned me at the same time that Air France's regulations differed from those of Trans-World, and that from Paris onward the box would have to travel freight and not in the passenger portion of the aircraft.

Mij was sleeping on his back inside my jacket, and I had to steel myself to betray his trust, to force him back into that hateful prison and listen to his pathetic cries as he was nailed up in what had become to me suddenly reminiscent of a coffin. There is a little-understood factor that is responsible for the deaths of many wild animals in shipment; it is generally known as 'travel shock', and the exact causes have yet to be determined. Personally I do not question that it is closely akin to the 'voluntary dying' of which Africans have long been reputed to be capable; life has become no longer tolerable, and the animal *chooses*, quite unconsciously no doubt, to die. It was travel shock that I was afraid might kill Mijbil inside that box, which to him represented a circumstance more terrible than any he had experienced, and I would be unable even to give him the reassuring smell of my hand through the breathing-holes.

We disembarked in torrential rain that formed puddles and lakes all over the tarmac and had reduced my thin, semi-tropical suit to a sodden pulp before even I had entered the bus that was to take me and the three other London-bound passengers across Paris to Orly Airport. I clung to the unwieldy box all this time, in the hope of reducing Mij's unavoidable period of despair after I became separated from it; together with the personal impedimenta that I could not well lose sight of it rendered movement almost impossible, and I felt near to voluntary death myself.

After an hour's wait at Orly, during which Mij's cries had given place to a terrifying silence, I and my three companions were hustled into an aircraft. Mij was wrested from me and disappeared into the darkness on a luggage transporter.

When we arrived at Amsterdam instead of London the company was profusely apologetic. There was no flight to London for a further fifty-five minutes.

I had lost sight of Mij's box altogether and no one seemed to have a very clear idea of what had happened to any of the luggage belonging to the four London-bound passengers. A helpful official suggested that it might still be in Paris, as it must be clearly labelled London and not Amsterdam.

I went to the Air France office and let the tattered shreds of my self-control fly to the winds. In my soaking and dishevelled condition I cannot have cut a very impressive figure, but my anger soared above these handicaps like an eagle on the wind. I said that I was transporting to London a live animal worth many thousands of pounds, that unless it was traced immediately it would die, and I would sue the Company and broadcast their inefficiency throughout the world. The official was under crossfire, for at my elbow an American businessman was also threatening legal action. When the shindy was at its height another official arrived and said calmly that our luggage was now aboard a B.E.A. plane due for take-off in seven minutes, and would we kindly take our seats in the bus.

We deflated slowly. Muttering, 'I guess I'm going to cast my personal eyes on that baggage before I get air-borne again. They can't make a

displaced person out of me,' my American companion spoke for all of us
waifs. So we cast our personal eyes into the freight compartment, and
there was Mij's box, quite silent in a corner.

It was the small hours of the morning when we reached London
Airport. I had cabled London from Amsterdam, and there was a hired
car to meet me, but there was one more contretemps before I reached the
haven of my flat. In all my travels I have never, but for that once, been
required by the British Customs to open a single bag or to do more than
state that I carried no goods liable to duty. It was, of course, my fault;
the extreme fatigue and nervous tension of the journey had destroyed
my diplomacy. I was, for whichever reason, so tired that I could hardly
stand, and to the proffered *pro forma* and the question, 'Have you read
this?' I replied, with extreme testiness and foolishness, 'Yes – hundreds of
times.'

'And you have nothing to declare?'

'Nothing.'

'How long have you been out of this country?'

'About three months.'

'And during that time you have acquired nothing?'

'Nothing but what is on the list I have given you.' (This comprised my
few purchases in Iraq; two uncured otter skins, a Marsh Arab's dagger,
three cushion covers woven by the Beni Lam tribe, and one live
otter.)

He seemed momentarily at a loss, but he had retired only *pour mieux
sauter*. The attack, when it came, was utterly unexpected.

'Where did you get that watch?'

I could have kicked myself. Two days before, when playing water
games with Mijbil in the bath, I had forgotten to screw in the winding
handle of my Rolex Oyster, and it had, not unnaturally, stopped. I had
gone into Basra and bought, for twelve shillings and sixpence, an
outrageous time-piece that made a noise like castanets. It had stopped
twice, unprovoked, during the journey.

I explained, but I had already lost face. I produced my own watch
from a pocket, and added that I should be grateful if he would confiscate
the replacement forthwith.

'It is not a question of confiscation,' he said, 'there is a fine for failing
to declare dutiable goods. And now may I please examine that
Rolex?'

It took another quarter of an hour to persuade him that the Rolex was
not contraband; then he began to search my luggage. No corner was left
unexplored; Mijbil himself could not have done better, and when he had
finished none of the cases would close. Then he turned to the last item on

my list, one live otter. He pondered this in silence for perhaps a minute. Then, 'You have with you a live otter?' I said that I very much doubted whether it was still alive, but that it had been when at Paris.

'If the animal is dead there will be no duty payable on the uncured skin; if it is alive it is, of course, subject to the quarantine regulations.'

I had taken the trouble to check this point before leaving Iraq, and at last I was on firm ground. I told him that I knew there to be no quarantine regulations, and that since he had now cleared my luggage I proposed to leave with the otter; if he tried to detain me I would hold him legally responsible for the death of a valuable animal.

Just how long this battle would have lasted I do not know, for at that moment he was relieved by an official who was as helpful as he had been hostile, as benign as he had been bellicose. Within three minutes the box and all my luggage had been loaded onto the waiting car and we were on the last lap of the journey. What meant still more to me was that from the box there now came a faint enquiring chitter and a rustle of wood shavings.

Mijbil had in fact displayed a characteristic shared, I believe, by many animals; an apparent step, as it were, on the road to travel-shock death, but in fact a powerful buffer against it. Many animals seem to me to be able to go into a deep sleep, a coma, almost, as a voluntary act independent of exhaustion; it is an escape mechanism that comes into operation when the animal's inventiveness in the face of adversity has failed to ameliorate its circumstances. I have seen it very occasionally in trapped animals; an arctic fox in Finmark, captive by the leg for no more than an hour, a badger in a Surrey wood, a common house mouse in a box trap. It is, of course, almost a norm, too, of animals kept in too cramped quarters in zoos and in pet stores. I came to recognize it later in Mij when he travelled in cars, a thing he hated; after a few minutes of frenzy he would curl himself into a tight ball and banish entirely the distasteful world about him.

On that first day that he arrived in England he had, I think, been in just such a barricaded state ever since the lid of the box was nailed down before reaching Paris; back, for all one may know, among the familiar scenes of his Tigris swamps, or perhaps in a negative, imageless world where the medulla had taken over respiration and the forebrain rested in a state bordering upon catalepsy.

He was wide awake once more by the time we reached my flat, and when I had the driver paid off and the door closed behind me I felt a moment of deep emotional satisfaction, almost of triumph, that I had after all brought back a live otter cub from Iraq to London, and that Camusfeàrna was less than six hundred miles distant from me.

I prised open the lid of the box, and Mijbil clambered out into my arms to greet me with a frenzy of affection that I felt I had hardly merited.

CHAPTER 8

I lived at that time in a studio flat near to Olympia, one large room with a sleeping gallery that opened onto the garage roof, and penthouse premises at the back containing kitchen, bathroom and box-room, each of diminutive size and resembling a divided corridor. Despite the absence of a garden, these unconventional premises held certain advantages for an otter, for the garage roof eliminated the normal difficulties of keeping a house-trained animal in a London flat, and the box-room opening from the bathroom provided quarters in which at any time he might be left for short periods with all his essential requirements. But just how short these periods would be – a maximum of four or five hours – had never struck me until Mij had already become the centre point round which, eccentrically, revolved my life. Otters that have been reared by human beings demand human company, much affection, and constant co-operative play; without these things they quickly become unhappy, and for the most part they are tiresome in direct ratio to their discontent. They can be trying, too, out of sheer inquisitiveness and exuberance of spirits, but not in the seemingly calculated way that is born of deprivation.

The spacious tile-floored bedroom of the Consulate-General at Basra, with its minimum of inessential furniture or bric-à-brac, had done little to prepare me for the problems that my crowded and vulnerable studio would present in relation to Mijbil. Exhausted as he was that first night, he had not been out of his box for five minutes before he set out with terrifying enthusiasm to explore his new quarters. I had gone to the kitchen to find fish for him, expected by prearrangement with my charlady, but I had hardly got there before I heard the first crash of breaking china in the room behind me. The fish and the bath solved the problem temporarily, for when he had eaten he went wild with joy in the water and romped ecstatically for a full half hour, but it was clear that the flat would require considerable alteration if it was to remain a home for both of us. Meanwhile sleep seemed long overdue, and I saw only one solution; I laid a sleeping bag on the sofa, and anchored Mij to the sofa-leg by his lead.

I have never been able fully to make up my mind whether certain aspects of otter behaviour merely chance to resemble that of human beings, or whether, in the case of animals as young as Mij was, there is actual mimicry of the human foster parent. Mij, anyway, seemed to regard me closely as I composed myself on my back with a cushion under my head; then, with a confiding air of knowing exactly what to do, he clambered up beside me and worked his body down into the sleeping-bag until he lay flat on his back inside it with his head on the cushion beside mine and his fore-paws in the air. In this position, such an attitude as a child devises for its teddy-bear in bed, Mij heaved an enormous sigh and was instantly asleep.

There is, in fact, much about otters that encourages humans to a facile anthropomorphizing. A dry otter at play is an animal that might have been specifically designed to please a child; they look like 'invented' animals, and are really much more like Giovannetti's 'Max' than anything else, a comparison that has instantly struck many people upon seeing my otters for the first time – the same short legs, the same tubby, furry torso, vast whiskers, and clownish good humour. In the water they take on quite a different aspect and personality, supple as an eel, fast as lightning, and graceful as a ballet dancer, but very few people have watched them for long below the surface, and I have yet to see a zoo that gives its otters a glass-sided tank – a spectacle that I believe would steal the show from the whole aquarium.

Mij and I remained in London for nearly a month, while, as my landlord put it, the studio came to look like a cross between a monkey-house and a furniture repository. The garage roof was fenced in, and a wire gate fitted to the gallery stairs; so that he could occasionally be excluded from the studio itself; the upstairs telephone was enclosed in a box (whose fastening he early learned to undo); my dressing-table was cut off from him by a wire flap hinging from the ceiling, and the electric light wires were enclosed in tunnels of hardboard that gave the place the appearance of a power-house.

All these precautions were entirely necessary, for if Mij thought that he had been excluded for too long, more especially from visitors whose acquaintance he wished to make, he would set about laying waste with extraordinary invention. No amount of forethought that I could muster was ever able to forestall his genius; there was always something that I had overlooked, something that could be made to speak with a crash for his mood of frustration, and it did not take me long to learn that prophylaxis was more convenient than treatment.

There was nothing haphazard about the demonstrations he planned; into them went all the patience and ingenuity of his remarkable brain and all the agility of his muscular little body. One evening, for example, after the contractors had departed for the third or fourth time, leaving, as I thought, an otter-proof situation at last, I had confined Mij to the gallery for an hour in deference to the wishes of a female visitor who feared for her nylons. He appeared, after a few moments, balancing adroitly on the top of the gallery railing, paying no attention either to us or to the formidable drop below him, for his plan was evidently already mature. At various points along the length of this railing were suspended certain decorative objects, a Cretan shepherd's bag, a dagger, and other things whose identity now eludes me. Purposefully, and with an air of enormous self-satisfaction, Mij began to chew through the cords from which these *objets d'art* or *de voyage* hung. After each severance he would pause to watch his victim crash to the parquet floor below, then he would carefully renew his precarious, straddling progress along the rail until he reached the next. We stood, my visitor and I, waiting to catch the more fragile items as they fell, and I remember that when the last fruit, as it were, had fallen from the bough she turned to me with a sigh and said, 'Don't you ever feel that this just simply can't go on?'

More usually, however, when he was loose in the studio, he would play for hours at a time with what soon became an established selection of toys, ping-pong balls, marbles, india-rubber fruit, and a terrapin shell that I had brought back from his native marshes. The smaller among these objects he became adept at throwing right across the room with a flick of his head, and with a ping-pong ball he invented a game of his own which would keep him engrossed for up to half an hour at a time. An expanding suitcase that I had taken to Iraq had become damaged on the journey home, so that the lid, when closed, remained at a slope from one end to the other. Mij discovered that if he placed the ball on the high end it would run down the length of the suitcase unaided. He would dash round to the other end to ambush its arrival, hide from it, crouching, to spring up and take it by surprise as it reached the drop to the floor, grab it and trot off with it to the high end once more.

These games were adequate for perhaps half of all the time he spent indoors and awake, but several times a day he needed, as much psychologically as physically, I think, a prolonged romp with a human playmate. Tunnelling under the carpet and affecting to believe himself thus rendered invisible, he would shoot out with a squeak of triumph if a foot passed within range; or he would dive inside the loose cover of the sofa and play tigers from behind it; or he would simply lay siege to one's person as a puppy does, bouncing around one in a frenzy of excited chirps and squeaks and launching a series of tip-and-run raids. It was the 'tip' that was the trouble, for his teeth were like needles, and however gently he might try to use them, such games used, I am bound to say, to end with a certain amount of visible proof of his success in tactics left on the human hand. It did not hurt, but it made a bad impression upon visitors, many of whom were ready in any case to accord him the distrust appropriate to an alien upstart.

But I soon found an infallible way to distract his attention if he became too excitable, a way whose success was, I think, due to the refusal to be baffled by obstacles that is an otter characteristic. I would take the terrapin shell, wrap it in a towel, and knot the loose ends tightly across. He came to know these preparations, and would wait absolutely motionless until I handed him the bundle; then he would straddle it with his fore-arms, sink his teeth in the knots, and begin to hump and shuffle round the room in a deceptively aimless-seeming manner. Deceptive, because no matter how complex the knots he would have them all undone in five or ten minutes. At the end of this performance he liked, and seemed to expect, applause, and he would then bring the towel and the terrapin shell to be tied up again. He brought the towel first, dragging it, and then made a second trip for the terrapin, shuffling it in front of him down the room like a football.

At night he slept in my bed, still, at this time, on his back with his head on the pillow, and in the morning he shared my bath. With utter indifference to temperature he would plunge ahead of me into water still too hot for me to enter, and while I shaved he would swim round me playing with the soapsuds or with various celluloid and rubber ducks and ships that had begun to accumulate in my bathroom as they do in a child's.

Outside the house I exercised him on a lead, precisely as if he had been a dog, and, like a dog, he soon showed preference for certain streets and certain corners at which dogs of all sorts and sizes had left stimulating messages; messages that were, perhaps, the more fascinating for being, as it were, in a foreign language. Whether or not he could decipher their purport, whether or not they conjured up for him the various erotic, impudent or pugnacious images intended, he would spend minutes at a time sniffing these clearing-houses of local canine information, and would occasionally add to them some liquid comment of his own, tantalizingly cryptic, no doubt, to the next comer.

I was too timid of the result to allow him to meet any dog so to speak nose to nose, and I would pick him up if we met unattended dogs in the street, but for his part he seemed largely indifferent to them. The only time that I was conscious of some mutual recognition taking place, some awareness of similarity between canine and lutrine values, was one morning when, setting out for his walk, he refused to be parted from a new toy, a large rubber ball painted in gaudy segments. This ball was too big for his mouth, so that he could only carry it sticking out from one side of his jaws like a gigantic gumboil, and thus encumbered he set off briskly up the street, tugging at his lead. Rounding the first street corner we came face to face with a very fat spaniel, unattended and sedately carrying in its mouth a bundle of newspapers. The respective loads of otter and dog made it difficult for either of them to turn its head far as they came abreast, but their eyes rolled sideways with what appeared to me a wild surmise, and when they were a few paces past each other both suddenly stopped dead for a moment, as though arrested by some momentary mental revelation.

Mij quickly developed certain compulsive habits on these walks in the London streets, akin, clearly, to the rituals of children who on their way to and from school must place their feet squarely on the centre of each paving block; must touch every seventh upright of the iron railings, or pass to the outside of every second lamp-post. Opposite to my flat was a single-storeyed primary school, along whose frontage ran a low wall some two feet high separating a corridor-width strip of garden from the road. On his way home, but never on his way out, Mij would tug me in the direction of this wall, jump up on it, and gallop the full length of its thirty yards, to the hopeless distraction both of pupils and of staff within. There was more than one street of which he would use one pavement only, refusing with dug-in toes to be led to the other side, and there were certain drain grilles through which he would peer motionless for long seconds before he could be led away from them. On return to the flat he would scrabble frantically to be let in, and the moment his lead was unhitched he would roll on his back and squirm with eye-bewildering speed and vigour before returning to his toys.

Many of his actions, indeed, appeared ritual, and I think that comparatively few people who keep wild creatures realize the enormous security-value of routine in the maintenance of an animal's contentment. As soon as routine is broken a new element enters, in however minute and unrecognizable a trace – the fear of the unknown which is basic to the behaviour of all animals, including man. Every living creature exists by a routine of some kind; the small rituals of that routine are the landmarks, the boundaries of security, the reassuring walls that exclude a *horror vacui*; thus, in our own species, after some tempest of the spirit in which the landmarks seem to have been swept away, a man will reach out tentatively in mental darkness to feel the walls, to assure himself that they still stand where they stood – a necessary gesture, for the walls are of his own building, without universal reality, and what man makes he may destroy. To an animal these landmarks are of even greater importance, for once removed from its natural surroundings, its ecological norm, comparatively little of what the senses perceive can be comprehended in function or potentiality, and the true conditions for insecurity are already established. As among human beings, animal insecurity may manifest itself as aggression or timidity, ill temper or ill health, or as excessive affection for a parental figure; unfortunately this last aspect encourages many to cultivate insecurity in their charges, child or animal, as a means to an end.

.   .   .

It was about this time that Mij delivered his first serious, intentional bite. He was fed now upon live eels – which I had learned to be the staple food of many races of otter – supplemented by a mixture of raw egg and unpolished rice, a sticky concoction for which he evinced a gusto no doubt influenced by his early life among the Arabs. The eels I kept in a perforated bucket under the kitchen tap, and fed them to him in the bath; it had become an established way of quieting him when he was obstreperous, to shut him in with a full bath of water and three or four eels. On this occasion I had closed the bathroom door imperfectly, and Mij elected to bring his second eel through and eat it in the studio. To this, though he was sodden with water and the eel very slimy, there seemed no alternative, for it is folly to try to take away from a wild animal its natural prey; but when after a few mouthfuls he decided to carry it upstairs to the gallery I determined to call a halt, visualizing a soaking and eel-slimed bed. I put on three pairs of gloves, the outermost being a pair of heavily-padded flying gauntlets. I caught up with him half-way up the stairway; he laid down the eel, put a paw on it, and hummed at me, a high continuous hum that could break out into a wail. Full of euphoric self-confidence I talked away quietly to him, telling him that he couldn't possibly hurt me and that I was going to take the eel back to the bathroom. The humming became much louder. I bent down and put my heavily-gloved hand upon the eel. He screamed at me, but still he took no action. Then, as I began to lift it, he bit. He bit just once and let go; the canines of his upper and lower jaws passed through the three layers of glove, through the skin, through muscle and bone, and met in the middle of my hand with an audible crunch. He let go almost in the same instant, and rolled on his back squirming with apology. I still held the eel; I carried it back to the bath, where he refused to pay any further attention to it, fussing round me and over me and muzzling me with little squeals of affection and apparent solicitude.

There were two small bones broken in my hand, and for a week it was the size of a boxing glove, very painful, and an acute embarrassment to me in the presence of those who from the first had been sceptical of Mij's domesticity. I had been given a sharp and necessary reminder that though he might carry painted rubber balls through the London streets he was not a spaniel.

It was not lack of curiosity, so much as lack of time and opportunity, that made me delay for nearly three weeks before making any real effort to establish Mij's identity. It would, I thought, require a day's research in the library of the Zoological Society, and at that early stage Mij could not be left alone for more than an hour or so without fretting. But, as may be imagined, he caused no small stir in his walks through the streets of West Kensington, and it was increasingly borne in upon me that I could answer only in the most perfunctory and unsatisfactory terms the fire of questions with which our strolls were punctuated.

It is not, I suppose, in any way strange that the average Londoner should not recognize an otter, but the variety of guesses as to what kind of animal this might be came as no less of a surprise to me than the consistent accuracy with which a minority bracketed the bull's-eye without once touching it. Otters belong to a comparatively small group of animals called Mustellines, shared by the badger, mongoose, weasel, stoat, polecat, marten, mink and others; the official at Cairo airport had set an early precedent of outer scoring when he asked whether Mij was an ermine – which is, of course, a stoat in winter coat. Now, in the London streets, I faced a continual barrage of conjectural questions that sprayed all the Mustellines but the otter; wilder, more random fire hit on practically everything from 'a baby seal' to a squirrel. The seal heresy had deep root, and was perhaps the commonest of them all, though far from being the most bizarre; 'Is that a walrus, mister?' reduced me to giggles outside Harrods, and 'a hippo' made my day outside Cruft's Dog Show. A beaver, a bear cub, a newt, a leopard – one, apparently, that had changed his spots – even, with heaven knows what dim recollections of schoolroom science and a bewildering Latinized world of sub-human creatures – a 'brontosaur'; Mij was anything but an otter.

But the question for which I awarded the highest score – a question evading with contemptuous dexterity any possible inaccuracy on the part of the speaker; putting the blame, as it were, for the creature's unfamiliarity squarely on my own shoulders; hinting, or doing more than hint, that someone had blundered, that the hand of the potter had shaken; containing, too, an accusation of unfinished work unfit for exhibition – came from a Herculean labourer engaged, mightily and alone, upon digging a hole in the street. I was still far from him when he laid down his pick, put his hands on his hips, and began to stare. As I drew nearer I saw that this stare held an outraged quality, one of surprise, certainly, but also of affront, as though he would have me know that he was not one upon whom to play jokes. I came abreast of him; he spat, glared, and then growled out, "'Ere, mister – *what is that supposed to be?*'

It was, I think, his question more than any other that reminded me of my own ignorance; I did not, in fact, know what Mij was supposed to be. I knew, certainly, that he was an otter, but I also knew that he must be one of a species which, if known to the scientific world, was at least not known to live in the delta marshes of the Tigris and Euphrates, for the scant zoological literature that had accompanied me to Iraq made it plain that the only known otter of the Mesopotamian marshes was the Persian sub-species of the common European otter, *Lutra lutra*. Chahala, the cub that had died, had clearly belonged to that race; she had longer fur with 'guard hairs' in place of Mij's sleek, darker velvet; she was lighter on her throat and belly than upon her back, whereas Mij's body seemed to have been slipped into an evenly-dyed plush bag; the underside of her tail was not, as was Mij's, flat like a ruler.

In a village of the marshes between the Tigris and the Persian frontier I had bought two otter skins from the householder with whom we had been staying; both were, apart from any possible scientific interest, objects of fascination, for they had been 'case' skinned, the whole carcass having been removed, without a single incision, through the mouth. One of these skins belonged to Chahala's race; the other, contrast heightened by juxtaposition, was plainly of Mij's, a much larger and darker creature, whose fur was short and shiny and the colour of milkless chocolate. These two skins now reposed in my flat, pregnant with possibility and as yet unexamined by competent authority.

I telephoned to the Natural History department of the British Museum, in Cromwell Road, and the same afternoon Mr Robert Hayman arrived at my flat to examine the two skins and the living specimen. There is in the serious zoological world a deadpan-ness, an unwillingness for committal, that must rival the most cautious of consulting physicians. Hayman was far too competent a zoologist, far too encyclopaedic in his knowledge, to have been unaware in those first moments that he was looking at a skin and a living animal from a habitat that made the race quite unfamiliar to him, but he did not betray it. He took such measurements as Mij would permit, examined him closely, peered at his formidable array of teeth, and left bearing the two skins for comparison with museum series.

But in due course, after the slow, precise, painstaking processes of the taxonomic world, Mij's new race was proclaimed. Hayman summoned me to the muscum to see the cabinets of otter skins from all over Asia, where the larger of mine lay, unlabelled and conspicuously differing from any other, in a drawer by itself, but in apposition to its nearest relatives. These, various sub-species of *Lutrogale*, a short-coated otter with a flat underside to the tail, ranged over most of Eastern Asia; according to their geographical race they were of a variety of hues from pale sandy to medium brown, but none had been recorded west of Sind, in India, and none resembled my specimens in colour.

There are very few people, and even fewer amateur zoologists, who stumble upon a sizeable mammal previously unknown to science; in the nursery world of picture-books of birds and beasts the few who had given their own names to species – Steller's Eider and Sea Eagle, Sharpe's Crow, Humboldt's Woolly Monkey, Meinerzthagen's Forest Hog, Ross's Snow Goose, Grant's Gazelle, Père David's Deer – had been surrounded for me with an aura of romance; they were the creators, partaking a little of the deity, who had contributed to the great panorama of bright living creatures in which, unshadowed and uncomplicated by knowledge, my childish fancy wandered. Now, when Hayman suggested that the new otter should bear my name, I experienced a sharp, brief conflict; I felt that it should bear his, for he, not I, had done the work; but something small and shrill from the nursery days was shouting inside me that I could be translated into the hierarchy of my early gods and wear, however perilously, the halo of a creator. ('Can I have it for my own?' we used to ask when we were small. 'For my *very* own?' Here, surely, was an animal of my very own, to bear my name; every animal that looked like it would always bear my name for ever and ever, unless some odious taxonomist of the future, some leveller, some jealous, dusty scribe of the backroom and the skeletons, were to plot against me and plan the destruction of my tiny, living memorial.)

So Mij and all his race became *Lutrogale perspicillata maxwelli*, and though he is now no more, and there is no ostensible proof that there is another living specimen in the world, I had realized a far-off childish fantasy, and there was a Maxwell's otter.

CHAPTER 9

It was now early May, and I had been in London for more than three weeks, three weeks of impatience and nostalgia for Camusfeàrna, and I felt I could wait no longer to see Mij playing, as I visualized him, under the waterfall, or free about the burn and the island beaches. I went by way of my family home in the south of Scotland, where Mij could taste a partial but guarded liberty before emancipation to total freedom in the north.

Travelling with otters is a very expensive business. There was now no question of again confining Mij to a box, and there is, unfortunately, no other legitimate means of carrying an otter by train. For the illegitimate means which I followed then and after, I paid, as do all who have recourse to black markets, highly. He travelled with me in a first-class sleeper, a form of transport which for some reason he enjoyed hugely; indeed from the very first he showed a perverse predilection for railway stations, and a total disregard for their deafening din and alarming crowd scenes.

At the barrier the railway official punched for me a dog ticket (on which I had noticed the words 'Give full Description') and had already turned to the next in the queue before his eyes widened in a perfect double take; then Mij was tugging up the crowded platform at the end of his lead, heedless of the shouts and the bustle, the screaming train hooters and rumbling luggage trolleys.

I had planned this operation with some care, visualizing each hazard and circumventing it as far as possible in advance; my hush money was already paid; the basket I carried contained everything conceivably necessary to Mij for the journey; over my left arm was an army blanket ready to protect the sheets from Mij's platform-grimed paws as soon as he entered the sleeper. When the initial penetration of the citadel, as it were, passed off without the slightest hitch, I felt that I had reaped no more than the just rewards of my forethought.

Mij had an instant eye for anything connected with water, and the most cursory inspection of the sleeping compartment convinced him that in the wash basin, however dry at the moment, lay the greatest pleasure-potential; he curled up in it, his form fitting its contours as an apple fits a dumpling, and his paws began increasingly feverish experiments with the chromium tap. It was, however, of a type entirely new to him, operating by downward pressure, and not a drop could he draw from it for a full five minutes; at last, trying to lever himself into an upright position, he put his full weight on the tap handle and found himself, literally, in his element.

There was only one incident that evening, an incident, however, that for a moment bade fair to bring the whole train to a stop and to expose to the outraged eyes of officialdom my irregular travelling companion. My attention had wandered from Mij; the train was roaring up through the Midlands in summer dusk, and I was watching out of the window the green corn and the blackthorn hedges and the tall trees heavy with leaf, and thinking how effectively the glass and the movement of the train insulated one from any intimacy with these desirable things while seeming to offer no protection against the impact of drab industrial landscapes. Thus occupied, it had not occurred to me that Mij could, in that very confined space, get into any serious mischief; it had not crossed my mind, for example, that by standing on the piled luggage he could reach the communication cord. This, however, was precisely what he had done, and when my eye lit on him he already had it firmly between his teeth while exploring with his paws the tunnel into which its ends disappeared. It was probably nothing but this insatiable curiosity as to detail that had so far saved the situation; now as I started towards him he removed his fingers from the recess and braced them against the wall for the tug. It takes a surprisingly strong pull to ring the communication bell (I have once done so, when the only other passenger in my compartment died while lighting his pipe), but Mij had the necessary strength, and, it seemed, the determination. I caught him round the shoulders, but he retained his grip, and as I pulled him I saw the chain bulge ominously outward; I changed my tactics and pushed him towards it, but he merely braced his arms afresh. It seemed a deadlock, and one that might end in ignominy, until suddenly inspiration came to me. Mij was extremely ticklish, particularly over the region of the ribs. I began to tickle him feverishly, and at once his jaws relaxed into the foolish grin that he reserved for such occasions and he began to squirm. Later that evening he tried several times to reach the cord again, but by then I had redisposed the suitcases, and it was beyond the furthest stretch of his elastic body.

It was in unfamiliar surroundings such as these that Mij appeared most often to copy my actions; that night, though by now he had become accustomed to sleep inside the bed with his head to my feet, he arranged himself as he had on the first night at my flat, on his back with his head on the pillow and his arms outside the bedclothes. He was still so disposed when the attendant brought my tea in the morning. He stared at Mij, and said, 'Was it tea for one, or two, sir?'

                            .   .   .

During his stay at Monreith, the home of my family, Mij's character began to emerge and to establish itself. At first on farm mill dams, then in the big loch over which the house looks out, and finally in the sea – which, though he had never known salt water, he entered without apparent surprise – he demonstrated not only his astonishing swimming powers but his willingness to reject the call of freedom in favour of human company. At first, guessing the urgency of the summons that his instincts would experience, I allowed him to swim only on the end of a long fishing line. I had bought a spring reel, which automatically took up the slack, and attached this to the butt end of a salmon rod, but the danger of underwater snags on which the line might loop itself soon seemed too great, and after the first week he ran free and swam free. He wore a harness to which a lead could be attached in emergency, but its function was as much to proclaim his domesticity to would-be human aggressors as one of restraint. The design of this harness, one that would neither impede movement nor catch upon submerged branches and drown him, was a subject that occupied my imagination for many months, and was not perfected for nearly a year.

This time of getting to know a wild animal on terms, as it were, of mutual esteem, was wholly fascinating to me, and our long daily walks by stream and hedgerow, moorland and loch, were a source of perpetual delight. Though it remained difficult to lure him from some enticing piece of open water, he was otherwise no more trouble than a dog, and infinitely more interesting to watch. His hunting powers were still undeveloped, but he would sometimes corner an eel in the mill dams, and in the streams he would catch frogs, which he skinned with a dexterity seemingly born of long practice. I had rightly guessed that his early life in a Marsh Arab household would have produced an enlightened and progressive attitude towards poultry – for no Ma'dan would tolerate a predator among the sparse and scrawny scarecrows that pass in the marshes for chickens – and in fact I found that Mij would follow me through a crowded and cackling farmyard without a glance to right or to left. To most domestic livestock he was indifferent, but black cattle he clearly identified with the water buffaloes of his home, and if they gathered at the edge of water in which he was swimming he became wild with excitement, plunging and porpoising and chittering with pleasure.

Even in the open countryside he retained his passion for playthings, and would carry with him for miles some object that had caught his fancy, a fallen rhododendron blossom, an empty twelve-bore cartridge case, a fir cone, or, on one occasion, a woman's comb with an artificial brilliant set in the bar; this he discovered at the side of the drive as we set off one morning, and carried it for three hours, laying it down on the bank when he took to water and returning for it as soon as he emerged.

In the traces left by wild otters he took not the slightest interest. Following daily the routes for which Mij expressed preference, I found myself almost imperceptibly led by his instinct into the world in which the otters of my own countryside lived, a watery world of deep-cut streams between high, rooty banks where the leaves of the undergrowth met overhead; of unguessed alleys and tunnels in reedbeds by a loch's edge; of mossy culverts and marsh marigolds; of islands tangled with fallen trees among whose roots were earthy excavations and a whisper of the wind in the willows. As one may hear or read a strange, unusual name, and thereafter be haunted by its constant coincidental recurrence, so, now that I had through Mijbil become conscious of otters, I saw all around me the signs of their presence where I had been oblivious to them before; a smoothed bank of steep mud which they had used for toboganning; a hollowed-out rotten tree-stump whose interior had been formed into a dry sleeping place; the print of a broad, capable, webbed foot; a small tarry dropping, composed mainly of eel-bones, deposited upon a stone in midstream. In these last I had expected Mij to show at least an equal interest to that which he had displayed in their canine counterparts, but whether because otters do not use their excreta in an anecdotal or informative way, or because he did not recognize in these the product of his own kind, he treated them as if they did not exist.

During all the time that I had him he killed, so far as I know, only one warm-blooded animal, and then he did not eat it, for he seemed to have a horror of blood and of the flesh of warm-blooded animals. On this occasion he was swimming in a reedy loch when he caught a moorhen chick of a few days old, a little black gollywog of a creature half the size of a day-old chick. He had a habit of tucking his treasures under one arm when he was swimming – for an otter swimming underwater uses its fore-limbs very little – and here he placed the chick while he went on in a leisurely way with his underwater exploration. It must have drowned during the first minute or so, and when at length he brought it ashore for a more thorough investigation he appeared disappointed and irritated by this unwarrantable fragility; he nuzzled it and pushed it about with his paws and chittered at it in a pettish sort of way, and then, convinced of its now permanent inertia, he left it where it lay and went in search of something more co-operative.

In the library at Monreith I explored what natural historians of earlier generations had to say about otters. There were no recent works, for the relevant section of the library had received no addition for many years past. That garrulous eighteenth-century clown, the Comte de Buffon, whose nineteen volumes had acquired a petulant flavour by his contemporary translator's insistence on the use of the English word 'pretend' for the French *prétendre*, did not, on the whole, approve of otters. He was a whimsical man, much concerned with the curious, and credulous as to the existence of most patently improbable creatures, which he himself tried assiduously to produce by arranging monstrous matings (after much experiment he was disappointedly forced to the conclusion that a bull and a mare 'could copulate neither with pleasure nor profit'); furthermore he appeared to attach some mystic significance to whether an animal could or could not be persuaded to eat honey. Otters, he found, could not.

'Young animals are generally beautiful; but the young otter is not so handsome as the old. A head ill shaped, ears placed low, eyes small and covered, a lurid aspect, awkward motions, an ignoble and deformed figure, and a kind of mechanical cry, which he repeats every moment, seem to indicate a stupid animal. The otter, however, acquires industry with age, sufficient, at least, to carry on a successful war against the fishes, who, both with regard to sentiment and instinct, are much inferior to other animals. But I can hardly allow him to have the talents of the beaver ... All I know is, that the otters dig no habitations for themselves, ... that they often change their places of abode; that they banish their young at the end of six weeks or two months; that those I attempted to tame endeavoured to bite; that some days after they became more gentle, perhaps because they were weak or sick; that, so far from being easily accustomed to a domestic life, all of them that I attempted to bring up, died young; that the otter is naturally of a cruel and savage disposition ... His retreats exhale a noxious odour, from the remains of putrid fishes; and his own body has a bad smell. The flesh is extremely fishy and disagreeable. The Romish Church permits the use of it on maigre days. In the kitchen of the Carthusian convent, near Dijon, Mr Pennant saw one preparing for the dinner of the religious of the rigid order, who, by their rules, are prohibited, during their whole lives, the eating of flesh.'

This description might perhaps have proved somewhat discouraging had I not such abundant first-hand evidence to refute it, but if Buffon had been the otter's principal detractor, the great American naturalist Ernest Thompson Seton was certainly champion in chief. Writing soon after the turn of this century he said, 'Of all the beasts whose lives I have tried to tell, there is one that stands forth, the Chevalier Bayard of the wilds – without fear and without reproach. That is the otter, the joyful, keen, and fearless otter; mild and loving to his own kind, and gentle with his neighbour of the stream; full of play and gladness in his life, full of courage in his stress; ideal in his home, steadfast in death; the noblest little soul that ever went four-footed through the woods.' In his writings I recognized the animal that I knew, 'the most beautiful and engaging of all elegant pets. There seems no end to its fun, its energy, its drollery, its good nature, and its postures of new and surprising grace. I never owned a pet otter, but I never yet saw one without shamelessly infringing article number ten of the Decalogue'.[1] While noting that in its structural affinities 'the otter is nothing but a big water weasel', he adds, writing of

[1] *Life Histories of Northern Animals* (Constable, 1910).

the tobogganing habit: 'It is a delightful proof of growth and uplift when we find an adult animal setting aside a portion of its time and effort for amusement, and especially for social amusement. A large number of the noblest animals thus relax from sordid life and pursue amusement with time and appliances after a fashion that finds its highest development in man.'

Yet another early writer, whose name I find elusive, remarked, with a certain quaint charm in choice of words, that 'the Otter is of course a giant amphibious stoat whose nature has been softened by the gentling and ennobling influence of the fisher life'.

We arrived at Camusfeàrna in early June, soon after the beginning of a long spell of Mediterranean weather. My diary tells me that summer begins on June 22nd, and under the heading for June 24th there is a somewhat furtive aside to the effect that it is Midsummer's day, as though to ward off the logical deduction that summer lasts only for four days in every year. But that summer at Camusfeàrna seemed to go on and on through timeless hours of sunshine and stillness and the dapple of changing cloud shadow upon the shoulders of the hills.

When I think of early summer at Camusfeàrna a single enduring image comes forward through the multitude that jostle in kaleidoscopic patterns before my mind's eye – that of wild roses against a clear blue sea, so that when I remember that summer alone with my curious namesake who had travelled so far, those roses have become for me the symbol of a whole complex of peace. They are not the pale, anaemic flowers of the south, but a deep, intense pink that is almost a red; it is the only flower of that colour, and it is the only flower that one sees habitually against the direct background of the ocean, free from the green stain of summer. The yellow flag irises flowering in dense ranks about the burn and the foreshore, the wild orchids bright among the heather and mountain grasses, all these lack the essential contrast, for the eye may move from them to the sea beyond them only through the intermediary, as it were, of the varying greens among which they grow. It is in June and October that the colours at Camusfeàrna run riot, but in June one must face seaward to escape the effect of wearing green-tinted spectacles. There at low tide the rich ochres, madders and oranges of the orderly strata of seaweed species are set against glaring, vibrant whites of barnacle-covered rock and shell sand, with always beyond them the elusive, changing blues and purples of the moving water, and somewhere in the foreground the wild roses of the north.

Into this bright, watery landscape Mij moved and took possession with a delight that communicated itself as clearly as any articulate speech could have done; his alien but essentially appropriate entity occupied and dominated every corner of it, so that he became for me the central figure among the host of wild creatures with which I was surrounded. The waterfall, the burn, the white beaches and the islands; his form became the familiar foreground to them all – or perhaps foreground is not the right word, for at Camusfeàrna he seemed so absolute a part of his surroundings that I wondered how they could ever have seemed to me complete before his arrival.

At the beginning, while I was still imbued with the caution and forethought that had so far gone to his tending, Mij's daily life followed something of a routine; this became, as the weeks went on, relaxed into a total freedom at the centre point of which Camusfeàrna house remained Mij's holt, the den to which he returned at night, and in the daytime when he was tired. But this emancipation, like most natural changes, took place so gradually and unobtrusively that it was difficult for me to say at what point the routine had stopped.

Mij slept in my bed (by now, as I have said, he had abandoned the teddy-bear attitude and lay on his back under the bedclothes with his whiskers tickling my ankles and his body at the crook of my knees) and would wake with bizarre punctuality at exactly twenty past eight in the morning. I have sought any possible explanation for this, and some 'feedback' situation in which it was actually I who made the first unconscious movement, giving him his cue, cannot be altogether discounted; but whatever the reason, his waking time, then and until the end of his life, summer or winter, remained precisely twenty past eight. Having woken, he would come up to the pillow and nuzzle my face and neck with small attenuated squeaks of pleasure and affection. If I did not rouse myself very soon he would set about getting me out of bed. This he did with the business-like, slightly impatient efficiency of a nurse dealing with a difficult child. He played the game by certain defined and self-imposed rules; he would not, for example, use his teeth even to pinch, and inside these limitations it was hard to imagine how a human brain could, in the same body, have exceeded his ingenuity. He began by going under the bedclothes and moving rapidly up and down the bed with a high-hunching, caterpillar-like motion that gradually untucked the bedclothes from beneath the sides of the mattress; this achieved he would redouble his efforts at the foot of the bed, where the sheets and blankets had a firmer hold. When everything had been loosened up to his satisfaction he would flow off the bed onto the floor – except when running on dry land the only appropriate word for an otter's movement is flowing; they pour themselves, as it were, in the direction of their objective – take the bedclothes between his teeth, and, with a series of violent tugs, begin to yank them down beside him. Eventually, for I do not wear pyjamas, I would be left quite naked on the undersheet, clutching the pillows rebelliously. But they, too, had to go; and it was here that he demonstrated the extraordinary strength concealed in his small body. He would work his way under them and execute a series of mighty hunches of his arched back, each of them lifting my head and whole shoulders clear of the bed, and at some point in the procedure he invariably contrived to dislodge the pillows while I was still in mid-air, much as a certain type of practical joker will remove a chair upon which someone is in the act of sitting down. Left thus comfortless and bereft both of covering and of dignity, there was little option but to dress, while Mij looked on with an all-that-shouldn't-really-have-been-necessary-you-know sort of expression. Otters usually get their own way in the end; they are not dogs, and they coexist with humans rather than being owned by them.

His next objective was the eel-box in the burn, followed, having breakfasted, by a tour of the water perimeter, the three-quarter circle formed by the burn and the sea; shooting like an underwater arrow after trout where the burn runs deep and slow between the trees; turning over stones for hidden eels where it spreads broad and shallow over sun-reflecting scales of mica: tobogganing down the long, loose sand slope by the sand-martin colony; diving through the waves on the sand beach and catching dabs; then, lured in with difficulty and subterfuge from starting on a second lap, home to the kitchen and ecstatic squirming among his towels.

This preamble to the day, when Mij had a full stomach and I had not, became, as he established favoured pools and fishing grounds which had every morning to be combed as for a lost possession, ever longer and longer, and after the first fortnight I took, not without misgiving, to going back indoors myself as soon as he had been fed. At first he would return after an hour or so, and when he had dried himself he would creep up under the loose cover of the sofa and form a round breathing hump at the centre of the seat. But as time went on he stayed longer about the burn, and I would not begin to worry until he had been gone for half the day.

There were great quantities of cattle at Camusfeàrna that year, for the owner of the estate was of an experimental turn of mind, and had decided to farm cattle on the lines of the Great Glen Cattle Ranch. The majority of these beasts were black, and, as at Monreith in the spring, Mij seemed to detect in them an affinity to his familiar water buffaloes of the Tigris marshes, for he would dance round them with excited chitterings until they stampeded. Thus massed they presented too formidable an appearance for him, and after a week or two he devised for himself a means of cattle-baiting at which he became a past master.

With extreme stealth he would advance *ventre à terre* towards the rear end of some massive stirk whose black-tufted tail hung invitingly within his reach; then, as one who makes a vigorous and impatient tug at a bell-rope, he would grab the tuft between his teeth and give one tremendous jerk upon it with all his strength, leaping backwards exactly in time to dodge the lashing hooves. At first I viewed this sport with the gravest alarm, for, owing to the structure of the skull, a comparatively light blow on the nose can kill an otter, but Mij was able to gauge the distance to an inch, and never a hoof so much as grazed him. As a useful by-product of his impish sense of humour, the cattle tended to keep farther from the house, thus incidentally reducing the number of scatological hazards to be skirted at the door.

I had a book to write during those summer months at Camusfeàrna, and often I would lie for hours in the sun by the waterfall; from time to time Mij would appear from nowhere, bounding up the bank from the water, to greet me as though we had been separated for weeks.

There is a patron saint of otters, St Cuthbert – the eider duck, too, shares his patronage; clearly he was a man who bestowed his favours with the most enlightened discrimination – and there exists an eye-witness account of his converse with them.

'It was his way for the most part to wander in those places and to preach in those remote hamlets, perched on steep rugged mountain sides, where other men would have a dread of going, and whose poverty and rude ignorance gave no welcome to any scholar ... Often for a whole week, sometimes for two or three, and even for a full month, he would not return home, but would abide in the mountains, and call these simple folk to heavenly things by his word and his ways...

'(*He was, moreover, easily entreated, and came to stay at the abbey of Coldingham on a cliff above the sea.*)

'As was his habit, at night while other men took their rest, he would go out to pray: and after long vigils kept far into the night, he would come home when the hour of common prayer drew near. One night, a brother of this same monastery saw him go silently out, and stealthily followed on his track, to see where he was going or what he would do. And so he went out from the monastery and, his spy following him, went down to the sea, above which the monastery was built: and wading into the depths till the waves swelled up to his neck and arms, kept his vigil through the dark with chanting voiced like the sea. As the twilight of dawn drew near, he waded back up the beach, and kneeling there, again began to pray: and as he prayed, straight from the depths of the sea came two four-footed beasts which are called by the common people otters. These, prostrate before him on the sand, began to busy themselves warming his feet with pantings, and trying to dry them with their fur; and when this good office was rendered, and they had his benediction they slipped back again beneath their native waters. He himself returned home, and sang the hymns of the office with the brethren at the appointed hour. But the brother who had stood watching him from the cliffs was seized with such panic that he could hardly make his way home, tottering on his feet: and early in the morning came to him and fell at his feet, begging forgiveness with his tears for his foolish attempt, never doubting but that his behaviour of the night was known and discovered.

'To whom Cuthbert: "What ails you, my brother? What have you done? Have you been out and about to try to come at the truth of this night wandering of mine? I forgive you, on this one condition: that you promise to tell no man what you saw, until my death." And the promise given, he blessed the brother and absolved him alike of the fault and the annoyance his foolish boldness had given: and the brother kept silence on the piece of valour that he had seen, until after the saint's death, when he took pains to tell it to many.'[1]

Now it is apparent to me that whatever other saintly virtues St Cuthbert possessed he well merited canonization by reason of his forbearance alone. I know all about being dried by otters. I have been dried by them more times than I care to remember. Like everything else about otters, it takes place the wrong way round, so to speak. When one plays ball with a puppy, one throws the ball and the puppy fetches it back and then one throws it again; it is all comparatively restful and orderly. But when one plays ball with an otter the situation gets out of hand from the start; it is the otter who throws the ball – to a remarkable distance – and the human who fetches it. With the human who at the beginning is not trained to this the otter is fairly patient, but persistent and obstinate refusal meets with reprisals. The same upside-down situation obtains when being dried by otters. The otter emerges tempestuously from the sea or the river or the bath, as the case may be, carrying about half a gallon of water in its fur, and sets about drying you with a positively terrifying zeal and enthusiasm. Every inch of you requires, in the view of a conscientious otter, careful attention. The otter uses its back as the principal towel, and lies upon it while executing a series of vigorous, eel-like wriggles. In a surprisingly short space of time the otter is quite dry except for the last four inches of its tail, and the human being is soaking wet except for nothing. It is no use going to change one's clothes; in a few minutes the otter will come rampaging out of the water again intent upon its mission of drying people.

[1] Helen Waddell, *Beasts and Saints* (Constable, 1934).

I have but little doubt what the good brother of Coldingham monastery really saw. St Cuthbert had been praying at the water's edge, not, as the brother thought (it was, one must bear in mind, night, and the light was poor), up to his neck in the waves; and it was entirely the condition of the saint's clothing after he had been dried by the otters that led the observer to deduce some kind of sub-marine devotion. Clearly, too, it was an absolution rather than a simple benediction that the now shivering and bedraggled saint bestowed upon his tormentors. In the light of my interpretation St Cuthbert's injunction to silence falls neatly into place, for he could not know of the brother's misapprehension, and not even a saint enjoys being laughed at in this kind of misfortune.

While otters undoubtedly have a special vocation for drying human beings they will also dry other objects, most particularly beds, between the sheets, all the way from the pillows to the bed-foot. A bed dried by this process is unusable for a week, and an otter-dried sofa is only tolerable in the heat of summer. I perceive why St Cuthbert required the ministrations of the eider ducks and the warm down of their breasts; the unfortunate man must have been constantly threatened with an occupational pneumonia.

This aspect of life with an otter had never really struck me before I brought Mij to Camusfeàrna; in London one could run the water out of the bath, and by using a monster towel could render him comparatively harmless before he reached the sitting-room, while at Monreith the loch was far enough from the house for him to be dry before reaching home. But at Camusfeàrna, with the sea a stone's throw on one side and the burn on the other, I have found no satisfactory solution beyond keeping the bedroom door closed, and turning, as it were, a blind posterior to wet sofas and chairs.

The manuscript that I was writing that summer became blurred and stained as though by tears; I would lie, as I have said, sunbathing and writing in the grass by the burn, and every now and again Mij's busy quartering of the stream's bed from the falls to the sea and back again would bring him to the point above which I lay. With delighted squeaks and gurgles he would rush through the shallows and come bounding up the bank to deposit his skin-load of water indiscriminately upon myself and my manuscript, sometimes adding insult to injury by confiscating my pen as he departed.

In the sea, Mij discovered his true, breathtaking aquabatic powers; until he came to Scotland he had never swum in deep waters, for the lakes and lagoons of his native marshes are rarely more than a fathom or two deep. He would swim beside me as I rowed in the little dinghy, and in the glass-clear waters of Camusfeàrna bay, where the white shell sand alternates with sea-tangle and outcrops of rock, I could watch him as he dived down, down, down through fathom after fathom to explore the gaudy sea forests at the bottom with their flowered shell glades and mysterious, shadowed caverns. He was able, as are all otters and seals, to walk on the bottom without buoyancy, for an otter swims habitually underwater and does not dive with full lungs, depending for oxygen – we must presume in the absence of knowledge – upon a special adaptation of the venous system. The longest that I ever timed Mij below the surface was almost six minutes, but I had the impression that he was in no way taxing his powers, and could greatly have exceeded that time in emergency. Normally, however, if he was not engrossed, he would return to the surface every minute or so, breaking it for only a second, with a forward diving roll like that of a porpoise. Swimming at the surface, as he did if he wanted to keep some floating object in view, he was neither very fast nor graceful, a labouring dog-paddle in amazing contrast to his smooth darting grace below water. For hours he would keep pace with the boat, appearing now on this side and now on that, sometimes mischievously seizing an oar with both arms and dragging on it, and from time to time bouncing inboard with a flurry of water, momentarily recalled to his mission of drying people.

Only when I was fishing did I have to leave Mij shut up in the house, for he was a creature who must test everything with his mouth, and my worst nightmare was the vision of a mackerel hook in his jaw. At first I fished little, having no great liking for the lythe and coal fish that are all one may depend upon in early summer round the Camusfeàrna skerries. Though by mid-June there are all the signs of summer; the teeming, clangorous bird life of the islands established for many weeks and the samphire and goose-grass alive with downy chicks, it is not until July that with the coming of the mackerel the sea appears to burst into life; for following them come all the greater creatures that prey upon them, and the mackerel in their turn force up to the surface the lesser fishes upon which they feed, the small, glittering, multitudinous fry of many species, including their own. When far out on the blank face of the summer sea there are screaming patches of gulls that dip and swoop, half running, half flying, alighting with wings still open to grab and to swallow, one may guess that somewhere beneath them lies a great shoal of mackerel, who are pushing up to the surface and the waiting gulls the little fish fleeing in panic from, perhaps, their own parents. Sometimes there are curiously local patches of fry at the surface, and at sunset when the sea is really as smooth as glass – a much misused simile, for it rarely is – I have seen, miles from shore, little dancing foot-wide fountains of blue and silver mackerel no longer than a man's thumb, and have found no predator below them.

After the mackerel had arrived I fished for a few minutes in the cool of every evening; for them Mij, though he never caught one himself, so far as I knew, had an insatiable passion, as had Jonnie before him; and I too welcomed them, perhaps because of childhood associations. When I was a child in Galloway we used to fish for mackerel by trolling from a sailing-boat a single hook baited with bright metal, or with a sliver of flesh and skin sliced from a mackerel's flank (how well I recall the horror of seeing for the first time this operation performed upon the living fish; the tears, the reassurance, all among the blue waves and the spindrift and the flapping brown sail). We caught our fish singly and rebaited the hook each time, and if we caught twenty or thirty fish in an afternoon we chattered about it for weeks. It was not, I think, until shortly before the war that the murderous darrow came into general use in the West Highlands, and at Camusfeàrna, where there is no means of disposing of surplus fish but dumping them, it has the disadvantage of limiting fishing time to a few minutes. A darrow consists of a twelve-foot cast carrying up to twenty-two flies of crudely-dyed hen's feathers, weighted at the bottom with a two-pound sinker. The boat is stationary in anything from six to twenty fathoms of water, and the darrow and line are allowed to run out until the sinker bumps the bottom. By that time, as often as not in Camusfeàrna bay, there are half a dozen or so mackerel on the hooks. If there are not, it is simply a question of hauling in two fathoms of line and letting it run out again, and repeating this process until either the boat drifts over a shoal or a moving shoal happens to pass beneath the boat. Sometimes the mackerel are in shallower water, clear water where one can see fathoms down to pale sand and dark sea-tangle and rushing shoals of aquamarine fish as they dart at the bright feathers. Quite often every single fly is taken at once; then at one moment the line is lead-heavy, tugging and jerking, and at the next light as floating string as the mackerel swim upward carrying the sinker with them. There is a great art in dealing with a full darrow, for twenty-two large fish-hooks flipping wildly about the hold of a small boat catch more than fish. In the days of the Soay Shark Fishery I saw many barbs sunk deep in hands and legs of mackerel fishers; there was only one way of extraction, and a very painful one it was – to push the hook clean through, as opposed to pulling on it, then to snip off the barb with wire cutters and work the hook all the way back again.

It is not always mackerel that take the darrow flies; there are saith and lythe and the strangely heraldic gurnards, so fantastically armoured with spikes and thorns as to make their capture by anything but man seem nothing short of impossible, yet I have watched, with the same sensations as a man might view a big snake swallowing an ox whole, a shag swallow a large gurnard tail first – against the grain, as it were. This extraordinary and surely gratuitously painful feat took the shag just over half an hour of grotesque convulsion, and when the stunt was at last completed the bird had entirely changed its shape. From being a slim, graceful, snake-like creature with a neck like an ebony cane, it had become an amorphous and neck-less lump – its crop so gigantically distended as to force the head far back down the spine and flush with it – unable to rise or even to swim without danger of ridicule.

Mij himself caught a number of fish on his daily outings; and week by week, as his skill and speed grew, their size and variety increased. In the burn he learned to feel under stones for eels, reaching in with one paw and averted head; and I in turn learned to turn over the larger stones for him, so that after a time he would stand in front of some boulder too heavy for him to move, and chitter at me to come and lift it for him. Often, as I did this, an eel would streak out from it into deeper water and he would fire himself after it like a brown torpedo beneath the surface. Near the edge of the tide he would search out the perfectly camouflaged flounders until they shot off with a wake of rising sand-grains like smoke from an express train – and farther out in the bay he would kill an occasional sea trout; these he never brought ashore, but ate them treading water as he did so, while I thought a little wistfully of the Chinese who are said to employ trained otters to fish for them. Mij, I thought, with all his delightful camaraderies, would never offer me a fish; I was wrong, but when at last he did so it was not a sea trout but a flounder. One day he emerged from the sea onto the rock ledge where I was standing and slapped down in front of me a flounder a foot across. I took it that he had brought this for congratulation, for he would often bring his choicer catches for inspection before consuming them, so I said something encouraging and began to walk on. He hurried after me and slammed it down again with a wet smack at my feet. Even then I did not understand, assuming only that he wished to eat in company, but he just sat there looking up and chittering at me. I was in no hurry to take the gesture at its face value, for, as I have said, one of the most aggressive actions one can perform to a wild animal is to deprive it of its prey, but after perhaps half a minute of doubt, while Mij redoubled his invitation, I reached down slowly and cautiously for the fish, knowing that Mij would give me vocal warning if I had misinterpreted him. He watched me with the plainest approval while I picked it up and began a mime of eating it; then he plunged off the rock into the sea and sped away a fathom down in the clear water.

Watching Mij in a rough sea – and the equinoctial gales at Camusfeàrna produce very rough seas indeed – I was at first sick with apprehension, then awed and fascinated, for his powers seemed little less than miraculous. During the first of the gales, I remember, I tried to keep him to the rock pools and the more sheltered corners, but one day his pursuit of some unseen prey had taken him to the seaward side of a high dry reef at the very tide's edge. As the long undertow sucked outward he was in no more than an inch or two of marbled water with the rock at his back, crunching the small fish he had caught; then, some forty yards to seaward of him I saw a great snarling comber piling up higher and higher, surging in fifteen feet tall and as yet unbreaking. I yelled to Mij as the wave towered darkly towards him, but he went on eating and paid no heed to me. It curled over and broke just before it reached him; all those tons of water just smashed down and obliterated him, enveloping the whole rock behind in a booming tumult of sea. Somewhere under it I visualized Mij's smashed body swirling round the foot of the black rock. But as the sea drew back in a long hissing undertow I saw, incredulously, that nothing had changed; there was Mij still lying in the shallow marbled water, still eating his fish.

He rejoiced in the waves; he would hurl himself straight as an arrow right into the great roaring grey wall of an oncoming breaker and go clean through it as if it had neither weight nor momentum; he would swim far out to sea through wave after wave until the black dot of his head was lost among the distant white manes, and more than once I thought that some wild urge to seek new lands had seized him and that he would go on swimming west into the Sea of the Hebrides and that I should not see him again.

As the weeks went by his absences did grow longer, and I spent many anxious hours searching for him, though as yet he had never stayed away for a night. When I had drawn blank at the falls and at all his favourite pools in the burn or among the rock ledges by the sea, I would begin to worry and to roam more widely, calling his name all the while. His answering note of recognition was so like the call of some small dowdy bird that inhabits the trees by the waterside that my heart would leap a hundred times before I knew with certainty that I had heard his voice, and then my relief was so unbounded that I would allow him to dry me without protest.

The first time that I found him in distress was in the dark ravine above the waterfall. The waterfall divides, in some sense, the desert from the sown; the habitable world from the strange, beautiful, but inhospitable world of the dark gorge through which the burn flows above it. In summer, when the water is low, one may pick one's way precariously along the rock at the stream's edge, the almost sheer but wooded sides rising a hundred feet at either hand. Here it is always twilight, for the sun never reaches the bed of the stream, and in summer the sky's light comes down thin and diffused by a stipple of oak and birch leaves whose branches lean out far overhead. Here and there a fallen tree-trunk spans the narrow gorge, its surface worn smooth by the passage of the wildcats' feet. The air is cool, moist, and pungent with the smell of wild garlic and watery things such as ferns and mosses that grow in the damp and the dark. Sometimes the bed of the stream widens to deep pools whose rock flanks afford no foothold, and where it looks as though the black water must be bottomless.

Once Morag asked me, in an offhand way behind which I sensed a tentative probing, whether I felt at ease in that place. It was a question that held a tacit confession, and I replied frankly. I have never been at ease in it; it evokes in me an unpleasant sensation that I associate only with the unfurnished top floor of a certain house, a sensation which makes me want to glance constantly over my shoulder, as though, despite the physical impossibility, I were being followed. I catch myself trying to step silently from stone to stone, as though it were important to my safety that my presence should remain undetected. I should have been abashed to tell Morag of this had she not given me the lead, but she told me then that she had had a horror of the place ever since she was a child, and could offer no explanation.

To conform to the spirit of my confession the gorge ought, of course, to be shunned by bird and animal alike, but it has, in fact, more of both than one might expect. There are foxes' and badgers' and wildcats' dens in the treacherous, near-vertical walls of the ravine; the buzzards and hooded crows nest every year in the branches that lean out over the dark water; below them there are the dippers and grey wagtails (a crass ornithological misnomer for this canary-yellow creature), and, for some reason, an unusual number of wrens that skulk and twitter among the fern. Whatever makes the gorge an unpleasant place to some people does not extend its influence beyond human beings.

The deep pools spill in unbroken falls a few feet high, and after two hundred yards or so there is the second real waterfall, dropping fifty feet interrupted by a ledge pool half-way down. That is the upper limit of the 'haunting', though the physical details of the gorge above the second falls differ little from those of the stretch below it; then, a further hundred yards up the burn's course, the way is blocked by the tall cataract, eighty feet of foaming white water falling sheer.

Mij, certainly, found nothing distasteful in the reach where my ghosts walked, and he had early used his strength and resource to scale the

Camusfeàrna waterfall and find out what lay beyond. Thereafter this inaccessible region had become his especial haunt, and one from which his extraction presented, even when he was not in difficulties, almost insuperable problems. The clamour of the falling water effectively drowned the calling human voice, and even if he did hear it there was little chance of the caller perceiving his faint, bird-like response. On this occasion there was more water in the burn than is usual in summer, and there had been, too, a recent landslide, temporarily destroying the only practicable access from above. I lowered myself into the ravine on a rope belayed to the trunk of a tree, and I was wet to the waist after the first few yards of the burn's bed. I called and called, but my voice was diminished and lost in the sound of rushing water, and the little mocking birds answered me with Mij's own note of greeting. At length one of these birds, it seemed, called so repeatedly and insistently as to germinate in me a seed of doubt, but the sound came from far above me, and I was looking for Mij in the floor of the burn. Then I saw him; high up on the cliff, occupying so small a ledge that he could not even turn to make his way back, and with a fifty-foot sheer drop below him; he was looking at me, and, according to his lights, yelling his head off. I had to make a long detour to get above him with the rope and all the while I was terrified that the sight of me would have spurred him to some effort that would bring tragedy; terrified, too, that I myself might dislodge him as I tried to lift him from his eyrie. Then I found that the trees at the cliff-top were all rotten, and I had to make the rope fast to a stump on the hill above, a stump that grew in soft peat and that gave out from its roots an ominous squelching sound when I tugged hard on it. I went down that rock with the rope knotted round my waist and the feeling that Mij would probably survive somehow, but that I should most certainly die. He tried to stand on his hind legs when he saw me coming down above him, and more than once I thought he had gone. I had put the loop of his lead through the rope at my waist, and I clipped the other end to his harness as soon as my arm could reach him, but the harnesses, with their constant immersion, never lasted long, and I trusted this one about as much as I trusted the stump to which my rope was tied. I went up the rope with Mij dangling and bumping at my side like a cow being loaded onto a ship by crane, and in my mind's eye were two jostling, urgent images – the slow, sucking emergence of the tree roots above me, and the gradual parting of the rivets that held Mij's harness together. All in all it was one of the nastiest five minutes of my life; and when I reached the top the roots of the stump were indeed showing – it took just one tug with all my strength to pull them clean out.

But the harness had held, though, mercifully, it broke the next time it was put to strain. Mij had been missing, that day in the ravine, for nine hours, and had perhaps passed most of them on that ledge, for he was ravenously hungry, and ate until I thought he must choke.

There were other absences, other hours of anxiety and search, but one in particular stands out in my mind, for it was the first time that he had been away for a whole night, the first time that I despaired of him. I had left him in the early morning at the burn side eating his eels, and began to be uneasy when he had not returned by mid-afternoon. I had been working hard at my book; it was one of those rare days of authorship when everything seemed to go right; the words flowed unbidden from my pen, and the time had passed unheeded, so that it was a shock to realize that I had been writing for some six hours. I went out and called for Mij down the burn and along the beach, and when I did not find him I went again to the ravine above the falls. But there was no trace of him anywhere, though I explored the whole dark length of it right to the high falls, which I knew that even Mij could not pass. Just how short a distance my voice carried I realized when, above the second falls, I came upon two wildcat kittens at play on the steep bank; they saw me and were gone in a flash, but they had never heard my voice above the sound of the water. I left the burn then and went out to the nearer islands; it was low tide, and there were exposed stretches and bars of soft white sand. Here I found otter footprints leading towards the lighthouse island, but I could not be certain that they were Mij's. Later that summer his claws became worn so that his pad-marks no longer showed the nails, but at that stage I was still unsure of distinguishing his tracks from those of a wild otter, unless the imprints were very precise. All that evening I searched and called, and when dusk came and he still did not return I began to despair, for his domestic life had led him to strictly diurnal habits, and by sundown he was always asleep in front of the fire.

It was a cloudy night with a freshening wind and a big moon that swam muzzily through black rags of vapour. By eleven o'clock it was blowing strong to gale from the south, and on the windward side of the islands there was a heavy sea beginning to pile up; enough, I thought, for him to lose his bearings if he were trying to make his way homeward through it. I put a light in each window of the house, left the doors open, and dozed fitfully in front of the kitchen fire. By three o'clock in the morning there was the first faint paling of dawn, and I went out to get the boat, for by now I had somehow convinced myself that Mij was on the lighthouse island. That little cockleshell was in difficulties from the moment I launched her; I had open water and a beam sea to cross before I could reach the lee of the islands, and she was taking a slosh of water over her gunwale all the way. If I shipped oars to bale I made so much leeway that I was nearly ashore again before I had done, and after half an hour I was both wet and scared. The bigger islands gave some shelter from the south wind, but in the passages between them the north-running sea was about as much as the little boat would stand, and over the many rocks and skerries the water was foaming white and wicked-looking in the half light. A moment to bale and I would have been swept onto these black cusps and molars; the boat would have been crunched on them like a squashed matchbox, and I, who cannot swim a stroke, would have been feeding the lobsters. To complete my discomfort, I met a Killer whale. In order to keep clear of the reefs I had rowed well north of the small islands that lie to landward of the lighthouse; the water was calmer here, and I did not have to fight to keep the nose of the boat into the waves. The Killer broke the surface no more than twenty yards to the north of me, a big bull whose sabre fin seemed to tower a man's height out of the water; and, probably by chance, he turned straight for me. My nerves were strung and tensed, and I was in no frame of mind to assess the true likelihood of danger; I swung and rowed for the nearest island as though man were a Killer's only prey. I grounded on a reef a hundred yards from the tern island, and I was not going to wait for the tide to lift me. Slithering and floundering in thigh-deep water over a rock ledge I struggled until I had lifted the flat keel clear of the tooth on which it had grated; the Killer, possibly intent upon his own business and with no thought of me, cruised round a stone's throw away. I reached the tern island, and the birds rose screaming around me in a dancing canopy of ghostly wings, and I sat down on the rock in the dim windy dawn and felt as desolate as an abandoned child.

The lighthouse island was smothered in its jungle-growth of summer briars that grip the clothing with octopus arms and leave trails of blood-drops across hands and face; on it I felt like a dream walker who never moves, and my calling voice was swept away northwards on gusts of cold, wet wind. I got back to the house at nine in the morning, with a dead-weight boat more than half full of water and a sick emptiness in my mind and body. By now part of me was sure that Mij too had met the Killer, and that he was at this moment half digested in the whale's belly.

All that day until four o'clock in the afternoon I wandered and called, and with every hour grew the realization of how much that strange animal companion had come to signify to me. I resented it, resented my dependence upon this sub-human presence and companionship, re-sented the void that his absence was going to leave at Camusfeàrna. It was in this mood, one of reassertion of human independence, that about five in the evening I began to remove the remaining evidence of his past existence. I had taken from beneath the kitchen table his drinking bowl, had returned for the half-full bowl of rice and egg, had carried this to the scullery, what the Scots call the back kitchen, and was about to empty it into the slop pail, when I thought I heard Mij's voice from the kitchen behind me. I was, however, very tired, and distrustful of my own reactions; what I thought I had heard was the harshly whispered 'Hah?' with which he was accustomed to interrogate a seemingly empty room. The impression was strong enough for me to set down the bowl and hurry back into the kitchen. There was nothing there. I walked to the door and called his name, but all was as it had been before. I was on my way back to the scullery when I stopped dead. There on the kitchen floor, where I had been about to step, was a large, wet footprint. I looked at it, and I thought: I am very tired and very overwrought; and I went down on my hands and knees to inspect it. It was certainly wet, and it smelled of otter. I was still in a quadrupedal attitude when from the doorway behind me I heard the sound again, this time past mistaking – 'Hah?' Then Mij was all over me, drenched and wildly demonstrative, squeaking, bouncing round me like an excitable puppy, clambering on my shoulders, squirming on his back, leaping, dancing. I had been reassuring myself and him for some minutes before I realized that his harness was burst apart, and that for many hours, perhaps a day or more, he must have been caught like Absalom, struggling, desperate, waiting for a rescue that never came.

I am aware that this scene of reunion, and the hours that for me had preceded it, must appear to many a reader little short of nauseous. I might write of it and subsequent events with a wry dishonesty, a negation of my feeling for that creature, which might disarm criticism, might forestall the accusation of sentimentality and slushiness to which I now lay myself open. There is, however, a certain obligation of honesty upon a writer, without which his words are worthless, and beyond that my feeling for animals that I adopt would, despite any dissimulation that I might essay, reveal itself as intense, even crucial. I knew by that time that Mij meant more to me than most human beings of my acquaintance, that I should miss his physical presence more than theirs, and I was not ashamed of it. In the penultimate analysis, perhaps, I knew that Mij trusted me more utterly than did any of my own kind, and so supplied a need that we are slow to admit.

. . .

When I missed Mij from his accustomed haunts I would go first to the waterfall, for there he would spend long hours alone, chasing the one big trout that lived in the big pool below the falls, catching elvers, or playing with some floating object that had been washed down. Sometimes he would set out from the house carrying a ping-pong ball, purposeful and self-engrossed, and he would still be at the waterfall with it an hour later, pulling it under water and letting it shoot up again, rearing up and pouncing on it, playing his own form of water polo, with a goal at which the human onlooker could but guess. Once, I remember, I went to look for him there and at first could not find him; then my attention was caught by something red in the black water at the edge of the foam, and I saw that Mij was floating on his back, apparently fast asleep, with a bunch of scarlet rowanberries clasped to his chest with one arm. Such bright objects as these he would often pick up on his walks, and carry them with him until some rival attraction supplanted them. I never performed any tests to define his degree of colour vision, but whether by chance or selection his preferred playthings were often of garish hue.

I was watching him at the waterfall one day, trying to take photographs of him as he frolicked with his ping-pong ball in the deep pool, when I lost my footing on the sloping rock and found myself in beside him, camera and all. I had just started back for the house to change my clothes when I heard voices. A dry-stone wall runs between the waterfall and the house, and when I reached this with Mij at my heels I saw a figure approaching me whom I recognized with difficulty as the literary editress of the *New Statesman*; with difficulty, because her clothes were far from conventional, and I had not previously seen her away from city surroundings. We exchanged greetings over the wall, and began to talk. Mij climbed onto the wall top beside me and watched.

Now Mij had an especial vice that I have not yet mentioned; a vice that I had been unable to cure, partly, anyway, because I did not understand its cause or motivation. To put it bluntly, he bit the lobes of people's ears – not, certainly, in anger nor in spite; not, apparently, as a conscious act of aggression or ill will, but simply because he liked doing so. He collected them, so to speak, not as David collected the foreskins of the Philistines, in enmity, but as an amiable hobby. He just nipped through them like an efficient ear-piercer, and apparently felt the better for it. It was now so long since he had met strangers and had the opportunity to add an ear to his list that I had momentarily forgotten this deplorable proclivity. My visitor leaned an arm on the wall as she talked, with her head a mere foot from Mij's, and Mij reached out, without comment, and pierced the lobe of her left ear with surgical precision.

It was her finest hour. I had seen many lobes pierced by Mij; I was a connoisseur of reaction to the situation, ranging from the faint shriek, through gabbling reassurance, to the ominous flushed silence; I thought I knew them all, but I was wrong. Not by the smallest interruption in her flow of speech, not by so much as a hint of an indrawn breath did she betray that she had perceived the incident; only her eyes, as she continued her sentence, assumed an expression of unbelieving outrage entirely at variance with her words.

One of the few people who escaped this hallmark, as it were, of Mij's acquaintance, was Morag. I myself had had both ears pierced early in my association with my namesake, and now enjoyed immunity. To only two other people did he extend the tempestuous affection that he accorded to me, to Morag and to Kathleen Raine; but though the degree of demonstrative love to each of us did not greatly differ it was quite unlike in kind – with each, that is to say, he formed an entirely different relationship. With Kathleen, whose mere proximity would send him into ecstasies, he was rough and rumbustious, fiercely possessive, and he took advantage of her whenever and however he could; she in turn found some strange community with him, and was prepared to put up uncomplainingly with his most exuberant horseplay. With Morag he was gentler, less bullying, in his love, and with me more deferential, more responsive to the suggestion of command. But it remained around us three that his orb revolved when he was not away in his own imponderable world of wave and water, of dim green depths and tide-swayed fronds of the sea-tangle; we were his Trinity, and he behaved towards us much as Mediterranean people do towards theirs, with a mixture of trust and abuse, passion and irritation. In turn each of us in our own way depended, as gods do, upon his worship; I, perhaps, most of all, because he belonged to the only race of living creature that was ever likely to bear my name.

CHAPTER 10

I returned to London with Mij in the autumn, and with his usual good humour he adjusted himself quickly to the absence of his beloved burn and foreshore. During the car journey from Camusfeàrna to Inverness he seemed, in a long deep sleep, to shed his wild nature and to awake metamorphosed as a domestic animal. In the station hotel he lay beside my chair while I had tea, and when a waitress brought him a saucer of milk he lapped it as delicately as any drawing-room cat, spilling never a drop. He entered his first-class sleeper as one long used to travel, and at the studio next morning he seemed actively pleased to be among his old surroundings. He settled quickly, too, into his earlier routine: eels in the bath; walks round the grubby London streets; even, not without trepidation on my part, an afternoon's shopping in Harrods. By one local shop he was allowed to make his own selection before purchase; he had, as I have mentioned, a passion for rubber toys, more especially such as would squeak or rattle when manipulated. Near by to my flat was a shop devoted entirely to such oddities; india-rubber fruit and buns, explosive cigars, apparently full glasses from which no drop of liquid could escape, even papier mâché imitations of dog and cat excrement – the whole practical joker's compendium. Here I was hesitating one day between a chocolate éclair that whistled and an india-rubber mackerel that wheezed when the assistant said, 'Why not let him make his own choice, sir?' and placed both on the floor. Mij plumped for the éclair, to the assistant's surprise, and thereafter Mij chose his own toys and himself bore them home in triumph. It was a very realistic éclair, and as we passed the door of the pub on the corner a figure emerged swaying slightly, focused Mij, and stood riveted. 'Good God!' he said, quite quietly, and behind him a voice shouted, 'You've got 'em again, Bill – you've got 'em again!'

Mij seemed in those days to possess a quality of indestructibility, an imperviousness to physical hurt, that was little short of miraculous. He succeeded, despite all my precautions, in falling from the gallery to the parquet floor below, but he might, for all the notice he took of the incident, have fallen upon a feather bed; his head was caught, without protest, in a slamming door; and, finally, he chewed a razor blade into fragments. I had been out for the evening, and had left him the premises beyond the kitchen, the bathroom, that is to say, with a full bath, and beyond it the box-room where he had a tattered armchair of his own and an electric fire that shone down upon it from the wall. When I came in I opened the bathroom door and called him, but there was no response. I went in and saw that the bath was empty of water; at the bottom of it my safety razor was in two pieces, lying among splintered pieces of the blade. It did not at that instant strike me that the total absence of blood indicated, however improbably, an intact otter; I went through into the box-room expecting to find a corpse in the chair beneath the warm glow of the fire. But there among the cushions he was squirming with self-satisfaction, as though conscious of having carried out a difficult task with initiative and acumen, and there was not, as far as I could discover, so much as a scratch on him.

·   ·   ·

I cannot now remember whether, when I had been in Iraq, I had ever seriously considered what was to be done with an otter during such times as I was unable to look after him myself; when, for example, I was again abroad, or even when I wanted to be away from my own premises for a day or two. Perhaps I had thought that at any rate in the latter case he could accompany me, for I had not yet learned that an otter is not at its best as a guest in a strange house – or rather that the house would be very strange indeed at the end of the visit. Mij was content to be alone for four or five hours, but for no longer unless those hours began in the evening, and now I found my activities so hamstrung by this dependence that I was forced to take the problem seriously.

In November I had to be away from London for three days, to lecture in the Midlands, and this was Mij's first and only imprisonment away from the people and surroundings that he knew. I arranged for him to be boarded for those three days at the zoo sanatorium, and took him up to Regent's Park in a taxi. Once inside the gardens he plodded sturdily ahead at the end of his lead, and for all his reaction the teeming animal voices and smells around him might not have existed. Only when he passed by the aviaries containing the great birds of prey did he cower and tug his lead the other way; a memory, perhaps, of his native marshes where, winter long, the eagles wheel above the wastes of water, and where they must be the otter's only natural enemy; or perhaps an inborn instinct that his race's foes came from the skies. I left him in a grim cage whose last occupant had been a sick wart-hog, and when the door was closed on him and he found himself alone his wails went to my heart. I could hear him long after I had closed the gate of the sanatorium yard.

On the evening of the next day I telephoned from the north to enquire if he had settled down. Too much, I was told; in fact he has insulated himself from the world by the same deep coma into which he had sunk when shut into a box on the air journey. He had refused all food, and after digging at the iron and cement that enclosed him until his feet bled he had curled up in my sheepskin coat and refused to be roused. I was advised to come back for him as soon as possible; not rarely pet animals in such surroundings would pass almost imperceptibly from such a coma into death.

I left for London very early the next morning, but there was a dense white fog which slowed me to a bicycle's speed for the first hundred miles. Then if furled up suddenly to reveal a bare blue sky and bright autumn sunshine. My car was a ferocious vehicle, converted from a single-seater Grand Prix racing car, and in her distant prime speeds in excess of 160 m.p.h. had been claimed for her, but at this moment I was running-in a set of new pistons that she seemed to require about as often as more modest conveyances need refilling with petrol. With the last hundred miles the running-in distance was, on the milometer, completed, but in my anxiety to reach London and my pining otter I left out of account that they had been covered so slowly as to be valueless for the purpose. I came out onto the long straight north of Grantham, and unfortunately there was not another car in sight to slow me down. I had been driving at about 90 m.p.h.; now, I thought, I would go very much faster, and, for a short time, I did. The supercharger screamed, dial needles moved with incredible rapidity towards red zones; I had a glimpse of the speedometer hovering at 145 m.p.h., and I was still accelerating briskly. Then there was a rending sound, the cockpit filled with a great puff of blue smoke, and in the mirror I saw a thin black trail of oil stretching away behind me. I came to rest opposite to a farmhouse, and all I could think of was whether a train could get me to London before the staff of the zoo sanatorium went off duty for the evening. The farm had a telephone; the only possible train left Grantham in thirty-eight minutes, and I caught it as it was moving out of the station.

Back at the zoo sanatorium, I could not at first even see Mij in his cage. There were a lot of dead fish lying about untouched, and a big basin the size of a hip bath had been slopped about so that there was water everywhere; the sheepskin jacket was lying in a huddle in the middle of this, and there was no movement anywhere. I came in through the steel-barred door and called his name, but nothing stirred. I put my hand into the jacket and I felt him warm and breathing, as far into the arm hole as he could push himself. Only when I thrust my hand in beside him until I could touch his face did he begin to awaken, with a slow, dazed air as if he were emerging from a trance; then suddenly he was out and leaping in a frenzy of joy, clambering over me and inside my coat, and rushing round and round that barren cage until he threw himself down panting in front of me.

In those two days he had taken on the sour small-cat-house odour of stale urine and dejection and indignity that is the hallmark of the captive; he had lost his self-respect and fouled his own bed, so that his usually sweet-smelling fur stank like an ill-kept ferret. It was not an experiment that I ever repeated, but his boarding was clearly a problem to which I had to find a solution.

He paid one more visit to the zoo, but this time not as a captive. I had for long wanted to have a clear, eye-level view of his performance underwater, and to this end I was allowed by the Zoological Society to erect in the back premises of the Aquarium a large glass tank that I had hired for the day. Had I known that there was never to be another opportunity I would have arranged for a cinema camera, but as things were I asked Michael Ayrton to come and make drawings of him. With the tank I was provided with a number of goldfish for Mij to catch and consume; I could have wished that there had been something of more feral appearance, something associated less in the mind's eye with the parlour and the aspidistra and the loving care of an old maid, or with the cosy, unpredatory world of the nursery, where only in fiction was nature permitted to be red in tooth and claw. Mij, however, was untroubled by any such connotations, and set about their destruction with a zeal and a display of virtuosity for which even my long hours of watching him from above had left me unprepared. His speed was bewildering, his grace breathtaking; he was boneless, mercurial, sinuous, wonderful. I thought of a trapeze artist, of a ballet dancer, of a bird or an aircraft in aerobatics, but in all these I was comparing him to lesser grandeurs; he was an otter in his own element, and he was the most beautiful thing in nature that I had ever seen.

As with his toys, he was not content to be in possession of only one fish at a time; having captured the first he would tuck it under one arm, and, apparently utterly unhandicapped by this awkward parcel, would swoop, sometimes 'looping the loop' as he did so, upon another; at one moment he had fish under both arms and a third in his mouth. At the conclusion of this display, which had cost me in hire charges some ten shillings a minute, I felt that I had seldom been so richly rewarded for financial outlay on visual experience, and I determined that I must have a glass tank of my own for him in London.

I began my own search for emancipation by inserting an advertisement in *Country Life*, the *Field*, and *The Times*, requesting in gist a temporary home for Mij where he could be left for anything from days to months as necessity demanded. Altogether I received some forty replies to this somewhat egregious demand, and conscientiously followed up every one of them, but one by one the prospective guardians were weighed and found wanting. Few of them had any idea of what they would be taking on; fewer still had premises in any way suitable; some turned out to be schoolchildren applying without their parents' knowledge. At the end of two months I was no further on than on the day I had drafted the advertisement.

Then I began to interview retired zoo keepers, but a few weeks of this convinced me that a retired zoo keeper has an implacable intention to remain retired. Meanwhile the book that I had been writing was finished, and I should in the normal course of events have begun again to travel. It seemed an impasse. Though I found a temporary solution – to return to Camusfeàrna in the spring and there to write a book about Mij – these were clearly no more than delaying tactics, and with friends in the zoological world I left an urgent plea to find me, by hook or by crook, a whole-time otter-keeper. But by the time he was found and engaged, Mij was dead.

·   ·   ·

What little there remains to tell of this story I shall write quickly, for anyone who in reading it has shared a little of my pleasure in his life must share, too, a little of my unhappiness at his death.

I had arranged to go to Camusfeàrna to spend the spring and summer alone in his company, and there to write the book about him that I had projected. I was to leave London early in April, but I needed a fortnight's freedom from his incessant demands upon my time, and I arranged that he should precede me to Scotland in the charge of a friend. I packed his 'suitcase', a wicker basket whose essential contents seemed ever to become more and more elaborate – spare harnesses, leads, tins of unpolished rice, cod-liver oil, toys partially disintegrated but long favoured, and I travelled with him in the hired car from my flat to Euston station. It was a big Humber, with a broad ledge between the top of the back seat and the rear window; here, I recall with a vividness that is still in some sense painful, he sprawled upon his back and rolled my fountain pen to and fro between his forepaws, or held it clasped with one of them against his broad, glossy belly. I called my companion's attention to the rich sheen of his coat reflecting the neon lights. He was in his most domesticated mood.

At the station he tugged purposefully at the lead all the way up the astonished platform to the sleeper, where he made straight for the wash basin and accommodated his plastic body to the curves. His left hand reached up and fumbled vaguely with the tap. That was the last I ever saw of him.

During the next ten days I received letters telling me of Mij's delight in his renewed freedom; of the fish that he had caught in the river and in the sea; of how he would come in dog-tired and curl up before the fire; of anxious hours of absence; of how it had been decided at last that he would be safer without his harness, which, despite the care and experiment that had gone to its design, might still catch upon some underwater snag and drown him.

On April 16th I had packed my own luggage, and was to be at Camusfeàrna myself the following afternoon, when I received a telephone call from the estate agent of the property to which Camusfeàrna belonged. It was rumoured, he told me, that an otter had been killed at the village four miles north of Camusfeàrna, and Mij was missing. There was, however, a discrepancy; the otter that had been killed was said to have been so mangy and scabby that the killer had not thought it worth while to preserve the skin. There was no detailed information.

Nor was there to be any yet; no tidy end, no body to identify, no palliative burial at the foot of the rowan tree; no human kindness that would spare to those who had been fond of him the day-long search, the door standing open all through the night.

I arrived at the village the following afternoon. I had heard conflicting tales at the railhead station, on the launch that took me to the village, at the village pier. Some said that a very old wild otter had been killed, but that Mij was already safely returned, others that he had been seen in a village miles to the south of Camusfeàrna. I did not believe them; I knew that Mij was dead, but I was driven by a compulsive desire to know by whom and how he had been killed.

A roadman, I was told in the village, had been driving his lorry past the church when he had seen an otter on the road where it bordered the sea, and had killed it. The skin was partly hairless and he had not kept it.

I found out where this man lived, and drove some four miles inland to see his family. I arrived furtively, for I expected to find Mij's pelt nailed out to dry somewhere in the environs of the house – a thing I should not be allowed to see if I made my enquiry first. For me it would have felt like finding the skin of a human friend, but I had to know.

The family denied all knowledge of it. The skin, they said, had been so mangy that the killer, Big Angus, had thrown it away before reaching home. No, they didn't know where. Big Angus was not back yet – he would come riding on the pillion of a motor-cycle; if I was to wait in the village I might see him.

I waited. The motor-cycle came at last. Yes, it was true that he had killed an otter yesterday, but it was also true that the skin was half bald, and he had not thought it worth keeping. He was soft-spoken and ingenuous.

I asked him to show me where it had happened. I walked back with him some two hundred yards to a sharp bend where a little churchyard lay between the road and the sea. He had come round the corner with his lorry, and the otter had been there, just above the road, in the ditch. He had stopped his lorry.

I could see it desperately plainly. 'How did you kill him?' I asked. 'With a stick?' 'No, Major,' he said, 'I had a pick-head in the back of the lorry.' He thought that a wild otter would wait in the road while he went to fetch the instrument of its death. He stuck to his story; by his account the otter he had killed could not have been mine. 'He was very old and skinny,' he said again and again. 'I threw the carcass in the river, and I don't remember where.' He had been well briefed and well rehearsed, as I learned much later, when he had gone in panic to seek advice. Brave murderer; for his lies and deceit I could have killed him then as instinctively and with as little forethought as he had killed the creature I had brought so many thousands of miles, killed him quickly and treacherously, when he was expecting it no more than Mij had, so that the punishment would fit the crime.

Instead, I appealed foolishly to the quality he lacked; I pleaded with him to tell me; I tried to make him understand what it would be like for me to remain at Camusfeàrna waiting day after day for the return that I did not believe possible. He did not give way an inch.

I learned later, from someone else with more humanity.

'I felt I couldn't sit by and see you deceived,' he said. 'It's just not a decent action in a man, and that's the truth. I saw the body of the beast on the lorry when it stopped in the village, and there wasn't a hair out of place on the whole skin – except the head, which was all bashed in. If he didn't know fine it was yours he knew then, because I told him; "You want to get your head seen to," I said, "if you think that's a wild otter, or if you think a wild one would wait for you to kill it in broad daylight." It's just a pack of lies he's telling you, and I couldn't think of you looking and calling for your pet up and down the burn and by the tide every day, and him dead all the while.'

I got the story little by little. Mij had been wandering widely for some days past, and though he had always returned at night he must have covered great distances, for he had turned up one day at a hamlet some eight miles south by sea. There he had been recognized and gone unmolested; the next day he had journeyed north up the coast to the village where he was killed. Earlier in the day he had been recognized there too; a man who saw an otter in his hen run had fetched his gun before he was struck by the otter's indifference to the chickens, and made the right deduction. Mij had been on his way home when he had met Big Angus, and he had never been taught to fear or distrust any human being. I hope he was killed quickly, but I wish he had had one chance to use his teeth on his killer.

He had been with me for a year and a day on the night he had left London.

CHAPTER 11

I missed Mij desperately, so much that it was a year before I could bring myself to go to Camusfeàrna again. I mourned for my fallen sparrow; he had filled that landscape so completely, had made so much his own every yard of the ring of bright water I loved, that it seemed, after he had gone from it, hollow and insufficient; for the first time all the familiar things in which I had taken joy appeared as a stage backcloth against which no player moved. I did not stay there after I knew that he was dead; instead, I returned at once to Sicily, and resumed a work that had by now been long interrupted. As the slow summer months passed under that scorching sun the year during which I had had an otter for a companion, and even Camusfeàrna itself, seemed at times like a dream. I could not deny to myself how much I had been affected by the death of one wild animal, but some part of me stood aside and questioned the validity, the morality, perhaps, of such an attitude in face of the human misery surrounding me. Like my occupancy of the Isle of Soay, that year now appeared to me episodic, sharply defined at beginning and end, and without possible extension; but, as in that other instance, I was wrong.

I came back from Sicily in the autumn, and moved house to Chelsea, partly, I must confess, because I found the elaboration of otter-proofing devices that now composed my premises to be too constant and nagging a reminder of my failure to keep alive an animal to which I had given so much attention. But I had grown accustomed to the continual prox- imity of an animal, and when one day in Harrods I found a ring-tailed lemur, lately the property of Cyril Connolly, not even the price of seventy-five pounds could discourage me from my folly. Kiko, as she was called, came to live in my new flat. Kiko was an exceedingly beautiful animal rather larger than a very large cat, an *haute couture* creation in soft blue-grey fur, with a foxy black-and-white face, a great bushy tail of alternating black and white rings, golden eyes, monkey hands with straight needle-pointed claws, and habits that were both insanitary and obscene. For the greater part of the time she remained almost per- petually on heat; what was noticeable, however, was not so much the heat as the humidity. For the rest, she had some deep-seated psychosis that made her about as suitable a pet as a wild-caught leopard. For nine hundred and ninety-nine minutes out of every thousand she was as loving and gentle as any child might wish; for that remaining minute she was a killer, attacking without warning or *casus belli*, and always from behind. Her technique of inflicting grievous bodily harm was to spring from some high bookcase to one's shoulder – she could leap twenty feet without apparent effort – and claw for the eyes with the rending pins on her fingers. Whatever the early traumatic experience responsible for this hideous treachery, it was, I deduce, concerned in some way with windows, for each of her three attacks was launched when I was standing at a window, and, for one purpose or another, touching it; at the moment of the third and final outrage I was talking through the window to someone on the pavement outside.

I think I was fortunate not to have been killed by Kiko, for I ignored the danger signs for far too long. I chose to regard my slit eyelid as an accident, thinking that she had lost her balance and clawed without intent. The next time I defended my eyes with my hands, and as a result bear scars that I shall never lose, for her teeth were slashing instruments with razor-sharp edges. I excused this on the ground that she had interpreted my movement as a gesture of aggression. The next time I used my arms rather than my hands to cover my eyes, and Kiko lost balance and fell to the floor. She seemed to me to be making angry feints at my legs, but I was unaware of any actual contact before I noticed, with something very like panic, that I was standing in a large and rapidly widening puddle of blood. I knew that nothing but an artery could have produced that astonishing volume; I got out of the room somehow, and made for the bathroom, leaving behind me a trail of blood that appeared appropriate to a slaughterhouse. There I found that my tibial artery was sticking out of my calf like a black cigarette end, and spouting blood to a distance of more than a foot. I soaked a handkerchief and tried to apply a tourniquet, but my knowledge had deserted me; I could not remember the pressure point. At the end of several minutes' trying here and there I estimated that I had by now lost something like two pints of blood, and I wasted several more seconds trying to calculate how soon I should lose consciousness, for I was already beginning to feel weak and shaky. I made out that at the present rate of loss I had a little over five minutes, and I was searching wildly for some thread to tie the artery when I suddenly had a perfect mental picture of a huge wall chart showing the venous system in red and the arterial in blue. The tibial artery, of course, only surfaced at the groin. I got the tourniquet on and a cigarette lit and began to think about Kiko. The psychoanalysis of a lemur, I realized, would present insuperable problems. She now shares spacious accommodation with three other ring-tailed lemurs in the Chester Zoo. She is still mine, and once I hoped that she would breed and I might rear her offspring well sheltered from trauma, but now I feel that lemurs, sharing as they do a common ancestor with man, might require as careful choosing as do human friends.

After Kiko came a bush-baby, who, apart from the wholly misleading blood-curdling shriek with which he would nightly challenge the sleeping jungle of Chelsea, turned out to be a really crashing bore; his hobbies, moreover, were solitary and embarrassing. Later, after he had moved onto less exacting ownership than mine, I was offered another with the curious but most appropriate name of Hitchcock; though he proved, in fact, to have been christened by the surname of his owners, it was a reminder, and I declined.

I did not experiment with any other animals; none of these creatures, had, anyway, the least affinity with Camusfeàrna. I acquired, instead, a baker's dozen of small, brilliant tropical birds, who flew at liberty about my sitting-room; they proved to be both less insanitary and less dangerous than Kiko.

If Camusfeàrna had lacked one obvious element of conventional romance it was buried treasure, not symbolic treasure, but the hard practical glitter of coins in the peat. Now, but alas during my year of absence, the lily was thus gilded. Two forestry workers, digging ditches on the hillside above the house, came upon a small hoard of coins, hidden or dropped, together with fragments of hide in which they had been once contained. The were for the most part coins of the sixteenth century, of Mary Tudor, Philip and Mary, Elizabeth, and James I, and one, the largest of them all, a dollar piece of Frederick Ulric Duke of Brunswick and Luneburg; the savings, probably, of some soldier of fortune, a mercenary who, like many Highlanders of old, had sold his sword and his courage to the service of foreign commanders. The cache, if cache it was rather than a purse hurriedly hidden when the enemy was already in sight, must have been a secret kept to himself; and whether he died fighting in some far-off land or in the bitter, vicious skirmishes of clan warfare, his treasure had thereafter remained undisturbed for more than three centuries.

In the early spring of the following year I made up my mind to go back to Camusfeàrna. There, with the cold, bright March weather shining on the landscape that had long become my real home, I found myself assailed again by echoes of the emptiness that I had experienced when Mij was killed; dimly at first, and then clear and undisguised, came the thought that the place was incomplete without an otter, that Mij must have a successor; that, in fact, there must always be an otter at Camusfeàrna for as long as I occupied the house.

Having at last made up my mind, I turned all my attention to this end. With vivid recollection of my slavery to Mij's exigence, I wrote first to the zoological friends who had offered to find an otter-keeper for me, and then began a systematic examination of all the holts I knew up and down the coast from Camusfeàrna. One of the chain of islands leading out from the bay is called Otter Island, and on it is a tumbled cairn of big boulders forming a system of low caves much used by otters; in an earlier year, before I had become as it were otter-conscious, there had been a litter of cubs there. But now, though several of the inner chambers had been well ordered and lined with fresh bedding, there was no sign of young, and the public lavatory was little used. There is a lavatory at every otter holt, and the excrement (which is known as 'spraint', and has no offensive odour, being composed almost entirely of crunched fish bones, or, in the case of shore-living otters, of fragments of crab carapace) often forms a high pyramidal pile; on the very top of one such I remember seeing, in that year when the cubs were on Otter Island, a tiny caterpillar of spraint whose deposition must have been an acrobatic feat for the tottering cub.

One by one I visited all the holts of which I knew, but there seemed no otters breeding in the Camusfeàrna area. I did not despair of acquiring a cub locally, for otters have no 'breeding season', and cubs have been found in every month of the year, but as a second string I wrote to Robert Angorly in Basra, and asked if he could arrange with the Marsh Arabs to get me another of Mij's species.

In response to Angorly's request the Marsh Arabs brought in a succession of cubs, three of which were *Lutrogale perspicillata maxwelli*, but each in turn died within a few days of arrival. This he at last put down to the fact that for days before arrival they had been tended by ungentle and inexpert hands; now he said flatly that he would accept no cub that had been more than twelve hours captive. As a result, the next cub lived, and in late June he wrote to tell me that I could arrange her transport to England when I liked. She was not, he said, a Maxwell's otter, but he personally believed her to belong to yet another undiscovered race. She lived in the house, and was as playful and friendly as any dog.

With this apparent certainty of a successor to Mij, I began to make elaborate preparations, for I was anxious to make the fullest use of my hard-earned experience. My early enquiries for an otter-keeper had at last borne fruit, and now I was able to engage Jimmy Watt, a boy leaving school, who, though without first-hand knowledge of otters, had a profound natural feeling for animals and a desire to work with them. In London I had a large glass tank erected in the garden.

I had arranged for the otter to be flown from Basra to London on Thursday, July 10th, but the glazing of this tank was still uncompleted on the preceding Monday, and I telegraphed to Angorly asking him to postpone despatch until the same flight on Tuesday the 15th.

On Monday, July 14th, revolution swept Iraq, and on that Tuesday they were playing football with the Crown Prince's head in the streets of Baghdad. Of Robert Angorly, who by nature of his office as chief game warden numbered as one of the tyrant's personal entourage, I have heard no word since.

.   .   .

One incident stands out from that golden, Mediterranean summer at Camusfeàrna, a summer spoiled only by my own small vacuum of frustration, my little foxes that spoiled the vines and robbed my loved landscape of its full stimulus.

This was a spectacle of such magnificence and magnitude that it should, perhaps, have quelled in me an obsession as freakish as the desire for the companionship of a particular species of wild animal. Often before I had seen the Northern Lights, the Aurora Borealis, flicker and tremble across the silent night sky above the mountains, but never, until that night, had I understood their fearful majesty, or the sense of utter negation that they could bring.

Tex Geddes, who had been my fellow harpoon-gunner in the Island of Soay Shark Fisheries, had come over to visit me from Soay, which he had bought when the venture was over. He left his boat anchored in the bay before the house, and we found so much to talk about that it was late at night when he remembered the time. The curtains were drawn and the lamps lit, and we had no knowledge of anything strange taking place in the outside world. Tex went out of the door in front of me, and I was still inside when I heard his voice.

'For Christ's sake! This must be the end of the world – they're shooting down the moon with Sputniks or something!'

Over his shoulder I looked out upon a sky that seemed, indeed, alight with some awful doom. We were standing, it appeared, under a stupendous conical canopy, in the arena, perhaps, of a cosmic circus, where infinitely far overhead a multicoloured tent of light hung from a single point; or a tremendous magnification of a sight familiar during the war, when one stood at the centre of a circle from all of whose circumference searchlights were trained upon a single aircraft. But now the beams of the searchlights were each miles wide, shot with red and purple and green and blue, sheets of ice and of fire moving and merging with a terrible and remote grandeur.

Here and there the rays were interrupted and jagged, like the splintered wood of a snapped plank, but they soared up always towards that central point to join a coppery, dully-glowing ring of light. As we watched, the colours began to slide and to change; now the whole northern sky was red, while to the west it became a cold splendour of glacial green. Of all the natural sights that I have seen it was at the same time the most beautiful and the most terrible; it awoke in me some ancient racial animism, so that I felt that I could throw myself prostrate to worship and to placate.

. . .

In the autumn I made another attempt to acquire an otter, but by now with diminishing hope. A friend arranged to import, through a London dealer, two Indian Clawless otters; he was to keep one and I the other. They were described as being young and tame, a male and a female.

They were due to arrive at London Airport at about one o'clock in the morning, and such was our anxiety for their welfare that we were there to meet them. There was, however, no trace of them, and, reflecting that they were consigned to a dealer to whom they represented hard cash, we returned to bed. We telephoned to the dealer as soon as his premises were open, and were told that the otters had arrived and would be ready for collection at any time after two o'clock. We got there, more from eagerness than from any suspicion, at one-thirty; the crate was standing still unopened, as it had stood since the small hours of the morning. The two occupants were feeble, shivering, soaked in their own dung and urine, and almost too weak to stand. They died early the next day, mine in the new zoo hospital, and my friend's in his wife's lap; she had sat up all night trying to coax the pathetic little creature back to life.

. . .

It is, of course, precisely those people who find such incidents the most repugnant that by their patronage keep alive the nauseating market in wild animals, and after this I was determined that I would try no more importing of otters through normal channels.

These misfortunes might in themselves have deterred one less obsessed than I, but there was yet another in store, more tantalizing even than its predecessors, for this time all obstacles seemed already to have been surmounted. A veterinary officer from Singapore presented a hand-reared, house-living pet otter to an English zoo. The news of this action reached me immediately, and I at once offered an exchange for the abominable Kiko, whose market value was some four times that of the otter. My offer was accepted in writing, and I travelled south from Camusfeàrna to take delivery. During the twenty-four hours occupied by my journey, however, a friend of mine, all unaware of the transaction, set about trying to obtain the otter for me, and to this end contacted the previous owner, who was spending a brief holiday in the north of England. For some reason this gentleman was determined that his pet should remain behind bars (with no more water, incidentally, than it could drink); and there, owing to the resulting fracas, and a regrettable timidity on the part of officials of the zoo concerned, it remains to this day.

After this third disappointment I made up my mind to rear a cub in Scotland, and with that end in view I returned to Camusfeàrna, for a prolonged stay, in the spring of 1959.

I had been there for no more than a week when there occurred by far the strangest episode in the saga of my efforts to replace Mijbil, a coincidence so extravagant, partaking so insolently of the world of fiction, that had it been unwitnessed or in another land I should hesitate to record it.

On April 19th I motored to the station, thirty-odd miles away, to meet an arriving guest, a foundation guest, as it were, who over many visits had constructed much of the Camusfeàrna furniture, and who with me had watched the house grow from an empty shell. I arrived very early in the village, to do some necessary shopping, and had lunch in the hotel, a large and exceedingly glossy hotel that caters for the most moneyed element of the tourist trade; in the summer it is loud with Cadillacs and transatlantic accents. Now, however, it was comparatively empty; and on falling into conversation with the hall porter I found that we had many acquaintances in common. He remembered my shark-fishing boat the *Sea Leopard*; we shared affectionate memories of Captain Robertson of the island steamer *Lochmor*, who, because of a voice pitched in an almost supersonic key, had been commonly known as Squeaky.

We exchanged stories about Squeaky, and it transpired that I knew one that he had never heard. It dated from the war years; Squeaky had been sailing northwards from Barra in a thick white mist, and there was among his passengers a certain admiral, spending his leave in the Hebrides. Peering from the boat deck into the enveloping white screen, the admiral thought the ship on a course to lead her into a minefield, and as the minutes passed and the *Lochmor* churned on unheedingly he grew more and more apprehensive. At length his alarm became so acute that he decided to beard the captain on the bridge. The two had never met, and Squeaky was quite unaware that he was carrying a high-ranking naval officer. Gazing glassily ahead with his remarkably protuberant blue eyes, and dreaming perhaps of happy deals in coupon-free Harris tweed at the northern extremity of his run, he was suddenly outraged to observe standing at his elbow a stocky little man in a raincoat and a Homburg hat. Squeaky was an habitually irascible man, and he exploded.

'Ket off my plutty pridge, you pugger!' he shouted in a voice like that of an angry wren.

The admiral remembered that he was in civilian clothes, apologized, and introduced himself. Squeaky, though by nature no respecter of persons, was impressed.

'An Atmiral, is it? And what could I be toing for you, Atmiral?'

'Well – Captain Robertson – I wondered whether you would be kind enough to give me our position.'

'Position? Ach, well, we're chust here or hereabouts.'

'No, no, Captain, I meant our position on the chart.'

'Is it a chart?' shrilled Squeaky. 'I haven't seen a chart for forty years!'

The admiral was insistent. 'Ach, well, Atmiral, if you're so keen to be

seeing a chart, come down to my capin and have a wee tram, and we'll
see what we can find you.'

The two went below to the captain's cabin, and after the 'wee tram'
Squeaky began to rout about in his chart drawer. There were charts of
the Indian Ocean and the China Sea, charts of Polar seas and of the
Caribbean, of the English Channel and the Skagerrak; at last, seemingly
at the very bottom of the drawer, he discovered a chart of the Minch. He
spread this on the table, adjusted his spectacles, and at length planted a
stubby foreinger a few miles north of Eriskay.

'Well, Atmiral, it's hereabouts we are, and this is our course
northwards.'

The admiral stared ominously at a sparkling of black dots right in the
ship's path. 'What,' he asked bleakly, 'are these?'

Squeaky peered. 'Those plack tots? Well, if they're rocks we're
puggered for sure, but if they're what I *think* they are, which is fly-shit,
we're right as rain!'

I have digressed to recount the whole of this anecdote, partly because
it is irresistible, and partly because the sharing of this joke and of other
memories with the hall porter had a direct bearing upon the dream-like
happenings of two hours later. Had we not in those few minutes
discovered the bond of mutual friends and recollections, those extraordinary events would never have taken place.

I met my guest on the station platform, and we returned to the hotel
for what Squeaky would have called a 'wee tram' before setting off for
Camusfeàrna. We sat in the sun-lounge that overlooks the sea, but we
were well back from the window, and out of sight of the gravel sweep
beyond the glass. Suddenly the hall porter came running over to us from
the hall.

'Mr Maxwell!' he called. 'Mr Maxwell! Come quick to the door and
tell me what's this strange beast outside – quick!'

I have an open mind on the subject of so-called telepathy and
extrasensory perception in general; I have had one or two curious
experiences, but none quite as strange as the overwhelming and instant
certainty that I felt then of what I was going to see. Whether that
certainty communicated itself from me to my guest, or whether he had a
separate moment of clairvoyance, he too had a sudden and vivid
knowledge of what was outside the door.

Four people were walking past the hotel, making for a car parked near
to the jetty. At their heels lolloped a large, sleek otter, of a species that I
had never seen, with a silvery-coloured head and a snow-white throat
and chest. I had a deep feeling of unreality, of struggling in a dream.

I rushed up to the party, and began to jabber, probably quite incoherently, about Mijbil and how he had been killed, and about how time and time again my efforts to find a successor had been frustrated at the eleventh hour. I must have been talking a great deal, because what they were saying in reply took a long time to sink in, and when it did the sense of dreaming increased almost to the point of vertigo.

'. . . only eight months old and always been free, house trained, comes and goes as she likes . . . brought her up myself with a bottle. In six weeks we've got to go back to West Africa, so it looked like a zoo or nothing – what else could we do? Everyone admires her, but when they come to the point of actually owning her they all shy off . . . Poor Edal, it was breaking my heart. . .'

We were sitting on the steps of the hotel by this time, and the otter was nuzzling at the nape of my neck – that well-remembered, poignant touch of hard whiskers and soft face-fur.

By the time I had taken in what her owners, Dr Malcolm Macdonald and his wife, from Torridon, were saying, the party had dwindled by two; it transpired that the only reason why they had been in the village at all was to give a lift to two foreign girl hikers whose destination it was. And the only reason that I was there was to meet my guest, and the only reason that the Macdonalds and I had met at all was that two hours earlier I had made the acquaintance of the hall porter and exchanged reminiscences about Squeaky Robertson. I had not sat near enough to the window to see the otter for myself, and if he had not called me they would have passed by the hotel and gone home to Torridon, and I should have finished my drink ten minutes later and gone home to Camusfeàrna.

Ten days later Edal became mine, and there was once more an otter at Camusfeàrna, playing in the burn and sleeping before the hearth.

CHAPTER 12

Malcolm Macdonald has set down for me the circumstances of Edal's early life, and the chain of events that led, on his side, to the strange climax of our meeting, the meeting of the only man in the British Isles who was trying desperately to find a home for a pet otter with the only man who was searching, with equal desperation, for an otter.

'She came on August 23rd 1958.
'For the past year we had been living, my wife Paula and I, on a mature rubber plantation in the Niger Delta region of West Africa. Our

nearest town was Sapele, two miles away and across the Benin river. The house we lived in was old, and built in the rambling barn-like style of half a century ago. It stood in a compound which generations of planters had filled with a profusion of flowering shrubs and fruit trees. We shared it with a motley collection of animal waifs and strays, and in their company we were never lonely.

'Paula had been shopping in Sapele that morning, and she came back from the riverside like the Pharaoh's daughter with a little bundle in her arms.

'"Just look what I've got!"

'The bundle parted and there was a plump broad silvery muzzle spiked with stiff translucent whiskers. Two hazy puppy eyes were struggling to open.

'We gazed down on her enraptured and smoothed her velvety coat.

'Under the funny flat face a little pink mouth appeared with brand-new needlepoints of teeth. It emitted an astonishingly loud demand to be fed. While Paula set off on a frantic rush to collect feeding-bottle and teat, milk and boiled water, I tried to comfort this strange new waif.

'Priscilla came up and looked on in calm enquiry. Priscilla was a half-Alsatian bitch. The composition of the other half was open to speculation and she was about a year old. Very soon after our arrival at Sapele she had turned up from God knows where, a spindly-legged, pot-bellied, thoroughly ugly and very sick puppy. We took her in, and she recovered to stay with us and grow into a beautiful animal, a constant friend and a natural guard dog.

'Now Priscilla took upon herself a most important function, which was probably vital to the successful rearing of the newcomer.

'Responding to the little creature's cries for help, gently but firmly and with a somewhat officious air, she nuzzled the cloth aside and licked. She was rewarded with a positive explosion of wind and a stream of excrement. The cub's cries became less desperate, though they persisted until feeding was accomplished, and Priscilla sat back and looked smug.

'Disappointment is all too often the lot of people who attempt to rear very young animals, and frequently it is due to lack of the very necessary maternal service which Priscilla so kindly provided. In the absence of an obliging bitch gentle massage with a moist finger will serve.

'In due course the bottle was prepared. Paula took the cub into the crook of her arm and offered her the rubber teat; as soon as she tasted the milk she sucked avidly, but she was soon satisfied, taking little more than an ounce, and fell into a deep contented sleep.

'While she slept we took stock of the situation.

'At the end of her morning's shopping in Sapele Paula had noticed

several Africans standing arguing around one of their number who held
a box containing, it seemed to her at first, a couple of very young
puppies. Their talk caught her interest.
' "Which kind of beef dis?" said one.
' "Na tree-bear," answered another.
' "At all," said a third. "Dis na rabbit." (Rabbit is the local name for a
species of big rat.) A fourth was emphatic in his disbelief.
' "Na lie," he said.
'Paula's curiosity overcame her and she went to see for herself. At the
same time a senior African joined the group. "This be the piccin of
water-dog," he intoned, settling the controversy for good.
'It transpired that two young fishermen had come upon the holt in a
river bank and heard the cubs inside. So the cubs were dug out, and it is
certain that if they had been old enough to show the least hostility they
would have been done to death there and then. However, being
obviously harmless and too small to be of much consequence as "beef"
they were carried off unharmed to Sapele. It is well known there that
some Europeans have a kind of "craze for head" which induces them to
part with ludicrously large sums of money for useless beasts – particularly if the beasts are small and helpless and sure to die if left.
'There were two cubs, a male and a female. The female was larger and
lighter in colour than the male. It seemed somewhat stronger and more
advanced, too, in that its eyes were beginning to open. Both cubs were a
silvery-grey colour, lighter at the head, with creamy white throats and
"shirt-fronts". At each side the white was sharply divided from the grey
at a line which extended from the angle of the jaw to the shoulder. Their
tails were no thicker than an ordinary pencil.
'After much palaver Paula secured possession of the female cub for the
single pound note she had with her and extracted a promise that should
the other cub not be sold to a European within a very short time it would
be brought to our house. The other cub was, in fact, bought by an
amateur animal collector who, a few weeks later, took his entire
collection to a zoo in England which he held in high esteem. The cub,
however, died later of a cerebral haemorrhage.
'Now we had an otter to bring up. Our knowledge of otters was
virtually nil. They are rarely seen in West Africa, for cover is abundant
and they are mainly nocturnal in habit; once, however, we had had the
good fortune to see a pair of Cameroons otters. We were staying at an oil-
palm plantation in the southern part of the British Cameroons, and one
evening we stood upon a promontory of high ground at a remote edge of
the plantation. Below us on our left there was a big river running in
spate. From its far bank the dense black rain forest stretched for endless

unknown miles into the heart of Africa. Directly below us, from a waterfall to our right, a clear stream flowed through deep pools to join the river. The brief equatorial dusk was beginning.

'Among the rocks below the waterfall two brown figures were playing, indistinct at that distance. For several minutes they sported together, sometimes upright, sometimes rolling on the smooth bare rocks. Then taking cleanly to the water, they swam with magnificent sinuous grace through the clear calm pools a hundred feet below us. Unmistakably otters they were then, but so big that our native otters must seem pygmies by comparison. They were not less than five feet from nose to tip of tail, lithe and powerful, a breathtaking sight.

'We wondered if our little cub might grow so big. We guessed then that she was two weeks old; now we think that she had been born a month.

'Two hours after her first meal with us she wakened and struggled free of the towel which was her temporary bed. Using her stubby loose-jointed limbs as oars she rowed herself along on her sleek belly. She was pleased to receive our attentions and took another small feed, made up of one part of ordinary canned evaporated milk with two parts of boiled and cooled water added. This was a pretty strong mixture and when, as did occur in the first two or three weeks, the cub had diarrhoea we diluted it by simple rule of thumb reckoning. In any case we came to the conclusion that some looseness of the bowels with mucus is normal to an infant otter. The mixture was served at a little above body heat, i.e. perceptibly warm to the touch at elbow or back of wrist.

'In the first two or three weeks she slept most of the time, as infants do. She grew rapidly, and almost with every awakening one could see the development of her strength and co-ordination of movement. In all five senses her range of perception increased in proportion; her eyes opened wider and rounder and their smokiness cleared. Movements attracted her; she came to recognize her bottle and would stretch out her hands to hold it.

'They were fascinating, those hands. The stubby fingers were strong and mobile and only slightly webbed. At the tip of each pink finger there was a tiny depression, the vestigial representative of a claw. Her hands were important to her; she used them to investigate every new object, and as she grew older they developed amazing dexterity.

'Edal, as we called her, had an instinct for cleanliness, and always on waking she would struggle away from her bed for toilet purposes. We occupied only the cool upper floor of our house, and feared for her safety, so we made her a day-bed in a beer crate. Crumpled copies of the airmail *Daily Telegraph* made an excellent disposable, absorbent base, and soft cotton cloths made the bed proper. There she had comfort and freedom from draughts and room to move about and keep dry.

'The nights at that season were chilly, and when we went to bed she slept in a nest between our pillows. There was many a frantic rush when a squeaky "Whee, whee" proclaimed that she was stirring.

'For the first two or three days we fed her two-hourly, with one or more feeds in the night as she demanded them. And those feeds had to be just right. An indignant crescendo "Wheeeeeeeee" soon told us if the bottle were cold. Time passed; the intervals between feeds extended to four hours, and the night feeds were stopped. The quantity she took at each feed increased to six ounces.

'When feeding, Edal liked to lie on her back in the crook of one's arm. Tightly holding the neck of the bottle she would squirm with pleasure as she sucked, thrusting back hard with her little round head. Priscilla and the kitten Stinky Pooh and sometimes the elegant black tom-cat Sooty would gather round, waiting for the milk that would be left when Edal was satisfied. Squeezing the Polythene feeding-bottle produced a fine stream of milk. Stinky Pooh was expert at catching the jet; with tongue oscillating briskly and ears pinned back she never missed a drop. Poor Priscilla just could not compete. With her tongue flapping wildly and her bottom shuffling with embarrassment she would get milk up her nose, into her eyes, anywhere but into her big mouth. Sooty was none too clever either and would stalk away angrily, flipping a disdainful paw.

'Edal now slept all night in her own little bed beside ours. At about six o'clock the first houseboy to come in would carry her out to join Priscilla for a short time, whilst her first feed and our own morning tea were prepared. Throughout this time Priscilla devotedly assisted with her personal hygiene, and I am sorry to say that Edal responded only with indignation and base ingratitude.

'We were particularly pleased with our "boys". They had been accustomed enough to tending our animals, but to Edal they became almost as devoted as we.

'We were more than amply rewarded for those broken nights. As she grew and took on her proper otter shape and became an active member of the household she was delightful. By the end of September she was about eighteen inches long, a scampering, merry little otter cub.

'When first introduced to the bath Edal yelled with fright. It took a great deal of talking and soothing to convince her that an otter should like water, but soon she found that it was great fun to splash about in an inch or two of cool water. Not bad stuff to drink, either.

'Over a period of days we made her baths gradually deep enough for real swimming. With a supporting hand at first she learned that she could swim. Industriously paddling round she would look up with the most comical expression. Well! Just look at me!

'As we laughed back at her she positively grinned. "Wheee-eee." This was living.

'How she loved that bath. She learned to swim under water and do corkscrew rolls. With a thrust of her broad webbed feet she would lunge forward out of the water and belly-flop. She loved, too, to play peek-a-boo over the edge of the bath, diving quick as a flash. She gathered a collection of bath toys, all sorts of odds and ends, though her favourite was a plastic pint measure. First she would sink it; then, drawing a deep breath, she would thrust her head into it and swim with it clattering around the bath.

'When she tired she would come to the side to be lifted out and dried. Sometimes she would take over-long in tiring and the bath attendant for the occasion would take the plug out. This was an eternal mystery to Edal. Where did that water go? She would thrust her muzzle into the hole, poke her fingers through the grid, sit on it. Finally, the water gone, she would peer wistfully after it and look up enquiringly. Then, accepting the situation with her usual good humour, she would come and be dried.

'She loved laughter and would positively join in, grinning and prancing.

'Her basic conversational vocabulary was a high-pitched whistling "Whee". With loud and soft, short and long and other variations of "Whees" she had quite a lot to say and said it. We came to understand much of it. Two expressions in particular we knew. "Wheeeee-uk" said "I want some water in the bath", and several anxious chirping "whees" suggested a swift trip to the garden.

'She had to be introduced gently to the out-of-doors. It was just too BIG out there. From her lavatory patch she would toddle anxiously back to the safety of the doorway. There she would pause and turn, head down and wary, as ancestral memories stirred of the lurking enemies of her race. Then her white throat would gleam as her head rose high and she would stand poised with one arm flexed for a final reassuring look round.

'She very quickly learned to scramble up the stairs to our living-room, one laborious step after another, and was always patently glad to be back. This was her home, and she accepted us as her parents who loved her and laughed with her and provided all she required. And her greatest requirement was our company. In her waking hours she would never willingly let us out of her sight. It was a requirement we found easy to fulfil, for we never tired of hers.

'Her playmates lived here too. Priscilla played with Edal kindly and patiently, but it was in Stinky Pooh that she found a real kindred spirit. Stinky Pooh was one of those starry-eyed fluffy sedate-little-girl kittens who surprise you by behaving like tom-boys. She and Edal would roll and tumble in ferocious mock battles, and their greatest joy was a friendly squabble over a ball of screwed-up paper.

'The grey parrot wasn't really a playmate. A glutton for petting himself he was jealous of the little stranger. He had come to us as "dash" – pidjin English for a present – and, not knowing at first that he was a cock bird, we called him Polly. As the youngsters roistered on the floor Polly would watch them with his pale cold eyes. Like a crotchety old Giles schoolmaster he would hobble across the room and, pecking them indiscriminately, would take away their paper ball. Carrying it to his perch by the window he would moodily tear it to shreds.

'Poor Polly; when Edal grew a little older he met his deserts. One day he fled squawking while she, munching on a mouthful of red tail feathers, registered sheer delight.

'We kept three monkeys then. Two were mere lodgers whom we looked after whilst their mistress was away, and they spent nearly all their time in a big wire cage in the compound. The third was a Mona monkey we had reared ourselves.

'She had been found clinging to the thick back hair of her mother's corpse. The native hunter who slew the mother for sale as "beef" brought the pathetic infant to our house. Paula, ever an easy victim to this form of moral blackmail, gave him a few shillings for her. She was a tiny wizened creature, almost bald and toothless, with terror standing in her shiny brown eyes, and her little body was chafed and sore with the coarse raffia string that bound her. It is a hard-hearted person indeed who will not spare a shilling or two to take such unfortunates from their pedlars – if only to grant them the mercy of dying in peace.

'We called the tiny monkey Oweenk, from her own plaintive cry. She snuggled into Paula's neck, grateful for a little love and protection.

'Paula fed her on very dilute milk from an eye dropper and she thrived. By the time Edal came Oweenk was nearly a foot tall and a pain in the neck. We could allow her full liberty for only a short time each day and then only under close supervision. She wore a small dog-collar around her waist and spent the greater part of each day on a long string in the garden.

'These monkeys are very affectionate in their own crazy way. They love to cling to one and hate to be alone. But they are full of sin. At liberty in a house they leave a trail of devastation, and little can be done to teach them good behaviour. In illustration of this there is a story of a man who set about house-training one. Diligently, when the monkey messed, he would seize it, slap its backside, and toss it out of the window. After some weeks his efforts bore fruit. The monkey would mess on the floor, slap its own backside, and jump out of the window.

'When Oweenk was first allowed to meet the toddling Edal she danced and chattered with delight. She cuddled Edal in her arms and searched in her fur – much to Edal's chagrin – and wailed when they were separated. All too soon, monkey-wise, the loving turned to mischievous teasing and eventually they became enemies.

'To me the much-vaunted human affinity of the monkey wears thin in the presence of an otter, and as these two young creatures grew up together the comparison of their behaviour made a fascinating study.

'Edal's tactile handling of objects contrasted with Oweenk's frenzied manipulations; her joyful play with the monkey's staccato caperings. Gay friendliness contrasted with urchin familiarity, and innocent interest with acquisitive seeking. The contrasts were legion, but they all favoured the otter.

'With the month of October came tribulation. Edal shed her front incisor milk teeth and little buds of new white enamel appeared in their place. At the same time she became dissatisfied with her bottle. One afternoon when I went to the kitchen refrigerator for a cold drink she tried to scramble into it, snorting loudly and greatly excited. The cook had left some herring roes there and Edal wanted them. I cut them into strips for her and she ate them all. Soon the mystified manager of the Sapele Kingsway Shop wanted to know why on earth we wanted so many of his cold-store herrings. Edal was weaned.

'With proper parental pride we applauded these events, but then her eye teeth, the canines of her upper jaw, began to give her much trouble, and our jubilation changed to concern. For a week and more she was fretful and nagged with pain. She would lie on the floor or in her bed "wheeing" plaintively and rummaging in her mouth with her hands. She would come and plead for help and comfort, gnawing one's fingers. At night she sought comfort in Paula's bed; her sleep was fitful and disturbed, and many times a day she called to be put in the bath to cool her fevered body and soothe her aching mouth. Her body lost its sleek roundness and her fur its silvery sheen. She ate little and that without enthusiasm, and blankly refused to return to bottle feeds. And yet, in her easier moments, she would find a little toy and feebly play.

'Nor was this all. At the same time we were horrified to see that her right eye was badly inflamed, the cornea blue and swollen. But this condition too was transitory, for it responded satisfactorily to an eye-drop formula and after a few more wretched days the tooth on the left side came away. She took on a new lease of life, eating prodigiously, playing gaily, and sleeping soundly. She grew sleek again, and her coat gleamed. There were minor recurrences of her eye trouble into the early part of November; then the last recalcitrant tooth separated, and her childish ailments were over.

'We engaged a local native fisherman, an old man with a permanently disgruntled expression. His fish he caught in basket traps set overnight, and each morning he brought them alive in a bucket from the Jameson river. Edal had usually demolished them all by night, and we supplemented her diet with butter, eggs, and fresh liver.

'The only people I met who had seen otters, other than the nocturnal fishermen, were workers upon an oil-palm plantation which I visited. Part of the plantation lay close to the Benin river bank and sometimes at dawn they surprised "water-dogs" foraging for the oil and vitamin-rich palm fruit. Edal, however, preferred butter.

'The diet we gave her seemed satisfactory, for she grew well, and was always bursting with high good humour. Nothing escaped her interest, and everything was examined for its possibilities as a plaything. Bottles were just made to be rolled upon and a box of matches was treasure-trove. She appeared to derive enormous satisfaction from scattering a boxful of matches and then packing them, one by one, into the toe of a slipper. Finally she would thrust her arm through the cover of the box and wear it like an outsize bangle. All this made life pretty lively when I settled down to relax with a drink and cigarettes at night.

'Her appetite was astounding. She took a great interest in our own meals and attended regularly at table for titbits. She rejected all cooked meats except pork and ham, liked some vegetables, especially runner beans, enjoyed pastry, and was frantically fond of ice cream. She would take a piece in both hands and cram it into her mouth, making ecstatic little mewing noises and getting thoroughly messy. When offered a tasty morsel she really wanted she would moan softly and "hurrrh" through her nose before taking it.

'She drank frequently and spent a great deal of her time in the bathroom, for when not actually in the bath she liked to take her day-time naps there. She liked a towel to sleep on, and if one were not already provided she would help herself, pulling one down from the towel-rail and dragging it off to a quiet corner. Bunching it up beneath her she would worry at it until she found a suitable part to suck; then she would suck at it with tremendous fervour, eyes shut tight, mewing and snuffling and waggling her rump until she fell asleep.

'By now the stairs were no longer an obstacle to her, and she could go out and in at will. From Priscilla she learned to recognize the sound of my car, and when I returned home in the afternoons they both would come rushing out in a riotous welcome, competing to be first. Edal would seize Priscilla by a hind paw, making her turn around, then dash between her legs to gain a yard or so.

'She joined our evening walks with Priscilla and Oweenk and the cats. When we left the house she became very wary, staying close to heel and snorting in alarm at any sudden movement, with an inborn awareness, it seemed, of the persecution to which her race is subject.

'Even at home she was apt to wail and squirm with apprehension when a stranger entered the house, and she would have to be reassured with a few soothing words and the touch of a hand, for she looked to us at all times for protection and guidance.

'In nature she would have enjoyed a relatively long period of parental care; now the responsibility was ours to see that she did not want for understanding and sympathy.

'So long as she felt safe she was the most charmingly amiable and playful of creatures, but there was nothing submissive about her friendliness; it was always on a basis of mutual esteem. She made many friends, for there were few visitors to our house who were not captivated by her, and she was gentle and affectionate with children.

'The New Year came, and we began to be anxious for the future of our protégée. We were due to return to the United Kingdom at the beginning of March, and although several kind people offered to keep her we hated the thought of abandoning her. She had no tradition of domesticity behind her, and, although her wild instincts were so well reconciled with her life with us, she might not be able to establish the same harmony with others. She was still very young; her reactions in those circumstances were unpredictable, for she was deeply attached to us, as indeed were we to her. At that time we were half-persuaded that the best eventual home for her would be a good zoo, where she would receive the best of care from professional animal-keepers, but we have since been sadly disillusioned on that score.

'One afternoon I was to meet Paula at the Sapele ferry. Edal followed me to the car so I took her along with some idea of accustoming her to travelling. At first she was nervous in the car, clinging anxiously to my neck and pressing hard against me. I drove slowly down to the waterside, talking to her all the while, and persuading her that she had nothing to fear.

'We sat waiting near to the ferry pier, at peace with the world. An African girl with a basket of peppers on her head sauntered by singing.

'As she saw Edal the basket teetered and her eyes dilated wide. She yelled.

'"Yah! Look um! Look de beef!"
'In seconds a jabbering crowd surrounded us.
'"Eh! Look um!"
'"Look 'e'n teeth!"
'"Dem pass dog own!"
'"'E fit to bite man proppah!"
'"How 'e no de bite white man?"
'"Ah! Dis na docitah. I t'ink say 'e gie um injection."
'A seamy-faced character in tattered shorts, evidently a fisherman, pushed into the crowd.
'"Eh Heh! Na watta-dog! 'E keel feesh fo' watta! 'E bad fo' we! If 'e get chance 'e savvy bite man too much!"
'I had started the engine, and as I let in the clutch our knowledgeable friend was expounding the culinary properties of young otters.
'"As 'e dead now, 'e sweet to chop ..."

. . .

'It was decided that Edal should come with us. Polly was to come as well. In the short time remaining I obtained the import permit from London and booked aircraft space. Edal was required to travel in a ventilated box and Polly in a light travelling cage.
'We started the journey on an appallingly hot day in early March with a flight from Benin to Lagos. The small aircraft was like an oven in the blistering midday sun. Throughout the flight the air was turbulent, and the plane was tossed about like a small boat in a storm. We were terribly anxious for Edal.
'At Lagos she was unconscious and on the point of death. We rushed her to our rest home; her limp body was fiercely hot, her breathing intermittent and gasping, and her heart fluttered feebly as she struggled for life in the last stage of heat exhaustion. We placed her on her back in the bath in an inch of cool water, moistened her parched mouth, and bathed her limbs with iced water from the refrigerator.
'When her condition became a little less desperate we placed her on a wet towel under the fan in our shaded bedroom. While Paula went into the city for some essential shopping I stayed beside Edal and went on bathing her and moistening her mouth with iced water. Very slowly the raging heat left her; she breathed more steadily, and her heart beat less frantically; then she lapsed into a deep sleep.
'In the evening I had to leave the room for a few minutes. The closing of the door must have disturbed her, for when I returned she had crept under a chair where she crouched bewildered and fearful. As I knelt to speak to her, relief and recognition shone in her eyes; weakly she reached up to cling to my neck, and mewed and nuzzled against my face.

'The following evening we joined a B.O.A.C. Stratocruiser bound for London. Edal was rested and well again, and I had given her a tranquillizing pill. She was to travel in a pressurized compartment below the forward passenger cabin. There was a refuelling stop at Kano before the long night flight across the Sahara and onto Rome.

'When we took her out at Kano we were delighted and relieved to find her sleepy and quite unperturbed. She followed us nonchalantly to the airport buildings, where she made friends with the aircraft's captain, and in the middle of a plot of grass – to call it a lawn would be flattery – she found a watering point and played happily with the jet.

'We gave her another tranquillizer and she must have slept throughout the night, for we heard no more of her until we were over the Channel and descending towards London. Then she began to whistle and cry; the steward was sympathetic but Edal's compartment was inaccessible in flight.

'In the Customs hall there was the usual milling throng of sleepy passengers and bustling baggage porters. A saturnine Customs Officer looked through our sheaf of import and export licences and veterinary certificates and chalked our baggage without spoken comment. Friends were waiting outside with a car. Polly was quite debonair, fluttering his flame-red tail and wolf-whistling wickedly at the passers-by. A voice called, "Look out mate, yer arse is on fire!"

'Edal was in a pitiful state, thirsty and hungry and worn out from her struggles to escape; her fingers were raw and bleeding and there was an angry worn patch on her muzzle. Her ordeal was nearly over now, but there remained an overnight train journey to Inverness.

'At Euston the guard was understanding and helpful. He could not allow Edal to join us in the sleeping accommodation but he took her box into his own warm section of the van where a stove burned, and we were duly grateful.

'At Inverness the morning was crisp and bright. I took delivery of my car at the station and we headed for the country, pausing only to buy some fish for her. The day was fine and clear with the warmth of spring in the air, and we dawdled along towards the mountains of the western seaboard, revelling in the pastel highland hues after Africa's garish colours, and stopping often to let Edal investigate her new homeland. She was happy to be free with us again, and bore us no ill will for the horrors of the journey. She travelled well by car but was a restless passenger, scrambling from side to side to peer out of the windows.

'In the next few weeks, as the spring unfolded, I explored anew with Edal the seashore and the mountain burns that I had known in my childhood. Although she had recoiled at first from the biting chill of the water, our colder climate seemed to agree with her. On the ebb tides we dug the succulent clams from the sand and she learned to hunt for crabs and cobbler-fish among the rocks and tangle. She was still growing fast. When we left Nigeria she was three feet long and weighed fifteen pounds; by May she had grown by ten pounds and a good half dozen inches, and was immensely strong.

'Those were happy weeks indeed, but we were due to go to Ghana in June and again we began to worry about her future. Dearly as we loved to have her with us, the necessity for many more thousands of miles of travel made parting with her, at least for a time, inevitable. We were anxious to see her properly settled and in good hands before the time came for us to go.

'One beautiful morning in late April we set out to motor to the village of Plockton, near Kyle of Lochalsh. For most of the previous evening we had discussed what we might best do for Edal, and were miserable at the prospect of parting with her. We had been urged to lodge her in a particular zoo, and had been assured that she would be given every care and attention there. Still we recoiled from the idea, and could reach no decision.

'On the road to Plockton two foreign girls on a youth hostelling holiday hitched a lift with us. They wanted to go to Skye, and since the ferry was but a few miles off our route we elected to take them there.

'We made our usual intermittent progress, stopping every twenty miles or so to let Edal out for a while. In the early afternoon we stopped at the Lochalsh Hotel and wandered along the terrace, looking across to the hills of Skye. The gods were smiling on us that day, for they had taken the nagging question of Edal's future into their own hands. As we came abreast of the hotel door a figure bolted from it like a ferreted rabbit, laying a trail of whisky from the glass clutched forgotten in his hand, his whole attention fixed delightedly and incredulously on Edal.'

CHAPTER 13

Nothing was decided at that first meeting; Edal's owners not un-naturally wanted to satisfy themselves that this extraordinary co-incidence was all it seemed on the surface, and that she would find with me the home they wanted for her. They promised to write during the next few days; Edal jumped into their car with the ease of familiarity, and as they drove away she appeared leaning far out of the passenger window, one hand delicately shielding her windward ear.

A week later she visited Camusfeàrna for an afternoon; then, after an interval of ten days Malcolm and Paula came to stay for a week-end, to leave Edal with me when they went. I had not been idle during those ten days; I was determined to repeat none of the mistakes that had led, directly or indirectly, to Mij's death. I sent to Malcolm Macdonald a harness that had been made for Mij just before he was killed; with the help of Jimmy Watt I enclosed the house with a fence that might not, perhaps, have foiled Mij, but which would, I thought, be barrier enough to baffle this apparently more docile, less self-willed creature if she should think in the first days to seek her late foster parents; within these confines we dug a pool and piped to it water that rose in a fountain jet appropriate to more formal surroundings. The entrance to this enclosure, and thus to the house, we guarded by a double gate, the lowermost wood of which met a sheet of metal sunk into the ground against digging. I did not think that these precautions would be necessary for long; they were to make certain that during the period when she would inevitably fret and believe herself to belong elsewhere I should not lose her through any fault of my own.

Even during that first week-end, while I was still a stranger to her and her surroundings were unfamiliar, I was so enchanted by Edal that I found it difficult to believe my own good fortune. Because she did not feel herself to be in her own home I was able to see in those first days only a fraction of her fascination, a mere corner of the piquant personality I came to know later, but I saw enough to know that if I had searched the world over I could have found no more perfect successor to Mijbil.

· · ·

On the third day, while Edal was sleeping soundly on the sofa, Paula and Malcolm left silently. Our goodbyes were hushed, almost tacit, both because we did not want to awaken that softly-breathing ball of fur, and because something of their own feeling of unhappiness and betrayal had communicated itself to me, and in my long-postponed moment of triumph I felt not jubilation but sadness for the sundered family.

After they had gone Jimmy and I sat beside Edal on the sofa, waiting miserably for her awakening and the panic that we thought would follow the realization of her abandonment. An hour passed, two, and still she slept on. Presently Morag arrived; the Macdonalds had called at Druimfiaclach as they left, and told her that Edal might feel less lost and despairing in feminine company. So we three sat silently and anxiously, as around a sick bed, and my thoughts wandered between the sleeping animal and her late owners, for I had recognized in them the same obsessional feeling for their otter as I had experienced for Mij, and for nothing in the world would I have changed places with them as they drove home desolate now.

When Edal awoke at last she appeared to notice little amiss. Paula's jersey lay beside her on the sofa, her own towel and toys were on the floor, and if she was aware of her owners' absence she was too well-mannered a guest to comment upon it so early. Also, as was to be expected, she got on extremely well with Morag.

. . .

It is time to give a more detailed description of Edal as she was when she came to me early in May 1959.

By far the strangest and most captivating aspect of her was that of her hands. Unlike Mij, whose forepaws were, despite the dexterity he contrived with them, true paws with wide connecting webs between the digits, hers were monkey-hands, unwebbed, devoid of so much as a vestige of nail, and nearly as mobile as a man's. With them she ate, peeled hard-boiled eggs, picked her teeth, arranged her bed, and played for hours with any small object that she could find.

Once in a hospital in Italy I watched a cripple child practising the use of artificial hands. She had before her a solitaire board and a numbered set of marbles; the holes were numbered too, but the marbles had been wrongly placed, and her task was to transpose them until each ball and socket corresponded. She worked with complete absorption, oblivious of onlookers, and with each passing minute she discovered new powers. Once, too, I had watched a ball juggler practising his act with the same withdrawn inturned eye, the same absence of irritation or impatience at failure, the same apparent confidence of ultimate success.

Of both these Edal reminded me as she juggled with such small objects – marbles, clothes-pegs, matches, Biro pens – as could be satisfactorily contained within her small, prehensile grasp; she would lie upon her back passing them from hand to hand, or occasionally to the less adept grip of her webbed but almost nailless hind feet, working always with two or more objects at a time, gazing fixedly at them all the while, as though these extremities of hers were in some way independent of her and to be watched and wondered at. At moments it was clearly frustrating for her to require four feet upon which to walk, for she would retrieve a lost marble clutching it firmly in one hand – usually the right – and hobbling along upon her other three limbs.

Because, it seemed, of her delight in her own dexterity, it was her practice to insert her plaything of the moment into some container from which it had then to be extracted, a boot or a shoe for choice, and it mattered little to her whether this receptacle already contained a human foot. She would come hobbling across the room to me with some invisible treasure clenched in her right fist and thrust it into my shoe just below the ankle bone; on more than one occasion the foreign body thus introduced turned out to be a large and lively black beetle. She was also an adept, if not entirely imperceptible, pickpocket; with impatiently fumbling fingers she would reach disconcertingly into the trouser pockets of any guest who sat down in the house, hardly waiting for an introduction before scattering the spoils and hurrying away with as much as she could carry. With these curious hands she could, too, throw such playthings as were small enough to be enclosed by her fingers. She had three ways of doing this; the most usual was a quick upward flick of the arm and forepart of the body as she held her clenched fist palm downward, but she would also perform a backward flick which tossed the object over her shoulder to land at her other side, and, on occasion, usually when in a sitting position with her back supported, she would throw overarm.

Like Mij, she was an ardent footballer, and would dribble a ball round the room for half an hour at a time, but she had an additional accomplishment that Mij had not learned, for when she shot the ball wide or over-ran it she would sweep her broad tail round with a powerful scoop to bring it back within range of her feet.

For the rest she was a small, exceedingly heavy body inhabiting a rich fur skin many sizes too large for her. It cannot be described as a loose fit; it is not a fit at all. The skin appears to be attached to the creature inside it at six points only: the base of the nose, the four wrists or ankles, and the root of the tail. When lying at ease upon her back the surplus material may be observed disposed in heavy velvety folds at one or other side of her, or both; a slight pressure forward from the base of her neck causes the skin on her forehead to rise in a mountain of pleats like a furled plush curtain; when she stands upright like a penguin the whole garment slips downwards by its own inertia into heavy wrinkles at the base of her belly, giving her a non-upsettable, pear-shaped appearance.

She is thus able to turn, within surprisingly broad limits, inside her own skin, and should one attempt to pick her up by the scruff of the neck one is liable to find oneself gripping a portion of skin rightly belonging to some quite different part of her body, merely on temporary loan, so to speak, to the neck. The colour of the fur is the best guide to what really belongs where; her chest and throat are of yellow-tinged white – not pure white as I had thought when seeing her first in the sunshine – and here the pelt hangs in such positive bags of redundancy that she has a habit of gathering up this bib in her two hands and sucking it with an enjoyment that the fine plush texture makes wholly understandable. The bib is divided from a silvery, brocade-texture head by a sharp line of demarcation immediately below the ears; the body and the enormous tail are pale mauvish-brown, velvet above and silk below. Beyond the points of attachment at the four wrists the fur is of an entirely different character; it changes from velvet to satin, tiny, close-lying hairs that alter colour according to how the light falls upon them. The tightly gloved hands and the enormous fullness above the wrists give her the appearance of wearing heavy gauntlets; watching her lolloping out for her morning walk with Jimmy Watt I have thought that she resembled nothing so much as a very expensive woman taking no chances on the weather at a point-to-point meeting.

Her comparative babyhood, and her upbringing by human beings, had left some strange gaps in her abilities. To start with, she could not lap water or milk, but only drink from a dish as does a bird, lifting her head to allow the liquid to trickle down her throat, or sucking it noisily with a coarse, soup-drinking sound punctuated with almost vocal swallowing. She possessed, however, an accomplishment probably unchallenged among wild animals – that of drinking milk from a spoon. One had but to produce and exhibit a cup and spoon for her to clamber onto one's lap and settle herself with a heavy and confiding plump, head up and expectant. Then she opened her mouth and one poured the spoonfuls into it, while the soup noises reached a positive crescendo. At the end of this performance she would insist upon inspecting the cup to make certain that it was indeed empty; she would search into it with enquiring fingers and abstracted gaze; then, belching and hiccuping from time to time, she would lift the spoon out in one clenched hand and lie upon her back, licking and sucking it.

It came as a shock to me to discover that she was the most precarious of swimmers. Even in the wild state otter cubs have little if any instinct for water, and their dam teaches them to swim against their better judgement, as it were, for they are afraid to be out of their depth. In the water Edal preferred to keep her feet either in surreptitious contact with the bottom or within easy reach of it, and nothing, at that time, would tempt her into deep water. Within these self-imposed limits, however, she was capable of a performance that even Mij might have envied; lying on her back she would begin to spin, if that is the correct word, to revolve upon her own axis, to pirouette in the horizontal plane, like a chicken on a spit that has gone mad.- In this, as in the novelty of new aquabatic powers that she quickly learned, she took a profound delight, and if she had not yet apprehended that otters should swim underwater and only return to the surface for refreshment, she knew all the joys of a great disturbance upon it.

Her language was at first an enormous problem to me. While she shared a certain number of notes with Mij they were, whether by reason of her different species or because she had not been taught to speak by parent otters, used in so utterly different contexts as to produce, at the beginning, acute misunderstanding. Thus the singing hum that had proclaimed Mij's extreme anger she employed to ask for food that a human was holding, and she later learned to do this at request. Mij's interrogatory 'Hah?' was, with her, also a request for some piece of food held in the human hand, a confirmation that she had smelled it and found it acceptable. The high, snarling wail that had, very rarely, marked the end of Mij's patience and the probability of a bite, she produced in response to any stranger who came near her, and appeared apprehensive rather than aggressive, for she never bit, but only ran to the safety of her friends. All through the first two nights I suffered, intermittently, from this terrifying din screeched into my very ear-holes. She had been wont to share a bed with her late owners, and to pass most of the night upon the pillow; now she chose the foot of my bed, and, heavy and forgetful with sleep, came ambling up every half hour or so to take her accustomed position. At the discovery of a strange head on the pillow, one that seemingly never lost its dismaying novelty, she put her mouth against my ear and vented her feelings in wails and screams of abandoned anguish. I could not, perhaps, be blamed for finding this alarming; I also was recalled each time suddenly to consciousness, and to me those sounds had in the past been precursors to a bite like a leopard's.

Her call note was basically the same as Mij's, but less resonant and assertive, more plaintive and feminine. Beyond these similarities, she had a whole range of then unfamiliar expressions denoting affection, pleasure, greeting or casual conversation; notes strongly reminiscent of the human infant; most of these might, unflatteringly, fall into the category of squeals rather than chirps – unflatteringly, for they had none of the ugliness that the word connotes. Like the other otters I had owned she had a note used only when suddenly and extremely alarmed; I had heard it first from Chahala in the Tigris marshes, when the door of the reed hut was suddenly darkened by a human figure. The sound was exactly like that produced by a human being who fills his cheeks with air and expells it violently through half-closed lips. I heard it once from Mij and once from Edal.

From the very first she formed an entirely different relationship with Jimmy Watt from that which she established with me; it was, with him, a violently vocal friendship on her side, while with me, though she quickly became deeply affectionate and demonstrative, much remained tacit. Jimmy she would greet, crow over, harangue, nag, scold, caress and croon to, yell at if he disturbed her while she was sleeping, squeal with pure joy when he first appeared in the morning; with me, while she would perform the same actions, she spoke hardly a word. 'It's youth,' said Morag. 'She thinks he's another otter.' A little later other differences between the two relationships were evident, for on her daily walks she would come anywhere with me, but would not follow Jimmy if he appeared to her to be setting off in a dull or distasteful direction.

. . .

We had intended that for a full fortnight Edal should remain within the confines of the fence that enclosed the house and the pool. At first this did not seem difficult, for the pool was a new delight to her, and her moments of fretting were rare, mainly in the evenings. Then one day our attention strayed from her for a moment or two and she was gone. Where the wire joined the little shed at the north end of the house, nearest to the bridge and the route by which she had arrived with Malcolm and Paula, she had found that she could force the barrier. By the time we had made sure of her absence she had perhaps ten minutes' start.

We guessed rightly the route that she had taken; when we reached Druimfiaclach she had already been there for five minutes. Morag was away, and her husband had been unable to establish rapport with this preoccupied creature all of whose thoughts were suddenly for the past. She lay at the top of the stairs (I have found that if there is a stairway an otter is possessed of an inalienable instinct to ascend it) and wailed piteously. She seemed pleased to see us, and greeted Jimmy with notes almost as loud of those of her distress, but she did not want to come back to Camusfeàrna. We had never put the lead on her before, but now there seemed no alternative.

The return journey took more than an hour. She would trot happily ahead for perhaps fifty yards; then she would sit down, dig in her toes, and wail. I did not realize that it would have been the easiest thing in the world to have picked her up and carried her home, with no inconvenience beyond the weight of her ponderous person, for I was still under misapprehension as to the threat contained in this item of her repertoire. As it was, the nervous strain was more exhausting than any load could have been.

A few days later she repeated this escape for the second and last time; but on that occasion Jimmy, unhampered by my conditioning to other otter language, caught her up half-way and carried her home round his neck like a lead-weighted fur collar.

At the end of a fortnight there was no further danger of her straying. We had provided her with so many distractions, so many novelties –

and the greatest of these was certainly constant access to running water – that she had been suborned. It was, perhaps, fortunate for us that this period of acclimatization coincided with the migration of the elvers. For these transparent morsels, who swarmed and wriggled in the rock pools below the waterfall and formed a broad snail-paced queue up the vertical rock beside the white water, she discovered a passion that obscured every other interest. Hour after hour she would pass about these pools where Mij had hunted before her, scooping and pouncing, grabbing and munching, reaching up the rock face to pluck the pilgrims as they journeyed, and from these lengthy outings she would return surfeited to play and to sleep in the kitchen as if she had known no other home.

These elvers, however, proved no small embarrassment to us, for over a period of several weeks they intermittently blocked our water supply and reduced us once again to carrying water in buckets from the burn. In our anxiety to keep Edal occupied and amused during her period of acclimatization we scooped buckets full of the elvers and tipped them into her pool. The pool was fed by a branch of the same Alkathene piping that carried our water from the top of the falls to the house; the elvers, quick to discover the only upstream exit from the pool, took up their interrupted migration with the same inflexible determination that had inspired them for the past two years, ascending the hundred-and-twenty-yard length of pipe until they reached the perforated 'rose' at the top. The perforations in the metal were, however, just too small to allow passage to their bodies, and there they stuck and died, each hole blocked by the protruding head of an elver, a pathetic and ironic end to so long and brave a journey. The 'rose' in the pool above the waterfall was accessible to us only by rope descent into the ravine; a dozen times a day we would go there and extract the dead elvers, but it was like sniping at a swarm of locusts, for behind them there were ever more of the journeying host to strangle on the very verge of liberty.

Routine is, as I have explained, of tremendous importance to animals, and as soon as we saw that Edal was settled we arranged a daily sequence that would bolster her growing security. She had her breakfast of live eels, sent, as they had been for Mij, from London, and then one or other of us took her for a two-hour walk along the shore or over the hills. During these walks she would remain far closer at hand than Mij had done, and we carried the lead not so much as a possible restraint upon her as a safeguard against attack by one of the shepherds' dogs, for Edal loved dogs, regarded them as potential playmates, and was quite unaware that many dogs in the Western Highlands are both encouraged and taught to kill otters.

On one of these morning outings with her I had a closer view of a wild otter than ever before. Edal was hunting rock-pool life on a ledge two or three yards from the sea's edge and a few feet above it; she had loitered long there among the small green crabs, butter-fish and shrimps, and my attention had wandered from her to an eagle coasting over the cliffs above me. When I turned back to the sea I saw Edal, as I thought, porpoising slowly along in the gentle waves just beyond the pool where she had been. I could have touched her with, say, the end of a salmon rod. I whistled to her and began to turn away, but as I did so the tail of my eye perceived something unfamiliar in her aspect; I looked back, and there was a wild otter staring at me with interest and surprise. I glanced down to the pool at my feet, and saw Edal, out of sight of the sea, still groping among the weed and under the flat stones. The wild otter stayed for a longer look, and then, apparently without alarm, resumed his leisurely progress southward along the edge of the rocks.

In those rock pools along the shore Edal learned to catch gobies and butter-fish; occasionally she would corner a full-grown eel in the hill streams, and little by little she discovered the speed and the predatory powers of her race. Her staple diet was of eels sent alive from London, for probably no otter can remain entirely healthy without eels, but she was also fond of ginger nuts, bacon fat, butter, and other whimsical hors-d'œuvre to which her upbringing by humans had conditioned her. Among local fish she disdained the saith or coal fish, tolerated lythe and trout, and would gorge herself gluttonously upon mackerel. We put her eels alive into her pool, where after early failures in the cloud of mud that her antics stirred up, she proved able to detect and capture them even in the midst of that dense smoke-screen. This is achieved, I think, by the hypersensitive tactile perception of her hands, for when in the shallow end of the pool she would appear deliberately to avert her gaze while feeling round her in the opaque water; the palms, too, are endowed with a 'non-slip' surface, composed of a number of round excrescences like the balls of fingers, which enable her to catch and hold between them an eel that would slither easily through any human grasp.

By the end of June she was swimming as an otter should, diving deep to explore dim rock ledges at the edge of the sea-tangle, remaining for as much as two minutes under water, so that often only a thin track of bubbles from the imprisoned air in her fur gave guide as to her whereabouts. (This trail of bubbles, I have noticed, appears about six feet behind an otter swimming a fathom or so underwater at normal speed; never, as the eye subconsciously expects, directly above the animal.) But though she lost her fear of depth she never felt secure in great spaces of water; she liked to see on at least one side of her the limits of the element as she swam, and when beyond this visual contact she was seized with a *horror vacui*, panicking into an infantile and frenzied dog-paddle as she raced for land.

Hence our first experiments with her in the rowing boat were not a success; the boat was to her clearly no substitute for terra firma, and in it, on deep water, she felt as insecure as if she were herself overboard $-$ more so, in fact, for she would brave a wild rush for the shore rather than remain with us in so obvious a peril.

· · ·

Edal was not the only newcomer to Camusfeàrna that summer. Years ago I had formed, at Monreith, a great collection of wild geese; after the war they represented the only major collection of rare wildfowl left in all Europe, and in 1948 they went to form the nucleus of Peter Scott's Wildfowl Trust at Slimbridge. By then, however, the commoner varieties had bred in such numbers and were so elusive to the pursuer that they were not thought worth the trouble of transporting; and the flock of full-winged greylags remained about Monreith Loch, intermittently harried for sport or as vermin to the grazing parks, semi-feral, and unwary only in the breeding season, for ten years after the collection was a thing of the past. By 1959 there were still some two or three pairs nesting at the loch, and I arranged for one brood to be hatched under a hen at Monreith and sent up to Camusfeàrna. After a long and circuitous journey by train and boat five goslings arrived, feathered but not fledged, gawky, uncouth and confiding, displaying a marked predilection for human company at variance with the traditional characteristics of their race. This paradox was pleasing to me, for like many others I had come to a fondness for wild animals and birds by way of bloodthirstiness; in my youth I had been an ardent wildfowler, and these five goslings were the direct descendant of birds I had shot and wing-tipped or otherwise lightly wounded at the morning flight years before. It had, in fact, been the keeping and taming of a few wounded greylags shot in blustering winter dawns on the salt marsh and mud-flats of Wigtown Bay that had initiated my attempt at a living collection of all the wild geese of the world, and these gabbling flat-footed five who tried so persistently to force their way into the house at Camusfeàrna were the twelfth generation, or so, in descent from the victims of my gun. Perhaps it was from some obscure part of the guilt under which, unrecognized, we labour so often, that I wanted these birds to fly free and unafraid about Camusfeàrna, wanted to hear in the dawn and the dusk the wild music of those voices that long ago used to quicken my pulse as I waited shivering in the ooze of some tidal creek with the eastern horizon aflame.

As a daily delight and as an ornament to Camusfeàrna these

particular wild geese exceeded my most optimistic expectations. To begin with they were, as I have said, as yet unable to fly; only the very tips of their sprouting pinion feathers peeped out of the casing of blue blood-quill, but day-long they would stand flapping hopefully and grotesquely, lifting themselves a foot or so into the air and progressing in a series of ill-co-ordinated and ungainly hops. As it had fallen to Jimmy Watt and myself, neither of whom can swim, to teach an otter to do so. so now as the geese grew and their wing feathers became long enough for flight, but their imagination remained too small to compass the attempt, it was we who taught the wild geese to fly. Jimmy would run in front of them wildly flapping his arms in a mime of flight, until one day the goslings, performing much the same action as they hurried after him, found themselves, to their consternation, to be airborne. The immediate result was a series of most undignified crash landings, but in those few seconds they had found their powers; within a week they were strong and certain on the wing, and in answer to a call from the house they would come beating up the wind from the beaches of the distant islands.

At night we kept them shut up in a wire enclosure, wire floor and roof, too, as a safeguard against wildcats and foxes, and when we let them out in the morning they would rise with a great clamour and wing their way down the burn to the sea, twisting and turning in the air, 'whiffling' as wildfowlers call it, in the pure joy of their flight.

I must admit that for all their charm and beauty these five wild geese displayed, in some matters, a truly astonishing want of intellect, a plain stupidity, indeed; the very opposite of the sagacity usually ascribed to their race. Even after months of familiarity with the precincts of the house it was doubtful whether they could enter the garden gate without one or other of their number getting left behind; a goose would as often as not find himself on the wrong side of the open gate, and instead of walking round it to rejoin his companions, would concentrate upon moronic attempts to penetrate the wire that divided them from him.

More striking still was their behaviour in the pen which confined them at night. Every morning I would go to open the wire-netting door and release them; as soon as I appeared they would set up a gabble of greeting which reached crescendo as I lifted the barrier and they stalked out. One morning in September, being up at first light, I opened their door (which formed the whole of one side of the enclosure) some two hours earlier than the time to which they were accustomed. They greeted me as usual but did not immediately emerge, and I went back to the house thinking that they would move only when the sun was up, and pondering afresh on the role of routine in animal behaviour. It was nearly three hours later, and thus long past the time when they would normally have flown down to the sea, that I caught sight of them from the kitchen window. They were still inside the pen, chattering irritably, and walking up and down in front of the open door as if some invisible barrier separated them from the grass outside. Deciding that they could only be liberated by some symbolic gesture, I went out to them exactly as if we had not met that morning; I closed the door and then re-opened it with a flourish, talking to them the while as I was wont. With profound relief apparent, one would have said, in their every action, they came trooping out at my heels and almost at once took wing for the shore.

From the last days of May until early September the summer, that year, took leave of absence; while England panted in equatorial heat and the coast roads from London were jammed by twenty-mile queues of motionless cars, Camusfeàrna saw only sick gleams of sunshine between the ravings of gale and rain; the burn came down in roaring spate, and the sea was restless and petulant under the unceasing winds. The bigger dinghy dragged her moorings and stove a plank, and there were few days when the little flat-bottomed pram could take the sea without peril. Because of this, and because, perhaps, I welcomed Edal's fear of the open sea as a factor in favour of her safety, it was not until the first of September that we renewed experiments with her in the boats.

She had gained much confidence meanwhile, both in us and in her proper element, and she gambolled round us in the warm sunshine as we dragged the pram across the sand into a still blue sea that reflected the sky without so much as a ripple. The geese, ever companionable and anxious to share activity, followed us in a chuckling procession down the beach, and the whole strange convoy set off from the tide's edge together; Edal shooting through the clear, bright sea, grabbing and clasping the oar blades or bouncing inboard with a flurry of aerated water, the geese paddling along a few yards astern with mildly disapproving eyes behind their orange bills. We rowed for a mile down the coastline, with the glorious ochres and oranges of tide-bared weed as a foreground to the heather, reddening bracken, and the blue distances of mountain heights. All the magic of Camusfeàrna was fixed in that morning; the vivid lightning streak of an otter below water; the wheeling, silver-shouldered flight of the geese as they passed to alight ahead of us; the long, lifting, blue swell of the sea among the skerries and the sea-tangle; the little rivers of froth and crystal that spilled back from the rocks as each smooth wave sucked back and left them bare.

Edal, finding herself from time to time swimming above an apparently bottomless abyss, would still panic suddenly and rush for the boat in a racing dog-paddle, her head above water and not daring to look down; her instinctive memories, it seemed, alternated between those of the dim mysterious depths and forests of waving weed, and the security of the hearth rug, lead, and reassuring human hands. So she would turn suddenly for the boat (of which she had now lost all fear and felt to be as safe as the dry land), a small anxious face above furiously striking forefeet, cleaving the surface with a frothing arrow of wave, and leap aboard with her skin-load of water. Then she would poise herself on the gunwale, webbed hind feet gripping tensely, head submerged, peering down on the knife edge between sea and terra firma, between the desire for submarine exploration and the fear of desertion in the deep unknown. Sometimes she would slide, soundlessly and almost without ripple, into deep water, only to panic as soon as she had submerged and strike out again frantically for the boat. Yet in the moments when her confidence had not yet deserted her, when the slim torpedo of her form glided deep below the boat's side , weaving over the white sand between tall, softly-waving trees of bright weed, or darting in sudden swift pursuit of some prey invisible from above, it seemed as if the clock had been set back and it was Mijbil who followed the dinghy through the shining water.

After the first of these paradise days among the islands the geese failed for the first time to return at nightfall. In the morning I called for them, but there was no greeting chorus in reply. It was as yet early for them to have felt any migratory instinct, which I thought would in any case have probably been extinguished by some generations of static forebears, and when I had seen no sign of them by the afternoon I feared that they had wandered too far and fallen prey to some tourist with a .22 rifle. I had, indeed, given up all hope of them when in the early evening I landed with Edal upon one of the white-sand beaches of the islands, drawn there by the desire to make the acquaintance of some visitors who had landed from a sailing dinghy. I was talking to them when I saw, half a mile or so to the northward, the long unhurried beat of goose wings against the sky, and recognized, with an absurd surge of joy, my missing greylads. I called to them as they made to pass high overhead in the sunshine, and they checked in mid-air and came spiralling down in steep, vibrant descent, to alight with a flurry of pinions on the sand at our feet.

It never ceased to give me delight, this power to summon wild geese from the heavens as they passed, seemingly steady as a constellation upon their course, or to call to them from the house when the sun was dipping behind the hills of Skye, to hear far off their answering clangour, and see the silhouette of their wings beating in from the sea against the sunset sky. I found more enjoyment in that brood of humble greylags than ever I had in the great collection of exotic wildfowl of which their ancestors had been the discarded dregs, the lees, not worth removal; more pleasure, perhaps, in their peaceful, undemanding coexistence than had any medieval nobleman in the hawk who at his bidding rose to take the wild duck as they flew or hurl the heron from the sky.

Though the greylags gave little trouble and much reward, they produced on occasion, as do all creatures for whom one is responsible, moments of acute anxiety. The worst of these was the sight of one of the number, out of my reach, doing its utmost to swallow a fish hook. Edal, as I have said, was fed upon live eels sent from London; this was a costly procedure, and as she grew and her consumption of eels rose beyond the original order for six pounds a week, I had begun experiments to supply her from the Camusfeàrna burn, in which eels abounded. But despite much advice I had failed signally to devise a satisfactory eel trap, and one afternoon we set a number of short lines from the bridge, baited with worms. This proved effective, and we had several eels in a few hours, but I had forgotten the geese. They were not often at the bridge, and I had not thought, in any case, that they would be inquisitive enough to investigate the almost invisible lines. Some two hours later, nevertheless, they chose perversely to fly in there from the sea, and by the time that I saw them one had a foot-length of trout cast dangling from its bill. At the end of the cast was the hook, a small hook taken from a stripped trout fly, and the goose, unaware of danger, was trying hard to swallow what remained. The fineness of the cast was all that impeded the intention, but while I watched in an agony of suspense another two or three inches disappeared from view. The other geese gathered round my feet, but this one, intent upon its personal problem, kept obstinately to the centre of the pool, while the hook, in response to the gobbling movements of the bill, mounted steadily higher. In the nick of time we lured it to the bank with an offer of food, and when I gripped the cast and pulled I found myself hauling it out hand over hand, for the bird had some five feet of line in its crop. The incident put a temporary full stop to my efforts to supply Edal with eels from the burn.

For the same reason the geese became an embarrassment, too, to fishing expeditions at sea; when they did not actually accompany the boat out from the beach they would discern it from afar, long after we thought to have eluded their pursuit; they would come winging out over the waves and alight, gabbling, alongside, pressing in close, round the darrow line, fascinated by the fish hooks and the dancing blue-and-silver glitter of fish hauled in over the gunwale, so that often it became necessary to control a darrow-full of mackerel with one hand and fend the geese from danger with the other. It was at such moment that I understood how difficult life would be if all wild animals and birds were unafraid of man; how complicated the everyday business of living must have become to St Francis.

CHAPTER 14

The house had been much transformed since Edal's arrival. While there had been no otter at Camusfeàrna I had concentrated upon improving the décor and comfort of the rooms; now that the whole premises were once more, as it were, in a state of siege this aspect had perforce to be abandoned for more practical considerations. Every table and shelf had somehow to be raised above the range of Edal's agile inquisition; every hanging object upon the walls moved upward like the population of a flooded town seeking sanctuary upon the rooftops. No longer could there be a paper-table at the end of the sofa, for this recently constructed innovation she appropriated for her own on the first day, tearing and crumpling the effete reading matter until it formed a bed suited to her exacting taste. There she lay upon her back and slept, her head pillowed across a headline describing traffic jams on the roads out of London.

It was exceedingly difficult to elevate every vulnerable object above her reach, for by standing on tiptoe she could already achieve three foot six inches. When wet she would pull down a towel, or several towels, upon which to dry herself; when bored she would possess herself of any object that caught her wayward fancy, and, deeply absorbed, set about its systematic disintegration. These moods would come and go; there were days when she was as sedate as a lap dog, but there were days, too, when there simply was not room enough on the walls for the fugitives from her depredations. By nature of its surroundings Camusfeàrna is heavily-stocked with rubber boots, both Wellingtons and sea-boots; many of these have over a period of years been patched with red-rubber discs, and Edal early found a fiendish delight in tearing these off and enlarging the holes they hid.

Thus the rooms to which she had access acquired the look of country-house parks whose trees display the 'browsing line' so much deplored by late eighteenth-century writers on landscape gardening. From the height above ground to which the trees were branchless it was, in those parks, possible to deduce whether the owner kept fallow deer, cattle, or horses, and by much the same process I was able to compare the relative sizes of Edal and Mij. If there was any doubt at first, at the end of her first month with me she was certainly a much larger creature, and yet she was still a full six months younger than he had been when he was killed. Her growth was almost visible. In May Malcolm Macdonald had estimated that she was some forty-two inches long and weighed twenty-five pounds; by August she was close on fifty inches, and I estimated her weight as not far short of forty pounds. She was then a year old, and since she had not yet come into season it was clear that her growth was far from complete. In equatorial America there are otters the size of seals; if they have ever been domesticated the rooms of their owners must present a most curious appearance.

.   .   .

Because of the limitations of wall space in the kitchen-living-room it was not advisable to leave Edal quite alone there for long periods. She was more accommodating in this matter of being left alone than Mij had been, and if she had been exercised and fed she was content for five hours or more. When we went by boat to the village or over to Skye we would leave her shut into a room given up entirely to her, the unfurnished room over the kitchen, that had served the same purpose in Mij's day. Here she had her bed, made from a motor tyre covered with rugs; her lavatory in a corner, composed of newspapers laid on American cloth (to this somewhat remote convenience she would dutifully ascend from the kitchen whenever necessary); a host of miscellaneous toys; and dishes of water. This room had one great disadvantage: it had a single-plank floor and it was directly above the living-room. Though her water bowls were of the non-upsettable variety made for dogs, they were far from non-upsettable to her, for having tried and failed to tip them by leverage she would simply pick them up in both hands and overturn them; and the ceiling was, as I have indicated, far from waterproof. In the early days, too, her marksmanship at her lavatory was none too accurate, and this was unfortunately situated at a point roughly above the chair where any casual guest would normally sit.

Water multiplies its value to an otter as soon as it is falling or otherwise on the move, and Edal discovered that having overturned her bowl upstairs it was possible to scamper down to the kitchen and receive the double dividend of the drops falling through the ceiling; I have seen her on the kitchen floor, head up and mouth wide open, catching every drip as it pattered down from above.

.   .   .

It was a source of great disappointment to Edal that the few dogs she was allowed to meet fell far short of her standards as playmates. In general their attitude towards her reminded me of nothing so much as the colour-bar, and she clearly felt hurt and chagrined at their failure to accept her as one of themselves. With few exceptions they growled, barked, and snarled at her overtures. The first, a sedate Golden Labrador bitch, sat in front of the fire with her back turned to Edal in a most marked manner; every now and again Edal, discouraged from more direct approach by an unequivocal snap, would tentatively stretch out one of her monkey-like hands and touch the unresponsive yellow rump, making, the while, little plaintive, yearning whines in the back of her throat. She was plainly puzzled by her failure to establish friendly relations, for she was unused to rebuff.

Two dogs only achieved with her a temporary *bonhomie*, but both, after a short time, found her personality too overpowering. A peculiarly zany, yellow-eyed pointer bitch, brought over by James Robertson Justice, entered to begin with into the true spirit that Edal required of her playmates, racing round and round in dazzling circles while Edal displayed remarkable judgement in the matter of short cuts – too remarkable for the pointer, who ended upon her back in the burn while Edal mocked her from the bank. This incident produced a coolness that their relationship did not survive; the pointer became wary and then frankly hostile. When I expostulated at this deplorable lack of stamina her owner replied, 'Well, she never thought she was going to be called upon to make sport for an otter, least of all one called Crumpet.' (Like most curious pets Edal had, since her arrival at Camusfeàrna, acquired a variety of alternative names, among which this was perhaps one of the least regrettable.)

Eric Linklater introduced a great rangy English Setter, a gorgeous beast named Tops'l, and he, too, was at first prepared to chance his arm playing with an otter, this time on the sand; but like the pointer, he found his ability to make rings round her set at nought by her unerring eye for radii. Thus consistently outwitted, he took refuge in hysterical barking, and Edal took refuge in the sea. I still hope some time to find a dog who will play with her as Priscilla did in Africa.

The otter and the five greylag geese were the resident familiars of Camusfeàrna, though during the course of the summer there were other, more transient visitors; a young Slavonian Grebe that from all the multitudinous waters of that landscape chose to alight upon the tiny pool that we had dug behind the house for Edal, and found the surrounding wire-netting too high to permit take-off; a miserable blind young vole dropped by its parent as she carried it in torrential rain from the suddenly-flooded ditches of forestry drainage, and which survived for four days fed from a laborious replica of a mouse's teat; a wounded and scarcely fledged herring gull, picked up near to the house, dying in deluge and gale, who recovered to develop both flight and a degree of dependence upon household scraps; and a water rail, that arrived from the village in a cardboard box on the back of whose label was written, 'What bird is this, and is it usually found perched by the fire-side?' It had, inexplicably, been discovered squatting by the empty hearth when the householder came down in the morning. It was a great surprise to me, this bird of which a more usual view is in short flimsy flight low over the rushes of some snipe bog, the most unambitious of aerial enterprises, ending abruptly in a landing that, though invisible, one feels can only be ungraceful and inept. A thoroughly undistinguished bird, one would say, nondescript in plumage, gauche in action, and in habits retiring to the point of nonentity. Yet the specimen in the cardboard box, thus forced as it were into propinquity and social contact with mankind, revealed itself as dapper, even dressy, in personal appearance, with irascible ruby-red eyes and an aggressive, choleric temperament. He flew like a fighting cock at any hand that approached him, and the deceptively slender red bill had a grip like a pair of pliers. He clearly resented every detail of his ignominious captivity, but he had arrived in the evening and I did not want to set him free until I was sure that he was uninjured; he spent the night in my bedroom, whose floor was for the occasion littered with earthworms and other unsavoury offerings; either in pursuit of these or in simple self-assertion he stamped about all night making, as the occupant of the room beneath put it, a noise like a mouse in hob-nailed boots. Daylight showed him to be sound in wind and limb, and he resumed anonymity in a larger landscape.

Finally, producing a more lasting impression, came a wildcat kitten. Late one afternoon we had discovered that the Calor-gas cylinder (an innovation that year) was almost exhausted, and we decided to take the boat up at once to the village five miles away. It was a blue-and-gold September afternoon, with the sea between the islands as smooth as the face of a cut and polished stone. The tide was ebbing and the tops of the sea-tangle showing between the skerries, so that had we not been pressed for time before the village shop would close we should have passed outside the lighthouse point; now the possible saving of ten minutes seemed a worthy gamble against the danger of running aground, and we decided to try the channel between the lighthouse island and its neighbour. I was at the tiller, and Jimmy Watt was kneeling in the bows, directing me between the rocks. Suddenly he called my attention excitedly to something at the surface on our port bow.

There, fifteen yards away, was a half-grown wildcat kitten, swimming uncertainly in the direction of the farther island. (I have since learned that it is no rarity for wildcats to take to the water, even when they are not pursued, but at the moment it seemed as strange as would a fish progressing over land.) The cat was in about two fathoms of water, and swam slowly and very high, so that the whole back and tail were above water and dry. I tried to turn towards it, but at the precise moment the outboard engine bracket, which in our hurry to set off had not been tightened securely on the transom, came adrift on one side and left me without steering. To our amazement the cat then appeared to turn towards the boat as if towards rescue, and by forcing the engine into the water with one hand I was able to bring the bows alongside it. I had never handled a living wildcat, and I thought the least that Jimmy was in for was a bad scratching, but there was not as much as a snarl as he grasped it round the body, lifted it from the sea, and dumped it into a wicker hamper. It was difficult to associate this meek, fluffy, lost kitten with the untameable ferocity of all reports, and I thought that here was the opportunity to test the rumours at first hand. But it was difficult to see how Camusfeàrna could contain with any placidity both a wildcat and an otter, and my thoughts turned to Morag; she, I thought, would welcome this ghost of her childhood days, for long ago she had kept, and mourned the loss of, a hybrid with a wildcat sire. She was at that time housekeeping, during the daylight hours, for the lodge by the river four miles up the coast, so we abandoned our idea of replenishing the Calor-gas supplies and headed for the river. Morag, however, had already left by the mail Land Rover for Druimfiaclach; at the lodge we were lent a car, and continued to her home by road. The calm of the cat within the hamper had by now given place to a low but almost continual growl, a menacing sound that suggested a curbed ferocity hardly held in rein.

While I learned that Morag felt herself too cramped by household duties to commit herself to the care of a wildcat, I should, no doubt, have released it, but despite all that I had heard and read of the untameable nature of wildcats I had met no one who could personally contribute to the picture; I knew, too, that it was very rare to capture an undamaged kitten and I felt that an opportunity to test the validity of the myth was not to be thrown away. I returned to the lodge, and from there telephoned to Dr Maurice Burton, a zoologist who at his home in Surrey keeps and observes a great variety of wild creatures, and who has in the course of a lifetime devoted to the study of animal behaviour acquired experience of most British fauna. Curiously, however, he proved never to have kept a wildcat, and knew no one who had ever tried to tame one, though he did know someone whose lifelong ambition it had been to acquire a healthy kitten for the experiment. He proposed telephoning to this friend, who would in turn telephone to me during the next half hour, and in due course I spoke to Mr William Kingham, who was prepared to leave London by car at dawn the next morning to collect the cat. It was then Friday evening; he expected to complete the seven-hundred-mile journey by Sunday morning.

I carried the now distinctly vocal hamper back by boat to Camusfeàrna. There was only one way of bridging the next thirty-six hours: to evacuate my bedroom in favour of the kitten and to sleep in the kitchen. This I did with some reluctance, not because I envisaged the shambles to which my room would be reduced, but because it had been but three nights before that I had returned to it after the departure of my last guest.

It was already dark when we beached the boat below the house, and there was no means of obtaining any suitable food for a wildcat that night. I left the hamper open in my bedroom beside a saucer of tinned milk and some sea-trout roes. As an afterthought I blocked the chimney with a screwed-up ball of wire-netting.

In the morning, after a far from novel night in a sleeping-bag by the kitchen fire, a cursory inspection of the bedroom discovered no cat. One of the trout roes and all the milk had disappeared, and there was an odoriferous mess in the centre of my bed, but of the perpetrator of this outrage there was no sign whatever. Just so, I remember, would we as children incarcerate hedgehogs in rooms that would not have offered exit to a mouse and yet find on awakening, eager and unwashed, not so much as a single spine to tell us that it had not been a dream. I have since suspected the adult world of some nocturnal interference in the matter, but in those days we were both fatalistic and ingenuous.

A more detailed examination revealed the cat, in the chimney. It had pulled out the inadequate cork of wire mesh, and was ensconced, owl-like, on a ledge some two feet above and to one side of the grate. My first tentative fumblings drove it up higher into the dim funnel, into regions accessible only to weapons of remote control such as chimney brushes.

I was distressed by this, for recapture was clearly necessary, and equally clearly would be a traumatic experience for the subject of an experiment in domestication. But there was no alternative, and Jimmy Watt, armed with a long string and a weight, scaled the roof while I waited, heavily-gloved, to grasp the kitten when it should descend within range.

The gloves proved, in fact, to be encouragingly unnecessary; there was a certain amount of snarling and spitting, but no retaliation whatsoever. Liberated, the cat made one bound for the darkest corner of the room, and remained there, eyes glowing dully, while I made the chimney impregnable.

Sunday morning came and there was devastation in every corner of my bedroom, but there was no sign of any relief party from the south.

During the night, it seemed, my captive had enjoyed the greatest of high spirits; it had concentrated not upon escape but destruction, tearing up letters, playing ball with inkbottles, ascending with airy grace to remote shelves beyond the wildest dreams of any otter. It had dined well upon the carcass of an oyster-catcher, of which nothing but the wing feathers and the bill remained. The insult on the centre of the bed had been repeated, louder and clearer, so to speak, than before. The cat had taken up daylight quarters in a peat creel, a wicker pannier designed to be carried by a pony, that we had found washed up on the beach, and which now hung on the wall as a wastepaper basket beyond the reach of otters.

The necessity for shooting birds locally in order to feed this creature worried me. Many of the birds in the immediate vicinity of Camusfeàrna were tamer, more trusting, than in areas where someone or other was constantly on the prowl with a gun; not only was I reluctant to disturb this tranquillity, but I felt, as I set out from the house with a loaded weapon, like a deliberate traitor to the small sanctuary that I had long respected. The situation was made no easier for me by the geese, who insisted on accompanying me, sometimes on foot, sometimes locating me from afar and flying in to join me as I crouched, camouflaged, on the rock of some outlying skerry; by them I was embarrassed, obscurely ashamed that they should witness this predatory side to my nature. I found myself, as I crouched there in the salt wind and spray, repeating a childish little litany: 'I am only doing this so that the kitten may live'; this, by some absent-minded transposition, reshaped itself into the words and tune of a forgotten hymn 'He died that we might live'; and then I realized that my subconscious mind had jumped a gap at which my intellect had jibbed – for after all Christians do eat the body and blood of their God.

So, with distaste, I kept the wildcat supplied with birds that I would rather have seen alive; a turnstone, a shag, an oyster-catcher, and a curlew, and my unwilling guest consumed them all with relish and went on defecating squarely in the middle of my bed. I put a box of earth on the floor, but though it was much dug by morning and smelled strongly of ammonia the bed remained the major receptacle.

On the Monday a telegram arrived explaining that Mr Kingham had reached Glasgow a day earlier, only to be overtaken by sickness that had compelled him to turn back. Unaware that the number from which I had spoken to him was five miles by sea, he asked me to telephone to him in Surrey that evening.

The relief that I had hourly awaited being thus indefinitely postponed, I set off again for the village with a faltering outboard motor which completed the northward but not the return journey. By intermittent use of the oars I got home late at night, with the promise of an immediate telegram about the future of the wildcat.

There were further delays and misunderstandings, but a week after the original capture an emissary arrived at the railhead twelve miles north by sea, and despatched a hired launch to Camusfeàrna. He did not accompany it himself; I had assumed that he would arrive to stay for the night and receive such information as I could give him about the wildcat's habits, so that I was quite unprepared for boxing the animal at once with the launch waiting outside on an ebb tide. However, though the human escort was absent he had sent a stout and commodious crate filled with straw, at the back of which lay a plump unplucked pullet.

To the cat this third and necessarily hurried capture was still further trauma. He – for excremental reasons I vaguely supposed it to be a male – was crouched on a high shelf in the shadow of my typewriter (already knocked down and smashed by the otter), and the first advance of a gloved hand produced a tigerish and highly intimidating snarl of warning. On the second attempt he bounded from the shelf to a table in the window and crouched there growling with his back to the glass.

At this point Jimmy, who had been out in the boat fishing for mackerel when the launch came, arrived and demanded to take control. He put on the gloves and entered the arena with all the confidence of inexperience. At his first near approach the cat became transformed; almost, I had said, transfigured. The last trace of resemblance to a fluffy domestic Persian kitten vanished utterly; in its place was a noble, savage wild animal at bay before its ancestral enemy. Laying his ears not back but downward from the broad flat skull, so that the very tips and the tufts of hair that grew from within them were all that turned upward, baring every fang and gum in his head so that the yellow eyes became slits of rage and hate, swelling his ringed tail to twice its previous girth, he reared himself back against the glass of the window pane. But while one paw was lifted high with extended talons, the other still rested on the table, for the forelegs seemed to have elongated like telescopes; those velvet limbs had in an instant changed from instruments of locomotion into long-reaching weapons to rake and to slash. As an image of primordial ferocity I had seen nothing to equal it; it was splendid, it was magnificent, but it was war.

Jimmy, as yet accustomed only to handling creatures whose bluff was easily called, was undismayed by this display of *Furchtbarkeit*, but retired after an instant with a bite clean through glove and thumb-nail.

It seemed as if deadlock had been reached, until it occurred to us that we could as it were bottle the cat between the open end of the crate and

the window glass; this manoeuvre was instantly successful, and he bolted
to the dim interior behind the straw and was silent. That was the last I
saw of him; it is, however, not improbable that we shall meet again, for
his new owner undertook that if the cat followed the pattern of legend
and proved untameable it should be returned to Camusfeàrna and freed
where wildcats enjoy the privilege of protection.

· · ·

It is October, and I have been for six unbroken months at
Camusfeàrna. The stags are roaring on the slopes of Skye across the
Sound, and yesterday the wild swans passed flying southwards low over
a lead-grey sea. The ring of tide-wrack round the bay is piled with fallen
leaves borne down the burn, and before a chill sea-wind they are blown
racing and scurrying up the sands. The summer, with its wild roses and
smooth blue seas lapping white island beaches, is over; the flower of the
heather is dead and the scarlet rowanberries fallen. Beyond are the brief
twilit days of winter, when the waterfall will thunder white over flat
rocks whose surface was hot to bare feet under summer suns, and the
cold, salt-wet wind will rattle the windows and moan in the chimney.
This year I shall not be there to see and hear these things; home is for me
as yet a fortress from which to essay raid and foray, an embattled
position behind whose walls one may retire to lick new wounds and plan
fresh journeys to farther horizons. Yet while there is time there is the
certainty of return.

Camusfeàrna
October 1959

Thank you, my friendly daemon, close to me as my shadow,
For the mealy buttercup days in the ancient meadow,
For the days of my 'teens, the sluice of hearing and seeing,
The days of topspin drives and physical well-being.

Thank you, my friend, shorter by a head, more placid
Than me your protégé whose ways are not so lucid,
My animal angel sure of touch and humour
With face still tanned from some primeval summer.

Thanks for your sensual poise, your gay assurance,
Who skating on the lovely wafers of appearance
Have held my hand, put vetoes upon my reason,
Sent me to look for berries in the proper season.

Some day you will leave me or, at best, less often
I shall sense your presence when eyes and nostrils open,
Less often find your burgling fingers ready
To pick the locks when mine are too unsteady.

Thank you for the times of contact, for the glamour
Of pleasure sold by the clock and under the hammer,
Thank you for bidding for me, for breaking the cordon
Of spies and sentries round the unravished garden.

And thank you for the abandon of your giving,
For seeing in the dark, for making this life worth living.

THE END

A Cat
in the Window

Derek Tangye

To
JEANNIE'S MOTHER

CHAPTER 1

The opening paragraph of my book, *A Gull on the Roof*, which told how we came to live in Cornwall, was about our cat Monty of whom I said: 'He was, for both Jeannie and myself, the repository of our secret thoughts.' I am writing the story of Monty in *A Cat in the Window*.

I first met Monty in Room 205 of the Savoy Hotel. He was six weeks old and, when I came into the room, was tumbling, chasing, biting an old typewriter ribbon dragged temptingly across the carpet by Lois, Jeannie's secretary. He was the size and colour of a handful of crushed autumn bracken. At the time I did not notice the distinguishing marks I was later to know so well – the silky white shirt-front, the smudge of orange on the left paw, the soft maize colour of the fur on his tummy. I did not notice his whiskers, nor his tail with its dark rings against cream, the rings graduating in size to the tip which, in his lifetime, was to flick this way and that, a thousand, thousand times. I saw only a pretty kitten with great big innocent eyes gambolling in the incongruous setting of Jeannie's office, and I wondered why.

'What's this?' I said to Lois, looking down at the two of them. 'What on earth is this kitten doing here?' I had seen Ambassadors, film stars, famous journalists, politicians of all parties, in Jeannie's office, but I had never before met a cat. It made me suspicious.

'Come on,' I said, 'come on, Lois, tell me what it's all about?' But Lois, the perfect secretary, went on playing as if she hadn't heard me. 'Lois, you're hiding something from me. Where's Jeannie? What's she been up to? Both of you know I dislike cats and if . . .'

'She'll be back soon.' Lois was smiling and refusing to be drawn. 'She had to go over to Claridge's. General Montgomery has just arrived and nobody is allowed to know. She won't be long.' As Public Relations Officer of the Savoy Group it was part of Jeannie's job to keep certain news from the Press, just as much as it was on other occasions to get other news widely publicized.

But on this occasion, on this particular warm, summer afternoon as I awaited her return with Lois and the chocolate box cover of a kitten, her task was specially important.

Monty had arrived to make a progress report to Churchill on the Battle of the Desert.

. . .

I came from a dog family. In the walled garden of my rambling Cornish home was a row of wooden crosses with painted cries of Victorian sentiment. 'Alas, poor Rosa,' 'Sweet, gentle Cara,' 'Farewell Little Gyp.' And in my own childhood I remember the crosses going up again. My parents had no desire to disclose their emotions so, in their day, only the birth and death and name of the dog appeared on the cross. Rex, Bulger, Bruce, Mary, Lance, Roy, Gay. These sparse tributes to devotion were sometimes countered in my mind by unexpectedly finding my father standing opposite a cross quietly puffing his pipe. Young as I was, it touched me to feel the memories that were passing through him.

My personal friends were first Bruce and then Lance; or Sir Lancelot by which, until I found the name too much of a mouthful, I first called him. Bruce was a mongrel of indescribable parentage while Lance, an Old English Sheepdog, brought with him from the kennels where he was born a list of relations bearing the name of sheepdog royalty. Bruce was in our family before I was born and by the time I was seven I thought he was immortal. He was to me a brother of my own age, and for hours on end I would tease him or wrestle or play hide-and-seek with him among the gorse- and tamarisk-covered land around our home. Bruce was the answer to any doubts of my mother as to how I could spend my time.

Then he died and grief being suddenly to me an emotion instead of a word, my father countered by producing Lance. He moved subtly. He knew that what I needed was a dog I could call my own, and he devised a means that would make me, the small boy, feel he was my own. He told me one evening after I had gone to bed that he was driving to London the following morning and that, if I liked, I could go with him to Exeter, then return to Newquay by myself on the Cornish Riviera. He made me feel grown up and, unsuspectingly, I excitedly accepted. But when we reached Exeter station and the Riviera rolled in I found I was not to be alone on my return journey; for in the guard's van curled timidly in a wicker basket was Lance.

I matured with Lance. First the same childish games I had with Bruce, then the tearful partings before school terms, wild barking reunions, and soon the long walks of doubtful youth, Lance at my side in the winding lines sharing my puzzlement. I was a man when Lance died. Dogs, then, had been entities in my life. Cats, as if they were wasps with four legs, had been there to shoo away. They did not belong in my life nor in my family's life. All of us were united that whenever we saw a cat the most important thing to do was to see it out of sight.

But as I moved slowly out of the environment of my family, I found naturally enough people and homes who accepted cats as we accepted dogs. Cats were not vulgar as, in some mysterious way, I had been led to believe. I began to note that cats were able to bestow a subtle accolade upon their apparent owners which made these owners rapturous with delight.

I resented this. Dogs, and by this I mean well-mannered, full of character, devoted dogs who did not snarl or bark unnecessarily, were to me the true tenants of a home. Cats were vagrants. They did not merit affection.

I sensed, of course, that my attitude in a home where there was a cat or cats was unsatisfactory; so I developed a pose that after a while I made myself believe was genuine. I was allergic to cats. The proximity of one produced asthma. I felt dizzy. I behaved so strangely that any owner of a cat who was entertaining me was convinced that if I were not to prove a sickly embarrassment the cat had to be removed. I know there are some people who genuinely feel like this, but I was not one.

It was in this mood that I paid my first call on Jeannie's parents in their handsome house on the hill of St Albans. I sat down in the sitting-room and promptly Tim, Jeannie's cat, a huge blue Persian, jumped on my lap. Unthinkingly I played my customary part. I gave Tim a violent push and, in so doing, knocked over a small table upon which was my untouched cup of tea. From that moment I began to realize it was dangerous to appear to dislike cats.

For Jeannie is a cat lover, not only the slave of an individual, but an all-embracing cat lover. If she sees a cat on the other side of the street she will want to cross over to talk to it. Any pretty little thing, any handsome Tom, will receive her caressing and cooing. She fawns on the breed. Little wonder her mother after my visit had ended cast a humorous doubt on a successful marriage. Could a cat lover live happily with a cat hater?

My future dealings with Tim were, therefore, cautious. I was careful not to cause offence by throwing any make-believe tantrums, yet I was equally careful not to appear affected by the lofty gaze he sometimes cast on me. I was polite but distant. I was determined to hold fast to my traditional dislike of the species. I was not going to be hypnotized by gentle purrs, soft kneading of paws, an elegant walk across the room and a demand to jump on my knees. I disliked cats. I most certainly would not have one in our home after we had married.

This was my mood as I waited for Jeannie to return from Claridge's. We had been married three months.

CHAPTER 2

But I made no scene except a mock one. It was an inevitable defeat. I could only bluster. I could not enter my married life with an argument about a cat.

Monty chose the moment of Jeannie's return to pounce upon the toe of my shoe; then disappear up my trousers, except for a tail. He tickled my leg until I had to stoop and, for the first time, touch him. Jeannie and Lois watched hopefully the effect this would have on me. He was very soft, and the wriggle with which he tried to escape me was feeble, like the strength of my little finger. I felt the teeth nibble my hand, and a tiny claw trace a tickle on my skin; and when I picked him up and held him firmly in front of me, the big eyes stared childishly at me with impotent resentment. I had never held a cat in my hands before.

'This is diabolical,' I said in pretence fury, addressing Jeannie and Lois, 'and don't think I haven't a card up my sleeve ... I'm going to chuck this thing over Hammersmith Bridge on the way home.' I spoke so vehemently that Lois seemed half to believe me. 'Yes I am,' I said, rubbing it in, 'I'll stop the car and fling the cat over the parapet.'

'Kitten,' murmured Lois.

'Monty,' said Jeannie.

There is no defence against women who sense your heart has already surrendered. The head, however astute in presenting its arguments, appears hollow. If Jeannie wanted Monty she had to have him. How could I deny her? The best I could do was to learn to tolerate his existence; and make an attempt to impose conditions.

'All right, I won't do *that*,' I said, and was immediately irked by the gleam of victory in their eyes, 'but I'll tell you what I *will* do ...' I looked defiantly at both of them. 'I'll make quite certain he is a *kitchen* cat. There'll be no question of him wandering about the house as if he owns it.'

This display of authority eased me into seeing the situation in a more comforting perspective. Jeannie would be happy, Monty out of sight, and I could continue my aloofness towards the species as before.

'But if he doesn't behave himself,' I added, looking at the little ball of fur in my hand, 'he'll have to be found another home.'

The weakness in my attack was my responsibility for Monty's arrival. It was indirect, but a fact. We had mice in our cottage at Mortlake; and when, at Jeannie's request, I set traps and caught the mice, I was so sickened by the task of releasing the dead mouse from the trap that I preferred to throw both the mouse and the trap into the river.

The cottage, with a roof the shape of a dunce's cap, was within a few yards of the finishing post of the Boat Race, and only the towpath separated the front steps and the river. On the ground floor was the dining-room, the kitchen and the spare bedroom; on the first, two bedrooms, one overlooking the river, and the other the garden; and on the top floor were the bathroom and the sitting-room which stretched the breadth of the cottage. Across this room at door level stretched two massive old oak beams and from them, dove-tailed by wooden pegs, were two spans ancient as the beams, triangular, supporting the inside of the dunce's cap which was the ceiling. In one corner was the fireplace and opposite, along the length of the room, were the windows from which we watched the Thames flowing to the curve at Barnes Bridge; and beyond, the silhouette of London.

The cottage was once upon a time an inn, and one of the innkeepers was a waterman who married a Shakespeare player. I used to dig up broken old clay pipes in the garden, sometimes part of a stem, sometimes a bowl, and when I sent a sample to the British Museum they confirmed they were Elizabethan. From then on I used to hand pieces to visitors, telling them the story of the cottage. 'You had better keep this,' I would say, 'Shakespeare may have used it.'

It was a small walled garden the length of a cricket pitch and the width of half a tennis court. At the top end was the concrete shelter in which we crouched during bad air raids ... except the night we were celebrating our first wedding anniversary with a party in the cottage; and the roof was blown off.

On the other side of one wall was the garden of the Ship, the pub next door; on the other side of the opposite one was a passage-way from the river to Mortlake village; and within a hundred yards of both were Sandy Lane and West Road with the Brewery towering in the background. Along the river bank were three or four houses and beyond them, three minutes from the cottage, was Chiswick Bridge. In time, in the early morning, Monty used to walk with us to the Bridge but he would go no further. He would sit down when we reached the archway and, however much we coaxed him, would not budge. He was never, in fact, to be a wanderer while he lived at Mortlake. His world, for seven years, was to be the small walled garden; except after the bombing when he came with us to Jeannie's old home at St Albans. And it was from St Albans in the first place that he came.

I complained once again one morning to Jeannie about my trap task. In retrospect I know, of course, I was being ridiculous, but at the time, when I had to perform the task, I felt disgusted.

'Now if we had a cat,' replied Jeannie, and she gave no sign that she was trying to influence me unduly, 'you wouldn't have to worry about traps at all ... you see, the very smell of a cat keeps mice away.'

In due course I was to find this statement to be untrue, but at the time, in the frame of mind I was in on that particular morning, it interested me.

'You mean to say that a mouse never comes into a house where there's a cat, and all that catching and squealing takes place outside?'

'Oh, yes,' said Jeannie blandly, 'mice are very intelligent and they know they haven't a chance if a cat finds them in a house.'

'And what about birds?' Jeannie, I knew, once had a favourite cat called Tubby who spent much of her time in the spring climbing up trees to catch nestlings for her kittens. Jeannie, when she could, would gently take the little bird from Tubby's mouth when she reached her kittens and return it to the nest.

'Well,' she said, making the answer sound very simple, 'all you have to do is to have the cat doctored. Cats only catch birds for their families.'

Here again the ardour to convert me misled her sense of accuracy. True, Monty was seen to catch only one bird in his life, and that was a wren which annoyed him and which he promptly let go when we advanced on him; but he, I think, was an exception. Most cats, if they don't catch for their families, will catch for the fun of it, or because they are bored. You can't blame them. They are no worse than the man who takes out his gun for an hour or two of rough shooting.

'Anyhow,' I said, by way of ending the conversation, 'I still don't like them.'

On reflection, I believe my dislike was based on their independence. A dog, any dog, will come to you wagging its tail with friendliness if you click your fingers or call to it. There is no armed neutrality between the dog world and the human race. If a human is in need of affection and there is a dog about, he is sure to receive it, however frail affection from a stranger may be. Dogs are prepared to love; cats, I believed, were not.

I had observed, too, that cat owners (but who, I wondered, would call himself the owner of a cat?) were apt to fall into two types. Either they ignored the cat, put it out at night whatever the weather, left it to fend for itself when they went away on holidays, and treated it, in fact, as a kind of better-class vermin; or else they worshipped the animal like a god. The first category appeared callous, the second devoid of sense.

I had seen, for instance, a person sit rigid and uncomfortable in a chair because a cat had chosen his lap as the whim of its own particular comfort. I had noticed, and been vexed by her, the hostess who hastens away at the end of a meal with titbits for the cat which has stared balefully at her guests during the course of it. Cats, it seemed to me, aloofly hinted the power of hypnotism; and as if in an attempt to ward off this uncanniness, their owners pandered to them, anxiously trying to win approval for themselves by flattery, obedience, and a curious vocabulary of nonsensical phrases and noises. A cat lover, I had found, was at the mercy of the cat.

I was now to learn for myself whether this was true. My education was about to begin. My morning conversation with Jeannie had made her believe there might be a gap in my armour; and by the time I had forgotten the conversation, she had already rung up her mother to disclose her hopes. 'I think he's weakening,' she said. 'We must seize the chance.'

And so no time was lost. Her mother had an appointment at the hairdresser's and she promised that immediately afterwards she would go to the pet shop to see what kittens were available. The visit never took place. At the hairdresser's she confided her mission to the girl who attended her. 'But I've got a kitten that nobody wants,' the girl said. 'It's a ginger, the last of a litter, and if we don't find a home by tomorrow he'll have to be put away.'

I would not have agreed if my advice had been sought. One less kitten in the world would not have seemed very important to me. But my advice wasn't sought and Monty was saved.

For the price of my mother-in-law's weekly chocolate ration, he entered our lives.

CHAPTER 3

As soon as I picked him out of the wicker basket in which we had brought him home, I explained to our housekeeper that Monty was to be a kitchen cat. 'I don't want to see him at all,' I said. 'He's here to catch mice and although he may be small for that yet, I've been told the very smell of a cat will keep them away.'

I looked at Jeannie. She was busily unwrapping a small paper parcel. 'Isn't that true? Didn't you say that?'

'Oh yes … yes.'

An object had now appeared from the paper. A small *sole bonne femme*. It was freshly cooked and succulent.

'Good heavens, Jeannie,' I said, 'where did you get that?'

'Latry gave it to me,' she said. Latry was the famous maître chef of the Savoy. 'He's cooked it specially as a celebration present for Monty.' I looked at the fish and then at Monty. Only a few hours before, the girl in the hairdresser's was frightened he would be put away on the morrow.

'Really, Jeannie,' I said crossly, 'you can't go cadging food for the cat.'

'I wasn't cadging. Latry *gave* it to me, I tell you. He loves cats and felt honoured to cook Monty's first meal.'

'Honoured,' I murmured to myself, and shuddered.

Jeannie mashed the fish up in a saucer, put it on the floor and began cooing at Monty who, never having seen a fish before, tottered off in the opposite direction.

'There you are,' I said, as if I had achieved a minor triumph, 'he doesn't like fish.'

Of course he was soon to do so; and during the course of his life he was to eat vast quantities of it, although sole was not his favourite. It was whiting. The cottage, and also in due course our cottage in Cornwall, was often to reek with the stink of it when the water in which it was cooked boiled over from the pan onto the stove.

But on the first morning of his life with us, the morning on which I awoke to a disquieting awareness that the pattern of my life was about to be readjusted, the sole from the Savoy kitchens awaited him. 'I wonder whether he has eaten it,' pondered Jeannie aloud as she dressed.

Oddly enough I found myself wondering too. It was as if time being momentarily dull I was awaiting the B.B.C. News to hear if the announcer had anything to say to stir the pulse. 'I'll go down and see,' I said, and was off through the door in my dressing gown.

The stairs were narrow and steep, of polished wood and slippery; and on the third step from the bottom, too frightened to go up or down, was Monty. 'How have you got there?' I said; and my voice was as firm as could be allowed when a child gets caught in a predicament. 'Your place is in the kitchen. It's no use you trying to learn to climb stairs.' The tiny miaows did not protest against my firmness, they appealed for my help; and so I picked him up in one hand and took him to the saucer of the night before where it had been placed under the kitchen table. It was empty.

Jeannie was encouraged by my apparent gentleness on this occasion; and I observed, during the days that followed, how she cunningly began to use Monty to help pierce my utilitarian attitude towards him. The process continued from days into weeks until one afternoon an incident took place which, she considered, set the seal on her triumphant tactics.

The first of these tactics was her good sense in realizing it was unwise to make too much fuss of Monty in my presence. She made up for this apparent coolness in my absence, but this I was not to know; and I was not to know, for instance, that Latry, the chef, continued to supply her with delicacies which she fed to Monty surreptitiously while I was in the pub next door.

Nor when, as he grew older, he began successfully to climb the stairs, did she encourage him to do so; and on the evening he was found for the first time in a tight ball on the bed, she impressed me with her scolding. Indeed I felt a twinge of sympathy for Monty as I carried him, on Jeannie's instructions, back to the kitchen. I found myself wondering against my will whether it was fair he should be banished when it was so obvious he was prepared to give both of us his affection.

Monty played his own part very well because from the beginning he made it plain he liked me. It was a dangerous moment of flattery when I realized this and I believe, had it not been for my entrenched posture of dislike for the species, I would have fallen for it without more ado. There was, however, a thick enough layer of prejudice inside me for me to hold out.

He would seek to play with me. I would be sitting at dinner and feel a soft cushion gently knocking my foot, and when I put down a hand to stop it my fingers were enclosed by small teeth. In the garden he would perform his most bewitching tricks in front of me, the clumsy chase of a butterfly, the pounce on an imaginary demon leaving a spreadeagled posterior to face me. And when at the end of the day we returned to the cottage, unlatched the door and went inside, it was strange how often he came to me instead of paying court to Jeannie. Did I perhaps impose an intuition upon him that my prejudice, once defeated, would leave a vacuum that he alone could fill? My prejudice has long ago disappeared, but I am still a one-cat man. I have never developed a taste for a household of cats, each with a colourful name, each having to share the affection accorded to them all, each leading a life so independent that one of them can disappear for a few days without causing undue worry. It is a taste in cat worship I will never share. I am incapable of spreading my affection so widely. Monty needed only to vanish for a few hours and we both would fill ourselves with imaginary fears.

But the talk of these cat lovers among Jeannie's friends was part of my education. She enlisted their aid. I listened to the language they used, both spoken and unspoken, and became aware there was a streak of connoisseurship in this world of cats. It was the snobbery of an exclusive club; and if the flavour of conversation was an acquired taste, it was no more so than learning to like jazz or Bach. They perused Monty and unanimously pronounced he would grow into a beautiful member of the fraternity; and fraternity henceforth replaced for me the words of species or breed. They admired his head and foretold, quite correctly, it would become like that of a miniature tiger, not snouty and elongated like some ginger cats. They assessed his mother as a tortoiseshell and his father as a tabby. They liked his whiskers which at that age were wisps of white. They forecast, as he had been doctored, that he would become a huge cat. They discussed him, men and women of distinction in various walks of life, in the tone one associates with relations probing the future of an infant of noble heritage. Would his appearance measure up to his responsibilities? Young as he was, did he show signs of a strong character? Would his movements prove elegant? How thick would become his coat? Monty was fussed over and cooed at as if to win his favour was an ambition far outweighing in importance any achievement in the daily task. I watched amused, comforting myself with the knowledge that Jeannie's friends were not as serious as they appeared. Monty was only a diversion. He was a toy for temporary enjoyment. A cat could never possess a personality which could be remembered except by those with whom he lived.

In any case, during the initial period of this homage bestowed on him, Monty did not appear very attractive. He would not wash. His body was dull and dusty, the white on his left paw a dirty cuff, the crescent of white on his little chest a grey, soiled shirt. 'He looks like an alley cat,' I taunted Jeannie.

My coolness towards him, my inclination to niggle at any of his failings, naturally increased the sense of protection she had for him; and during this phase of unwash she was afraid I might have the excuse to get rid of him. Yet, to my surprise, I did not feel that way at all. I too, felt a sense of protection; and the evening, Jeannie having gone home before me, I returned to find Monty on a chair in the kitchen his fur shining bright, I was as delighted as Jeannie. I did not know she had damped him all over with plain water; and he had licked himself dry.

It was another homecoming a few weeks later, an unexpected one, which finally witnessed my capitulation. I had spent the day in the cottage and was not thinking of Jeannie's return till the evening. I was in the top room alone when there was a noise at the door as if it were being kicked by a soft boot. I opened it and Monty came scampering in. He rushed to the sofa, jumped up, climbed on the back walking along it tail up, then down again to the floor and across to where I was standing, arching his back, rubbing his head against my leg and purring. All this in less than a minute, and performed with such *élan* that it made me wonder whether he was telling me in his particular fashion that I had been making an ass of myself. I bent down and stroked him, and he thereupon carried out a manoeuvre which he was often to do when he aimed to be especially endearing. He twisted his head as if he were going to fold up in a ball, collapsed on the floor and turned over, and lay with his back on the green carpet, paws in the air, displaying his silky maize underparts while a pair of bright yellow eyes hopefully awaited the pleasure the sight would give me. The reward he expected was a gentle stroke until he decided he had had one too many when there would be a savage mock attempt to bite my fingers.

But on this first occasion I was holding a pipe cleaner in my hand and I tickled him with that, which led to a game, which led half an hour later to his sitting on my desk, a large kidney-shaped Regency desk with a top like a table, performing ridiculous antics with a pencil.

I was sitting there roaring with laughter when the door opened. In walked Jeannie.

CHAPTER 4

My capitulation was complete, and within a few weeks there was no pretence that Monty was a kitchen cat. Every room in the cottage was his kingdom; and at night, if his fancy was to sleep on the bed, I would lie with legs stiff so as not to disturb him while he curled in a ball at the bottom. I endlessly wanted to play with him, and felt put in my place when he was not in the mood, stalking away from me tail in the air showing he had something more important to do, like a vigorous if temporary wash of the underparts.

Sometimes my games were gently malicious, as if taking a friendly revenge on the way he had captured me. I used to lift him onto the beam in the sitting-room where he glared down at me, then ran along the beam to find a place from which to leap onto the floor, only to find I had moved along too and was there to stop him. I would put up a hand and receive a slap from a paw.

There was another game with an ulterior purpose or game perhaps is the wrong word for it. Three months had gone by and there was still no evidence that he had caught a mouse; no remains had been found, no victory bellow heard, no sign that there were fewer mice than before. It was disturbing. His presence had brought no fear to the mice and so he seemed as useless as a dog for the purpose required of him. 'Perhaps he left his mother too soon,' said Jeannie, apologizing, 'and she didn't have time to teach him.'

I no longer wished to prise Jeannie's defences and whereas in the beginning I would have ridiculed such a remark, I now said nothing. Monty was growing fast and his appetite enormous, so the best thing to do, I decided, was to keep him hungry for a while and let his natural cat's instinct develop out of necessity. After twenty-four hours he was prowling around like a tiger, and Jeannie was yearning to yield to his fury. 'You're cruel,' she said, 'to do this to him.' It was often to be like that, Jeannie always ready to surrender to his whims while I, my anti-cat upbringing still somewhere within me, endeavoured to insist on discipline.

But my plan on this occasion was to put him up in the attic, a dark, forbidding world of rafters, cobwebs and, without doubt, mice. Standing on a chair, my arms outstretched above me, I shoved Monty through the trapdoor, and returned to the sitting-room to await results. After half an hour Jeannie argued it was time to let him out. After an hour I was restraining her from standing on the chair. She was furious. I was anxious less my plan had misfired. Another ten minutes and I admitted I was wrong. I stood on the chair to push upwards the trapdoor. At that instant there was a wild scramble on the ceiling, followed by squeak, squeak, squeak ... and a few seconds later peering down from the opening above me was Monty with a mouse like a fat moustache, in his mouth.

As Monty grew larger Jeannie's lap became too small for his comfort, and he transferred to mine. He would approach where I was sitting, arch his back, claw for a brief second at the chair's fabric, leap up and settle down, then turn his head upward to me as if he were saying: 'Thank you very much.' That was not, however, the moment when I required any thanks because I always felt flattered he had chosen me, above all other comfortable spots in the house, to rest on awhile. It was later when I deserved the thanks, when my feet had gone to sleep, my legs had got cramp, and I had refrained from doing any job I had intended to do. I never dared move him. I would watch him comfortably dozing, occasionally adjusting his posture while I sat stiff as a ramrod: such a gesture as selecting my lap was an accolade I could not refuse. I was to spend hours, days, weeks of my life like that, while Jeannie sat opposite watching the two of us.

There were times, however, when first he paid me this attention, that circumstances forced me to move him. It was the period of the little blitz, the bitter late winter when Hitler again attacked London. The sirens would wail while we sat upstairs in the sitting-room and we would wait, pretending we were not tense, until the guns began firing. 'They're not very busy tonight,' I would sometimes say, which only meant I had not heard any bombs fall in the neighbourhood. But there were other times when a stick would fall uncomfortably close, and then I would tuck Monty under my arm and we would all hasten to the shelter at the top of the garden. We would crouch there, the dark being flashed into brilliance while Jeannie, a hand clutching Monty, would declare she was more afraid of the spiders than she was of the bombs.

On the night a near miss blew the roof off, leaving our sitting-room facing the stars, we were not in the shelter. It was the evening of our first wedding anniversary and a number of friends were celebrating with us when we heard the stick coming . . . one, two, three, four and wham! The Brewery had a direct hit and the fire that followed lit the night into daylight, and we knew that this tempting sight might lead to another attack. None of us was hurt, only covered with plaster, but the room we loved so much was a terrible sight; and Jeannie and I were standing at the door looking at it, thinking how only an hour or two before we had spent such care getting it ready when suddenly she said: 'Where's Monty?'

We ran down the stairs asking as we went whether anyone had seen him. We ran into the kitchen shouting his name, then into the dining-room, then into the spare bedroom that led from the kitchen. No one had seen him. I ran into the garden calling his name, the guns still firing, the flames in the Brewery leaping into the sky; and I remember how even in that moment of distress I found myself marvelling at the silhouette of a fireman's ladder that was already poised high against the fire, a pin-point of a man at the top of it. 'Monty,' I yelled, 'Monty!' No sign of him there so I went back to the house asking everyone to look, then out onto the river bank where I knew Jeannie had gone. I found her, but no Monty; and after searching for a while we felt our task hopeless, nothing to do except go home and wait. 'He'll turn up,' I said, trying to encourage her.

And half an hour later into the kitchen came one of our guests, a burly Australian war correspondent, with Monty held in his arms like a child. His fur was powdered with plaster, as white as if he had spent the night in a bakery house.

'He'd got in his foxhole,' the Australian said with a grin on his face, using the phrase of a soldier. 'I found him upstairs in the airing-cupboard!'

He was unharmed except for the temporary mess of his fur; and later, when dawn was breaking and the raiders had gone, he decided to sit on the kitchen table and receive the homage of the firemen for whom

Jeannie was pouring cups of tea. The powdery plaster had been licked away; and he sat, tail gently flicking, eyes blinking, dozing like a miniature tiger in the midday sun, utterly sure of himself amidst the hubbub of chatter. He was calmer than any of the humans around him.

And when, to commemorate this end of our first year of marriage, we asked the firemen to sign their names in the visitors' book, one of them scrawled alongside his signature:

'Monty, the handsomest cat I ever saw.'

CHAPTER 5

We left Mortlake two days later to become evacuees with Jeannie's father and mother at St Albans; and within an hour of arrival at his temporary home there was an incident which had an effect on Monty for the rest of his life. He had always been suspicious of dogs, but until St Albans, he had never come face to face with one in the same room.

Bryher Lodge stood on the hill facing east towards London; and on nights when duties did not perforce make us stay in the city we would stand on the terrace above the garden which sloped down to the wood at the bottom, and watch the inferno in the distance. First the little blitz, then, a few weeks later and shortly before we returned to the cottage, the beginning of the flying bombs. We would watch for a few minutes this insanity of the human race, then return indoors to the private war between Judy the Scottie in the house, and Monty.

With Judy, when we came, was Tim the Persian. Tim was the placid old cat with blue grey fur so thick that it made him look as if he was wearing a muff, whose unwelcome attention on my first visit resulted in my knocking over the table on which stood my cup of tea. I was friends with him now, of course, and he was so placid that even Monty's sudden appearance could not annoy him. Tim and Monty tolerated each other from the beginning but Judy, after one look at the evacuee, decided she would not give him a moment's peace. Monty was an interloper, and Judy was never to allow him to forget it.

My own opinion is that Jeannie and her mother were partly to blame because of the method of introduction they chose to arrange. I myself favoured a gradual acclimatization, an interchange of left-over sniffs after one or the other had left the room, a sight of each other in the garden with one of them safely behind a window. I was cautious, I had an instinct of inevitable trouble if suddenly they were placed nose to nose.

I expect trouble was inevitable in any case, but it certainly exploded with the least delay. I unloaded our luggage, lumbered it up to the bedroom and then heard Jeannie cry out: 'Come on downstairs, we're going to introduce Monty to Judy.' Their theory, and I suppose there was some sense in it, was that as Judy and Monty were going to live in the closest proximity, they might as well learn to be friends as quickly as possible; and I arrived in the room just as the introduction was made.

It was over within thirty seconds. Judy leapt at Monty and snapped at his paw. Monty then jumped on a table crashing a vase, remained there for an instant with fur like an upturned brush, then onto the floor dashing between the legs of Jeannie's mother who grabbed him, holding him until he freed himself, whereupon he raced across to the blue velvet curtains, up them like a monkey and remained on the pelmet, snarling like a mad thing at Judy yapping hysterically below.

We ourselves, for a moment, were quite silent. Each of us was thinking how such enmity could possibly be handled during the weeks to come. Jeannie and I, and Monty, despite it being her old home were guests in the house and we could not be expected to be popular if we brought chaos along with us; and Jeannie's mother was saying to herself that at all costs the welcome of our arrival must be brought back to normal. She did so by never disclosing that Monty had gashed her so sharply with his claws that the following day she had four stitches in her arm.

Monty and Judy never came face to face again, yet the atmosphere of their hate remained. If one was allowed free in the house, the other was shut in a room; and the one which was free would be aware of the door behind which was the other. Judy would scratch, Monty would sniff and his fur rise up. It was an unhappy period for both of them, and the immediate effect on Monty was to lessen the affection he had for Jeannie and me. He became remote from us. There were no purrs. It was as if he had lost his personality and was just an animal on four legs which had no thought in its head except to eat and sleep. He would not play. He would not sleep on the bed. His behaviour, in fact, made me lose interest in him. He was a silly, characterless cat.

This zombie attitude continued for four months until, the cottage repaired, we returned home; and within a few minutes of our arrival Monty's old self returned too. He proved it by jumping out of the kitchen window. The window had been his own private entrance, not the main casement window but the small one above it, open and shut by a lever. We had always kept it half open for him, day and night, and he would leap to its frame, pause a moment and disappear outside; or at night we would be in the kitchen and become suddenly aware that Monty had silently appeared from the darkness without and was poised up there,

watching us. On this occasion he had not been in the kitchen a minute
before he jumped up to this window, then down to the garden; and
without waiting he was up again to the window and into the kitchen. We
watched him repeat this act, as if it were a celebration dance, four or five
times; and as we watched we could sense the dull attitude which had
developed disappearing, and the old relationship becoming real again.
'He's actually glad to be home,' I said to Jeannie, as if I were surprised
such a feeling could exist within him. 'He really *knows* he's home.'

My simplicity had its reaction later that night when I was lying
awake, I found myself thinking that as I had learnt to get on perfectly
well without considering Monty while at St Albans, I had better do the
same now at home. I was retracing my steps. I was having a midnight
revolt against my over-indulgence of the cat. I had been hastening to
become as cooing as the cat lovers I used to despise, submerging my own
personality for Monty's benefit, becoming a slave to his wayward habits;
and it was time for me to stop.

St Albans had taught me that one could give a roof to a cat without
losing one's own identity; and although Monty had been plainly
uncomfortable he did not run away, he remained clean, he had a good
appetite. He could, therefore, lead a useful but negative life with us at
the cottage, have his meals and his freedom to wander about, but, as at
St Albans, there was no need for him to enter the stream of our life.

I would not, for instance, become excited just because he jumped in
and out of the kitchen window. I would not consider myself favoured
when he sat on my lap; I would push him off if it suited me. Lying there
in the dark I realized I had been showing all the faults of the convert, all
the undisciplined enthusiasm the novice displays. I had been behaving,
before the change at St Albans, like a fawning servant before its master.
It was ridiculous and tomorrow I must set out to regain my independence whatever tricks Monty might produce. Of course Jeannie was
going to be difficult; but if I were cunning, if I did not take any positive
action against Monty, if I were polite but distant, she would have no
need to suspect the great change that had suddenly taken place inside
me.

She was sound asleep, and Monty was also on the bed, down at the
bottom alongside my feet. I suddenly thought: why not set the pace of
my new attitude towards him immediately? My legs were cramped and
had he not been occupying so much room, I could have stretched them
and been comfortable, and I might even have fallen asleep. Here goes, I
said to myself; and gave him a shove. A second later there was a thud on
the floor, then, a few seconds later he was on the bed again. Another
shove. Another thud.

And at that moment Jeannie woke up, shouting excitedly as one does when alarmed from a dream: 'What's wrong? What's wrong?' 'Nothing at all,' I said soothingly, 'only Monty fell off.'

CHAPTER 6

Monty's memory of Judy, had he been human, might have been eradicated on a psychiatrist's couch; but as it was the rage he felt against her simmered inside him, erupting in an explosion at intervals during the rest of his life. He was determined to fight a ceaseless battle of revenge.

His first victory, soon after our return, was over a bulldog pup belonging to a friend who lived close by. Outside our front door was a tiny garden, enclosed by a three-foot wall to help keep out the high tides of the Thames; and we went over this wall from the garden to the towpath by a ladder of stone steps. These steps were never a particular favourite of Monty's, indeed he usually avoided the tiny front garden as if he disliked the bustle of the towpath on the other side of the wall; but on occasions he liked to sun himself there, and one pleasant morning he was lying on the top step when along came the bulldog pup.

The pup was a bandy-legged brindle and he came jauntily down the alleyway from his home with a sniff here and a sniff there, up to the pillar-box and across to the lamp-post. I was standing myself by the open front door and I watched him amusedly; he looked like a schoolboy on holiday without a care in the world.

But Monty was watching as well. He watched until the pup was within five yards of the steps, then crouching as if to spring at a mouse, he waited for it to come another yard nearer ... and pounced. I was so surprised that I just stared; but the pup, thank goodness, had been attracted the same instant by the railings on the other side of the towpath; and he moved away as Monty sprang, so his stumpy stern met the onslaught instead of his back. A yell of fright from the pup and it set off at a gallop for Chiswick Bridge. It was still galloping long after Monty had stopped the chase; for Monty, as if to put fear into a bulldog was victory enough, returned nonchalantly to the steps after a chase of a few yards and unconcernedly began an elaborate wash. He never attacked the pup again, it never came near enough to let him.

Monty did not seek out his battles with dogs, creating a quarrel because he had nothing else to do. I often, for instance, saw him sitting in contemplation while a dog passed by without his ever making a move. It was when we were about that he became enraged. He either considered himself our protector or, more likely, the memory of Judy ground such jealousy in his mind that for a few moments he reverted to the wild cat of the jungle. No dog was safe whatever the size or breed and, for that matter, no human was safe who tried to stop the attack.

The first human to suffer was an elderly lady who arrived at the cottage with a small terrier on a lead. We did not fully appreciate Monty's temper at the time, and we had taken no steps to shut him in a room when the lady and the terrier entered the downstairs hall. Bang! Monty was hurtling out of the kitchen straight at the terrier and in the shambles that followed the poor lady was gashed in the leg. I had to take her to hospital.

This incident, of course, put us on our guard. We had so to speak to put a notice outside the front door: 'Beware of the Cat.' We had to meet anyone who arrived with a dog and shout: 'Wait out there a minute while we put Monty away.' And if Monty could not be found, the visitor and the dog had to be sneaked in, then rushed upstairs to the sitting-room, and the door firmly shut. Then, when the visit was over, I would act as a scout and see whether Monty was lurking anywhere on the stairs. I had to act like a conspirator, and I used to be thankful when the visitor and his dog were safely waved away.

Yet I never met a dog owner who did not at first believe we were playing a joke. Dog owners inflict their doggy devotion on others more officiously than their cat counterparts, or some of them do. Some dog owners I have found, for instance, are either deaf or peculiarly insensitive. They shut a dog in a house or shed in the garden, and have a sadistic relish in the barks that follow for hour after hour, bringing despair and wild exasperation to the neighbours. It is a form of torture to which I am particularly vulnerable. I lie awake at night and each bark is a hammer blow, and if it comes from a distance, from somewhere unknown to me, I have an uncontrollable desire to get dressed and go searching for the exact source of the hell. The daytime yap, the yap, yap, yap on some afternoon in high summer has seen me seize a stick and march towards the noise, only to halt a few minutes later and go back. For what is the use of action? It is a strange thing about such dog owners, if you complain, if you say you cannot sleep, or get on with your work, or that you are being driven slowly mad, you are seldom met with apologies. You are made to feel it is your fault, certainly not that of the dog or its owner.

Cats, of course, make a hullabaloo on the tiles but only if other cats are there too. Cats on their own are silent while a dog on its own will still bark. Cats may impose their personalities on visitors to their homes but, as they are too independent to go on visits themselves, strange homes are spared them. Dogs bounce out of the car on arrival, go galloping over the flower beds in excitement, ignoring the cries of discipline; or come on a rainy day, shaking their wet coats, mapping the carpet with muddy paws. In our case, however, we had Monty; and so whenever a dog appeared one of us would cry out the alarm: 'Look out, Monty's about!'

The snag lay in the fact that unless the dog owner had visited us before, the reaction was not what we intended. The answer to our alarm was a display of supreme confidence.

'Oh don't worry,' would come the lofty reply, 'Our dog *never* chases cats!' We would try to explain how it would be Monty who did the chasing. 'Don't you understand?' we pleaded, 'Monty will chase *your* dog!' Meanwhile the dog would be running around and, in the distance, we would see a menacing Monty approaching.

At Mortlake we had the front door as the barrier, and so a clash was comparatively easy to avert. But when we came to live at remote Minack, our cottage in Cornwall, Monty could be lying in wait anywhere. Hence the attacks at Minack were more frequent. Monty was only making certain he would never again share his life with a dog.

It was also at the time of his return from St Albans that he developed a growl. Most cats growl at some time or other but it is a sound that is a close cousin to a purr. Monty's growl was a deep-throated challenge of such resonance that he might have acquired it from one of the larger dogs he hated. Yet it was not a weapon of war, a threat to frighten an opponent.

It was a means of self-reassurance, a method of bolstering himself when he found himself in a situation not to his liking. Any odd noise he did not understand would bring forth the growl and, for that matter, any big noise too. He growled at the guns which fired at the flying bombs, and at thunder, and when rockets took the place of flying bombs he growled at them. The first rocket which ever landed in Britain landed within a mile of Mortlake; and it is Monty's growl I remember, not the explosion.

Sometimes the growl made us laugh because he uttered it when caught in a predicament. There was an elm tree close to the cottage at Mortlake and up it he went one day, leaping from branch to branch, higher and higher, showing no sign he was soon to lose his nerve. I have never understood this particular blind spot of cats, how time and again they will climb to inaccessible places with the greatest of ease, then become transfixed by the height they have reached. I hate heights myself. I have an occasional nightmare which has me racing to the top of

Everest; nothing hinders my climb, no hint of fear, until there I am looking out above the world ... and quite incapable of descending. Monty too was incapable of descending and I had to fetch a ladder, and when the ladder did not reach him I had to climb up to him branch by branch. He was obviously terrified but he was not miaowing. He was growling.

A time came when we had chickens at the top of the garden, a dozen Rhode Island Reds penned in a small compound by wire netting on the side that faced the garden. On the other sides were high walls and on some point on these walls Monty would sit looking down on them while they clucked in troubled excitement. He was fascinated by their antics. Hour after hour he would crouch like a Buddha, eyeing them, trying to make up his mind what could be the purpose of their presence. At last he decided to make a closer investigation and he descended from the wall to the compound. I did not see him make his descent but I was in the garden reading a book when I heard the cacophony that hens make when a fox is among them. It was only Monty, an embarrassed Monty, surrounded by twelve furious ladies whom he was keeping at bay with his growl.

CHAPTER 7

My midnight revolt, my show of independence when I kicked Monty off the bed, was in retreat by next morning. It takes two to sustain a revolt. You cannot keep up a revolt if the opposition insists on showing affection. Monty ignored my off-hand behaviour, forcing himself on my lap whenever he wished to do so, kneading my knees with his claws, letting me watch his back bulge like bellows with his purrs. For my part I could not refrain from stroking his silky fur, gently massaging his backbone and tracing a finger round his beautiful markings. I would have been of stone if I hadn't. His presence was therapeutic, and he brought a calm to the hectic life we led.

In the years which followed the end of the war we were seldom home in the evenings except at week-ends. The nature of our work rushed us from party to party and we used to return home increasingly exhausted as the week developed. One becomes casual in such circumstances. One is so absorbed in fulfilling the basic responsibilities, that one is inclined to be blind to the subtleties that enrich life. Monty was a subtlety, and although we were always sure to give him a rapturous greeting whatever hour of the night we got back, he was, I think, treated by us more as a toy than an animal. It was a period that I look back upon as distressing; and yet it had its value. It helped us in due course to form our decision to pack up our jobs and leave London. It helped us, for instance, to realize it is more important to be true to oneself than to accept unthinkingly the standards of others.

Monty, in this period, was like a toy because the haste in our life only spared us the time to bestow affection on our own terms. He was like a child in a Victorian family who was shoved into the drawing-room by a nurse only at times when the parents were in a mood to see him. He would be used as a receptacle of our emotions, hugged and kissed in times of distress, expected to play games if we demanded them, shown off like an exhibit to appropriate friends. I have seen many cats, and dogs, treated in this way, and have disliked the sight of it. When human beings use their pet animals as agents of their own exhibitionism it means humiliation both for the human being and the animal; except that the human being concerned is too dumb to feel it. Often, of course, there are people who are frightened to show affection, or think it a curious kind of bad form either in themselves or in others; hence they consider pets should be treated as if behind bars in a zoo. These are the people who bury a cat or a dog one day, and buy a substitute the next, preferably of the same colour or breed so that the sequence of outward appearance remains undisturbed. Sometimes, of course, this is done not because of callousness but of fear, a fear of being unable to live a while with a memory. Either case provides an attitude which is unfair to the pet; for the first suggests it was no more important than an old kitchen chair while the second proposes that the death of a friendship can be swopped for a physical resemblance. I do not advocate a mourning, but I suggest that as a pet is a giver during its life and a human is usually a taker, a human should not accept an animal in his home unless he is prepared to make sacrifices which deserve affection.

One can also go to the other extreme and behave to an animal like a neurosis-ridden parent to his child; who must not swim because the sea might be dangerous, or own a bicycle, or stay out after dark, or who is fussed over like an invalid. Pampered animals can be observed any day of the week. Yet this other extreme need not be a form of neurosis or, for that matter, of exhibitionism. One can love an animal overmuch because of its vulnerability, because it makes one feel secure in an insecure world, because as it grows older it reflects the years of one's life. In due course we loved Monty overmuch but at this time, at this brittle period of our life, he was a toy; which had the merits of an anchor in our restless existence.

He would glare at us from inside the dining-room window as we arrived home, the sweep of the headlights shining on his fierce face. 'We're in trouble again,' I would say as I put the key in the door. It was perfectly true that he had the knack of making us feel we had misbehaved, that two o'clock in the morning was a disgraceful hour to return home. We would switch on the light and hurry into the dining-room ready to gush a greeting, only to find he had not moved, that he was still staring out of the window pretending to be unaware of our arrival except for the sharp flicks of his tail.

Jeannie used to come ready to bribe on these occasions and after she had purposely clattered plates in the kitchen and unwrapped some small paper parcel that had been donated by the Savoy restaurant, Monty would enter with the air of a cat who was ready to let bygones be bygones. He would devour the delicacy, lick the pattern off the plate but, unfortunately, would not pay the price expected of him. Jeannie's caresses were spurned and he would struggle free from her arms, jump first on the sink then up through his private entrance above the kitchen window, and disappear into the night. He was an opportunist, not a weak character open to a bribe.

There were other times when there was no doubt he had become unhappy in our absence. I knew the sign when we stood at the front door and heard him come thumping down the bare wood stairs, wakened by the sound of the car as we drew up. 'He's only hungry,' I would say to Jeannie, mocking his greeting. But if he was hungry it was not the hunger which was the result of a bribe. He did not bellicosely clean the plate, then away into the night. He would eat a little then look up at us watching him; and I defy the person who does not believe he was saying thank you. And afterwards he would not refuse to pay the price of his meal. Jeannie was permitted to hug him, as many hugs as she wanted, and carry him upstairs and deposit him on the bed where he lay curled through the night. There was now no fear of my kicking him off.

He was not on his own all the time. We did not leave him at nine in the morning and let him fend for himself until our return at any old hour. He had his friends. There was our daily, Mrs Hales, who had to queue for his whiting before she arrived at the cottage; whiting the staple diet, with the stink that hung for hours in the cottage. Mrs Hales was ill one day but as she lay in her bed she realized that the whiting, bought and cooked two days before, must have been consumed. 'Oh dear,' she said, explaining the situation to us later, 'oh dear, there I lay thinking of poor Monty. Whatever will he do, I said. All by 'imself and nothing to eat. It mustn't be I said. So I got up and called a neighbour through the window. "Our Monty," I said, "'asn't got 'is whiting. Do me a favour, will you?" I said. "Go to the fish shop and get three nice whiting. I can manage to cook 'em ... then I'll send me 'usband up to Monty when 'e comes 'ome from work."'

There were Mr and Mrs Foster who lived next door at the Ship. The Fosters had been landlords since 1912, through the times when the Ship, as the pub at the finishing post of the Boat Race, was a pivot of the great day. Maharajahs, Cabinet Ministers, famous actors and actresses, as Gus and Olivette Foster never ceased telling us, used to be their customers then, shouting the crews to victory between glasses of champagne. There was none of that now; the bars were crowded on the big day, the steps of the pub and the towpath in front were jammed with people, but for the Fosters it was a poor imitation of what they remembered.

A high wall divided our small garden from theirs; and theirs was large enough for Gus Foster, in the distant past, to tether the trotting ponies the racing of which was once his hobby. This wall was Monty's favourite and he would reach it by way of the kitchen window and the flat roof of our spare room which ran along a short way beside it. Thus Monty, as he patrolled the top of this wall, could be observed not only from our side but also from the back windows of the Ship by anyone, such as the Fosters' son with the nickname of Whiskers, who might be at work in the garden.

Both Whiskers and his sister Doris had a particular interest in Monty, but as Doris worked in London during the day, it was Whiskers, the barman in the pub, who mostly kept a watch on his outside activities. He was in his garden one day digging a patch of ground when he heard a terrific hullabaloo on the other side of the wall as if it came through an open window from inside the house. Quite obviously the noise was of two fighting cats and one of them, presumably, was Monty.

Now the Fosters kept the key of our front door for just this kind of emergency, and Whiskers we always considered as a guardian of Monty in our absence. He was about to rush in for the key when the noise suddenly rose to a crescendo, followed a few seconds later by a huge tabby racing along the top of the wall with Monty at his tail. Whiskers said afterwards he was so delighted to see such a victory that he shouted: 'Well done, Monty!' at the top of his voice. But Monty, left alone on the wall after the tabby had fled over another, was obviously hurt. He lifted up a paw, looked down at Whiskers and miaowed loudly.

So Whiskers fetched the key and went inside our cottage and into the garden, and coaxed Monty down from the wall and into his arms. It was a nasty bite and we had the vet for him that evening; for Whiskers had immediately rung up Jeannie to tell her of the battle.

And what was the battle about? Instead of the stink of fish in the kitchen there was the stink of a tom cat. The tabby had stolen the whiting.

CHAPTER 8

Not only the Fosters but others along the river bank kept a watch on Monty. He was a talisman to the passers-by as he sat in the dining-room window, hour after hour, waiting for our return. One autumn we spent a month in Paris and when we got back we were looked at reproachfully by those who had seen him day after day in the window. 'You should have seen him late at night when the street lamp lit up his face,' said a neighbour, 'he looked so mournful.' We hated to hear such remarks because we felt we were in the wrong. Of course he had been well looked after by his guardians but he had been very lonely. And yet what does one do if ever one wishes to go away for a holiday with an easy conscience? Deposit a cat at the vet and you may think it is safe but you cannot possibly persuade yourself that the cat in such strange surroundings does not believe it has been deserted and has been left in a prison. There seems to be no answer except never to take a holiday.

Monty's big day in the dining-room window was Boat Race day. The Boat Race party, as far as we were concerned, came round each year much too quickly. An annual affair which had such raucous results as a Boat Race party, is apt to dissolve in some mysterious way with its predecessors. Time stands still. The guests have never left, or they are always just arriving or saying goodbye. Hence my old friends Mr and Mrs X are greeted by me at the door and I feel I am simultaneously greeting them this year, last year and the year before. Ours used to be a bottle party and as the Boat Race generally took place at some unearthly hour in the morning, guests began to arrive with their bottles at 9 a.m. The trouble with a bottle party is the stress it puts on the host and hostess who are inclined to greet their guests with graduated enthusiasm, according to the importance of the bottle. We had one guest who regularly brought a bottle of milk. I never found out whether this was a joke, for he consumed alcohol like everyone else; but I remember how our greeting became dimmer each year until it would have become extinct had we not departed for Cornwall.

The preparations, of course, began at the crack of dawn and as it was always a marathon day of festivity, large quantities of food were prepared to cope with late breakfasts, lunch, tea and those who still had the stamina to stay for supper. For Monty these preparations were a nuisance and this might be considered surprising because, with so much food about, one might have expected him to be the official taster. But he was never a greedy cat. He ate his requirements and no more, although like all of us he had certain favourite dishes, chopped pigs' liver, for instance, which he gobbled faster than others. He considered these preparations a nuisance, I think, because he wanted to get on with the party. He had a role to play, and it was a role which he enjoyed.

He would keep out of sight, the airing-cupboard was the ideal hiding-place, until he had the good sense to realize the towpath was waking up; shouts of small boys who without reason for loyalty to either University were violently partisan on behalf of one or other of the crews, odd couples booking places on the railings, then the appearance of hawkers with dark and light blue favours. There was a pleasant atmosphere of impending excitement, and it was now that Monty appeared and expected attention.

Both Jeannie and I were Cambridge supporters and before our first Boat Race party Jeannie had bought Monty a large light blue ribbon which she tied in a bow round his neck. I did not approve. I thought such a gesture was ostentatious and silly and I anticipated confidently that Monty would wriggle free from the encumbrance as soon as he had the chance. He did not do so. True the ribbon became more and more askew as the day wore on with the bow finishing up under his tummy, but this had nothing to do with any action on his part. It was the attention he received which caused that.

Hence the light blue ribbon became an annual ritual and invariably, after the bow had been tied, he would sit in the dining-room window staring with a lordly air at the crowds; and the crowds looking for a diversion until the race began would call to him and shout to their friends about him. He adored this period of glory. So much on his own but now at last receiving his due. And when our guests arrived, a hundred or more packing the cottage, a cacophony of laughter and talk, cigarette smoke clouding the rooms, people sitting on the floor and the stairs, glasses everywhere, Jeannie and I rushing around with bottles and plates of cold food, Monty was as cool as a cucumber. He would stroll from room to room, pausing beside a guest when the praise was high, even deigning to jump on a lap, ignoring the cat haters, refusing with well-bred disgust any morsel dangled before him by some well-meaning admirer. He was unobtrusively sure of himself; and when the rackety day was over, when Jeannie and I had gone to bed feeling too tired to sleep and we put out a hand and touched him at the bottom of the bed, we both felt safe. Safe, I mean, from the tensions among which we lived.

Sometimes I wonder if we would ever have come to Cornwall had it not been for Monty. Decisions are often based on motives which are not obviously apparent, and cool intellects certainly would not believe that two people could change the mainspring of their life because of a cat. Such intellects, however, are free from turbulent emotions. They are the human version of the computer; to be envied, perhaps, because they are spared the distractions of light and shade. They can barge through life indifferent to the sensibilities of others because they have none themselves. Materialism in their view, is the only virtue.

Monty became a factor in our decision because he reflected, in his own fashion, stability. It did not matter how tired we were when we reached home, how irritated we might be by the day's conflict of personalities, how worried by inflated anxieties, how upset by apparent failures, Monty was solidly there to greet us. His presence, you might say, knocked sense back into us. He thus gave a clue to the kind of reward we might have if we exchanged our existing way of life for one that had a more enduring standard of values. We did not say this self-consciously at the time, too many other factors were involved; but on reflection I realize his example helped us to take the plunge.

The process of changing over from a city to a country life was spread over a year and more. We made several sorties to the cottage near Land's End during that time, and Monty was usually a companion. He appeared to be quite unconcerned by the long car journey except once, and that was my fault. I was naturally on guard against him jumping out of the car in a panic whenever on the route I had to slow down or stop; but there came a time when I exchanged my ordinary car for a Land Rover. A saloon car you could shut tight but a Land Rover with its canvas hood had potential gaps through which a determined cat might escape. I therefore bought him a basket and at the instant of leaving Mortlake I pushed him in it, banged down the lid and tied it, and set off. It was an appalling miscalculation. Instead of appreciating my action as a gesture towards his own safety, he took it as an insult. He was enraged. He clawed and spat and cried and growled. I was half way to Staines when the noise of his temper forced me to stop, and I gingerly lifted the lid up an inch. A pair of eyes of such fury blazed through the slit that I hastily banged down the lid again.

Now Jeannie was with me on this occasion and inevitably this incident developed an argument. She wanted to take him out of the basket. I was too scared that once allowed to be free there would be no holding him. My imagination saw him gashing us with his claws as he fought to escape, then away like a madman into the countryside. She, however, insisted that only the basket angered him and he would be his old gentle self as soon as he was let out. So the argument went on, past Staines, past Camberley, past Basingstoke; it was not until we reached the outskirts of Andover that I gave in. Monty was released and, with a look of disgust in my direction, the purrs began.

There was another occasion when he travelled as a stowaway on the night train from Paddington. Jeannie was always very proud of this exploit as she was the architect of its success. She was due to join me for the week-end and was dining at the Savoy before catching her sleeper when she suddenly decided she would like Monty to accompany her. She dashed back to Mortlake, found him, after a five minute desperate search, crouched on the wall at the end of the garden, and arrived at Paddington with three minutes to spare. Monty was an admirable conspirator. He remained perfectly still as she rushed him along the platform wrapped in a rug. Not a miaow. Not a growl. And nobody would ever have known that the night train had carried a cat, had Jeannie been able to curb her vociferous enthusiasm when she arrived at Penzance.

But she behaved as if the Crown Jewels were in her compartment. She was in such a high state of excitement when I met her that she did not notice the car attendant was directly behind me as she slid open the door to disclose her secret.

Monty's aplomb was superb. He stared at the man with regal indifference from the bunk. And as I recovered from my surprise and Jeannie muttered feeble excuses, all the car attendant found himself able to say was: 'Good heavens, what a beautiful cat!'

Five minutes later we were in the car on the road to Minack.

CHAPTER 9

Monty was wary in the beginning at Minack. He did not relax on those initial short visits, seldom put his nose outside the cottage, making even a walk of a few yards in our company a notable occasion. He was seven years old and needed time for readjustment.

Minack is a cottage a few hundred yards from the cliff and cupped in a shallow valley with a wood behind it. The walls grow up from great rocks which some crofter a few centuries ago decided would make the ideal foundation. The stones of the walls are bound together with clay and, when we first came, the floor inside the cottage was of earth layered over by thin boards. There are two rooms; one, which is the length of the cottage is our living-room and kitchen, the other a tiny one, is our bedroom; and there is a third room which we added as an extension along with a bathroom that became known in his lifetime as Monty's room. On one side of the cottage the windows stare out undisturbed, except for the old barn buildings, across moorland to the sea and the distant coastline rimming Mount's Bay; on the other, two small windows on either side of the door face a pocket of a garden. The old crofter, the architect of Minack, wished to defend the cottage against the south westerlies; and so this little garden, and the cottage, were set in the hill that rose away to the west. Thus, if we walk up the hill fifty yards and look back, the eye is level with the massive granite chimney; the chimney which to fishermen sailing back to Mousehole and Newlyn in a stormy sea gives the comfortable feeling they are near home.

There is no house or eyesore in sight; and this freedom amid such untamed country provides a sense of immorality. As if here is a life that belongs to any century, that there is no harsh division in time, that the value of true happiness lies in the enduring qualities of nature. The wind blows as it did when the old crofter lived at Minack, so too the robin's song, and the flight of the curlew, and the woodpecker's knock on an elm. This sense of continuity may be unimportant in a world with the knowledge to reach the stars; but to us it provided the antidote to the life we had led. It was a positive reminder that generations had been able to find contentment without becoming slaves of the machine. Here around us were the ghosts of men and animals, long forgotten storms and hot summer days, gathered harvests and the hopes of spring. They were all one, and our future was part of them.

Our plan was to earn a living by growing flowers and, the speciality of the district, early potatoes in pocket meadows on the cliff. We were, however, more influenced by the beauty of the environment than by its practical value; hence we presented ourselves with difficulties which had to be borne as a sacrifice to our whim. There was, for instance, no lane to the cottage. A lane ran from the main road a half mile to a group of farm buildings at the top of the valley; but once past these buildings it became rougher and rougher until it stuttered to a stop amid brambles and gorse. In due course we cut a way through and made a road, but in the beginning the nearest we could take the car to Minack was the distance of two fields; and across these two fields we used to carry our luggage ... and Monty.

Jeannie on the first visit put butter on his paws. There had been a sad, remarkable case in a newspaper of a cat that had been taken away from his home near Truro to another near Chester from which he had immediately disappeared. Several weeks later he arrived back to his old Truro home but so exhausted and close to starvation that he died a day or two later. I do not pretend to believe this story, documented in detail as it was, but Jeannie did, and she had a vision of Monty dashing from Minack and making for Mortlake. Thus she used the old wives' recipe for keeping a cat at home by buttering his paws; the theory being of course that the cat licks off the butter and says to himself that such a nice taste is worth staying for. A slender theory, I think, though comforting.

But it was soon made clear on that first visit and repeated on succeeding ones that Monty had no intention of running away. It was the opposite that provided us with problems. He never had the slightest wish to leave.

During this period, as I have said, he distrusted the outside around the cottage, made nervous perhaps by the unaccustomed silence and the unknown mysterious scents; and when we urged him to come out with us, he would usually turn tail as soon as we dropped him to the ground and rush back indoors. He was, in fact, sometimes so timid that he annoyed me, and I would pick him up again, deliberately deposit him a hundred yards from the cottage, then, impotently, crossly, watch him race back again.

Why, then, did he always disappear when we were due to start back for Mortlake? The bags would be packed, one load perhaps already lugged across the fields to the car, and there would be no sign of Monty. Obstinately remaining inside the cottage when we wanted him to be out, he was now out when we wanted him to be in. But where? The first disappearance resulted in a delay of two hours in our departure for we had no clue where to look. He had no haunts to which he might have sneaked, because he had never been long enough out of the cottage on his own to find one; no haunts, that is, that we knew of. Yet apparently on one of his brief excursions he had made a note of the barn, and how at the bottom of the barn door was a hole big enough for him to wriggle through; and that as the barn at the time was not ours and the door was kept locked, and the key kept by a farmer ten minutes away, it was a wonderful place to hide in. It became a ritual for him to hide there at the end of each visit. The key fetched, the key returned, and in between I would have had to climb to a beam near the ceiling where Monty glared balefully down at me. Or was he saying: 'I like it here. Hurry up and make it my home?'

It became his home one April evening when the moon was high. We had now cleared a way through the brush of the lane and though the surface was too rough for ordinary cars, it was suitable enough for a Land Rover. On this particular evening we bumped our way along it, the canvas hood bulging with our belongings. Monty alert on Jeannie's lap, both of us ecstatically happy that at last the time-wasting preliminaries had been completed. We drew up with a jerk and I switched off the engine. It was a beautiful moment. No sound but that of the surf in the distance. The moon shimmering the cottage as if it were a ghost cottage. Here was journey's end and adventure's beginning. All we had worked for had materialized.

'Good heavens, we're lucky,' I said, then added briskly as if to foreshadow the practical instead of the romantic side of our life to come, 'I'll get the luggage out ... you go ahead with Monty and light the candles.'

But it was Monty who went ahead. He jumped from Jeannie's lap, paused for a moment to see she was ready to follow, then sedately led the way up the path. A confident cat. A cat who knew he was home. A cat, in fact, who was happy.

CHAPTER 10

Monty's transition into a country cat was a gradual affair. An urban gentleman does not become a country gentleman simply by changing his clothes. He must learn to adopt a new code of manners and a new approach to the outdoors; to be less suave and to show more bluster, to accept the countryside as a jungle which has to be mastered by skill and experience. Monty, as an urban cat, had therefore a lot to learn.

He first had to acclimatize himself to having us always around and he showed his delight in various ways. There was, for instance, the in-and-out window game, a game which was designed not only to display his affection but also to confirm his wonderment that we were now always present to obey his orders. Thus he would jump on a windowsill and ask to be let out, only, a few minutes later, to be outside another window asking to be let in. This performance would continue for an hour until one of us lost patience, saying crossly: 'For goodness' sake, Monty, make up your mind what you want to do.' He would then have the good sense to stop the game, replacing it probably by a short, though vigorous, wash.

There were the unsolicited purrs. A cat has to be in a very bad mood if a human cannot coax him to purr. There is little honour in this achievement, only the satisfaction that a minute or two is being soothed by such a pleasant sound. But the unsolicited purrs belong to quite another category. These are the jewels of the cat fraternity distributed sparingly like high honours in a kingdom. They are brought about by great general contentment. No special incident induces them. No memory of past or prospect of future banquets. Just a whole series of happy thoughts suddenly combine together and whoever is near is lucky enough to hear the result. Thus did Monty from time to time reward us.

My own preference was for the midnight unsolicited purr. For the first years, until we found a fox waiting for Monty to jump out, he had the freedom of the window at night. He used to go in and out and we were never disturbed if he chose to spend the night outside, perhaps in the barn. But when he did choose to remain indoors, and instead of settling on the sofa, preferred a corner of our bed, we felt flattered. It was then that I have relished when sometimes I lay awake, the rich, rolling tones of an unsolicited purr.

In those early days the unsolicited purr was bestowed on us frequently. Later, when country life became to him a continuously happy routine it became rarer; but in the beginning the new pattern of his life was so ebulliently wonderful that he could not restrain himself. There he would be on the carpet in the posture of a Trafalgar lion and suddenly the music would begin. For no reason that we could see. Just his personal ecstasy.

There were other times when his show of affection was awkward. It was then that he posed a question that as a cat hater I used to find easy to answer, but now as a cat lover I found most difficult. How do you summon up courage to dismiss a cat who is paying you the compliment of sitting on your lap?

If you have a train to catch, if your life is governed by rules not of your own making, the excuse for removal is ready made. But in my case time was my own, the work to be done was the product of my own self-discipline, I could not blame anyone else if I shoved off Monty who was comfortably enjoying a rest on my lap. I would gingerly start to lift him up, my hands softly encircling his middle, with the intention of placing him gently on the spot I was about to vacate; and he would hiss, growl and very likely bite my hand. True this was a momentary flash of temper with more noise than harm in it; but the prospect of its display, the certainty I was offending him, were enough time and again for me to postpone any action.

My subservience was made to look even more foolish when Jeannie, as she often did, served a meal on a tray. My seat was always the corner one of the sofa and so I used to endeavour to balance the plate-filled tray partly on the sofa arm, partly on Monty's back; trying, of course, to take great care not to put any weight on Monty. If, however, he showed signs of annoyance, if he woke up from his sleep and turned his head crossly round at me, I would edge the tray further over the arm so that it balanced like the plank of a see-saw. I enjoyed many meals this way in the greatest discomfort.

Rational people would not behave like that. I can imagine my own sneers if a few years before I had seen into the future and found I was going to behave in such a fashion. But there it was, I enjoyed it. I was glad to be of some service, and I used to be tinged with jealousy if he chose on occasions to honour Jeannie instead. Such occasions were rare because her lap was not up to his measurements. He overfilled it. He was like a large man on a small stool. She would sit, transfixed into immobility, and if at the time anything was being cooked in the oven it was sure to be burnt. Pleasure is relative to the desire of the individual. I do not know what pleasure Jeannie could have been offered in exchange for such moments with Monty.

These incidents may suggest that, now that the three of us were always together, Monty was spoilt. But is not a cat's nature, any cat, impervious to being spoilt? You can spoil a child and it can become a nuisance. You can spoil a dog and everyone except its owner is certain to suffer. A cat on the other hand, however luscious may be the bribes, remains cool and collected. Indulgence never goes to its head. It observes flattery instead of accepting it. Monty, for instance, did not consider himself an inferior member of the household; a pet, in fact. Thus he loathed it when condescension was shown to him; and many a misguided stranger trying to lure him with snapping fingers and 'pussy talk' has seen his haughty back. He was co-tenant of the cottage. He was not to be treated in that imbecile fashion so many people reserve for animals. The compliments he wished for were of the kind we gave him; we set out to implement any decision he made on his own by helping to make the result as successful as possible. We played the role of the ideal servants and we won our reward by watching his enjoyment. And there was another reward which Jeannie called 'paying his rent'.

His rent was making him do what he did not want to do. Hence this was the reward we forced him to give us when we felt in the mood to assert our authority. Jeannie might suddenly pick him up, hold him in her arms and hug him, when it was perfectly obvious that he wished to be left by himself. He would lie in her arms, a pained expression on his face, as she talked sweet nothings to him; and then, the rent paid, he would rush across the room to a windowsill and sit there, tail slashing like a scythe, demanding to be let out.

I always maintained that Jeannie demanded more rent than I did. I think she had good reason to do so because she was responsible for his catering; and she was always filling plates or picking up empty ones or asking him to make up his mind what he wanted. 'Oh really, Monty,' she would say in mock fierceness, with Monty looking up at her as she stood by the sink, 'I've just thrown one saucer of milk away, you can't want another!' Or it might be one more morsel of fish required, and out would come the pan and down would go the plate.

His menu, now that we lived near a fishing port, was splendidly varied, and twice a week Jeannie would collect from Newlyn a supply of fresh fish. None of that shop-soiled whiting he used to have but sea-fresh whiting, boned megram sole or a little halibut or, what became his most favourite of all – John Dorey, the fish which fishermen themselves take home for their suppers. He would gobble John Dorey until he bulged, one of the few things which lured him to greed; and to satisfy this greed he would try to show his most endearing self to Jeannie. The spot where his saucers were placed was opposite the front door on the carpet at the foot of a bookcase which hid one corner of the sink. When he was hungry, a normal hunger not too demanding, he would sit on this spot, upright with front paws neatly together and the tip of his tail gently flicking them. His eyes would be half closed and he would sway imperceptibly to and fro. A meal was due but he was in no hurry.

Yet if John Dorey was on the menu and was simmering in a pan on the stove he could never restrain his impatience. He would walk excitedly up and down the room, roaring with anticipated pleasure, rubbing himself against Jeannie's legs, looking up at her as if he were saying: 'I love you, I love you.' Here was a cat who was no longer retaining his dignity. Nothing could hide the fact that at this particular moment Monty was thinking that Jeannie was the most wonderful cook in the world.

He would then have been ready to promise her, I am sure, all the rent she required.

CHAPTER 11

Monty's hunting at Mortlake had been limited to indoor mice, or indoor mice which happened to be outside. He soon began to find at Minack a variety of potential victims the like of which he had never seen before; and in some cases he was at a loss to the technique of attack required. I found him once, for instance, staring at a patch of ground under which a mole was digging.

My own first experience of a mole digging was the morning after a night out. It upset me. I was walking across a field, my head down, when I was suddenly aware that a patch of soil the size of a hat was moving. I stopped, stared and pinched myself. The soil circled like a slow spinning top, rising upwards, the texture of a seed bed. Monty saw this for the first time and was as startled as I had been. He put out a paw as if he were thinking of touching a red-hot coal, then leapt backwards with a growl. 'It's only a mole, old chap,' I said knowledgeably, 'only a mole digging a mole hill.' He was reassured enough to advance again. He touched the soil with his paw, then, meeting with no reaction, in fact finding there was no danger or excitement for him at all, he walked away with nonchalant composure; as cats do when they suspect they have made fools of themselves.

Another puzzle for him was what to do when he found an adder. A lizard, a slow worm or an ordinary grass snake was an easy excuse for a few minutes' play, but an adder he sensed was a danger; and he was certainly right. We have too many of them about. We are always on guard during the summer wearing wellington boots whenever we walk through the undergrowth; although it is in a warm spring when they are at their most viperish. I have been happily picking Scilly Whites on the cliff when I have suddenly seen the poised head of one within a few inches of my hand, hissing like escaped steam. In the summer they will wriggle away as you advance towards them and will whip up their heads and strike only if you step on them or tease them. In the spring they will attack at the slightest provocation and, as they have been hibernating through the winter, the venom injected into the wounds made by the fangs is a dose built up over the months. I learnt my lesson after the Scilly Whites, but Monty never learnt his lesson not to tease.

I have seen him touching the tail of an adder with his paw as if he were playing a dare game. It might have been even a form of Russian roulette because an adder can kill a cat, though this is very rare. As an adder is thirty inches long, perhaps he was deceived into thinking that the head was too far away to catch him, or perhaps I was worrying unnecessarily. He certainly never was bitten by an adder, nor for that matter did he ever kill one. He flirted with the danger. It was a game ... and yet, I wonder. There is a tradition in Cornwall that the capture and killing of an adder is the peak of a cat's hunting career; and when the rare victory is achieved the trophy is ceremoniously dragged whatever distance to the home and deposited on the floor of the kitchen for all to admire. Perhaps this was Monty's secret ambition. Perhaps above all he longed for the plaudits awarded to an adder killer. If so, the fates were against him.

I will not, fortunately, ever know the differences in flavour of mice – indoor mice, harvest mice, long-tailed mice, short-eared mice and so on. Shrews must be unpleasant because Monty, although he would catch them for fun, never ate them. But it seems obvious to me after watching the attitude of Monty that outdoor mice have a far better flavour than the ordinary household mice. At Mortlake, he became, without being flamboyantly successful, a sound indoor-mouse catcher. At Minack he spent so much time outside on the alert that often he lost the desire to fulfil his inside duties; and since the excitement of the chase should be the same both in and out, it occurred to me sometimes that the cause of his extraordinary behaviour may have been a bored palate.

I would be quite wrong to suggest that we were riddled with mice at Minack. For months we would be totally free of any sign of a mouse but at intervals one or two would arrive and cause us annoyance. They would make an unwelcome noise on the boards which provided our ceiling, and on occasions would descend to the sitting-room. Here Monty was often sleeping on the sofa. 'Monty!' I would say sharply. 'There's a mouse in the cupboard.' And Monty would go on sleeping.

The cupboard concerned was the shape of a large wardrobe, shelves climbing two sides while the back was the wall of the cottage. Apart from the china on the shelves with cups on hooks, there was a table in the cupboard on which stood a Calor gas refrigerator; and under the table was the gas cylinder, pots and pans, a bread bin and various other household paraphernalia. Thus the cupboard was crowded and a mouse had a wonderful place to hide unless we set about clearing a space by removing the chattels into the sitting-room. We would perform this tedious task, then wake up Monty, carry him to the cupboard, and deposit him there. He was alone, except for the gas cylinder which was too much trouble to move, with the mouse.

Here, then, was a situation that was often repeated. Monty one side of the gas cylinder and the mouse on the other, and Monty had only to race once round the cylinder to catch it. Yet he would not budge. He would sit looking at me as if he were trying to tell me the mouse was his dearest friend. 'Go on, Monty!' my voice rising to a crescendo. 'Go on, you ass. Catch it!' The mouse would move its position and I would push Monty towards it so that they met nose to nose. Still not a whisker of interest. Nor any sign of fear from the mouse. I would push and exhort and be angry and in the end give up in despair. Monty had a pact with the mouse and nothing I could do would make him break it.

But why? He was swift as a panther when outside. He would be across the land and into the hedge and back again with his capture inside a few seconds; and when necessary he had infinite patience. I always found it an endearing sight to look through the window and see him in the distance perched on a rock, staring intently at the grass a yard away; then begin to gather himself for the pounce, shifting the stance of his paws,' swaying gently forwards and backwards, until he gauged the great moment had come. And when he missed, when by some miscalculation he ended up in the grass with his back legs spreadeagled and a waving tail denoting his failure, I sensed with him his disappointment. His successes, of course, were loudly trumpeted. He consumed his victims not at the place of execution but on a square yard of ground on the edge of the path leading up to the cottage. No matter how distant the capture he would return with it to this spot; and I would see him coming jauntily up the lane, a mouthful of grass as well as the mouse. A few minutes later when nothing was left he would let out the bellow of victory. 'Well done, Monty,' we would say, 'well done!'

He was a wonderful hunter of rabbits, and he had an earnest idea that these should always be brought into the cottage and left under my desk until I had seen them. This behaviour was prompted by my enthusiasm for the first rabbit he caught. It was a baby one and the incident took place within a month of his arrival at Minack; and because I was so anxious to see him settle down, my enthusiasm and that of Jeannie was far too vociferous.

I was writing a letter and never knew he had entered the room until I heard a soft jungle cry at my feet; and there was Monty, like a retriever, looking up at me with the rabbit beside him. He was inordinately proud of himself. He strode up and down the room as we praised him, with purrs loud enough for three cats, rubbing against us, then scampering back across the room to have another sniff. He never forgot the glory of this moment, and time and again we had to suffer a repeat performance. If we saw him coming we shut the door, and there was always plenty of time to do so. A rabbit was far too big for him to carry in his mouth, and he would pull it along on the ground. 'Poor rabbit,' Jeannie would say, dead though it was.

Monty never touched birds, except once when I saw him catch a wren which annoyed him. Wrens can be foolish and this one was foolish. They are so small that if they kept themselves to themselves no one need know their whereabouts; instead they proclaim their presence by the cross rattle of warning and, in spring, enjoy baiting any objects they dislike. There was Monty lying somnolent in the garden while a pair of wrens rattled around him until he lost his temper and snatched one. I dashed forward, caught him, and put a hand to his mouth; and as I did so, he let the wren go and it flew safely away to a bush where it began its rattle again. And Monty went back to doze.

Monty's docile attitude to birds met its response from them. They showed no fear of him. It was I, if anything, who felt fear. I was always waiting for the incident that never happened.

CHAPTER 12

I become vague when I try to isolate the years. I would like to have them arrayed in my mind in neat compartments but I find instead they merge into each other, and incidents connect themselves by haphazard association rather than by dates. Thus the flower seasons here at Minack, each of which has a slow-moving yet mounting dramatic entity of its own, become dissolved in my mind into all flower seasons. The hours I have crouched weeding anemones or picking violets, lugging baskets of daffodils to the packing shed, rushing the flower boxes in the morning to Penzance Station, these hours do not belong to one year but to all years. So also appear the storms that have battered Minack, and the lazy pleasure of hot summer days, the first scent of the may, the arrival of the chiff chaffs, the wonder of an angry sea with a fishing boat fighting for home. I have grown older not by passing each incident as if it were a milestone, but by being absorbed by them.

As Monty grew older his contentment was so obvious for all to see that we felt part of it. If something had gone wrong, if we had suffered some defeat which left us despondent, the sight of his magnificent person poised perhaps on some wall with the sun glinting on his red-bracken coat, his head alertly surveying the scene around him, would be enough to quell our momentary fears. His example was a positive contribution to the life we had chosen for ourselves.

I suppose it was this contentment that produced in him his calm attitude to birds. There was no need for him to kill for the sake of killing because he had so much else to do and, for that matter, so much else to think about. He was a great thinker. We have seen him so many, many times blinking away in the sun, not asleep, not awake, sitting upright with paws bunched, a shining white shirt-front, tail round his haunches, the tip flicking delicately. 'Look at Monty,' Jeannie would say. 'He's having his million and one thought.'

And while he was contemplating, the birds would be hopping around him. We had a bird table in the pocket garden opposite the front door and inevitably the crumbs we put on it used to be blown off onto the ground; neither Monty nor the birds were perturbed as they collected them. Of course if you live in the country you are certain to make friends with individual birds which respond to your approach with more trust than others. In our case we had two particular friends who hopped around Monty collecting the crumbs, whom we called Charlie and Tim.

Charlie was a chaffinch and Tim was a robin, and they both treated Monty as if a cat was the most harmless thing in the world. Charlie was a bossy character who, in the spring and summer, used to follow us around cheeping all day. Even a bird's voice can sometimes sound too persistent and we used to chafe Charlie for the monotony of his cry. A gentleman chaffinch, if you look at it closely, is a beautiful bird. There is a touch of the tropics about its plumage of slate-blue, pink, chestnut, black and white wings and tail; only its voice is humdrum. Thus Charlie's voice as he perched on certain favourite places was a high-pitched note repeated over and over again, until I marvelled sometimes that Monty was not irritated into action.

He would hop, for instance, at the entrance of the flower house while Monty was dozing on a bench and we were bunching the daffodils, piping away on and on until in exasperation I would say: 'For goodness' sake, Charlie, think up another song.' Or he would perch on a certain stunted old apple tree under which in the lush grass Monty used to like to slumber; there would lie Monty curled in a ball while above him, with the monotony of a pneumatic drill, sang Charlie. But it was when we sat out of doors having breakfast or lunch that Monty was put most to the test.

We used to sit on a white seat, the scent of a verbena bush pervading the air, the sea in the distance, Monty at our feet, and Charlie a few yards away on the gravel path determinedly demanding crumbs from our plates. Nor would Charlie be alone, for he would have with him the dim little person who was his wife; and thus Monty had two to look at, to be tempted by, and yet to ignore.

In winter Charlie was a more silent individual, as if the summer had consumed his song. His feathers would lose their sheen, he would crouch rather than perch on a branch as if days were made to be borne instead of enjoyed. Sometimes he would disappear for weeks on end, and there was one winter when he was so long away that we made up our minds that he was dead. We missed his perky presence. We regretted our rudeness about his voice. We yearned to see his busy little nature once again. And we did. In the spring he suddenly appeared one day in the wood while Jeannie was feeding the chickens, the same old song, the same old Charlie, bossy as ever.

Tim was a gentle robin, if you can think of a robin as gentle. At least we ourselves never saw him attacking another or trying to assert his personality at the expense of other birds. Charlie would drive him off the bird table at any time. Tim simply did not fancy a battle. He preferred to wait cunningly until Charlie had had his fill, then he would return and stay there until perhaps a tom tit would harshly tell him to go; Tim, in fact, believed in appeasement. This possibly was the reason why he liked so much to be indoors with us, or in the flower packing shed when we were there. He found life less troublesome, felt safer, if he sat on a corner of my desk, despite the fact Monty might be wandering about the room. It was a remarkable sight seeing Tim on the back of a chair while Monty was on the chair itself. Or looking for crumbs on the carpet while Monty lay stretched by the stove. Or just flying around the room while Monty appeared not to take the slightest notice. Of course, Monty knew he was there. He observed Tim out of the corner of his eye, but it was an eye that never had the suspicion of a glint.

Yet Tim at times became so over-confident that he seemed to be going out of his way to court attack from Monty. I remember him once in the flower packing shed standing delicately on one leg on the cup of a daffodil that rose from a galvanized pail. The pail was with others on the floor and there was Monty threading his way between them until he reached the spot where Tim was on the daffodil looking down on him, while a paw-stretch away he was looking up at Tim; but neither bothered to show any interest.

The height of Tim's foolishness was when he urged his lady of the year to build a nest at ground level among a bed of polyanthus. Heaven knows what caused him to choose such a place because it was in an area fifty yards from the cottage which Monty had found a particularly fruitful hunting-ground. Perhaps Tim had done so because it was so near to the packing shed, which meant he could have an idle time indoors without being too far from his mate. Anyhow I found the nest while I was picking the polyanthus, flushing the mate away as I did so.

At that moment, I saw Monty coming towards me, walking earnestly between two rows of plants, tail erect, a benign expression on his face which suggested that for some reason I was particularly popular. This was a moment to enjoy not to spurn, but I hastened towards him, swept him up in my arms and carried him, now cross, away to the cottage. Then I returned with bamboo sticks and a coil of wire netting and proceeded to encircle the nest in a cage. It looked safe when I had finished, but my activities had upset even Tim. The nest was never used again.

A third friend was Hubert the gull. He was far too superior, of course, ever to use the bird table, and he would stand on the rim of the roof waiting for us to throw food to him. Quite often Charlie would be there too, hoping to pinch a bite from under Hubert's beak; and Charlie would look ridiculous, so tiny beside Hubert yet so importantly awaiting us, that I used to call out: 'Charlie seagull is up on the roof!'

Our postman saw them up there together one day, and he told us the story of a seagull at Mousehole who paraded every day on a certain balustrade. A sparrow used to like it there too for visitors passed frequently by, and thus the sparrow and the seagull were regularly fed. One day, however, after the end of the season and the visitors had gone and food was no longer thrown to them, the gull suddenly eyed the sparrow, waddled quickly towards it, snapped it up and swallowed it whole. For a while after hearing that story we kept a watch on Hubert when Charlie was up there alongside him ... just in case.

Hubert behaved towards Monty in his large way as Charlie and Tim did in their small way. Monty himself, at first was not sure of him. Hubert would sweep down from the roof, land on the path and advance towards Monty who retreated nervously, looking round every few seconds and curling his mouth in a soundless snarl. I feel sure Hubert had no intention of attack. He was curious perhaps. He succeeded, however, in those first weeks after his arrival at Minack in establishing a moral superiority for a while over Monty:

Yet if a cat and a gull can like each other these two did, or at least they learnt to tolerate each other. I have seen them both on the flat rock that stretches out from one side of the cottage like a sacrificial stone, Monty at one end, Hubert at the other, and neither of them appeared to be perturbed.

Hubert never behaved so calmly when another gull arrived on the roof. The roof was his personal kingdom and if a gull swooped down and settled at one end, Hubert exploded in fury, half ran, half flew towards it, lunged out with his beak, then sailed into the sky in a storm of squawks chasing the offender this way and that until both disappeared over the fields towards the sea. A few minutes later he would return, fluff out his feathers and be at peace again as king of the roof.

There were times when Monty was certainly jealous of him. During those meals outside when Charlie and his squeak were ignored, Monty would watch Hubert suspiciously as he stood with the presence of an eagle a little way off; and as soon as he began to come too close, Monty would advance timidly but surely until Hubert decided it was wise to retreat. But it was when Hubert accompanied us on our walks that Monty became most annoyed for he liked to have us to himself on these occasions and Hubert spoilt his pleasure.

Hubert would leave the roof as we set off down the lane, come swooping low over our heads, then up again into the sky, wheeling with the grace of a swallow; and when he came low again, his wings hissing the air with their speed, Monty would crouch and look up and glare. At other times we would be wandering around our meadows and fields with Monty trotting along with us when Hubert would dive from the sky, land on the ground twenty yards away, then strut on a parallel course; or if we had paused he would remain stationary, looking at us as if he were saying to himself, 'I wonder what they are up to?' These moments particularly infuriated Monty. He would begin to creep along the ground, stalking Hubert as he would a mouse, getting nearer and nearer, making a weird noise which was neither a growl nor a miaow. It was a comical sight. Both knew there would be no attack. Both knew the parts they had to play. It was a question of split-second timing. As soon as Monty had arrived within a few feet, Hubert, to save him the embarrassment of coming any nearer, flew off.

In spring, Monty's thick coat began to moult and we used to give him a daily combing. He would lie on my lap as I traced the comb up and down his back, on his sides and up around the jowls of his neck. He loved it. He purred happily until I turned him over and began the same task on his underparts. There would now be silence except for a series of little grunts. He found it awkward to purr on his back.

And when it was all over I would collect the silky fur in my hand, go outside and throw it into the wind. It floated into the air soaring and billowing, eddying in the end to some thorn bush or tussock of grass or entangling itself in the sea pinks on the wall. It did not stay in any of these places for long. The fur was much sought after. Most nests around Minack were lined with it.

CHAPTER 13

As the years went by we became increasingly sensitive to the hazards that faced Monty. In the beginning we were so content with our new way of life that we foresaw the possibility of trouble neither for ourselves nor for him. Then, as the nature of our struggle became clear, we realized that we were going to have anxiety as well as contentment. The defeats and shocks we suffered, the lost harvest of daffodils, a field of beautiful anemones destroyed in a night by a southerly gale, a drought at a time when moisture for cliff potatoes was vital, brought home to us the extent of the battle in which we were engaged. Hence there were times when nervousness was substituted for calm and the foolish mood of anticipating trouble created unnecessary fears.

This foolish mood developed one evening at dusk when I saw an owl chasing Monty, diving at his upturned startled face as if it were aiming to peck out his eyes. I rushed forward shooing it away, only for it to come back ten minutes later, and again the following evening, and the evening after that. I treated it as Monty's enemy, obsessed with the idea that it might blind him. 'That damn owl is there again,' I would say, and hasten to frighten it away.

Jeannie's attitude towards it was quite different. She viewed my actions as utterly stupid and whenever I hurried to perform them she would crossly say: 'Leave it alone. It's perfectly harmless ... It's *fond* of Monty.' This streak of romanticism had its origin in her childhood when she first came upon the rhymes of Edward Lear. A famous one had caught her fancy and she now saw the opportunity of watching its particular theme come to life.

The owl and the pussy cat went to sea
In a beautiful pea green boat.
They took some honey and plenty of money
Wrapped up in a five pound note.
The owl looked up to the stars above
And sang to a small guitar:
'Oh lovely pussy, oh pussy my love,
What a beautiful pussy you are, you are,
What a beautiful pussy you are.'

Nothing would shake her conviction that the owl pursued Monty out of a curious kind of affection; and I had to admit when several weeks had passed and no unpleasant incident had occurred that my fears were probably groundless. I refused to accept, however, that the owl *liked* Monty; and yet there were certain features of the relationship which were a puzzle. The tawny owls at Minack, and this was a magnificent tawny owl, nest at the top of the elms which surround a meadow close to the cottage. Very few cats could climb the specially favourite elm, and Monty was certainly not one of them. But the annual nest in this elm, just a cleft in the tree-trunk, was a very foolish one and, usually, one or other of the nestlings would fall out. I would find one on the ground, a bundle of white feathers and two large unhappy eyes, and then laboriously climb up the tree and replace it beside its fellow. During this particular spring, however, I found no bewildered baby owl and as, later in the summer, I frequently saw the two sitting together like identical twins on various trees in the wood, it was clear no casualties had occurred. Hence Monty, against his nature and in a fit of madness, could not have climbed the elm and attacked the nest or killed a fallen nestling. He had, in fact, done nothing to incur the ire of the parent.

Yet there it was, the owl haunted him. It pursued him like a large dog with wings, swooping up and down as he walked innocently down the lane, cracking the evening air with its harsh cries of *kewick, kewick*. Nor would it leave him alone if he were happily curled on a chair indoors. It wanted Monty to be out with it. It would demand his presence by perching on the wall outside the front door harshly repeating again and again *kewick, kewick*. 'Didn't I tell you?' Jeannie would smile and say. And I would reply abruptly: 'For goodness' sake don't be so whimsy.'

In the end I learnt to take the relationship for granted. It went on throughout the summer and as I never saw the owl make a direct attack on Monty I lost my concern that it might do him harm. But there was one incident which surprised me. I was coming up the path from the cliff one evening when there was still another hour or two of daylight, when on turning the corner close to the cottage I saw the owl perched on the back of the white seat. It stared unblinkingly back at me, incongruous in such a daylight setting as if it belonged to another world. But what surprised me was that Monty was only a few feet away, lying comfortably like a Trafalgar lion in front of the seat. He saw me coming, got up and stretched, and walked slowly forward; while the owl heaved itself into the air and flapped off into the wood. I felt as if I had disturbed two people having a gossip.

I had other fears for Monty which were to prove more tangible. He was too like a fox, for instance. I did not appreciate this until a farmer one day came hurrying up the lane to warn me he had seen a fox in the field close to where we kept the chickens. It was Monty, of course, a Monty with a burnished bracken-coloured coat which, I thereafter realized, certainly did make him look like a fox. The same mistake was made at another time by a man with a gun whom I saw stalking beside the hedge which ran up from the wood. I charged across the field shouting at the top of my voice and when I reached the fellow, flustered and out of breath, he looked at me with disdain. He was about to shoot a fox. Up there in the corner where the winter gorse was in bloom. Can't you see it? Look it's moving ... and Monty, alert at seeing me, came quickly through the grass towards us. These alarms put us on guard about the Hunt. The hounds might mistake Monty for their quarry and so when the Meet was at St Buryan or Lamorna Turn or anywhere else nearby, we used to keep him in all day.

But the hounds only once rushed through Minack and Monty was curled up on the bed at the time; and the reason we have been so lucky is that it is obviously dangerous for the hounds when they run for the cliff.

Thus when a fox makes for our area the hounds are called off and the fox, sidling along the hedges of our fields to the impenetrable brambles and thorn trees which slope steeply to the sea, is safe. My instinct is always to be on the side of the fox. I suppose I have found that when one lives as we live, our daily existence posted like that of the ancient grey rocks which heave out of the untamed countryside everywhere around us, one is incapable of killing for sport. We share our life with the wild. We are part of it. Hence I will kill should an animal become an enemy, but never for fun.

Yet a fox, as everyone knows, can become an enemy; and one summer when Monty was growing old, a fox's earth was found by a neighbour outside of which were the skeletons of four cats. The discovery thus explained why cats over a period of time had been disappearing from the homes of our neighbours, disappearances which hitherto had been blamed hopefully on the wandering instincts of farm cats. Then, two or three weeks later, a friend of mine saw a fox catch a cat. He saw the cat three fields away from where he was standing, intently looking at a point in the hedge, then poising himself for a jump, so full of concentration that it was deaf to the fox that was stalking through the grass behind it. My friend yelled at the top of his voice but the sound disappeared in the wind. He could do nothing but watch the fox pounce, then hurry away.

I do not believe that all foxes are cat-killers. You get a rogue which develops the taste for them, just as you get a rogue badger which brings calumny on his race by developing a taste for chickens; but whatever the case, whether one fox or two were guilty, a cat-killer was at large around Minack and Monty was in danger. We kept watch on him within the limit of ever being able to keep watch on the peregrinations of a cat; and although he did not usually wander far, he obstinately chose this period to do so. 'Have you seen Monty?' I would ask Jeannie, and when the answer was no we would forget the importance of what we were doing, and set out to search. We used to hasten around his known hide-outs, a dozen or so of which found favour in rotation, and when he was in none of these we were inclined to develop a panic.

On one such occasion I ran one way towards the sea and Jeannie another up the field towards the farm buildings at the top of the hill. When I rejoined her she had Monty in her arms, holding him tight and telling him what a fool he'd been. This is what had happened. She had reached the entrance to the field that faced our lane and was looking across the field to the far side when to her horror she saw a red object chasing another red object. She instantly guessed a fox was chasing Monty, and she began to run across the field calling his name; and she had run only a few yards when the second red object stopped and looked

back at her. It was Monty. He was chasing a cub. Of course he did not
know that it was running back to the earth where the cats were killed.

Soon after this we realized the killer was after Monty. We had proof of
this one evening when we heard a fox barking as if on the doorstep
followed by Monty flying in through the window. He plummeted at my
feet and then turned glaring at the open window, growling. I ran to the
door and out to the corner of the cottage which looks down the lane. I
saw nothing and all I could do was to make a noise, the human version of
an angry animal, which I thought would frighten the fox away. But
Jeannie and I were now to behave extraordinarily foolishly.

We accepted the fact we had been stupid enough to allow him out at
night without keeping him company, and so we decided from then
onwards he would be kept indoors after dusk. Monty was furious. He
had lived at Minack for six years and was over thirteen, and for the first
time in his life he was forbidden the freedom of the night. He made such
a hullabaloo, woke us up so often with his miaowing demands to be let
out that three days later – and this was our foolishness – we gave in. 'All
right, you go out,' I said. 'I'm not going to be kept awake by your fuss.
I'm tired. I want to sleep. But you look out for that killer. He was after
you last week. He'll be after you again.'

Our bed lay alongside the window so that if Monty was lying on it,
then decided he wished to investigate what adventure awaited him
outside, he had only to creep from the bedclothes to the sill and jump
down onto the flower bed below. There he was tucked in on the bed when
on the very next night after his freedom had been foolishly granted, he
woke me up with the noisiest growl I have ever heard. I put out my hand
and felt him creeping for the window. And then, from the daze of my
sleep, I suddenly sensed there was danger. I grabbed Monty with one
hand, and with the other found my torch. It was a torch with a new
battery; and when I shone it out of the window I saw a magnificent sight.

A fox, the size of an Alsatian. At first directly beneath the windowsill.
Then gliding away down the lane, so silently, so superbly a thorough-
bred that for a moment I forgot he was a killer and I called out to
Jeannie:

'Quick! Wake up! You'll never see such a beautiful fox!'

And up to now, I have never done so again.

CHAPTER 14

There were other hazards beside foxes; and there are two episodes in Monty's life at Minack that I would like to forget, but which remain painfully in my mind. Yet, and this is the paradox, I like also to remember them because of the happiness which followed, that magical sense of happiness when someone you love is reprieved.

The first took place the year before myxomatosis swept the rabbits away from our area, and when the gin trap was still the method used for their elimination. Such was our isolation at Minack that the fields where the traps were set were in a ring around us; and we were so far from other habitations that we alone suffered the hell of the traps' successes. We heard the momentary screams and the silence which followed. We lay in bed awaiting the next anguished cry, as we awaited once the next stick of bombs. A long way away those who were responsible for setting the traps would be pursuing their evening enjoyment while Jeannie and I, as if in the midst of a battle, listened.

A chill went through us whenever we heard the signal of traps being laid, the metallic sound of the trapper's hammer; and if Jeannie heard it first she would run looking for me, and we would both then go looking for Monty. I admit that rabbits had in some way to be controlled but it was the manner in which gin traps were used which was so barbarous. It was seldom that any steps were taken to cut short the pain of the trapped. The traps, set perhaps an hour before dusk, reaped most of their harvest in the first half of the night as the rabbits came out of their burrows. The screams then followed each other as if they were an endless series of echoes and we would have little time to remain tense, waiting for the next; but after midnight we had to wait, ten minutes, half an hour, or suddenly two or three, one after the other, then silence. It was not often that anyone considered it humane to come at midnight and kill those caught during the evening flush. We had to lie there thinking of them.

It was late one lovely May afternoon that Monty got caught in a trap. We knew that traps had been laid in the field adjoining the cottage but traps were not supposed to be actually set until dusk; and thus Monty should still have had an hour or two in which he could have wandered around in safety. Nevertheless we were nervous for him. We were in the mood to anticipate trouble and I said to Jeannie: 'I don't think we ought to let Monty out of our sight for an instant this evening.' There seemed to be no reason why we should. Our day's work was ended and we were both pottering about the garden and the cottage while Monty was in one of his benign moods. He was lying half-hidden among the wallflowers outside the front door, blinking sleepily, as if he were relaxing after a large meal. He was the epitome of contentment, a much-loved, magnificent ginger cat who was at peace with his private world; and heaven knows what prompted him suddenly to go somewhere he had never been before.

Unseen by us, he left his nest under the wallflowers, entered the field where the traps were laid and walked the length of it, miraculously threading his way through the traps until he was caught by one at the far end, close to a gap in the field which led down to the cliff.

I do not think five minutes had elapsed before I noticed his absence from the garden; and instinctively I knew what had happened. I shouted to Jeannie to follow me, then ran the few yards to a bank which rose above the field. I stood on it for an instant while my eyes peeled along the base of the hedge where the traps were set. I saw nothing but young green corn; until suddenly in the far distance I saw an object at ground level languidly flopping up and down. It was Monty's tail.

The next twenty minutes are a jumble in my memory. We raced across the field, enraged that our care for him had cheated us; and when we reached him and saw his yellow eyes looking trustingly up at us while his little front paw with the white smudge on it was squeezed in the gin, we broke out with curses against those responsible for setting it.

'I'm going to throw it away!' Jeannie cried, 'right away in the sea.' But this outburst did not help us release Monty. He began to struggle so I put my hands firmly round his body while Jeannie tried to open the gin; and as only a few weeks before she had released a trapped dog she could not understand why, on this occasion, the fangs had stuck fast. Poor Monty; sweat began to moisten his fur and his mouth frothed, and then panic seized him and for an instant he freed himself from my hold.

'Look out!' I shouted. He lashed out with his three free legs, claws like spikes, too quick for Jeannie to move away in time and I saw a line of blood on her arm. A second later he was quiet again, lying panting on his side, tongue lolling, uttering little cries, and his paw still trapped.

I do not wish to remember again the ten minutes which followed. A hideous time against the background of a sea-scented evening, larks exultant in the sky, early swallows skimming in from the south, the pilchard fleet chugging out into Mount's Bay. I do not wish to remember the anguish of those ten minutes; only the sweet relief we had when at last we had him safe. He lay exhausted for a while on the sofa while Jeannie tried to tempt him with warm, sugared milk and we angrily discussed what we should do.

The trap would go into the sea. I would make a complaint. We both, in fact, blistered with fury; and yet, maddeningly enough, there was nothing we could righteously be furious about. We did not possess the field concerned, and so Monty, in the legal sense of the word, was trespassing. Thus the whole incident revolved around the question of standards. The countryman had grown up to expect a layer of cruelty in his life. We had not. Thus when Jeannie threw the trap away and I made my angry complaint, it was inevitable that a feud should begin. We did not mind of course. We at least had proclaimed our indignation against cruelty. And in any case the vet had seen Monty. No permanent harm had come to his paw.

The other episode took place when he was fourteen years old. We now had a splendid greenhouse a hundred feet long and twenty feet wide, and during this particular winter we were growing sweet peas for early spring flowering. We spent hours of our time pinching them out and layering them and it was only natural that Monty should be with us during these sessions. He amused us while we pursued the monotonous task. For no reason at all he would race up and down the rows or ridiculously treat a sweet pea tendril as an enemy, or interrupt the flow of our work by turning upside down at our feet, requesting his tummy to be tickled. There were no signs that he was an old cat. He looked in magnificent condition and when one day we put him in a basket which hung on the potato scales, he weighed eighteen and a half pounds net.

Yet there were a couple of incidents during the daffodil season – it begins with us late in January and ends according to the warmth of the spring in the latter part of March – that made us puzzle about him. On each occasion he appeared momentarily to stagger and yet so briefly that it could have been an accidental lack of balance and not a signpost to coming illness. In between times he was completely normal, the usual large appetite and as agile as ever.

Then one day at the end of March we went out and did not return till after dark; and as so often happened, the headlights as we came up the lane to the cottage lit up his fierce face as he glared at us from the bedroom window. He had the gift of making us feel we had neglected him. It was an echo of those late Mortlake nights. 'Where have you been?' he seemed to be crossly saying.

On this occasion we performed the inevitable rites of apology, picking him up and hugging him, and hastening to bribe him to return our affection by the obvious method of filling his plate with fish. Jeannie had turned to the sink to collect the fish pan when I suddenly saw Monty begin to stagger and half stumble across the carpet to a spot under my desk, where he collapsed.

'Look at Monty!' I shouted, and rushed over and knelt beside him, stroking him; and because I met with no response, his eyes seemed to be glazed and unseeing, I picked him up and carried him to our bedroom. He was desperately ill.

'You stay here,' I said to Jeannie, not certain whether I was asking her to carry out the best or the worst of the two tasks, 'while I race up to the farm and telephone the vet. If he's in he'll be here within half an hour.' And miraculously he was in and, within half an hour, he was at Minack. We both looked at his face as he carried out his examination, seeking to read the signs we hoped to see. 'Is it a heart attack or a stroke?' I murmured, fearing his answer.

He was a quiet Scot with the comforting assurance of his race; and goodness knows why but I always prefer it when advice comes in a Scot's accent. 'I don't think so,' he said slowly, 'you see his eyes are rolling, and look how he's struggling.' He paused for a moment. 'You haven't been putting any poison down, have you?' I hadn't, but I suddenly remembered the sweet peas and the dust we had been using on them to check disease, and I rushed out into the night to find the tin. I brought it back and the vet slowly read the instructions and list of chemical ingredients.

'That's the trouble all right,' he said, 'he's been poisoned, though there's no mention here the dust is dangerous. The fact is he's absorbed the dust in his fur and body over the months and now he's got enough inside to hit him.'

He was in a coma for two days and nights. He lay on the pink bedspread in the spare bedroom while one of us sat always with him. The treatment was bicarbonate of soda every four hours and as it required both of us to pour the dose down his throat the one who was on night duty woke up the other when the fourth hour came round. About six o'clock on the second morning we had carried out our duty and we were standing together watching him . . . and suddenly there was a purr.

'Oh Monty, Monty!' cried Jeannie. 'You're safe. You're safe!'

For us the remaining year of his life had the delicate pleasure of borrowed time.

CHAPTER 15

In previous years we had occasionally to go away, never for more than three or four days, and elaborate arrangements of course were made for Monty's welfare. A travelling fish salesman supplied fish from his van, and whoever it was we had helping us at Minack at the time would cook it, and keep a saucer filled with milk from the farm. Monty was allowed to wander about as he liked during the day but in the evening he would be locked indoors; and when we were going to bed three hundred miles away in London, there was comfort in the thought he was safely ensconced within the cottage. We hated leaving him and he in his turn throughly disapproved of our absence; and on one occasion he nearly made us miss our train.

We were going by night, and while in the afternoon Jeannie was packing, he sniffed around the suitcases in that apprehensive fashion that both dogs and cats are apt to show when travel is scheduled. He then quite suddenly began to limp. I had never seen him limp before but there he was hobbling about as if he had only three legs. This continued for an hour; and so theatrical were his gestures that Jeannie declared she would not catch the train unless he was seen by the vet. The vet was fetched and he pronounced Monty a malingerer. There was nothing wrong with him at all; and Monty, admitting his bluff had been called, promptly began walking normally again.

Our returns usually had a chilly reception. He liked at first to pretend that he could get on perfectly well without us and it was immaterial whether we lived at Minack or not. The pretence lasted until we went out for a stroll to see how things had been growing while we had been away; and as we walked we would suddenly hear a bellow of a miaow, then see Monty running towards us. We would continue our stroll with him at our heels, while at intervals the bellow was repeated. It was a touching experience for in the sound was the agony of loneliness. We knew then how much he had missed us.

But in the last year of his life there was no need to go away, and although sometimes we were absent during the day we were always with him at night. He recovered splendidly from the dust poison, and by the early summer he was his usual beautiful self. 'Oh, what a beautiful cat!' some hiker would say as he passed through Minack seeing Monty perched aloofly on a stone. 'How old is he?'

No one believed he was nearly fifteen. Nor did I for that matter. Time deceives in its pace, luring years into yesterdays, garlanding memories without intervals, seeping the knowledge of age into one's mind. I did not want to say how old he was. I did not want to remember that for so long he had been the recipient of our secret thoughts. Each of us had talked to him in that mood of abandon which is safe within friendship. Maybe it was only a cat's friendship, but secure never to be tarnished, easing problems because the aftermath of confession did not breed the fears of disclosure.

He was an integral part of our failures and successes at Minack, and a hulky miner from St Just whom we once had helping us called him the foreman. 'Look out, the foreman's coming,' he would shout as he lunged away with his shovel in a potato meadow. 'We'll get our cards if we don't do our job properly.' Monty would appear and walk leisurely down the row where he had been digging, sniffing the discarded potato tops which spreadeagled on the side as if he were checking that all the potatoes had been collected from the plants. It was always a solemn inspection. There were no games. And when he had completed it, and had left the meadow, disappearing out of sight, the hulky miner would stab his shovel into the ground, rub his hands together and call out: 'All clear, boys. We can have a smoke now.'

He was sometimes an inconvenience when we were picking flowers. At daffodil time the pace of picking has to be so fast that there is no time for distractions; and yet Monty would often insist on accompanying us, walking ahead between the daffodil beds at a very slow pace of his own choosing so that our feet tumbled over him. 'Hurry up, Monty,' I would say, but at the same time I did not want to sound too brusque. I was glad that he wished to be with us; and so I would stop the rhythm of my picking and bend down and stroke him. Then, if he did not move, I would step over him.

He had a passion for violet plants and, in his time, we used to grow three or four thousand every year. The variety was called Bournemouth Gem and each plant bushed dark green leaves that perfumed the meadow in which they were grown even before the violets themselves appeared. Monty liked rolling among them. The rich orange of his fur against the dark green was a pretty sight and although you would have expected him to do damage, little damage was done; the plants were such fat cushions that the few broken leaves had plenty waiting to replace them. So we let him roll and only became alarmed when he jumped on a plant, gathered as much of it as he could with his four paws, turned on his side, and proceeded furiously to disembowel it. The fact is he liked the smell of violets. I have often seen him walking on his own down a row, his tail pointing like a periscope above the leaves, smelling the plants on either side of him. 'Monty's picking violets,' I would say to Jeannie as a joke.

He enjoyed sitting on the bench in the packing shed hemmed in by galvanized tins of wallflowers or jars of violets or anemones. He would sandwich himself in a space and if you looked in from the outside you would see through the window a splendid array of early spring flowers and in the midst of it all the dozing face of Monty. I remember a flower salesman coming to see us one day who was so amazed by what he saw in the packing shed that he nearly forgot to discuss his business; for there was Monty among the daffodils, and Tim the robin up on a shelf warbling a song from a jar of anemones, while Charlie the chaffinch was looking up at us, calling his monotonous note from the floor. These three had three flower seasons together and this particular occasion was the last. First Monty, then Tim eighteen months later, and Charlie six months after that. And all the while up there on the roof was Hubert, observing everything, majestic, so compelling a character that neither of us would dare to let him remain hungry if he were demanding a meal, however busy we might be. 'Jeannie!' I would call out as I was stacking flower boxes in the Land Rover ready for Penzance Station. 'Hubert's hungry. Have you got anything?'

Monty was always tempted by boxes. If a parcel arrived and Monty was in the room and we unpacked it, he was certain to fill the vacant space. Perhaps he was born in one. Perhaps a psychiatrist would be right in saying that parcels and cardboard boxes recalled exquisite incidents of kittenhood. He certainly loved flower boxes and the tissue paper we put in them; and many a time we used to relieve the intensity of our work by pretending Monty, lying in a flower box, was indeed a flower. 'Shall we send him to Covent Garden?' one of us would say absurdly. 'They'd certainly call him a prize bloom,' the other would reply equally absurdly. When we were working at great pressure, it was a relish to have Monty to distract us, in so kind and pleasant and trivial a way.

CHAPTER 16

One of Monty's lovable characteristics was the way he enjoyed going for walks with us, trotting along like a dog at our heels. Sometimes when we wanted to go on a proper walk, a walk far longer than he could manage, we would sneak down the path planning to get out of sight without him realizing we had gone; but from some hide-out in which he was spying upon us, he would suddenly appear, all smiles as if he were saying: 'Going for a walk? Good idea, I'll come too.' Then, of course, we had to cancel our plans and go on a limited walk instead.

He played games on these walks, some of which were vexing, some charming. He had the usual whim of a cat to tear up trees as if the wind were in his tail, but as many of the trees were elders he never climbed high. It was at night that these climbs were annoying.

We would be taking a late-night stroll and wishing to return to go to bed when he would race up the elder which is opposite the old barn and obstinately stay there. My voice would at first sound coaxing, then commanding, and then frankly I would lose my temper. 'Come on, Monty, come down!' I would shout at him. He would not budge so in the end, with Jeannie standing beside me holding the torch, I would climb the tree towards the pair of phosphorescent eyes which stared down from above. I would be up there among the branches trying to grab him, while Jeannie was laughing at both of us in the darkness below.

He had an endearing game he played when he thought a walk required livening up; or perhaps because he decided we were not giving him enough attention. He would wait until we had gone several yards ahead of him, crouching meanwhile on the path and shifting his paws as if he were about to spring ... and then race at terrific speed up to and past us, coming to a full stop a couple of yards away. Thereupon we inevitably bent down and made a fuss of him. Then we would go on, and soon the game would be repeated.

The longest walk he used to take was to the Carn we can see from our windows at Minack and which stands above a cascade of rocks that fall to the sea below. It is a rough walk most of the way, a track through gorse and brambles and bracken while on either side of a long stretch of it there is a whole series of badger setts. In springtime the land around is sprayed with bluebells while may trees plume white from among them; and ahead is the Carn and the panorama of Mount's Bay.

We used to make it an early morning walk when the dew was still wet on the grass, and a peaceful one if Monty was in a docile mood; but there were times when we would pass the badger setts thinking he was behind us, and suddenly find he had disappeared down one of the cavernous holes. It would take us a few minutes before we found which hole he had chosen, then we would see him looking up from the dark, just out of reach. I found myself thinking on these occasions he was taking a mischievous revenge on the only time I ever had power over him ... when he wanted me to open a door or a window; for there he would be holding up the walk, and nothing we could do except await his decision to rejoin us.

His favourite walk, or stroll I should call it, was fifty yards down the lane to the stream; a stream which rushed water from November to June, then dried up and became a dip in the roadway. It was a stroll that now has a significance for Jeannie and myself because it represents in our memories the joy of his first stroll and the sadness of the last.

The first night on which we came to live at Minack the moon was high, and after I had transported our luggage to the cottage, we celebrated the freedom we had captured by taking this stroll. The moon was shining, except for the murmur of the sea and the hoot of owls, on silence.

Monty, who in the first week or two was going to be shy in daylight, came with us, nosing his way down the lane which to him was full of imaginary dangers, sniffing, hesitating, taking no action except to advance steadily towards the sparkling water that ribboned ahead of him. And when at last he reached it and put out a paw in puzzlement I felt this was an occasion when I must not allow him to have any further apprehension; and so I bent down to pick him up and carry him over. He was quick to expose my foolishness. He slipped from my hold, and with the grace of a gazelle he leapt the stream. From that moment, this miniature valley across the lane has been called Monty's Leap.

It was in daffodil time that his illness began to threaten the normality of his days. Nothing sudden, no pain, just a gradual ebbing of strength; so that first the bluebell walk to the Carn had to be abandoned, then the one we used to take along the top of the cliff, and then even the strolls to the Leap became less frequent. I would watch him from the corner of the cottage wending his way down the lane, and my heart would yearn to see a spring in his movements I knew I would never see again. He would reach the stream, drink a little, then turn and come slowly back. This stroll was the yardstick of our hopes, and sometimes Jennie would come running to me: 'He's been twice to the Leap this morning!' ... and her voice would have the tone that the inevitable was going to be defeated.

But I knew sooner than Jeannie that there was nothing we could do, nothing that her loving care and nursing ever could achieve. Each time I saw him set off for the Leap I was on guard; and there was one evening, the last evening, when on seeing him, from our window, start down the lane we ran to follow him only to find that after a few yards he had lain down. Then on a few yards and down again; and yet he was such an old warrior that when I picked him up he tried weakly to struggle free ... as if he were saying: 'Let me be, I can make it!' I gently gave him to Jeannie to take home to the cottage, and as I watched her I realized that she too now knew that our life with him was over.

He died on a lovely May morning in his sixteenth year. I had hurried to fetch the vet and on my return I found Jeannie had taken him out into the warm sun and he was breathing gently on a bed of lush green grass. Up above on the roof was Hubert, quite still, his feathers bunched, as if he were waiting for something; and within a yard or two of Monty were his friends, Charlie and Tim. No sound from either of them. Tim on a rosebush, Charlie on a grey rock. They were strange mourners for a cat.

The next day, soon after the sun had risen above the Lizard far away across Mount's Bay, we carried him down the lane to the stream and buried him beside it. Between his paws we placed a card:

Here lies our beloved friend Monty who, beside the stream that crosses the lane and is known as Monty's Leap, is forever the guardian of Minack.

THE END

Elephant Bill

J.H. Williams

FOREWORD
by
FIELD-MARSHAL SIR WILLIAM SLIM
G.B.E., K.C.B., D.S.O., M.C.

In the XIVth Army our soldiers varied in colour from white, through every shade of yellow and brown, to coal black. The animals we used reflected a similar variety. Pigeons, dogs, ponies, mules, horses, bullocks, buffaloes and elephants, they served well and faithfully. There were true bonds of affection between men and all these beasts, but the elephant held a special place in our esteem. It was not, I think, a matter of size and strength. It was the elephant's dignity and intelligence that gained our real respect. To watch an elephant building a bridge, to see the skill with which the great beast lifted the huge logs and the accuracy with which they were coaxed into position, was to realize that the trained elephant was no mere transport animal, but indeed a skilled sapper.

I could never judge myself how much of this uncanny skill was the elephant's own and how much his rider's. Obviously it was the combination of the two which produced the result, and without the brave, cheerful, patient, loyal Burmese oozie our elephant companies could not have existed. And we should have had no oozies had it not been for men like 'Elephant Bill' and his assistants. It was their jungle craft, elephant sense, dogged courage, and above all the example they set, which held the Elephant Companies together under every stress that war, terrain and climate could inflict on them.

They built hundreds of bridges for us, they helped to build and launch more ships for us then Helen ever did for Greece. Without them our retreat from Burma would have been even more arduous and our advance to its liberation slower and more difficult. We of the XIVth Army were – and are – proud of our Elephant Companies whose story 'Elephant Bill' tells so modestly but so vividly.

A Goodbye to the Elephants and their Riders, and to the Up-country Staff of Timber Assistants in Burma. Also as an appreciation of two Sappers, Bill Hasted and Tich Steedman of the XIVth Army, who did everything possible to help the Elephants in War

PART ONE

CHAPTER 1

I have always got on well with animals. I like them and, with one or two notable exceptions, they always seem to have liked me. When I was a boy in Cornwall my first animal friend was a donkey. He had free range over the moors, but I always knew where to find him. Then, during the World War of 1914–18, I was in the Camel Corps, and then, later on, Transport Officer in charge of a lot of mules. These experiences taught me much about animals, for both camels and mules are temperamental beasts, and mules have also a remarkable sense of humour, so that in dealing with them one gets plenty of exercise for one's own. That was valuable. My life has been spent east of Suez in places where if you lose your sense of humour you had much better take the first boat home.

And in one respect camels were a preparation for elephants, since the male camel, like the male elephant, is subject to coming into 'season', or going on must. In all other animals it is only the female that comes into season.

Like millions of other fellows, when the war was over I began to think about finding myself a job. A friend told me that he knew a man who knew someone else who knew a chap who did something or other with elephants in Burma. This sounded to me as though it would be just what I wanted, particularly as when I was in the Camel Corps I had read a small book called *The Diseases of the Camel and the Elephant*, by Hawkes. I took for granted that such a job would mean living in the jungle, shooting, riding ponies and putting up with a good deal of loneliness, though no doubt I should meet a fine crowd when I went on leave.

We looked up Burma in an atlas, and that night both of us wrote letters. My friend wrote to the fellow he knew, introducing me as a suitable candidate for elephant management, and I wrote direct to the head of the Bombay Burma Trading Corporation – the company concerned.

It was 1920 before I got back to England, but my letter led to an interview, and before the year was out I was in Burma.

My first vivid memories of Burma are not of the pagodas and rice-fields and all I had read about, but of my first *jungle salt*, Willie, the man under whom I was to begin my training. It is said that 'you can take a man out of the jungle, but if he is born to it you cannot take the jungle out of a man'. No man I ever met was a better example of the truth of this saying, or believed it more than he did.

I met him at his camp on the banks of the Upper Chindwin River, Upper Burma. He was, in his own words, down with fever, but he was sitting at a table, about midday, outside his tent, drinking a whisky and soda and smoking a Burma cheroot with as much loving care as if it had been a very fine Havana.

His welcome – if welcome it could be called – was icy, and I immediately guessed that he jealously resented anyone sharing his jungle life. I hoped that I should be able to break down that attitude and that then all would be well. It was, however, to take me some time to do so.

Although it is nearly thirty years ago, the following incidents seem to have happened yesterday. About four o'clock in the afternoon I asked for a cup of tea – and was laughed at for not drinking whisky and soda. I vowed, privately, that I would see him under the table later on. About five o'clock seven elephants arrived in camp, and were paraded in line as though for inspection. Willie did not speak one word to me as he got up from his camp chair and walked off to inspect them. However, I followed him, uninvited. Judging by appearances, there was one worn-out animal which looked as though it might be the mother of the other six. Each animal was closely inspected in turn, and Willie entered some remark about each one of them in a book. This took up about half an hour, during which he did not address a single word to me. I was careful not to ask any questions as I saw that I should only be called a damned fool for my pains. However, when the inspection was over, Willie turned on me, saying: 'Those four on the right are yours, and God help you if you can't look after them.'

For all I knew, I was supposed to take them to bed with me. However, I saw no more of them till the next evening, when Willie told me to inspect my own four myself and to see that their gear was on their backs comfortably – as though I could tell! However, I followed a lifelong rule when in doubt: I trusted to luck.

After the inspection that first night, as my tent had been pitched near his, I joined Willie at his camp table. On it were two bottles of Black Label – one of his and one of mine.

After half an hour or so Willie thawed sufficiently to ask me: 'Are you safe with a shotgun?' – not 'Do you shoot?' as is more usual.

Silence reigned after my answer. Willie emptied and refilled his glass several times. At last he suddenly opened up, and, passing his bottle to me, remarked: 'I drink a bottle a night, and it does me no harm. If I never teach you anything else, I can tell you this: anything to do with the jungle, elephants and your work you can only learn by experience. No one but a Burman can teach you, and you'll draw your pay for ten years before you earn it. Tomorrow I'll give you some maps, and the day after you must push off for three months on your own. You can do what you damned well like – including suicide if you're lonely – but I won't have you back here until you can speak some Burmese.'

After this speech he walked off to his bed without even saying 'Goodnight'. Unfortunately the following day he heard me address a few words of Urdu, that I had picked up in India, to my Burmese cook. Willie just sacked him on the spot as being a hindrance to my learning Burmese.

At dinner that night he gave me some chili sherry of his own brew. The bottle had a sprinkler top, and I gave it two shakes, as though it were ordinary tabasco sauce. When I had swallowed a few mouthfuls of my soup he asked me if I were homesick. His chili sherry burned a hole in the roof of my mouth, but I finished the soup, and then, wiping the tears out of my eyes, replied: 'No. But I'd like to start off on my jungle trip tomorrow.'

That remark got inside his guard. For the time being his hostility collapsed, and he kept me another two days in camp.

Going to bed that night he was staggery; and when he got up from table he corked his empty whisky bottle and turned it upside down, saying:

'By dawn it will have drained its last pau peg into the neck. It'll do to lace my early morning cup of tea.'

He ignored my 'Goodnight' as he staggered off. The new recruit was not to be allowed to forget that he had disturbed the peace of jungle life.

I greeted him with 'Good morning' at 6 a.m. next day.

He looked at me and replied: 'Good Lord! You still here?'

He had become just like the jungle – as hard and as unyielding and unfriendly as a tree seems when one is lonely. But a few years later he had become a great friend of mine. He accepted me slowly, as the trees and forests did.

After four and a half years' service in the Army I believed that I was past the age of adventures; but leaving on my first jungle trip certainly gave me a thrill. With four elephants carrying my kit, a cook, two bearers and two messengers, I was on my own again. After going nine miles it dawned on me that my life in charge of elephants had begun.

.   .   .

I started that trip in November, when every day was like a perfect English summer's day. Every evening a log fire beside my tent gave me the companionship of its warmth and the homeliness of its glowing embers. I moved camp for the first four days, so as to put sufficient distance between myself and Willie for me to feel reasonably sure that he would not pay me an unexpected visit – then I stayed in camp for a day to sort out my possessions.

I had been well equipped in England before leaving, with a new shotgun and a new 450/400 high-velocity rifle, and the Bombay Burma Corporation had issued me with excellent camp equipment. Among the treasures and curios it contained was a teak office box filled with books, circulars and papers for my information. The most interesting of them was a small textbook on elephant management by Hepburn, a young veterinary surgeon who had spent a few years as an Assistant with the firm, but who unfortunately had died of enteric. The book did not contain either a photograph or a diagram of an elephant, being concerned only with a brief account of the treatment of various accidents and diseases to which elephants are liable. My first impression was that they were likely to get every possible complaint to which man, woman and child are subject, except whooping-cough.

The book was, however, a gold mine, and all too soon I had to put it into use. For before I arrived at my destination the ancient female elephant known as Ma Oh (Old Lady) was discovered dead an hour before I was due to move camp. Willie had, I now know, somewhat unscrupulously palmed her off on me – and his terrible words, 'God help you if you can't look after them,' now rang in my ears. Seeing her enormous carcass lying in the jungle – just as she had died in her sleep – was a terrible sight, and it was awful that she had died within a few days of my being made responsible for her. How on earth, I wondered, should I get out of this mess? This was the nadir of my misfortunes. Willie's reception of me, the dead elephant, and his threat ringing in my ears, combined to fill my cup with bitterness. 'At the worst,' I thought, 'I can only lose my job. I'm damned if I'll buy them a new one!' It was a bad business, but as I had no one to help me out, I had to help myself, and I decided that the best thing I could do was to hold a post-mortem and see what I could find inside to account for her death.

Tragedy soon turned into farce. The 'Old Lady' was scarcely cold before I was literally inside her, with her arching ribs sheltering me from the sun. I learnt a good deal about elephant construction from her. Spare parts galore had been hauled out and arranged neatly in a row before tea-time. Her carcass proved to be a cave full of strange treasures, such as the heart, the gizzard and the lungs. The only snag was that, do what I would, I could not find any kidneys, and I was almost tempted to conclude that she must have died for lack of them. However, when I came to write out a report that evening I decided that 'no kidneys' might not be an acceptable cause of death – so, in desperation, I left it at 'found dead', and did not even mention my Jonah's journey. Later on I found out that many strange explanations of the the deaths of elephants were made by Assistants, and that most of them were taken with a grain of salt. The unwritten law of the Bombay Burma Corporation was that some cause of death had to be given if the deceased animal was under fifty-five years of age. Over that age the explanation of 'old age and general debility' was accepted. If one is lucky one may get away with the explanation, 'struck by lightning', once in one's career of twenty years – but one cannot try it twice. The Assistant who described an elephant as dying of 'broken heart' did not get away with it, though he may have thought he had good reason if he examined the heart and found it looked as though it had been split in two, with two apexes instead of one, as in man and the lesser mammals. This formation of the heart is a peculiarity not only of the elephant, but of some of the other large mammals as well.

The loss of one transport elephant seemed to make no difference with the type of pack being used. Ma Oh's load was easily divided among the remaining three animals, and on I went. My instructions were to march to a certain village in the Myittha Valley, where I was to meet a head Burman named U Tha Yauk. I shall never forget his welcome. I was on foot with my messengers and the two bearers, and we had outdistanced the elephants by several miles by taking a short cut up the bed of the creek. U Tha Yauk had come some way out of the village to meet me, and was squatting on a rock beside the creek up which we were travelling. I think that he formed his first impressions of me before I had ever seen him. He heard me laugh with the Burmans before he saw me, and he watched me eagerly bounding from rock to rock before I had seen him. Then he saw my quick reaction on seeing him, and noticed the tone of friendly authority in my greeting. I think these little things may have counted in my favour.

I greeted him with my three words of Burmese and laughed because I could say no more, and he laughed back; then we marched on in single file until we came into a big open clearing around which there were about ten bamboo huts, all standing on bamboo stilts and thatched with grass. A Burmese girl dressed in her best, with a pretty little white coat, and a flower in her hair, came forward with a cane basket-work stool for me to sit on. Three men came up with green coconuts and, cutting them open at one end, poured the juice into a cup of hand-beaten copper and gave it to me with the reverent gestures of priests administering the sacrament. I drank off at least six cups of the cooling drink before I realized that a dozen people had gathered round to stare and gaze at me.

Unfortunately, I attracted quite as much attention from all the biting bugs and flies as from the Burmans. But at once a small boy came forward, and offered me a fan to keep them off. In order to interest him and make some return, I first showed him a handkerchief on which there was a design of a fox, with hounds and a huntsman, and then tied it round his head. The watching crowd laughed with delight. I was relieved when U Tha Yauk and his son-in-law, who could speak a few words of English, reappeared and explained that the elephants would soon arrive, but that, as it was already late in the afternoon, it would be better if I were to sleep in the hut reserved for my occupation during the monsoon rains.

Directly the elephants turned up, the crowd moved off to help unload them, and my cook was at once installed in his hut. In a few minutes a chicken had been killed and plucked, a fire lit and cauldrons filled with water. My kit was soon piled up in one corner of the big room twenty-four feet by sixteen, which was divided into my bedroom on one side and living-room on the other, by a bamboo matting wall.

In a quarter of an hour the room was furnished – with a ground-sheet covered with bright blue cotton dhurries on the floor, my camp bed, camp tables and camp chair; my bedding roll was undone and the mosquito net put in position. Meanwhile other Burmans were filling my tub in a bathroom at the back of the hut with tins of water from the brook. After dismissing the other helpers, my personal servant unlocked my basket packs and took out photographs to arrange on my dressing-table, and my revolver, which he put carefully under my pillow. Then, when all was ready, he asked me to come in. As soon as I had looked round and sat down, he took off my puttees and boots, and then disappeared. When I had undressed and gone to the bathroom, I found a Burmese boy, who poured two buckets of hot water into my tub and swirled it around, giving me a smile, as though to say: 'Bath ready, sir.'

I bathed, and by the time I went back into my hut I found the table was laid with a spotless white cloth, and that flannel trousers, socks and white shirt were spread out on my bed, but that my perfect valet had once more vanished.

My dinner was ready, and as I finished each course hands of unseen attendants passed up the meat and vegetables, the sweet and savoury to my valet, who stood silently behind my chair as I ate. While I drank my coffee, he drew down the mosquito net and tucked it in, and then gave a graceful bow saying, though I could not understand him:

'By your leave I will now go.'

Left alone, I was overcome by a great homesickness. The overpowering kindness of the Burmans was too much for me, and I asked myself what I had done to deserve it. Surely life in the jungle would not continue on such a pattern? It never dawned on me that the Burmans wanted to show their sympathy with me in my loneliness and my ignorance of their language and all the difficulties that lay ahead.

CHAPTER 2

Next morning a new life began – my life as a pupil of U Tha Yauk. Fortunately, he was as eager to teach me and to show me everything as I was enthusiastic to learn. Every waking moment I had to study jungle lore, to observe every detail and, in particular, to observe elephants and all their ways.

That morning I woke to the sound of elephant bells of varying notes, and the camp was astir before I had dressed, shaved and had my breakfast. While I was drinking my tea I could see that the camp was already full of elephants standing about unattended, and that three or four groups of Burmans were squatting round having their early morning meal of boiled rice. Each man had a heap of it, steaming hot, served on a wild banana leaf instead of a plate. Not a word was spoken while they ate, and as each man finished he rinsed his mouth and washed his hands from a coconut-shell cup of water. Then he walked off to his harnessed elephant, mounted in silence, and in silence the elephant and its rider vanished into the jungle to begin their day's work. But before they had all gone U Tha Yauk was waiting for me.

With the aid of a good map of the Indaung Forest Reserve, he made me understand I was to go on a tour with him from the valley, crossing the creeks and climbing over the watersheds, and so on, up and down, crossing in all five parallel creeks flowing from east to west into the Myittha River. On the sides of each of the watersheds he had a camp of elephants, ten camps altogether, each with an average of seven elephants, or seventy working animals all told.

Judging from the map, the distance between the camps was six to seven miles, with hills three to four thousand feet high between each. No tracks were marked, the whole area of about four hundred square miles was divided into numbered and demarcated areas, though the boundaries were irregular, as they followed the natural features of creeks and ridges.

At the first camp we reached I found about twenty Burmans, including a carpenter of sorts, erecting a set of jungle buildings. It was explained to me that this camp was to be my headquarters during the coming monsoon months. I soon realized that the elephant was the backbone of the Burmese teak industry.

The history of the Bombay Burma Corporation went back to the time of King Theebaw, when a senior member of the firm, who visited Burma, appreciated the great possibilities of the teak trade and was able to obtain a lease of certain forest areas on agreeing to pay a fixed royalty per ton of teak extracted.

As a result, sawmills were established at the ports, and forests previously regarded as inaccessible were opened up, a system of rafting teak-logs down the creeks and rivers was organized and elephants were bought on a large scale. Teak is one of the world's best hardwoods, partly because of the silica it contains. In the mixed deciduous forests of Burma, teak grows best at heights between two thousand and three thousand feet in steep, precipitous country, though it is also found in the rich valleys. The trees often stand ten or twelve to the acre, but usually only one tree – the largest – is selected, and the remaining trees, which are immature or under the girth limit, are left for the next cycle of felling, which is probably twenty-five or thirty years later. Under this system the teak forests would never be exhausted. The tree chosen is killed by ringing the bark at the base, and the dead tree is left standing for three years before it is felled, by which time the timber is seasoned and has become light enough to float; for green teak will not float. As teak grows best in country which is inaccessible to tractors and machinery, elephant power is essential for hauling and pushing the logs from the stump to the nearest stream that will be capable of floating them during the flood-waters of the monsoon months.

When the logs reach the main waterways they are built up into rafts, which are floated down the rivers to Rangoon or Mandalay. There they are milled and the squared timber shipped to the world markets.

Not only do the streams, creeks and rivers vary very much in size, but the degree of flooding during the monsoon spates varies with each, and depends on the size and situation of the catchment area feeding it. A great deal of experience is required to judge how high the flood will reach – or, in other words, below what level the logs must be hauled. There are all sorts of natural indications to enable one to judge this, that one learns in time. Debris from last year's floods caught up in bushes is a good guide, but often does not last from one year to the next. Less obvious indications are that jungle weaver-birds, which build near the creeks, never let their pendulous nests hang low enough to touch flood-water, and that lower down, near the rivers, turtles lay their eggs only above the level of the highest flood.

All such pointers are invaluable, for much work will be wasted if the logs are hauled far below flood-level. On the other hand, an error of judgement in leaving them too high may make all the difference between the logs taking eight years instead of one to reach Rangoon, a thousand miles away.

The value of the logs depends greatly on their being cut up at the stump to the best advantage. There are specialized demands for different types of logs. The 'English Square' for shipment to Europe and South Africa requires the greatest length possible without defects, while for 'White Star' – the old ship-building term – logs yielding large flitches are required, and son on. A lot of clearance work is necessary in the jungle. Gorges have to be blasted clear of the huge boulders in their beds, which if left would trap the logs in jams when they were coming down on a spate. Dragging-paths have to be cut through the jungle for elephant haulage, and these have to circumvent natural obstacles such as cliffs, ravines and waterfalls. The Bombay Burma Corporation had to build up herds of elephants. Some were bought, mostly from Siam, but a few also from India. The majority were, however, obtained by capturing wild elephants in Burma and breaking them in. This process is known as 'kheddaring', and Burmans, Karens and Shans employ rather different methods in carrying it out.

When, however, the Bombay Burma Corporation had built up con-siderable herds of elephants, it realized the importance of the elephant calves born in captivity. These could be broken in and trained much more easily than captured wild elephants. Finally, when the Corpora-tion's herds had nearly reached a strength of two thousand animals, it was found that births balanced the deaths, and that new supplies of elephants were required only on rare occasions. The kheddaring of wild elephants, on any extensive scale, thus came to an end, as it was unnecessary.

The health, management and handling of the elephants in this enormous organization impressed me as the factor on which everything else depended. I well remember wondering how many people who had waltzed on the teak deck of a luxury liner had ever realized that the boards of which it was built had been hauled as logs from the stump by an elephant in the Burma jungles.

The routine work of elephant management in camp consisted in checking up gear-making, getting to know the oozies, or elephant-riders, inspecting elephants and dressing any galls caused by gear rubbing or wounds caused by bamboo splinters in the feet, and other common injuries.

For my early training in all these tasks I am indebted to U Tha Yauk. After our first trip we spent several days in camp. During these early days there often seemed no hurry to teach me anything, but I mixed freely all day with everyone, for ever asking questions and being given answers packed with information that I had to remember. I went back to my hut for a curry lunch and for a cup of tea, and it was on such an occasion, I remember, that I first watched a most fascinating sight. About a hundred yards below my hut was a large pool in the brook.

Two elephants, each with her rider sitting behind her head, entered the pool, and then, without any word of command that I could hear, they both lay down in the water. The riders tucked up their lungyi skirts so that they were transformed into loincloths, slipped off their mounts into the water, and began to scrub their respective elephants from head to tail with a soap which lathered freely. Then they washed it off the elephants, splashing water over them with their hands. The soap they were using turned out to be the soapy bark of a tree. Soon I was standing on the bank of the pool, and from there I watched five elephants being washed in the same way. Two of them were cows with young calves, which rolled over and over and played in the water like young children. There were also two large males, with gleaming white tusks, which were scrubbed with handfuls of silver sand.

After they had all been washed and dried off, the elephants were paraded for inspection – all drawn up in line abreast – with each of the riders dressed in his best.

U Tha Yuak advanced with military precision and, after bowing instead of saluting, handed me the books, all ragged and torn, but on the covers of which each elephant's name was written.

I looked at one book and called out the name of the elephant; and the rider, hearing me, rode it up to me at a fast, bold stride. Rider and elephant both had a sort of natural magnificence. Then the oozie halted the animal just before me. He was a splendid beast, with his head up, his skin newly scrubbed but already dry in the sun, a black skin with a faint tinge of blue showing through it, which seemed to make it so alive. The white tusks, freshly polished, gleamed in the evening sunlight. The rider was motionless, with one leg bent, on which he appeared to be sitting, and the other dangling behind the elephant's ear. On his face was an expression of intense pride – pride in his magnificent beast.

Suddenly he gave a sharp order and the elephant swung swiftly round to present his hindquarters, on which there was a brand, made with phosphorous paint when the animal was six years old.

I opened the book and read a number of entries, each with the date when he had been inspected during the last ten years. On the front page was the history of the animal with his registered number and all sorts of details – such as that he had been born in Siam, bought when he was twenty-years-old, badly gored by a wild tusker, but had fully recovered after being off work for a year.

Thus I inspected each of the animals in turn and read their histories. As each inspection was finished the rider and elephant left the clearing and disappeared into the jungle.

When they had all gone I was taken round the harness-racks – just a row of horizontal branches of trees on each of which hung one of the animals' gear. All the harness except the heavy dragging-chains was hand-made by the riders. There were great cane basket panniers, woven breast-straps of fibre, wooden breeching-blocks, padding from the bark of the banbrwe tree, ropes of every kind twisted from the bark of the shaw tree.

One evening, as I passed the camp huts on the way back to my own, I noticed a Burmese girl unlike any Burmese girl I had seen. Her skin was a different colour and she looked ill. She was rocking a bamboo Moses basket hung in the shade of one of the huts.

She gave me a pleasant smile, so, plucking up all my courage, I went up to her, gave the cradle a swing and peeped inside at a newborn baby which was fast asleep.

Now that I was close to the girl, I saw that her peculiar yellow colour, so unlike the natural pale bronze of the Burmese, was due to something smeared over her skin – a saffron lotion used by Burmese women after childbirth.

In those first three months on my own I did most of the things worth doing in Burma. U Tha Yuak helped me to achieve my ambition of shooting a wild bull elephant. My main reason for shooting him was not to secure the tusks, much as I coveted them, but to carry out a post-mortem so as to see what the organs of a really healthy elephant looked like and make another attempt to find the kidneys. This second post-mortem taught me a good deal about what had been wrong with Ma Oh. In fact it showed me half a dozen sufficient reasons why she must have died.

After three months, which passed all too soon, I returned to Willie, having learned a great deal since I had left him. Naturally, when I arrived I got the greeting I expected: sarcastic remarks about my having let one of my elephants die in the first two days – no doubt by having overloaded her with all my blasted new kit.

I replied that I was surprised that she had lived as long as she had. Her liver was riddled with flukes, and her heart was as big as a rugger ball.

'How do *you* know how big an elephant's heart ought to be?' snorted Willie.

'I shot a wild tusker that U Tha Yauk told me was forty years old, and I did a post-mortem on him in order to see how the organs of a healthy elephant compared with hers. His heart was only the size of a coconut.'

Willie's whole attitude to me changed after I said this. What pleased him was that I had shot an elephant, not for its tusks, but in order to learn more about elephants. For Willie, like most men who live long in the jungle, hated big game to be shot. He felt far more sympathy with any creature which was part of his jungle than with any new arrival, armed with all his new kit.

That evening I became a companion with whom he could enjoy rational conversation, instead of an interloper who had to be bullied and kept in his place. What I told him about shooting helped, for he was a magnificent jungle-fowl shot. I showed him my diary, and the bags of jungle fowl I had made in the evenings, using my elephant-riders as beaters, surprised him. I had found a very good ground for jungle fowl in an area where he had not shot, and he saw we had something to talk about. What this really led to was gin before our whisky and then double rations of that. We had jungle fowl that I had brought back with me for dinner, and we sat up drinking for a long time afterwards. I did not see him under the table, as I had once promised myself, because he gave up the contest by falling asleep in his chair.

I did not dare wake him, and went slowly to bed. At last I saw him get up and move over towards the fire, as though to shift a log. Next moment he had overbalanced into it. I raced from my tent to save him. He had rolled out of the fire, and I pulled him to his feet. He stood up perfectly to attention and said very sternly:

'What the hell are you doing? Do you insinuate that I am drunk?'

To this I replied: 'No. But you've burned your arm badly.'

He then ordered me to my tent and told me to mind my own business. This was more than I would stand and I turned on him, saying:

'Well, if you fall in again, I shall let you sizzle.'

He appeared absolutely sober at once. The shock of being spoken to in such a way by a young subordinate had been greater than that of the red-hot embers.

Next morning we were back where we had started, but I could see that he was feeling sorry for himself. It was two days before he was forced to swallow his pride and ask me to dress his arm for him. The ground lost over the bottle was regained by tactful bandaging, and I think it was from that time that our friendship really began.

But the way in which I had pleased him was by my interest in elephants. His great ambition had been to get someone who would take up the subject of elephant management seriously, and it seemed to him that I might be the man he wanted.

Before I left him, two or three days later, he had advised me to take up elephants and to make them my chief concern and my life's work. I thus owe a great debt of gratitude to Willie.

The job of extracting teak and delivering it a thousand miles away has many branches, and European Assistants took up different aspects of the work. Up till that time nobody had specialized in trying to improve the management of elephants. Most of the details concerning it had been left to the Burman.

The average European Assistant joining any of the large teak firms in Burma was put in charge of a forest area bigger than an English county. In it were scattered a total of a hundred elephants, in groups of seven. By continually touring during all the seasons of the year, he might be able to visit every camp about once every six weeks. In such conditions it would be a long time before he learnt to know his elephants even by name, still less by sight; and it would be a very long time indeed before he knew their individual temperaments and capacities for work.

I was more fortunate, as I was made responsible for seventy elephants, all working in a fairly small area. I was thus often able to visit my camps twice a month and to spend longer in each of them.

What follows is largely the result of my having the luck to start in conditions that enabled me to get to know my elephants really well.

CHAPTER 3

There are three distinct species of elephant, one Asiatic and two African.

The Asiatic elephant is the one most frequently seen in zoos and circuses, as it is easily tamed. African elephants are rarely seen in captivity and are very rarely broken in for work, but the large African elephant is well known by sight from photographs and films of African safaris.

Four races of the Asiatic elephant are recognized: the Indian or Burman, the Ceylonese, the Malayan, and the Sumatran. All these are very similar, and differ from the African elephant in having much smaller ears and a smooth, tapering trunk; the female Asiatic elephant has no tusks.

In the Ceylonese race tusks are absent in both male and female. This has been attributed to the fodder available on the island. The Ceylonese elephants do not work in harness, but will drag a rope gripped in the mouth and teeth.

The African elephant is a taller and more lanky animal than the Asiastic. It is easily recognized by the large ears and the segmented trunk. One exhibited by Barnum and Bailey was ten foot nine inches' high at the shoulder.

There are four races: the Central, Sudanese, Eastern and Southern varieties.

It is often stated that the African elephant is not capable of being domesticated. This is not entirely true, but specimens kept in captivity have usually had more uncertain tempers than the average Indian elephant. The reason why African elephants are so seldom domesticated is partly because the Negro races have not the temperament to attempt the task and have no tradition of working with elephants. The elephant, moreover, is far more useful for dragging or pushing heavy weights than as a beast of burden. The African elephant is not so well proportioned for dragging heavy weights as the Asiatic animal. It lacks the short hind leg, and the hindquarters do not fall away to the same extent. The tusks of the African elephant are far more massive. A pair on exhibition in New York weigh two hundred and ninety-three pounds, being eleven feet five and a half inches and eleven feet in length, respectively, and eighteen inches in circumference at the base.

At the time of writing a movement is on foot for importing Burman or Karen elephant-men into Tanganyika in order to capture and train African elephants. If this is undertaken as a last attempt to effect jungle clearing for the British Government Groundnuts Scheme, I shudder to think what the eventual cost will be to the British taxpayer.

It is true the Portuguese East African elephant has been used in harness, and I have seen photographs and read an account of this successful experiment. But the work done was never heavy, and did not go beyond dragging small cultivators and ploughs, and it required little expenditure of energy by the animal.

The African pigmy elephant is a distinct species, limited to the equatorial and Congo region. The largest males are said never to exceed seven feet in height. Specimens of the pigmy elephants have been kept in captivity, and I have seen all three species in America. The ears of the pigmy are similar in shape to those of the ordinary African elephant – like enormous cabbage leaves. The ears of the Indian elephant are triangular, like the map of India, and when cocked never protrude above the head, like those of the African.

The African elephant is confidently stated to have been the species domesticated by the Carthaginians who employed it in their wars against Rome.

In 218 B.C. Hannibal began his invasion of Italy with an army of ninety thousand foot, twelve thousand horse and thirty-seven elephants. He is believed to have crossed the Alps by the Little St Bernard Pass. If this is correct, he at first made his way over the Mont du Chat through the Chevelu Pass and up the valley of the Isère before climbing the Little St Bernard. He descended by the valley of the Doria to Aosta. Part of his route was through a narrow defile, and there he was threatened by the mountain tribes who appeared on the heights. At the white rock, still known as 'La Roche Blanche', he halted his infantry and sent his cavalry and beasts of burden ahead to the top of the pass. The next day, the ninth, he stood with his army on the highest point and addressed cheering words to his half-frozen Africans and Spaniards.

The descent was difficult and dangerous. The Italian side is steeper than the French, and the slopes were covered with freshly fallen snow. Three days were spent in constructing a road for the elephants and horses. Three days later the army reached the valley of Aosta. But his army had shrunk to twenty thousand infantry and six thousand cavalry. The casualties among the elephants are not recorded.

Hannibal's feat of taking the elephants over mountain passes and along narrow mountain tracks is of immense interest to me, as I have faced and overcome a similar problem myself. Since Hannibal crossed the Alps during the autumn, and early snow had only just fallen on the Italian side, there must have been fairly plentiful fodder for the elephants for the greater part of the time. Thus they did not have to rely entirely upon a grain ration.

It is not clear what his object was in taking the elephants with him. They cannot have been for pack purposes, unless for some special load such as bullion, since their total load could not, at a maximum, have exceeded forty thousand pounds.

The chief use of elephants in Indian wars was in battering open fortified defences during the final assault on beleaguered towns, and in particular in knocking down gates. The gates of Indian cities and fortified places were frequently covered with enormous iron spikes three to five feet long, so as to prevent elephants from battering them with their heads. It is possible Hannibal wanted the elephants for sieges. But it is more probable that they were taken as a form of psychological warfare. Among the ancients, rumours and news became even more exaggerated than they do today, and the appearance of unknown gigantic beasts trained to warfare would have been terrible in the extreme.

The most puzzling thing, and the only part I find difficult to believe, is that the elephants were African. It was physically quite possible for the Carthaginians to import young domesticated elephants by sea from India to Iraq, and then to march them overland, either to Tyre for reshipment to Carthage, or overland through Egypt and Cyrenaica. The Carthaginians were a maritime race of traders, and not Africans. One would expect them to buy elephants and mahouts and to ship them. One would not expect them to explore Africa, and discover the secret of capturing wild elephants and of breaking them in. If elephants were being captured, broken in and trained for warfare in Africa it is extraordinary that the Egyptians did not continue the practice.

But no tradition of elephant training has survived in Africa, and there is no record of elephants being used by any indigenous African people, whereas Indian history is full of accounts of the use of elephants in war. In India the elephant has been domesticated from time immemorial. There were elephants in the armies which sought to repel Alexander the Great. But, however formidable looking, they could not withstand the dash of his well-armed and disciplined troops.

If an elephant's trunk is injured the animal becomes unmanageable, and wounded beasts probably did more damage to their own side than to the enemy. Sometimes elephants carried great wooden towers capable of holding, it is said, thirty-two soldiers. These were archers.

From A.D. 1024 onwards elephants are mentioned in trains of thousands in the Wars of the Princes; and those who are familiar with the subject find no reason to question such figures. After the battle of Delhi, Prince Timour is stated to have captured three thousand elephants from Prince Mohammed. It is said that they all had snuff put into their eyes so as to make them appear to weep tears of grief at having been defeated.

Indian elephants were on the strength of the Royal Engineers up till 1895, when Daisy, the last and oldest pensioner, died.

In India itself elephants have gradually disappeared. Only a few are kept by the princes for ceremonial purposes and shikar. The elephant is, however, and animal in which every Indian is interested, and it is invested in a haze of myth and legend which delights children and is a source of pride to the descendants of India's ancient warriors.

It is impossible to understand much about tame elephants unless one knows a great deal about the habits of wild ones. The study of wild elephants usually entails shooting a few of them at some period, either deliberately for sport or ivory, or in self-defence. Most men who have shot elephants come afterwards to regret having done so – but 'to hunt is to learn'.

The only attempted census of wild elephants in Burma is contained in

Big Game in Burma by E. A. Peacock, who puts their number at three thousand. If I were to hazard a guess, I should double that figure, but all one can really say is that they are plentiful.

Wild elephants normally live in herds of thirty to fifty, and during the year cover great distances, chiefly in search of fodder. During the monsoon months – from June to October – they graze on bamboo in the hilly forest country, sometimes remaining on one watershed for a week or ten days, after which they suddenly move ten miles for another week's stay on another slope. After the monsoons are over they move into the lower foothills and the swamp valleys, feeding more on grass and less on bamboo.

It is at this time that the full-grown male tuskers join the herd, though they seldom actually enter it, preferring to remain on its outskirts, within half a mile or a mile of it. At this season they do their courting and mating, in the course of which the older bulls often have to fight some youngster who is pursuing the same female.

The herds know their yearly cycle of grazing grounds, and in their annual passage wear well-defined tracks along the ridges of the hills. In places where they have to descend from a precipitous ridge down the side of a watershed they will move in Indian file, and by long use will wear the track into a succession of well-defined steps.

Wild elephants hate being disturbed on their feeding-grounds, but they do not usually stampede suddenly, like many other herds of big game. With an uncanny intelligence, they close up round one animal as though they were drilled, and their leader then decides on the best line of retreat. He leads, and they follow irresistibly, smashing through everything, like so many steam-rollers.

If they cannot exactly locate the danger which threatens them, they invariably retreat along the track from which they have come while grazing, with their trunks on each other's backs, but in a formation of three or four abreast.

I once had the unpleasant, but exciting, experience of being a member of such a stampeding party, when I was mounted on one of my own elephants. The wild elephants were fortunately quite oblivious of the fact the Elephant Bill and tusker Po Sein (Mr Firefly) were among them. Fortunately my rider was able to extricate us from the party before they reached a muddy nullah with banks eight feet high. The leading elephants plunged their forefeet into the edge of the bank, broke it away, and, sitting on their haunches, made a toboggan slide for the herd following them.

Most wild elephant calves are born between March and May. I believe that, if she is disturbed, the mother elephant will carry her calf, during its first month, holding it wrapped in her trunk. I have seen a mother pick up her calf in this way. On two occasions I have found the tracks of a newly born baby calf in a herd. Later on, after I had disturbed them, there were no tracks of the calf to be found among those of the stampeding animals, nor could the calves have kept up with a stampeding herd. But there was no possibility of the calf being hidden or abandoned.

The birth of a calf is quite a family event in a herd of wild elephants, and I have on several occasions camped close to what I may call the maternity ward. For many years I could not understand the bellowing and trumpeting of wild elephants at night during the hot weather, when most calves are born. The fuss is, without any doubt, made by the herd in order to protect the mother and calf from intruders – in particular from tigers. The noise is terrifying. The herd will remain in the neighbourhood of the maternity ward for some weeks, until the new arrival can keep up with the pace of a grazing herd. The ward may cover an area of a square mile, and during the day the herd will graze all over it, surrounding the mother and her newly born calf, and closing their ranks round her at night. The places chosen, which I have examined after the herd has moved on, have been on low ground where a river has suddenly changed its course and taken a hairpin bend. These spots were thus bounded on three sides by banks and river. The kind of jungle found in such places is always the same. They are flooded during the rains, but during the hot weather – the normal calving period – they are fairly dry, with areas of dense kaing, or elephant grass, eight to twelve feet high, with an occasional wild cotton tree giving shade. They are eerie spots, and to explore them is an adventure. Wild pig breed in the same type of jungle, and harbour their sounders of sucking pigs under huge heaps of leaves and grass which in size and appearance resemble ant-heaps four feet high.

It is common practice for a Burman oozie, or elephant-rider, to ride his elephant silently up to such a 'pig's nest' of leaves and grass and then, silently controlling the elephant by movements of his foot and leg, to instruct him to put one forefoot gently on the mound.

Squeals and snorts usually follow from the old sow, and three or four sucking pigs join in a stampede.

Once while an elephant did this I had the good luck to bag a right and left of sucking pig for the camp pot from an elephant's back. It was ridden by an oozie called Kya Sine, who knew every trick of the jungle and became my gun-boy until his death.

It is a peculiar thing that the elephant, which becomes so accustomed to man, and has such confidence in him once it has been trained, should be so afraid of him in its wild state. Owing to this fear of man, they do surprisingly little damage to village crops, considering the vast numbers of wild elephant. They much prefer their own deep jungles, and seldom leave them. The damage that they do has been greatly and most unfairly exaggerated, and the extermination of wild elephants in Upper Burma was actually started on unreliable advice. Solitary animals may, however, do great damage and become bold enough to drive off any human intruder who shows himself. They will do this almost as though they thought it was a joke. Such animals, however, are always eventually declared rogues and are killed – or at least shot at, or caught, or injured in traps.

Before the Japanese came into the war in 1941 we made it difficult for the Burmese cultivators to obtain arms. It was not that we distrusted the villagers themselves, but if one of them was known to own a firearm, the local robbers or dacoits were likely to steal it. Many robberies were carried out with one firearm in order to obtain a second. Rightly or wrongly, when a villager was allowed to possess a gun, it was usually a twelve-bore shotgun, which is scarcely an ideal weapon with which to kill a wild elephant. The Burmese villagers did their best with what they had, and a common practice was to remove the shot from a twelve-bore cartridge and then plug it with a pointed roasted cane about three inches long. It protruded about two inches from the cartridge-case, and was firmly fixed in with molten wax to make all as gas-tight as possible. Such a cane dart carries fairly accurately for about thirty yards, and if an elephant is wounded in the foot by one, the dart usually becomes deeply embedded and sets up such severe inflammation that the animal goes dead lame. In such a case it abandons cultivated crops and takes shelter in the jungle. I have sometimes had my own elephants wounded by these darts, and, indeed, have had to employ the same unpleasant method to capture savage animals that had gone wild after being loose for a long time. The operation of removing one of these darts from the foot is extremely difficult to perform and, like all operations on the foot, is exceptionally painful to the animal.

Ordinary fences round crops are no good as a protection against elephants. The Burma Posts and Telegraphs know only too well that an elephant has merely to lean against a telegraph post in order to push it over, and has only to grip it with its trunk and give a heave to pull it up with ease. And no ordinary fences have posts stronger than telegraph poles. The only effective fence against elephants is what is called the punge. This is often used as a trap, and it was a godsend to the XIVth Army, which often employed it instead of barbed wire. The punge fence, or trap, is made of a series of sharpened and lightly roasted, or smoked, bamboo stakes of varying lengths. One end of each is stuck into the ground at an angle of thirty degrees, with the point upwards and facing outwards. On the outside of the fence, concealed in the undergrowth, are very short stakes, protruding only three or four inches out of the ground, and behind these are stakes gradually increasing in length, the longest sticking out four or five feet. The depth of the fence may be as much as eight or ten yards.

I have seen wild boar stampeded down a track across which a punge fence had previously been erected. They were killed outright, skewered through the chest and out between the shoulder-blades.

If an elephant charges a punge fence, a stake may easily pierce right through the foreleg before snapping off. On one occasion I had to extract such a stake, gripping the point with a pair of blacksmith's tongs and pulling it right through the leg. For, like a barbed fish-hook, a piece of bamboo cannot be withdrawn by the way it has entered.

Pit-traps which occur so frequently in books about elephant-hunting are very uncommon in Burma. I think the Burmese elephant is too intelligent to fall into them. An effective and heinous trap which killed one of my own elephants was a spear, about the size of a ship's spar or a light telegraph pole, heavily weighted and suspended in a tree over a game track. The release was by means of a trip-wire rope, and the spear came down with such force as to transfix the elephant, smashing his ribs and piercing his intestines. It must have taken at least a dozen men to erect this trap. I never traced the culprits. When I tackled them on the subject, all the villagers within a hundred miles round would only say that the tree must have grown like that.

Wire ropes of all sizes have become common in the jungle, and the simple wire noose can be very dangerous, and terrifies elephants, as the trunk is often caught; and if an elephant's trunk is seriously injured it will die of starvation, since everything it eats has to be torn down or pulled up and handled by the trunk.

The noose-trap is set with a very stiff but flexible sapling bent over as a spring. When anything is caught in the snare the sapling springs up and pulls it tight.

I was once confronted by a full-grown Himalayan black bear hanging by the neck, with his hind legs dangling three feet off the ground. The spring of the sapling jerking the wire noose must have broken his neck, as there were no signs of a struggle. I was glad it was the bear and not me, for I might easily have put my foot through the noose.

Herds of wild elephants are not always suspicious of danger. I have on many occasions ridden on one of my own tuskers into a herd of somtimes as many as fifty animals. Sitting on my own elephant, I have passed so close to a wild one that I could have struck a match on his back. Without being detected, I have watched and photographed wild calves of different ages playing in a mud wallow, like children playing at mud pies.

The mating of wild elephants is very private. The bull remains, as usual, outside the herd, and his lady love comes out where she knows she will find him. She gives the herd the slip in the evening, and is back with them at dawn. Sometimes a rival tusker intervenes, and a duel ensues. This is why elephant fights are always between two bulls. There is never a general dog-fight within the herd.

Elephant bulls fight head to head and seldom fight to the death, without one trying to break away. The one that breaks away frequently receives a wound which proves mortal. Directly one of the contestants tries to break off and turn, he exposes the most vulnerable part of the body. The deadly blow is a thrust of one tusk between the hind legs into the loins and intestines where the testicles are carried inside the body. It is a common wound to have to treat after a wild tusker has attacked a domesticated one.

Some males never grow tusks, but these tuskless males are at no disadvantage in a fight, although to outward appearances they are the eunuchs of the herd. This impression is quite wrong. From the age of three all that the animal gains by not having to grow tusks goes into additional bodily strength, particularly in the girth and weight of the trunk. As a result, the trunk becomes so strong that it will smash off an opponent's tusk as though, instead of being solid ivory, it were the dry branch of a tree.

From the time that a male calf is three years old there is always interest among the oozies as to whether it is going to be a tusker with two tusks, or a tai (with one tusk, either right or left), or a han (a tuskless male, but with two small tushes such as females carry), or, lastly, a hine, which has neither tusks nor tushes.

One of the most delightful myths about wild elephants is that the old tuskers and females drop out of the happy herd life when they realize they are no longer wanted, and that they finally retreat to die in a traditional graveyard in some inaccessible forest. This belief has its origin in the fact that dead elephants, whether tuskers or females, are so seldom found. I wish I could include a description here of how I had discovered one of these graveyards. But since I cannot, I shall try to explain away the myth by describing what really happens. I will take the case of a fine old bull that has stopped following the herd at about the age of seventy-five and has taken to a solitary existence. He has given up covering great distances in a seasonal cycle, and remains in the headwaters of a remote creek. It has become enough for him to devote all his time to grazing, resting and taking care of his health. His cheeks are sunken, his teeth worn out. Gathering his daily ration of six hundred pounds of green fodder has become too great a tax on his energy, and he knows he is losing weight. Old age and debility slowly overtake him and his big, willing heart. During the monsoon months he finds life easy. Fodder, chiefly bamboos, is easily gathered, and he stays up in the hills. As the dry season approaches, fodder becomes scarcer, and the effort of finding food greater, and he moves slowly downhill to where he can browse on the tall grass. Then, as the hot season comes on, and there are forest fires, he is too tired and too old to go in search of the varied diet he needs, and his digestion suffers. Fever sets in, as the showers of April and May chill him, and he moves to water – to where he knows he can always get a cool drink. Here, by the large pool above the gorge, there is always green fodder in abundance, for his daily picking. He is perfectly happy, but the water slowly dries, until there is only a trickle flowing from the large pool, and he spends his time standing on a spit of sand, picking up the cool sand and mud with his trunk, and spraying it over his hot, fevered body.

One sweltering hot evening in late May, when there was not a breath of air stirring in this secluded spot, to which he had come again for a drink, he could hear that a mighty storm was raging ten miles away in the hills, and he knew the rains had broken. Soon the trickle would become a raging torrent of broken brown water, carrying trees and logs and debris in its onrush. Throwing his head back, with his trunk in his mouth as he took his last drink, he grew giddy. He staggered and fell but the groan he gave was drowned by peals of thunder. He was down – never to rise again – and he died without a struggle. The tired old heart just stopped ticking.

Two porcupines got the news that night, and, in spite of the heavy rain, attacked one of his tusks, gnawing it as beavers gnaw wood.

They love the big nerve-pulp inside near the lip. They had only half eaten through the second tusk when the roar of the first tearing spate of the rains drove them off.

A five-foot wall of water struck the carcass – debris piled up while the water furiously undermined and outflanked this obstruction – at last the whole mass of carcass, stones and branches moved, floated, and then, swirling and turning over, went into the gorge down a ten-foot waterfall and jammed among the boulders below. Hundreds of tons of water drove onto it, logs and boulders bruised and smashed up the body, shifting it further, and the savage water tore it apart. As the forest fires are God's spring-cleaning of the jungle, so the spates of the great rains provide burial for the dead. That elephant never had to suffer months of exhausting pilgrimage to reach a common graveyard.

By dawn the floods had subsided and the porcupines had to hunt for their second meal of tusk. Other jungle scavengers had their share of the scattered parts, taking their turns in the order of jungle precedence. But the spate came again the next night, and in a week all traces of the old tusker had disappeared.

In South Kensington Museum there are three petrified mammoth's teeth, one canine and two molars, which I found in a gorge in Burma. They are entirely different in kind from elephants' teeth, which are larger, serrated dentals on either side of the jaw. These mammoth teeth are all that is left of an incident similar to the one I have described, which must have happened many centuries ago.

Existing species of elephants are all that remain of a rich and varied family. Fossils bones of fourteen species of the genus *elephas* are known, and there are a still larger number of the allied genus *mastodon*, which had tusks in both jaws and more numerous teeth. The most interesting of all the extinct forms is undoubtedly the mammoth. It coexisted with primitive man, whose drawings and engravings of it are well known, and it may have survived to a late period in Siberia. Its remains are frequently found throughout northern Europe, America and Asia, and are so abundant in Siberia that the tusks form an important article of trade. Mammoths have been found frozen in almost perfect preservation. The remains of elephants have been frequently found in England, and in Malta remains of two pigmy elephants have been discovered.

CHAPTER 4

As civilization eats into the jungle with its roads and railways, the herds of elephants grow fewer. The number of elephants in India has shrunk enormously for this reason, and I fear the same thing will happen in Burma. Fortunately, there are vast forests in the north of Burma into which the herds will gradually withdraw, and where they will, for a long time to come, find that peace characteristic of the jungle of which they are a symbol.

Low-flying aircraft are a new danger. They disturb and terrify herds of elephants, and may seriously affect their breeding for some generations.

The elephants which piled the teak in the sawmills of Moulmein,

Mandalay and Rangoon were hand fed, and so are the great majority of ceremonial elephants kept in India. Such animals are kept in stalls, like horses, just as they are in the London Zoo. Sawmill elephants were at one time quite a showpiece in the mills where they were used, and those invited to see them were usually asked to come by 12.30 p.m.; for at one o'clock, when the siren blew for the midday break, the elephants, like the men, just downed tools. They flatly refused to place the piece of timber they were holding between tusks and trunk on the stack, but just dropped it.

The fact that very few, if any, of these animals ever bred in captivity is sufficient proof of the unnatural conditions in which they lived. Very little could be learned from elephants kept in such conditions which was of any use in improving the general management of the thousands of up-country elephants. The conditions of these up-country elephants are completely different. They are far nearer to the wild state than any other domesticated animals. Indeed, one might say that they are domesticated for only eight hours out of the twenty-four. The great difference is that these elephants feed on their natural fodder in the jungle, and gather it for themselves. They are not hand fed. As a result of the liberty which this involves, they breed readily.

A conservative figure of the numbers of elephants working in the mixed deciduous forest areas of Burma before the Japanese invasion is six thousand. Seventy per cent of them were born in captivity.

The purchase of newly captured kheddared elephants was more often than not left to a Burman who was reputed to be a good judge of elephants. But the purchase of kheddared elephants was never really successful. A kheddared elephant seldom works as well, or as reliably, as one brought up from a calf to be familiar with man and with work, and it can be immediately recognized by the terrific training scars on its legs. It was soon realized that it was increasingly desirable to keep up the numbers by taking greater care of mothers and newly born calves, of which the death-rate was very high. I arrived in Burma just as a determined effort had been started to improve the management of these elephants and their calves. In order to do this, it was first necessary to improve the conditions of the oozie, who must be considered as part and parcel of the Burmese timber-working elephant which he rides. These men are born with a knowledge of elephants. Their homes are in camps in the most remote parts of the jungle. They can sit an elephant from the age of six, and they grow up learning all the traditional knowledge, the myth and legend, the blended fact and fiction, which is attached to this lovable animal. At the age of fourteen the average boy in an elephant camp is earning a wage. He starts life as a paijaik – that is, the man who hooks the chains to the logs – a ground assistant of the oozie who rides on the elephant's neck.

It is a proud day in that boy's life when he is promoted to oozie and has an elephant in his own charge. There is no more lovely sight than to see a fourteen-year-old boy riding a newly trained calf elephant of six. The understanding between them is only equalled by that of a child with a puppy, but the Burmese boy is not so cruel to his elephant as most children are with puppies. The Burman oozie is cruel to his elephant only if he loses his temper, but usually he has the patience of Job. He has a pretty hard life. In the first place, he has to catch his elephant every morning and bring it to camp. The camp is often a hundred miles from his village, and may consist of a few jungle huts, or even no more than a couple of tarpaulins making a shelter on the bank of some creek in the densest jungle. Catching his elephant involves tracking the animal a distance of about eight miles, starting at dawn through jungles infested with all types of big game. That in itself is a lonely job, and to do it successfully the oozie has to become one of the jungle beasts himself – as alert and as wary as they are.

He knows the shape, size and peculiarities of his own elephant's footprints with such certainty that he can recognize them at once and distinguish them from all other elephant footprints. Once he has picked them up, he sets off, following the trail. While he is doing so he notices many things: he finds the spot where the animal rested in the night, he observes its droppings, and, after giving one heap of dung a kick, can tell that his elephant has been eating too much bamboo and, for that reason, will probably have headed for a patch of kaing grass that grows on the banks of the creek over the watershed.

When he has gained the ridge he will halt and listen, perhaps for ten minutes, for the sound of the bell his particular animal wears round its neck. He can hear a bell perhaps two miles away but he decides it is not the note of the bell that he made himself, hollowing it from the teak with such intricate care. So he goes on again, descending to the creek, and when he is half a mile from the kaing grass he listens again and this time he recognizes the sound of his own kalouk. Elephant bells are made with two clappers, one on each side, hanging outside the bell, which is made from a hollowed-out lump of teak. No two bells ever have the same note, and the sound of fifteen or more can only be compared to the music of a babbling brook.

As the oozie approaches his beast he begins to sing, so as to let her know that he is coming. He has taught her, or she has taught him, that it is dangerous for them to startle each other in the jungle. So, instead of bursting through the kaing grass that stands nine feet high, he sits down on a boulder beside the creek and fills his home-made pipe and lights it. Between the puffs he keeps calling 'Lah! Lah! Lah!' (Come on! come on! come on!) But no sound comes from where his elephant is grazing, so he changes his words to: 'Digo lah! Digo lah!' (Come here! Come here!) And he will sit and smoke and call for fifteen minutes without showing impatience. He gives her time to accept the grim fact that another day of hard work has begun for her. If he hurried her, she might rebel.

Presently the elephant emerges from the kaing grass, and, chatting away to her, he says: 'Do you think I've nothing else to do but wait for you? You've been eating since noon yesterday, and I haven't had a bite of breakfast.'

Then his voice rings out with a firm order: 'Hmit!'

Dropping first on her haunches, then reposing with all four legs extended, she allows him to approach her.

'Tah!' (Stand up!), he orders, and she does so, keeping her front legs close together. He then bends down and unfastens her fetter-chain and throws it over her withers. These hobbles are either chain or cane, and are put on fairly tight and with little play between the legs. When the animal is hobbled it can either shuffle slowly on easy ground or progress by a series of hops. But in spite of this it can go fast: for short distances it can go as fast as a man can run.

After unfastening the hobbles the oozie orders her to sit down, then he climbs onto her head, and away they go, back to camp, by the route she has been feeding along ever since the previous day.

When they reach camp the oozie has his first meal of the day, washes his elephant in the creek, and then harnesses her for work. Their job for the day is to climb a ridge two thousand feet above the camp and to drag a log from the stump to the creek.

When the oozie reaches the log with his elephant and his paijaik, he will trim it, cutting off knots where there were branches with his axe, so as to make it easier for dragging. He also cuts a hole in the thinner end of the log, through which the dragging-chains are passed. This hole, called a nepah, is so useful in handling the log when rafting, as well as in dragging, that though it is wasteful of good timber it is preferred to fastening the chains round the log in a clove hitch, or to any other form of attachment.

Then he will make sure the chains are securely fastened. After that there begins the wearisome task of dragging a log twenty-nine feet long and six or seven feet in girth – that is to say, over a hundred cubic feet of timber, or four tons dead weight. For a mile the path follows the top of the ridge. 'Patience! patience! patience! Yoo! yoo! yoo!' (Pull! pull! pull!), calls the oozie. As the elephant takes the strain, she feels what power she must exert besides that of her enormous weight. Tremendous energy is necessary. The ground is ankle-deep in mud, and there are dozens of small obstructions which must be levelled out by the log's nose – sapling stumps, bamboos, stones, even rocks. So the elephant puts out her first effort and, bellowing like hell, pulls the log three times her own length and then stops. She rests then to take breath, and her trunk goes out sideways to snatch at a bamboo. It is her chewing-gum as she works, but it earns her a sarcastic comment from the oozie: 'My mother, but you are for ever eating!' However, his patience is quite undisturbed. The elephant takes her time. 'Yoo! yoo! yoo!' calls the oozie, but there is no response. 'Yoo! yoo! yoo!' Then the elephant pulls again, but this time, as it is slightly downhill, she pulls the log six times her length before she halts. So it goes on, until they reach the edge of a precipice – a four-hundred-foot drop. The elephant knows the margin of safety to a foot, and when the log is ten feet from the edge she refuses to haul it any closer. The chains are unfastened, and the elephant is moved behind the log. The oozie gives his orders by kicks and scratches with his bare feet behind the elephant's ears. So he coaxes her to bend down her massive head in order to get a leverage under the log with her trunk. Working like that, she moves it first four feet at one end, then rolls it from the middle, then pushes the other end, until she has got it almost trembling on the balance onto the very edge of the cliff. She will then torment her oozie by refusing to touch it again for ten minutes. Finally, when the oozie's patience is almost at an end, and the elephant can foresee that she will get a cursing and a vigorous toe-nail scratching behind her ears if she refuses any longer, she puts one forefoot out as calmly as if she were tapping a football; and the log is away – gone. There is a crash in the jungle below, and then a prolonged series of crashes echoing through the jungle, as the log tears down bamboos, until it comes to rest four hundred feet lower down, leaving the elephant standing on the edge of the precipice above, with a supercilious expression on her face, as though she were saying: 'Damned easy.'

Half an hour later elephant and oozie have reached the log again, having gone round by a circuitous game-track to the foot of the precipice. Once down there, she has again to drag the log with the chains along a ledge, which has been roughly blasted out of the hillside around a precipitous waterfall.

Such blasting is often done by a more primitive method than using dynamite. The rock is heated with a fierce brushwood fire and then cracked by pouring water over it. After that the fractured rocks are again broken with crowbars, and the big pieces disposed of by elephants.

Dragging a log weighing four tons while negotiating a not very wide ledge is a risky business, for the log might roll. But the elephant can judge what is safe to the inch – not to the foot – and she works with patience, patience, patience. Both oozie and elephant know that should the log start to roll or slide over the edge, all the gear and harness can be got rid of in the twinkling of an eye. The elephant has only to whip round in her tracks, step inside her chain, and bend down her head for all the harness to peel off over her head as easily as a girl will strip a silk slip off over her shoulders. For this reason it is very rare indeed for an elephant to be dragged over a precipice by a log suddenly taking charge.

After negotiating the ledge there is an easy downhill drag for half a mile to the floating point on the side of the creek. By that time it is about three o'clock in the afternoon. The oozie unharnesses his elephant, puts on her fetters, slaps her on her backside, and tells her that she must go off in search of food. For neither of them is their day's work really over. The elephant still has to find her fodder; not only to chew it, but to break off, pull down, or pull up, every branch, tree, creeper or tuft of grass that she eats. The oozie has to repair his gear, trim logs or weave a new laibut, or breast-strap of bark. This bit of harness takes the full strain of the elephant's strength when dragging, and has to be made accordingly. It gets a tremendous lot of wear.

Such is the oozie's day's work – and with it all he is a very happy man.

His chief relaxation is gambling. He does often literally lose the shirt off his back. I have seen one particular shirt worn by six different owners in a year. But they don't wear their shirts at work, but only dress up in the evening and when showing their elephants for inspection.

The hardest work, described above, lasts from June until March. Then for three months the oozie gets a rest from logging, but has still to look after his elephant every day.

He is, as I know Burma, all that is left of the real Burman – the cheerful Irishman of the East. I have watched him fraternize with all who played a part in the evacuation of Burma in 1942 and with those who recaptured it in 1945 – the British soldier, the Gurkha, the Sikh, the Punjabi, the West African and the East African. He even fraternized with the Jap, because he would not abandon his elephant, and for a time both had to work for a new master.

One gets to know one's riders at the same time, and in the same way, as one gets to know the elephants. They are so much part of one another.

Living under such primitive conditions, not only the oozie but also his wife and family need frequent medical attention, and they have no one to look to but the European Assistant who lives nearest. Apart from all the diseases, accidents are constantly occurring in the jungle, and the Assistant has to be a bit of a doctor, and ready to take decisions which would make an ordinary medical man's hair stand on end. One may come into a new camp and find six people down with beri-beri – and one has to decide at once what one is going to do about it. One has to be ready to tackle a girl with a bad afterbirth haemorrhage, or a man scalped by a bear, with his long hair tangled deeply into the wounds and one eye out of its socket. Malaria is more common than are colds in the head in England, and is often followed by pneumonia. Dysentery, and even cholera and smallpox epidemics are all liable to break out in the jungle. I am convinced that life in such conditions would be impossible if it were not for the elephants, which exert a fascination over the Burmese, a fascination which Europeans soon begin to feel as well.

Like the elephant, the jungle Burman makes a marvellous patient. Both, when they are ill, have an implicit trust even in the most amateur of doctors, whose equipment is all too often only a first-aid box the size of a biscuit tin. Luckily, faith helps to make up for its deficiencies.

CHAPTER 5

The fact that men and elephants live about as long as one another and come to maturity at much the same ages means that they can live together all their lives. They can thus acquire a lifelong mutual knowledge of each other's characters. With no other domestic animal is this possible. A baby boy may be born in an elephant camp, and at the same moment an elephant calf may be being born a mile or two away in the jungle; and that child and that calf may grow up together, play together, work together all their working lives, and they may still be familiar friends when sixty years have passed.

Elephants are not bred in captivity. The captive animals breed naturally in their natural surroundings. During the war I was talking about elephants to two war correspondents, one American and the other an Australian. The latter asked me: 'Is it true that elephants are very shy about their actual love affair?' Before I could answer, the American chipped in with: 'Of course they are: aren't you?' The mating of elephants is a private affair, and even the oozies of the tusker and the female concerned may not know that it has taken place. Often they know, but regard it as none of their business, and do not talk about it.

The most fantastic tales are told, and even believed, about the mating habits of elephants by Europeans. The tallest story that has come my way was told by a young Sapper officer to a very attractive nurse whom he took to the Rangoon Zoo, after the recapture of Rangoon in May 1945. Among the few animals left behind in it by the Japs were two young elephants, a male and female, which led very boring existences hobbled and tethered by the hind legs to two posts in the elephant-shed. While watching this melancholy pair, the young Sapper described how the female elephant turns to thoughts of love in the spring time, and prepares for her honeymoon by digging a deep pit, round which she stacks a month's supply of fruit and fodder for herself and her young bridegroom. When she has completed these preparations, she lies down in the nuptial pit and trumpets a love-call to her mate. After his arrival they live in one unending embrace for the whole month, and do not separate until they have shared their last pineapple or banana! No doubt the Sapper hoped that his attractive listener would take the hint and act likewise. The pretty girl to whom this story had been told afterwards applied to me for confirmation of the story. I felt sorry to have to disillusion her, though the love-making of elephants as I have seen it seems to me more simple and more lovely than any myth. It is beautiful because it is quite without the brutishness and the cruelty which one sees in the mating of so many animals.

Without there being any appearance of season, two animals become attracted by each other. In other words they fall in love, and days, and even weeks, of courtship may take place, the male mounting the female with ease and grace and remaining in that position for three or four minutes. Eventually the mating is consummated, and the act lasts five or ten minutes, and may be repeated three or four times during the twenty-four hours. The pair will keep together as they graze for months, and their honeymoon will last all that time. When they have knocked off from the day's work they will call each other and go off together into the jungle. My own belief is that it lasts until the female has been pregnant for ten months – that is, until she has become aware that she is pregnant. The act of mating can be performed as easily by an elephant wearing hobbles as without them, as the position of the male's forelegs lying along the barrel of the back of the female is not interfered with by the hobbles. In the final mating position the male is standing almost vertically upright, with the forefeet resting gently on the female's hindquarters.

The average female first mates between the ages of seventeen and twenty. She shows no sign of any particular season, but apparently feels some natural urge. It has recently been noticed that female circus elephants become moody in periods of approximately twenty-two months. Gestation lasts twenty-two months, and she does not appear to realize that she is pregnant until the end of the first ten months. After that the period of mating comes to an end, and the companionship of the male is replaced by that of a female friend or 'auntie'. From that time onwards the expectant mother and her girl friend, or 'auntie', are never apart. They graze together always, and it becomes difficult to separate them. It is, indeed, cruel to do so. Their association is founded on mutual aid among animals, the instinctive knowledge that it takes two mothers to protect a calf elephant against tigers, which, in spite of all precautions, still kill twenty-five per cent of all calves born.

After the calf has been born, the mother and the 'auntie' always keep it between them as they graze – all through the night – and, while it is very young, during daylight hours as well.

To kill the calf the tiger has to drive off both the mother and 'auntie' by stampeding them. To do this he will first attack the mother, springing on her back and stampeding her; then he returns to attack 'auntie', who defends the calf, knowing that in a few moments the mother will return. On many occasions I have had to dress the lacerated wounds of tiger-claws on the backs of both a mother elephant and her friend.

A mother elephant in captivity has no suspicions that man will injure her calf. I have only once been attacked by one of the many mothers whom I have congratulated by a pat on the trunk, often within an hour of the actual birth. That was an accident. I was patting a calf so young that it could not focus me with its little piggy eyes, and it bumped hard against my bare knees and yelled out the cry for danger. As I jumped back, the lash of the mother's trunk missed me by inches. She then chased me, but only for twenty yards, as she had to return to her squealing babe. On the other hand, I have handled a newly born dwarf elephant under the mother's belly, lifting it up so that it stood on a small platform, so as to reach its mother's nipples, and the mother seemed to consider this as much of a joke as I did.

A baby calf follows its mother at heel for three or four years. It is suckled by the mother for that period, from the breasts between her forelegs.

This position, between the forelegs, affords the calf perfect protection. At birth the calf's trunk is a useless object, or membrane, growing rather to one side, so as to allow the calf to suck more easily through the mouth. It does not become flexible and useful for three to four months. When the sacred white elephant of Mandalay Palace was a calf its mother died, and it was suckled by twenty young Burmese women daily as wet nurses, and so reared.

At the age of five or, at most, six years, the calf has learnt to gather its own fodder, and gradually gives up sucking its mother. Female elephants have an average of four calves in their lifetime. Twins are not uncommon, and two calves of different ages following their mother at heel is quite a usual sight. Larger families are not uncommon.

'Accidents' happen in the elephant world, and elderly females occasionally spring a surprise. Thus Main Hpo (a Shan name) gave birth to her eighth calf just after the Japanese War, in the Gangaw Valley, when she was sixty-one years old. All her previous calves had lived and had been trained – in fact her eldest son, a tuskless male named Hine Pau Zone (Mr Laziest), was the only elephant ever recorded as having killed a Japanese soldier. This incident took place at a Chin village in 1945, during the Japanese withdrawal.

After weaning, young elephants go through an awkward stage, becoming a bit truculent owing to the desire for independence – much like human boys and girls.

At fifteen or sixteen they become very much like human flappers and young stalwarts. They have reached the same adolescent stage of not knowing quite what they want. Some soon find out, others do not; for their temperaments vary.

Young male elephants do a lot of flirting with the females from the ages of sixteen to twenty, sometimes being most enterprising. But the average animal does not show any signs of must until the age of twenty. A male elephant will mate when he is not on must, in fact he usually does. But when he is on must all the savage lust and combative instincts of his huge body come out.

From the age of twenty to thirty-five must is shown by a slight discharge of a strongly smelling fluid from the must-glands near the eye, directly above the line of the mouth. In a perfectly fit male it occurs annually during the hot months, which are the mating season. It may last about two weeks, during which time he is very temperamental.

From the age of thirty-five to forty-five the discharge increases and runs freely, eventually dribbling into his mouth, and the taste of it exasperates him and makes him much more ferocious. He is physically in his prime at that age, and unless he is securely chained to a large tree while on must, he is a danger to his oozie and to other elephants. His brain goes wild, as though nothing would satisfy him, and nothing will.

From forty-five to fifty must gradually subsides, and finally disappears. Tuskers that have killed as many as nine men between the ages of thirty-five and forty-five will become docile during must in the later years of their lives. But no elephant on must can be trusted unless he is over sixty years old.

Poo Ban, a magnificent tusker, was normally a friendly animal, and would allow me to walk under his head and tusks, but he went on must in the Taungdwin Forest area, killed his oozie and another man, then killed two female elephants, and attacked on sight any man who came near him. Finally he entered villages, tore rice granaries open, and became the terror of the valley. I offered a reward of three hundred rupees for his capture, and decided to destroy him if he could not be captured.

He was marked down in a dense patch of bamboo jungle in Saiyawah (the Valley of Ten Villages), four marches away. With Kya Sine, my gun-boy, I set out, lightly loaded with two travelling elephants as pack. The evening before I was to tackle Poo Ban I was testing my rifle with a half charge, i.e., with half the cordite removed, and with a soft-nosed bullet in the left barrel, keeping a normal hard-nosed cartridge in the right. I wanted to wound Poo Ban in one of his forefeet with the half charge, and then recapture him, break his spirit and heal his wound. At a hundred yards my practice-shooting was so accurate that I felt hopeful of success. Kya Sine, however, begged and implored me to let him go ahead and attempt to recapture him without shooting, so that he could earn the three hundred rupees. He intended to tackle him boldly, face to face, relying on his own authority and the animal's habits of obedience. Unfortunately, I gave in, and before dawn he had gone on ahead. I arrived at 3 p.m. next day to be met by men who said: 'Kya Sine is dead.' Poo Ban had killed him during his attempt at recapture.

That night I bivouacked in an open place which had at one time been paddy-fields. It was a brilliant moonlight night, and before I went to sleep I made my plans to recapture Poo Ban. I had no desire to avenge the death of Kya Sine – to whom I was devoted, and who had the greatest knowledge of jungle lore of any man I have ever known. The idea of revenge on an elephant would have been very distasteful to him.

I was asleep, lying in the open, when I was woken by a clank! clank! clank! Luckily for me, a piece of chain had been left on Poo Ban's off forefoot. I came suddenly to my senses out of a dream, and, jumping up, saw the finest sight of my life. Two hundred yards away, in the open, a magnificent tusker was standing, with his head erect in challenge, defiant of the whole world. He was a perfect silhouette. I did not dare move an eyelid. He was a bigger man than I was, and while I held my breath he moved on with a clank, clank, clank, which at last faded away like the far sound of the pipes over the hills.

At dawn I tried to put my plans into action. When he had been located, I took up my position, while twenty Burmans, with four shotguns between them, tried to drive him past me.

Poo Ban faced the lot, defying them four times. Shots rang out, but at last he changed his mind and, turning, came towards me. I was perched on a broken-down, dilapidated brick pagoda, a heap of rubble about six feet high, behind which was the hundred-feet-high bank of the Patolone River. Directly in front of me was a clearing of disused paddy-fields, and my hopes were that Poo Ban would cross it. I still meant to wound him in the foot, recapture him, break his spirit and then heal the wound.

Poo Ban came out of the jungle with his head held high. He halted, and then made a bee-line across my front, travelling fast over the open ground.

Kneeling, I took the shot at his foot on which my plans depended. The bullet kicked up a puff of dust in front of his near forefoot as he put it down in his stride. I had missed!

Poo Ban halted and swung round to face me, or the bark of my rifle which he had heard. Then he took up the never-to-be-forgotten attitude of an elephant about to charge, with the trunk well tucked away in his mouth, like a wound-up watch-spring or the proboscis of a butterfly. As he charged it flashed through my mind that I had no time to reload. I depended on the hard-nosed bullet in the right barrel. At twenty-five yards I took a chest shot. At twenty yards Poo Ban fell. His head dropped; his tusks drove nine inches into the ground. For a few seconds he balanced, and then toppled over, dead.

I dropped my rifle and was sick, vomiting with fear, excitement and regret. Poo Ban was dead, and I had failed to catch him alive. There was no court of enquiry. My report was accepted, and I was given the tusks as a souvenir, a souvenir of a double failure that I bitterly regretted, and of the death of the finest and bravest Burman hunter I have known.

CHAPTER 6

There is undoubted cruelty in breaking the spirit of and training wild elephants after they have been captured by kheddaring. The ideal age at which to capture a wild elephant is usually considered to be from fifteen to twenty, as it is then only a few years before it is sufficiently mature to do heavy work and to earn its original cost. But the spirit of a youngster of that age, whether male or female, takes a lot of breaking. It often takes a matter of weeks, while it is tethered to a tree with chains; and its continual struggling and fighting to break free cause the most shocking galling of the ankles and neck. Food is thrown to the tethered animal, but insufficient and unsuitable food leads to great loss of condition, and the oozie, or attendant responsible for feeding and watering, often retaliates with a spear-stab in the cheek after the captive has lunged at him with its trunk. The wounds it receives are almost impossible to treat, and they naturally become fly-blown and ulcerated. In the end the young animal becomes heartbroken and thin. Finally it realizes that it is in captivity for the rest of it days, and after the last heartbreaking struggle will put up with a man sitting on its head. By then it is usually covered with sores and wounds.

But a calf born in captivity in the nearest possible surroundings to those of a wild elephant is far more easily trained. From the day it is born until it leaves its mother at five years old it is in contact with its mother's oozie. It flirts with him like a child, it pretends to chase him, then runs away again. But, though so playful, it seldom trusts him much beyond accepting a titbit of fruit or a handful of rice from his hands.

In November of its fifth year the calf is weaned, and from that moment becomes more independent. Five or six calves are trained at a time in one camp. A Burman specially picked as a trainer is in charge, assisted by two men per calf, with eight other men to do general work. A training camp should be in flat country near a stream. An area of a hundred yards square is cleared, except for a few trees to give shade, leaving only a carpet of earth. In the middle a 'crush' or triangular-shaped pen is built of logs of about the height of the average five-year-old calf. The logs of which it is built are fastened with wooden pegs; no nails are used in its construction. The bark is stripped from the logs, which are rubbed smooth and smeared with grease – all precautions against galling the calf's hide while it is in the crush under training. In addition to the calves with their mothers in camp is an elephant known as the koonkie (schoolmaster). This animal is usually a tuskless male between forty-five and fifty years of age, chosen for his docility and patience.

There is a great deal of superstition connected with the whole business of training young elephants. Before any attempts at actual training have begun, offerings are made to the Nats or spirits of the jungle. A small shrine is built near the crush, and the actual day on which training is to be begun is chosen by the manner in which a series of candles burn out. All the ropes for training are made from raw buffalo hide, preferably woven, and kneaded in lard until they are soft and pliable. Stocks of fruit, such as bananas and tamarinds, are also laid in at the camp, so as to provide the calf with titbits while it is in the crush. These help to keep its mind occupied and soften the shock of its finding itself in a cage.

On the morning when the first calf is to be weaned, the mother and the calf are brought into the clearing and made familiar with the crush and its surroundings. Some calves are so unsuspicious that they will follow a man into the crush if he holds out a banana as a bait. Once the calf is inside, the attendant Burmans quickly slip two stout bars in behind its hindquarters. More often than not, however, the calf is suspicious, and has first to be caught by one foot when in the open. This is done by placing a number of raw-hide running nooses on the ground where the calf is likely to walk. Each man is responsible for one of these lassoes, and has to twitch the noose tight once the calf has stepped inside it. A short struggle and a good deal of yelling on the part of the calf follow, but provided its mother is near at hand, it soon quietens down. It is then gradually pushed and pulled into the crush. In obstinate cases the koonkie, or schoolmaster, has to be brought up, and, with no fuss at all, he puts his head against the calf's fat little rump and gently butts it forward. The mother is quite content to stand by watching these proceedings, and makes no attempt to charge the Burmans so long as she is loose. But she becomes terribly agitated if she is tied up, and will make every attempt to snap her chain to get free and go to its rescue.

Once the calf is inside the crush, the forefoot which is still in the noose is tethered to the apex of the triangle. Bribery is begun at once, but the calf is at first far too intent on getting out of the cage to take the titbits offered to it. It will usually struggle and kick for about two hours. Then it sulks, and finally it will take a banana from the oozie out of sheer boredom and disgust. The expression on its face is like that of a child who eventually has to accept just one sweet after it has sulked for half an hour because it cannot have the whole bag.

While the calf is being cajoled and persuaded that it will do better to make the best of what is offered it, instead of struggling and sulking, its future rider has been attached to a pulley a few feet over its head. Two men on the ground, on either side of the crush, control this pulley, and on a signal from the rider he is lowered slowly onto the calf's head.

'Damn you, get off!' screams the calf, bucking like a bronco. The would-be oozie has soon to be hauled up again, but no sooner has the calf quieted down and accepted another banana, than the rider is lowered once more – and so on, again and again and again, until the poor little calf seems to say: 'All right, damn you. Sit there if you must.

When it has finished the bananas it will buck again; but directly it starts eating, down comes the inevitable oozie.

So far, so good. By that time it will be nearly midday. The poor calf is tired, but the Burmans, stripped of all but their tucked-up lungyis, are thoroughly enjoying the game, though they are dripping with sweat, which shows up their gleaming copper skins and rippling muscles.

Suspended from another pulley above the centre of the calf's back is a heavy block of padded wood. This is also lowered onto its back and provokes more bucking bronco antics, with sideways rollings and strugglings against the greasy bars. A moment or two later the block is lifted, but directly the calf stands still, down it comes again. Once more there are determined struggles to get free, and so it goes on, and all the while the calf is being offered food and spoken to with kind and soothing words. Finally, in utter disgust, the calf sits down with its front feet straight out, hoping that it will get rid of the pests riding on its back in that way.

A cheer goes up from the Burmans: a cheer which soon becomes a chant of 'Tah' (Get up), 'Hmit!' (Sit down). As the weight is lifted, the calf gets up, and all the Burmans chant, 'Tah!' As the weight comes down, and the calf sits, all of them chant, 'Hmit!' in chorus.

After a time the rider, still attached to the pulley, remains comfortably seated on its head. By evening, unless the calf is a really obstinate young devil, the rider can turn and, putting his hand on its back intead of the log of wood, order the calf to sit down by pressure and by saying, 'Hmit.'

Once that is possible, the calf is considered as broken. Often it takes less than twelve hours, with no cruelty whatsoever. Sometimes, however, in dealing with obstinate and truculent young tuskers, the game has to be kept up, by the light of bamboo torches, far into the night. Occasionally it may last even till the morning of the next day. But however long it may take, the Burmans never give in and never give the calf any rest until their object is achieved. The great lesson is that man's will-power is stronger than its own, and that man will always get his own way, however long it takes him.

Before the calf is taken out of the crush on the following morning it is hobbled with well-greased buffalo-hide thongs, and it is then tied to a tree for twenty-four hours, being caressed and cajoled all the time by its future rider. He makes it sit down each time he approaches. He mounts on its head, remains there ten minutes, orders the calf to sit again, and dismounts, and sometimes keeps it in the sitting position for five or ten minutes. Extraordinary patience is needed throughout. Once the Burman starts, he goes on until he gains his point. He never lets the calf win a victory, however temporary. Meanwhile the calf's mother has been taken away. No doubt she misses it, as it is common for her to call her calf for a couple of nights after their separation. But the tie between them has grown slender at that age. She does not really want the calf with her, though she may feel some anxiety on its account. The calf is then taken for its first walk, attached to the koonkie by a buffalo-hide girdle. The koonkie has a surcingle over the withers and behind the forelegs, while the calf walks alongside. He thinks the whole thing a bore, but he stands no nonsense. If the calf jibs, sits down, or lags, he gives him one wrench that pulls him along. On occasion he will give him a real welt with his trunk, as though to say: 'Come on, you wretched urchin.'

It soon becomes a decorous walking-out, and at a later stage the koonkie can mange two calves – one on each side of him. By the time they are really well-behaved the koonkie puts on the airs of a stuffy old nurse taking a pair of well-behaved and terribly bored twins out in the Park. As they approach other calves, one can imagine him saying: 'Don't you dare speak to those common children over there.'

I once had a camp with nineteen calves in training in it. They were a joy to watch. Each had a different temperament, and their innate differences of character were enshrined in a lovely lot of names. The trainer really has the right to name calves, and long discussions go on among the assembled riders and the trainer over the camp-fires at night before the calves are finally christened. Often some incident which occurs in the initial stages of training will suggest the name. One such instance I well remember. On the third night after the calf had been taken out of the crush, and while it was tethered to a tree, some little way off from the riders' camp, it was attacked by a tiger, which sprang upon its back.

The calf threw the tiger off, and managed to keep it at bay for twenty minutes, until men from the camp arrived with bamboo torches. That calf naturally became a hero, and the next day it was christened Kya M'Nine (Chyarmanine), which means 'The tiger could not overcome him' – as lovely a name for an elephant as Black Beauty for a horse.

Sometimes there is humour in the name, such as: Ma Pin Wa (Miss Fat Bottom). One young elephant of that name could scarcely have been called anything else. How she wobbled as she walked!

The name given to a calf sticks to it for life, but it never knows its name, as a dog does; for the oozies do not usually call their elephants by name. The real reason why they are christened is so that men can talk about them to each other.

Some of the names are most attractive: Po Sein (Firefly), always given to an animal with a bright fiery eye; Ma Hla (Miss Pretty), always a good-looking calf with a perfect figure; Ma Palai (Miss Pearl), an animal with a pearl-coloured eye; Maung Kyaw Dan (Mr Straight-back); Bandoola (the name of a famous Burmese General), rarely given except to an animal of most outstanding temperament and build. In a herd of two hundred animals in a forest area, it is rare that any two have the same name.

On occasions the trainer will pay a European Assistant the compliment of asking him to christen an animal. In one forest I had a Hitlah and a Musso. In another I had a solitary female calf named Susan Ma after my wife. Twelve years later, by an extraordinary coincidence, I spoke to the rider of a fine young elephant seventeen years old – the first animal to be recovered from the Japs after the evacuation of Burma.

'What's the name of your elephant?'

'Susan Ma,' he replied, and smiled all over his face, for he knew what the name meant.

Less than a year later Susan Ma was lost again when we were overrun by the Japs – but seven months after that, when the Japs retreated, Susan Ma became mine once more, and her namesake still is.

From the age of breaking, young elephants are kept under training until the finishing age of nineteen. For about two years they remain in the camp nursery, merely being caught daily and taught the simple words of command and the 'aids' of the rider and by foot control, behind their ears.

Perhaps this is the place in which to explain what these 'aids' are. Their nature will be familiar enough to polo-players. They are simply movements of the rider's body by which he translates his wishes, almost instinctively, to his mount. Thus an intense stiffening of his limbs and leaning back will be at once understood as halt. A pressure on one side will be understood as turn to the left, on the other as turn to the right. Leaning forward and forcing downwards will mean stoop or kneel. A dragging up on the right side will be correctly interpreted as lift the right foot – on the other, as lift the left.

At about eight years old, young elephants carry their first pack and become 'travellers', accompanying a European Assistant when he tours the forest areas. They thus become accustomed to going over the mountains and down the streams, carrying light weights, such as camp cooking-pots, or a light roll of bedding.

In camp the young traveller is learning something new and useful all the time, even if it is only to pick up the branch of a tree in his trunk and carry it into camp as firewood, or to disentangle his chain if it should get caught in some bamboos.

Such travelling, and all the odd jobs which accompany it, continue until the calf is nineteen years old, after which he joins a working camp and starts hauling timber.

During the early years the elephant never really earns its keep or does enough to pay the wages of its oozie, but is learning all the time. By the time it is nineteen its temperament is fully known, and it has developed physically sufficiently for its future value as a working animal to be gauged.

Up to the age of nineteen or twenty it will have cost about one thousand pounds, when the wages of the oozie, training costs and maintenance are added up. Any earning capacity it might have had during those years would be small, even if used for rice transport. Moreover, any attempt to increase its earnings during the early years is very bad policy, and likely to involve its being overloaded and its whole future usefulness put in jeopardy.

We may assume that the elephant has on the average a working life from its twentieth to its fifty-fifth year. In this period it may cost another one thousand five hundred pounds in the wages of its oozie and in maintenance.

Each working year consists of nine months' work and three months' rest, necessary both to keep it in condition, and on account of the seasonal changes. From June to the end of February are the working months; whilst during the hot weather season, from March to May, animals should not work, there being insufficient fodder and water for them in the teak-bearing and deciduous forest areas.

Each month consists of only eighteen working days and twelve rest days, animals working three days in succession and then resting two. Thus, during the nine months of the working year there are only one hundred and sixty-two working days. Each day averages about eight hours. Thus an elephant works thirteen hundred hours a year. During this time an average animal delivers one hundred tons of timber from stump to a floating-point in a creek. This is only one of the steps in the transport of the teak to the mill.

CHAPTER 7

By the time it is twenty-five years old, a well-trained elephant ought to be able to understand twenty-four separate words of command, quite apart from the signals or 'foot-aids' of the rider. He ought also to be able to pick up five different things from the ground when asked. That is to say, he should pick up and pass up to his rider with his trunk a jungle dah (knife), a koon (axe), his fetter or hobble-chain, his tying-chain (for tethering him to a tree) and a stick. I have seen an intelligent elephant pick up not only a pipe that his rider had dropped, but a large lighted cheroot.

He will tighten a chain attached to a log by giving it a sharp tug with his trunk, or he will loosen it with a shake and a waggle, giving it the same motion with his trunk as that given by a human hand.

An elephant does not work mechanically, like many animals. He never stops learning, because he is always thinking. Not even a really good sheep-dog can compare with an elephant in intelligence.

I don't believe that 'an elephant never forgets', but I should scarcely be surprised if he tied a knot in his trunk to remember something, if he wanted to. His little actions are always revealing an intelligence which finds impromptu solutions for new difficulties. If he cannot reach with his trunk some part of his body that itches, he doesn't always rub it against a tree; he may pick up a long stick and give himself a good scratch with that, instead. If one stick isn't long enough, he will look for another which is.

If he pulls up some grass, and it comes up by the roots with a lump of earth, he will smack it against his foot until all the earth is shaken off, or, if water is handy, he will wash it clean, before putting it into his mouth. And he will extract a pill (the size of an aspirin tablet) from a tamarind fruit the size of a cricket ball in which one has planted it, with an air of saying: 'You can't kid me.'

Elephants can also detach a closely clinging creeper, like ivy, from a tree far more skilfully than can a man working with two hands. This is due to their greater delicacy of touch.

Many young elephants develop the naughty habit of plugging up the wooden bell they wear hung round their necks (kalouk) with good stodgy mud or clay, so that the clappers cannot ring, in order to steal silently into a grove of cultivated bananas at night. There they will have a whale of a time, quietly stuffing, eating not only the bunches of bananas, but the leaves and, indeed, the whole tree as well, and they will do this just beside the hut occupied by the owner of the grove, without waking him or any of his family.

Catching a young animal at this is just like catching a small boy among the gooseberry bushes. For some reason stolen fruit is always sweetest.

Oozies are not always as innocent as they pretend on such occasions. I once had to pay a fine to the Forest Department for damage done by my elephants to some experimental plantations of teak saplings. Naturally, I gave the oozies a reprimand for their slackness in allowing their animals to stray into these plantations. A month afterwards I happened to meet the Forest Officer who had fined me, near a large village, where we both camped for the night. He had four elephants with him, and I had eight. Next morning his annoyance can be imagined when the village headman arrived to ask for compensation for no less than a hundred banana trees, destroyed by his four elephants. Strangely enough, not one of my eight elephants had been involved in the mischief, a fact which made it even more annoying for him. It was not until a week after we had parted company that I found out that though my elephants were innocent, my oozies were quite the reverse. They had taken the bells off the Forest Officer's four elephants and during the night had led them quietly into the banana groves – and had thus paid him out for fining me for the damage to the teak plantation.

I have personally witnessed many remarkable instances of the quick intelligence of elephants, though I cannot claim that they equal the famous yarns which delight all of us, whether we are children or grown-ups – such as that of the circus elephant who saw a man who had befriended him sitting in a sixpenny seat, and at once picked him up with his trunk and popped him into a three-and-sixpenny one!

But the following incidents seem to me to denote immediate brain reaction to a new situation, rather than anything founded on repetitive training.

An uncertain-tempered tusker was being loaded with kit while in the standing position. On his back was his oozie, with another Burman in the pannier, filling it with kit. Alongside, on the flank, standing on the ground, was the paijaik attendant, armed with a spear which consisted of a five-foot cane, a brightly polished spear-head at one end and a spiked ferrule at the other. Another Burman was handing gear up to the Burman in the pannier, but got into difficulties with one package and called out to the paijaik to help him. The latter thrust the ferrule of the spear into the ground so that it stood planted upright, with the spear-head in line with the elephant's eye. Then he lent a hand. The oozie, however, did not trust his beast, and said in a determined voice, 'Pass me the spear.' The tusker calmly put its trunk round the cane at the point of balance, and carefully passed it up to his rider. But, unthinkingly, he passed it head first and held it as though waiting for the rider to catch hold of it by the head.

The rider yelled at his beast in Burmese: 'Don't be a fool – pass it right way round!' With perfect calm and a rather dandified movement, the elephant revolved the spear in mid-air and, still holding it by the point of balance, passed it to his oozie, this time ferrule first.

The oozie did not say thank you, but gave him a curse with a touch of endearment – as though saying, 'You are a damned ill-mannered wild elephant, and I want no more of it.' Then, with a quick movement, he moved the spear-head beside the elephant's eye, an action which meant that he would suffer for it if he tried any tricks with his tusks on those engaged in loading him up. The loading was completed without incident.

Sometimes an elephant will show its intelligence by divining what its oozie wishes.

A case I remember concerned an animal which would not work with a rider on its head, but was obedient to the words of command given by its oozie walking alongside. I was watching this beast straightening logs in a creek – that is to say, placing them in rows of eight or twelve parallel to each other and pointing down the bed of the stream, in readiness for the first floods to carry them away. The oozie was sitting on the bank; work was almost finished, but, because I was around, he knew every log had to be straight in line with the others before they broke off.

There was one noticeable and unshapely log, and the elephant came to the last row in which it lay. He was a big tusker, and was doing all the work with his tusks and head, free of all chains. Without any word of command being given, he let the first log alone, and began shifting the second, keeping one eye on his oozie, as though saying: 'Come on, wake up and tell me what you want!'

The oozie soon told him, shouting: 'You old son of a bitch! What's wrong with that one? Leave it.'

The elephant moved onto the next log, keeping his eye cocked on his oozie, like an old man looking over a pair of spectacles.

'No,' shouted the oozie. 'You know as well as I do,' and made a gesture of picking up a stone to throw at his beast.

The elephant gave a squeal of pure delight at having pulled his oozie's leg, and, without hesitation, disregarded the next five logs and, without pausing, bent down and rolled the one irregularly placed log over four times, leaving it exactly parallel with the others and about a foot from them. Then he walked up to his master, as though to say: 'Enough fooling, let's break off!' and the day's work was finished for man and beast.

But one of the most intelligent acts I ever witnessed an elephant perform did not concern its work, and might just as well have been the act of a wild animal.

One evening, when the Upper Taungdwin River was in a heavy spate, I was listening and hoping to hear the boom and roar of timber coming from upstream. Directly below my camp the banks of the river were steep and rocky and twelve to fifteen feet high. About fifty yards away on the other side, the bank was made up of ledges of shale strata. Although it was already nearly dusk, by watching these ledges being successively submerged, I was trying to judge how fast the water was rising.

I was suddenly alarmed by hearing an elephant roaring as though frightened, and, looking down, I saw three or four men rushing up and down on the opposite bank in a state of great excitement. I realized at once that something was wrong, and ran down to the edge of the near bank and there saw Ma Shwe (Miss Gold) with her three-month-old calf, trapped in the fast-rising torrent. She herself was still in her depth, as the water was about six feet deep. But there was a life-and-death struggle going on. Her calf was screaming with terror and was afloat like a cork. Ma Shwe was as near to the far bank as she could get, holding her whole body against the raging and increasing torrent, and keeping the calf pressed against her massive body. Every now and then the swirling water would sweep the calf away; then, with terrific strength, she would encircle it with her trunk and pull it upstream to rest against her body again.

There was a sudden rise in the water, as if a two-foot bore had come down, and the calf was washed clean over the mother's hindquarters and was gone. She turned to chase it, like an otter after a fish, but she had travelled about fifty yards downstream and, plunging and sometimes afloat, had crossed to my side of the river, before she had caught up with it and got it back. For what seemed minutes, she pinned the calf with her head and trunk against the rocky bank. Then, with a really gigantic effort, she picked it up in her trunk and reared up until she was half standing on her hind legs, so as to be able to place it on a narrow shelf of rock, five feet above the flood-level.

Having accomplished this, she fell back into the raging torrent, and she herself went away like a cork. She well knew that she would now have a fight to save her own life, as, less than three hundred yards below where she had stowed her calf in safety, there was a gorge. If she were carried down, it would be certain death. I knew, as well as she did, that there was one spot between her and the gorge where she could get up the bank, but it was on the other side from where she had put her calf. By that time, my chief interest was in the calf. It stood, tucked up, shivering and terrified on a ledge just wide enough to hold its feet. Its little, fat, protruding belly was tightly pressed against the bank.

While I was peering over at it from about eight feet above, wondering what I could do next, I heard the grandest sounds of a mother's love I can remember. Ma Shwe had crossed the river and got up the bank, and was making her way back as fast as she could, calling the whole time – a defiant roar, but to her calf it was music. The two little ears, like little maps of India, were cocked forward, listening to the only sound that mattered, the call of her mother.

Any wild schemes which had raced through my head of recovering the calf by ropes disappeared as fast as I had formed them, when I saw Ma Shwe emerge from the jungle and appear on the opposite bank. When she saw her calf, she stopped roaring and began rumbling, a never-to-be-forgotten sound, not unlike that made by a very high-powered car when accelerating. It is the sound of pleasure, like a cat's purring, and delighted she must have been to see her calf still in the same spot, where she had put her half an hour before.

As darkness fell, the muffled boom of floating logs hitting against each other came from upstream. A torrential rain was falling, and the river still separated the mother and her calf. I decided that I could do nothing but wait and see what happened. Twice before turning in for the night I went down to the bank and picked out the calf with my torch, but this seemed to disturb it, so I went away.

It was just as well I did, because at dawn Ma Shwe and her calf were together – both on the far bank. The spate had subsided to a mere foot of dirty-coloured water. No one in the camp had seen Ma Shwe recover her calf, but she must have lifted it down from the ledge in the same way as she had put it there.

Five years later, when the calf came to be named, the Burmans christened it Ma Yay Yee (Miss Laughing Water).

In 1930 it fell to my fortune to do fieldwork with a brilliant veterinary surgeon named Pfaff. He was a research officer who had been appointed to stamp out anthrax among domesticated elephants in Burma. Having isolated the germ from an elephant's whole ear which had been sent him, he cultured it and prepared vaccines from both oxen and horses. Then came the experiments in inoculating elephants. The first of these was carried out under perfect conditions, with picked animals in a special camp with a 'crush' to hold the elephants while being inoculated, and with ample time and all that one could wish for. The first experiments were disastrous, a large proportion of the elephants inoculated either were very seriously affected or died. It was some time before he could get the dosage right. But he was determined, and we went on. But when inoculation had proved its value, the work fell on European Forest Assistants working under very different conditions.

Baby-trained calves, savage and dangerous animals, nervous females were all in the day's work for the Assistant working hundreds of miles away from the nearest help. But one had to overcome all difficulties and treat them as child's play, just because one had enough self-confidence to ignore or to forget any risk attached to the work – and the animals knew it. One cut out all the fuss and just walked up boldly to the animal, gave it a good smack with the left hand and exclaimed: 'Hullo, old chap!' while with the right, one thrust the needle through the hide and squirted in the vaccine. Then one gave it another smack and turned away, exclaiming, 'Come on!' to the next elephant. With that technique one could inject fifty animals in the morning and have them back in their working camps during the afternoon.

An Assistant working under me at that time once sent me a frantic message that while he was struggling to inoculate a particularly restive elephant he had unfortunately broken off three needles, and had not been able to recover the broken pieces. He asked for immediate instructions as to whether he should operate and try to extract them.

I replied at once, pointing out that the age of the animal was forty, and we might hope that, considering the size of the elephant and its circulatory system, it would take another fifty years before the needles reached its heart. By then the animal would be getting on for a hundred, so there was no reason for operating now. Moreover, three needles in the heart would result in a most interesting post-mortem on an elephant of ninety! He went on with his work of inoculation, and, so far as I know, he lost no more needles.

Another Assistant had to report that inoculation had been held up, as a truculent elephant broke away on feeling the injection, and carried off the hypodermic syringe and needle firmly planted in his hide. The elephant was not recaptured for a fortnight.

Such humorous incidents helped us to make light of our difficulties in the early experimental days. But only those who have known and experienced the effects of an epidemic of this terrible disease can appreciate what it meant to overcome it. Wholesale inoculation, carried out in this cheery way, brought with it immense relief – one of the nightmares was banished.

I lived through such a nightmare once when thirty-seven elephants, out of the seventy in my charge, died in three weeks.

At nine o'clock one morning I inspected a camp of seven elephants and entered all of them, in their inspection books, as 'fit and fat'. That evening, when I was camped ten miles away, I received an urgent message from the Burman in charge of the elephants I had inspected to say that one of them was down with anthrax. I went back immediately, and reached the elephant camp well after dark, to find that the sick animal was dead and that another one was down.

Veterinary treatment of the disease in those days was amateur indeed, and I was working in the dark in more senses than one, as I started operations on a prostrate elephant by the light of a bamboo fire kept stoked by three Burmans.

Running along under the belly of the elephant was a swelling the size of a bathtub. I made an incision about two feet long in this with a large knife, and poured almost pure carbolic acid into the wound. At that time the accepted cure was to get carbolic to circulate with the blood. There must be a providence that looks after honest fools. Going to my tent that night, sweating and tired and very gory, I prayed earnestly for success.

Strange to say, that animal did recover, but next morning anthrax was reported from another camp ten miles off. And so it went on for that week, until the map of my forest area was closely dotted with crosses in red ink, marking where my elephants had died.

One night, after vainly pondering on how the disease could spread from one camp to the next, ten miles away, and from animal to animal, although by that time I was keeping them isolated, each tethered to a tree a mile from its nearest neighbour, I fell asleep, sitting at my camp table, and dreamed that I myself was the dread carrier of the disease.

When I woke up I found the two table candle-lamps were almost burned out, and in their guttering light I decided to take no action when the next case was reported, no matter how near or how far away it might be. Then I went to bed. I did not move camp for a week, and I shall never know whether my unconscious intuition had been correct, and whether I, like many others, had been the carrier of the disease. For then the rains broke, and the epidemic, mercifully, died out.

I once returned a pony-saddle that I borrowed, but advised that it should be burned, as I had used it touring the anthrax area. The owner did not burn it, which caused great indignation on the station among all who owned polo-ponies. But nothing happened.

Just before the war, experiments in the use of local anaesthetics, and even of general anaesthetics, on elephants were carried out. No doubt these will be resumed one day. But up till the time of the reconquest of Burma, after the Japanese invasion, all elephant surgery was on old and somewhat primitive lines.

It needs confidence to walk under an elephant's jaw and tusks, armed with a bellied knife with a ten-inch blade four inches across in one's left hand, and a six-pound wooden club in the right hand, and then to tell him to hold up his head while you drive the knife up to the hilt into a huge abscess on his chest with one blow of the mallet.

One blow of the mallet is all you can get – if you try another, you must look out for squalls. The elephant does not like it. But if you do the job properly and make a quick and quiet get-away to his flank, he will let you go back ten minutes later to clean out the abscess with your hands and then syringe it with disinfectant. Abscesses on the back are dealt with in the same way, when the animal is sitting down in the 'Hmit' position. Elephants will bear a great deal of pain patiently and appear to understand that it is being inflicted for their own good. But they will only put up with it when the operator is full of confidence in himself and feels he is making a good job of it. For an elephant can sense the absence of self-confidence quicker than any other animal in the world – and when one loses confidence it is high time to hand the knife and the club to someone else.

Wounds caused by tigers, most often received by mother elephants protecting their calves, are exceptionally difficult to heal and frequently do not respond to the most modern antiseptics.

The Burman has cures for all the ills that may befall an elephant. Some are herbal, some are mystic spells and incantations, and some of them have had to be vetoed as being definitely harmful. But I have so far found no treatment for tiger-wounds that comes up to the traditional Burmese method of plugging the wounds with sugar. The Burman also used maggots to clean up gangrened wounds for centuries before the method was rediscovered in modern surgery.

It has been quite truly said that once an elephant goes down, owing to exhaustion or severe colic, he has only a twenty-five per cent chance of getting onto his legs again unaided. Any method of keeping him on his legs improves a sick elephant's chances of survival. The Burman will do this by putting chili-juice in his eye – a counter-irritant that must be agony. But it is effective and about doubles the animal's chances of recovery. No matter how far modern research goes in the veterinary treatment of elephants, we shall always rely to a certain extent upon the Burman's knowledge.

I know, without question, that an elephant can be grateful for relief given to it from pain and sickness. For example, I remember Ma Kyaw (Miss Smooth, an expression often used to describe any Burmese girl with a strikingly good figure). She had fearful lacerations on the barrel of her back from tiger-claws, and I treated her for them every day for three weeks. In the early stages she suffered great pain, but although she made a lot of fuss – rather as an eight-year-old child might have done – she always gave way, because I was determined, and she let me go on. When she was sufficiently healed I sent her back to camp under a reliable Burman, with instructions that she was to be given light dressings of fly repellent on the wounds. I did not see her again for two months, when I was having a cup of tea in camp outside my tent, while seven elephants were being washed in the creek near by, preparatory to my inspecting them. The last animal to come out of the creek and to return to camp to dry off before inspection was Ma Kyaw. As she passed me, about fifty yards away, with her rider on foot, following at her heel and not on her head, I called out, more in order to greet him and show that I recognized him than because of any interest in the animal, which I was anyhow going to inspect in less than an hour's time, 'How is Ma Kyaw's back?'

Her rider did not reply, as he had not caught what I said, but Ma

Kyaw swung round, at right angles to the direction in which she was going, and came towards me.

She walked straight up to me where I was sitting. I patted her on the trunk and gave her a banana off my table, and then, without any word of command, she dropped into the sitting position and leant right over towards me, so as to show me her back. Having patted her I told her to 'Tah' (get up), and away she went, leaving me with the agreeable conviction that she had come to say 'thank you'. Then I began to suspect that perhaps, on hearing my voice – with which she had become familiar – she had done it merely from habit.

But later on, when I inspected her, I got a surprise. She was the last in the row, and I went over her back very carefully, kneading the wounds with my hands, and I found one little hole which still suppurated. There was great tenderness along a line nine inches long where the wound had healed over. There was undoubtedly a sinus. Ma Kyaw let me open it up to its full length there and then, although my doing so obviously gave her great pain. But she was a good patient.

This made me think over the incident again. I can never be quite sure that she came and showed me her back in order to tell me that it was still painful. But I am sure that she liked me, trusted me, and was grateful, and that we were very good friends.

Besides the surgical side of looking after elephants, there is the medical side. This is not so much administering drugs and medicines as keeping the animals healthy so that they never need them. This means understanding the particular needs of individual animals. The elephant is not a ruminant, and has only one stomach. He has to collect about six hundred pounds of green fodder to fill that every day, and the most likely thing to go wrong is his digestion. To keep well he needs variety, but one has to see he doesn't pay too high a price for it. For example, an animal may be working in a place where there is nothing but bamboo fodder. To get the variety of food he needs, he may have to travel eight miles, and this he will do. But to do this every night after a hard day's work and to come back in the morning will soon pull him down. And in three weeks he may lose condition that will take him at least three months to recover. It needs a really experienced man to spot any loss of condition when inspecting an elephant. A good man ought to be able to answer the very frequent question, 'Do you know every animal by name?' by replying, 'Yes, and by its digestion too.'

To divide up a herd of elephants into bunches of seven at random and allot each group to a different camp would soon be disastrous to the health of the herd. Animals have to be chosen so that the fodder available in the part of the forest in which they will work corresponds to their individual needs. The type of ground, rocky or otherwise, precipitous or undulating, has to be taken into account. Moreover, the work they are expected to do must be adapted to their strength. Some can handle large timber, others only small logs.

Elephants' feet vary as much in size and shape as do those of human beings, although practically all of them have five toe-nails on the front foot and only four on the hind. But, in selecting animals for certain areas, one has to take their feet into account. Only elephants with well-shaped feet with thick ankles should work in mud.

Lastly, the sex of the animal is of the greatest importance in allocating work. Tuskers are needed more than females in forest areas where the timber is large and the country is very precipitous. Special tuskers, known as htoking elephants, do the work of clearing the log away from the stump and getting it to the dragging-path. Sometimes a tree, when it is felled, will skid three or four hundred feet into deep ravine. Powerful animals with tusks are then required to htoke it up to the dragging-path after it has been cut into logs.

CHAPTER 8

In 1931 I had the good fortune to be selected as one of a party which was to explore the forests of the North Andaman Islands.* There were three other officers in the party, and we were given forty-eight convicts from the penal settlement as our labour. Part of my job was to discover whether the native flora, grasses, etc., would provide sufficient natural fodder to enable elephants to be completely self-supporting, as in Burma. I decided, before embarking on this adventure – for it really was an adventure – to collect all the plants on which elephants feed in Burma, for purposes of comparison. The one and only way to do it seemed to me to live with an elephant, continuously, for three days and three nights. I did this, moving with the animal as she browsed, and collecting specimens of every plant she ate. Altogether I gathered forty-eight species of common plants: the few rare plants I ignored. I had my collection classified for me by the Botanist of the Forest Department School, and the specimens were pressed into a two-volume herbarium, which later fell into the hands of the Japs, together with the rest of the contents of my bookcase, when I left Burma in 1942. With them was my diary of the four months' trip in the Andamans, which showed

* See map on p. 485.

how valuable that knowledge of fodder proved, as it enabled me to decide that the North Andaman Islands provided sufficient natural fodder to support elephants. Elephants are not indigenous to the Andaman Islands, but the Forest Department had, some years previously, imported eighty into the South Islands, where it was erroneously believed that natural fodder had to be supplemented by a ration of paddy – that is, rice in the husk.

During a trek across the largest island of the Northern group, I was amazed to discover the tracks and droppings of an elephant which I could only suppose was a wild one. Judging from the impressions of the pads and the size of the droppings, I came to the conclusion that it was a young animal, about twenty years old. I got quite close to him on two occasions, but, owing to the dense jungle, was unable to see him before he winded me. Thus I was left guessing, until the end of our exploring trip.

My enquiries then revealed that a seven-year-old calf elephant, one of the South Andaman Forest Department's elephants, had been missing twelve years before. It had been 'written off' in the Forest Department records as 'believed drowned', having been seen attempting to swim from island to island. The age of this animal coincided pretty well with my estimate, and there can be no doubt it was the same. It was a remarkable swim, for it was over two hundred miles from where he was last seen to where I found him, and some of his swims from island to island must have been at least a mile in the open sea, which is seldom without a swell, and in a country where there are two monsoons a year. Of course, he had twelve years in which to do it, and no doubt he had a good sojourn on each island before moving to the next. An elephant thoroughly enjoys swimming, and will entirely submerge for brief periods when in deep water. He must have been a considerable surprise to any of the wild Jarawa tribesmen who saw him, and he must have seemed to them like a sea monster. These Jarawas are sea gipsies who live entirely on fish and shellfish. They are still wild, and in the past, if they were in large numbers, used to shoot their poisoned arrows at anyone they met. Now they are practically extinct, and there are less than a hundred of them left. They are of Negro type, and are said to be the only link between the African Negro and the Australian Aborigine. I was lucky enough to meet a small party of five, consisting of three men and two young girls. They were all small in stature, but the men were muscular and healthy, and the girls had exceptionally good figures. The men were naked, and the girls wore nothing but a leaf, the shape of a fig leaf, which was traditionally designed for that very purpose. The amusing part was that the girls each had two spare leaves, which they carried rolled up, above each ear. Thus they were able to change their frock twice a day, once during the midday heat, and again in the cool of the evening. The whole party attached themselves to our camp for a few days, during which time the men were most useful in showing us the few fresh-water springs that existed on the coasts of the islands.

No doubt the young elephant was just as surprised, on emerging from the sea after swimming from a distant island, at being confronted by a modern Eve, as the Jarawa Eve was to see a sea monster rise up out of the sea and disappear into the jungle.

But the Jarawas are used to strange animals. They helped me to catch a dugong, the warm-blooded mammal which some suppose to have given rise to the myth of the mermaid. This dugong was a female, and it certainly had a more uncanny resemblance to a human being than any monkey. It had a repulsive little nose, human-looking teeth, well-formed breasts the size and shape of inverted teacups, flippers like deformed arms and fat fists like little hands.

While I was on this exploring trip I learned a great deal about Burman dacoits, or robbers, which confirmed all that I had imagined them to be from my experiences in Burma. We had working for us, during the four months of our trip, forty-eight convicts with life sentences.

Before I set off to the Andaman Islands I stuffed the bladders of two Rugby footballs full of opium, as I knew that half of the dacoities which are committed are done in desperation by opium addicts, in order to obtain money to buy it.

I picked up our convicts – most of them dacoits – at Port Blair, and from there I took them to the North Islands, where we were dumped for four months. The leader of them was a Burman called Nga Moh, with a grey moustache, like a mandarin's, hanging to below his chin. During the first week I never saw a smile on his face. He had wonderful control over his companions, who were a bunch of the biggest cut-throats I had ever seen. The only precaution I took with regard to them was to immobilize our two motor launches offshore every night. They included men of all sorts of trades: mechanics, fitters, elephant-riders, and even goldsmiths; and every one of them had that wild look in the eye which indicated he would take any risk in order to see his native land again. They were all either murderers or accessories to murder, but they had a sense of humour, and we often had the camp ringing with laughter after the day's work was done – and it was at that hour that I gave out the opium ration. I heard the most astounding tales from them about the crimes they had committed, which eventually earned each of them a life sentence in a penal settlement.

Nga Moh told me he was one of a gang of eight dacoits when he was twenty. They attacked a mule caravan on the Burma–Siam border, but had no intention of using the one firearm they possessed, except to fire a couple of shots in order to stampede the mules. Unfortunately for him, the attack did not go as planned, and the leader of the dacoits had to fire his gun at a muleteer, killing him outright, in order to avoid being struck down with a Gurkha kukri-knife.

Nga Moh was unlucky, as he got badly knifed in the leg and was captured. The only two spare rounds of ammunition that the dacoits possessed were found on him. He told us the story round the camp-fire on the sands of a lovely and uninhabited island, set in the middle of the Indian Ocean, where he was spending the twenty-fifth year of his exile, at the end of which he would have served his time and would regain his freedom. He did eventually follow me to the Upper Chindwin in Burma, but he soon felt a nostalgic longing for the sea and the islands of his exiled years, and he went back to them.

These four months were months of freedom for the convicts, and they enjoyed every minute of them like children. Many of them were, no doubt, still prisoners there when the islands were occupied by the Japanese after 1942, but they will all have got their freedom by now.

The penal settlement on the South Islands is to be abolished, and the forests I explored in the North Islands are to be exploited. It is a melancholy thought that the peace of those islands should be disturbed. The spotted deer we encountered, right in the depths of the untrodden jungle, came up to meet one without fear, to sniff at one's clothes with nervous inquisitiveness. They greeted the unheard-of stranger, whose bad reputation was unknown to them, with friendship, as I greeted them. I did not disillusion them, and then, stepping softly and gently through the jungle, they went their ways.

I had known many dacoits intimately before I went to the Andamans. Sometimes I knew what they were, but sometimes I was quite oblivious of the truth and employed them believing they were good fellows and trustworthy. But, on the whole, the average Burman dacoit has earned a good name for himself as a gentleman outlaw, like Robin Hood. He has a sporting instinct, and plans his crimes with roguish humour. And, if it is at all possible, he tries to avoid combining dacoity and murder.

Once I set out from Paungbyin in the Upper Chindwin for the Kanti forests, with ten pack-elephants carrying over one hundred thousand rupees in silver, packed in specie boxes, each of which weighed about three hundred pounds. The trip was planned to take me eighteen days. The daily loading of each of these boxes on to the elephants was a real feat of strength, and the day after I left Paungbyin my head Burman suggested that I should hire a man from the village where I had camped who had the reputation of being as 'strong as an elephant'. I agreed that such a man would be useful, and sent for Maung Ngapyaw (Mr Banana Tree), as he was called. He was a man of magnificent physique, and a really pleasant rogue with a most cheerful temperament – and he could handle those boxes of rupees as though they weighed only fifty pounds apiece. Thus loading up in the morning became easy work. He accepted an offer of sixty rupees for the trip, and soon gained everyone's confidence and became the wag of the camp. We felt we had made a good find.

After a particularly hard trip, as we had been caught by the first break of the rains, I reached Kanti, my jungle headquarters, where there was a safe. I made it my first job to roll the money into hundred-rupee packets and put it in the safe. Ngapyaw became one of my chief helpers, and proved most expert at the job. Just as I had finished, and felt quite happy that all the money had been checked and made secure in the safe, the first jungle messengers since my departure arrived with the ever welcome mails. It was 6 p.m., so having called for a tub, I decided to read my mail after bathing, by which time it was late evening and peg time. I opened the mail-bags alone on the bamboo veranda of my hut, sorted home mail and private letters into one pile and official in another. As was my habit, I ran through the official first, so as to get the worst things done with. Among them was an envelope marked *Urgent and important*. I wasn't in the Army, and knew that only something really urgent and important would be marked in this way by the Corporation, so I opened it at once. It was to inform me that the police had reason to believe that a renowned dacoit named Ngapyaw, alias San Shwe, alias San Oo, was following my camp, and that every precaution was necessary. In my private mail was a note from my Forest Manager, a man of few words, which merely read, 'Forewarned is forearmed'.

I was not at all perturbed by the news, though I was extremely grateful for the warning. After I had had a meal, I debated with myself whether I should give him the shock of arresting him that night, or wait till next morning when I paid him off. Eventually I decided on the second course.

My position in this lonely forest camp was a perfect setting for a real armed dacoity, and as the night wore on I was not too easy in my mind. However, I eventually dropped asleep, keeping one eye and one ear cocked, but I was not disturbed.

In the early hours of the morning, when I got up I decided to send for Ngapyaw, but when I asked for him, my head servant informed me that he had disappeared from the camp during the night, together with one of the messengers who had brought the mails. Thus all of us had been forearmed and forewarned! The police and Forest Manager had written to warn me by letter, and the spare messenger had come along to warn Ngapyaw! It then became my turn to send messages off, warning one of my neighbours in the jungle. Ngapyaw was not heard of again for another year, when he was shot by the police in the notorious Shwebo dacoit area. He had, however, passed on all the necessary information as to the lie of the land and the lay-out of the safe in Kanti jungle headquarters to some confederates, as my successor in this district had his safe robbed, two years later, of twenty-five thousand rupees in notes.

The dacoits who did it had a really enviable sense of humour, as before they departed with their booty they impaled a ten-rupee note on each post of the fence round jungle headquarters. There were one hundred and twenty posts altogether, so they returned one thousand two hundred rupees as a jest.

One of the most interesting of my experiences, or close approach to an experience, with dacoits, was when I was forearmed and forewarned of their proximity by the behaviour of a common brown rat.

I was moving camp, travelling in a large dug-out country boat up the Myittha River from Kalewa, sleeping on the bank at convenient staging bungalows. I was bound for Kalemyo, where I was to be joined by some travelling elephants.

As usual, I had a considerable quantity of specie with me, and was not at all comfortable about it, during that stage of the trip. It would be safe enough after I joined my elephants and riders, for I always had great confidence in them. I was camped for the night at the Chaunggyi Rapids bungalow, a poor apology for a rest house, consisting of one small room and a veranda, raised about four feet above ground-level. The walls, door and floor were all made of bamboo matting. While I was having an early meal about seven o'clock, my head servant reminded me that I was some distance from where my servants were sleeping, and the sound of the rapids would make it difficult for them to hear me call. Also I was to remember that there were no elephant-men in camp, and that it would be as well if I kept a sharp watch on the boxes of rupees. He knew something was in the wind, and his vague warnings were, no doubt, intended to put himself right with me after the event, but I did not tumble to it at the time.

It had been raining heavily, and it was one of those nights when every kind and shape of bug with wings had seemed to decide to commit suicide against my one and only hurricane lamp. Their varying stings, bites, stinks and noises eventually drove me to seek shelter on my camp bed under my mosquito net. I left the lamp on a specie box beside the bed, intending to read for an hour before I went to sleep. I had got settled comfortably under the net with a book, lying propped on my left elbow with the only weapon I had in camp, a .45 revolver, lying beside my knee. Keeping it handy was as much habit as anything else, as the very last thing in my mind was the possibility of a dacoity, although it was a lonely and isolated spot.

Presently a slight movement in a corner of the twelve-feet-square room caught my eye, and a very pleasant, cheeky-looking rat appeared. I watched him without moving my head, and his movements fascinated me. He first of all sat up on his hind legs and washed his face with his forepaws, then he came out into the room and picked up a small piece of biscuit I had dropped. I was watching him thoroughly enjoying nibbling it, when he suddenly dropped it and scuttled off to a corner where I could not see him, so I decided to remain absolutely still, hoping he would come back. While I waited, I wondered whether it could have been the movement of my eye that had scared him. Presently he came back, and again repeated his trick of picking up the biscuit. I fully expected he would finish it this time, but, more suddenly than in his first scurry, he dashed off again, dropping the biscuit half-way to his dark corner.

As he did so, a sense of fear gripped me. I knew that the rat and I were not the only occupants of the little hut and veranda. My heart pounded in my throat, and for a fraction of a second my arms and legs felt paralyzed, as though I could not move them. But my adrenalin glands pumped their stuff into my blood, and my voice barked out in Burmese, 'Who is it?' I then heard distinct whispering outside the wicker-bamboo door and a movement under the floor of the hut. Without further hesitation, I fired two rapid shots through the roof. A frightful confused stampede from the veranda and from underneath the hut followed instantly.

My four camp servants heard the shots and joined me by the time I had got on to the veranda myself, and we soon tracked the would-be dacoits by torchlight to the river bank, whence they hurriedly made off downstream in a dug-out canoe which they had waiting. They were a party of six, and had undoubtedly followed me with the intention of rushing my hut that night. I was never able to find out whether they were armed or not.

Before I went away next morning I left an open tin of Kraft cheese for my little pal, the rat, not on the floor, where some dacoit might get it, but hidden in the roof. A month or so later, when I passed that camp again, I found the empty tin. Not only had the cheese gone, but there was an empty nest inside. Mrs Rat had reared her babies in it.

I was very glad to join my elephant-men at Kalemyo, and from there sent off word that a party of river dacoits was at large.

These experiences, and all the various mysterious stories which I discovered my elephant-men believed about dacoits, helped me when I came to handle my crowd of forty-eight of them in the Andaman Islands. My riders believed that dacoits had acquired immunity to gunshot wounds by secret tattoo marks known only to themselves, and that they could carry out their dacoities in absolute silence, as a result of drinking the warm blood of the slow loris.

Superstitions of this kind, when firmly believed in, change human behaviour, and they naturally influence the European Assistant living alone among people to whom what we call superstitions are established truths. One of the most puzzling cases concerned a Burman called San Shwe Oo. I think I liked him better then any Burman I knew. He was really a Kadu gipsy. With his very fair skin and long black hair, which hung down to his waist when he let it down, he always looked a bit out of place among the other elephant-men. He rode one of the most dangerous of my animals, a tuskless male called Han Po. He was particularly friendly with me whenever I visited the camp where he worked, and took pains to bring himself to my notice. I often met him unexpectedly, alone by some creek near camp, and he was always eager to accompany me, if I went out in the evening with my rifle for a shot at something. He liked talking to me, and I found him very good company, for he had a lovely sense of humour.

The headman of that camp, U Po See, was a man of the deeply religious, old-fashioned type who was regarded with respect by all his men. He had always discouraged the presence of women in his camp except for his own family, who lived in one hut, while his ten other men lived in one long hut twenty-four feet by sixteen, the bamboo floor of which was raised six feet above the ground.

The incident occurred in September, and although, since the war, enthusiastic Chindits have stated that the Burmese jungle is not 'a green hell', I thought it was, there, at that time of the year. During a nine-mile march I had to swim the Kanti seven times, and I got into camp shivering with malarial ague like an aspen leaf. I was my own doctor, taking thirty grains of quinine a day, as long as the fever lasted. There was no question of my going sick, I had to carry on with my job. It was just part of the normal life of every Forest Assistant, until he finally developed immunity to malaria.

I had just got into my camp bed, and was almost delirious with fever, when I felt powerful sinewy hands working up and down the vertebrae of my spine. No one who has not been down with malaria and given massage can imagine the relief it gave me. I opened my eyes, saw San Shwe Oo bending over me and smiling. I blessed him in silence. By midday next day I was up and about, and U Po See came to see me. After enquiring about my health and telling me his news, in a happy and contented way, he suddenly changed his position by sitting down and falling into a shiko posture, with his hands together on his knees. He then asked me to dismiss San Shwe Oo from his camp. I enquired, with a pained expression, what his reasons were, and for five minutes had to listen to a long rigmarole in high Pali Burmese, which he used on purpose to confuse me. I did, however, gather that the camp was in terror of supernatural vengeance on account of San Shwe Oo's complete disregard of every tenet of the Burmese faith, and that, unless he were removed, a tragedy would ensue, owing to the presence of a Nat tiger, or Spirit tiger, which the men said was prowling round the camp.

I pretended that I had understood every word he said, and told him not to worry – I owed Sna Shwe Oo a considerable sum in wages, and would go into it when settling up, before leaving camp.

San Shwe Oo came to see me again that evening with a present of three minute chicken's eggs in a little bamboo basket, which looked like a child's Easter-egg present. He had come to ask me if I would like another massage for my malaria, as he was recognized as the most skilful man in camp. I gladly accepted his offer, as the aches and pains of another bout of fever were upon me. He persuaded me to let him tread the small of my back with his bare feet. I was already in a new malarial rigor. San Shwe Oo's company and sympathy and understanding of the loneliness I felt in this outlandish jungle camp where the torrential rain was falling incessantly, strumming endlessly upon the large teak leaves, while I was in the grip of continuous bouts of malaria, made his dismissal the very last thing I would have agreed to. He had nothing to say about any unhappiness in camp, but, strangely enough, he did say that I should be quite fit again in a day or two, and then added, as a joke, 'You might even have a shot at the Nat tiger.' With those words he departed. Later that night I asked my personal servant Maung Aung Net – a dear, faithful, simple fellow, if ever there was one – when he came, about midnight, to change me from my clothes soaked in sweat into dry ones, what all the tommy rot was in camp about a Nat tiger. He told me that he had heard in camp that when it was San Shwe Oo's turn to do the cooking and washing up of the rice-bowls he treated it as a joke, and had even played boats in the brook with the rice-bowls and ladles, as a child might have done. And it was also said that he did not take any rice that was left over to the Nat Shrine, or present it to the fishes in the creek, but would actually scatter it in the mud. I thought this was probably a true account of San Shwe Oo's offences in U Po See's eyes, and the explanation of why he would like to banish such an atheist from his camp. The European Assistant has to respect all these jungle superstitions, even if he is not in some degree influenced by them. I had another three days in that camp, performing my ordinary duties, and on the last day, having got rid of my fever, settled up the men's wages. To my surprise, Maung San Shwe Oo asked that the balance of the money owing to him – sixty-eight rupees – should be retained by me. I granted his request and gave him a credit note, though it complicated my accounts. He gave me no reason for this request, and I asked for none, but it occurred to me that perhaps he intended leaving the camp after my departure. I did not at all want him to, as it would not have been easy to find his equal as a rider for Han Po. At the same time, I did not wish to get involved in any way with a breach of their superstitious beliefs.

I saw U Po See alone again late that evening, telling him that I should leave at dawn and be back in six weeks. I gave him orders and said, '*Au revoir*,' and there was no mention of either San Shwe Oo or the Nat tiger. I went to bed feeling I had been very successful in dodging a domestic complication in the camp.

Dawn had not quite broken, when I was aroused by an excited camp servant calling out to me, 'Hurry, Thakin, hurry. A tiger has just killed Maung San Shwe Oo.'

There was a faint glimmer of the green light of dawn, breaking through the jungle saturated by rain. By the time I had got on a few garments and a pair of gum-boots, I could hear an excited commotion going on in the camp, three hundred yards away. The first person I met, as I stumbled through the mud down the slope, was U Po See. 'Nat kyah, Thakin!' (A Nat tiger, sir) he exclaimed. He appeared terrorstricken. When I got to the oozies' hut I found an excited party of five men, all examining the indisputable pug-marks and tracks of a tiger that had sprung up into the hut and down again. There were clear tracks of a dead body having been dragged through the mud down the slope to the creek, which was half in spate, but only a foot deep. On the near bank, fifty yards away, was another group of Burmans examining the marks and on the far bank a third group. All were yelling to each other. The interior of the hut was a mass of dishevelled blankets and clothes. A wailing friend of San Shwe Oo's told me some sort of story, of how two men had woken up, scared, and found him gone, but no one had heard him scream or any sort of scuffle. Every spear in camp had been got out, and U Po See was carrying his single-barrel shotgun. Even in the excitement of the moment, I got hold of it and unloaded it, as I knew that there would be no need for a supernatural explanation if an accident happened with that weapon. I then plunged on, down through the mud, to the edge of the brook, which was sandy. The tracks led into the water, but when I crossed to the other side there were no tracks of pug-marks or of a dragged body coming out. Apparently the tiger and San Shwe Oo's body had evaporated into thin air after going into the stream.

The men, who were all skilled trackers, were dispersing – small parties going upstream and downstream on both banks, which were sandy for a very long way. The air was filled with the cries of excited men, calling 'Cheeyah m' twai boo!' (Can't find a track), and their excitement grew into hysteria. I fired two rifle-shots in the air, with a faint hope that the tiger might drop his kill and leave it where he was hiding. Every minute I expected one of the men to cry that he had found the track, but the minutes passed by . . . half an hour later it was broad daylight.

Someone made the suggestion that the tiger must have swum away with the body and travelled a long way. I set off barefoot, with five spearmen, downstream, while another party, under U Po See, went upstream. It was clear that the tiger could not have kept to the river below a place called Kyauk Shin, as at that point there are boulders, rapids and broken water. I felt sure we should find something when we got there. It was less than a mile from where the track had disappeared, but there was an unaccountable absence of tracks, and, when we got there, no trace at all. Judging from the river banks, there might not have been a wild animal in the jungle.

After that I went upstream, and again there was not a tiger pug, new or old, to be seen.

In camp there was still an uproar going on. U Po See sat with his gun beside him, perfectly satisfied that the tragedy was due to a supernatural cause. It made me angry to hear him speak so confidently of a Nat Kyah.

I cancelled orders for my departure and went to the hut to be alone – drank some hot tea, which I laced with whisky, and lay back in a long camp chair.

U Po See soon appeared. He was a pathetic sight, a dear old deeply religious Burman of the old school, stunned by the event, but quite disposed to accept it unquestioningly.

I sent him away, and told him to join the other men, who were still continuing the search.

I drank several more cups of tea and whisky, before I rejoined the camp. By evening all the men had returned to camp, and no trace of San Shwe Oo's body had been discovered. I was beyond attempting any further investigation myself, but I was angry and depressed at having to accept something, of which I knew there must be an explanation, which I had failed to discover. All San Shwe Oo's possessions were intact. I stayed three more days at the camp, in order to restore the morale of the men and convince them that the Nat Kyah would pay no further visits. Nor did it, and during the two years following which I spent in that forest area I never heard any explanation other than that San Shwe Oo had been taken by a Nat Kyah or Ghost tiger. My name was often mentioned by the Burmans in connection with the affair, as evidence of the truth of the story. I have heard the facts discussed by dozens of men and women and various explanations put forward. A jungle man whom I greatly respect summed up one view by saying:

'Billy, my boy, in spite of your knowledge of the jungle and the presence of your men, I believe that U Po See and some of his men murdered San Shwe Oo and provided perfect evidence to convince you that a tiger had taken him. Yet, who are you and I to decide what strange gods or supernatural forces are not masters of the jungle?'

I replied: 'San Shwe Oo was never murdered, and you, and every other man who knows the jungles of Burma intimately, have often to accept things that you cannot understand.'

He drained his glass and nodded his acceptance. There are thousands of unexplained and unsolved stories, but not all of them are gruesome or tragic.

I was once moving camp through jungle which had not been crossed for many, many years, if ever, by a European. I camped one evening in a creek that my Burmans called Yauk Thwa. The name puzzled me, and I was told that it meant 'Oyster'. I was a young Assistant then, and I was quite thrilled when, strolling down to the creek, I found dozens and dozens of petrified oyster-shells in its bed. In spite of being fifteen hundred miles from the nearest point on the sea coast of Burma, I sat up late pounding them open, hoping to find a fossil pearl. When I went to bed at last, I was no richer.

Next day I moved camp in a direction far away from any traces of Burmese village life. I knew from my map that I should have to follow a well-defined ridge for one or two marches, before I dropped down into the watershed for which I was heading. When I reached it I found it was more of a razor edge than the map indicated. The progress of my pack-elephants was impeded by thick undergrowth, which was uncommon on a ridge.

Towards the end of the second day's march I was becoming anxious, because there seemed to be no way down. It was already near sunset, I was ahead of my elephants, when I suddenly came to an open glade, where there was an obvious drinking-pool used by game. It was only a few square yards in area, but it was large enough to water my travelling elephants, and I knew we could camp there. I waited an hour, and rejoiced as the sound of the elephants bells grew nearer. Well before dusk we were settled in, and my men were pleased with me for having called a halt. I pitched no tent, but bivouacked under a spread tarpaulin. I gave orders that the elephants should be tethered after they had been watered, as otherwise they might wander down two thousand feet on either side of the ridge. My last order was that we were to be moving before the mists of dawn had risen.

My servants were camped within a hundred yards of my bivouac. I was near enough to hear their chatter, but they were silent, and insisted on giving me my evening meal before my usual hour. When I had eaten I soon turned in. But an air of uneasiness lay over the camp; there was a strange eerie silence. The drip of the night dew from the great leaves seemed to begin unusually early and was unusually heavy, so that it soon pattered steadily on to my stretched tarpaulin. I was comfortable and happy but for some reason I lay awake. The elephants must have been motionless, although tethered, for not a bell sounded. The last glow of the camp fire died down. At last I fell asleep, feeling perfectly confident of my safety, for all around me were men whom I trusted, elephants and the jungle that I had come to love.

I woke suddenly, feeling that I had only been to sleep for a short time, and found myself listening with fear, such as the European alone in the jungle often experiences. I sensed it was near dawn – but what had woken me? Was it one of my servants moving about to light a fire or put on a kettle?

I sat up in bed. The camp was still wrapped in sleep. Not a sound or movement came from my men. Then, as I sat listening, I heard a village cock crowing, and almost at once after it, I could distinguish the sounds of a baby crying. There was no question about it. I was wide awake. A village pungyi kyaung gong chimed clear as crystal, and the wailing of half a dozen pi dogs took up the echo of the chimes. Then I could hear someone begin chopping a log for the village fire. I could swear that I heard the voices of children and, at last, all the sounds of an awakened Burmese village in the early morning, and the distinctive sound of a Burmese girl, treading backwards and forwards on the board that shells the rice-paddy free of its husks, for the morning meal.

And then there was silence, and suddenly I heard someone stirring, and saw the flame of a lighted lamp, and could see the silhouettes of my servants moving in front of it. I dropped back, pretending I was asleep. My man would be bringing me a cup of tea in ten minutes. He would never wake me with a touch, for the Burman thinks that if a European is woken up suddenly there may not be time for his spirit to return from visiting his own land. He calls the spirit of sleep a butterfly which takes wing silently and slowly, and which must be given time to return.

I saw my servant approach, through my half-shut eyes, and watched him bump on purpose into something; then he coughed and scraped with his feet. I turned over, and he murmured to me, 'The mist has lifted.' I drank my tea at once, dressed instantly, and was only too willing to get away from that place in record time. There was no chatting among my men. The elephants loomed up like ghosts out of the mist, in silence, as they arrived to load up. I led the way along the ridge, with my headman following me. We did not say a word, until, after an hour's travelling, I realized we had reached the Upper Myaingyaung drainage, and it became clear that I was quite off the track. I halted then, and asked my Burman where the hell we had camped the previous night.

'That, Thakin, was the deserted village,' was his answer.

I made no comment at the time, but that evening I asked my servant if he had heard any noises during the night.

'No,' he replied, 'we did not. But we were frightened this morning when we were loading your kit. One of the oozies said that your bivouac under the nyaung tree was where the Nats lived, but where we camped under the zeebyn fruit trees was the site of the old village.'

I asked what had happened to the people who lived there, and he said that he had been told they had been wiped out by cholera. My men had known that a village, called Ywasoe, had existed thereabouts, but had never found the site before.

'You found it. Say no more. You are lucky. The Nats like you, and you respect them as we do.'

He said no more, purposely avoiding any further discussion, obviously holding something back. I was left with the feeling that I had not been alone with the Nats of Ywasoe. Curiously enough, this strange incident made a recording of the pleasant village sounds of Burma that I can almost hear again at will, and transformed them into an unforgettable memory of Burma.

CHAPTER 9

Elephants are good swimmers and extremely buoyant. When the oozie is going to cross a large river, such as the Chindwin or the Irrawaddy, with his elephant, keeping it under control, he fits a surcingle under its belly and over the withers, kneels on the animal's back and grips the rope in front of him, using a small stick, instead of his feet, to signal his 'aids', behind its ears. In this position he is on top of the highest point of the elephant.

Once they are under way and in deep water, it is most amusing to watch. For a time the elephant will swim along gaily, with a rather lunging action. Then, all of a sudden, the oozie will snatch a deep breath, as his mount goes down, like a submarine, into fifteen feet of water. The animal, for pure fun, will keep submerged, almost to bursting point, trying to make his rider, who goes down with him, let go.

But the oozie knows that an elephant can only stay under water for the same length of time as a man. So he holds on. The elephant, meanwhile, is doing a fairy-like dance on tiptoe along the bottom, while the poor old oozie is wondering if he will ever surface. Suddenly both reappear, blowing tremendously and taking great gasps of breath.

In crossing a wide river, where the elephant has to swim a thousand yards downstream. He does not make any strenuous effort to make the crossing where the river is narrowest, or to reach a particular point on the opposite bank.

Although elephants are such good swimmers, they are not infrequently drowned, a fact which I can only put down to heart failure. The Burmans, however, always attribute the loss of an elephant, when swimming, to the Nat Shin, a water-snake which no one has ever seen. The bite of the Nat Shin produces instantaneous death. A jungle Burman will tell you that a Nat Shin is just like a yay shin, only enormously larger. A yay shin is an unpleasant pale-green object, like a bootlace, about nine inches long and pointed at each end. It is very active in water, but when one pulls it out, looks like a fine strand of seaweed. One can tie it into as many knots as one likes, and it will have untied itself within five minutes of being dropped back into water. The yay shin is disliked for the practical reason that the water in which it lives is not fit to drink. But it seems uncanny to the Burmese, and they all accept the existence of its bigger, more deadly, brother, and give thanks that they have never had the misfortune to see one.

When elephants have to be moved long distances by water, they are frequently taken on rafts, or on river barges, which are towed alongside a paddle-steamer. Getting elephants onto such flats needs endless patience. First one has to find a leader which the other beasts will follow, and then one has to camouflage the gangway with tall grasses, or palms, on either side of it to a height of ten or twelve feet.

The flats usually have steel decks, which get terribly hot in the sun, and if elephants are standing on them for twenty-four hours, their feet swell to such a size that the fetters or chain hobbles have to be removed. Once I had to ship two flat-loads of twenty elephants from a river station on the Irrawaddy. I was assisted by a very capable Anglo-Burman, and we started work at dawn, but had only got one flat loaded by noon. The irate old skipper of the paddle-steamer was due to leave at 2 p.m. and to proceed up river on a three-day trip, tying up each night to the river bank. By 5 p.m. we got the last elephant on board the second flat, and the skipper's temper was as bad as mine. Just when I thought my job was finished and the skipper's had begun, he blew the steamer's siren – of all the damn fool things! And at the same time the enormous side-paddles started to churn alongside the loaded flats full of elephants, on either side of the steamer.

The captain's shock was greater than mine, as sixteen elephants trumpeted and roared, drowning every other sound. I think he thought half of them had broken loose and were boarding his steamer and after his blood, whereas only sheer terror kept them in their places. He had to reckon with me, however.

These particular animals had been transferred and marched from the Salween, via the Mawchi–Taungoo road, and had had about enough of it. All our tempers were on edge. We eventually got them settled down and under way, and put in an hour's steaming before tying up for the night. Leaving my Anglo-Burman Assistant to check up that all chains were secure and to supervise the hand-feeding of the elephants, I made for the saloon to make it up with the skipper over a peg.

At 9 p.m. I visited both flats, and found all remarkably quiet, no sound but a flapping of ears and the occasional movement of a foot, rattling a chain. At midnight I was still yarning with the skipper in the little saloon, when my Assistant arrived to say that a young tusker had collapsed. His doing so had caused little or no commotion among the others. As far as I could discover, he had fallen down dead beat, from fatigue. To get anywhere near him, one crawled through a forest of elephant legs.

After I had given him half a bottle of brandy, without results, I decided there was nothing more I could do but let him lie and wait for the dawn. I went back to the saloon for a night-cap, but my Assistant was still unhappy, and went to have another talk with the elephant-riders. I had gone to my cabin when he came back, looking very shy, to say that the Burman oozies wanted to put a temple candle for each year of the elephant's life round the prostrate body, and might they try it?

The theory was, that when all the candles were alight but before they burned out, the animal would get on its legs. My reply was: 'Yes, by all means. Buy twenty-one blinking candles, but don't set fire to the ship!'

That was the last I saw of him that night, but at dawn he came to my cabin to say, 'It's worked, sir. The animal is up. But you were one year out in his age. We had to do it a second time and use twenty-two candles!'

He was so sincere that I did not like to say what I thought, which was that the elephant was a young animal which liked sleeping with the light on. When I went to see him he was certainly up, bright, and eating banana leaves. My Assistant little guessed that I had probably worried far more about him than he had. As regards sleep, elephants are rather like horses. They get most of it standing up, and they will only go down when they think that, for a brief period at night, all the world is asleep. It is an uncanny period in the jungle night, and, for some reason, never seems to come at just the same time two nights in succession.

I have sat up with several elephants throughout the night, purely to find out when they did sleep, and for how long. The time is never the same, but it is always at that eerie hour when even the insects stop their serenades. It never lasts longer than half an hour if the animal is fit, but while it lasts he sleeps very soundly. For an hour previously the elephant stands absolutely motionless without feeding. There is not a flap of the ear or a swish of the tail. It seems as though he were intently listening for any sound. Then he seems satisfied that all is well, and down he goes in a slow, silent movement, as if overcome by some unseen jungle god. In bright moonlight it is a most beautiful but uncanny sight.

A full-grown elephant has little to fear in the jungle, unless it is protecting a calf, yet one can always notice that it is on the alert for uncommon sounds or scents. An elephant hates being startled, but it is startled only by things which are not part of its normal life. A prowling tiger will not worry a tusker elephant. He knows that no tiger would ever attack him in the jungle.

Elephants and ponies do not get on together. Not only are ponies frightened of elephants, but the elephants sometimes become so scared of ponies that a whole train of them will stampede at the sight of one, with the result that oozies are injured, gear is smashed and camp pots are broken. I was once away from my district for ten days with a severe attack of malaria. During my absence my Forest Manager toured my area and visited a training camp of which I was particularly proud. Fourteen calves had gone through the crushes, had been named, and were being put through their daily paces.

When I received a copy of the Forest Manager's report, I found to my astonishment that he was extremely critical of the training of these calves, which had been nervous and disobedient when he was inspecting them. His remarks almost brought on another attack of fever, but I did not stop to take my temperature. I at once went back to my forest, and travelled direct to the training camp. I felt certain there must be some explanation. Two marches from the training camp I was met by my trainer, Maung Chit Poo. I told him at once how displeased I was that he had failed to show my babies satisfactorily during my absence. But he was too loyal to question the Forest Manager's criticisms. I sensed that he had something to tell me, but that I must wait and find out indirectly what was in his mind. Nevertheless, there was a feeling of unpleasant tension during our two marches back to the training camp. I inspected the calves on the evening of my arrival, but only ten of the fourteen paraded. They were perfect. Not one of them had a mark on him from training, all were well under control, and each of them took a tamarind ball from my hand as sweetly as a puppy will take a titbit from its master.

It was disappointing that four of them were missing from the parade, but I accepted Maung Chit Poo's excuse that the oozies did not get their orders to parade early enough, and not all had been in camp. I gave orders, however, that as each of the four came into camp, it should be brought over to my camp, without waiting to bring all four at once. Not one of these calves had arrived by dusk. My camp was pitched on the site which had been used by the Forest Manager during his visit, in a large clearing, which was well laid out for the purpose.

I sent for Chit Poo, dropping the polite prefix of Maung when I greeted him. It was obvious that he was worried, and had something to tell me, but that he could not bring it out.

I suddenly asked him sharply: 'What is your game, Chit Poo? What is wrong?'

He gave me a broken-hearted look and answered: 'Please, Thakin, come out of camp to look at them. They are only fifty yards away, on the elephant track. But we cannot bring them in to camp.'

'Why not?' I asked. 'Don't be foolish; they are only babies.'

'They are not babies. That is the trouble,' he said.

I at once went to see what was the matter. But the green light of evening was already going, and it was becoming too dark to inspect elephant calves. When I had walked about twenty yards I spotted some pony droppings on the path. I hit one of these with my stick and at once said to Chit Poo: 'Take the calves back to camp. I will see them tomorrow.' I knew well enough that the calves would not pass the spot where those stinking animals – ponies – had camped, only ten days before. Chit Poo realized that I had discovered the real trouble, and that it mattered little what he told me.

Suddenly he dropped on his knees and exclaimed piteously: 'How can I be expected to parade trained calves in the presence of a white man, a white woman and three of their dogs, with two ponies shaking their coats only twenty yards away?'

Using a term which exalted his position I replied: '*U* Chit Poo. You are not expected to do so. Go back to camp, and don't worry about it any more.'

That evening I tried to write my report, and tore up a dozen sheets of paper, wondering whether I dared criticize my superior. Next morning I wrote a report ending with Chit Poo's words which I inserted as my own, and gave the presence of the ponies as the explanation of the restive behaviour of the calves. My report came back to me after a month of anxious waiting. In the margin the Head Forest Officer had written in red ink: 'You never know, you know.'

I did not forget this lesson, although before I left Burma I had inspected calves in the presence of my own wife, my assistant and his wife, with three children and four dogs running about, and a wireless set mercilessly bawling out Bow Bells. But I made allowances, for I knew how the baby jumbos loathe such conditions. Bad as they were, it would have been worse if we had had ponies.

Quite apart from the dislike of elephants, ponies are out of place in the jungle. In the cold season it is quite possible and pleasant to ride them, but the anxiety experienced on account of tigers scarcely makes it worth while. Tigers have a passion for ponies, and the only way to keep them off is to keep fires up all night, and to have syces or attendants with lanterns sleeping with the ponies.

Ponies know immediately when there are tiger round the camp. There are few camps in the deep jungle where tiger pug-marks are not as common, along the banks of the creeks, as are water-rat footprints in the mud of a Thames backwater. Naturally, there is perpetual anxiety, and the fear of the ponies is most distressing. Those who have handled horses in a burning building can best imagine what it is like. When tiger are about, ponies shiver continuously with terror, their eyes become staring, they appear hypnotized; and nothing one can say or do will calm them. One thinks that at any moment they will stampede into the black night of the surrounding jungle, but they remain shivering and glued to the ground on which they stand. No lover of horses who has watched this, for night after night, without being able to help, will willingly take his ponies into deep jungle again.

The dislike which elephants feel for ponies is exceeded only by their hatred and fear of dogs. In fact, a dog is one of the few animals at which an elephant will lash out with its trunk. I can remember once that a group of six travelling elephants had arrived in camp and were waiting to be unloaded. One of them had on its back a basket containing four lively fox-terrier puppies, just at the age when they are most mischievous, but not able to keep up on a journey. Their mother, Twigs, who was one of the principal figures in my camp at that time, was sitting beside me on a fallen tree, waiting to join her precious family when they were unloaded, when suddenly there was a shout of 'The puppies are out,' after the basket had been put on the ground.

There they were, walking around under the bellies and among the legs and feet of the six elephants, quite fearless and thinking it great fun. The elephants were stupefied. They hunched up their backs, rolled up their trunks and put them out of harms way in their mouths and lifted their feet up like cats on hot bricks. Not one of the elephants made the slightest attempt to injure a puppy. On the contrary, they were doing their best to avoid hurting them. Poor little Twigs was watching all this, shivering with excitement and terror, and at last, unable to stand it any longer, she broke away from me and dashed out, hoping to retrieve her puppies. With one yelp she stampeded five out of the six elephants. Only one young tusker hit at her with his trunk. Luckily he missed, or he would have broken every bone in her body. Twigs rushed back to me for protection, with the elephant following her up. But on seeing me he turned and bolted after the others, as I had an alpine stick with a spearhead in the ferrule. There was definitely some natural instinct which forbade the elephants injuring the puppies. But they would have taken delight in killing Twigs, whom they all knew by sight and hated.

In spite of this hatred, almost every jungle camp has two or three dogs in it. They are useful as watch-dogs or guards and also as scavengers. Dogs are seldom used for hunting in the jungle, as they soon fall victims to panther if they once leave the main elephant timber-dragging paths. It is a very common occurrence to hear that a camp dog has been taken by a leopard. One usually enquires if the dog's carcass has been found, as if so one has a good chance of bagging the leopard, by sitting up over it the following night. In nine cases out of ten, however, the leopard gobbles up the dog at one meal and leaves nothing for the next day.

I have never known a dog and an elephant make friends. Elephants will eventually become accustomed to certain dogs in camp, and dogs learn not to bark at them and always to keep out of reach of the slash of a trunk or the kick of a leg. The hatred of elephants for dogs cannot easily be explained. It is possible that they are afraid of dogs biting their trunks, though I do not think such a thing can ever have happened. Sometimes it has occurred to me that it might be an instinctive dread of hydrophobia, which has been recorded in elephants, and which is the dread of everyone who keeps a dog in camp, Burman and European Assistant alike.

Nevertheless practically every European Assistant keeps a dog, and I have almost always had one myself. The elephants hate them, and one is always losing one's dog, owing to leopard, tiger, bear and snakes. The tragedies of lost dogs are often an Assistant's first experiences of real grief.

It is easy to ask why, under such conditions, do you keep a dog? But I know of no other existence where a dog is so necessary as a companion to share every moment of one's life and to drive away loneliness.

In my years in Burma I had many: Jabo, Chin, Juno, Bo, Sally, Karl, Basso, Rhoda, Cobbler and Molly, to mention but half of them, ranging from a Burman pariah, Chow, Bull Mastiff, Alasatian, Bassein Fishing Dog of Bloodhound extraction, to a Red Cocker Spaniel and a Labrador, the last of which shared the war years with me, as the mascot of the Elephant Companies. Each of these few, named here, was as different in character as in breed; each was obtained in different circumstances, and came by his death in a different way.

Jabo chose me, not I him. His name means Piebald in Burmese, and he was something between red and white in patches, with a bobtail, for at some time, when he was a puppy, a Burman had slashed at him with a jungle knife, or dah, and cut his tail off. He was a powerful dog, built for the jungle, deep ribbed and deep chested and with small, well-shaped feet for his size.

I had reached camp with my elephants with a violent bout of malaria on me. While I was waiting for them to be unloaded I called for a deck-chair, and sank into it and dozed off, oblivious of my surroundings, until I should be able to crawl into my camp bed.

Suddenly I was startled, almost to death, by the shock of what seemed to be the coldest thing on earth being pressed against my fevered body. It was a dog's cold nose, and as I sprang forward I saw a dog wagging his hindquarters at me in default of a tail. I was new to the Burmese jungle and in one of my first bouts of high fever. The Cornish cliffs had never seemed so far away, and all my gratitude went out to this friendly, sympathetic creature. By the time my camp was pitched we were close friends. I was feeling too ill for anything but bed, but I called my servant and asked for a glass of whisky, sugar and boiling water before I tried to sleep. In a few moments the Burman had brought the kettle, and as he was mixing my drink Jabo thrust forward his head inquisitively. The servant called out: 'Get out, Jabo,' and turned a stream of water from the kettle onto him. There was a yelp of pain and a curse from me.

'You uncivilized devil! What do you mean by it?' I exclaimed, and ordered him to prepare food for Jabo twice a day so long as the dog would stay with me, though I was beyond eating anything myself.

That evening, when I had sweated out my fever a bit and was feeling like death warmed up, Jabo came to lick my hand again, but he was painfully nervous and badly scalded. My servant brought him a whole boiled chicken with rice in a wash basin, which he put beside my bed. I tore up the fowl with my own hands and mixed it in the rice, so that he should learn my smell. I hoped that he would sleep in my tent with me; but he never did, and always disappeared at dusk. I kept that formerly ownerless, roaming dog that was known in all the camps, five years, and never once did he sleep in my tent. He was too wise, for he was terrified of leopard, and always went to sleep in the midst of the elephant-men, or the camp servants, for better protection. Jabo became a character well known in the Chindwin jungles and riverside stations, where he had the reputation of being the father of more illegitimate puppies than any other dog in Burma.

He would be ashore from a river launch as soon as the mooring-rope, to search for a lady love before the siren sounded. He was usually last on board, but he almost always just made it before the gangway came up. If, however, he found a bitch, he would let the launch go without him and take the next one either upstream or down, according to the direction in which I had gone.

He always turned up, though he was often three days late. His end came when I was away, ill with fever, on two weeks' leave. I had left him with my head elephant-man, who greeted me when I got back with the news that poor old Jabo was dead. 'A Nat Shin took him when he was following a canoe, swimming across the Chindwin at Yuwa.'

I had to accept this story, though reluctantly, for one has to accept everything relating to the gods or Nats. The Nat Shin is the cursed water-spirit, and even more mythical than the jungle Nats themselves.

For some reason unknown, then, I could not forgive that Burman. I did not believe that a Nat Shin had killed Jabo, or could kill him, though I have more than once had to accept the tale that a Nat Shin has taken an elephant swimming across the river. I sacked the fellow.

Two years later a young Burmese girl told me the true story, as all girls will on certain special occasions.

Six of my elephant riders, led by the one I had dismissed, were crossing the Chindwin for a gambling bout in a village on the opposite shore. They were overloaded in their canoe, but Jabo wanted to visit that village also, for his own ends, and, although told, in no very sweet tones, to stay behind in camp, he followed them swimming, and drew close to the canoe, as though bent on climbing in. The head Burman feared he would upset them, and gave him a crack on the head with the paddle, to make him keep off. The paddle must have stunned him, or split his hard old skull, and Jabo sank, and was not seen to rise again.

The girl told me how the elephant-men had hunted for days for Jabo's body. That showed me that they had not meant to kill him. So I sought out the man responsible, and made him confess the whole story. He told me all, in tears; I forgave him and took him on once more.

Jabo was no ordinary pi dog. He was a grand companion, though he was no protection, since he would never sleep in my tent or hut. He knew the courses of my evening meal as well as any of my servants, who brought them fifty yards from the cookhouse. He would come with the soup, watch it being served, go back, to return again with the joint, and once more go back, to return with the savoury. But he would not travel those fifty yards after dark, except in company of a servant, for fear of leopard.

A dog that sleeps in one's hut or tent is a protection from dacoits, but is a great worry. For only if it is fenced in behind chairs and boxes under one's camp bed can one feel reasonably sure that a leopard will not take it from under one's very nose while one is asleep.

One Assistant had his black cocker spaniel snapped up by a leopard, when it was sleeping, chained up beside his bed, in his bamboo hut. He did not wake until it was too late to do anything. The chain was broken, and both had vanished. He could find no trace of his dead pal next day, but determined to try to have his revenge. So the next night he borrowed a dog from the elephant-men, fed it, and tied it up to his office box beside his bed. Then he put out his lamp and sat up in an upright chair in one corner of the room, determined to wait all night if need be.

The familiar sounds of chatting ceased in his servants' camp, the glow of the fires died down, the sound of the brook seemed to increase slightly in the night and the heavy dew began to drip steadily in an incessant ping, ping, ping, from the leaves overhanging the roof of his hut.

A porcupine called, 'Pyoo! pyoo!' A samba deer 'belled' to call its mate, an occasional elephant-bell sounded from across or down the stream, an owl cried, 'Zee-gwet, zee-gwet,' later followed by the mellow hoots of his bigger brother – calls which the Burmans associate with death and ill-luck.

The Assistant's chief worry was that he might shoot his bait-dog instead of the leopard.

The hour of stillness arrived, when all sounds seemed to cease. Even the stream seemed to stop babbling. Then there was a sudden tension in the room in which he could feel his heart pounding. The dog suddenly tore at his chain, pulling the heavy specie box to which it was tied across the bamboo floor.

The Assistant raised his shotgun, loaded with buckshot, and switched on his torch; on the bamboo steps in the doorway stood a leopard, blinded by the light. He fired both barrels, and it fell, mangled and dead. In a moment the camp was stirring with lights and his servants were uttering exclamations of delight. One of them, who had always prepared his spaniel's food, ripped up the white belly of the the leopard and disembowelled it; then he opened the intestines and pulled out a black knot of the curly coat of his master's beloved spaniel.

This was too much for my friend, who turned away and ordered his people back to bed, telling them to take the terrified camp dog with them. He told me that he cried himself to sleep that night, and that he thought it had done him good. He moved camp next day, with the leopard's carcass on one of his elephants. I met him at his next camp, and while we were talking after a day's work an elephant oozie and his wife approached us. They were a rather older couple than most camp Burmans, and real jungle-dwellers. The man was holding a baby honey-bear in his arms. It was quite small – about the size of a coffee-pot. They squatted down side by side in front of us, she with her shoulders bare and her tamain tucked across above her breasts.

I asked him where he had got the little creature, and he told me that the tree-fellers had killed its mother three weeks before, and that she had mauled Maung Chit Poo. The mother bear and her cub had been hidden in the branches of a teak tree they were felling, and, just as the last strokes were being given and the tree was about to fall, had dropped among the tree-fellers. Maung Chit Poo's son had rushed to his father's help and hit the mother bear on the head with his axe, killing her outright.

'Would you like to have the baby, Thakin Galay?' he asked my friend, for they had heard of the loss of his spaniel.

It was a charming expression of sympathy, which they did not put into any other words.

'No,' my friend and I both said together.

The little bear seemed to understand, and began to make queer babyish squeals and fumble about; and, with a perfectly simple and natural movement, the Burman passed it to his wife, who put it in her lap, while she untucked her tamain from under her arm, and fastened it again with a tuck in round her waist, exposing two perfectly shaped breasts. Then she lifted up the little bear and put her nipple in its mouth.

When we had thanked them again for the offer of their pet, they rose, bowed and departed with the bear cub still at her breast. She had been feeding it three or four times a day, filled with all the Buddhist pride that they were doing something of importance in their lives, by preserving life, and convinced that their action would put them on a higher plane in Nirvana.

There was nothing unusual in this. The jungle women will suckle baby fawns and any young creature which inspires them with pity. 'It deserves pity' are words often on their lips, and their pity at once moves them to succour and keep alive the orphan. Thus they will adopt newborn tiger or leopard cubs, and bears, not hesitating to save the lives of the hated enemies of their menfolk, which would become dangerous if they were reared. There is a wonderful gentleness in these jungle people.

No woman, however, would nurse a snake, if snakes could be taught to suck. The Burman thinks all snakes are better dead, a view which is justified by a legend of Buddha. Disease came into Burma from the north, down the Chindwin River. Buddha slew it near Meegyaungyay (the Crocodile Water), cutting off its head, which lay in Lower Burma, and leaving its tail in Upper Burma. The head was venomous, and for that reason, there are few poisonous snakes in Upper Burma, whereas Lower Burma is full of them.

With the example of Buddha to fortify his hatred, the Burman has no sympathy with any eccentric European who keeps a snake as a pet.

I have been told the story of one *jungle salt* in the Pyinmana Forest who did keep such a pet. She was a seventeen-foot python, whom he called Eve. She had a silver collar and chain, and he took her on all his tours in a basket, carried on one of his elephants.

Eve did little except sleep and eat, at longish intervals. She lived entirely in his hut or tent, at his headquarters, finding warmth during the day between the blankets of his bed, and at night getting what warmth she could from her master. But he kept her lying outside his bedclothes.

In the end familiarity bred contempt of danger. One cold night when her master was asleep, Eve glided under the bedclothes, and lay beside him, seeking not love, but warmth. While he slept, she gradually twined her coils around his body. The Assistant woke to find his legs and hips in a vice-like embrace. The more he struggled, the tighter Eve drew her constricting coils. His yells for help brought his camp servants running to his bedside, but he was not released until Eve had been cut into several pieces.

Snakes such as hamadryads and Russell's viper are common, but are seldom seen in heavy jungle, as they usually avoid man. But an extraordinary coincidence occurred to a friend of mine and myself, as each of us was chased by the same snake within a period of two years. Brian wrote to me from the Upper Kanti, describing how he had had the

unpleasant and rather terrifying experience of being chased by a
hamadryad snake at the confluence of the Big and Small Kanti Creeks,
where a game-track led up to the ridge from a ford, where game
habitually came down to drink.

The snake had suddenly slid down out of a large clump of bamboo.
The Burman with him gave the alarm, and the snake chased them along
the track, for at least fifty yards. The Burman, of course, insisted that it
was a Nat snake.

Two years afterwards I was just leaving the same creek junction, and
had just begun to climb up the game-track: I had quite forgotten the
incident which Brian had described, when suddenly my Burman
shouted a warning. I saw a large black hamadryad slithering down a
bamboo clump and coming for us. By the time it had reached the ground
I had overtaken my Burman, and we were in flight. It chased us, but I do
not think it followed us for any distance. I am afraid I did not stop to look
back until I was almost at the ridge. There was no question that the
incident occurred at the exact spot where Brian had been chased two
years before. It occurred during the same month, in the hottest season of
the year. My conclusion is that it was the spot always used by a pair of
hamadryads for breeding. The Burmans heard all about both stories,
and no doubt a magnificent legend of a Jungle Nat by now attaches itself
to the spot.

Strangely enough, the Burman who was with me at the time was
bitten by a poisonous snake some months later. In those days I was quite
ignorant of the proper treatment for snake-bite, and employed exactly
the worst methods. I first made him drink a bottle of whisky and then
lanced the place where he had been bitten on the leg with a razor blade,
making criss-cross cuts, like a Union Jack. I then found I could not stop
the bleeding, and spent a most anxious night, thinking he was going to
succumb to alcoholic poisoning, loss of blood or snake-bite. Fortunately
he survived both the snake-bite and my treatment of it.

So far as I know, elephants don't worry about snakes, though the
oozies believe that a number of elephant calves die of snake-bite. I have
had this reported to me many times, but in no instance could I find any
proof. The Burmans believe that the hairs of an elephant's tail pull out
very easily after it has been bitten by a snake. But, as this has also to be
proved, I was never able to accept it as conclusive evidence that an
elephant had been killed by snake-bite.

There is a widespread belief that an elephant is really terrified of a
mouse. The idea makes an obvious appeal to the human love of paradox.
But, if it is true, I can see no reason for it. It certainly cannot be because
the elephant is afraid of the mouse getting inside his trunk, since, with

one snort, he could eject it like a cork from a popgun. However, many women are terrified of mice, with as little reason. After all, most fears are imaginary, and there is no reason why elephants should be immune from such terrors.

Elephants are not, however, usually frightened by natural phenomena without very good reason. They do not mind thunderstorms in the way that dogs do, and they remain calm in the face of forest fires.

Forest fires are not by any means as terrible in the jungles of Burma as they are described as being in other parts of the world. Practically every mixed deciduous forest area in Burma has an annual spring-cleaning of fire, during the latter part of April or the early part of May. It is sometimes due to spontaneous combustion of the rotting leaves of the preceding autumn. The result is usually a carpet fire of leaves, dead twigs and fallen branches, which does not involve the living trees themselves. These carpet fires travel very slowly against any breeze there may be, at a rate not exceeding two miles an hour. Once they have started, they fan out, and become a narrow ribbon of flames, usually quite low, but occasionally catching hold of any tree with dead leaves or dry branches within their reach.

The only areas in which one gets really fierce raging conflagrations are stretches of dry kaing grass. But, as this grows by water, the stretches of grass are usually intersected by creeks, or by the beds of dry streams, which form natural fire-lines, barring its progress.

Elephants have no fear of the carpet type of fire. Domesticated elephants can be marched straight at the line of flame and through it. Their lack of fear and their immunity are due to their weight – for the weight on their pads extinguishes any burning leaves they tread on, and, as long as they keep moving, the underside of their pads will not scorch or blister.

It is a different matter in conflagrations of kaing grass. These fires travel fast, and elephants and all other wild animals recognize the sound and smell of fire immediately, and at once cross the nearest creek. Their understanding of wind direction, and how it will make the fire travel, is far greater than man's.

On many occasions I have set areas of kaing grass on fire on purpose, so as to clear the ground for a new growth. It is quite unnecessary to try to clear animals out of such areas before setting fire to them; directly they hear and smell the fire, the animals move out, at a steady pace, without any panic or excitement. In fact they remember what areas have been burnt earlier on, and return to them. Within a very short space of time, after heavy showers have fallen the blocks of blackened, fire-swept swamp become emerald-green with the fresh young grass.

I have only once seen elephants really frightened by natural phenomena, and that was due to their realizing that they were in a gorge
where water was rapidly rising in a spate. Rain was coming down as
though it would never cease, and in the distance there was a rumbling of
thunder, which added to the anxiety.

I had decided to take a short cut through the Kanti Gorge. I was
travelling with eight young pack-elephants, and it would save us a climb
of two thousand feet from one watershed to another. After passing down
the gorge, I meant to move up a side stream. It was during the month of
September, and I was almost at the end of my tether. I had been on my
own since the previous May, with daily fever, and I was making my way
back to jungle headquarters, where I should at least get a week in the
same camp. My spirits were high, the oozies were whistling and singing,
and our circus was travelling in Indian file down the hard, sandy bottom
of the stream.

Both banks of the gorge were sheer rock, to a height of about thirty
feet, with dense overhanging jungle and bamboos along their tops. The
gorge was three miles long, and the stream was about ankle-deep when
we started down it. By the time we had gone a mile one could hear the
unmistakable sound of a heavy thunderstorm breaking in the headwaters of the stream. The elephants showed their nervousness by half-
turning round. An elephant cannot see behind it by merely turning its
head; it has to half-turn its body. The bore of water eventually overtook
us, after which there was broken water well above my knees, and it was
lapping under the bellies and round the flanks of the smaller female
calves.

For a time it seemed as though the water would rise no higher, and we
were making good progress. But, by some instinct not shared by man,
the elephants knew there was more water coming down. They began
what would have become a stampede, if they had not been hindered by
the depth of the water and kept under partial restraint by their riders. It
became a terrifying experience, as there was no possibility of turning
back, and no hope of getting up the sides. During the last mile all the
elephants began bellowing; that, with the sound of the torrential rain,
and the raging muddy water around, made it seem a pretty grim
situation. I kept expecting to see one of the calves lose its balance at any
moment. At the end the water was up to my armpits, and I was holding
my rifle in both hands above my head.

I never knew a mile to seem longer. Bend after bend came in view,
with never a sign of the mouth of the creek I knew, which would provide
for our exodus from the black hole in which we floundered. Logs were
floating past, and, though I had no time to be amused then, I noticed

how the elephants' hindquarters seemed to have a magnetic attraction for the logs that floated down and overtook us. Just as a log was about to strike its hindquarters, the elephant would swing its rear end to one side, giving the log a glancing blow, so that it cannoned off like a billiard ball from the cushion, and passed on to the chap in front – and so on all down the line.

We were fortunate really, as the smaller animals were just afloat when we went round the bend to go up the side creek. Moreover, the side creek only came down in spate half an hour after we had started up it. If we had met the combined spates at the confluence, all out kit would certainly have been lost.

The elephants scrambled up the first feasible bank after turning in off the main river, and at a general halt they seemed to look at me as if to say: 'And you call yourself a jungle man!'

CHAPTER 10

Savage elephants are as rare as really wicked men, but those that are not savage sometimes give way to moments of bad temper. They are particularly liable to do so when they are in harness dragging a very heavy weight. Their most tiresome and dangerous habit at such moments is to pick up a large stick or stone with the trunk and throw it with great force and accuracy at some onlooker, particularly at someone in authority, whom they guess is responsible. One has to be prepared to jump, and jump quickly, when this happens.

A young European Assistant of my acquaintance visited the London Zoo with his mother and his sister on his first leave home. They went straight to the elephant house. After explaining all about the female elephant on view, he was emboldened to suggest: 'Shall I make her sit down?'

His mother and sister were delighted at the idea, and the onlookers were most impressed.

'Hmit!' he shouted, in close imitation of a Burmese oozie.

The elephant merely swished her tail and tickled her mouth with imaginary bananas.

'Hmit!' he shouted again, and, as the elephant ignored him, he grew angrier and more determined with the disobedient animal. 'Hmit! hmit! hmit!'

At last the elephant condescended to notice him, swinging her head round, cocking her ears, and eyeing him with an expression as though she were saying, 'So you come from Burma, too, do you?' Then, with lightning swiftness, she seized a lump of her dung the size of a cottage loaf and slung it at the young Assistant. It missed him, but it knocked a feather out of his mother's hat and exploded against the wall behind them. No one laughed, but the elephant house was soon empty.

Savage elephants – whether male or female – are rare, and the few exceptions are usually of a savage temperament from birth. Of course, during the must period all males are of uncertain temper. My interpretation of must is that it is an instinctive desire in the male elephant to fight and kill before mating. His blood is up, and his brain is affected. The mere act of mating does not cool his passion. He would rather fight for his chosen mate before he wins her, and drive off and kill an intruder during the time that he is making love.

The great majority of cases in which oozies are killed by their elephants take place when their charges are on must. For some unknown reason, the animal may then suddenly attack his rider, first striking him with tusk or trunk, then crushing him to death with a knee, when he is on the ground. A vicious young animal will throw his rider, and then attack him on the ground. Once he has done this he is classed as dangerous and given a metal bell, as he is likely to repeat such an attack. For three years he may never show a sign of viciousness – then suddenly he will catch his new rider off his guard, and so kill his second man.

Strange as it may sound, there is very little difficulty in finding a new rider for such an animal. Many riders take pride in riding an elephant known to be dangerous, and take such a job in a spirit of bravado. Such men find life easy; they care nothing for anything or anyone. They are usually opium-eaters, but in spite of that they work well. Every village girl knows them by name. But, though they gain in reputation and importance, they do not get spoilt, as they are not paid much more for such work than the ordinary riders.

In addition to the rider, a dangerous animal has a really good type of spearman attached to it as an attendant, whose duty is to cover every movement of the rider when he lies entirely at the mercy of the elephant – undoing his fetters, for example. Although the spearman carries a spear, the secret of his control is by the eye. He keeps his eye fixed on the elephant's. The two men together are usually sufficient to keep a savage elephant under control.

The temperament of a nasty-tempered elephant is somewhat like that of a Burman. The animal loses its temper and kills, and realizes too late what it has done. In just the same way a Burman will lose his temper about some trivial gambling debt and will draw his dagger and stab his best friend – ten minutes later he will realize with most bitter regret what he has done.

I have known one case of something that seemed like remorse in an elephant. He was a tusker who killed his rider. But he guarded the body, and would let nobody get near it, for a whole week. He grazed all round it, and charged in mad fury at anyone who came near. When the body had quite decomposed he wandered away from it, and ten days later was recaptured, without any difficulty, and behaved quite normally. He was not on must.

An animal named Ah Noh (a Siamese name) killed nine riders in a period of fifteen years, but there was never any difficulty in getting a new rider for him. He was peculiar in that he always killed his man with his tusks, actually goring him to death. He was never in harness unless there was a rider on his head and two spearmen, one on each side, with their spears at the ready.

It was finally decided to saw his tusks right off to the lip, or as near as possible to the lip. This involved overpowering him completely, and a description of it would make very painful reading, as it was cruel. But the job was done, under my supervision, and we cured him. The two great nerves were almost exposed by the sawing. They healed in a remarkable way, for the tusks did not grow again, but formed a rosette of ivory at each end. He was one of those exceptional and magnificent animals which are rarely seen, either in the wild state or in captivity. One could walk up to him and give him a banana, and he was so beautifully behaved one would think butter would not melt in his mouth. I have come across him feeding alone in the jungle many times, and have stopped to admire him. He never made the slightest attempt to attack me.

The wickedest elephant I ever knew was called Taw Sin Ma (Miss Wild Elephant). I never knew her when she was a calf, but she cannot have been greatly loved, to have earned herself a name like that, and she must have been very truculent in the crush. She was about twenty-five years old when I first knew her, and there was nothing in her recorded history which gave any explanation of why she should just loathe every European she saw. She had never been operated on, and could never have been ill-treated by a European. Even when she was had up for inspection she had to be chained to a tree, and when one was a hundred yards away would begin to lunge and strain at her chains, in order to attack one.

She recognized a European by his appearance quite as much as by smell, because she would attack a Burman rider if he were wearing a khaki shirt. I had a nasty experience with her, when she first attacked me on sight, and then chased me, following my trail by scent for four miles, from one catchment area over the watershed to the next. It was terrifying.

I met her by chance, when I was walking from one camp to another. We came on her suddenly, and she went for us at once. The Burman I had with me stampeded in one direction, and I in another, and for two miles I was not sure whether I was on the right track back to the camp I had left. There would have been no hope for me if her hobbles had snapped or come undone, unless I had found refuge up a tree. But I knew well that if I had done that I might have had to stay there for twenty-four hours or longer. As she was hobbled, my pace was a little faster than hers. She wore a brass danger bell around her neck (docile elephants wear wooden bells). Often it sounded from the bell as though she were nearly up to me, at times as though she had cut me off. Of course, I know that sounds in the jungle are deceptive, and play tricks; but it was not pleasant. This experience gave me the first opportunity I had ever had of trying out a trick for delaying a pursuing elephant, by dropping an article of clothing, in the belief that the animal will halt and attack it, and so give one a chance of gaining ground.

I first dropped a haversack, but I heard no check in the sound of the clanking bell on the elephant hurrying after me. When I had climbed to the top of the ridge I halted for a few moments, to locate her whereabouts. Then, after going as fast as I could along the ridge, I chose the steepest place for my descent, hoping she would hesitate to follow, and there I dropped my khaki shirt, for her to savage, or to chew to her heart's content. But I had no sooner reached the small spur reaching to the drainage area below than I heard an avalanche of crashing trees and bamboos, and it needed very little imagination to visualize Taw Sin Ma sitting on her haunches and tobagganing down the steep incline, much faster than I had done. My shirt had not delayed her a moment. Perhaps she was holding it in her mouth, to chew after she had first caught me. On I plunged, trying to remember to act on the law of the jungle, that one must never hurry and always keep cool. Once one breaks that rule every thorny bush that grows reaches out a tentacle to impede one, to tear and scratch, or even trip one up. I thought of discarding my once white, and very wet, vest, but I thought that if I was eventually treed, I might need something on. My relief was great when I met two men, busy with a crosscut saw on a fallen teak tree. But I had only to shout out the words: 'Taw Sin Ma!' and they joined me in my flight, without asking questions. They soon took the lead, and as I followed I at least had the satisfaction of knowing I was on the right track to camp and safety.

One of them got into camp, well ahead of me, and gave the alarm on my account. When I got in I met a chattering group of elephant-riders and their families, all of them doubled up with laughter, or smacking their hands on their hips in mirth at the sight of me – all, that is, except Maung Po Net (Mr Black as Night), who tucked up his lungyi skirt, as he prepared to go out and meet his 'pet'.

There was no alternative but to join the Burmans in their joke – for I often wanted them to share in mine. So I joined in their laughter and their hip-smacking.

Within an hour a rider came back with my shirt and haversack, quite undamaged and not even trodden on, and Po Net rode Taw Sin Ma back into camp. The expressions on both their faces seemed to indicate that the same incident might be repeated next day. It did not, as I at once issued twenty-five feet of chain, for Taw Sin Ma to trail behind her, whenever she was at large, grazing, in addition to her hobbles.

As far as I know, she was the only animal we never inoculated against anthrax. She was the type that never gets it!

Some riders teach their charges tricks that give a wrong impression of the real disposition of the animal. Bo Gyi (Big Man), a young elephant, which became well known, always charged his rider, as soon as he appeared to catch him and bring him to camp. But at ten paces the animal would stop dead, and sit down for his fetter to be undone, as gently as a lamb. Any other rider would bolt when the elephant charged him. The secret, that it was just a matter of standing one's ground, was only discovered after the rider who had taught him the trick had been killed by a bear. The elephant was at large for a month after his rider's death; nobody would face him. Finally a reward of three hundred rupees was offered for his recapture. A young village lad turned up one day, saying he could capture him, but asking if he would get the reward, since he was not one of my riders. I told him that of course he would. Two days later he came into camp riding the animal and smiling gaily, and was paid his three hundred rupees. Two of my own men had gone with the lad, and had watched the whole procedure, from a hiding-place near by. The secret had come from a young Burmese girl, a former sweetheart of the dead rider. The young lad was her new lover, and no doubt boy and girl found the three hundred rupees a useful start in life.

After a strike among eighty elephant-riders, in the early days, at a time when there had been political agitation in the neighbourhood, I was left with the job of capturing what appeared to be six savage elephants, simply because none of the men left with me knew the tricks that had to be employed with each animal. These tricks were just the result of habitual methods employed by their riders. In some cases the approach had to be made from the near side, in other cases from the off, or from in front, or behind, or when the animal was sitting, or standing. The approach to each animal had to be learned separately.

The last one to be caught was Toe Hline (The Destroyer). I got the information of how to catch him by bribing the rider who was on strike, through an agent of my own, who confided to the rider a long story of how he wanted a job so as to get enough money to marry a certain girl in camp. If he could catch Toe Hline he would get that money reward and the job of riding him.

I watched this recapture with great relief, as Toe Hline had a bad reputation for tearing down jungle rice godowns (storehouses), and he had taken up his grazing quarters near my jungle hut, which was by no means substantial, being built of bamboo, with very flimsy posts, and it looked just like a godown. The volunteer to catch Toe Hline was 'attacked' twice, on getting within one hundred and fifty yards of the animal. It looked pretty hopeless, but I soon discovered that these 'attacks' were merely a method of getting the elephant and the rider in full view of each other. Once this had been achieved, the rider designate sat down on his haunches and began calling in a very persuasive voice: 'Hmit! Hmit! Hmit! Hmit!' This went on for at least fifteen minutes, with the elephant taking no heed, but just going on feeding, keeping one eye on the rider, all the time. Quite abruptly, he stopped feeding, and stood perfectly still. Then, slowly moving his head towards where the rider sat, and, setting his ears forward inquisitively, he decided to 'Hmit'.

Even then it needed great pluck for the rider to go up to him. As he advanced, he repeated the same word, and, bending down, unfastened the fetter, which is normally done when the animal is standing up. Then he climbed on the elephant's head and said: 'Tah!' Toe Hline rose, and proceeded to camp, and I proceeded to get myself a peg, to celebrate the recapture of the last elephant. I had them all equipped with eighty new riders, and the strikers were left wondering.

The rider married his girl and got his money reward. Then Po Lone, the original rider, who was the pleasantest of rogues, came in to say that now he had enabled his friend to win the reward, and get his girl, he would like to ride his old elephant again himself. He got him, for the two riders had fixed it all up between themselves, while I thought I was breaking the strike. They are lovable rogues.

Young calves, if they have not been properly trained, are apt to get savage if not well handled afterwards. One particular calf, named Soe Bone (Wicked Bone) – the name of the creek where he was born – delighted in chasing me whenever he got an opportunity. I thought at first it was only rough play, but my head Burman assured me it was not, so we decided he was not too old to learn his manners. 'Shoot him in his toe-nails with roasted rice,' was the suggestion. So I emptied two cartridges and, after filling them with rice instead of shot, I wandered out of camp to find Soe Bone. He was in a sandy creek, throwing wet sand over his body with his trunk, and was under a bank, only three foot high.

'Hullo little chap!' I said, greeting him.

'Little chap to you,' he seemed to reply, and charged me on sight, as though determined to see me off.

I stood my ground, and gave him a left and right in the forefeet, so as to sting his toe-nails. Did it stop him? I nearly lost my precious shotgun as I made my getaway. He was up that bank with his fetters on almost as quickly as I could turn to run. And did he love me next time he saw me?

'What's the next move?' I asked.

'Oh well, we'll put him back into a crush and cane the little devil.'

A substantial crush was made, and into it he was enticed and trapped. My head Burman came to fetch me, carrying in his hand a six-foot whippy cane.

At least a dozen Burmans were there to witness the caning of this naughty schoolboy, as even Soe Bone's own rider had no use for this tiresome game of chasing people.

I was asked to give him the first twenty strokes. And what a behind it was to whip! I went to his head first, and showed him the cane. He showed me the whites of his eyes, as if to say: 'Wait till I get out of here,' but I changed his mind for him, and he squealed blue murder. Then everyone present, except his rider, was ordered to give him half a dozen, whereas his rider was permitted to stay behind and give him lots of titbits, after we had all gone.

I saw him next morning being loaded with some light kit as we were moving camp, and he looked rather ashamed of himself. Suddenly he saw me, carrying a stick, and, instead of pricking his ears, as he did when he was going to chase me, he gave one shrieking trumpet and bolted into the jungle for his life.

Shortly afterwards I left him for another forest, and did not see him again for fifteen years. By that time he was a magnificent beast of twenty-five, and quite docile. I won't say that he had forgotten, but he had certainly forgiven me.

One of the most remarkable incidents I ever had with savage elephants concerned a young Shan woman of about twenty. I was sitting in my hut near the camp one evening, very worried over a seriously injured spearman, Maung Chan Tha, who had been gored that afternoon by an elephant named Kyauk Sein (Jade-coloured Eyes) while he was trying to save the life of the rider, Maung Po Yin, who had been killed instantaneously by the elephant, who had then attacked the spearman. The animal had gone on must, and was at large in the neighbourhood of the camp.

I was discussing with my head Burman how we were going to get the wounded spearman away to hospital. To put him on an elephant would kill him, as he had a serious abdominal wound and a broken leg. To carry him on a bamboo stretcher to hospital would take five days, and was the only alternative.

Suddenly, quite unannounced, a tall, fine-looking girl walked into my bamboo hut, and I immediately recognized her as the widow of the dead rider. She was not wailing, or weeping or carrying her youngest child, which is the custom on such occasions, nor did she kneel and sit before me, in the customary manner. She just stood erect and in a firm, unemotional voice said: 'May I have a dismissal certificate from you for my husband Maung Po Yin, who was killed today by Kyauk Sein?'

'Yes,' I replied. 'And your compensation, if you will wait till tomorrow, as I am busy arranging to get Maung Chan Tha to hospital.' I added how grieved I was, and, in sympathy, asked her if she had any children.

My head Burman answered, instead of her, that she had none, and then, addressing her as though he were most displeased with her for coming to see me in such an unceremonious way, said:

'You can go now. I shall be coming back to the camp presently.'

She moved quietly out of the room, a tall and graceful figure.

When she was out of earshot I turned to my head Burman and asked: 'Is that Po Yin's wife?'

'Yes,' he replied, 'but she takes more opium than Po Yin did, and that is the reason why she has no children.'

I was very much surprised, as it was the first time I had ever heard of a Shan girl taking opium. I was even more staggered when my old Burman said in a quiet voice, 'Give me ten ticals of opium tonight, and she will recapture Kyauk Sein tomorrow, because she has often caught him for Po Yin, when he was in a heavy opium bout.'

I gave him the opium he asked for, but I went to bed that night with a very disturbed conscience. To add to my troubles, Chan Tha died before dawn.

I met my old Burman very early the following morning, but I asked him no questions, and waited to see what the day would bring forth.

By ten o'clock, however, he came to me saying:

'Kyauk Sein is coming in, with Ma Kyaw riding him. Come and look.'

I could scarcely believe my eyes when I saw Kyauk Sein passing through the camp, with the Shan girl riding him, oblivious to every-thing, and her eyes fixed straight in front of her. Her long black hair was hanging loose down her back, and she wore her blue tamain girdled above her breasts, leaving her beautiful pale shoulders bare. Again I did not interfere, and by noon I was informed that Kyauk Sein was securely tethered to a tree, as is customary for elephants on must.

That evening Ma Kyaw was brought to me, to receive the com-pensation due to her. She was dressed in her best, wearing a multi-coloured tamain, a little white coat, and a flower in her jet-black hair. She knelt and shikoed three times, and then sat down in front of me. She kept her eyes lowered, looking at the mat she sat on, and she toyed with a matchstick in her right hand, as though she were drawing something.

After paying her the compensation due to her for the loss of her husband, I gave her an extra bonus for recapturing Kyauk Sein. When I told her this, I could see a wisp of a smile at the corners of her mouth. I then wrote for her a certificate, such as is customarily made out for all men killed in accidents. These certificates are for the benefit of the Jungle Nats, who require them before admitting the spirit of the dead rider to their domains. The certificate ran, 'I hereby give leave to Maung Po Yin, rider of Kyauk Sein, to go where he wishes, as he has been dismissed from my service', and I signed it.

When I had risen from my table and given the money and the certificate into her hands, she wiped away two crocodile tears, did three shikos with her hands, got up and went quietly out into the dusk, back to the camp, three hundred yards away, on the other side of the creek.

I was only left guessing what the future developments would be for another twenty-four hours, for then, when I asked my old Burman about finding a new rider for Kyauk Sein, he told me:

'Oh, that is all arranged. Maung Ngwe Gyaw is an opium-taker, too. He has "taken on" (not married) Ma Kyaw, and they tell me that the biggest opium-taker of the lot is Kyauk Sein, the elephant. Another ten ticals of opium would be useful.'

By that time I would willingly have given him twenty, if he had asked for them.

I do not believe to this day that the girl took opium, but she was a resolute character, and the elephant Kyauk Sein knew her well enough to take opium out of her hand. He probably knew the smell of her hand, because she was the wife of his rider. I think she completely stupefied the animal before she caught him.

The ways of the jungle are strange, but all is not savage, hard and cruel in it. For every savage elephant that attacks or kills his rider there are ninety-nine that are docile and friendly.

CHAPTER 11

I find it hard to realize now, after living for twenty-five years in the jungle with the most magnificent of all animals, that for the first three and a half years my eyes were blinded by the thrill of big-game shooting. I now feel that elephants are God's own, and I would never shoot another.

However, it was as a result of these three and a half years that I reached my present views, and because of my experiences then that I developed as deep a reverence for the jungle and all the jungle creatures as anyone possibly could.

Of course, the big cats are a nuisance. There are too many tigers and leopards in the jungle – so many, indeed, that the few which are shot make scarcely any impression on their numbers. Quite apart from seeing them, when sitting up for them in a tree over a kill, hoping to get a shot, the European Assistant almost invariably has some memorable incident in his career, when he sees tiger in more natural conditions. I once jumped into a creek, ten yards from a tiger that was lying down eating a freshly killed samba deer. He was magnificent. I could not jump back from the boulder I had alighted onto the bank behind me. For what seemed quite half a minute we stared at each other, and he snarled at me. Then he jumped up and, with the most graceful movements, bounded from boulder to boulder up the creek. He whoofed twice as he went, as though disgusted that the stench of a white man should interrupt his lunch.

Willie, whose reception of me when I first arrived in the jungle will be remembered, first came out to Burma in the early years of this century. Although he belonged to a good family and was a good shot, he arrived with very little equipment, for I fancy he had exhausted his father's purse and patience before he was sent East. If he was anything like his son, Willie's father must have been a formidable disciplinarian in his day. On Willie's arrival he was at once invited to a big shoot, at which high jungle fowl were expected. Poor Willie had to confess that he had not got a gun. However, as it was obvious that the lad was very keen, one of the party took pity on him and lent him a small-calibre rifle, saying it was possible that the beaters might put up some ground game, and that Willie might get a shot. He was told, however, that he must not fire in front of him towards the line of beaters, but must wait until the game had passed through the line of waiting guns. The first two beats were most successful, with numbers of high birds, which were brought down brilliantly by the guns. But poor Willie did not get a shot.

The third beat was a blank. Not a single jungle fowl rose to meet the line of waiting guns, and the beaters were almost up to them and had ceased rattling their sticks on the bamboos, when there was the crack of a rifle, and Willie's neighbours were horrified to see that he had disobeyed instructions, and fired in front of him, towards the beaters.

'What the hell do you think you are doing, young man?' demanded 'Growler' Moore, going up to him in a fury. 'What on earth are you firing at?'

'I saw a tiger,' said Willie.

'Tiger? What d'you mean, tiger? Don't talk nonsense!' shouted Growler, intent on ticking off the offender.

'Well, there it is, and it's dead,' said Willie.

And there, twenty yards from them, was a fine tiger, with a bullet through its head. Willie could not make out why the other guns made such a fuss about it when they came up and inspected it, for he had assumed that tigers were a normal part of the bag in a Burmese jungle-fowl shoot.

Although I now dislike the thought of shooting big game, I can still recall, and live over again, the thrill when I was young enough to take any opportunity that offered which gave me even chances of life or death.

I remember how for two whole months I spent day after day near the mouth of the Manipur River, trying to get a solitary wild bull elephant – and every day was hard, and ended in disappointment. He was well known by the name of Shwe Kah, which my elephant-riders had given him.

These words are used to describe the pose of a Burmese girl's arms and hands when she is dancing: a pose in which the forearms and the hands and extended fingers are gracefully curved upwards and outwards. In the beautiful and perfectly symmetrical tusks of this wild elephant my riders had seen the same lovely upward and outward curve. Shwe Kah had gored two of my tuskers badly, and had continually worried my elephants. He was far too bold for the liking of my riders, particularly when they were catching their beasts deep in the jungle. Many of them had seen him, and they described the dimensions of his tusks outside the lip, by stretching both arms out horizontally, to show their length, and by encircling their legs above the knee with the outstretched thumbs and forefingers of both hands to indicate their girth. Some tusks!

I had numerous opportunities to bag other wild elephant at that time, but I was set on getting Shwe Kah. I saw him twice, but not in a position for a shot. I then went on leave for a month, knowing I should be back in the same area during May, the best month in Burma for big game.

If I got him, Shwe Kah would be my fourth elephant, and I had learned quite a lot about tracking and all that big-game shooting entailed. One night during my leave, a very pleasant Sapper Major joined our small party at the bar of the Maymyo Club (now no more). While we were chatting, he mentioned that he had just purchased a rifle from someone going home, and that he was more than keen to bag an elephant before he left Burma. It was a case of finding him somewhere where he could shoot. I did not like the description of his purchase. It was a magazine rifle with a high-velocity bullet, but on the small side. My opinion was (and is) that a double-barrel breech-loader 400/450 was the right weapon for Burma big game. This difference of opinion led to a hot argument, as it usually does, but we ended up such good friends that finally I said: 'Can you get a month's leave, from the twenty-fifth of April, as I am going back for a tour of jungle camps, during which I hope to get some big-game shooting in my spare time?' He jumped at it, but, to make it quite square, I explained that I would do all that I could to put him onto the track of a decent wild tusker, but that it must be understood that Shwe Kah was to be mine only. This he fully appreciated.

He had never done any big-game shooting, and he was thrilled with the idea of the trip, even apart from the chance of getting an elephant. He was a man of thirty-seven. I was just twenty-six. I worked out that he might expect to get ten days' actual shooting, and that, with any reasonable luck, working from my little jungle headquarters, he ought to bag an elephant, and stood a good chance of getting a bison and other game.

He joined me on the appointed date, and we set off, poling up the Myittha River in a country dug-out. One evening we had a bathe after I had been out with a rod. While I was drying my feet, he said: 'Lord, I wish I had feet like yours!'

Laughingly I replied: 'Why, have you got corns?'

'No,' he replied. 'But I have eight hammer toes.'

Looking at them, I saw eight tightly clenched toes, in spite of his feet being flat on the boat boards. I howled with laughter, and asked him how on earth he thought he was going to trek all day through the jungle. He was quite honest, and said he had hoped to sit quietly in one spot and wait for the game to go by. This rather damped my hopes that he would have any great success. But he was quite happy, as he was much enjoying all my routine work of inspecting elephant camps.

When we reached Sinywa (Wild Elephant Village), late one evening, I was told by my men that Shwe Kah was about, and had been seen the previous day, two miles away, on the other bank of the river. My shikar companion insisted on accompanying me the next day, without his rifle, purely to see what would happen. He had a morning which quite cooked him, but he saw two female wild elephants, and was thrilled to the marrow of his aching toes.

We eventually got on the tracks of a big tusker, which I imagined to be those of Shwe Kah. These led us back to the Myittha River bank, where it was quite obvious that during the night the animal had crossed the river, to the side on which we were encamped. It was then well after noon, and was sweltering hot. As we should pass near our camp, I suggested that we should have a cup of tea and something to eat there, and then continue our attempt to find Shwe Kah. My friend was all for the cup of tea and the cold Green Pigeon pie, but candidly admitted he was far too cooked to leave camp again, but said he'd excuse me if I went.

I had just eaten a first mouthful of pie when a Burman arrived to say there was an enormous wild tusker, believed to be Shwe Kah, not three hundred yards from their camp, a mile away from where we were.

Without any hesitation, I was off. No tea, no pie – I left my companion resting his weary bare feet on a box by our camp table. As I left, he graciously said: 'I'll leave some pie for you.'

By 3 p.m., under a sweltering tropical sun, I had got near enough to this wild elephant to hear an occasional flap of his ear. There was no other sound, as he was browsing in elephant grass, twelve feet high, through which I had ventured, following up his tracks. I knew that the river bank could not be far to my left, I knew only too well that if he were suddenly disturbed he would stampede back, direct on his tracks. I therefore decided to get off them into the tall grass on one side. There I rested my rifle against a small tree, and wiped the sweat from my face and brow. I took a quick swallow from a water-flask, as that was probably the last refresher I should get. I was determined to get a shot that afternoon.

I was suddenly alarmed by realizing that my presence had been detected by the elephant, probably, as so often happens, by scent. There was a never-to-be-forgotten noise of the animal cracking the end of his trunk on the hard ground – it makes a sharp, clear, metallic, ringing sound, owing to the trunk being hollow. Then there followed that awful silence. I had no alternative but to stand my ground. Both of us were left guessing, but the elephant broke first, and made away from where I was standing, whereupon I made direct to where I imagined the river bank to be. It was closer than I had realized, and I reached it where the tall kaing grass grew to the very edge, which was eight feet high above the water, and had recently fallen in. The edge was unapproachable without risk of further collapse, but not many seconds passed before I heard a tremendous splashing, and through the tall grass I saw a magnificent tusker elephant, crossing the river fifty yards below me, moving at a fast ambling trot, the splashes of water covering his body.

Without hesitation, I jumped down the eight feet, landing in three feet of water, but sinking into the mud to the tops of my boots. I was bogged. It was now or never for a shot. I decided on a heart shot, as he was moving quickly, water splashing, and I was unsteady.

Crack! He was quite seventy-five yards away when I fired. He stumbled a bit, recovered, and then swung round, like a polo pony, and came back on his tracks, not twenty-five yards below me. He was wild with rage – so wild that he did not see me. I was stuck, and had no hope of regaining the bank. As he climbed up, where he had slid down a few minutes before, I realized that he was mortally wounded, and noticed that his tusks did not appear as big as those of Shwe Kah, nor as tilted.

I gave him another heart shot, and there was no mistake this time. He collapsed stone dead against the top of the bank. Before I had extricated myself from the mud, my gun-boy, who had remained behind in a tree on the bank, went off to inspect him, and came rushing back to me yelling: 'Amai! (Oh Mother) Amai! You have shot a Kyan Zit.'

I was far too excited and occupied to appreciate what he meant. It was about half-past four in the afternoon, and sweltering hot. I well remember my feelings when I realized that I had not bagged Shwe Kah, as I so much wanted his tusks as the trophy of my last wild elephant. For I could not get a licence to shoot another for a year. However, all my disappointment vanished as soon as I saw the head of the magnificent beast I had shot. For he was something very rare, and was already causing great excitement among all the elephant-riders, who had come rushing along from their camp.

'Kyan Zit! Kyan Zit! Kyan Zit!' was all they could repeat as if one of the strangest myths of the jungle had been proved.

I could not have been more astonished if I had shot a unicorn. The words Kyan Zit describe a rare type of elephant tusk, that has grown in rings or corrugations, like the sections of a piece of sugar-cane. The Burmans speak of such an animal as such a rarity as to be almost mythical, but in existence, and they believe that a Kyan Zit is a king of elephants, to whom all other elephants do obeisance, in terror of his strength.

The tusks were corrugated, in rings, from the tip to the lip where they entered the head; after they were extracted the corrugations were found to continue, but faded out gradually, right up to the socket and root. A photograph of the tusks was afterwards published in the *Bombay Natural History Journal*, but no explanation of the cause of their formation was forthcoming. It was not a malformation, as the rings were symmetrical in both tusks. I have never seen comparable tusks amongst any of the thousands of captive elephants I have known in Burma.

I rested on the leg of the dead beast and had a drink of water, and looked at him with a mixture of excitement and remorse, and I asked myself what had the King of Elephants with the Kyan Zit tusks done to me? – What had I done to him?

Long discussions followed among the riders standing round and admiring the rare tusks. A head man arrived from camp to supervise their removal with small axes and sharpened knives. Then the women of the camp arrived with children and babies in arms, all to be shown Kyan Zit.

Up to this time I had not allowed any of them to touch him, as I knew that once those Burmans started on a dead elephant they combined the qualities of Americans after souvenirs and vultures after flesh.

I then heard someone yelling my name. It was my guest, who, on hearing my two shots in camp, had just hopped off his camp bed and, without waiting to put on his shoes, had come along, with two or three of the men from my camp. Hammer toes or no hammer toes, he wanted to see the result of those two rifle-shots. When he emerged from the tall kaing grass he nearly collapsed with surprise.

'Lord, how magnificent!' was his only remark, as he opened up his camera and took several snapshots.

Not till he had finished did I get the chance to explain that it was not Shwe Kah but Kyan Zit – and I explained the whole story, as we stood beside the tusks.

'Oh! I am sorry!' he exclaimed.

But I assured him that I was more than content. So pleased, in fact, that our next job must be for him to bag Shwe Kah, as he was now his game. My guest was beginning to be a little doubtful about having to take on anything the size of such a monster, but I told him he could borrow my rifle for the job, which seemed to relieve his mind a little.

I had not noticed that he was barefoot, until I suddenly looked down. 'Good Lord, man! Your feet will be blistered to hell!' I exclaimed.

So I sent back to camp for his shoes, and for tea and sandwiches for myself, and we settled down to supervise the removal of the rusks, taking also the hairs from the tail and one forefoot, as the Kyan Zit had the most perfect feet and toe-nails I have ever seen on an elephant. The toe-nails looked as though they had just been manicured, and the oil sweat-glands between the nails showed that he was an animal in his prime. The forefeet were perfectly circular, and my shikar companion was quite ready to take a heavy bet that twice their circumference was not equal to the animal's height at the withers. He was astonished when I measured it up and showed him that it was.

By this time the human vultures had started operations. Whole baskets of meat were carried off to camp, to be dried in the sun. There was enough to last them many months. It was my Burman hunter's perquisite to have the two aphrodisiac snips, which consist of the triangular tip of the trunk and the tip of the penis, also the big nerves out of the tusks, which are a native medicine for eye troubles, as well as a coveted aphrodisiac.

By the time we had removed the tusks and the forefoot it was almost dusk. More men and women from Sinywa village had arrived, to carry away meat. It was a really savage-looking party, with a lot of jokes and chatter. My Burman hunter came in for a great deal of chipping and cross-chat from the girls on the subject of his special perquisites.

As dusk fell we left them to it and went back to camp. Before we went to bed I had many things to tell my guest, as he was thrilled with all this, and was one mass of questions. The last thing he said to me, after I had done what I could for his poor feet by anointing them with Zam-Buk, was: 'You know, I am so enjoying this that I don't mind if I don't shoot anything.'

I had work to do the next day, and left my guest to watch my men cleaning the tusks and the forefoot for curing.

That evening news came into camp that there was a small herd of wild elephant feeding in a swamp area three miles from camp, and that it was more than likely that Shwe Kah was hanging round.

Next morning my guest insisted that his feet were not fit for marching that day, but I overcame his objections by saying we would ride an elephant of mine as far as the swamp, so as to have a look round, though I did not think it sounded very promising. The swamp was about half a mile wide – of tall, dense kaing grass, flanked on either side by fairly open jungle with big trees.

On the west side there were all the signs that the herd had entered the swamp during the night, and about half a mile to the north there were tracks of two solitary and separate bulls, which had gone in also. Either of these tracks might have been those of Shwe Kah.

We talked it over with my hunter, and agreed that very little could be done in this dense swamp area, but that if my guest remained on the west side, and we stampeded the animals from the east, he might have the luck of a novice in seeing a tusker pass him.

I explained everything, and placed my guest in the fork of a large tree, fifteen feet from the ground. His farewell remark was to whisper: 'What a host! This is what I call a sitter.' I left my rifle and gun-boy with him, and skirted the whole swamp on my own elephant, with an expert rider.

It was two hours before I got into position on the eastern side. I had warned my guest that he would have a long wait, and that he was to take no notice of any calling or talking he might hear. I moved up and down on the edge of the swamp, from north to south and back again, speaking as loudly as I could to my rider. Unfortunately, my elephant was completely silent as it strode up and down, as there was no fodder for it to snatch at whilst walking.

Presently I heard a wild elephant 'chirping', at short intervals. It is a beautiful note of warning, rather than a signal of real danger, as though to say: 'Keep in together. There are voices from the east side.'

We halted our elephant for a short time on high ground, and from its back I could overlook the sea of kaing grass covering the swamp.

My elephant, Chit Sia Yah (Lovable), who was trained to stand a rifle-shot fired from his back, stood facing west, with his ears cocked forward, listening. He could hear something that we could not. Then my rider pointed to the sea of kaing grass, and said in a quiet voice: 'See the grass tips moving. Wild elephant are closing in.'

I was particularly anxious that they should move west without any panic or stampede, so we remained perfectly quiet for fifteen to twenty minutes.

It was all most exciting to watch – there was silent movement without a sound. Here and there I could see the grass stirred, as though by a fitful breeze, though there was not a breath of wind.

Then from the very centre three or four elephants' trunks appeared above the sea of kaing. They kept moving from side to side in an uncanny fashion, like cobras poised to strike.

My rider whispered: 'They have scented either you or the other Thakin on the other side.'

Without hesitation, I gave a series of shouts, in which my rider joined. This left the herd in no doubt as to our position. One animal trumpeted, and then the whole herd began moving west towards my guest in the tree. It was like watching a silent, slow roller, as the herd moved in a body through the tall grass. One could see it going down, as they moved steadily, not in a stampede, but in an organized stream. Their leader had undoubtedly decided to leave the swamp, which was a small area and a poor hiding-place, as it was surrounded by open jungle.

It seemed an hour before they passed out of sight and hearing, but really it was only ten minutes. Then there was an overpowering silence, while we waited to hear a shot. Even my elephant seemed in a state of tension, and to be expecting it. I had very nearly come to the conclusion that all the elephants must have passed either to the north or to the south of my guest in his tree, when two rifle-shots echoed through the jungle. I began to move towards him on my elephant, when 'Crack! crack!' came another couple of shots, shortly followed by two more.

I began to wonder whether my guest was having a stand-up fight with Shwe Kah, or whether he was shooting down the whole herd – males, females and calves – and was also wondering if there would be any rifling left in the barrels of my precious rifle!

Suddenly Chit Sia Yah, my elephant, pulled up, motionless. I then heard, and immediately afterwards saw, a magnificent bull elephant with a pair of finely shaped tusks about three hundred yards away on my left, moving rapidly into the jungle behind me. I thought it was Shwe Kah, and that beginner's luck had not favoured my guest.

Complete silence reigned once more. The pageant was over as far as we were concerned on the eastern flank. But what was happening on the west?

I yelled and shouted to my friend, but could get no answer, although I knew he was within hearing. I was still uncertain if there were a wounded animal in the sea of kaing grass, and did not dare to take Chit Sia Yah through it until I knew. One thing I did know, and that was that my friend would not come down from his perch if he had only wounded an elephant.

Finally I could not wait any longer so, dismounting from Chit Sia Yah, I told the rider to wait till I called, and started to cross the swamp on foot, heading towards my friend. The going was fairly good, as it was the month of May, and therefore fairly dry, and the wild elephant had made a wide trail through the tall, heavy grass.

I occasionally halted and called, forgetting my rider would follow up, so I had a severe shock when he appeared behind me. I hailed him, as I thought that if my guest had downed all the beasts he could in the wild herd, he was quite capable of finishing off his day's sport by shooting Chit Sia Yah by mistake. The track I followed was that along which the herd had avalanched, leaving a roadway fifteen to twenty feet wide through the kaing grass, as though a reaping-machine had gone through it.

Finally I came out, calling to my friend before I did so, and found him sitting twenty yards away in his tree.

'Why the hell can't you answer?' I asked him.

'You told me not to,' he replied, adding: 'But look out, I've shot an elephant.'

I did not know what that meant, or stop to enquire, but dashed forward to the protection of the nearest big tree. From there, however, I saw a magnificent dead tusker on the edge of the kaing grass directly in front of my friend. The shape of his tusks left no doubt that he was Shwe Kah.

'He's dead, isn't he?' I shouted.

'I think so, but I'll make certain again,' replied my friend, and gave the carcass another couple of rounds.

'For God's sake have some respect for my rifle,' I shouted, and then Kya Sine, who was with him in the tree, called to me in Burmese:

'It has been dead nearly an hour. It must be cold by now, but he won't let me come down the tree.'

I went up to the dead elephant, and saw the largest and most magnificent pair of tusks I have ever seen in Burma. My guest was so thrilled by all that had happened to him that he could not get it out, but Maung Kya Sine gave me a wonderful description. The whole herd of twenty-two animals had walked directly under their tree, and they had had a circus view of them. According to Kya Sine, my guest had the rifle at his shoulder the whole time, pointing it in turn at every animal with the least sign of a tusk. As the parade was coming to an end, Kya Sine spotted the back of an enormous beast which was following up at the tail of the herd, and indicated by nods and shrugs that my friend must wait. My guest had then dropped the rifle from his shoulder, thinking he had lost his chance, when this enormous tusker had appeared and halted with his head projecting from the kaing grass.

My friend dropped him first shot and wisely gave another. But, being determined not to let him rise again and escape, he began to try to get a heart shot. I had discussed this with him, telling him it was often more advisable than one through the brain. It was, however, an impossible shot from the angle at which he was up the tree. My gun-boy went back to camp on Chit Sia Yah to give the news, and soon the scene was the same as that we had watched two days before when I had shot Kyan Zit. My friend had quite forgotten his blistered feet and hammer toes, as we went back to camp. He spent the next two days with his trophy, while I continued my daily work. On the fifth day in camp I sent him off to hilly jungle, in spite of his feet, to see if he could find a bison. Before they left, my gun-boy told me that he knew the whereabouts of a bull. They reappeared by noon. My visitor had again had the most phenomenal luck. He had come across a bull bison, which was lying down chewing the cud, like any dairy bull in an English meadow, and he had bagged him. I rather regretted this, as it would have given him a real shikar thrill if he had met the great beast face to face, for it stood five feet ten inches at the withers.

My visitor left me to return to his unit, in a country dug-out, piled high with elephants' feet, tusks measuring six feet two inches in length, a bison's head and two hoofs, not to mention all sorts of curios that he had collected in camp, such as elephant bells, rings and bracelets of elephant's hair, and bamboo gongs. He waved goodbye to me, with a smile spreading from ear to ear, and wished he might return.

He never came back, and with his visit my own big-game shooting came to an end. I never shot big game again, and never catered for others who might want to do so.

Nevertheless, though I dislike it now, I have no regrets in regard to those early years. For it was those years that laid the foundations of a love and understanding of the jungle and the elephants in it. I shot four elephants; but on the other side of the account is all I have tried to do for hundreds of their fellows. I fought for their well-being for years, and fought with them during the years of war.

PART TWO

CHAPTER 12

During the open season of 1925–26 I had to run a shoot for General Sir William Birdwood, as he then was, the Commander-in-Chief, India, and his staff on the Upper Chindwin River. I met him and his party at Sittaung.

Burma was at that time under India Command, but the significance of the Commander-in Chief trekking into India from Imphal to Tamu on foot can scarcely be linked with the subsequent events over the same track, eighteen to twenty years later.

As far as I can remember, the trek took him five days, during which time he made every member of his staff swim in the coldest mountain streams imaginable. The track was then a six-foot ungraded bridle-track; it had, apart from any strategical importance in the future defences of India, a political interest, as at that time the question of the separation of Burma from India was very much to the fore.

Opinion in Burma was strongly against any development of this road to India. It was pointed out that a good road might serve as a backdoor entrance through which a flood of undesirable Indian immigrants might pour. It would be more difficult to control than immigration by sea. The road would have no value as a trade route, and it was concluded that it would be of no advantage to Burma.

The whole of the Burma Campaign from 1942 to 1945 depended on the existence of this route. For there are only two ways of reaching India from Burma – by sea, and by this, and one or two other mountain tracks leading from the tributaries of the Upper Chindwin into Northern Assam. In other words, there is an impenetrable mountain barrier running down the Burma–India frontier, which completely seals off the valley of the Irrawaddy from Assam; and there is no feasible coast-road along the Burmese seaboard province of Arakan. Thus, to reach India from Burma overland, one has to go up the Chindwin as far as Kalewa, go up the Kabaw Valley to Tamu, and cross the mountains into Manipur and the Imphal plain.

The strategic importance of the road is therefore immense. But so long as it was believed that Britain had undisputed command of the sea, the strategic importance of the road was subordinate to the political disadvantages to which it might lead.

The impression I gathered from General Birdwood at that time was that he favoured the improvement of the road, as a strategical communication of great importance. He had enormously enjoyed trekking over it, as during the trip he had escaped entirely from the world of red tape and official receptions. He obviously felt as though he were a subaltern again on a month's leave. Lady Birdwood came by sea from Calcutta to Rangoon, and then proceeded to Mandalay, where she painted some water-colours, and later on joined her husband on the Chindwin.

The object of the shoot was to get duck and geese, and there was no question of big game or elephant.

I remained with the Commander-in-Chief and Lady Birdwood for two days, having at my disposal the Bombay Burma Corporation launch *Chindwin*, which had been suitably victualled. It made a very enjoyable break for me.

Little did I guess then that during the war years of 1942 and 1944 I should lunch informally with Lord Wavell when he was Commander-in-Chief, and dine informally with Sir Claude Auchinleck when he was Commander-in-Chief, on the same road between Burma and India.

The Japanese invasion was not the first time that the Kabaw Valley and the bridle-track from Tamu to Imphal had been a scene of war, and of all the miseries that go with it. As far back as the sixteenth century this route was used by the Burmese General, Ba-Yin-Naung, to lead his army from Burma to Manipur.

Again in 1812 the Burmese King Bo-Daw-Pa-Ya annexed the Kabaw Valley, after intervening to decide the succession to the throne of Manipur.

It is one of those valleys which impress one either as a miniature paradise or as a green hell. During the years I have lived there, in peace and in war, I have known it in both aspects. The Manipuris and Burmans look on it as an ideal grazing ground for their cattle and buffalo herds, during the hot and dry seasons of the year, when pasture has been dried up elsewhere. And in the cold season it is a sportsman's paradise. The wild jungle fowl provide almost ideal high driven birds, and the gin-clear waters of its streams abound in mahseer up to eight pounds in weight. But in the monsoon it becomes a squelching swamp, generally overgrown by heavy unhealthy jungles.

In describing the withdrawal of the British Army in 1942, the Chief of Staff said that 'death dripped from every leaf'. That phrase might damn it for ever, but, visiting it today, one would not guess that his words had ever been true. Nor would one find many signs that the largest British Army of the Second World War, the XIVth Army, had fought its way down it.

In 1938 I was at home on leave and, as war seemed imminent, was for some time undecided whether I should return to Burma and my elephants. However, I finally made up my mind to go back, as I thought that if war did come, Japan would join our enemies, and that I should be of more use East of Suez than in the West.

With the outbreak of war in 1939, teak became as important a munition of war as steel, and all those employed in its extraction were regarded as engaged in work of national importance. Vast quantities of it were shipped to England during the first period of the war. When the Italians came in, supplies of timber were required in the Middle East. India's demand for teak alone was greater than could be supplied from Burma, and work in the forests was accelerated. Elephants were required for the extraction not only of teak, but of other kinds of timber as well.

After the Japanese came into the war, India's demands increased still further, and vast projects were put in hand after December 1941. Practically every officer concerned with teak extraction was away in the jungle in the three months which followed. Many of them were accompanied by their families. Their only link with developments in the war was by wireless. In spite of the rapid advances of the Japs, everyone was confident they would be held at Singapore and in Malaya. However, things were going so badly that a hurried warning was given by the Bombay Burma Corporation that it might, as a private firm, have to arrange for the evacuation of its European officers and their families from the Upper Chindwin into Manipur, and thence to Assam. A scheme for this was therefore prepared. If we had not had elephants for transport, it is unlikely that the scheme would have been put forward.

At that time I was on tour with my wife and family in the Shan states, right up the Shweli River.

By the same mail runner I received a confidential letter, strongly advising that all wives should return to headquarters, and a telegram instructing me to proceed to Monywa, on the Chindwin River, and to be ready to proceed beyond. I had no knowledge of the scheme for evacuation, but knew the country so well that I guessed what might be coming. My first thoughts, however, were that my instructions might be due to internal troubles in Burma. By forced marches with elephants to the river, followed by two days' voyage downstream in my own launch,

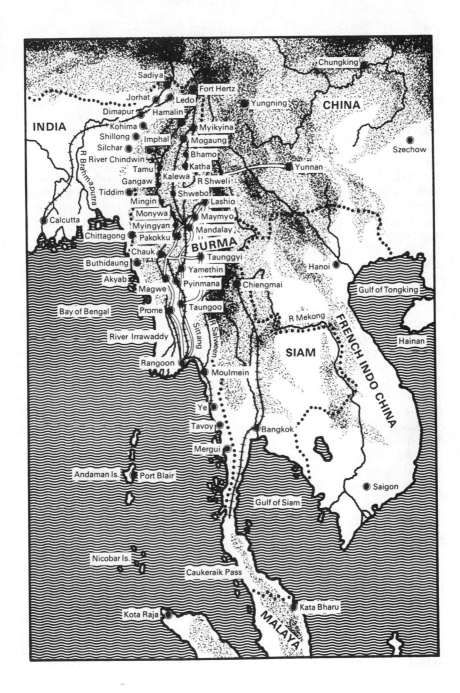

7

we reached the Irrawaddy. I little thought that I was saying goodbye to my Shweli elephants.

At Mandalay I found that the conditions, to which one had become accustomed since the war, were unchanged. But all wives and children, except those who were members of the Women's Auxiliary Forces, had proceeded up the Chindwin. There was great tension, and the wealthy Indians were already on the move.

I was instructed to go direct from Mandalay to Monywa, but I decided to go first to my home and headquarters at Maymyo, for one night, to dump my camp kit and collect the light kit my wife would require while up the Chindwin. I felt sure that even if she were forced to leave Burma, I should have an opportunity of returning to Maymyo myself.

Even at this stage the trains to Monywa and the steamers to Kalewa were crowded by Indians. The Bombay Burma Corporation had been the first to move all the European women and children of its employees up the Chindwin, from which they could get a good start if the worst should happen. A few of the more far-sighted Government officials had privately made the same arrangements for their wives. The Government had formed no plans to deal with such an emergency. The Bombay Burma Corporation was severely criticized at the time for its policy of partial evacuation of women and children. But it had the excellent effect of stirring the Government to action, at a time when the situation was becoming grave. Quite apart from the fact that the policy of women and children first was the right one, it relieved the married men among the employees of their heaviest responsibility, and greatly increased their usefulness.

At Monywa I overtook the second batch of women and children. The first batch had travelled up the Chindwin River by launch, as far as Mawlaik, where it had been decided to assemble, to await a final decision. It had been my intention to return from Monywa, but when I reached it I was instructed to proceed to Mawlaik on the launch, in charge of the second party.

When I reached Mawlaik, and had handed over the party in my charge, I was instructed to stay there, to help organize preparations for the trek to India, via Manipur State, in case it finally became necessary. If it was decided on, I was to accompany the party of women and children with elephant transport. The elephants were not for them to ride on, but to carry their food and a minimum of camp kit and their personal belongings.

From that time forward the elephants began to play an important part. Geoff Bostock, the senior member of the Forest Staff up-country, ordered all elephant work in timber extraction on the west bank of the Chindwin, north of Kalewa, to be stopped, and the elephants to be used to assist evacuation wherever possible. It was February 1942.

Rumours had spread that a road was being hurriedly constructed from Imphal to Kalewa, for the use of some phantom army which was coming from India to check the rapid advance of the Japanese on the Sittang River on which we were falling back from the border of Malaya. Some people believed these rumours. Work had in fact been begun on the road, from the Kalewa end, and on to Tamu, from where the ranges of hills towered up to the west – an effective bottleneck. Elephants were used in road-making, dragging timber to the bridge sites. The riders and elephants worked very hard for long hours, but with great willingness, and were quite unperturbed by the stream of Indians going past them.

Other elephants were being used to start a shuttle service to carry aged and sick people from Sittaung on the Chindwin to Tamu. There was a Forest Assistant in charge at each of the temporary camps at which they stopped on the way. Other elephants were being used to carry up rations for the evacuee rest camps. In the final stages the Bombay Burma scheme was handed over to the Government, together with the Forest Staff and elephants necessary for its operation.

The elephants and their riders continued on the work until the end of April, after which date there was no water left to water the animals. Those working on the Kalewa–Tamu road stayed there, until the retreating Army in Burma crossed the Chindwin at Kalewa, on its way out.

Our women and children were to reach Tamu by forest paths, as I thought that it would have created chaos to have travelled on the main track, with elephants among the packed crowds of refugees. I left Mawlaik with Bostock on February 14th 1942, in charge of a party of twenty women and fifteen children, with a train of elephants. The second party, under Parker and Jones, left with twenty women and twelve children, two days later. There were, altogether, forty women, twenty-seven children and one hundred and ten elephants. The reports sent us from Tamu were that it would be impossible to take elephants beyond that point. However, I was certain it could be done, even if it meant destroying them at the end of the trek, after we had reached the Imphal Plain.

In general, Bostock's job was to look after the women and children, and mine to manage the elephants. Both of us were married, and our families were with the party. Parker was also married, with his wife in the party, but Jones was a bachelor and, no doubt, glad to be put in charge of elephants only.

Fortunately, during the whole of the trek from Mawlaik to Tamu, over the route we took, there was ample fodder. We were thus able to tie the elephants up by night, and their riders were able to cut enough bamboos, branches, grass, etc., to hand-feed them. The camps from Kalewa to Tamu were well off the beaten track, and were pleasant places for the women and children. For me they were rather a nightmare, as the elephants were continually breaking loose at night, and I felt the responsibility. We reached Tamu in six marches without any incidents except one bad stampede of elephants at night, when it was lucky no one was killed. The spirit of the women was remarkable, as every one of them had had to leave a comfortable home and abandon all her possessions at a few hours' notice. The novelty of roughing it in camp kept them from brooding over their misfortunes. Their chief worry was that their husbands were remaining in Burma, no scheme having been organized for withdrawing them, even with the Army. I got very exasperated on being told by several women that I was lucky to be in charge of them, and I found it more and more difficult to return a polite answer.

Tamu had become a congested bottleneck, filled with thousands of Indians, all wondering how they would negotiate the next fifty miles, along a rough bridle-track, and over mountains five thousand feet high.

During the one day we halted there I thought it necessary to throw out all the tuskers and proceed with only thirty-two female elephants, all of them between twenty and forty-five years of age. Kit and personal luggage were cut to sixty pounds per head, as sufficient supplies of food had to be carried. A head Burman was killed on our arrival in Tamu. He was standing ten yards from me at the time, taking an air-travel suitcase, covered with labels from voyages in more civilized quarters of the globe, from an oozie sitting on an elephant's head, when the animal suddenly attacked him. I privately thought we were extremely lucky to have got so far with nothing worse happening, but the camp was greatly upset for the rest of the day.

From Tamu onwards the women became less talkative and their tempers more strained. However, I don't think any of the women in our two parties travelling on foot, but with elephant transport for kit and food, could describe the journey as anything worse than uncomfortable at times. For others it was a hellish nightmare, which became worse and worse as time went on.

I had many worries with the elephants, but the oozies remained serene. At one camp eight refugees had died of cholera and the elephants had to drop one thousand six hundred feet down from the ridge before they could get water. The women and children, however, camped on the ridge, although the ground had been fouled under every tree by the hordes who had preceded us.

We pushed on, although we were warned that it would be worse ahead. The warning proved only too accurate. The elephants were without water or fodder for thirty hours, except for twelve wild plantain stalks each, which were cut for us by some Lushai Chins from a Chin village. This just saved the situation. The elephants had to be tied up directly we reached our bivouac, and they could do no foraging for themselves. It was a big undertaking to have embarked on a sudden march, with women and children, without any rehearsal. However, every day things became better organized, and a routine was established.

Before dawn the children were pulled out of their blankets, and the camp resounded with their pathetic wails. They wondered why they were there, and what it was all about. Then, after they had been given some food, they set off on their long and weary trek with Bostock in charge. I remained behind, and supervised loading the elephants. When I had seen the last of the elephants fall into the line of march, I set off at a rapid pace, to overtake the party of women and children, and forge ahead to pick the next halting-place about nine miles farther on. The presence of water was usually the reason for my choosing it.

On the third morning, when I was passing the party, and trying to make a cheerful remark to each family as it trailed along, my wife called me back, as though she had something important to say to me; but it was to show me something. In her hand she held half a dozen wild white violets. It was a tremendous thrill for us both that she should have found them growing at five thousand feet, among the mountains of Manipur, and for a moment we were able to forget all that this march meant to us, leaving Burma and our home. The sight and scent of those fresh, perfect little flowers was a wonderful stimulus to my morale, as I walked on up the line of straggling children. Some were singing, some crying. The track was narrow, and the sides so precipitous that it was easy to roll any dead who collapsed in their journey over the edge and down into the jungle. But a tell-tale stench lingered, and at such places mothers hurried the children on, leaving their questions unanswered.

At Tengnopal the country ahead to the saddle appeared a little less trying to the elephants; and the two young Assam tea-planters, who had just arrived to set up some sort of rest camp for the hordes of refugees, told us that things were not so bad ahead to Palel. It was, however, between Tengnopal and the saddle that the elephants met the first of the bulldozers, monsters which were to become their workmates in the months and years to follow. It was what was known as a D4, which had been sent forging ahead to reconnoitre the track which was later to become the Burma Road. We had all heard rumours that some phantom engine of war lay ahead of us, but late one night Major Murray Lees came to see me in our camp, in order to ask me what was likely to happen next morning, when his baby bulldozer encountered my train of elephants, going in the opposite direction. I was quite as scared that his bulldozer would make my elephants stampede, as he was that they would charge his mechanical pet and hurl it down the precipitous slope, or khudside, with their tusks. I was careful not to give away, in our discussion, that my fears were more realistic than his.

Since we seemed to hold equally strong cards, we compromised, and decided that he should start up his bulldozer at dawn and jockey it into a position which would allow my elephants room to get by. The track where it was working was the width of an ordinary single bed, and was cut out of the side of a precipitous slope.

I went ahead to have a look at my first bulldozer, and thought that if anyone ever deserved a knighthood it was the subaltern who was working it. I watched him for ten minutes, expecting that he would crash two thousand feet with every bladeful of earth, stones and shrubs his machine excavated and pushed over the edge. I found a spot where my elephants could pass round his machine, and work was stopped while they did so, leaving the engine idling. I have been informed that in one of the stages of D.T.s the sufferer sees visions of green elephants with yellow braces. But I am sure that if elephants have D.T.s, they see bulldozers. The look on the faces of both the elephants and the oozies riding them, as they sidled round this yellow-painted D4 bulldozer, with a British subaltern perched upon it like an oozie, while it blew out a blue diesel engine exhaust from its head, was that of sufferers in the most acute stages of D.T.s, seeing things. When we reached the saddle, the roar of the larger bulldozers working up the hill could be heard, but we were able to avoid passing them, by dropping down to a foot-track to the plains from Sita. As far as the eye could see, it was marked by an irregular line of refugees, walking in single file, each with a bundle, or a child, on shoulders or head. From above it looked like a line of black ants.

We halted for an hour or so on the saddle, so as to get women and children well ahead. Eventually the word was given for us to push on, as within a few hours another larger tide of refugees was expected. I went ahead. I had been told that the track crossed many small ravines, which had been roughly bridged. There were dozens of them, and we had continual trouble in getting the elephants into the ravines and then out again, as the bridges were only made of the branches of trees, and none of them would have stood an elephant's weight. I watched all the animals pass alongside a particularly bad one, and as they went by gave orders that no one was to risk trying to cross over any bridge ahead. I then followed the last elephant, and stopped for a moment to speak a few cheering words to an unfortunate Anglo-Burman family.

Suddenly terrific yells and shouts burst out ahead of us, and, looking down the steep path, I saw odd refugees and stragglers jumping this way and that, bundles rolling into a ravine, and signs of chaos. Then I saw a riderless elephant, with its pack gone, coming up the slope towards me at a fast stride. Her ears were forward and she had an expression on her face which, I thought, meant that she was off back to Burma.

The path had cleared by magic, and I faced her alone, armed with an alpine stick fitted with a spear-head. I thought there would be an awful tragedy if I did not stop her, as there were hundreds of Indian women and children coming down the slope behind me. The valley below was ringing with shouts and yells. But she came straight at me, without hesitation, and only by hurling my spear at her and rolling down the khud did I escape being crushed. Only one of the deep narrow ravines behind me would check her.

I collected myself and my spear, and had regained the path, when I saw her come tearing back upon me at a high speed. Between us lay a deep, narrow ravine, which she must have crossed going up, though I had not seen her do so. To my amazement, I saw her 'jump' it, with an action I had never seen an elephant make before, except a hobbled animal in slow motion. But there was no slow motion here. She was over the obstacle like a 'chaser over a brook, and I jumped clear of the track. I followed her down as fast as I could, and found she had been caught, and a batch of men were helping an injured oozie out of a deep ravine. He was in charge of the last elephant in the train, and it was obvious that he had disobeyed my orders, for fear of being left too far behind. He had tried to force his mount across the bridge, but she had refused, and had pushed it down with her forefeet, with the unfortunate result that the rider and pack went headlong into the ravine, while she kept her balance on the brink. Then, like a convict making a bold bid for liberty, she had stampeded up the hill, hoping to return from the barren hills to a land of bamboos. She stood quietly to be saddled, and went on with her work. She is the only elephant I have ever seen jump something wider than it could step across, but she must have hurt herself in doing so, as she went dead lame on both fore pads within two days. But by then the trek was over.

All the way to Palel, in the Imphal Plain, we could hear the bulldozers, coming up the new road they were cutting from that end.

But was it for an army to march into Burma, or to help an army march out? The news from Burma was very grave. From Palel we were able to get motor transport to Imphal, but instead of destroying my tired and run-down elephants, I decided to march them back again, as there was more work for them to do. There was quite fair fodder and water for them near Palel, and while Bostock and I took the women and children to Dimapur, on the Assam Railway, the elephants had a well-earned rest for five days.

It was a relief to see the families off by the train on the Assam–Bengal Railway, and after we had waved goodbye, Bostock and I returned, against the tide of evacuees, to Palel and our elephants. The second party did not use elephants for the hill section from Tamu, but engaged Chin coolies.

The Assam tea-planters were travelling in the same direction, coming up with thousands of their coolies to help in constructing the road, while others were putting up relief camps for the increasing numbers of homeless Indian refugees.

We were asked if on our return journey we would take supplies, by elephant, for a projected camp for evacuees at Konkhan and build it when we got there. This we did successfully, and when we had completed it and stocked it with food we went back to Tamu and Burma.

The elephants all got back, none the worse for their journey to Manipur, and at once went on to help in the work on the Kalewa – Tamu road. The riders were still game to carry on, though by that time they realized that the fall of Burma was imminent and that India was threatened.

In this terrible upheaval big men became petty. I do not wish to blame anyone, for the struggle against odds was appalling. One night there were two thousand four hundred Indian refugees in Tamu, and only eight sacks of rice to feed them on. But the more I saw of men during those last days in Tamu in 1942 the better I liked my elephants. I don't want to criticize others, for I have no doubt I was criticized myself.

I made one final bid to get two hundred elephants out, but it was too late. I was told that if I had carried on with my plan I should have congested the one remaining walking-track for the wretched Indians, and so have caused even greater hardship and greater loss of life.

Mr Justice Braund, of the Allahabad High Court, did much stalwart work in those dark days, and in an article on the evacuation over the Manipur road said: 'It was an affair of "tea" to the rescue at one end, and "teak" to the rescue at the other. But for the help of the planters, the Indian Tea Association and the men of the Bombay Burma, it would never have been possible.'

There are few occasions in life when one is in such a tight place that one is unable to help others. But I can record two incidents, which happened when I moved out for the last time as an evacuee myself. I left Tamu on April 9th 1942, under a scorching midday sun, carrying all the kit I possessed, and leading a friend's faithful old Labrador – for I had lost my own dogs. As I turned a bend where the track took off for the first ascent into the Manipur hills, I found two sobbing little Indian children, a girl of about seven and a boy of about four. Against the bank lay an Indian girl mother, aged about twenty, dying of thirst, hunger, exhaustion and grief. I could do nothing less than give her a drink out of my water-bottle, and in her eyes I read gratitude and a terrible question: 'What will happen to my children?'

While I was looking at her, in despair of doing anything, the change came suddenly, and a moment later I realized that I was left alone with the responsibility of these children, and that every man and woman coming up the road was fighting for his or her own life, and many of them would be lucky if they could save themselves. I could not carry one child, even if I were to leave the other. Something made it impossible for me to go on, and so I turned back instead. Providence came to my aid, for within a mile I met a jeep – one of the first jeeps we had seen on that road. It was being driven by a Staff Captain, whom I had met a few days previously in Tamu.

I stepped out in front of him, blocking the track, and taking the risk that he would drive over me or send me spinning down the khudside. But he recognized me, and pulled up. Then he greeted me with the words: 'Can't be done, old chap. If I pick you up, I'll never get through, and I have to get over the mountains before dark.'

I told him I would rather die by the roadside than be seen in such a car, or take the risk of being driven by him, but I begged him to take the two children, packed under his kit in the back, and to drop them at the evacuee camp at Imphal. I was determined he should take them, and I think if he had refused I would have tried to shove his car off the road, down the khudside. But he did not, and when I had loaded the two children and watched them being driven off, there was a lump in my throat. Then I plodded on after them with a lighter heart, while the noise of the jeep grew less and less. When I had crossed the mountains for the second time, I went along to the evacuee camp at Imphal, and found both children being properly looked after in the Orphan Section.

But before then I saw many heart-rending sights, when I could give no help. At one of the wayside camps, which would obviously be washed away when the rains broke, a young Anglo-Indian spoke to me. He was sitting in a ditch near the camp, with his wife and a little girl of six huddled beside them in a blanket. They all seemed ill, and had that look that one sees only on the faces of refugees and lost animals.

The man's voice sounded as though he were delirious with fever, as he asked me if I had passed a little boy of eight, lying dead on a blanket. Without waiting for me to answer, he poured out his tragic story. He had carried his son, who was dying of pneumonia, until his wife had collapsed and could carry the little girl no farther. Then he had abandoned his dead, or dying boy, to carry the little girl and enable his wife to continue. He was haunted by the fear that the little boy wasn't actually dead, and might have been saved. By the end of the trek over the mountain both the man and his wife were casualties with pneumonia, and I discovered that when he spoke to me he had been describing what had happened to them five days before. So there could have been no question of turning back.

That road was full of tragedy and tears. But it was rapidly becoming a road. We met the bulldozers coming down, clearing a real road to Tamu, just in time to enable the Army to get out from Burma. When the elephants saw them they must have felt their day was over – but if so they were wrong, for they were needed in all the stages of the campaign.

The first army lorry reached Tamu from Manipur just before I started to walk out, and for a time the Army tried to clear the road of evacuees before the retreating troops arrived from Burma. I remember one big lorry passing me, loaded with forty people, and as it reached the bend I saw it fail to turn, and take a headlong dive, keeping upright for an amazing distance, before it was shattered on a tree. I went down to help. There were four dead and any number of broken arms and legs. This sort of accident was always happening.

When I was climbing to the saddle overlooking the Palel Plain, on my second walk out, a staff car going towards Tamu along the newly cut roadway pulled up. A Major-General got out, spoke a cheering word to me, and admired my Labrador. The wise old dog wagged his rudder and looked eagerly at the car, as if asking him to give us a lift. The General told his A.D.C. to turn his car round, at a perilous spot on the edge of the precipice, and took us as far as where the old bridle-track diverged from the new road, overlooking the Palel Plain. There the General dropped us with the words, '*Au revoir*.' His farewell words came true, for within six months I was serving under him in the Army at Tamu, when he was commanding the 20th Indian Division.

CHAPTER 13

With the fall of Burma the demand for timber in India became of increasing importance, and I was employed until the end of October in making timber surveys in Bengal and Assam, and in helping to raise a labour corps for timber extraction, for the Assam Government. If I could have laid my hands on a hundred of my timber elephants, I have no doubt my war job would have been the extraction of timber in Assam. But I could not, and I felt a gnawing ache to get back to those we had left behind in Burma. I knew well that, once we advanced down that new road, elephants and their oozies would play a big part.

Luckily I was not the only person to think so. In October 1942, I had a letter from the General Officer Commanding, Eastern Army (which later became the XIVth Army), asking me to come to see him, in order to discuss elephants, my knowledge of the Chindwin forests and the topography of Burma.

I did so, and, at his personal request, I joined his staff as Elephant Adviser, though at that time the Army had no actual elephant for me to advise him on. On November 8th 1942, I was posted to 4th Corps Headquarters, then at Jorhat in Assam. I was quite a novelty at 4th Corps Headquarters. I could speak Burmese, I knew the roads, rivers and railways of Burma, I knew the Irrawaddy river area and, most marvellous of all, I knew the jungle tracks! Intelligence Branch secured a room in which to install me, as a living ready-reference library. No doubt they intended to allow me out for a breath of fresh air at stated intervals, but on one of these airings I greatly shocked them, and indeed the whole of Headquarters, by going direct to the Commander.

'Might I disturb you for five minutes, sir?' I asked.

'Yes, sit down. What can I do?'

'I want a jeep of my own, and I want to get down to Tamu to find out if there are any elephants not yet in the hands of the Japs.'

I got my jeep within three days, a feat which had been regarded by everyone as an impossibility, but even that was easier than getting out of the clutches of Intelligence Branch. Eventually they let me go, on the understanding that I might be recalled at any moment to meet an important personage.

I was free again, this time with my own jeep, and on my way to Tamu I got in contact with the Forward Division Headquarters, and from the General Officer Commanding got permission to pull out Harold Browne, a great friend of mine. I had known Harold from his first days as a Forest Assistant. He was a South African by birth and a man of magnificent physique, with broad shoulders and narrow hips, Scandinavian blue eyes, and hairy all over, like a gorilla. On his arrival in Burma he had taken to the jungle like a duck to water, and he never minded the loneliness of the life; indeed, he often preferred to be alone, even when he was on leave, though at other times he threw himself into riotous parties and entertained lavishly. He was a man without vices, though certain of his characteristics almost ranked as such. One of them was always over-calling his hand at bridge or poker, another was an inordinate passion for crossword puzzles, and the third was that he was an impenitent practical joker. I remember at one gala dance at Maymyo he put sardine sandwiches into the handbags of all the women who were dancing, and had the audacity to sympathize with various girls who pulled them out when they stopped to powder their noses after that dance was over. He even went about saying: 'Some awful cad must be at large.' He had made the mistake, however, of putting one in my wife's bag; she instantly recognized his handiwork and exposed him. On a similar occasion he let loose an enormous number of mole crickets of the largest size in the ladies' room and on the dance-floor. They at once took wing and settled everywhere, exhibiting a particular fondness for seeking shelter for their silky bodies in the bosoms and down the backs of the girls wearing the lowest frocks. Panic reigned and modesty disappeared, as the girls' partners helped, with nervous fingers, to track down the bolder and more enterprising insects. Harold, however, had not waited to watch the results of his crime, but had gone off for a solitary moonlight swim.

Not long after he became my Number One officer he gave way once more to his propensity for practical joking. Part of his duty in forward areas was to pick up anything suspicious and send it back to Intelligence Headquarters for investigation. Sometimes when nothing turned up he used to scribble mysterious messages in Burmese on scraps of paper and plant them where they would be found and sent back. In this way he kept the wretched interpreters busy. But as these efforts produced no visible reaction, he came to me one day with a much-crumpled bit of paper on which something or other was printed in Japanese characters. I told him to send it back to Intelligence Headquarters, and he remarked with perfect sang-froid. 'I bet it will give that little schoolmaster who taught English in Tokyo something to scratch his head over.' I had forgotten the incident when, about a month later, Harold brought me in a young Intelligence officer who had come up from Headquarters to speak to me. Unlocking an important-looking despatch-case, the officer produced a sealed envelope, and from the envelope he extracted the scrap of paper printed in Japanese characters, which I recognized. I leant forward hoping to hear something of real interest. Browne, however, gave a howl of laughter the moment he saw it, and I then saw a piece of paper attached to it with the words written in red ink: 'Advertisement for Eno's Fruit Salts. Ascertain who sent in this document'. By laughing too soon, Harold had almost given himself away. In Burma bottles of Eno's used to be wrapped in an advertisement extolling their merits in various Oriental languages, and when he was taking an early morning dose, Harold had noticed that one of them was in Japanese. The Intelligence officer was more than suspicious, and I had to take the matter up on a much higher level than I should have liked before I could smooth it over.

It was difficult to talk to Harold Browne seriously, for though he was thirty-five years old he had remained a mischievous schoolboy who would not grow up. However, I did my best, and he regretfully abandoned manufacturing suspicious objects with which to plague Headquarters and pull the legs of the experts.

Harold Browne was one hundred per cent loyal to me as an officer and as a friend, and he would fight tooth and nail to secure fair play for our Burman oozies.

During the war the Kabaw Valley became his estate, and he was a wonderful host for the senior officers who visited my camp.

In the first months, before I got hold of him, Harold Browne had volunteered to remain behind as a liaison officer with No. 1 Brigade, and had done a sterling job of work for them between May and October.

During these months he was the only officer with a knowledge of Burma who kept in contact with the Kabaw Valley right down to the banks of the Chindwin. On occasions during his patrols he had used a few straggling elephants recruited with their oozies from villages to which the Japs had not yet penetrated.

During the rains of 1942 the Japs had not penetrated as far as Tamu even with patrols. At Lokechao we met the Headquarters of No. 49 Brigade, the then forward brigade.

Just before we arrived at Tamu, a young Anglo-Burman, named Goldberg, who had joined Civil Affairs, had accompanied a patrol to Auktaung, near Sittaung on the Chindwin, in an endeavour to make contact with a party of Burmese with forty elephants which, it was said, had been ordered to march to Mawlaik by the Japanese.

The headman at Auktaung turned out, unquestionably, to be working for the Japs, and he had ordered the oozies of these elephants to march them to Mawlaik. The officer in charge of the patrol – quite rightly, I think, in this case – showed him no mercy, while Goldberg, on his own initiative, went and talked to the Burmese elephant-riders. They were due to march next day, to join the Japs, but Goldberg, who knew many of them, persuaded them to march as hard as possible to the Upper Teelaung Creek and then head west for Tamu. There were more elephants than there were oozies, and it had been planned to leave these behind, if they had joined the Japs. But, on hearing that we should be at Tamu to meet them, the oozies' women volunteered to ride the riderless elephants and bring them along. They set off by night, and showed great boldness, as the oozies and their families ran a big risk of running into Japanese patrols in the jungles of the Teelaung Creek, which were a no-man's-land, but which Japanese patrols visited more frequently than ours did.

It was wonderful to be able to welcome these oozies in Tamu. This batch of elephants was the nucleus of what eventually became No. 1 Elephant Company, Royal Indian Engineers.

There was sufficient timber-dragging gear to equip twenty-five of them. Some of the others were trained calves under twenty, only fit for transport work, and the remainder were either thin and out of condition, heavy with calf, or with babies at heel, and would, from an Army point of view, have been better out of the way at that time.

Experiments had been made by an Anti-Aircraft Bofors Gun Regiment with an adaptable platform that made it possible to break the Bofors gun down sufficiently for transport on elephants. I was ordered to experiment and report on the type of gear necessary for loading it on elephants. It did not take long, for we found that the standard pack, known as the Siamese pack, would take the gun. It was also found that the Burmese oozies and their attendants could load and unload the elephants very quickly without assistance. The gun-crews did not, therefore, need training in loading elephants. A section of eight elephants took one gun, with the spare barrel, reserve ammunition and all the kit of the British gun-crew, without difficulty.

These experiments were not followed up. Had the necessity arisen, the elephants would have provided invaluable transport, for they could have negotiated the most precipitous forest tracks over the hills, where no mechanical transport could have been taken.

The elephants used in the experiments remained quite unperturbed seventy-five yards from where the Bofors gun was firing. This was the only foundation for a tale the Gunners told the Infantry – that we had plans to have elephants in close support of the infantry, each with a gun fired off its back!

A signal I sent to the Commandant Royal Artillery, that I was supplying a certain regiment of anti-aircraft gunners with 'eight good weight-carrying females, for experiment', was interpreted in many ways, which I need not go into in detail. Such hopes were disappointed when the female elephants turned up.

At this early period an incident occurred which made my plans of getting in touch with my former elephant-riders in the no-man's-land between Mawlaik and Tamu far more difficult to realize. A patrol had gone down to Yuwa, unfortunately without Goldberg, and had shot the only village elder of any importance there, U Nwa.

This was a great blow, and a set-back to all my hopes.

U Nwa was a Burman, aged sixty, who had worked in the closest contact with Europeans engaged in teak extraction in the jungle for forty years. He was possessed of all the instincts of a gentleman. His name was known to practically every Burman from the Upper Chindwin down to Mandalay, and it was never mentioned without the word 'Auza' cropping up, a word which is not easily translatable. 'Authority with labour' is the nearest I can get. U Nwa was a born leader of the Burmans. He was always naturally at ease with Europeans, and was completely without any inferiority complex. At the time of the evacuation he was believed to be wealthy for a jungle Burman. He had twelve thousand rupees in the Provident Fund, and private savings in the hands of his wife, who was one of the leading traders in Yuwa. U Nwa had remained quite unperturbed by visits of Japanese and British patrols to his village.

The only reason for suspecting him was that he had not fled into the jungle when a British patrol arrived. U Nwa was bewildered by all that had happened during the last six months, but he had never doubted our promise that we should return, and had been waiting patiently for someone to arrive. He came up to welcome the British, but, to his amazement, found that not one of them could speak Burmese.

U Nwa was tied to a tree at ten o'clock at night, and shot at dawn.

The effect of this action was electric. The news at once spread back to the Japs, who were employing jungle Burmans and elephants in every way they could, and of course it was a piece of heaven-sent propaganda for them.

But no time was lost in ensuring that the officer responsible got no more chances of going out with patrols. Luckily Tommy Thomas of the

Burma Civil Service was at Tamu, and both he and I put in red-hot reports on the incident.

Only someone who, like myself, has had the difficult task of making contacts with the Burmese elephant-riders during the two years of stalemate on the Burma–India border can possibly realize the lasting consequences and repercussions of this disastrous beginning to our work. The dearth of Burmese-speaking British officers in forward areas in those days of late 1942 and early 1943 was a tragedy. It was due to the disastrous 'reconstruction' organized in the Simla Hills, which took away many qualified men from where they could be most useful.

A journalist who visited Tamu in November 1942, described it as 'a city of the dead', but in reality it was a jungle village, in which hundreds of private cars, lorries and buses had been abandoned by refugees, since the road came to an end, and they could take them no farther. When I had last seen these cars they were all empty, and their owners were struggling to climb the mountain side.

But now, when I came back, I saw that these abandoned, derelict cars were filled with grisly figures, unbelievably emaciated, with rags still clinging to them here and there. Some sat rigid in the seats, some were tumbled into shapeless heaps, some were bent, some bowed, some sat behind the steering-wheels, gazing through the windscreens from the empty sockets of their skulls.

These were our rearguard from Burma, unfortunates who had reached Tamu after the withdrawal of our Army, when the monsoon had broken; unfortunates too worn out to tackle the mountain crossing in the floods and without food; unfortunates who had no hope left and, unable to find other shelter from the torrential rain, had climbed into the deserted cars and died in them, six months ago.

One landmark which stood in Tamu for some time, untouched, was a military ambulance, with four stretcher beds, each with a skeleton lying on it. Something had gone wrong with the engine, and the retreating Army had abandoned it, transferring any casualties it may originally have carried. Four poor wretches had found shelter in it, and perhaps had even felt that they were luckier than their neighbours, in being able to lie down, at full length, on well-slung stretchers to die.

Harold Browne eventually rid us of that gruesome reminder of the previous summer, by setting fire to it. He made away with hundreds of similar ghastly sights, all along the trail, by the same method.

In such surroundings we pitched camp at Moreh, close to Tamu, to wait for the coming of a new army. Occasionally we saw one of our patrols going out.

Almost every day representatives of all sorts of different Army services visited us, but all of them had to return to their headquarters at Imphal every night. One of the first to arrive was the Commandant Royal Engineers of the forward division, who called on me at our camp at Moreh to ask if we could help with elephants, to drag a few logs, and assist the sappers in building a bridge over the Lokechao River at Moreh, as a brigade was to move forward, but could not possibly do so until it had been bridged. I replied that of course we could, but asked what kind of bridge did the sappers mean to build, and where were they? Blue prints, pink prints, and even white prints were produced from a pigskin portfolio. My first impression was that I was being shown a design for the new Ava–Mandalay bridge! All these plans were merely to cross a river four feet deep and two hundred feet wide, full of fast-flowing, clear water. He told me the sappers would not be able to get up for some time, as they were busily engaged on a hill section farther back, but that timber was required in readiness.

I picked up a pencil and drew him an 'elephant bridge', and after making a rough calculation of the number of logs that would be wanted and the number of elephants available, told him it would take me fifteen days to complete it without any assistance from the sappers, and that it would take anything in the Division on wheels or tracks.

'What class will it be, and what width?' asked the officer.

'First class, and twelve foot wide,' I answered.

'No, I mean what tonnage vehicle will it take? The Chief Engineer wants it to be twenty-two foot wide.'

'What is your heaviest load?' I asked.

'About ten tons.'

'Well, I will guarantee it will take a twenty-ton load, and you can tell the Chief Engineer that he can't have it twenty-two foot wide. When we've finished this bridge, we'll build another one for vehicles going in the opposite direction. In any case there would not be enough timber for a twenty-two foot bridge at the site you've chosen. But we'll find another site nearby, for the second bridge. Moreover, Indian drivers are safer if they have a bridge to themselves – from what I've seen of our lorry-drivers, we shall do better without two-way traffic over rivers.'

The Commandant Royal Engineers put his plans away reluctantly, and was obviously somewhat doubtful about these new methods of bridging rivers. Then he said, 'It's O.K. by me, but I must be getting back, and will see the Chief Engineer and let you know the day after tomorrow.'

Before his jeep was out of earshot I was giving orders to my head elephant-man to arrange for the felling and logging of trees, four to six feet in girth with boles twenty-five feet long. All the riders were to make dragging harness for twenty-five elephants.

Browne had the work under way before ten o'clock next morning.

Shortly after this the Brigadier of the 49th Brigade arrived to have a look at this circus camp in front of him. He had come out of Burma, in command of a Scottish regiment with the Burma Army. I explained the whole thing to him, and he cheered me up a lot by saying: 'Don't worry a damn about anyone. Build your bridge, and if the sappers want another, they can build another.' It was then December 2nd, and he told me confidentially that the bridge would be needed by the nineteenth.

Actually the whole of his brigade transport passed over that bridge on the fifteenth. The elephants were of great interest while they were building this bridge, and many visitors to Tamu came forward to watch them.

On December 20th, much to my annoyance, I received à signal to return to Corps Headquarters at Jorhat in Assam for another conference on the carriage of Bofors guns on elephants. This started up another war on the subject of whether elephants were transport or bridge-building animals. Fortunately, on Christmas Eve I went into the Planters Club at Jorhat, and there I met Stanley White.

He was, until the war, a River Captain of the Irrawaddy Flotilla Company. His jub, buoying the Chindwin River, brought him into contact with the Bombay Burma staff. Our Forest Assistants often travelled on his launch, and he shared their interest in jungle life, and, as he was a very keen shot, joined in all the shoots up and down the banks of the river.

White and I were often referred to as 'the long and the short of it', as White was not more than five foot four inches high. He was a powerfully built, square-shouldered little man who could keep up with the best of us on a long trek. He delighted in dressing himself up like a Christmas tree, carrying a gigantic rucksack, with an enormous revolver-holster hiding half of one side of him, and an outsize in jungle knives bumping up and down in its sheath over his fat little stern. White always walked like a sailor, with a salt-sea roll. He was a typical Scot, with a sense of humour which sparkled in his blue eyes. He had a very large fund of general information, and if by any chance there was something he did not know, he could bluff so well that he was seldom detected. I once heard him telling an innocent Colonel in the Royal Veterinary Corps how to castrate an elephant, and White was so glib and so convincing with his nonsense that I was quite impressed myself.

He spoke fluent Hindustani and good Burmese, and was thus a very useful interpreter at Corps Headquarters. During the evacuation of

Burma and the final period of 'scorched earth', White did a great job in scuttling launches up and down the river. He was naturally intensely eager to get back to his river, and soon after joining me became known to everyone as 'Chindwin White'.

I had not known him particularly well before the war, but we had many interests in common, and as he was a great friend of Harold Browne's, we soon became as inseparable as the Three Musketeers.

White shared the greater part of the rest of the Burma Campaign with me. We sometimes got separated, but, as he was exactly the man I wanted, I left no stone unturned to get him back on the job I knew he could do best. I got the very best out of him, and he stuck to me.

Harold Browne and Chindwin White made a grand team. Their intimate knowledge of all Burmans was extraordinarily useful.

They had the same love of practical jokes, and had one trick in particular, which they often brought out if they thought it would perturb some visitor to our camp.

They would start an argument in Burmese, which at first amused visitors who did not understand a word. Then their faces would grow grimly serious, and English words would creep into the dispute – unpleasant English words and phrases which are not often employed by one man to another. For they translated freely the foulest Burmese abuse of each other's families and particular relatives.

One night they started this, after having several drinks, and, though I had heard them at it before, it seemed to me they were getting a bit hot. They were sitting on opposite sides of a long bamboo table with a hurricane lamp in the middle. Each was holding a tin mug full of rum and lime juice in his hand, and they took turns, one sipping his drink and glaring over the top of his mug, while the other treated him to the foulest abuse.

Suddenly Chindwin brought out a grossly offensive remark about Harold Browne's sister, and I felt he had gone too far. Mothers and aunts are fair game, but I felt this remark about Harold's sister was beyond a joke – and Harold seemed to think so, too, for he dashed the contents of his mug in Chindwin's face. There was a dead silence, and Chindwin sat for a moment with his eyes tightly shut, while the precious rum and lime juice streamed down his face. Then he suddenly flung the contents of his mug in Harold's face, and, grabbing the hurricane lamp in his other hand, swung it at Harold Browne's head. There was a crash of broken glass, and the lamp went out. I felt sure Harold had been badly hurt, but peals and peals of laughter came from them both as they sat in the darkness, and a convivial evening followed after we lighted up again, much to the relief of our visitors, who had thought that they were witnessing a very ugly scene.

Chindwin White always tried to give the impression that he thought everyone he met was a fool, but he had most loyal feelings and a real respect for anyone who really knew his job, and for such people he would work his fingers to the bone.

When I met him at Jorhat he was a round peg in a square hole, and he pleaded that the obvious place for him was with me up at Tamu.

I much enjoyed a convivial Christmas Eve with him, but on Christmas morning I decided that Intelligence Branch would be a useful lever with which to extract him from his square hole. I put it up to them, and got the answer: 'The very man we want immediately.'

Within an hour I had got him into my cage, and we were busy on a job of work passed on from the Commander. This kept us busy for half Christmas night, but we finished the bottle and finished the job about simultaneously, and then sang a carol. White was soon christened 'Chindwin White', while I was commonly known as 'Sabu', which changed later on into 'Elephant Bill'.

CHAPTER 14

My one idea was to get away to Tamu again, taking White with me. This led to another battle with Intelligence Branch. It ended by my telling them that the only information I possessed which might be of use to them was the female elephant's period of gestation. I have reason to believe that they took this personally, as an obscure reflection on themselves.

On White's being asked the depth of the Chindwin River opposite Sittaung, he replied that it all depended whether the tide was in or out; at which a young Intelligence Officer exclaimed: 'Oh, is it tidal up there?' As Sittaung is fifteen hundred miles from the nearest tidal stretch, the innocent question gave us an advantage which we pressed. However, we remained friends with them, and for a long time we made use of the Intelligence Office as a haven whenever we visited Corps Headquarters.

I think that even Intelligence Branch would admit we gave them some valuable information, which was lost or mislaid a dozen times, before it was eventually made use of three years later, by which time an elephant cow might have had a second litter.

I was just about to get away when the Commander sent for me and told me he wanted me to stay on at least another two days, as a visiting Brigadier wanted to see me. I suggested that White should also be called in, if any information about crossing the Chindwin were wanted. I was told I might take him with me if I liked.

On January 3rd 1943, I was told to wait in the anteroom of the Commander's mess at nine o'clock. White was with me. The mess was empty, and I had just picked up a magazine when a sullen-faced Brigadier came in, wearing only one ribbon – the D.S.O. and bar.

He threw his hat into a chair, and said, as though he were angry:

'Are you Williams?'

'Yes, sir.'

'Well, come on. Have you got the key of the War Room?'

'Yes,' I replied.

With that we moved off to the Commander's War Room. The Brigadier went in first, and, as I followed, White gave me a dig in the ribs from behind, from which I gathered that he guessed that my reaction had been that I was not going to be bullied.

Wingate, the name of the Brigadier, at that time meant nothing whatever, except to those of the Higher Command. He kept me for two hours standing in front of a very well-illuminated wall-map, on a scale of half an inch to the mile, and he stood directly behind me, with a pointer in his hand. His questions were abrupt, and my replies equally so. He had ignored White, with such rudeness that whenever he put a question concerning the Chindwin River I turned round and asked White to reply.

Wingate's manners were almost intolerably aggressive, but within an hour I was deeply impressed, and within another half-hour I was completely absorbed in what was obviously the general plan. I felt that if I did not go with him, the whole damned shooting-party would get lost in the Burmese jungles within a week. Most of it was.

Part of that story is told in Bernard Fergusson's beautiful book, *Beyond the Chindwin*.

While I was being questioned in detail, on jungle, streams, mountains and valleys, and my answers written down, I was making up my mind what I would reply if I were asked to join this wild-cat expedition, as I fully expected to be at the end of the interview. But the question never came, and I only afterwards found out that Wingate had been told that he could not have me, and that I was to continue with my job as Elephant Adviser, which lasted throughout the Burma Campaign.

The thing which impressed me about Wingate was the thought behind each of his questions. Pointing to some high ground on the map –

a hill I knew – he would ask: 'Could troops live on that hill during the monsoon, and make it a strongpoint, if they had to?'

'All depends how many, sir. It is practically impossible to dig in, as it is mostly solid rock, only covered with very sparse jungle. It might water twenty-five men, but no more. Mules could not get up and down.'

'Could mules get down that creek?'

'Definitely not. Elephants could. But mules could take this ridge away to the east, by following Forest Department boundaries.'

'Right. I want that information later.'

Before he went away, leaving us to lock up, I asked him if he was likely to require any elephant pack on either side of the Chindwin. A decided 'No' was his reply.

White and I went off to Tamu next day, and discussed Wingate for most of the way.

When we got back we found that during our absence Browne had completed three more bridges – one going north to Myothit, one south to Witok, and one east towards Sittaung. White was to go off on a reconnaissance to Sittaung. By the end of January, 23rd Division had its Headquarters at Moreh, near Tamu. I found that the Brigadier of 49th Brigade had laid out Tamu and its surrounding roads and bridges, and had named our first bridge 'Williams Bridge', and the second 'Browne Low Bridge', with large placards bearing their names beside them. They stayed there, and the names stuck. Even the local Burmans used them, but I found it embarrassing. Later that season I saw Wingate's columns pass through Tamu. A personal friend of mine, Peter Buchanan, was with one of them. His exploits are recorded in *Beyond the Chindwin*.

Unknown to anyone but him, I arranged for elephants to help his party over the Tonhe track, to clear it for mules, and I provided twelve pack-elephants to help him as far as Tonhe. His was the only Wingate column that got its complete equipment as far as the Chindwin.

Wingate's own column got half-way from Tamu to the Chindwin, and came across a Burman, Maung Chit Gyi, building a bridge, with four elephants. He ordered him, at the point of his revolver, to remove their harness, and then loaded them up with everything that he would otherwise have left behind. Sticky bombs, boxes of grenades and other heavy equipment were tied on anyhow with rope. These four elephants did the journey to the Chindwin, with far less trouble than the mules, and Wingate was so satisfied that he swam them across the Chindwin with their full loads on. One badly loaded animal overturned in deep water, and was lost.

However, he had not gone far on the other bank when, greatly to his surprise, he received a signal ordering him to send my elephants back.

One went astray, and only two came back with Maung Chit Gyi. However, the stray one eventually swam across the Chindwin on her own, and rejoined her companions, with a fine story of adventure, if she chose to tell it.

Wingate only used one or two stray elephants on the east bank of the Chindwin during that campaign. In fact, his column came across very few, and gained no information concerning the herds left behind.

Two months later, parties of Wingate's expedition were recrossing the Chindwin, north of Yuwa as far as Homalin.

Malcolm Freshney, returning with his party – which included some Karens, who had come out with the Burma Army in May 1942 – met two Karen elephant-riders in dense jungle, about fifty miles east of the Chindwin. They said, when questioned, that they came from an elephant camp with twenty-nine elephants and forty-nine Karens, who were in hiding from the Japs, and that they had been there for six months. The Karens are a particularly loyal hill tribe. These two men were very friendly, were Christians and very pro-British, so Freshney decided to spend a night in their camp. There were two English-speaking Karens amongst those at the camp, and in the course of conversation they told Freshney that they had worked under me in the Moo and Shweli Forests. When he told them that I was at Tamu, three of them asked to join his party, as far as Tamu, so that they could see me.

He brought these three Karens along, and they were of immense importance to Intelligence Branch. One of them had travelled since the Japanese invasion as far south as Toungoo between Mandalay and Rangoon, in Lower Burma.

The Divisional Commander then gave help, in providing an escort to return with these men to their camp. I knew the country well enough to plan their route there and back when they would make an attempt to bring their elephants back to us across the Chindwin, and through territory occupied by camps working for the enemy.

Two young officers who knew Burma – Jonah Jones and Robin Stewart, both in an Intelligence Branch – reached Tamu at that time, and they both volunteered to go with the Karens and make the attempt. Browne was unfortunately not in camp at the time.

Wingate's expedition had, of course, stirred up the Japs, and their patrols were becoming increasingly difficult to elude, for they were following up tired parties of Wingate's men, or trying to intercept them during their withdrawal.

Stewart and Jones covered the fifty miles on the other bank of the Chindwin in two days, relying on their own irregulars, and leaving the escort party half-way, to cover their rear.

I had asked for two platoons to cover the Chindwin crossing, as at that time Pantha was occupied by the enemy, and our crossing was to be made just above Yuwa, at Kadun. Jones and Stewart performed a remarkable feat on the return journey, marching twenty-nine elephants, with forty-nine attendants and their irregular escort, fifty miles back to the Chindwin in two days, reaching the river at 6 p.m. There were no women with the party. Jones reached the river a few hours before the main body, and met a small party of Burmans, which was obviously a Japanese agent's scouting patrol from Pantha. They did not engage, but made off south towards Pantha. White was in charge of eight Lundwin country boats, for ferrying the escort and men. The two platoons of troops which were supposed to cover the crossing had not turned up. There was only a section of Indian troops, which was obviously considerably rattled. The forty-nine Karens were unarmed.

From the time of arrival until dark every effort was made to swim the elephants. But the animals were all too dead beat from their march to face the swim, and not one leader could be found among them. A decision was eventually made to tie up all the elephants on the east bank and to ferry all personnel across and sleep on the west bank. The expected platoons to cover the crossing had still not arrived.

All was quiet on both banks of the river during the night. At dawn White set off with his eight boats full of oozies and a small escort from the west bank to the east. Now that the elephants and men had rested, there was no doubt that they could cross without difficulty. White was in the leading boat with the head boatman holding the paddle-rudder, and two other Burmans rowing. The other seven boats were strung out at irregular intervals, and packed with Karen oozies.

When White's boat was about seventy-five yards from the east bank, a Japanese officer rushed onto the bank shouting, 'Banzai! banzai!' and then took cover behind a tree. At the same time Japanese machine-gun, rifle and mortar fire opened on the boats. A few shots were fired in return, but several of the leading boats at once capsized, and within two minutes everyone was in the water. Three sepoys and one Karen were killed, and two Karens were wounded. Everyone else swam successfully back to the west bank. White considers that he owed his escape to the Japanese concentrating their fire on his topee, which floated away downstream, whilst he was swimming underwater. He had never realized that a man could hold his breath for so long. The Japanese had been brought up from Pantha during the night and, finding our elephants unattended, had laid an ambush for the morning.

The Japanese showed great folly in not holding their fire. If they had waited until the boats were ten yards from the shore not one man of the party would have survived. Their shooting was also extremely poor. It was not until 1945, after our general advance down the Chindwin, that I heard the true story of the fate of these elephants.

A dacoit Burman from Pantha, who was with the Japanese, and was one of their agents, told them that as they were Karen elephants, no Burman would risk unchaining them. He therefore advised shooting them for their ivory. Fourteen were shot before some Burmans arrived, who said they could manage the remainder, all of which were young animals. Only one of these was eventually recaptured, after the Japanese had been finally defeated.

The whole incident, which with better management would have succeeded, was most unfortunate. I may add that it did not end there for those who should have provided the platoons to cover the crossing of the river, and had not done so.

Seventeen elephants were captured during the hot weather of 1943, bringing our strength up to fifty-seven animals. They were first employed in building bridges along the three roads in the Kabaw Valley, and later in making these bridges double width. By that time the elephants had established their reputation in the military mind as bridge-builders and road-makers of immense value.

There were patrol clashes with the enemy throughout the hot weather. We had only two brigades guarding the gateway from the Kabaw Valley to Imphal, so they were rather thinly spread out over the ground. Straggling parties of Wingate's columns were still coming back, through the screen of the 23rd Division, protecting the Tamu–Imphal road. The Japanese had been becoming more aggressive farther south, from Kalemyo up towards Tiddim in the Chin Hills.

The Mango showers of April gave the troops some idea of the effects of rain in the Kabaw Valley.

The 17th Division of the Burma Army on their withdrawal up it, the previous May, had nicknamed it 'The Valley of Death', because they were following the tragic trail of refugees, who were dying in hundreds along the road from exhaustion, starvation, cholera, dysentery and smallpox.

But the name stuck, and had an unfortunate psychological effect upon the health of the troops holding it later on. Actually malaria was no worse in the Kabaw Valley than in any other forest valley in the wet zone. But it had gained an evil reputation, and did not live it down until the 11th East African Division went down it, before the end of the 1944 monsoon, and showed that it could be faced with impunity, even in the worst weather.

I was living in our established elephant camp at Moreh, but I made periodic visits to Corps Headquarters in Assam. As a result, I was one of those who were kept informed of the general position. Only those who have had the experience of keeping up the morale and confidence of their men when privately aware that we were carrying out a strategy of mere bluff, which might at any time collapse, can understand the difficulties and embarrassments I went through at this time. In May 1943, I was called to Headquarters and told to write an appreciation of the elephant situation if all troops were withdrawn from the valley before the monsoon broke. My appreciation was expressed in very few words:

'The elephants must remain in the valley, and Browne and I will stay there with them. All we need is six months' rations for the riders and ourselves. We will keep the elephants ready to make their escape to Imphal, if the Japanese patrols come up far enough to threaten us.'

The value of the elephants when our troops re-entered the valley after the monsoon was over was fully realized. But I was not willing to take them out and upset the morale of my Burmans, by making them take part in another retreat by our Army. I was also doubtful whether I should be able to get the elephants back again at the right time, as directly our Army started to come back, the road would be packed with faster mechanical transport.

My proposal met considerable opposition, but I eventually got it sanctioned, and was told to make my own arrangements. Luckily I had plenty of time, as the withdrawal of the 23rd Division had not started.

Just at this time the inhabitants of Tamu and the surrounding villages in the valley gave a celebration pwai to welcome the return of our Army. They had been a little slow in organizing it, and, unfortunately, had timed it when we were on the point of abandoning them again. After I had taken an extra tot of rum, I danced with the Minthami, or Princess of the Show, and towards the end of the evening U Po Sine, my head elephant-man was presented with a beautifully engraved sword by the Commander of 23rd Indian Division.

It was a great night for the Burmans, and a cheery one while it lasted, but I went to bed with the bitter knowledge that the valley would be empty of troops again within two months, at most. As it fell out the withdrawal was delayed for a fortnight owing to events to the south-west, in which the 17th Division was involved. The monsoon broke early, and caught the 49th Brigade still in the valley at Witok. Within two days all motor transport was bogged. There was a small break in the rain, and then the vehicles were able to start crawling back. But they could never have done it except for my elephants. All along the road there were urgent requests for help, and the elephants were pulling the army lorries out of the mud like champagne corks out of bottles. Two or three lorries were wrecked owing to drivers starting up their engines, in order to help the elephants, by spinning the back wheels. But they found themselves and the lorry being taken for a fifty-yard stampede into the jungle, ending up with the lorry hitting a tree or overturning, or the elephant's chains snapping and releasing him from the jungle devil he was towing.

Besides pulling lorries out of tight places, the elephants laid causeways of logs in the mud in amazingly quick time, while whole convoys waited to pass over them. Elephants could not he hurried in their work, but they could, and did, work overtime until the job was finished. After seeing the last vehicle over the Moreh causeway, the Brigade Major walked along the logs to tell me that all the motor transport were out.

The elephants were standing near, in the fast-fading light, and gazing, with what I thought was bewilderment and disgust, at this new kind of jungle demon, the motor lorry. What the oozies thought of the withdrawal of our Army, I don't know. All I could tell them was that Browne and I were staying behind with them.

Those really were, I think, the filthiest rains that two Europeans ever weathered in Burma. There were weekly Gurkha patrols through our camp, and elephants were used throughout, on a shuttle system, to get them across that quagmire of a valley. The Gurkhas were grand little men, but, fit as they were, they often came back after a patrol of anything from eight to twelve days staggering with exhaustion and fever. No quinine or mepacrine was being issued to them at that time, owing to the mistaken order that only a doctor could administer it!

Our elephant camp was the first camp they reached on their way home, and for the last three marches they always rode elephants. The sick men had to be brought back on elephants, and in that swamp those that were still fit could not keep up with them. So we provided enough animals to carry all of them. Their rations were sent down, on a separate shuttle system, as far as Mintha, throughout the rains. No elephant or oozie ever let them down.

I found it rather a heartbreaking job at times trying to teach not only Indian soldiers, but also British officers, that an elephant is an animal which needs quite as much care as a mule. It was far more valuable at that time, as mules would have got bogged at once in the quagmire of mud.

At last, in desperation, I issued general notes on elephant management. In spite of that, elephants were still kept tied to trees for hours and hours on end, waiting at rendezvous points for patrols, instead of being allowed to graze on nearby fodder. As a result their digestions were upset for no good reason. Animals were also loaded in any fashion, with no attention to balancing the loads. The Gurkha, who is a jolly little man, thought it very funny to be riding an elephant, and it was quite common for me to catch as many as six of them on the back of one animal, with their rifle-slings looped round the animal's ears, as though on a hatstand. On several occasions when I caught them doing this they would slide off over the hindquarters *en masse* and bolt into the jungle, to hide from me, like schoolchildren caught climbing apple trees. I finally got my way, by a resolute refusal to supply elephants to any troops who would not co-operate in treating them properly.

The whole subject also led to a battle between the Royal Indian Army Service Corps and the Royal Engineers, partly to decide which of them could obtain priority in the use of elephants, and partly to determine the perennial military question of whether elephants were a branch of transport or of sappers. To those who knew conditions in the Chindwin areas and what lay ahead of us, it was a foregone conclusion that elephants would ultimately be used as sappers. However, in those early days it was a case of trying to be of the greatest use to both parties, and please them both.

Although the position was obvious to anyone working with elephants in the field, the problem was far too difficult for General Headquarters to decide. Elephant Companies were raised later on, and such questions as their war equipment and war establishment were involved, and the question of their status dragged on until after the war with Japan was over; and I am by no means sure that it is settled yet. I see now that I ought to have invoked precedent, and called up the ghost of Daisy, in the Royal Engineers, in 1895. At the time I was concerned only in getting on with the job and keeping the animals fit. I had no time to spend months arguing on paper in an Indian depot over Elephant Companies. But it was lamentable that our work should have suffered owing to the inability of someone to cut through red tape, or for the sake of what was a purely academic question, in a paper organization.

The elephants, however, were not the chief sufferers from this lamentable incompetence. After burying eight men and two officers in my own little private cemetery, and making the teak crosses for their graves myself in my hut in the evenings, I became so frantic about the idiotic order which prohibited their taking quinine that I secretly supplied each patrol as it was going out with sufficient supplies of it for any man going down with malaria. Even so, I had to make fourteen crosses by the end of those rains. Twelve of them were for men whose lives had been thrown away for no reason.

It was an eerie camp. Most of the time there was nothing between us and the Japanese but dripping jungle. My oozies were, however, in contact with all the small villages scattered up and down the valley. I had implicit faith in them as a screen which would give us early warning of the approach of any Japanese patrol.

Some changes took place in my party. Chindwin White went off to take up a job on the Arakan front, and C. W. Hann, an Anglo-Burman, joined Browne and me.

In July the log bridge over the Lokechao was swept away like matchwood, but a small Bailey bridge, which had been put up well above the gorge and over it, remained.

We had several scares, for the jungle is a land of rumours. But the Japanese made no attempt to interfere with the roadhead at Tamu, and my elephants were kept busy doing everything possible to prepare for the re-entry of the Army. But when?

CHAPTER 15

We prayed that in October 1943 we should launch the offensive to recover Burma. Elephant Camp became a hostel that autumn, where everyone dropped in. No place was ever visited by so many specialists. We remained a hostel until the following March. There was a field telephone connected, and we became a general information bureau as well. I was constantly being rung up and told: 'An important person is arriving tomorrow at 10 a.m. Apart from other things he would like to see the elephants at work. Will you put him up?'

Apart from the cheery company, the interest of it all provided me with the best memories I have of that camp. Everyone who stayed there will no doubt remember the friendly arguments over the camp-fire. There was no red tape. The General Staff must have been told a dozen times at least how and when to retake Burma! The earliest of my visitors were, however, malariologists and tank experts.

For me it meant spending whole days in jeeps, going right down the valley, as there was no way of imparting one's knowledge so well as on the ground. The malariologists tried to damp my enthusiasm by telling me that the lwins (small open marshes which occur in dense jungle) could not be breeding-grounds for malaria mosquitoes, as they were still and stagnant waters. But they found no answer when I told them that it was not still water, but that there was movement owing to seepage from one lwin to the next. The fauna and flora in the Kabaw Valley are completely different from those of Manipur and Assam, and the habits of the mosquitoes, and even their species, might differ. My final argument was that no jungle wallah and no Burmans would ever camp near lwins, and that, as for elephants, they avoided them like the plague.

Before the malariologists had taken their departure, in came the brigadier of a tank brigade, to have a cup of tea, and then to be taken round to visit the various types of jungle, and to learn that most of the common big trees were shallow-rooted and that a tank could push them over like ninepins. A simple little fact, but of some practical value. Then came the R.A.F., then Radar, then the Artillery. Besides these, the camp was never without at least one sapper. With all these visitors, I led a busy life, quite apart from looking after my elephants. Everything pointed to the Army's coming back quite soon. Souvenirs of tips of elephant tusks and hand-made pipes in teak, with ivory mouthpieces, made by the oozies were in great demand – these gave out but not the curry and rice.

The mud of the monsoons was fast drying in the valley, and before the motor transport of the 20th Indian Division arrived to take the place of the 23rd, a sufficient number of elephant bridges had been constructed over the rivers, creeks and nullahs to allow the brigades to fan out over the same fair-weather tracks which had been used before – north to Myothit, east towards Sittaung and south to Witok.

Elephants were still occasionally used for pack, but only to help in fording rivers, for it had become quite obvious to all that their chief function was in building log bridges.

I still had difficulty in persuading troops to handle elephants in the proper Burmese fashion.

The good humour of the oozies when working with Indian troops was the greatest help, and conditions never became unworkable. The oozies were not enlisted men. When the sun was boiling hot and the elephants needed shade and fodder, the oozies just went off with them where they could find it. They did not care a damn whether it was a Jemadar Sahib or the Officer Commanding a Field Company who was trying to stop them. The demands for elephants here, there and everywhere were more than I could cope with. A large percentage of them were busy in bridge-building; others were wanted to help with patrols and others dragging logs for building native boats. At that time I never had more than seventy-eight elephants. They had become accustomed to traffic much sooner than I ever imagined that they would. However, there were a lot of accidents before all drivers of motor transport learned to slow up before passing elephants at work.

There were casualties from the animals fighting, owing to our restricted quarters, and my finest male elephant, Bandoola, killed two other tuskers.

A Gurkha sentry heard a wandering elephant approaching his beat, and was fascinated by the tusks gleaming in the moonlight. He fired a well-aimed shot; the bullet entered just below the eye, passed through the cheek and after leaving a hole the size of a five-shilling piece in it, was deflected into the animal's chest. The bullet was extracted after an operation on the chest, and that elephant was back at work within three weeks.

This was the beginning of a new source of trouble, because once the habit started it would be repeated in any camp that happened to be disturbed at night by elephants. I began to get called to the telephone at all hours of the night, often from places many miles away.

'Hullo! We have an elephant here in the camp that is eating all our rations. Everyone is terrified of him. What are we to do about it?'

'Who are you?'

'Cascara' (or some such code name).

'Good Lord! but that is seven miles from here. He will have eaten them all before I can get to you. You had better let him carry on until he's finished.'

'Right ho! But he is making such a hell of a row opening the bully-beef tins!'

Such was the humour of the sappers, and it helped a lot to make the combination of elephants working with an army in the field possible.

If I had been told three years before that elephants would be working alongside pile-drivers and bulldozers, I should never have believed it. If I had interfered it would never have worked. The oozies took for granted that I expected it of them, so they made the best of it – and the elephants thought the same. This work was constantly within sound of gunfire, and we were all wondering what the next move would be, and waiting for it.

I cannot say I was altogether happy, for at the back of my mind I was always wondering what I could do with my men and elephants if the Japanese made a determined attack. I was continually being called up on the telephone and questioned on topographical points about jungles, hundreds of miles away, in the heart of Burma, but all I actually knew was that something big was due to start soon. It was tedious work, waiting for it, but at the end of December I had a stroke of good luck. Two days before Christmas, a friendly Corps Commander sent me a signal to report back from Elephant Camp to Corps Headquarters. I drove my jeep back up the Imphal road, every bend of which was by that time only too familiar to me. I reported, and gave the information for which I had been asked; then, just as I was about to salute and leave the room, he said, jovially, 'I've been given five days' leave to Shillong for Christmas.'

'Grand, sir,' I replied. Then, suddenly seeing how the wind lay, I added, 'Three would do me.'

'All right,' he replied. 'Take seven, and see the New Year in with your family.'

In less than ten minutes after leaving his room I was heading west in my jeep, accompanied by Abdul, my unnecessary Indian Army orderly, who, for some reason unknown to me, had by Indian Army regulations always to be hanging around at my heels, even when I was in Burma.

I drove four hundred miles non-stop, and arrived in Shillong, Assam, on Christmas Eve, in time to find my wife busily employed in filling the four children's stockings. It was a wonderful Christmas, but the grey dawn of January 1st 1944, came all too quickly, and at 4 a.m. I had to say goodbye. It was a cold, frosty morning up there in the hills, and the engine of my jeep seemed to purr with pride as I pushed down the hill road towards the plains of Assam. The headlights made the wall of the jungle on each side seem a sad and sinister green. The wretched Abdul was sitting at my side, with his rifle between his knees, and he and I were lost in our own thoughts when, swinging around a bend in the road at thirty miles an hour, I had to jam on the brakes hard. For what at first glance looked like a calf was lying in the middle of the tarred macadam road. As I came to a dead stop, my headlights were focused on a magnificent male tiger.

He sat up suddenly on his haunches, blinded by the lights, but yet quite unperturbed. Abdul sat frozen in his seat, with his rifle unheeded between his knees. I felt as though I were sitting in the toy jeep that I had seen an excited child haul out of his stocking on Christmas morning. The tiger slowly stood up on all fours, and I felt myself shrinking into a toy driver. In a moment of inspiration I blew the horn, and Stripes turned his back, and I noticed his furry quarters sway slightly as he walked away in a slow quiet gait down the road, to disappear round the next bend.

When he had gone Abdul and I awoke from our trance, and I heard him working the bolt of his rifle to bring a cartridge into the breech. I gave him a dig with my elbow, which he understood – it was an unflattering reminder that he could not hit a haystack, let alone a tiger. Otherwise he would never have been taken out of the ranks to be my servant.

I lit a cigarette, and sat thinking for a few minutes. If I shot that tiger it would almost serve as justification for taking another day's leave. But I made no move, and when I had given him enough time to slip away down the khudside I started off again on my journey. I had got into third gear and gone round another two bends of this picturesque hillside road, when I was once more faced with the same startling apparition. For there, lying in the centre of the black tarmac, facing me, with his pink tongue lolling out and his warm breath condensing as he breathed out into the cold morning air, framed against a background of green forest, lay this perfect animal, in his finest full winter striped coat. He was not twenty yards from us when we pulled up. It flashed through my mind that I must shoot or go back. I drew my .45 Colt from the webbing at my waist, and fired two shots, sideways, out into the jungle. I thought for a moment of taking Abdul's rifle and getting out, but thought better of it. Stripes remained unperturbed by my two shots. He slowly got up, and then, turning out of the glare of the headlights, broke into a gentle trot, until he had nearly reached the next bend. He then subsided into a walk, and looked back once at us over his shoulder. I have no doubt he was cursing us.

This time I waited at least ten minutes, lit a cigarette, and smoked it through. It was obvious that this tiger loved lying on the warm surface of the road, which still held some of the heat of the previous day, and was as reluctant to leave it as I had been to rise from my warm bed in Shillong.

I then followed him up again, and thought I had seen the last of him, when, after travelling about a mile, I overtook him once more. By this time I was becoming hardened, and did not pull up at once, but went on slowly towards him, slipping the clutch, roaring the engine, and keeping my finger on the horn. He got up again and turned broadside on to me, but before he slowly slipped over the khudside he turned his great painted head and looked at me, puzzled and angry, and I imagined he was growling out, 'Curse this blasted war.' I accelerated all I could as I went by the spot where he had disappeared, and so came back to Elephant Camp with mixed memories of Christmas trees and tigers.

At last, early in the New Year, the Army began to make a move. It seemed as though we intended to advance south, as every available elephant was put onto improving the main road from Tamu to Kalemyo. Bailey and Hamilton bridges and heavy road-construction mechanical equipment were arriving. Only a very few knew the true situation. The Japanese had been clearing the villages in their forward areas of all Burmese, and there were many rumours that they were preparing for an offensive up the Kabaw Valley.

Then one glorious evening something passed over our heads. It was our first airborne troops and gliders – Wingate's Chindits. Their passage made us believe that they would be followed by something more. But the expected army did not arrive. We went on building the road. It had been decided to add log-timber abutments to all the bridges, and the elephants were working twice their normal hours, in order to keep ahead of the sappers and have logs stacked in readiness for them at every bridge. It seemed a case of working desperately hard. The tanks were up, but there were only three months left before the break of the 1944 monsoon. Knowing the valley, I realized that it would need a gigantic effort to make that road passable in all weathers.

I was sitting at my table one evening in March, when the telephone bell went. I had just calculated that the elephants had delivered two thousand three hundred tons of timber at the road in three months. It was the Divisional Commander speaking, not with his usual cheerful personal touch, but giving me a grave invitation to lunch next day, to meet the Corps Commander. I could tell that the invitation meant something very serious. I walked across to Browne's hut, where, as usual, he was poring over a crossword puzzle. He suggested a rum peg and at the same time remarked that I looked tired. I accepted the drink, and told him that I could not come to Hlezeik next day, as the Corps Commander was expected. We ate our supper early, and talked about the Chindit gliders until bedtime.

At luncheon next day there was a tension, as though something very serious were the matter. After lunch the Corps Commander and the Divisional Commander took me alone into a tent and said to me: 'This is Top Secret. How many days' warning would you need to get all your elephants collected together, and how would you get them out of the Kabaw Valley?'

My heart missed a couple of beats, in bitter disappointment at the idea that the troops were going to be withdrawn again, and that this time my elephants would have to go with them. I got up and walked to the Divisional Commander's table, where there was a map. I knew the position of all the elephants in the valley, and could easily calculate that it would take five days to assemble all the animals. I suggested that there should be two rendezvous areas. The Corps Commander agreed, and ordered me to assemble them without delay. Details were discussed, and half an hour later they agreed that I could tell Browne my secret orders, as I pointed out that the success of this movement of elephants depended on complete co-operation, and that I should need his help.

Feeling very depressed and rather stunned by this development, I immediately drove off in my jeep to the elephant camp farthest away, and gave orders cheerfully for them to move up the valley next day. It was well after dark when I got back to camp. It was after midnight before I had explained everything to Browne and we had laid our plans for the following day. We fell asleep to the sounds of heavy gunfire.

For the next four days we kept out of the way of all our friends. But at this stage all our plans went well, and we even managed to get the oozies' women and children who were not already in the camp to come in from their jungle encampments.

On the fourth evening I telephoned to the Divisional Commander, to say that all elephant camps were assembled, with the exception of one which was centrally placed at Tamu. On the fifth day reserve rations for fifteen days were dumped at the assembly points. There were forty-six elephants at Kanchaung, eight miles north of Tamu, and thirty-three at Mintha twenty miles north of Tamu.

Rumours of Japanese activity on the east bank of the Chindwin and in the Kalemyo area, due south of Tamu, were now rife. My Burmans had realized by this time that there was something in the air. But they had no idea it would mean a move west, away from their beloved Chindwin. I was never in any doubt about their following me.

White, who had joined me again from the Arakan, was in charge of a shuttle service of country dug-out boats on the Yu River, which were manned by Burmese boatmen. He received orders to disband his Burmans and then rejoin me. However, without carrying out these orders, on his own initiative he packed eighty of his best men onto motor transport and sent them along, to live and fight another day. They turned out most valuable the following year.

I had put Hann in charge of the herd of forty-six elephants at Kanchaung, and had explained to him that he might be called upon to move suddenly, and told him to be in readiness.

Browne was to be in charge of the herd of thirty-three at Mintha. All the best animals which had been doing engineering work were at Kanchaung. All the young calves and thin or sick animals were at Mintha.

My Karens, who had lost their elephants when they were ambushed at the Chindwin River crossing, were at Elephant Camp with me. I formed them into two escort parties, one for Hann and one for Browne. On March 16th I sent Browne off to check up that Hann was ready to go on and visit Mintha, if he had time.

At noon the code signal to withdraw came over my telephone. I was further informed that the Japanese had crossed the Chindwin to the north of us, and were moving fast. Their patrols had already by-passed our troops on the Tonhe track.

I went off at once to Kanchaung in my jeep, and was lucky enough to find Browne still there with Hann. I told Browne to push on to Mintha to warn his party, and I explained to Hann, by the aid of maps, the route he was to follow.

Hann was rather staggered by these orders, but I explained to him that the only alternative was to shoot all the elephants. I told him to catch all elephants that evening and tie them up for the night, and then to push on as hard as he could at dawn. I then arranged that, with luck, I would next meet him in the Imphal Plain, with a supply of rations and our next orders.

My last words were: '*Au revoir*, and the best of luck. You can make it. You must. Don't worry if you lose any animals *en route*, but push on with your main body.'

I went back to the main road to wait for Browne. He was back by dusk, and we returned to Elephant Camp with much to do there that night, as we had to be back at Mintha by dawn, where he would find his herd ready to move off. I had picked out his route. Although shorter, as Mintha is rather nearer to the Imphal Plain, it was over the most frightful mountainous country. We both had confidence in our men and animals, and believed it could be done, although we knew nothing like it had ever been attempted before. But this was War.

At midnight, after Browne had turned in, I received news that the Japanese had crossed the Chindwin to the north in strength, and were pushing forward over two main tracks, and also that a brigade of ours would be going up the north road beyond Mintha at dawn. This last piece of news cheered me a good deal.

There had been a roar of traffic all through the night. Browne left at dawn. Things were obviously moving fast, and when I saw Browne off I felt a presentiment that he would not find things at Mintha as we had planned. There was no news by 11 a.m., so I telephoned Brigadier, General Staff, at Corps Headquarters, to say that all was going well at Kanchaung but things were not going as planned elsewhere. I was then instructed to get back to Headquarters at Imphal myself, with my remaining Karens, in order to prepare for the arrival of the elephants. My elephant camp was to become Tactical Headquarters for an anti-aircraft, anti-tank regiment, which was already moving in.

The head Burmans to whom I spoke were completely bewildered. But they took it like well-trained troops.

I was just about to destroy a pile of secret papers and maps, when I saw Browne coming into camp, covered with blood and bandages. Just when he was nearing Kanchaung, his truck had skidded, when going at forty miles an hour, and hit a tree head-on. He was in a hell of a mess as a result. Luckily, it occurred close to where a west-country regiment was furiously digging in. The medical officer of the battalion gave him first aid, and Browne, very much cut about and badly shaken, tried to borrow another truck in order to push on, as every minute counted. He was told no traffic was to proceed beyond the sector he was in, let alone to Mintha, and that fighting was expected there within two hours.

Browne came back to appeal to me. I rang up Divisional Head-

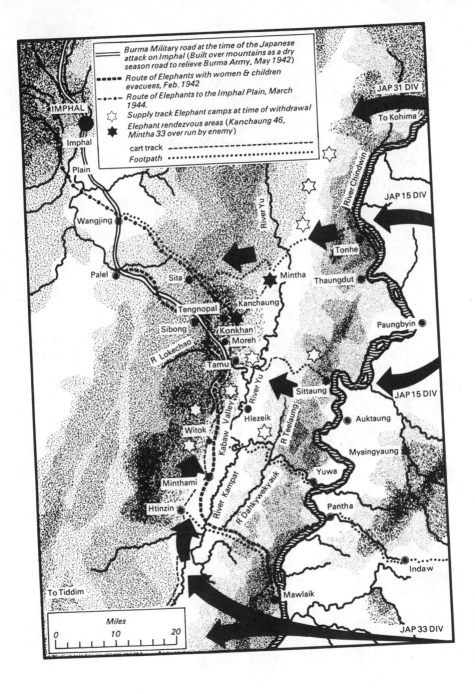

Burma Military road at the time of the Japanese attack on Imphal (Built over mountains as a dry season road to relieve Burma Army, May 1942)

▬▬▬▬ Route of Elephants with women & children evacuees, Feb. 1942

▬•▬•▬ Route of Elephants to the Imphal Plain, March 1944.

☆ Supply track Elephant camps at time of withdrawal

★ Elephant rendezvous areas (Kanchaung 46, Mintha 33 over run by enemy)

cart track ▬▬▬▬▬▬▬▬

Footpath ••••••••••••••••••

JAP 31 DIV

To Kohima

IMPHAL

Imphal

Imphal Plain

River Chindwin

JAP 15 DIV

River Yu

Wangjing

Tonhe

Palel

Sita

Mintha

Thaungdut

Tengnopal

Kanchaung

Paungbyin

Sibong

Konkhan

Moreh

R. Lokechao

Tamu

River Yu

Sittaung

JAP 15 DIV

Auktaung

Hlezeik

R. Teelaung

Myaingyaung

Witok

Kabaw Valley

Yuwa

Minthami

River Kampat

R. Dahkyweykyauk

Pantha

Htinzin

To Tiddim

Indaw

Mawlaik

JAP 33 DIV

Miles

0   10   20

quarters, and it was confirmed that a brigade was on its way up, so I told Browne we would change places. He should take over Headquarters and I would make an attempt to get up to the waiting elephants and set off with them. However, he begged me to let him go and try again, so I let him go.

I then heard that the movement of the brigade up the valley had been cancelled, so once more Browne could not get by. It was a good thing he was stopped, as he would have driven straight into the Japanese if he had pushed on. This happened to three Bren carriers an hour after Browne had come back and rejoined me.

It was pretty clear by this time that the Japanese had launched a large offensive. Our only hope was that the oozies at Mintha would have acted on their own initiative and moved west into the hills, when they heard our forward patrols engaging the enemy. However, this hope was disappointed. They just remained waiting at their posts, completely bewildered, as they had no orders. They had been cut off by Japanese patrols behind them before the main body of Japanese entered Mintha. We were completely cut off from hearing any news of them, but retained a faint hope we might come across them in the hills.

We made a gloomy departure from Elephant Camp that evening, leaving everything. A battle was fast developing on both sides of us. One could hear it to the south already.

Just as I was leaving, a serious young subaltern turned up, looking for me, saying he belonged to the Graves Commission, and could I please tell him how he was to get to Dahkywekyauk Wa, on the Yu River, in order that he might record the graves of men of the Northamptonshire Regiment who were buried there. I told him that it was not the moment to go there, unless he wished to remain there for ever, and that my experiences of Dahkywekyauk had convinced me that it was the unluckiest place in Burma.

We listened together to mortar fire, and, as he still seemed uncertain what to do, I added: 'Dahkywekyauk is eight miles beyond those mortars. Go back to Imphal and tell them I sent you back.'

He gave me the plan of the graves, and I put it in my pocket, feeling certain that some day I should have an opportunity of finding them, either when I went down next year with an offensive, or after the war was over. Then I could see that they were recorded. My presentiment came true.

As I climbed back towards Imphal, over the road from Tamu, I thought again about my experiences at Dahkywekyauk, and wondered why they should have been so disastrous. It is a jungle creek, and its name means 'the stream with knife-sharpening stones'. I first went there in

1925, and as I entered it from the mouth of the Yu River my first impression was of a dark, dismal tunnel, leading into the jungle, shaded impenetrably from any ray of sunlight by vast canopies of leafage.

For two years, in that dismal spot, I fought, all on my own, against considerable odds. I was stabbed by a Burman there in 1926. I was so ill with mud sores and high fever in 1927 that the only way to save my life was to get away by boat. This meant shooting the rapids in a dug-out, which had never been done before during flood-water of the monsoon. My elephant-men risked everything to get me out, and succeeded. My favourite dog, Juno, died there. One of my assistants was accidentally shot there. Another of them developed blackwater fever, and died shortly after we got him to Mawlaik.

That is a very brief list of some unlucky experiences there. But before I left in 1927 I did clear a hut site at the mouth of the creek, with a garden, from which I used to make sketches. I little guessed what use that habit of observation was going to be in 1943! Before the North-amptonshires had attacked the Japanese bunkers at Dahkywekyauk, in February 1943, I was able to sketch an accurate and detailed map for their Brigadier, even marking a tree, which I had planted to mark Juno's grave. That tree was the key point of the Japanese bunkers.

I made an impassioned plea, as an amateur soldier, that the attack on the bunkers should be launched from the hill and down the slope, instead of along the bank. It was the last and most important piece of information I could give them. But after I had listened, from a distance, to the air strike which preceded the attack, the news came through that our first attempt, led by a young officer of the Northamptonshire Regiment, had failed. They had attacked along the bank. That afternoon he led a second attack, this time from the hill behind it, and captured the enemy position brilliantly. He was killed, and awarded a posthumous V.C.

These thoughts filled my mind as I buzzed up the mountain in a jeep. The Japs were back, I was again on the run, and had lost touch with thirty-three elephants.

Browne and I spent the night at Palel in the Imphal Plain, arriving there after dark. The Japanese had launched their offensive. Perhaps it was just what our Higher Command had been expecting and praying for – or perhaps not. But my only concern just then was with the elephants on the march, and wondering what had befallen those we had left at Mintha. The worry of having lost thirty-three animals, and the uncertainty about the others, not to speak of what our next move would be, was very great.

The first news I got was that the Mintha elephants had never started on the march, but that the oozies had hastily dispersed them into jungle hiding-places, where they had their fifteen days' rations with them. This was a relief, as the Japanese would certainly have pursued them, and overtaken them, if they had moved off as a body. Had the Japanese captured them, they would have provided them with a transport column of immediate usefulness. It would be some time before the Japanese found all of them and assembled them for use.

It was five days before I got in touch with Hann and his party. One march after passing through Sita, on the main ridge, when all the elephants were already tied up at night, Hann received word that the Japanese had taken Sita. So they hastily loaded up, and pushed on again till dawn. In our eagerness to hear news of Hann and his party, Browne and I ran the gauntlet back to Konkhan in our jeep. But everyone had their own worries. All the troops were at action stations, and my constant question, 'Have you seen any elephants?' was usually regarded as a most untimely jest.

I was known intimately, and always greeted with a joke and a cheerful welcome, at Brigade Headquarters. Now when I went into their dug-outs all was serious. I stood silently listening to a telephone conversation about a counter-attack which was just going to be launched by a company of my old regiment in which I fought in the war of 1914–18. And as I listened I could not help feeling that I should have been happier if I had been an infantry subaltern again, leading a platoon to the attack, instead of worrying about my elephants, lost in the hills, through which the Japanese were infiltrating like yellow ants.

When the Brigade Major put down the telephone he looked at me and said: 'Sorry, Sabu. Your elephants were mistaken for Jap elephant transport in the high bamboo, and were shot up coming down the slope from Sibong.' He assured me, however, that he was speaking only of a small party of six, and I realized that they were animals which had been attached to a special patrol, not part of those I had assembled for evacuation. But there was no news of the main party with Hann. We were told to clear out as fast as we could.

I eventually got in touch with Hann, when his party was two marches from the Imphal Plain. I left Browne to deal with him when he arrived, and went to report at once to Corps Headquarters.

By this time we all knew that the Japanese had launched an offensive with three divisions, one against our 17th Division in the Chin Hills, one against our 20th Division at Tamu, and one in the north in the direction of Kohima, which was met by our 23rd Division, then in reserve in the Imphal Plain.

The Corps Commander sent for me, and told me that I must march the forty-five best animals, which I had saved, to the north of the Imphal Plain immediately, and then continue west out of the plain, as they were on no account to be lost.

No one knew better than he what those orders meant. He agreed that I would have to accompany them myself, and reconnoitre a route out. The Bishenpur track to the Silchar-Surma Valley could not be used, as the 17th Division had been cut off, and the Japanese were expected to cut that track as their next move.

Transport was impossible to get, but I knew that my only hope of moving on was to separate the oozies and their families, and send the latter to a place of safety – that is, down the Kohima road to the main railway. That would relieve all of us of a great responsibility.

It was a case of the devil helps those who help themselves. I made no attempt to get military transport, which I knew was impossible, but went direct to Steve Sutherland, an ex-officer of the Burma Forest Department, who was in charge of refugee supplies. He gave me the lorries.

When the train of elephants, with the oozies and their wives and families, arrived to cross the main road at Wangjing, I met them with eight lorries. I explained to the oozies that I would see that their families were all right. I then put the lorries of women and children into the charge of a young Anglo-Burman named McVittie and told him to proceed with them at once to the Manipur Road Railway and report to what was left of the Evacuee Camp there.

Browne and Hann continued north-west across the Imphal Plain with the oozies and the elephants, camping in Manipur villages, and feeding the elephants entirely on village banana trees. We calculated that it would take them another five days to reach the north-west end of the Imphal Plain, where I should meet them again. In the meantime, White and I were to do a reconnaissance of the route over the mountains to the west. The Barak River, which drains out into the Surma Valley in Assam, rises in Manipur, where it is but a stream. It is bridged at mile-post 102, on the main Imphal–Dimapur road. The first move was to reconnoitre its headwaters for fodder. The country through which it flowed was terrific, and to follow it one would have to negotiate a series of gorges and waterfalls. But water would always be available.

At 3 p.m. that day I sat with White at the bridge by 102 milestone, and decided that we would attempt to follow the Barak River route. I knew it would be a hellish trek. In front of us there were mountain ranges five to six thousand feet high, with cliff gorges engulfing the river.

I had, however, three officers to help me who would undertake anything I asked of them, whether it appeared possible or not.

Before six that evening, however, the road was cut by a strong party of the enemy, at the very bridge on which I had been sitting with White at three o'clock that afternoon.

With the Imphal–Tiddim road also cut, and the Bishenpur track seriously threatened, there was now no recognized track left out of the Imphal Plain, except a foot-track to Haflong to the west, to join the Lumding–Sylhet hill-section railway. This track passed through a village called Tamelong. Over this track, which was scarcely a footpath, it had been decided to march thirteen echelons of six hundred Pioneers at a time, so as to reduce the problem of rationing, which would be a big problem if our army were surrounded and besieged in Imphal.

My problem was to get from the Imphal Valley into the Surma Valley in Assam, due west of us, but divided from us by a series of five precipitous mountain ranges, five to six thousand feet high, over a country about which I knew nothing, except what I could gather from maps of a quarter-inch to the mile. Before dark I saw the Brigadier, General Staff, again, and explained that any more reconnaissances were out of the question. All I wanted was fifteen days' rations for ninety-six elephant personnel and *carte blanche* to get out as best I could. This he was not prepared to give me. However, the Corps Commander saw me again, and gave it, provided that I visited Tamelong *en route*, so that I could signal back that all was well as far as that. I also armed all my Karens with Sten guns and rifles.

The 17th Division broke through the Japanese block on the Tiddim road that day, and the very tragic news of Wingate's crash came through. With the 17th Division came sixty-nine women and children – mainly Gurkhas – who were refugees from the Chin Hills. They had been in the hands of the Japanese, and were a pathetic sight. Nobody had any time to deal with them, so I arranged with Supplies Branch that if they would fly out the pregnant women and old people I would attempt to take the others with me. There were sixty-four of them. I drew fifteen days' rations for them, and then took them in lorries to our starting-point. I was far from popular with my party. Not only was I tying this millstone of sixty-four strange women round our necks, but I had, only four days previously, almost forcibly separated my oozies from their own wives and children, who were at least familiar with elephants.

I returned to Imphal alone, after dumping my cargo, in order to have a tooth extracted, as toothache would not help me on the trip, and to pick up a red parachute, for ground signalling to the R.A.F. This was someone else's idea – not mine. Finally, I said *au revoir* to all those who had helped me and my attempt to get out.

The parting words of the Director Medical Services to me were: 'I'd rather stay here and starve, Bill.'

During the short run back to my elephant camp I was alone with my old Labrador dog, Cobber. He seemed to realize that sympathy was called for, and, leaning over the back of my seat, gave my face one slobbering lick, and wagged his tail cheeringly. Then he stared ahead through the windscreen, with his tongue hanging out and a broad grin on his face, as if he were saying: 'Next stop, Surma Valley.'

In the back of my jeep was a royal present of a case of rum. Steve Sutherland gave it me, saying as he did so: 'Say nothing, Bill. If there's nothing else you'll need on this Hannibal trek, you'll need this.'

Final plans were discussed that evening in camp. We were to start at dawn on April 5th 1944. It rained most of the night, and Imphal was in a state of siege next morning – what is known in the war histories as the Fourth Corps Box.

CHAPTER 16

The foothills to the west of Imphal Plain are treeless. From where we started there is a graded mule-track up to about two thousand five hundred feet, as far as Tamelong. Only one person saw us off on our departure: an R.A.F. pilot in a Harvard Trainer, who damned nearly stampeded the whole party of elephants, just as they were descending a very steep bit of the track. Whether he was just verifying the direction in which we were starting off, or whether he thought we were a horde of Japs, I can't tell. But he made off as quickly as he came, possibly because he realized how disastrous to us his presence would be, or possibly because he saw a few rifles being aimed in his direction! If our curses had any effect, he would have had a forced landing on his trip back.

We were a most extraordinary collection. I went ahead, with an armed vanguard of Karens, and when I looked back, down over the serpentine track, the collection looked like the 'Lame Host', and we were strung out to such an extent that it seemed possible that the first of the elephants would reach his destination before the last of them got started.

Our total strength was forty-five elephants, forty armed Karens, ninety elephant-riders and attendants, sixty-four refugee women and children, and four officers in charge. From where I was watching them, the elephants looked like slowly moving moles, followed by a trail of black ants. The cheerfulness of the Burmans was a great encouragement, and, provided that we escaped being attacked by Japanese patrols, we felt confident we should make the Surma Valley sometime and somehow.

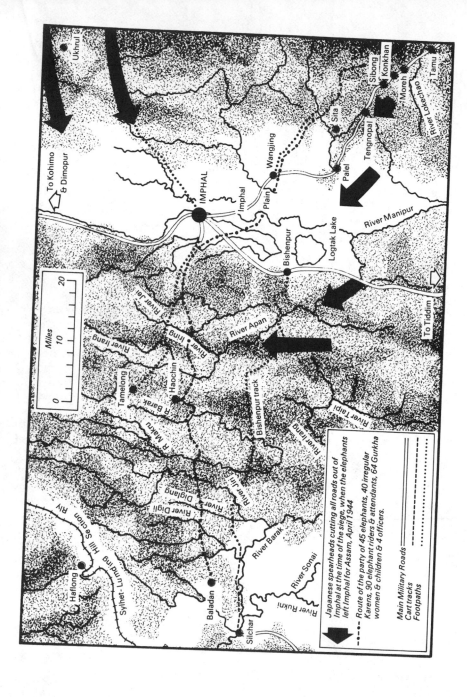

Ukhrul

To Kohimo & Dimopur

IMPHAL

Imphal Plain

Wangjing

Sita

Sibong   Konkhan

Tengnopal   Moreh   Tamu

Palel   River Lokechao

Bishenpur   Logtak Lake   River Manipur

To Tiddim

River Apan

River Iring

River Ian

River Iring

Tamelong   Haochin

R Naku   R Barak

Bishenpur track

River Taipi

River Iring

River Jiri

River Dijiang

River Digli

Haflong   Hill Section Lumding   Sylhet-Lumding Riv

Baladan   River Barak

Silchar   River Sonai

River Rukni

Miles 0 10 20

Japanese spearheads cutting all roads out of Imphal at the time of the siege, when the elephants left Imphal for Assam, April 1944

Route of the party of 45 elephants, 40 irregular Karens, 90 elephant riders & attendants, 64 Gurkha women & children & 4 officers.

Main Military Roads ━━━━━
Cart tracks ─ ─ ─ ─
Footpaths ⋯⋯⋯⋯⋯

Our first halt was the Iring River, after we had crossed the first watersheds. There was good water and ample fodder for the elephants at that halt. Half-rations were issued to all, and even the lamest of the lame ducks got into camp before dusk. That first evening, however, we were overtaken by the first echelon of six hundred Pioneers. They were carrying ten days' hard rations, and it was obvious that chaos, if not tragedy, was going to mark the whole of their route, as they could not cover the distance in that time.

I was, anyhow, anxious to get my party off their track as quickly as I could. I did not at all relish the company of seven thousand eight hundred Pioneers, and could visualize my elephants providing them with a most welcome supply of fresh meat if we remained with them. We were out of touch with any further orders, and had only one remaining duty – to visit Tamelong and send off a signal from there.

We therefore arranged that White and I should continue as far as Tamelong, and send off the signal, while Browne and Hann should proceed due west to Haochin, where we would rejoin them. However, we were still two marches from the point where we planned to part company, and during those two days I thought we should get an idea of what we might expect on the trek.

The women and children found the marches very exhausting, but on the whole they were marvellous. When we started off in the morning there would be three women and about four children riding on elephants, owing to various ills. When we got in at night ten to fifteen would be riding, the oozies having taken pity on them, although pity was a luxury we could ill afford, since the elephants were already over-loaded with rations and kit, and were making very severe marches. A few elephants showed signs of feeling it. These had to be nursed, by giving them lighter loads, which, in turn, meant that the others had to be still further overloaded. However, although every day the elephants would become more exhausted, every day we were eating a portion of their loads. That would make quite a difference after a week of marching. Before White and I separated from the elephant party, I gave orders that they should on no account delay during their march to Haochin, and any rest and reorganization of loading that might be necessary should take place after they had left it. For we were by no means out of range of Japanese patrols. I was to learn later that the very day on which the elephants left Haochin, a strong enemy patrol arrived in the evening and occupied the village, murdering a Political Officer, named Sharpe, who was following in the tracks of our party.

Tamelong was in the state of chaos which I had expected. A very young Political Officer, named Young, was in charge of thirty rifles, with one Indian officer. The fact that Sharpe did not arrive led eventually to a second tragedy.

The Pioneers were straggling deplorably. All the lame, the blind and the halt were just sitting there, and showed no disposition to push on. Young seemed to have been forgotten in the general confusion elsewhere, and was trying to manage against very heavy odds. I got a signal sent off, giving my intended route, and adding just what I thought of the Pioneer echelons marching out. This led to the departure of any further echelons from the Imphal Plain being stopped, and to an airdrop of food for the stragglers stranded there.

White and I rejoined the elephants, as planned. The night after that we had to camp for the first time on a ridge, where there was only a trickle of water for the elephants. But it was just enough.

From Haochin onwards we had to face the unknown, and travel due west over whatever was in front of us, until we reached the Surma Valley. The point nearest us on the map was marked Baladan Tea Estate, high up on the edge of the valley. We made jokes about it, and decided we should find a bungalow with a very old tea-planter living with a very lovely young wife, and there would be buttered toast and a telephone. Then, slapping my Labrador, Cobber, on the flank, one of us added that he was quite sure that this ideal couple had a very elegant Labrador bitch who would appreciate him.

We were by this time five thousand feet up, which is high above any normal 'elephant line'. In fact we were as high as Hannibal was when he crossed the Little St Bernard. The great beasts were painfully slow in climbing, and Browne had had difficulty, owing to some of the older animals nearly collapsing. It was magnificent scenery, which made a great deal of difference to us four officers, in spite of the hundred and one worries which continually beset us.

So far there was no doubt that there would be sufficient fodder for the elephants and, provided we could cross over a watershed each day, we should be able to find sufficient water for them at lower levels.

I had been given a compass by an Australian War Correspondent, who once spent a night at Elephant Camp, Tamu. It had originally been given to his father by Sir Alan Brooke, and it proved invaluable to us on that trek.

The cold, at the altitude we now were, brought on attacks of malaria amongst the women, and we soon had a number of fever patients to look after. There were heavy falls of rain at night, which made their lives miserable. In addition, there were cases of sore feet, dysentery, pneumonia and abscesses in the breasts. Some of the elephants were in need of first aid as well. But we could not let our invalids rest and recuperate; we had to push on. Every day we marched from dawn till after five o'clock in the afternoon, always in fear of a Japanese ambush.

From Haochin onwards we had to organize track-cutting and digging parties, each officer in turn starting off with a party, to clear the way ahead of the elephants. When, in climbing up from a creek or river, I had fixed on our reaching some particular point on that ridge from which to drop down into the next drainage area, I had to make certain that the leading party kept their direction to that ridge and did not drop into a side creek. Unfortunately game-tracks were non-existent, as there was very little or no game in those hills. Any small villages marked were usually non-existent also. This was because the people are nomadic agriculturists who move to new areas as they are cultivated for hill rice – and the land can be cropped only once in three years. When new areas are cleared in rotation the village moves on. The villages marked were, however, a guide, as we always found the headstones of the graves at the village site. The dead remained, though for the time being the living inhabitants had moved into another valley.

As we ate our rations, we could afford to carry more of the children, who had by this time quite lost their fear of the elephants. The mothers soon found that they need not walk beside the elephant, constantly expecting to have to catch a falling child. For the oozies were very good at looking after the children, and I rewarded them for their work with an extra cigarette ration. Thus the mothers were able to make an early start with the vanguard of path-finders. Many of the younger women even lent a hand with jungle-knives, clearing bamboos. I was constantly badgered by everyone for a day's rest. Then, on the ninth day of consecutive marching, the country decided the question for me.

We had reached a large creek with good fodder, far off the beaten track. It had been my day with the vanguard, and, as I reached the site for the camp a long while ahead of the elephants, I crossed the creek and went part of the way up the next ridge, so as to see what it was like for our start next morning. The map read as though there were a fault or escarpment running north to south, parallel with the creek, and on the west bank of it. The ridge I was climbing seemed the most likely to provide a way up to the top of the escarpment. I struggled up for about two miles of very steep climbing, through dense bamboo jungle, which would mean a very slow and exhausting climb for the elephants. Then I suddenly came out against a sheer rock face escarpment, three or four hundred feet high. My heart sank. I turned south and followed the foot of the cliff for a mile. There was not a single place where I could have possibly climbed it myself. There was no question of an elephant climbing a perpendicular cliff. I then came to a patch of old and very large bamboos, some of which had obviously been cut with a knife possibly a year before. This looked to me like the work of a Chin villager, who must have been there at some time, and who was more likely to have come down the escarpment, particularly as the map showed a deserted village on the ridge to the west of it.

Before I retraced my steps to camp I found a place where there had been a landslip in the escarpment. It looked a possible way for men to come down, but not at all the kind of place for elephants to go up. I marked the place with a large blaze on a tree, and went back to camp, exhausted. There could be no question of our turning back.

When the elephants and our party came into camp I was forced to announce that we would stay in camp for two days. The evacuee women and children actually cheered, and practically all the clothes they had on were immediately washed and hung up to dry, before the sun went down. I explained that there was a lot of hard work and serious trouble for us ahead. This was not because there was no path – we had not been following a path for many days – but because it was impossible to go on, until we found a place which it was possible to climb, and then dug a path up it. Next morning I sent Browne, White and Hann, each with a separate party, to explore the foot of the escarpment. Browne was to attempt to get up at the place I had found, Hann was to follow the escarpment to the north, and White to the south. I stayed in camp, and provided food for the party by blasting fish with grenades.

Much to my surprise, Browne was back in camp by noon. As I watched him crossing the creek I remembered his return to Elephant Camp at Tamu, after two attempts to reach the elephants at Mintha. Then I saw that among his party were two Chins, armed with spears, and I wondered if he could possibly have got up to the ridge. It was not long before I heard his story. He had climbed up the place I had found at considerable risk. It was, apparently, the route by which the Chins had gone up or down some time ago. But it developed higher up into a narrow ledge, with sheer cliff above and below it, until the top was reached. He knew how I hated heights, and said that I should have to be taken up blindfolded. He said also that he thought that unless White or Hann found something better we were stumped. He had, however, reached the main ridge above, and found the village marked on the map. On the ridge was quite a good path, which ran due south to join the Bishenpur track. This, however, was just the place we wanted to avoid, as, until we had crossed this path to the west, I thought there was quite a good chance of our running into a Japanese patrol. I wanted to keep out of trouble, not to look for it.

It was evening before White and Hann got back within half an hour of each other. They had found no place nearly as good as Browne's.

The only decision I made that night was to cut rations down still further. The strictest watch was set on our food dump. In fact, we officers slept on it, and I posted a guard over it during the day.

We spread the red parachute over some boulders on the bed of the creek, though we had seen no aircraft up to this time. Hann reported having heard a Harvard Trainer during the afternoon, but we had no wish to see our old friend again.

We agreed that the following day we should take our two head elephant-men to see the way by which Browne had got up. It was easy to understand, from the signs made by the two Chins, that there was no alternative route.

I was not actually blindfolded, but I preferred to crawl a good part of the way on all fours! I made sure of my hand-holds, knowing my feet could look after themselves.

Except for the one narrow and dangerous ledge round the face of the cliff, we considered that we could make it possible with two days' cutting and digging. Fortunately, it was sandstone. The question was whether elephants would face it. In some places it was so steep that the elephants would almost be standing on their hind legs.

Po Toke, who was not my head Burman, but in charge of a group of seven elephants, which included Bandoola, surprised us all by saying as we returned: 'Bandoola will lead, and if he won't face it, no other elephant will. He knows how to close his eyes on the khudside, and won't put his foot on anything that will give. Moreover, if he should refuse half-way up, he can back all the way down, as he has eyes in his backside!'

Bandoola was a magnificent tusker, but with a bad name as being dangerous.

I don't think he really believed half what he said, but I took care not to give him an opportunity for retracting. All of us agreed what a marvellous elephant Bandoola was, and we left it at that.

Apart from the narrowness of the ledge, or shelf of rock, and the occasional, almost impassable, outcrops of rock, the whole of the inner wall of the proposed track had to be cleared of jungle growth. This would widen it as a path, and was in any case necessary for the passage of the pack carried on the elephant's back. White went ahead to the village with the two Chins hoping to raise a party of men to help in bamboo-cutting. He brought a dozen, all with good jungle-knives, and they started work from the top that afternoon.

Every fit man and woman in the camp, oozies included, was at work on that road by dawn next morning. We divided our labour force into four parties, each working on a different section. I took charge of the one nearest camp, so as not to be working where I might get giddy and fall over!

The good humour of even the evacuee women in tackling what was more than a full day's hard work helped enormously. In the evening I went up again. Far less crawling on all fours was necessary, and a lot of the jungle growth cut from the inner wall had been piled up on the outer edge, so as somewhat to hide the terrifying drop below. One day's work had certainly made a vast difference. All the same, I rather doubted if we could do it. I knew, however, that there was no possibility of turning back.

We continued work throughout the following day, and by evening the head Burman and Po Toke were satisfied that we could not improve it any more. If we could not do it now, we never could. There were two particular danger spots, where the track was only about three foot wide, with a wall above, and a sheer drop on the outside, with nothing to blind it. I could not help wondering whether the whole of this ledge might not collapse under the weight of forty-five elephants passing along it.

I had worked up old Po Toke to the pitch of thinking he was practically in charge of the whole adventure, and that all our chances of success depended upon his elephant, Bandoola.

I arranged that all the refugees were to wait until the last of the elephants had gone up the track. Needless to say no women or children were to ride, and invalids who were unable to walk would have to be carried up later. There was to be no talking among the oozies. Po Toke was to lead the way on foot, in sight of Bandoola.

I myself had pushed on ahead of everyone as soon as all the elephants were loaded up.

Only those who know how silently a train of elephants can march can imagine what an eerie start we made that morning. From half-way up, where I turned to look down into the valley, I could hear nothing but the burble of the water of the creek rushing over its boulders far below, and at intervals the distant thuds of gunfire, coming from the direction of the Bishenpur track to the south.

I sat and waited for two hours on that ledge, and thought over many things. Before I left Imphal I had given a scribbled note for my wife to a Spitfire pilot, who was flying to Calcutta. In it I merely said, 'Starting to march tomorrow.' I knew that this would set her wondering, now that the news of the Japanese offensive on Imphal was coming through.

I had stopped just two hundred yards above the most dangerous spot, at which we had actually cut a series of steps in the sandstone, each just big enough to take an elephant's foot. Once I saw Bandoola pass that, I intended to push on up the next stretch.

I thought that Po Toke would never appear – nor, in fact, did he. Bandoola's head and tusks suddenly came round the corner below me. He looked almost as though he were standing on his hind legs. Then up came his hindquarters, as though in a slow-motion picture. The oozie was sitting on his head, looking down, and seemed to be directing the elephant where to place each of his feet. Then he had passed that worst place. I caught a glimpse through the elephant's legs of old Po Toke following. Without a word I pushed hurriedly on. We had got Bandoola up at least half-way. I just prayed for good luck, but had no faith in success.

It was more than two hours before I saw Bandoola again, and then he was practically at the top, and all danger of his slipping or refusing was over. He was up, at all events, and my relief and excitement cannot be expressed in words.

Behind Bandoola came Po Toke, and after him a female elephant. As he passed me, Po Toke behaved rather like a pall-bearer at a village funeral who unexpectedly gives one of the onlookers a wink. He was intensely solemn, and did not utter a word, but he gave me a queer fleeting look, that was as good as saying: 'Don't you worry. They'll all follow now.'

He was right. They all did. I waited, and ticked off forty-five adult elephants and eight calves at heel go by. The back legs of some of the animals had been strained to such a point that when they halted they would not stop quivering.

Much as I hated having to camp on a ridge, where there was a well-worn track to the south, up which the Japanese might come, there was no alternative. It was dark by the time we had got the last of the refugee women up to the top. No day ever seemed longer.

I learned more in that one day about what elephants could be got to do than I had in twenty-four years. Po Toke's intuition had been perfectly right, and I am certain that we should never have done it if we had led with any animal except Bandoola.

Our camp on the ridge that night was the last one where I put out pickets. From there onwards I felt no fear of the Japanese.

Our next move was down to the Barak River. The descent was almost as steep as the previous day's climb up to the ridge, but there was no escarpment or ledges of rock to follow. Again we had to have a day's rest, as the elephants were feeling the strain, and had to be allowed to recover.

From there we followed the course of the river; our obstacles were mud and swamp, and very dense bamboo, through which we had to hack a track. We should never have got through if we had not been using Siamese-pattern gear on our elephants. It is much stouter.

Time was now our enemy, and my chief worry was whether our rations would last out. We still had a long way to go, but from the map it looked as though we should move into better country once we had reached the Digli River. It was quite obvious that our trek would last twenty days at least, and not the fifteen I had allowed for. By that time we had two cases of pneumonia among the refugee women, as well as other things. The only food we four officers were getting, on which to do a day's march, was chappattis made by the refugee women, jam and half a cigarette-tin of rice in the evening. As might be expected, our tempers were getting a bit short. Cobber, my dog, enjoyed himself more than anyone, but even he found the food dull. The Burmans were down to half a cigarette-tin of rice a head per day, and were feeling the pinch. They eventually petitioned me to increase it. But I refused, and told them that it was my job to get them through this march alive, and that I was determined to keep three full days' rations as a reserve, in case of some miscalculation. About this time we came to a Chin village, and had some trouble over a pig. Po Toke paid forty rupees for a village pig, but it escaped to the jungle just before he could kill it. It was obvious that the villager would get it back after we had gone, as these pigs are left free to roam during the day, and come back to their pens at night. Po Toke naturally asked for his money back, and, just as naturally, the Chin villager refused to give it him. The dispute was therefore brought to me to settle, so I handed Po Toke a rifle and told him to go and shoot a wild one tomorrow instead. Before we left camp he had bagged two. Of course I knew they were not wild ones, but it did at least settle the argument in favour of my men.

Before we moved on that morning the head man of the village came and asked me for compensation for damage done by the elephants to banana trees during the night. He had actually got his bill down on paper, and brought with him a boy of seventeen, who could speak a few words of English and claimed that he had been educated. It was he who had put the head man up to this ruse to obtain money. I told White, who could speak Hindustani fluently, to deal with him. It did not take him long!

But from my point of view the incident was the first sign that we were reaching civilization again. However, as we were not going south to link up with the Bishenpur track, but west, it turned out there was a very long stretch of uncivilized country still to cover. Nevertheless, we had by this time at least left the mountains. In place of precipices we struck jungle swamp in which the animals got bogged. In trying to cut across country above the junction of the Digli and its tributary we were forced to turn back and follow down one river-bed to the confluence and then up the other river. It involved eight miles in water, knee-deep, with semi-quicksand bottom. It was just as slow going for the elephants as for the humans. All the children and the majority of the women had to ride, but the younger women were quite game to carry on. A few dropped out, and we had to send elephants back to pick them up.

Following elephants along a creek with a patchy quicksand bottom is an experience which thoroughly tests one's endurance and one's temper. It amounts to floundering along and continually losing one's balance, as one is always taking a step that meets with no resistance – as though one had stepped into a hole. It is next to impossible to carry anything, and the Gurkha girls soon discovered it was equally difficult to wear anything. It was not a time or place for false modesty and they were quite beyond caring about such matters. So they just handed up their garments, one after another, to the oozies and floundered on, naked, unimpeded and unashamed.

It was quite impossible to travel along the banks or to keep near them, as the dense jungle not only came down to the water's edge, but bamboos and canes grew right across. These had to be cut to allow the elephants to pass, and the sharp, twisted masses that resulted were awkward obstructions for those following.

I estimated that we covered only ten miles between 5 a.m. and 5 p.m. that day. Everyone was dead beat when we arrived at the confluence. It was an amazing sight to see the refugees sorting out their few wet rags of clothes on an open patch where we had decided to camp.

That last desperate day of floundering down the river had brought us, I reckoned, to within one day's march of the tea estate. But we agreed that to arrive there with our entire party might not be popular, so I decided to take the really sick along with me, on nine elephants, and to leave the remainder of the party camping as near the tea estate as we dared. I had the astonishing experience of walking right out of the wall of dense jungle into the open plain of the tea estate – an ocean of green tea, as far as the eye could see. I had come out exactly where I had planned on the map. There were doves cooing. I felt a lump in my throat, and could hardly believe my eyes. About a mile away was a large bungalow, typical of so many planters' bungalows in Assam. I went ahead to introduce myself to the old planter and the lovely young wife whom we had imagined.

It looked a homely bungalow. As I approached it I could see a figure in a white shirt on the veranda, for the bungalow was built on high ground, above the level of the surrounding tea bushes.

Before I reached it I was hailed by a man, speaking with a strong Scotch accent, 'What is the hurry? What about a cup of tea?'

'No hurry, and nothing I should like better,' I replied, and, swinging up his garden path, I walked on to a big open veranda with a breakfast table, with breakfast just laid. The planter was James Sinclair. He was a bachelor of forty-eight, and had no attractive young wife. He had mistaken me for one of the officers of a Commando unit, which had just arrived in that neighbourhood. Some of them were in the habit of dropping in to see him.

He asked me where I had come from and where I was going, so I gave him a brief account of my travelling circus. He then said that he had heard a rumour that there was a party of Japanese somewhere on the move with a few hundred elephants, but that he had not believed it. Now it turned out to be true, but, thank the Lord, we weren't Japs!

I breakfasted off new-laid eggs and hot coffee, and during the meal he told me that he had been expecting to hear of some refugees who were supposed to be coming through that way. Imphal had apparently signalled to Silchar about them. He was more than surprised when I told him I had brought them with me.

White arrived presently with the very sick on nine elephants, and Sinclair gave us every assistance, by handing them over to his tea-garden doctor.

We were still twenty miles from Silchar, but I was able to telephone to the civil authorities about the refugee women and children. It would be the greatest possible relief to hand them over, and have no further responsibility for them.

I was not able to communicate that day with the military authorities, and I was not particularly concerned to do so. I was already six days overdue, and had kept three days' rations in hand.

The refugee women were handed over that evening, so there was plenty of food left for my elephant-men. Two weeks later I was able to check up that all the sick among the refugees had recovered. I saw them in their camp, and they looked cheerful and happy. They were waiting to be sent farther on into India. They would have a fine story to tell their Gurkha menfolk when they met again after the war.

White and I stayed that night with Sinclair, and opened our last bottle of rum. Browne and Hann also had one at the camp. It had been agreed there was to be no rationing of their contents.

Next morning Sinclair invited all four of us to stay in his bungalow until I had got in touch with the Army and straightened everything out. The main elephant camp settled in about two miles from the tea gardens.

That was the twenty-fourth of April. We stayed with Sinclair for a period of four months.

The Sub-Area Headquarters at Silchar were so astonished at our arrival that I thought I detected a note of disappointment! Supplies Branch had made fabulous calculations as to the amount of fodder they would have to provide for the elephants, and there was already a file of signals about the lost host of forty-five elephants, four officers and Burman personnel. The R.A.F. had apparently been trying to find us for twenty consecutive days, but we had vanished, only to pop up again, just after we had finally and happily been written off.

My demands on Supplies for elephant rations were nil, and my other requests easy and simple. So we immediately became popular.

I flew to Army Headquarters at Comilla, where news of our arrival had caused quite a stir.

By the time I got there our bodies and elephants were already up to auction to the Assam Forest Department.

One of my first enquiries was to discover what had happened to the wives and families of my elephant-men. But it was a month before I ran them down, through the refugee organization of Assam, and discovered that they had been dumped at Parbuttipur, in Assam, on the Brahmaputra River. Being Burmese, they attracted considerable interest. As soon as it was possible, I sent Browne and White, with two of the most influential elephant-men, to visit them, so that they could bring back first-hand news to the oozies about their families. I have never known any two men who got on with children better than Harold and Chindwin, and their reception at Parbuttipur Camp was described to me later by the officer in charge. They were mobbed by the delighted children, whose excitement was indescribable. All in the camp felt that my promise had been kept. The families had to remain separated through the monsoon months. But they made the best of it, set up their own hand-looms, and were actually trading in Shan woven silk bags and hand-woven cottons before they returned to their homes.

They accepted their share of the upheaval in a wonderful spirit, and this helped me to hold their men together for four years, although they were not enlisted and I had no disciplinary authority over them. The difficulties for high-ranking officers in time of war can be very great, but to be in charge of Elephant Companies, without even an Establishment, could at times be far worse. My elephants could not be taken to Delhi and officially branded as the property of the Indian Army. My oozies could not be sent in a body to Simla to be certified as Burmans of good repute to those who resided there, and they were many!

However, an Imprest Account, written chiefly in Burmese, did confuse the Army Accounts Department to such an extent that they were forced to take it on trust. The advantages of our irregular position came when the war was over, as it enabled us to be demobilized at once, without waiting for all sorts of papers to come through.

CHAPTER 17

The battle for Kohima and Imphal, which proved decisive, and led on to the reconquest of Burma, was then in its first most critical stages. But my horizon was limited to my own job. Having got rid of the refugees, my concern was my elephants. A prolonged rest, so that they could get into good condition, was essential for them. Otherwise nothing would ever be got out of them again. They would also have to be refitted and re-equipped.

Expert timber-dragging elephants like these were almost worth their weight in gold in the forests of Assam. The Army authorities hoped to put them to good use with the Assam Forest Department. Fortunately we were in the wrong valley. The Forest Department needed us in the Brahmaputra Valley, near the main Assam railway and trunk-road. This involved a march of two hundred miles. The rains had broken, and I declared that it was impossible for us to undertake it before October.

I was very glad to be able to put off our working on timber extraction in India, for I knew that once we started it the elephants would not return to Burma during the war, and probably not for many years after it was over. If we could hold the Japanese attack during the monsoons, I felt certain that we should follow the enemy back into Burma when he cracked, and I knew that my elephants would be invaluable when that time came. I soon became involved in the usual type of Army paper war, of which I had little experience up till then. I rapidly learned the technique of obstructiveness in order to stave off the plan of sending us to work for the Assam Forest Department, which I determined to fight in every way I could.

Meanwhile, I took the opportunity to send each of my three officers on long leave, for I knew that there would be little chance of any later.

The Imphal battle turned in our favour, and soon afterwards an opportunity occurred for me to get the question of the employment of the elephants settled as I wished.

I was called to visit Army Headquarters at Imphal, to supply information on a subject unconnected with elephants. But the interview made it clear that the elephants might soon be able to return to the

Kabaw Valley. They were in the right place to do so directly the Bishenpur track was cleared. It was obvious, therefore, that the sooner any plans for employing them on timber extraction were dropped, the better. I therefore took the opportunity to ask for a definite ruling, and was given an interview by the Army Commander at Imphal, with results most satisfactory to me.

When I returned, the Burmans were delighted to hear my news of our future plans. Browne and White were to march the elephants back to the Kabaw Valley as soon as possible, and I planned to go back ahead of them, in order to pick up any stray elephants which our Army might have overrun or captured. The Japanese had been using large numbers of elephants in their offensive, and wholesale desertion by the oozies, complete with elephants, might be expected during their retreat.

I was, however, recalled to Headquarters with White, to be caged up in Intelligence Branch in Army Headquarters at Comilla with what would obviously be a ten-day job of work. I was rather amused by the manner of our return. We reached the large airfield near Silchar on a really dirty day of monsoon weather. The surrounding hills were enveloped in thick cloud, and while we were waiting Chindwin White said to me: 'I don't know that I wouldn't prefer to walk back.'

A few moments later a dirty yellow little Harvard Trainer came out of the rain-clouds and landed. Our names were called out, and we walked out to the aircraft, with our big rucksacks on our backs.

'Same damn machine that nearly stampeded the jumbos,' said White as we approached.

The pilot already had two R.A.F. passengers aboard, and called out to me: 'I can't possibly manage you, sir, but we might squeeze in the little fellow, if he would take that hump off his back.'

Chindwin was accordingly crammed in, and yelled to me: 'There's a new suicide game on here. Everyone else is strapped in and has got a parachute. But don't you kid yourself, I'll hang on to the legs of one of these chaps if we do have to jump.'

I joined him, an hour or two later, at Imphal, getting in on a Dakota in which there was plenty of room to spare. Chindwin went round telling everyone how I had got rid of him in a Harvard, and implied that I had been trying to get rid of him altogether.

It had been decided that, in spite of the monsoons, our Army would follow up the Japanese as fast as possible and keep them on the run. Unfortunately, White went down with a severe attack of malaria with complications. It was three months before he was well enough to come back. I was instructed to proceed to the Kabaw Valley to join the Commander of the 11th East African Division and, *en route*, to see the

General Officer Commanding the 33rd Indian Corps. Hann had gone off to join a formation of Intelligence Branch in the field, and Browne was left to bring the elephants back alone. He was quite confident that he could, and he did so successfully, but he did not really recover from the exhausting strain of being the only officer in charge of them, for a whole year. He then went on leave to South Africa, with his job completed, four days after the Japanese surrender. No man ever deserved leave more.

I arrived in Imphal and Tamu. No words can describe the conditions of the latter place.

McVittie, the young Anglo-Burman to whom I had entrusted the women and children of my elephant-riders four months before, had got back before me, and was already building bridges with eleven elephants he had collected, whose oozies had deserted from the Japanese. The importance of the work these animals were doing can be judged from the fact that the necessary gear and all requirements had been flown in and dropped by air, as a top priority, and demands for priorities were many at the moment. Other elephants were becoming available, as the oozies and elephants were escaping from their Japanese masters in their disorderly flight.

The lack of gear was the most serious problem which held up our using these animals, and, as Browne's party of elephants could not possibly reach us from the Surma Valley under six weeks, I decided to make use of all the equipment and hand-made harness which their oozies had made in the rest camp, near the Baladan Tea Estate. Fetching it took me three days in a lorry convoy.

The monsoons were by no means over in the Kabaw Valley, but nothing was to stop the East African Division going down it. Within three weeks I had collected and equipped sixty recaptured elephants, and sent up what reinforcements I could to McVittie. The rains were so violent that log bridges built one day were often washed away the next, only to be replaced the day after. Japanese lorries were bogged all along the valley of mud. The East Africans cut millions of saplings and threw them across the road to keep it open. They gave out a stench as they rotted which almost matched that of the bodies of the Japanese, who had dropped out, all along the line, and died of disease, starvation and exhaustion.

The streams were in such spate that it was next to impossible to keep log cribs in place for any length of time. We therefore used elephants to haul discarded Japanese lorries into the beds of the streams, and built our log cribs on top of them. Had it not been for the exceptionally heavy late rains in September and early October 1944, the Japanese retreating along the Tiddim road would have run into the spear-head of the East African Division, coming down the Kabaw Valley.

The sappers had now completely accepted elephants as part of the necessary equipment. Oozies whom I had not seen for seven months, and had since been made to work for the Japanese, were now back again under me, and were working with the East Africans. They were given the same rations as the troops, and realized that the Army had now really returned, and that there was no possibility of our withdrawing from the Kabaw Valley again. Air-drops were as regular as clockwork, and elephants were used to carry the supplies dropped from the dropping-zone to the distribution centre. These animals had been dive-bombed and machine-gunned from the air by the R.A.F., when they were being used by the Japanese as transport, on the tracks to Ukhrul and Jesami, in the Chin Hills surrounding Imphal. In one such bombing forty elephants had been killed, and elephants were being recaptured with gaping wounds which needed dressing. I therefore established a camp for sick elephants on the bank of the River Yu. To the best of my belief it was the first field veterinary hospital for elephants ever to be established. Some of the worst wounds on elephants' backs had been caused by acid spilt from wireless batteries, during transport. The Japanese had ignored the danger, and the oozies were not sufficiently familiar with acid to realize what the consequences would be. These cases were a warning to our own troops using elephants for transport, and enabled me to take precautions to prevent cases being caused by our own carelessness. In some beasts the flesh had been burned half an inch deep, and the elephants must have suffered slow torture while working in pack-harness. I treated them by dusting with M. & B. powder, and healing was remarkably quick. Many of our pilots have told me that they regarded attacking columns of elephant transport as a most loathsome job. The sincerity of these statements is beyond question, as I have also read reports from pilots, asking that elephants should not be a target for attack. Occasions arose, however, when there was no altenative but to stop the Japanese receiving supplies carried on elephants. This was particularly the case during the rapid advance of the Japanese to the Chin Hills and to Jesami and Ukhrul, preparatory to the offensive against Kohima. For had that succeeded they would have isolated China, and have overrun Assam and Bengal. The elephant transport trains were extremely difficult targets to find, as they marched by night, without lights, and were concealed in the jungle by day. The inspection of the sick and wounded elephants in my hospital camp was an extremely painful task – as painful for me as visiting field-dressing stations filled with wounded men would have been. The gun-horse has now been almost completely superseded by mechanical transport, and set free from the horrors of war. One can only hope that the unfortunate mule will also be superseded.

The Japanese had looted all the rice in the villages to the north and down the Chindwin; for their armies had been left without supplies after the failure of their plans to capture our dumps in the Imphal Plain. The villagers were therefore starving, and all my calf elephants under twenty were used to transport food supplies to these people. Demands came also for more elephants, to rebuild the road to the north to Myothit, and to the east to Sittaung. I was nearly at my wits' end in the valley, and so was Browne, who was travelling back with our original herd of forty-five. He arrived with them safely, after a journey of six weeks, but he was far from fit. He refused to leave me, however, and we struggled on, trying to meet all the demands that were being made on us.

The rains gradually came to an end and our troops were pouring into Burma. Roads were therefore needed over every track to the Chindwin, north, south, east and west.

Browne's arrival brought our strength up to one hundred and forty-seven elephants. Every fit animal was working full time. My head Burmans became my officers, and they managed remarkably well, considering what they had to put up with, in trying to please everyone.

I had no alternative but to attach parties of elephants to sapper companies, asking for one officer to be responsible for rationing the men and for general supervision. By this means I always had one man with whom I could deal direct. I owe these sapper officers a debt of gratitude. They got the best out of men and animals, by keeping calm under all circumstances, and by preserving their sense of humour.

One of these officers, named Alexander, who was a young civil engineer in peacetime, became so completely wrapped up in the elephants and oozies working under him that he learned all their names in a week, and struggled hard to learn Burmese, bribing the oozies with cigarettes to give him lessons in the evenings. All was going well when a sudden disaster occurred. Okethapyah (Pagoda Stone), one of his best animals, was blown up by a Mark 5 land-mine near his camp. Alexander came rushing over a most fearsome track in a jeep, arriving at 2 a.m., to tell me all about it. He said its back legs had been blown off, but he had seen it move, and was afraid it might be still alive! The Burmans who came with him assured me in Burmese that the animal was stone dead. I gave Alex a good tot of rum, and told him I could not amputate an elephant's legs, and we could only do our best to prevent such accidents in future. He abandoned the subject, but asked me to give him a lesson in Burmese – at 2.30 a.m.! I went back with him, starting before dawn, taking an anti-tank rifle, in case he had been right; but of course the elephant was dead – a sad sight in the early morning hours. The men had already discovered three more Mark 5 land-mines, and led us to them.

I knew that they had been put down by a British infantry battalion six months before, during the retreat, and never mapped. Having been exposed all through the monsoon rains, they were most uncertain things to handle. However, Alex, being a sapper officer, considered it to be his duty to pick them up there and then, and replace the safety-pins. He told me to take the Burmans away behind trees while he was doing this. Two of the men, however, flatly refused, saying that if Thakin (Alex) wasn't afraid, they weren't, and anyhow they wanted to see just how it was done. So we all stayed and watched. While Alex removed the claw-clamp and the lid, he asked me to explain the sheer wire and how the pin had to be replaced. 'Simple enough!' exclaimed Tun Myin, one of the Burmans who was watching. And next morning he brought in five more land-mines all with their safety-pins replaced, just as Alex had done them.

When Alex was not at hand I always felt that, but for the grace of God, there goes Elephant Bill! It was not long before this business of land-mine recovery began to get on my nerves.

It was a standing joke with the oozies that all they were doing was only for the cold-season months, after which our Army would leave the valley once more. But I was able to arrange with the Army authorities to bring their wives and children back from Assam by lorry. This gave them new confidence that this time we had come back to stay.

By early December there were four roads fit for transport to the Chindwin River during the open season. The elephants built all the bridges on each of these roads: Tamu to Tonhe to the north, Tamu to Sittaung in the east, Tamu to Yuwa to the east, Tamu to Mawlaik to the south-east, Tamu to Kalewa to the south.

One or two small Bailey bridges had been brought up, but no bridging programme had been possible for these roads, as all bridging materials were wanted for the crossing of the Chindwin at Kalewa. No less than two hundred and seventy log bridges and log culvert crossings were put in by elephants over these routes, thus allowing all motor transport and tanks to move forward, before the main bridging programme was undertaken.

As the roads to the Chindwin were completed, Forestry Companies arrived, to obtain the timber required for building assault craft and small barges at Kalewa. Five hundred assault boats were built at Kalewa, from timber extracted by elephants and cut up at the sawmills.

They also supplied the portable sawmill, with the timber required for decking the main bridges, for an all-weather road from Tamu to Kalewa.

During the war elephants had many jobs to do with timber, which they had never encountered in the routine of peacetime. One of these was to lift and pass logs up to a height of nine or ten feet – that is to say, from ground level to the bridge level. These logs weighed, on an average, a quarter of a ton each, and were often too heavy for the trunk to grip or hold. If the log were balanced on the outside of the trunk, on the tusks, there was always a danger that as the elephant raised its head to lift it the last foot or two the log would roll back, up its forehead, and endanger the life of the oozie, who was sitting on the elephant's neck at a lower level.

On one occasion I was watching, with one or two sapper officers, the last logs being handed up to a bridge under construction, and we witnessed a remarkable display of intelligence. The elephant was a particularly clever animal, and was beautifully handled by his oozie, but it was evening, and they were both tired. Several logs had slipped during their efforts to balance them, and it was quite obvious that the elephant was anxious about the safety of the oozie, who was placed in a dangerous position, just as the log was lifted to the highest point. There were still about three logs to be lifted. The largest of them was picked up by the elephant, and held in an endways position between the trunk and tusk, the signals for this being given to the animal by the oozie with his foot. The elephant then let it gradually slide, so that it lay across his trunk, at the point of balance, and the curving-up ends of his tusks acted as stops to prevent it rolling onto the ground, and then slowly lifted his head.

'God's truth! how marvellous!' said a Major, in a low voice.

'Hope to God it doesn't roll up his head,' murmured the Brigadier.

I held my breath, and then said, in a calm voice, in Burmese: 'Carefully now.'

The animal at once dropped his head, and let the log crash to the ground. The oozie looked disgusted, and then, acting entirely without instruction, the elephant used his brains to devise a safe method of handling the log – that is to say, he thought of something which we four men ought to have thought of ourselves.

He moved to one side rapidly, and picked up a stout piece of wood, which had been shaped for use as a maul or club to drive pegs into the bridge. He rammed it in a vertical position, jammed between his tusk and his trunk. I at once saw what he had in mind. The oozie also had immediately understood, and put him hard at the log again. With almost vicious strength, and certainly with determination, the elephant picked up the log endways, lowered it, and balanced it as before and then raised his head. But this time the club-shaped bit of wood was there, to act as a vertical stop, so that the log could not roll back over his forehead onto his rider.

An oath came from the Major, a murmur of admiration from the Brigadier. I could feel my heart beating, as the animal moved towards the bridge platform, carrying the balanced log, and then, putting his forefeet on to another log so as to gain a little extra height, lowered his head a little, at the same time curling the end of his trunk out of the way, so that it should not get pinched. The log rolled onto the platform, as gently and easily as if placed in position by an electric crane. It was one of the most intelligent actions I have seen an elephant perform. The remarks of the Major and the Brigadier as we returned to camp would have made that elephant purr with the complacent pleasure of a Persian kitten, if he had heard them, and he deserved them all.

Elephants were given strange jobs, and some strange sights were seen. As an experiment a landing-craft was built on the River Yu, in the hope of getting it down that waterway to the Chindwin. By the time it was completed, the water in the Yu was falling fast, which made the rapids more dangerous. The officer in charge, Connel, came to my camp one evening and asked if I could help get logs into place for his launching-slip, with elephants, and then help pull his craft over the shallows. Four tusker elephants were supplied for the job. They cleared the launching channel, and assisted in the launching, but when they started pulling his craft over the shallows there was a nasty noise, and they pulled her bottom out. However, he repaired her, and finally got her down to the Chindwin, where she was invaluable in helping a division to cross the river.

The DUKWS amused the Burmans a great deal. One of them broke down, and an elephant had to tow it to the nearest repair workshops. The next things that came along were locomotives loaded on low loaders. They looked out of place, four hundred miles from the nearest railway, travelling along a road through the jungle. Two tuskers pulled one loader up an incline, where wheelspin had been causing trouble. Elephants were also used for clearing forest trees off new air-runways. Often they were working quietly alongside bulldozers.

There were a number of humorous requests for elephants: such as for cranking up stalled lorries with their trunks, for spraying tar with their trunks, and ramming in loose earth on air-strips with their feet.

Their last job, for the 33rd Indian Corps, was to put a bridge over the Nayanzayah River for a squadron of tanks, which was engaged in taking Kalemyo. It was the only occasion on which I have seen elephants working under gunfire.

The bridge had to be finished by evening, and elephants worked from seven o'clock in the morning till seven o'clock at night. Five animals stampeded, but were recovered a few hours later. During the whole day Dakotas were circling two to three hundred feet above and air-dropping in a dropping-zone, not half a mile from where the animals were working. Three Dakotas were shot down by enemy fighters that day. By this time the elephants had become so accustomed to aircraft overhead that they took no notice whatever.

The elephants near the dropping-zone at Indaingyi soon realized that salt was being dropped. Their peacetime ration of fifteen pounds a month had come to an end in 1942, and they were in need of salt. Therefore as soon as they were released from work they went to the dropping-zone in search of the broken bags of salt which were lying about.

Indian troops, except the Gurkhas, were surprisingly timid in dealing with elephants. So were the East Africans. But the British troops would readily climb on their backs for a ride, and it tickled their sense of humour to do so. Their confidence, though born of ignorance, was usually justified, but not always. A sapper Major moved a stubborn tusker on must off a main road, by offering it bits of bread, as though it were a zoo elephant. When he told me about it afterwards I could only say he was lucky in war. On the other hand, an Indian Army Service Corps driver, who had his truck held up by a tusker on the road, after screaming his horn and revving his engine without effect, shot it in the leg with his rifle. The bullet smashed the bone, and the animal had to be destroyed. Luckily, there were very few such incidents.

After the crossing of the Chindwin River at Kalewa, new forest areas kept falling into our hands, and I kept hearing of more elephants being found. The brigades which captured them did all they could to keep these animals as part of their own transport. This was not practical, as they had no officers who understood how to handle elephants or what their requirements were. As a result, I had many private wars to win before I could get the elephants back for proper organization. On one occasion I exchanged six jeeps for ten elephants.

By the time the 4th Corps came down the Kabaw Valley every elephant in my hands which had been recovered from the enemy was fit and was equipped ready to start road construction on the line of advance south from Kalemyo to Gangaw, up the Myittha Valley, and over into the Yaw and Irrawaddy Rivers. By that time two experienced officers, Finch and Scanlon, had joined me. They at once took charge of one herd, and did a sterling job of work.

Browne at this stage had to give in at last, after a long struggle. He had a most fearful skin complaint, caused by his exposure for two years to the most filthy jungle living conditions.

I, too, was beginning to feel the strain of something wrong with me. I was suffering from an excruciating pain, high up in what some people call one's stomach. For two months I laughed with friends who tried to cheer me up by saying that the trouble was a few gin-corks I must have swallowed at odd times, by mistake, and that it would be a simple operation to have them extracted, once we were back in Rangoon. A Divisional Commander, however, who came to ask me to pop over the ridge to Mawlaik in an L.5, to give some information to a Brigadier who was about to cross the river there, spotted that it would be my last job for a time, and on my return from my flying visit sent one of his doctors to see me.

Red tape was put aside, and I was told that I should be flown from Htinzin strip in an L.5 to Army Headquarters at Imphal, where the Army Commander would see me. When I got to the strip, however, I found no waiting aeroplane, but only an urgent message from the new 4th Corps Commander saying that it was necessary for him to see me. Finch, my new officer, who was to deputize for me, was with me, so the jeep was turned to 4th Corps Headquarters. I had not then been told that the 4th Corps was to advance down the Gangaw Valley. Corps Headquarters staff was at lunch when I arrived, and the Corps Commander ordered me the one and only egg in their dug-out mess. For half an hour it seemed that that golden egg had cured me. It did at least give me enough energy to perform the task required of me before I left. This was to go forty miles up the Yu River Valley, and try to persuade six elephant camps to swim the Chindwin River, at noon the following day, as a blind for a force crossing higher up the Chindwin.

Finch went with me, and I have never known six more willing volunteers than the headmen of those camps. I spoke to the riders, and they, too, were full of enthusiasm, though they knew well enough what a difficult and dangerous task it was, at that time of the year.

They needed no one to go with them, and were ready to manage on their own, as I knew they would be. Finch and I then returned to Corps Headquarters, to assure the Corps Commander that it was all arranged, and would be carried out. He gave me a late cup of tea, and I was able to explain that Finch knew every yard of Gangaw Valley, and before nightfall the Commander realized that those six elephant camps would be far more use to him with his Corps, in the valley, than employed as a strategic deception, as he had originally intended. The order for their crossing the Chindwin was therefore cancelled at dawn the next day.

With a sad heart I left the Kabaw Valley, to drive to Imphal in the dark. I knew that road so well, but I had such a hell of a pain that the only relief seemed to be to lean against the driving-wheel of the jeep.

The Army Commander, who always gave one the feeling that he knew every man in his Army, saw me at once. I had no arrangements to make; I did not have to wait in any transit camp; I was told to go to a Hill Station hospital direct and to get back to my elephants as soon as possible.

For a brief period all the pundits thought they ought to remove my gall-bladder, but, by the grace of God, one of them who knew me spotted that it was a duodenal ulcer, and suggested that all I needed was three weeks in bed. This did the trick, and six weeks later I was driving back in my jeep from Shillong in Assam to Army Headquarters at Monywa in the Lower Chindwin.

The battle for Meiktala was then at its height. I shall never forget my return, and I shall never live down the story that I had been cut open in hospital so as to have a bunch of Gordon's Gin corks taken out of me.

On my return to the Kabaw Valley, and before pushing forward to Army Headquarters, which by that time had reached Monywa on the lower Chindwin, I at once saw Finch. There was much for me to learn of what had happened in the past six weeks, and I was prepared for the inevitable bad news, which is a part of war. Many of my friends, I knew, must have given their lives while I had been away. For the XIVth Army had forged ahead, and was already hammering on the gates of Mandalay.

Far in its rear, in the Kabaw Valley, Finch had been concentrating on feeding two sawmill units with seasoned teak and other hardwoods for boat-building. This was now of urgent importance, and Kalewa, on the Chindwin, had become an organized shipyard at which all sorts of river craft were being constructed. And no shipyard anywhere had ever been better supplied with the finest teak in the world cut to all necessary dimensions.

It seemed for those in charge of the elephants on that job that they had taken the first step back to their normal peacetime work. In one of the permanent camps of elephants engaged in this work was Bandoola, who had remained in perfect condition ever since he had led the great climb over the mountains into Assam, Old Po Toke was in charge of that camp, and Bandoola was employed in handling the largest pieces of timber. The camp was two miles away from the main military road, and in it one could only just hear the grind of the incessant stream of Army lorries.

Before I went forward to visit Army Headquarters, I told Finch I would visit Po Toke's camp and inspect elephants, for I thought that it would help to keep up the morale of the oozies, who were already becoming impatient for the war to be over, though the elephants had, I think, become completely inured to it.

To my surprise, Bandoola was absent from parade, and I naturally asked Po Toke where he was.

He replied: 'He has been missing for three days, Thakin Gyi.'

Whereupon Finch broke in with: 'Nonsense! You told me five days ago, when I was last here, that he had not been caught.'

I said no more, but, after inspecting the animals, went on into Po Toke's camp, where his men were quartered. I at once sensed that something was wrong, and collected all the elephant-riders and tree-fellers, and spoke to them as follows:

'You all know the difficulties we have with elephants getting lost in peacetime, and how far worse it is in war. Have you all been on an organized tracking party, looking for Bandoola?'

No one answered me, so, looking at Po Toke, I asked him: 'Have you not organized one?'

Old Po Toke looked pale and worried and replied in a low voice: 'There is no trace of his tracks anywhere.'

At the risk of incurring the wrath of all the Chief Engineers in Burma, I barked out: 'All dragging work here is stopped until Bandoola is found, and there will be no rations in camp either except plain rice; so get to work at once.'

Finch and I went back to camp with the feeling that what we had heard was no normal story of a missing elephant. I went on to Army Headquarters, and Finch arranged to send me a signal when Bandoola was found. But no signal came, and when I got back five days later, I heard that Po Toke had been taken ill, and that the whole camp seemed in a most depressed state, as there was still no trace of Bandoola.

I went straight off, and blasted old Po Toke to hell. The effect was electric. He burst into tears and, blubbering like a schoolboy, said to me: 'Bandoola is dead within four hundred yards of camp. Go and see him. I am too ill to walk, Thakin Gyi.'

Two of the oozies silently led me along a track leading from the camp towards the hills, and before long I could smell the frightful stench of a decomposing elephant. The two oozies suddenly stood aside, and I walked on into a cleared patch of short grass. There lay Bandoola, the hero of my march. I could scarcely believe my eyes when I saw him lying dead. But his enormous belly was distended with decomposition – and then I noticed something else was wrong also. His right tusk was gone, and there was only a butt of solid ivory, where it had been sawn off at the lip. The left tusk, half embedded in mud and earth, on the lower side, had not been taken.

My feelings were a terrible mixture of grief and uncontrollable anger. I was determined to find out the truth. Bandoola was a war casualty. He had been shot. There was a bullet-hole in his forehead, and the bullet must have gone straight through his brain; he had obviously dropped dead where he was standing. As far as I could see, there was no trace of the spot having been visited for several days by any living soul.

I at once put a guard of five Karens, armed with Sten guns, round his carcass, and there was no need to tell them how to act if occasion should arise, or if any intruders came back to get the other tusk during the night. I told them I would be back next morning.

All I could get out of poor old Po Toke was the pitiful statement that Bandoola's oozie had found him dead one evening, ten days before, and on going with the oozie to the spot next morning he had found that the right tusk had been sawn off. In his panic and grief, he had sworn all his men in camp to silence, and had forbidden any of them to go anywhere near the carcass, for fear of the Jungle Nats, which alone would have had the power to kill his unconquerable elephant, Bandoola. He pleaded that he had been unable to face breaking such terrible news, as he knew that my grief and Finch's would be as great as his own. It was useless calling him a bloody fool and cursing him because his prevarication made it far more difficult to discover the culprit. Such arguments meant nothing to Po Toke. Bandoola was dead, and his own interest in life was over. Nothing mattered to him any more. It was late that night before I turned in, and, to put it mildly, I was grieved, angry and perplexed. By noon next day the left tusk had been extracted cleanly from the skull by my Karens, and a .303 bullet extracted from Bandoola's brain. The slenderness of this, my only bit of evidence, can be realized. Thousands of lorries passed nearby along the Army's lines of communication every day. I had enquiries made at every unit in the neighbourhood, but it seemed most unlikely that any sepoy had been guilty, as most of them belonged to non-combatant units. Every check was reported to have been made on ammunition – with negative results that might have been expected.

There was, however, a Chin village only two miles from the spot. I went there with an armed party, and ordered the headman to produce all firearms within ten minutes. He did so, bringing the owners with their weapons. I disarmed six men, three of whom were armed with old .303-calibre rifles, and put them under close arrest while I made a house-to-house search of their huts, hoping I might find the sawn-off tusk. But I drew a complete blank.

The headman was extremely perturbed when I told him that all the firearms would be confiscated until he either produced the tusk or evidence as to which of his hunters had shot my tusker elephant. Again I drew blank.

I then gave orders to Finch to dismiss Po Toke and Bandoola's oozie, hoping this would produce some reaction by which I could discover the truth. Once more I drew blank.

Bandoola's death still remains an unsolved mystery. His left tusk is my most treasured souvenir of the war. I have often wondered whether old Po Toke had become so war-weary as to become slightly deranged in his intellect and whether he had shot Bandoola, rather than leave him to a successor when he resigned. The ways of jungle Burmans are strange, and it is just possible that he also has a souvenir of his beloved elephant. The secret, whatever it was, was buried with the body of that heroic tusker, who was exceptional in every way. Even his name was a most unusual one, being that of a Burmese general who fought heroically against us during the Burma War which resulted in the British annexation of Burma in 1886.

I insert here the official record of this remarkable elephant of which I was so proud.

BANDOOLA: No. S.K. 895

1897	NOVEMBER: Born.
1903	Trained. Branded 'C' both rumps.
1904–17	Travelling with Forest Assistants as pack animal.
1918–21	Ounging Moo River (i.e. salving logs from sandbanks in it).
1922	Transferred to Gangaw Forest.
1923–31	Timber camp of Maung Aung Gyaw.
1932	Injured in fight with wild tusker. Rested throughout the year. Fully recovered.
1933	Transferred to South Kindat Forest. Upper Chindwin River. Allotted to camp of Maung Po Toke. Extraction of heavy timber Mawku Reserve.
1934–41	Fit throughout. Prime Elephant of the forest.
1942	JANUARY–APRIL: Employed on Kalewa–Kalemyo road, before the retreat of the Burma Army. MAY–OCTOBER: Disbanded but kept in secret hiding from the Japanese in side creek of Kabaw Valley by Maung Po Toke living in Witok. NOVEMBER: Handed over again to Elephant Bill and Harold Browne at Tamu. DECEMBER: Enrolled as No. 1 animal, the nucleus, of No. 1 Elephant Company, XIVth Army. Employed dragging timber for bridges.
1943	MARCH–NOVEMBER: Employed near Tamu collecting timber ready for the return of the Army.

NOVEMBER–MARCH 1944: Bridge-building with the Army in Kabaw Valley.

1944 APRIL–MAY: Leading elephant in the march out of Burma from Kanchaung to Baladan in Assam.

JUNE–OCTOBER: Resting in Surma Valley, Assam. Loose for one day in pineapple grove, estimated to have eaten nine hundred pineapples. Severe colic. Recovered.

NOVEMBER–DECEMBER: Marched back to Burma.

1945 JANUARY–MARCH: Attached to Forest Sawmill Units. R.E., teak-dragging for Army boat-building.

MARCH 8: Found dead, shot by unknown person near Witok.

During my absence in hospital and while all this was taking place, the work had gone on with accelerated speed. A log bridge built by elephants had been constructed over the Manipur River near its junction with the Myittha. Similar bridges had been constructed, as required right through to Tiddim, and every tank going down passed over them without a hitch. No troops were maintained on the lines of communication behind this corps on this route, and no excavating machinery had to be used on the one hundred and twenty miles of this forest road.

I had a grand total of four hundred elephants working under my direction at this time, and I was making new contacts with oozies with their elephants who had deserted from the Japanese, and were hiding in the Mingin and Pakokku forests.

An American pilot, who had made a forced landing, had been given shelter and food and kept in hiding, for two months, in a camp of Karen elephant-men, who eventually brought him into our lines. The story was that when he was rescued by the Karens he gave them his money-belt, full of coins, as a reward. But, having nothing better to do during the two months he was in hiding, he taught the Karens how to play poker and won it all back. He gave it them a second time, and won it back again. But he went on with this once too often, for a Karen, called Po Doh, learned to play poker so well that he won all the money from the other oozies and the pilot's Colt .45 automatic from him too.

During their retreat the Japanese were pressing a party of Burmans, with a hundred elephants, forward into the dry zone beyond Saw, on the Irrawaddy River. The head Burman went to the Japanese officer in charge, and told him that even though the Japanese shot all the oozies and all the elephants they would go no farther. The Japanese officer referred the matter to his superior, but, without waiting to hear his decision, the whole party escaped with their elephants, and reached our lines after three forced marches.

This accession increased the number in our hands to seven hundred. Many of them had been so overworked by the Japanese during their retreat that they needed long rest and careful nursing.

Another fifty came into our hands on the Moo River after the fall of Shwebo. No more were recaptured in the dry zone, and it was not until the Prome, Pyinmana and Toungoo districts had been overrun by our troops that another three hundred fell into our hands.

The loyalty of these oozies to us was often strikingly shown. One Independent Brigade, crossing the divide between the Chindwin and the Moo Rivers, asked me if I could help in any way to provide transport for them down the Moo Valley.

It was quite impossible to get elephants over in time to assist the Brigade, which was desperately short of mule transport. So I suggested that a letter in Burmese, addressed to a contractor who had worked for me for seven years, should be dropped by one of our Spitfires. It was dropped on Naunggauk village, inhabited by men who had formerly worked for me. In the letter I asked that he should organize as many pack-elephants as possible, from those which had deserted from the Japanese, and as many bullock-carts as possible, for the use of British troops who would be reaching them very shortly.

When the Brigade arrived it was met by twenty-three elephants and thirty-four bullock carts, all organized as perfectly as though by one of our officers. The Brigade made a landing-strip for light aircraft, and shortly afterwards I landed there in an L.5, to meet the men who had acted so loyally. I took a large sum of money to distribute among them as a reward. But I found they were terrified of accepting it, owing to the lawlessness and dacoity prevalent in the district. So I made arrangements to arm them as well, and the money was soon in circulation.

After the 33rd and the 4th Corps had all gone down into the dry zone, and the hot season was almost at an end, elephants were kept working on only one main line of communication – that down the Kabaw Valley from Tamu to Kalewa. A new all-weather Bithess road was to be constructed there before the monsoon broke. A hundred and fifty elephants were employed in clearing all the culverts, in preparation for its construction. The Bithess road was an extremely expensive experiment, but it was the only possible method by which an all-weather road could have been constructed down that valley in the time available. It was, in its essence, a carpet of water-proof hessian material made in strips two feet six inches wide, treated with bitumen or tar. The strips overlapped eight inches and sealed the road surface. Camber was obtained by laying the two outside strips first, and building up with overlaps to the centre.

After it had been completely organized, the rate of progress in laying the road was one mile a day. The early storms of the 1945 monsoon had broken before it was completed, but the road carried seven hundred tons a day during the critical months.

By July 1945, the road had 'cracked'. Over some sections stretches of a mile were awash, and a quagmire resulted. After this the only hope of keeping the road in use was to build log causeway diversions. Five miles of such causeways were constructed by elephants during the 1945 monsoons. This meant laying two thousand five hundred logs per mile, or a total of twelve thousand five hundred logs, which had to be felled and cross-cut, and then dragged and put in position by elephants. All this work was done by No. 1 Elephant Company, under the most appalling monsoon conditions. At every flood the culverts were soon jammed with jungle debris, and the elephants were kept busy, continually clearing them. But they kept the road open. Over it, all the petrol for the Army was carried.

As the labour which had formerly been employed in taking rafts of teak-logs down the Chindwin became available, it was organized for taking rafts of petrol drums from Kalewa down to Monywa and Myingyan. The work had been well planned. A month before Kalewa had been captured, and the Chindwin bridged, Burmans were set to work on the Upper Chindwin, above Mawlaik, in cutting cane and bamboos to build rafts. These were then floated down to Kalewa, when the time came. A million bamboos were delivered to Kalewa by the jungle Burmans for this work.

A small group of officers operated in the forward areas of Kabaw Valley. Thomas and Keeley did most valuable work in this. They could, and should, have been reinforced by large numbers of others, who were sitting in Simla, waiting for the fall of Rangoon, which they seemed to imagine was the only gateway to Burma.

The fall of Rangoon, however, was in sight. There would undoubtedly be a great demand for timber. No one knew what supplies of it would be found there. Before the war there were about three hundred thousand teak-logs within easy call, at depots supplying the Rangoon mills. It turned out there were less than three thousand easily accessible logs within ten miles of the city when it was occupied. The elephants would be kept busy for some time in getting the teak-logs left in the creeks since 1942 forward to meet the demand for timber. They would be wanted immediately they could be released from Army work.

CHAPTER 18

Considerable information had been gathered from the Burmans and former employers of the timber firms on the use the Japanese had made of elephants during their occupation of Burma.

During their advance of 1942 the Japanese used elephants to transport mortars and ammunition over the Caukeraik Pass from Siam into Burma. It is probable that this had been planned in advance, and the operation was successful. It seems very unlikely, however, that the Japanese had intended to make other military use of elephants in Burma before their invasion. For we know that they had made preparations for an organization to work the forests under military control. A Japanese company, called the Nipponese Burmese Timber Union, was formed soon after the fall of Burma. The company did round up a considerable number of elephants and their oozies, who remained inseparable from their animals. They appointed as many of the Anglo-Burman assistants of the timber firms as they could find, as officers. But these Anglo-Burmans were never trusted by the Japanese. Such suspicions did not make for efficiency, even if the men had been trying to work. No British firm would have ever paid a dividend, unless it had done the same work in less than a third of the time that the Nipponese Burmese Company took over it. As a matter of fact, though they made an effort to show that they intended to develop the forests, they did very little extraction of timber from the forests, and relied almost entirely on what had already been hauled to the waterways or rafted to the depots. This may partly have been due to the fact that the Japanese military had a prior claim on elephants, and would send for working parties of a hundred elephants whenever occasion arose for their use. No Anglo-Burman was ever appointed to command thses columns of elephants for military purposes, and the Japanese had to rely on the small number of Burmese-speaking officers in their army to coerce the oozies. There were many causes of difficulty and trouble. The rations of the Japanese soldier were inferior to what the oozie was accustomed to, and this was undoubtedly a principal cause of discontent.

The Japanese also insisted on elephants being tied up after a day's work, and being hand-fed by the oozies. This meant more work for the men, who had to cut fodder, and less food for the elephants, which always do best when they can pick their own food. After feeding their animals, the oozies were themselves kept penned in camp under guard. I found that most of the oozies who had worked under the Japanese hated them so much that they preferred not to discuss them. They were eager to forget as soon as they could. 'They lived like dogs; they ate like dogs; and they died like dogs,' one of the oozies said to me, in summing up the invaders.

The elephants and their oozies were of the greatest military use to the Japanese. The big Japanese offensive to break into India via Imphal, Ukhrul, Kohima and Jesami from the Upper Chindwin, depended largely on elephant transport. This accounted for their rapid movement over jungle paths in very difficult country.

On March 13th 1944, the Japanese crossed the Chindwin by night, with a column of three hundred and fifty elephants, which they marched direct to the Chin Hills. A Japanese N.C.O. was in charge of every thirty animals. The elephants were used over precipitous and impassable country, linking up with motor transport and bullock-carts when they reached roads once more. Their transport system was improvised *ad hoc* from all available means and, though it did not look smart, it functioned and moved fast.

The Japanese did not ill-treat elephants in the sense of being cruel to the animals, as their management was left entirely to the oozies. But they pushed them hard, and never gave them opportunities to get the full amount of fodder they needed. I have already referred to the careless indifference which led to injuries from acid spilt on elephant's backs.

The Japanese had, however, a passion for ivory, and practically every tusker elephant which had been in Japanese hands had his tusks sawn off, as near to the nerve as possible. This work could not have been done by the Japanese themselves, as it demanded expert knowledge. It was no doubt done by Burmans of the toughest type, who wished to curry favour with Japanese officers, who were mad about ivory. No serious damage was done to the health of the elephants by this. I did not see a single case in which the nerve had been exposed. But, nevertheless, it was criminal, as it greatly reduced the value of a tusker for timber work, since the tusks left were not long enough for him to get under a log in order to move it. The Japanese, however, were more concerned with using elephants for transport than they were with timber extraction. Perhaps they thought the elephants looked less dangerous without their tusks. Early in 1943 I was present at the examination of a full pack, dropped by a Japanese soldier, when avoiding a patrol of ours on the east bank of the Chindwin. The pack weighed approximately seventy-five pounds, and contained two tips of tusks weighing six pounds in all. The soldier obviously valued his souvenir, to add it to such a heavy load. I don't think, however, that the Japanese got all the ivory obtained in this way, as the Burman also has a passion for it.

'Four thousand elephants used for hauling timber have disappeared in Burma.' This statement appeared in the *Daily Mail*, and was quoted in *Punch* with the query: 'Have you looked everywhere?' Well, the answer is that we had not, and nobody ever will. The statement appeared before we had completely cleared the Japanese out, and a few more may have come to light. I can, however, claim to have discovered the whereabouts of one of the missing four thousand. He is the Regimental Mascot of a famous Indian regiment, which captured him, and would not surrender him to me. On their return from the Burma Campaign he was marched across India to the Regimental Depot. Unfortunately, there is on his behind a capital C branded on with white phosphorous paint when he was seven years old. This proclaims his real ownership – the Bombay Burma Trading Corporation – and all the dhobies in the Punjab can never erase it. The Quartermaster is advised to get busy with the regimental tailor and fit him with cloth of gold trappings to cover it up. When the regiment reached Assam a language difficulty arose. The Burman oozie wished to return home and it was decided that an Indian mahout must be found among the ranks of the battalion. Not one could be found, so it became a Brigade request, and eventually a sepoy, who claimed to have been employed in a Rajah's elephant stable, was appointed.

The handing over of the Regimental Mascot by the Burmese oozie to the Indian mahout was planned to be a ceremony of importance. Many officers were present, including three Battalion Commanders and the Brigadier. There was considerable speculation among those on the parade-ground as to how the elephant would react to orders spoken in Hindustani, for the animal's understanding of Burmese words of command had become a byword in the regiment.

The new Indian mahout arrived on the parade-ground in bottle-green battledress, wearing boots, belt and sidearms. The Burmese oozie sat on the elephant's head, dressed as usual in his lungyi skirt and a Japanese cotton vest. The Indian wore a look of immense self-importance, the Burman one of complete indifference. Not a word was exchanged between the pair as the oozie ordered the elephant to sit down on all fours. As the Burman slipped down off the elephant's head, the Indian mounted, and the animal stood up. The Burman walked off the parade-ground, and then came the great test, as the Indian was left to prove himself. Drawing his bayonet from its scabbard with a flourish, he first held it at the sword present arms. Then he gave the elephant a probe with it behind the right ear, and, to the astonishment of everyone, exclaimed in English: 'Now, Mr Burma, come on!' – and off they marched.

In all, one thousand six hundred and fifty-two other elephants were recaptured from the Japanese between November 1942 and the date of unconditional surrender. They went back to their working lives. Before I left Burma I visited and said goodbye to four hundred and seventeen of them, working in the Kabaw Valley in Upper Burma, where they were still being employed in pulling out the tail of the XIVth Army. They were all that was left of Elephant Companies Nos 1 and 2. The rest had gone back to their pre-war work of timber extraction, and were soon happily scattered through the teak forests of Burma where they belong. Some were war-weary, some were battle-scarred, but they were in good hands, and would be nursed back to good health and good condition. Of the lost host of three thousand nine hundred and ninety-nine (according to the *Daily Mail*), many hundreds lost their lives owing to the folly and ruthlessness of man. There can be no roll call of the survivors. But there were numbers of wounded who, though they may have had a hard fight for existence to gather their food, would recover after they had treated their wounds in the traditional elephant fashion, by sealing them with mud two or three times a day. When they recovered they would set forth to leave the valleys which had become hells in the jungle during the war, for peaceful areas. But many must have escaped unhurt.

Those that had stampeded and those that survived their wounds must greatly outnumber those that lost their lives, and I know well enough where they are now. For the herds of wild elephants show no resentment when domesticated animals join them. They have none of that herd instinct directed against the stranger that one finds in cattle, in small boys and among many grown-up men. This tolerance is just one of the things about elephants which makes one realize they are big in more ways than one. No doubt some attempts will be made by the jungle Burmans to recapture branded animals from the wild herds. The only successful way to do this is for two very daring oozies to ride a really trustworthy animal into the wild herd as it is grazing in open kaing grass and to edge it alongside the animal they are trying to recapture. One of the oozies will then begin to talk to it, very quietly, and if it listens without alarm, he will slip across from the animal he is riding onto its back. A short stampede is almost certain to follow, but a good oozie will soon gain control as the wild herd disappears. But those that will be recaptured in this way are few indeed, and with Burma in its present condition I like to think of the hundreds that will remain leading their happy wild life, undisturbed by the restless demands of man.

Elephants have recently been nationalized in Burma, which means that they will lose their best friends in captivity, the European Assistants, many of whom would never have gone on with their work in the jungle but for their interest in the most lovable and sagacious of all beasts.

THE END

Encounters
with Animals

Gerald Durrell

INTRODUCTION

During the past nine years, between leading expeditions to various parts of the world, catching a multitude of curious creatures, getting married, having malaria, and writing several books, I made a number of broadcasts on different animal subjects for the B.B.C. As a result of these I had many letters asking for copies of the scripts. The simplest way of dealing with this problem was to amass all the various talks in the form of a book, and this I have now done.

That the original talks were at all popular is entirely due to the producers I have had, and in particular Miss Eileen Molony, to whom this book is dedicated. I shall always remember her tact and patience during rehearsals. In a bilious green studio, with the microphone leering at you from the table like a Martian monster, I am never completely at ease. So it was Eileen's unenviable task to counteract the faults in delivery that these nerves produced. I remember with pleasure her voice coming over the intercom with such remarks as: 'Very good, Gerald, but at the rate you're reading it will be a five-minute talk, not a fifteen-minute one.' Or, 'Try to get a little enthusiasm into your voice there, will you? It sounds as if you hated the animal ... and try not to sigh when you say your opening sentence ... you nearly blew the microphone away, and you've no idea how lugubrious it sounded.' Poor Eileen suffered much attempting to teach me the elements of broadcasting, and any success I have achieved in this direction has been entirely due to her guidance. In view of this, it seems rather uncharitable of me to burden her with the dedication of this book, but I know of no other way of thanking her publicly for her help. And anyway, I don't expect her to read it.

PART ONE

BACKGROUND FOR ANIMALS

I am constantly being surprised by the number of people, in different parts of the world, who seem to be quite oblivious to the animal life around them. To them the tropical forests or the savannah or the mountains in which they live, are apparently devoid of life. All they see is a sterile landscape. This was brought home most forcibly to me when I was in Argentina. In Buenos Aires I met a man, an Englishman who had spent his whole life in Argentina, and when he learnt that my wife and I intended to go out into the pampa to look for animals he stared at us in genuine astonishment.

'But, my dear chap, you won't find anything *there*,' he exclaimed.

'Why not?' I enquired, rather puzzled, for he seemed an intelligent person.

'But the pampa is just a lot of grass,' he explained, waving his arms wildly in an attempt to show the extent of the grass, 'nothing, my dear fellow, absolutely nothing but grass punctuated by cows.'

Now, as a rough description of the pampa this is not so very wide of the mark except that life on this vast plain does not consist entirely of cows and gauchos. Standing in the pampa you can turn slowly round and on all sides of you, stretching away to the horizon, the grass lies flat as a billiard-table, broken here and there by the clumps of giant thistles, six or seven feet high, like some extraordinary surrealist candelabra. Under the hot blue sky it does seem to be a dead landscape, but under the shimmering cloak of grass, and in the small forests of dry, brittle thistle-stalks the amount of life is extraordinary. During the hot part of the day, riding on horseback across the thick carpet of grass, or pushing through a giant thistle-forest so that the brittle stems cracked and rattled like fireworks, there was little to be seen except the birds. Every forty or fifty yards there would be burrowing owls, perched straight as guardsmen on a tussock of grass near their holes, regarding you with astonished frosty-cold eyes, and, when you got close, doing a little bobbing dance of anxiety before taking off and wheeling over the grass on silent wings. Inevitably your progress would be observed and reported on by the watchdogs of the pampa, the black-and-white spur-winged plovers, who would run furtively to and fro, ducking their heads and watching you carefully, eventually taking off and swooping round and round you on piebald wings, screaming 'Tero-tero-tero ... tero ... tero', the alarm cry that warned everything for miles around of your presence. Once this strident warning had been given, other plovers in the distance would take it up, until it seemed as though the whole pampa rang with their cries. Every living thing was now alert and suspicious. Ahead, from the skeleton of a dead tree, what appeared to be two dead branches would suddenly take wing and soar up into the hot blue sky: chimango hawks with handsome rust-and-white plumage and long slender legs. What you had thought was merely an extra-large tussock of sun-dried grass would suddenly hoist itself up onto long stout legs and speed away across the grass in great loping strides, neck stretched out, dodging and twisting between the thistles, and you realized that your grass tussock had been a rhea, crouching low in the hope that you would pass it by. So, while the plovers were a nuisance in advertising your advance, they helped to panic the other inhabitants of the pampa into showing themselves.

Occasionally you would come across a 'laguana', a small shallow lake fringed with reeds and a few stunted trees. Here there were fat green frogs, but frogs which, if molested, jumped *at* you with open mouth, uttering fearsome gurking noises. In pursuit of the frogs were slender snakes marked in grey, black, and vermilion red, like old school ties, slithering through the grass. In the rushes you would be almost sure to find the nest of a screamer, a bird like a great grey turkey: the youngster crouching in the slight depression in the sun-baked ground, yellow as a buttercup, but keeping absolutely still even when your horse's legs straddled it, while its parents paced frantically about, giving plaintive trumpeting cries of anxiety, intermixed with softer instructions to their chick.

This was the pampa during the day. In the evening, as you rode homeward, the sun was setting in a blaze of coloured clouds, and on the laguanas various ducks were flighting in, arrowing the smooth water with ripples as they landed. Small flocks of spoonbills drifted down like pink clouds to feed in the shallows among snowdrifts of black-necked swans.

As you rode among the thistles and it grew darker you might meet armadillos, hunched and intent, trotting like strange mechanical toys on their nightly scavenging; or perhaps a skunk who would stand, gleaming vividly black and white in the twilight, holding his tail stiffly erect while he stamped his front feet in petulant warning.

This, then, was what I saw of the pampa in the first few days. My friend had lived in Argentina all his life and had never realized that this small world of birds and animals existed. To him the pampa was 'nothing but grass punctuated by cows'. I felt sorry for him.

THE BLACK BUSH

Africa is an unfortunate continent in many ways. In Victorian times it acquired the reputation of being the Dark Continent, and even today, when it contains modern cities, railways, macadam roads, cocktail bars, and other necessary adjuncts of civilization, it is still looked upon in the same way. Reputations, whether true or false, die hard, and for some reason a bad reputation dies hardest of all.

Perhaps the most maligned area of the whole continent is the West Coast, so vividly described as the White Man's Grave. It has been depicted in so many stories – quite inaccurately – as a vast, unbroken stretch of impenetrable jungle. If you ever manage to penetrate the twining creepers, the thorns and undergrowth (and it is quite surprising how frequently the impenetrable jungle is penetrated in stories), you find that every bush shakes and quivers with a mass of wild life waiting its chance to leap out at you: leopards with glowing eyes, snakes hissing petulantly, crocodiles in the streams straining every nerve to look more like a log of wood than a log of wood does. If you should escape these dangers there are always the savage native tribes to give the unfortunate traveller the *coup de grâce*. The natives are of two kinds, cannibal and non-cannibal: if they are cannibal, they are always armed with spears; if non-cannibal, they are armed with arrows whose tips drip deadly poison of a kind generally unknown to science.

Now, no one minds giving an author a bit of poetic licence, provided it is recognizable as such. But unfortunately the West Coast of Africa has been libelled to such an extent that anyone who tries to contradict the accepted ideas is branded as a liar who has never been there. It seems to me a great pity that an area of the world where you find nature at its most bizarre, flamboyant and beautiful should be so abused, though I realize that I am a voice crying rather plaintively in the wilderness.

My work has enabled me, one way and another, to see quite a lot of tropical forest, for when you collect live wild animals for a living you have to go out into the so-called impenetrable jungle and look for them. They do not, unfortunately, come to you. It has been brought home to me that in the average tropical forest there is an extraordinary *lack* of wild life: you can walk all day and see nothing more exciting than an odd bird or butterfly. The animals are there, of course, and in rich profusion, but they very wisely avoid you, and in order to see or capture them you have to know exactly where to look. I remember once, after a six months' collecting trip in the forests of the Cameroons, that I showed my collection of about one hundred and fifty different mammals, birds and reptiles to a gentleman who had spent some twenty-five years in that area, and he was astonished that such a variety should have been living, as it were, on his doorstep, in the forest he had considered uninteresting and almost devoid of life.

In the pidgin-English dialect spoken in West Africa, the forest is called the Bush. There are two kinds of Bush: the area that surrounds a village or a town and which is fairly well trodden by hunters and in some places encroached on by farmland. Here the animals are wary and difficult to see. The other type is called the Black Bush, areas miles away from the nearest village, visited by an odd hunter only now and then; and it is here, if you are patient and quiet, that you will see the wild life.

To catch animals, it is no use just scattering your traps wildly about the forest, for, although at first the movements of the animals seem haphazard, you very soon realize that the majority of them have rooted habits, following the same paths year in and year out, appearing in certain districts at certain times when the food supply is abundant, disappearing again when the food fails, always visiting the same places for water. Some of them even have special lavatories which may be some distance away from the place where they spend most of their lives. You may set a trap in the forest and catch nothing in it, then shift that trap three yards to the left or right onto a roadway habitually used by some creature; and thus make your capture at once. Therefore, before you can start on your trapping, you must patiently and carefully investigate the area around you, watching to see which routes are used through the tree-tops or on the forest floor; where supplies of wild fruit are ripening; and which holes are used as bedrooms during the daytime by the nocturnal animals. When I was in West Africa I spent many hours in the Black Bush, watching the forest creatures, studying their habits, so that I would find it more easy to catch and keep them.

I watched one such area over a period of about three weeks. In the Cameroon forests you occasionally find a place where the soil is too shallow to support the roots of the giant trees, and here their place has been taken by the lower growth of shrubs and bushes and long grass which manages to exist on the thin layer of earth covering a grey carapace of rock beneath. I soon found that the edge of one of these natural grassfields, which was about three miles from my camp, was an ideal place to see animal life, for here there were three distinct zones of vegetation: first, the grass itself, five acres in extent, bleached almost white by the sun; then surrounding it a narrow strip of shrubs and bushes thickly entwined with parasitic creepers and hung with the vivid flowers of the wild convolvulus; and finally, behind this zone of low growth, spread the forest proper, the giant tree-trunks a hundred and fifty feet high like massive columns supporting the endless roof of green leaves. By choosing your vantage-point carefully you could get a glimpse of a small section of each of these types of vegetation.

I would leave the camp very early in the morning; even at that hour the sun was fierce. Leaving the camp clearing, I then plunged into the coolness of the forest, into a dim green light that filtered through the multitude of leaves above. Picking my way through the gigantic tree-trunks, I moved across the forest floor, so thickly covered with layer upon layer of dead leaves that it was as soft and springy as a Persian carpet. The only sounds were the incessant zithering of the millions of cicadas, beautiful green-and-silver insects that clung to the bark of the trees, making the air vibrate with their cries, and when you approached too closely zooming away through the forest like miniature aeroplanes, their transparent wings glittering as they flew. Then there would be an occasional plaintive 'whowee' of some small bird which I never managed to identify, but which always accompanied me through the forest, asking questions in its soft liquid tones.

In places there would be a great gap in the roof of leaves above, where some massive branch had perhaps been undermined by insects and damp until it had eventually broken loose and crashed hundreds of feet to the forest floor below, leaving this rent in the forest canopy through which the sunlight sent its golden shafts. In these patches of brilliant light you would find butterflies congregating: large ones with long, narrow, orange-red wings that shone against the darkness of the forest like dozens of candle flames; delicate little white ones like snowflakes would rise in clouds about my feet, then drift slowly back onto the dark leaf-mould, pirouetting as they went. Eventually I reached the banks of a tiny stream which whispered its way through the water-worn boulders, each wearing a cap of green moss and tiny plants. This stream flowed through the forest, through the rim of short growth and out into the grassfield. Just before it reached the edge of the forest, however, the ground sloped and the water flowed over a series of miniature waterfalls, each decorated with clumps of wild begonias whose flowers were a brilliant waxy yellow. Here, at the edge of the forest, the heavy rains had gradually washed the soil from under the massive roots of one of the giant trees which had crashed down and now lay half in the forest and half in the grassfield, a great hollow, gently rotting shell, thickly overgrown with convolvulus, moss, and with battalions of tiny toad-stools marching over its peeling bark. This was my hideout, for in one part of the trunk the bark had given way and the hollow interior lay revealed, like a canoe, in which I could sit well hidden by the low growth. When I had made sure that the trunk had no other occupant I would conceal myself and settle down to wait.

For the first hour or so there would be nothing – only the cries of cicadas, an occasional trill from a tree-frog on the banks of the stream, and sometimes a passing butterfly. Within a short time the forest would have forgotten and absorbed you, and after an hour, if you kept still, you would be accepted just as another, if rather ungainly, part of the scenery.

Generally, the first arrivals were the giant plantain-eaters who came to feed on the wild figs which grew round the edge of the grassfield. These huge birds, with long, dangling magpie-like tails, would give notice of their arrival when they were half a mile or so away in the forest, by a series of loud, ringing and joyful cries . . . caroo, coo, coo, coo. They would appear, flying swiftly from the forest with a curious dipping flight, and land in the fig trees, shouting delightedly to each other, flipping their long tails so that their golden-green plumage gleamed iridescently. They would run along the branches in a totally unbirdlike way and leap from one branch to another with great kangaroo jumps, plucking off the wild figs and gulping them down. The next arrivals to the feast would be a troop of Mona monkeys, with their russet-red fur, grey legs, and the two strange, vivid white patches like giant thumbprints on each side of the base of the tail. To hear the monkeys approaching sounded like a sudden wind roaring and rustling through the forest, but if you listened carefully you would hear in the background a peculiar sort of whoop-whoop noise followed by loud and rather drunken honkings, like a fleet of ancient taxicabs caught in a traffic jam. This was the sound of the hornbills, birds who always followed the monkey troops around, feeding not only on the fruit that the monkeys discovered but also on the lizards, tree-frogs, and insects that the movements of the monkeys through the tree-tops disturbed.

On reaching the edge of the forest, the leader of the monkeys would climb to a vantage-point and, uttering suspicious grunts, survey the grassfield in front of him with the greatest care. Behind him the troop, numbering perhaps fifty individuals, would be silent except for the wheezy cry now and again from some tiny baby. Presently, when he was satisfied that the clearing contained nothing, the old male would stalk along a branch slowly and gravely, his tail curled up over his back like a question-mark, and then give a prodigious leap that sent him crashing into the fig-tree leaves. Here he paused again and once more examined the grassfield; then he plucked the first fruit and uttered a series of loud imperative calls: oink, oink, oink. Immediately, the still forest behind him was alive with movement, branches swishing and roaring like giant waves on a beach as the monkeys leapt out of cover and landed in the fig trees, grunting and squeaking to each other as they plummeted through the air. Many of the female monkeys carried tiny babies which clung under their bellies, and as their mothers jumped you could hear the infant squeaking shrilly, though whether from fear or excitement it was difficult to judge.

The monkeys settled down on the branches to feed on the ripe figs, and presently, with loud swishings and honks of delight, the hornbills discovered their whereabouts and came crashing among the branches in the wild disorderly way in which hornbills always land. Their great round eyes, thickly fringed with heavy eyelashes, stared roguishly and slightly idiotically at the monkeys, while with their enormous and apparently cumbersome beaks they delicately and with great precision plucked the fruit and tossed it carelessly into the air, so that it fell back into their gaping mouths and disappeared. The hornbills were by no means such wasteful feeders as the monkeys, for they would invariably eat each fruit they plucked, whereas the monkeys would take only one bite from a fruit before dropping it to the ground below and moving along the branch to the next delicacy.

The arrival of such rowdy feeding companions was evidently distasteful to the giant plantain-eaters, for they moved off as soon as the monkeys and hornbills arrived. After half an hour or so the ground beneath the fig trees was littered with half-eaten fruit, and the monkeys then made their way back into the forest, calling oink-oink to each other in a self-satisfied kind of way. The hornbills paused to have just one more fig and then flew excitedly after the monkeys, and as the sound of their wings faded away the next customers for the fig tree arrived on the scene. They were so small and appeared so suddenly and silently out of the long grass that unless you had field-glasses and kept a careful watch they would come and go without giving a sign of their presence. They were the little striped mice whose homes were amongst the tussocks of grass, the tree-roots, and the boulders along the edge of the forest. Each about the size of a house mouse, with a long and delicately tapering tail, they were clad in sleek, fawny-grey fur which was boldly marked with creamy white stripes from nose to rump. They would drift out from among the grass stalks, moving in little fits and starts, with many long pauses when they sat on their haunches, their tiny pink paws clenched into fists, their noses and whiskers quivering as they tested the wind for enemies. When they froze thus into immobility against the grass stalks, their striped coats, which when they were moving seemed so bright and decorative, acted like an invisible cloak and made them almost disappear.

Having assured themselves that the hornbills had really left (for a hornbill is occasionally partial to a mouse), they set about the serious task of eating the fruit that the monkeys had so lavishly scattered on the ground. Unlike a lot of the other forest mice and rats, these little creatures were of a quarrelsome disposition and would argue over the food, sitting up on their hind legs and abusing each other in thin, reedy squeaks of annoyance. Sometimes two of them would come upon the same fruit and both lay hold of it, one at either end, digging their little pink paws into the leaf-mould and tugging frantically in an effort to break the other's grip. If the fig were exceptionally ripe, it generally gave way in the middle so that both mice fell over backwards, each clutching his share of the trophy. They then sat quite peacefully within six inches of one another, each eating his portion. At times, if some sudden noise alarmed them, they all leapt vertically into the air six inches or even more as though suddenly plucked upwards by strings, and on landing they sat quivering and alert until they were sure the danger had passed, when they once more started bickering and fighting over the food.

Once I saw a tragedy enacted among these striped mice as they squabbled amongst the monkeys' left-overs. Suddenly a genet appeared out of the forest. This is perhaps one of the most lithe and beautiful animals to be seen in the forest, with its long sinuously weasel-shaped body and cat-like face, handsome golden fur heavily blotched with a pattern of black spots and long tail banded in black and white. It is not an animal you generally see in the early morning, for its favourite hunting time is in the evenings or at night. I presume this particular one must have had a fruitless night's hunting, and so when morning arrived he was still searching for something to fill his stomach. When he appeared at the edge of the grassfield and saw the striped mice, he flattened close to the ground and then launched himself as smoothly as a skimming stone across the intervening space, and was in amongst the rodents before they knew what was happening. As usual, they all leapt perpendicularly into the air and then fled, looking like portly little businessmen in their striped suits, rushing through the grass stems; but the genet had been too quick and he walked off into the forest, carrying in his mouth two limp little bodies which had so recently been abusing each other as to the sole ownership of a fig and had consequently left it too late to retreat.

Towards midday the whole country fell quiet under the hot rays of the sun, and even the incessant cries of the cicadas seemed to take on a sleepy note. This was siesta time, and very few creatures were to be seen. In the grassfield only the skinks, who loved the sun, emerged to bask on the rocks or to stalk the grasshoppers and locusts. These brilliant lizards, shining and polished as though freshly painted, had skins like mosaic work, made up of hundreds of tiny scales coloured cherry-red, cream and black. They would run swiftly through the grass stalks, their bodies glinting in the sun, so that they looked like some weird firework. Apart from these reptiles, there was practically nothing to be seen until the sun dipped and the day became a trifle cooler, so it was during this period of inactivity that I used to eat the food I had brought with me and smoke a much-needed cigarette.

Once during my lunch break I witnessed an extraordinary comedy that was performed almost, I felt, for my special benefit. On the tree-trunk where I was sitting, not six feet away, out of a tangle of thick undergrowth, up over the bark of the trunk, there glided slowly and laboriously and very regally a giant land-snail, the size of an apple. I watched it as I ate, fascinated by the way the snail's body glided over the bark, apparently without any muscular effort whatever, and the way its horns with the round, rather surprised eyes on top, twisted this way and that as it picked its route through the miniature landscape of toadstools and moss. Suddenly I realized that as the snail was making its slow and rather vague progress along the trunk it was leaving behind it the usual glistening trail, and this trail was being followed by one of the most ferocious and bloodthirsty animals, for its size, to be found in the West African forest.

The twining convolvulus was thrust aside, and out onto the log strutted a tiny creature only as long as a cigarette, clad in jet-black fur and with a long slender nose that it kept glued to the snail's track, like a miniature black hound. It was one of the forest's shrews, whose courage is incredible and whose appetite is prodigious and insatiable. If anything lives to eat, this forest shrew does. They will even in a moment of peckishness think nothing of eating one another. Chittering to himself, the shrew trotted rapidly after the snail and very soon overtook it. Uttering a high-pitched squeak, it flung itself on that portion of the snail which protruded from the rear of the shell and sank its teeth into it. The snail, finding itself so suddenly and unceremoniously attacked from the rear, did the only possible thing and drew its body rapidly back inside its shell. This movement was performed so swiftly and the muscular contraction of the snail was so strong, that as the tail disappeared inside the shell the shrew's face was banged against it and his grip was broken. The shell, having now nothing to balance it, fell on its side, and the shrew, screaming with frustration, rushed forward and plunged his head into the interior, in an effort to retrieve the retreating mollusc. However, the snail was prepared for this attack and as soon as the shrew's head was pushed into the opening of the shell it was greeted by a sudden fountain of greenish-white froth that bubbled out and enveloped nose and head. The shrew leapt back with surprise, knocking against the shell as it did so. The snail teetered for a moment and then rolled sideways and dropped into the undergrowth beneath the log. The shrew meanwhile was sitting on its hind legs, almost incoherent with rage, sneezing violently and trying to wipe the froth from its face with its paws. The whole thing was so ludicrous that I started to laugh, and the shrew, casting a hasty and frightened glance in my direction, leapt down into the undergrowth and hurried away. It was not often during the forest's siesta time that I could enjoy such a scene as this.

At mid-afternoon, when the heat had lessened, the life of the forest would start again. There were new visitors to the fig trees, in particular the squirrels. There was one pair who obviously believed in combining business with pleasure, for they ran and leapt among the fig tree branches, playing hide-and-seek and leap-frog, courting each other in this way, and occasionally breaking off their wild and exuberant activities to sit very quietly and solemnly, their tails draped over their backs, eating figs. As the shadows grew longer, you might, if you were lucky, see a duiker coming down to drink at the stream. These small antelopes, clad in shining russet coats, with their long, pencil-slim legs, would pick their way slowly and suspiciously through the forest trees, pausing frequently while their large liquid eyes searched the path ahead, and their ears twitched backwards and forwards, picking up the sounds of the forest. As they drifted their way without a sound through the lush plants bordering the stream, they would generally disturb some of the curious aquatic mice who were feeding there. These little grey rodents have long, rather stupid-looking faces, big semi-transparent ears shaped like a mule's, and long hind legs on which they would at times hop like miniature kangaroos. At this hour of the evening it was their habit to wade through the shallow water, combing the water-weed with their slender front paws and picking out tiny water-insects, baby crabs and water-snails. At this time rats of another type would also come out, and these were probably the most fussy, pompous and endearing of the rodents. They were clad all over in greenish fur, with the exception of their noses and their behinds which were, rather incongruously, a bright foxy red, and made them look rather as though they were wearing red running shorts and masks. Their favourite hunting-ground was in the soft leaf-mould between the towering buttress roots of the great trees. Here they would waddle about, squeaking to each other, turning over leaves and bits of rock and twigs for the insects which were concealed underneath. Occasionally they would stop and hold conversations, sitting on their hind legs, facing each other, their whiskers trembling as they chittered and squeaked very rapidly and in a complaining sort of tone as though commiserating with one another on the lack of food in that particular part of the forest. There were times when, sniffing about in certain patches, they became terribly excited, squeaking loudly and digging, like terriers, down into the soft leaf-mould. Eventually they would triumphantly unearth a big chocolate-coloured beetle, almost as large as themselves. These insects were horny and very strong, and it took the rats a good deal of effort to subdue them. They would turn them onto their backs and then rapidly nip off the spiky, kicking legs. Once they had immobilized their prey, a couple of quick bites and the beetle was dead. Then the little rat would sit up on its hind legs, clasping the body of the beetle in both hands and proceed to eat it, as though it were a stick of rock, with loud scrunchings and occasional muffled squeaks of delight.

By now, although still light in the grassfield, it was gloomy and difficult to see in the forest itself. You might, if you were fortunate, catch a glimpse of some of the nocturnal animals venturing out on their hunting: perhaps a brush-tailed porcupine would trot past, portly and serious, his spines rustling through the leaves as he hurried on his way. Now the fig trees would once again become the focal point, as these nocturnal animals appeared. The galagos, or bush-babies, would materialize magically, like fairies, and sit among the branches, peering about them with their great saucer-shaped eyes, and their little incredibly human-looking hands held up in horror, like a flock of pixies who had just discovered that the world was a sinful place. They would feed on the figs and sometimes take prodigious leaps through the branches in pursuit of a passing moth, while overhead, across a sky already flushed with sunset colours, pairs of grey parrots flew into the forest to roost, whistling and cooing to each other, shrilly, so that the forest echoed. Far away in the distance a chorus of hoots suddenly rose, screams and wild bursts of maniacal laughter, the hair-raising noise of a troop of chimpanzees going to bed. The galagos would now have disappeared as quickly and as silently as they had come, and through the darkening sky the fruit-bats would appear in great tattered clouds, flapping down, giving their ringing cries, diving into the trees to fight and flutter round the remains of the fruit, so that the sound of their wings was like a hundred wet umbrellas being shaken amongst the trees. There would be one more shrill and hysterical outburst from the chimpanzees, and then the forest was completely dark, but still alive and vibrating with a million little rustles, squeaks, patters, and grunts, as the night creatures took over.

I rose to my feet, cramped and stiff, and stumbled off through the forest, the glow of my torch seeming pathetically frail and tiny among the great silent tree-trunks. This, then, was the tropical forest that I had read about as savage, dangerous and unpleasant. To me it seemed a beautiful and incredible world made up of a million tiny lives, plants and animals, each different and yet dependent on the other, like the many parts of a gigantic jigsaw puzzle. It seemed to me such a pity that people should still cling to their old ideas of the unpleasantness of the jungle when here was a world of magical beauty waiting to be explored, observed and understood.

LILY-TROTTER LAKE

British Guiana, lying in the northern part of South America, is probably one of the most beautiful places in the world, with its thick tropical forest, its rolling savannah land, its jagged mountain ranges and giant foaming waterfalls. To me, however, one of the most lovely parts of Guiana is the creek lands. This is a strip of coastal territory that runs from Georgetown to the Venezuelan border; here a thousand forest rivers and streams have made their way down towards the sea, and on reaching the flat land have spread out into a million creeks and tiny waterways that glimmer and glitter like a flood of quicksilver. The lushness and variety of the vegetation is extraordinary, and its beauty has turned the place into an incredible fairyland. In 1950 I was in British Guiana collecting wild animals for zoos in England, and during my six months there I visited the savannah lands to the north, the tropical forest and, of course, the creek lands, in pursuit of the strange creatures living there.

I had chosen a tiny Amerindian village near a place called Santa Rosa as my headquarters in the creek lands, and to reach it required a two-day journey. First by launch down the Essequibo River and then through the wider creeks until we reached the place where the launch could go no farther, for the water was too shallow and too choked with vegetation. Here we took to dug-out canoes, paddled by the quiet and charming Indians who were our hosts, and leaving the broad main creek we plunged into a maze of tiny waterways on one of the most beautiful journeys I can remember.

Some of the creeks along which we travelled were only about ten feet wide, and the surface of the water was completely hidden under a thick layer of great creamy water-lilies, their petals delicately tinted pink, and a small fern-like water-plant that raised, just above the surface of the water, on a slender stem, a tiny magenta flower. The banks of the creek were thickly covered with undergrowth and great trees, gnarled and bent, leant over the waters to form a tunnel; their branches were festooned with long streamers of greenish-grey Spanish moss and clumps of bright pink-and-yellow orchids. With the water so thickly covered with vegetation, you had the impression, when sitting in the bows of the canoe, that you were travelling smoothly and silently over a flower-studded green lawn that undulated gently in the wake of your craft. Great black woodpeckers, with scarlet crests and whitish beaks, cackled loudly as they flipped from tree to tree, hammering away at the rotten bark, and from the reeds and plants along the edges of the creek there would be a sudden explosion of colour as we disturbed a marsh bird which flew vertically into the air, with its hunting-pink breast flashing like a sudden light in the sky.

The village, I discovered, was situated on an area of high ground which was virtually an island, for it was completely surrounded by a chessboard of creeks. The little native hut that was to be my head-quarters was some distance away from the village and placed in the most lovely surroundings. On the edge of a tiny valley an acre or so in extent, it was perched amongst some great trees which stood round it like a group of very old men with long grey beards of Spanish moss. During the winter rains the surrounding creeks had overflowed so that the valley was now drowned under some six feet of water out of which stuck a number of large trees, their reflections shimmering in the sherry-coloured water. The rim of the valley had grown a fringe of reeds and great patches of lilies. Sitting in the doorway of the hut, one had a perfect view of this miniature lake and its surroundings, and it was sitting here quietly in the early morning or evening that I discovered what a wealth of animal life inhabited this tiny patch of water and its surrounding frame of undergrowth.

In the evening, for example, a crab-eating raccoon would come down to drink. They are strange-looking animals, about the size of a small dog, with bushy tails ringed in black and white, large, flat, pink paws, the grey of their body-fur relieved only by a mask of black across the eyes, which gives the creature a rather ludicrous appearance. These animals walk in a curious humpbacked manner with their feet turned out, shuffling along in this awkward fashion like someone afflicted with chilblains. The raccoon came down to the water's edge and, having stared at his reflection dismally for a minute or so, drank a little and then with a pessimistic air shuffled slowly round the outer rim of the valley in search of food. In patches of shallow water he would wade in a little way and, squatting on his haunches, feel about in the dark water with the long fingers of his front paws, patting and touching and running them through the mud, and he would suddenly extract something with a look of pleased surprise and carry it to the bank to be eaten. The trophy was always carried clasped delicately between his front paws and dealt with when he arrived on dry land. If it was a frog, he would hold it down and with one quick snap decapitate it. If, however, as was often the case, it was one of the large freshwater crabs, he would hurry shorewards as quickly as possible, and on reaching land flick the crab away from him. The crab would recover its poise and menace him with open pincers, and the raccoon would then deal with it in a very novel and practical way. A crab is very easily discomfited, and if you keep tapping at it and it finds that every grab it makes at you with its pincers misses the mark, it will eventually fold itself up and sulk, refusing to participate any more in such a one-sided contest. So the raccoon simply followed the crab around, tapping him on his carapace with his long fingers and whipping them out of the way every time the pincers came within grabbing distance. After five minutes or so of this the frustrated crab would fold up and just squat. The raccoon, who till then had resembled a dear old lady playing with a Pekinese, would straighten up and become businesslike, and, leaning forward, with one quick snap would cut the unfortunate crab almost in two.

Along one side of the valley some previous Indian owner of the hut had planted a few mango and guava trees, and while I was there the fruit ripened and attracted a great number of creatures. The tree-porcupines were generally the first on the scene. They lumbered out of the undergrowth, looking like portly and slightly inebriated old men, their great bulbous noses whiffling to and fro, while their tiny and rather sad little eyes, that always seemed full of unshed tears, peered about them hopefully. They climbed up into the mango trees very skilfully, winding their long, prehensile tails round the branches to prevent themselves from falling, their black-and-white spines rattling among the leaves. They then made their way along to a comfortable spot on a branch, anchored themselves firmly with a couple of twists of the tail, then sat up on their hind legs, and plucked off a fruit. Holding it in their front paws, they turned it round and round while their large buck teeth got to work on the flesh. When they had finished a mango they sometimes began playing a rather odd game with the big seed. Sitting there they looked round in a vague and rather helpless manner while juggling the seed from paw to paw as though not quite certain what to do with it, and occasionally pretending to drop it and recovering it at the last moment. After about five minutes of this they tossed the seed down to the ground below and shuffled about the tree in search of more fruit.

Sometimes when one porcupine met another face to face on a branch, they both anchored themselves with their tails, sat up on their hind legs and indulged in the most ridiculous boxing match, ducking, and slapping with their front paws, feinting and lunging, giving left hooks, uppercuts and body blows, but never once making contact. Throughout this performance (which lasted perhaps for a quarter of an hour) their expression never changed from one of bewildered and benign interest. Then, as though prompted by an invisible signal, they went down on all fours and scrambled away to different parts of the tree. I could never discover the purpose of these boxing bouts nor identify the winner, but they afforded me an immense amount of amusement.

Another fascinating creature that used to come to the fruit trees was the douroucouli. These curious little monkeys, with long tails, delicate, almost squirrel-like bodies and enormous owl-like eyes, are the only nocturnal species of monkey in the world. They arrived in small troops of seven or eight and, though they made no noise as they jumped into the fruit trees, you could soon tell they were there by the long and complicated conversation they held while they fed. They had the biggest range of noises I have ever heard from a monkey, or for that matter from any animal of similar size. First they could produce a loud purring bark, a very powerful vibrating cry which they used as a warning; when they delivered it their throats would swell up to the size of a small apple with the effort. Then, to converse with one another, they would use shrill squeaks, grunts, a mewing noise not unlike a cat's and a series of liquid, bubbling sounds quite different from anything else I have ever heard. Sometimes one of them in an excess of affection would drape his arm over a companion's shoulder and they would sit side by side, arms round each other, bubbling away, peering earnestly into each other's faces. They were the only monkeys I know that would on the slightest provocation give one another the most passionate human kisses, mouth to mouth, arms round each other, tails entwined.

Naturally these animals made only sporadic appearances; there were, however, two creatures which were in constant evidence in the waters of the drowned valley. One was a young cayman, the South American alligator, about four feet long. He was a very handsome reptile with black-and-white skin as knobbly and convoluted as a walnut, a dragon's fringe on his tail, and large eyes of golden-green flecked with amber. He was the only cayman to live in this little stretch of water. I could never understand why no others had joined him, for the creeks and waterways, only a hundred feet or so away, were alive with them. None the less this little cayman lived in solitary state in the pool outside my hut and spent the day swimming round and round with a rather proprietory air. The other creature always to be seen was a jacana, probably one of the strangest birds in South America. In size and appearance it is not unlike the English moorhen, but its neat body is perched on long slender legs which end in a bunch of enormously elongated toes. It is with the aid of these long toes and the even distribution of weight they give that the jacana manages to walk across water, using the water-lily leaves and other water-plants as its pathways. It has thus earned its name of lily-trotter.

The jacana disliked the cayman, while the cayman had formed the impression that Nature had placed the jacana in his pool to add a little variety to his diet. He was, however, a young and inexperienced reptile, and at first his attempts to stalk and capture the bird were ridiculously obvious. The jacana would come mincing out of the undergrowth, where it used to spend much of its time, and walk out across the water, stepping delicately from one lily leaf to the next, its long toes spreading out like spiders and the leaves dipping gently under its weight. The cayman, on spotting it, immediately submerged until only his eyes showed above water. No ripple disturbed the surface, yet his head seemed to glide along until he got nearer and nearer to the bird. The jacana, always pecking busily among the water-plants in search of worms and snails and tiny fish, rarely noticed the cayman's approach and would probably have fallen an easy victim if it had not been for one thing. As soon as the cayman was within ten or twelve feet he would become so excited that instead of submerging and taking the bird from underneath he would suddenly start to wag his tail vigorously and shoot along the surface of the water like a speedboat, making such large splashes that not even the most dim-witted bird could have been taken unawares; and the jacana would fly up into the air with a shrill cry of alarm, wildly flapping its buttercup-yellow wings.

For a long time it did not occur to me to wonder why the bird should spend a greater part of the day in the reedbed at one end of the lake. But on investigating this patch of reed I soon discovered the reason, for there on the boggy ground I found a mat neatly made of weed on which lay four round creamy eggs heavily blotched with chocolate and silver. The bird must have been sitting for some time, for only a couple of days later I found the nest empty and a few hours after that saw the jacana leading out her brood for its first walk into the world.

She emerged from the reedbed, trotted out onto the lily leaves, then paused and looked back. Out of the reeds her four babies appeared, with the look of outsize bumble-bees, in their golden-and-black fluff, while their long slender legs and toes seemed as fragile as spider's webs. They walked in single file behind their mother, always a lily leaf behind, and they waited patiently for their mother to test everything before moving forward. They could all cluster on one of the great plate-like leaves, and they were so tiny and light that it scarcely dipped beneath their weight. Once the cayman had seen them, of course, he redoubled his efforts, but the jacana was a very careful mother. She kept her brood near the edge of the lake, and if the cayman showed any signs of approaching, the babies immediately dived off the lily leaves and vanished into the water, to reappear mysteriously on dry land a moment later.

The cayman tried every method he knew, drifting as close as possible without giving a sign, concealing himself by plunging under a mat of water-weeds and then surfacing so that the weeds almost covered eyes and nose. There he lay patiently, sometimes even moving very close inshore, presumably in the hope of catching the jacanas before they ventured out too far. For a week he tried each of these methods in turn, and only once did he come anywhere near success. On this particular day he had spent the hot noon hours lying, fully visible, in the very centre of the lake, revolving slowly round and round so that he could keep an eye on what was happening on the shore. In the late afternoon he drifted over to the fringe of lilies and weeds and managed to catch a small frog that had been sunning itself in the centre of a lily. Fortified by this, he swam over to a floating raft of green weeds, studded with tiny flowers, and dived right under it. It was only after half an hour of fruitless search in other parts of the little lake that I realized he must be concealed under the weeds. I trained my field-glasses on them, and although the entire patch was no larger than a door, it took me at least ten minutes to spot him. He was almost exactly in the centre and as he had risen to the surface a frond of weed had become draped between his eyes; on the top of this was a small cluster of pink flowers. He looked somewhat roguish with this weed on his head, as though he were wearing a vivid Easter bonnet, but it served to conceal him remarkably well. Another half an hour passed before the jacanas appeared and the drama began.

The mother, as usual, emerged suddenly from the reedbed, and stepping daintily onto the lily leaves paused and called her brood, who pattered out after her like a row of quaint clockwork toys and then stood patiently clustered on a lily leaf, awaiting instructions. Slowly the mother led them out into the lake, feeding as they went. She would poise herself on one leaf and, bending over, catch another in her beak, which she would pull and twist until it was sufficiently out of the water to expose the underside. A host of tiny worms and leeches, snails and small crustaceans, generally clung to it. The babies clustered round and pecked vigorously, picking off all this small fry until the underside of the leaf was clean, whereupon they all moved off to another.

Quite early in the proceedings I realized that the female was leading her brood straight towards the patch of weeds beneath which the cayman was hiding, and I remembered then that this particular area was one of her favourite hunting-grounds. I had watched her standing on the lily pads, pulling out the delicate, fern-like weed in large tangled pieces and draping it across a convenient lily flower so that her babies could work over it for the mass of microscopic life it contained. I felt sure that, having successfully managed to evade the cayman so far, she would notice him on this occasion, but although she paused frequently to look about her, she continued to lead her brood towards the reptile's hiding-place.

I was now in a predicament. I was determined that the cayman was not going to eat either the female jacana or her brood if I could help it, but I was not quite sure what to do. The bird was quite used to human noises and took no notice of them whatever, so there was no point in clapping my hands. Nor was there any way of getting close to her, for this scene was being enacted on the other side of the lake, and it would have taken me ten minutes to work my way round, by which time it would be too late, for already she was within twenty feet of the cayman. It was useless to shout, too far to throw stones, so I could only sit there with my eyes glued to my field-glasses, swearing that if the cayman so much as touched a feather of my jacana family I would hunt him out and slaughter him. And then I suddenly remembered the shotgun.

It was, of course, too far for me to shoot at the cayman: the shot would have spread out so much by the time it reached the other side of the lake that only a few pellets would hit him, whereas I might easily kill the birds I was trying to protect. It occurred to me, however, that as far as I knew the jacana had never heard a gun, and a shot fired into the air might therefore frighten her into taking her brood to safety. I dashed into the hut and found the gun, and then spent an agonizing minute or two trying to remember where I had put the cartridges. At last I had it loaded and hurried out to my vantage-point again. Holding the gun under my arm, its barrels pointing into the soft earth at my feet, I held the field-glasses up in my other hand and peered across the lake to see if I was in time.

The jacana had just reached the edge of the lilies nearest the weed patch. Her babies were clustered on a leaf just behind and to one side of her. As I looked she bent forward, grabbed a large trailing section of weed and pulled it onto the lily leaves, and at that moment the cayman, only about four feet away, rose suddenly from his nest of flowers and weeds and, still wearing his ridiculous bonnet, charged forward. At the same moment I let off both barrels of the shotgun, and the roar echoed round the lake.

Whether it was my action that saved the jacana or her own quick-wittedness I do not know, but she rose from the leaf with extraordinary speed just as the cayman's jaws closed and cut the leaf in half. She swooped over his head, he leapt half out of the water in an effort to grab her (I could hear the clop of his jaws) and she flew off unhurt but screaming wildly.

The attack had been so sudden that she had apparently given no orders to her brood, who had meanwhile been crouching on the lily leaf. Now, hearing her call, they were galvanized into action, and as they dived overboard the cayman swept towards them. By the time he reached the spot they were underwater, so he dived too and gradually the ripples died away and the surface of the water became calm. I watched anxiously while the female jacana, calling in agitation, flew round and round the lake. Presently she disappeared into the reedbed and I saw her no more that day. Nor did I see the cayman for that matter. I had a horrible feeling that he had succeeded in catching all those tiny bundles of fluff as they swam desperately underwater, and I spent the evening planning revenge.

The next morning I went round to the reedbed, and there to my delight I found the jacana, and with her three rather subdued-looking babies. I searched for the fourth one, but as he was nowhere to be seen it was obvious that the cayman had been at any rate partially successful. To my consternation the jacana, instead of being frightened off by her experience of the previous day, proceeded once more to lead her brood out to the water-lilies, and for the rest of the day I watched her with my heart in my mouth. Though there was no sign of the cayman, I spent several nerve-racking hours, and by evening I decided I could stand it no longer. I went to the village and borrowed a tiny canoe which two Indians kindly carried down to the little lake for me. As soon as it was dark I armed myself with a powerful torch and a long stick with a slip-knot of rope on the end, and set off on my search for the cayman. Though the lake was so small, an hour had passed before I spotted him, lying on the surface near some lilies. As the torch-beam caught him, his great eyes gleamed like rubies. With infinite caution I edged closer and closer until I could gently lower the noose and pull it carefully over his head, while he lay there quietly, blinded or mesmerized by the light. Then I jerked the noose tight and hauled his thrashing and wriggling body on board, his jaws snapping and his throat swelling as he gave vent to loud harsh barks of rage. I tied him up in a sack and the next day took him five miles deep into the creeks and let him go. He never managed to find his way back, and for the rest of my stay in the little hut by the drowned valley I could sit and enjoy the sight of my lily-trotter family pottering happily over the lake in search of food, without suffering any anxiety every time a breeze ruffled the surface of the rich tawny water.

PART TWO

ANIMALS IN GENERAL

The way animals behave, the way they cope with the problems of existence, has always been a source of fascination to me. In the following talks I tried to show some of the astonishing methods they use to obtain a mate, to defend themselves or to build their homes.

An ugly or horrifying animal – like an ugly or horrifying human being – is never completely devoid of certain attractive qualities. And one of the most disarming things about the animal world is the sudden encounter with what appeared to be a very dull and nasty beast behaving in a charming and captivating way: an earwig squatting like a hen over her nest of eggs, and carefully gathering them all together again if you are unkind enough to scatter them; a spider who, having tickled his lady-love into a trance, takes the precaution of tying her down with silk threads so that she will not suddenly wake up and devour him after the mating; the sea-otter that carefully ties itself to a bed of seaweed so that it may sleep without fear of being carried too far away by the tides and currents.

I remember once, when I was quite young, sitting on the banks of a small sluggish stream in Greece. Suddenly, out of the water crawled an insect that looked as if it had just arrived from outer space. It made its laborious way up the stalk of a bulrush. It had great bulbous eyes, a carunculated body supported on spidery legs, and slung across its chest was a curious contraption, carefully folded, that looked as though it might be some sort of Martian aqualung. The insect made its way carefully up the bulrush while the hot sun dried the water off its ugly body. Then it paused and appeared to go into a trance. I was fascinated and yet interested by its repulsive appearance, for in those days my interest in natural history was only equalled by my lack of knowledge, and I did not recognize it for what it was. Suddenly I noticed that the creature, now thoroughly sun-dried and as brown as a nut, had split right down its back and, as I watched, it seemed as though the animal inside was struggling to get out. As the minutes passed, the struggles grew stronger and the split grew larger, and presently the creature inside hauled itself free of its ugly skin and crawled feebly onto the rush stalk, and I saw it was a dragonfly. Its wings were still wet and crumpled from this strange birth, and its body soft, but, as I watched, the sun did its work and the wings dried stiff and straight, as fragile as snowflakes and as intricate as a cathedral window. The body also stiffened, and changed to a brilliant sky-blue. The dragonfly whirred its wings a couple of times, making them shimmer in the sun, and then flew unsteadily away, leaving behind, still clinging to the stem, the unpleasant shell of its former self.

I had never seen such a transformation before, and as I gazed with amazement at the unattractive husk which had housed the beautiful shining insect, I made a vow that never again would I judge an animal by its appearance.

ANIMAL COURTSHIPS

Most animals take their courtship very seriously, and through the ages some of them have evolved fascinating ways of attracting the female of their choice. They have grown a bewildering mass of feathers, horns, spikes, and dewlaps, and have developed an astonishing variety of colours, patterns, and scents, all for the purpose of obtaining a mate. Not content with this, they will sometimes bring the female a gift, or construct a flower show for her, or intrigue her with an acrobatic display, or a dance, or a song. When the animals are courting they put their heart and soul into it, and are even, if necessary, ready to die.

The Elizabethan lovers of the animal world are, of course, the birds: they dress themselves magnificently, they dance and posture and they are prepared at a moment's notice to sing a madrigal or fight a duel to the death.

The most famous are the birds of paradise, for not only do they possess some of the most gorgeous courting dresses in the world but they show them off so well.

Take, for example, the king bird of paradise. I was once lucky enough to see one of these birds displaying in a Brazilian zoo. Here, in a huge outdoor aviary full of tropical plants and trees, three king birds of paradise were living – two females and a male. The male is about the size of a blackbird, with a velvety orange head contrasting vividly with a snow-white breast and a brilliant scarlet back, the feathers having such a sheen on them that they seem polished. The beak is yellow and the legs are a beautiful cobalt blue. The feathers along the side of its body – since it was the breeding season – were long, and the middle pair of tail feathers were produced in long slender stalks about ten inches in length. The feather was tightly coiled like a watch spring, so that at the end of each of these wire-like feathers shone a disc of emerald green. In the sunlight he gleamed and glittered with every movement, and the slender tail-wire trembled and the green disc shook and scintillated in the sun. He was sitting on a long bare branch, and the two females were squatting in a bush close by, watching him. Suddenly he puffed himself out a little and gave a curious cry midway between a whine and a yap. He was silent for a minute as if watching the effect of this sound on the females; but they continued to sit there, observing him unemotionally. He bobbed once or twice on the branch, to fix their attention perhaps, then raised his wings above his back and flapped them wildly, just as if he were about to take off on a triumphant flight. He spread them out wide and ducked forward, so that his head was hidden by the feathers. Then he raised them again, flapped vigorously once more, and wheeled round so that the two females should be dazzled by his beautiful snow-white breast. He gave a lovely liquid warbling cry, while the long side-plumes on his body suddenly burst out, like a beautiful fountain of ash-grey, buff and emerald-green that quivered delicately in time to his song. He raised his short tail and pressed it closely to his back, so that the two long tail-wires curved over his head and on each side of his yellow beak hung the two emerald-green discs. He swayed his body gently to and fro; the discs swung like pendulums and gave the odd impression that he was juggling with them. He lifted and lowered his head, singing with all his might, while the green discs gyrated to and fro.

The females seemed completely oblivious. They sat there regarding him with the mild interest of a couple of housewives at an expensive mannequin parade, who, though they admired the gowns, realized they have no hope of purchasing them. Then the male, as if in a last desperate effort to work his audience into some show of enthusiasm, suddenly swung right round on the perch and showed his beautiful scarlet back to them, lowered himself to a crouch and opened wide his beak, revealing the interior of his mouth which was a rich apple-green in colour and as glossy as though it had just been painted. He stood like this, singing with open mouth, and then gradually, as his song died away, his gorgeous plumes ceased to twitch and tremble and fell against his body. He stood upright on the branch for a moment and regarded the females. They stared back at him with the expected air of people who, having watched a conjurer performing one good trick, are waiting for the next. The male gave a few slight chirrups and then burst into song again and suddenly let himself drop, so that he hung beneath the branch. Still singing, he spread his wings wide and then walked to and fro upside down. This acrobatic display seemed to intrigue one of the females for the first time, for she cocked her head on one side in a gesture of enquiry. I could not for the life of me see how they could remain so unimpressed, for I was dazzled and captivated by the male's song and colouring. Having walked backwards and forwards for a minute or so, he closed his wings tightly and let his body dangle straight down, swaying softly from side to side, singing passionately all the while. He looked like some weird crimson fruit attached to the bough by the blue stalks of his legs, stirring gently in a breeze.

At this point, one of the females grew bored and flew off to another part of the aviary. The remaining one, however, with head cocked to one side, was peering closely at the male. With a quick flap of his wings he regained his upright position on the perch, looking a trifle smug, I thought, as well he might. Now I waited excitedly to see what would happen next. The male was standing stock-still, letting his feathers shimmer in the sunlight, and the female was becoming decidedly excited. I felt sure that she had succumbed to his fantastic courtship, which was as sudden and as beautiful as a burst of highly coloured fireworks. Sure enough, the female took wing. Now, I thought, she was going up to congratulate him on his performance and they would start married life together at once. But to my astonishment she merely flew onto the branch where the male sat, picked up a small beetle, which was wandering aimlessly across the bark, and with a satisfied chuck flew off to the other end of the aviary with it. The male puffed himself out and started to preen in a resigned sort of fashion, and I decided that the females must be especially hard-hearted, or especially inartistic, to have been able to resist such an exhibition. I felt very sorry for the male that his magnificent courtship should go unrewarded. However my sympathy was wasted, for with a squeak of triumph he had discovered another beetle, which he was happily banging on the branch. He obviously did not mind in the least being turned down.

Not all birds are such good dancers as the birds of paradise, nor are they so well dressed, but they have compensated for this by the charming originality of their approach to the opposite sex. Take, for example, the bower-birds. They have, in my opinion, one of the most delightful courtship methods in the world. The satin bower-bird, for instance, is not particularly impressive to look at: about the size of a thrush, he is clad in dark blue feathers that have a metallic glint when the light catches them. He looks, quite frankly, as if he is wearing an old and shiny suit of blue serge, and you would think that his chances of inducing the female to overlook the poverty of his wardrobe were non-existent. But he contrives it by an extremely cunning device: he builds a bower.

Once again it was in a zoo that I was lucky enough to see a satin bower-bird building his temple of love. He had chosen two large tussocks of grass in the middle of his aviary and had carefully cleared a large circular patch all round and a channel between them. Then he had carried twigs, pieces of string and straw, and had woven them into the grass, so that the finished building was like a tunnel. It was at this stage that I first noticed what he was doing, and by then, having built his little week-end cottage, he was in the process of decorating it. Two empty snail-shells were the first items, and they were followed by the silver paper from a packet of cigarettes, a piece of wool that he had picked up, six coloured pebbles and a bit of string with a blob of sealing wax on it. Feeling that he might like some more decoration, I brought him some strands of coloured wool, a few multicoloured sea-shells and some bus tickets.

He was delighted; he came down to the wire to take them carefully from my fingers, and then hopped back to his bower to arrange them. He would stand staring at the decorations for a minute and then hop forward and move a bus ticket or a strand of wool into what he considered a more artistic position. When the bower was finished it really looked very charming and decorative, and he stood in front of it preening himself and stretched out one wing at a time as if indicating his handiwork with pride. Then he dodged to and fro through his little tunnel, rearranged a couple of sea-shells, and started posturing again with one wing outspread. He had really worked hard on his bower, and I felt sorry for him, for the whole effort was in vain: his mate had apparently died some time previously and he now shared the aviary with a few squawking common finches that took no interest whatsoever in his architectural abilities or in his display of household treasures.

In the wild state, the satin bower-bird is one of the few birds that uses a tool, for he will sometimes paint the twigs used in the construction of his bower with highly coloured berries and moist charcoal, using a piece of some fibrous material as a brush. Unfortunately, by the time I had remembered this and had made plans to provide my bower-bird with a pot of blue paint and a piece of old rope – the bower-birds are particularly fond of blue – he had lost interest in his bower and not even the presentation of a complete set of cigarette cards, depicting soldiers' uniforms through the ages, could arouse his enthusiasm again.

Another species of bower-bird build an even more impressive structure, four to six feet high, by piling sticks round two trees and then roofing it over with creepers. The inside is carefully laid with moss, and the outside, for this bower-bird is plainly a man of the world with expensive tastes, is decorated with orchids. In front of the bower he constructs a little bed of green moss on which he places all the brightly coloured flowers and berries he can find; being a fastidious bird, he renews these every day, taking the withered decorations and piling them carefully out of sight behind the bower.

Among the mammals, of course, you do not come across quite such displays as among the birds. On the whole, mammals seem to have a more down-to-earth, even modern attitude, towards their love problems.

I was able to watch the courtship of two tigers when I worked at Whipsnade Zoo. The female was a timid, servile creature, cringing at the slightest snarl from her mate until the day she came into season. Then she changed suddenly into a slinking, dangerous creature, fully aware of her attraction but biding her time. By the end of the morning the male was following her round, belly-crawling and abject, while on his nose were several deep, bloody grooves caused by slashing backhands from his mate. Every time he forgot himself and approached too closely he got one of these backhand swipes across the nose. If he seemed at all offended by this treatment and lay down under a bush, the female would approach him, purring loudly, and rub herself against him until he got up and followed her again, moving closer and closer until he received another blow on the nose for his pains.

Eventually the female led him down into a little dell where the grass was long, and there she lay down and purred to herself, with her green eyes half-closed. The tip of her tail, like a big black-and-white bumble-bee, twitched to and fro in the grass, and the poor besotted male chased it from side to side, like a kitten, slapping it gently with his great paws. At last the female tired of her vamping; she crouched lower in the grass and gave a curious purring cry. The male, rumbling in his throat, moved towards her. She cried again, and raised her head, while the male gently bit along the line of her arched neck, a gentle nibble with his great teeth. Then the female cried again, a self-satisfied purr, and the two great striped bodies seemed to melt together in the green grass.

Not all mammals are so decorative and highly coloured as the tiger, but they generally compensate by being brawny. They therefore have to rely on cave-man tactics for obtaining their mates. Take, for example, the hippopotamus. To see one of these great chubby beasts lying in the water, staring at you with a sort of benign innocence out of bulbous eyes, sighing occasionally in a smug and lethargic manner, would scarcely lead you to believe that they could be roused to bursts of terrible savagery when it came to choosing a mate. If you have ever seen a hippo yawning, displaying on each side of its mouth four great curved razor-sharp tusks (hidden among which two more point outwards like a couple of ivory spikes) you will realize what damage they could do. When I was collecting animals in West Africa we once camped on the banks of a river in which lived a hippo herd of moderate size. They seemed a placid and happy group, and every time we went up or down the stream by canoe they would follow us a short distance, swimming nearer and nearer, wiggling their ears and occasionally snorting up clouds of spray, as they watched us with interest. As far as I could make out, the herd consisted of four females, a large elderly male and a young male. One of the females had a medium-sized baby with her which, though already large and fat, was still occasionally carried on her back. They seemed, as I say, a very happy family group. But one night, just as it was growing dark, they launched into a series of roars and brays which sounded like a choir of demented donkeys. These were interspersed with moments of silence broken only by a snort or a splash, but as it grew darker the noise became worse, until, eventually realizing I would be unlikely to get any sleep, I decided to go down and see what was happening. Taking a canoe, I paddled down to the curve of the river a couple of hundred yards away, where the brown water had carved a deep pool out of the bank and thrown up a great half-moon of glittering white sand. I knew the hippos liked to spend the day here, and it was from this direction that all the noise was coming. I knew something was wrong, for usually by this time each evening they had hauled their fat bodies out of the water and trekked along the bank to raid some unfortunate native's plantation, but here they were in the pool, long past the beginning of their feeding-time. I landed on the sandbank and walked along to a spot which gave me a good view. There was no reason for me to worry about noise: the terrible roars and bellows and splashes coming from the pool were quite sufficient to cover the scrunch of my footsteps.

At first I could see nothing but an occasional flash of white where the hippos' bodies thrashed in the water and churned it into foam, but presently the moon rose, and in its brilliant light I could see the females and the baby gathered at one end of the pool in a tight bunch, their heads gleaming above the surface of the water, their ears flicking to and fro. Now and again they would open their mouths and bray, rather in the manner of a Greek chorus. They were watching with interest both the old male and the young who were in the shallows at the centre of the pool. The water reached up only to their tummies, and their great barrel-shaped bodies and the rolls of fat under their chins gleamed as though they had been oiled. They were facing each other with lowered heads, snorting like a couple of steam-engines. Suddenly the young male lifted his great head, opened his mouth so that his teeth flashed in the moonlight, gave a prolonged and blood-curdling bray, and, just as he was finishing, the old male rushed at him with open mouth and incredible speed for such a bulky animal. The young male, equally quick, twisted to one side. The old male splashed in a welter of foam like some misshapen battleship, and was now going so fast that he could not stop. As he passed, the young male, with a terrible sideways chop of his huge jaws, bit him in the shoulder. The old male swerved round and charged again, and just as he reached his opponent the moon went behind a cloud. When it came out again, they were standing as I had first seen them, facing each other with lowered heads, snorting.

I sat on that sandbank for two hours, watching these great roly-poly creatures churning up the water and sand as they duelled in the shallows. As far as I could see, the old male was getting the worst of it, and I felt sorry for him. Like some once-great pugilist who had now grown flabby and stiff, he seemed to be fighting a battle which he knew was already lost. The young male, lighter and more agile, seemed to dodge him every time, and his teeth always managed to find their mark in the shoulder or neck of the old male. In the background the females watched with semaphoring ears, occasionally breaking into a loud lugubrious chorus which may have been sorrow for the plight of the old male, or delight at the success of the young one, but was probably merely the excitement of watching the fight. Eventually, since the fight did not seem as if it would end for several more hours, I paddled home to the village and went to bed.

I awoke just as the horizon was paling into dawn, and the hippos were quiet. Apparently the fight was over. I hoped that the old male had won, but I very much doubted it. The answer was given to me later that morning by one of my hunters; the corpse of the old male, he said, was about two miles downstream, lying where the current of the river had carried it into the curving arms of a sandbank. I went down to examine it and was horrified at the havoc the young male's teeth had wrought on the massive body. The shoulders, the neck, the great dewlaps that hung under the chin, the flanks and the belly: all were ripped and tattered, and the shallows around the carcass were still tinged with blood. The entire village had accompanied me, for such an enormous windfall of meat was a red-letter day for them. They stood silent and interested while I examined the old male's carcass, and when I had finished and walked away they poured over it like ants, screaming and pushing with excitement, vigorously wielding their knives and machetes. It seemed to me, watching the huge hippo's carcass disintegrate under the pile of hungry humans, that it was a heavy price to pay for love.

A notably romantic member of the human race is described as hot-blooded; yet in the animal world it is among the cold-blooded creatures that you find some of the best courtship displays. The average crocodile looks as though he would prove a pretty cold-blooded lover as he lies on the bank, watching with his perpetual, sardonic grin and unwinking eyes the passing pageant of river life. Yet when the time and the place and the lady are right, he will fling himself into battle for her hand; and the two males, snapping and thrashing, will roll over and over in the water. At last the winner, flushed with victory, proceeds to do a strange dance on the surface of the water, whirling round and round with his head and tail thrust into the air, bellowing like a foghorn in what is apparently the reptilian equivalent of an old-fashioned waltz.

It is among the terrapins or water-tortoises that we find an example of the 'treat 'em rough and they'll love you' school of thought. In one of these little reptiles the claws on the front flippers are greatly elongated. Swimming along, the male sees a suitable female and starts to head her off. He then beats her over the head with his long fingernails, an action so quickly performed that his claws are a mere blur. This does not seem to make the female suffer in any way; it may even give her pleasure. But at any rate, even a female terrapin cannot succumb at the very first sign of interest on the part of the male. She must play hard to get, even if only for a short time, and she therefore breaks away and continues swimming in the stream. The male, now roused to a frenzy, swims after her, heads her off again, backs her up to the bank and proceeds to give her another beating. And this may happen several times before the female agrees to take up housekeeping with him. Whatever one may say against this reptile, he is certainly no hypocrite; he starts as he means to go on. And the female does not appear to mind these somewhat hectic advances. In fact, she seems to find them a pleasant and rather original form of approach. But there is no accounting for tastes – even among human beings.

However, for bewildering variety and ingenuity in the management of their love affairs, I think one must give pride of place to the insects.

Taking the praying mantis – mind you, one look at their faces and nothing would surprise you about their private lives. The small head, the large, bulbous eyes dominating a tiny, pointed face that ends in a little quivering moustache; and the eyes themselves, a pale watery straw colour with black cat-like pupils that give them a wild and maniacal look. Under the chest a pair of powerful, savagely barbed arms are bent in a permanent and hypocritical attitude of prayer, being ready at a moment's notice to leap out and crush the victim in an embrace as though he had been caught in a pair of serrated scissors. Another unpleasant habit of the mantis is the way it looks at things, for it can turn its head to and fro in the most human manner and, if puzzled, will cock its little chinless face on one side, staring at you with wild eyes. Or, if you walk behind it, it will peer at you over its shoulder with an unpleasant air of expectancy. Only a male mantis, I feel, could see anything remotely attractive in the female, and you would think he would be sensible enough not to trust a bride with a face like that. But no, I have seen one, his heart overflowing with love, clasp a female passionately, and while they were actually consummating their marriage his spouse leaned tenderly over her shoulder and proceeded to eat him, browsing with the air of a gourmet over his corpse still clasped to her back, while her whiskers quivered and twitched as each delicate, glistening morsel was savoured to the full.

Female spiders, of course, have this same rather antisocial habit of eating their husbands; and the male's approach to the web of the female is thus fraught with danger. If she happens to be hungry, he will hardly have a chance to get the first words of his proposal out, as it were, before he finds himself a neatly trussed bundle being sucked of his vital juices by the lady. In one such species of the spider, the male has worked out a method to make certain he can get close enough to the female to tickle and massage her into a receptive frame of mind, without being eaten. He brings her a little gift – it may be a bluebottle or something of the sort – neatly wrapped up in silk. While she is busily devouring this, he creeps up behind her and strokes her into a sort of trance with his legs. Sometimes, when the nuptials are over, he manages to get away, but in most cases, he is eaten at the end of the honeymoon, for it appears that the only true way to a female spider's heart is through her stomach.

In another species of spider the male has evolved an even more brilliant device for subduing his tigerish wife. Having approached her, he then starts to massage her gently with his legs until, as is usual with female spiders, she enters a sort of hypnotic state. Then the male, as swiftly as he can, proceeds to bind her to the ground with a length of silken cord, so that, when she awakes from her trance in the marriage bed, she finds herself unable to turn her husband into a wedding breakfast until she has set about the tedious business of untying herself. This generally saves the husband's life.

But if you want a really exotic romance you need not go to the tropical jungle to find it: just go into your own back garden and creep up on the common snail. Here you have a situation as complex as the plot of any modern novel, for snails are hermaphrodite, and so each one can enjoy the pleasure of both the male and female side of courtship and mating. But apart from this dual sex, the snail possesses something even more extraordinary, a small sack-like container in its body in which is manufactured a tiny leaf-shaped splinter of carbonate of lime, known as the love-dart. Thus when one snail – who, as I say, is both male and female – crawls alongside another snail, also male and female, the two of them indulge in the most curious courtship action. They proceed to stab each other with their love-darts, which penetrate deeply and are quite quickly dissolved in the body. It seems that this curious duel is not as painful as it appears; in fact, the dart sinking into its side seems to give the snail a pleasant feeling, perhaps an exotic tickling sensation. But, whatever it is it puts both snails into an enthusiastic frame of mind for the stern business of mating. I am no gardener, but if I were I would probably have a soft spot for any snails in my garden, even if they did eat my plants. Any creature who has dispensed with Cupid, who carries his own quiverful of arrows around with him is, in my opinion, worth any number of dull and sexless cabbages. It is an honour to have him in the garden.

ANIMAL ARCHITECTS

Some time ago I received a small parcel from a friend of mine in India. Inside the box I found a note which read: 'I bet you don't know what this is'. Greatly intrigued, I lifted off the top layer of wrapping paper, and underneath I found what appeared to be two large leaves which had been rather inexpertly sewn together.

My friend would have lost his bet. As soon as I saw the large and rather amateur stitches, I knew what it was: the nest of a tailor-bird, a thing I had always wanted to see. The two leaves were about six inches long, shaped rather like laurel leaves, and only the edges had been sewn together, so that it formed a sort of pointed bag. Inside the bag was a neat nest of grass and moss, and inside that were two small eggs. The tailor-bird is quite small, about the size of a tit, but with a rather long beak. This is its needle. Having found the two leaves it likes, hanging close together, it then proceeds to sew them together, using fine cotton as thread. The curious thing about it is not so much that the tailor-bird stitches the leaves together as that nobody seems to know where he finds the cotton material with which to do the sewing. Some experts insist that he weaves it himself, others that he has some source of supply that has never been discovered. As I say, the stitches were rather large and inartistic, but then how many people could make a success of sewing up two leaves, using only a beak as a needle?

Architecture in the animal world differs a great deal. Some animals, of course, have only the haziest idea of constructing a suitable dwelling, while others produce most complicated and delightful homes. It is strange that even among closely related animals there should be such a wide variety of taste in the style, situation and size of the home and the choice of materials used in its construction.

In the bird world, of course, one finds homes of every shape and size. They range from the tailor-bird's cradle of leaves to the emperor penguin, who, with nothing but snow for his building, has dispensed with the idea of a nest altogether. The egg is simply carried on the top of the large flat foot, and the skin and feathers of the stomach form a sort of pouch to cover it. Then you have the edible swift who makes a fragile, cup-shaped nest of saliva and bits of twigs and sticks it to the wall of a cave. Among the weaver-birds of Africa, too, the variety of nests is bewildering. One species lives in a community which builds a nest half the size of a haystack, rather like a block of flats, in which each bird has its own nesting-hole. In these gigantic nests you sometimes get an odd variety of creatures living as well as the rightful occupants. Snakes are very fond of them; so are bush-babies and squirrels. One of these nests, if taken to pieces, might display an extraordinary assortment of inmates. No wonder that trees have been known to collapse under the weight of these colossal nests. The common weaver-bird of West Africa builds a neat, round nest, like a small basket woven from palm fibres. They also live in communities and hang their nests on every available branch of a tree, until it seems festooned with some extraordinary form of fruit. In the most human way the brilliant and shrill-voiced owners go about the business of courting, hatching the eggs, feeding their young, and bickering with their neighbours, so that the whole thing rather resembles an odd sort of council estate.

To construct their nests, the weaver-birds have become adept not only at weaving but at tying knots, for the nest is strapped very firmly to the branch and requires considerable force to remove it. I once watched a weaver-bird starting its nest, a fascinating performance. He had decided that the nest should hang from the end of a delicate twig half-way up a tree, and he arrived on the spot carrying a long strand of palm fibre in his beak. He alighted on the branch, which at once swung to and fro so that he had to flap his wings to keep his balance. When he was fairly steady he juggled with the palm fibre until he got to the centre of it. Then he tried to drape it over the branch, so that the two ends hung one side and the loop hung the other. The branch still swayed about, and twice he dropped the fibre and had to fly down to retrieve it, but at last he got it slung over the branch to his satisfaction. He then placed one foot on it to keep it in position and leaning forward precariously he pulled the two dangling ends from one side of the branch through the loop on the other and tugged it tight. After this he flew for some more fibre and repeated the performance. He went on in this way for the whole day, until by evening he had twenty or thirty pieces of fibre lashed to the branch, the ends dangling down like a beard.

Unfortunately I missed the following stages in the construction of this nest, and I next saw it empty, for the bird had presumably reared its young and moved off. The nest was flask-shaped – a small round entrance, guarded by a small porch of plaited fibre. I tried to pull the nest off the branch, but it was impossible, and in the end I had to break the whole branch off. Then I tried to tear the nest in half so that I could examine the inside. But so intricately interlaced and knotted were the palm fibres that it took me a long time and all my strength before I could do so. It was really an incredible construction, when you consider the bird had only its beak and its feet for tools.

When I went to Argentina four years ago I noticed that nearly every tree-stump or rail-post in the pampa was decorated with a strange earthenware construction about the size and shape of a football. At first, I believed they were termite nests, for they were very similar to a common feature of the landscape in West Africa. It was not until I saw, perched on top of one of them, a small tubby bird about the size of a robin with a rusty-red back and grey shirt-front that I realized they were the nests of the oven-bird.

As soon as I found an unoccupied nest, I carefully cut it in half and was amazed at the skill with which it had been built. Wet mud had been mixed with tiny fragments of dried grass, roots and hair to act as reinforcement. The sides of the nest were approximately an inch and a half thick. The outside had been left rough – unrendered, as it were – but the inside had been smoothed to a glass-like finish. The entrance to the nest was a small arched hole, rather like a church door, which led into a narrow passageway that curved round the outer edge of the nest and eventually led into the circular nesting-chamber lined with a pad of soft roots and feathers. The whole thing rather resembled a snail-shell.

Although I searched a large area, I was never lucky enough to find a nest that had been newly started, for it was fairly well into the breeding season. But I did find one half-completed. Oven-birds are very common in Argentina, and in the way they move and cock their heads on one side and regard you with their shining dark eyes, they reminded me very much of the English robin. The pair building this nest took no notice of me whatever, provided I remained at a distance of about twelve feet, though occasionally they would fly over to take a closer look at me, and after inspecting me with their heads on one side, they would flap their wings as though shrugging, and return to their building work. The nest, as I say, was half-finished: the base was firmly cemented onto a fence-post and the outer walls and inner wall of the passageway were already some four or five inches high. All that remained now was for the whole thing to be covered with the domed roof.

The nearest place for wet mud was about half a mile away at the edge of a shallow lagoon. They would hop round the edge of the water in a fussy, rather pompous manner, testing the mud every few feet. It had to be of exactly the right consistency. Having found a suitable patch, they would hop about excitedly, picking up tiny rootlets and bits of grass until their beaks were full and they looked as though they had suddenly sprouted large walrus moustaches. They would carry these beakfuls of reinforcement down to the mud patch, and then, by skilful juggling, without dropping the material, pick up a large amount of mud as well. By a curious movement of the beak they matted the two materials together until their walrus moustaches looked distinctly bedraggled and mudstained. Then, with a muffled squeak of triumph, they flew off to the nest. Here the bundle was placed in the right position and pecked and trampled on and pushed until it had firmly adhered to the original wall. Then they entered the nest and smoothed off the new patch, using their beaks, their breasts and even the sides of their wings to get the required shining finish.

When only a small patch on the very top of the roof needed to be finished, I took some bright scarlet threads of wool down to the edge of the lagoon and scattered them around the place where the oven-birds gathered their material. On my next trip down there, to my delight, they had picked them up, and the result, a small russet bird apparently wearing a bright scarlet moustache, was quite startling. They incorporated the wool into the last piece of building on the nest, and it was, I feel sure, the only Argentinian oven-bird's nest on the pampa flying what appeared to be a small red flag at half-mast.

If the oven-bird is a master-builder, whose nest is so solid that it takes several blows of a hammer to demolish it, members of the pigeon family go to the opposite extreme. They have absolutely no idea of proper nest-making. Four or five twigs laid across a branch: that is the average pigeon's idea of a highly complicated structure. On this frail platform the eggs, generally two, are laid. Every time the tree sways in the wind this silly nest trembles and shakes and the eggs almost fall out. How any pigeon ever reaches maturity is a mystery to me.

I knew that pigeons were stupid and inefficient builders, but I never thought that their nests might prove an irritating menace to a naturalist.

When I was in Argentina I learned differently. On the banks of a river outside Buenos Aires I found a small wood. The trees, only about thirty feet high, were occupied by what might almost be called a pigeon colony. Every tree had about thirty or forty nests in it. Walking underneath the branches you could see the fat bellies of the young, or the gleam of the eggs, through the carelessly arranged twigs. The nests looked so insecure that I felt like walking on tip-toe for fear that my footsteps would destroy the delicate balance.

In the centre of the wood I found a tree full of pigeons' nests but for some odd reason devoid of pigeons. At the very top of the tree I noticed a great bundle of twigs and leaves which was obviously a nest of some sort and equally obviously not a pigeon's nest. I wondered if it was the occupant of this rather untidy bundle of stuff that had made the pigeons desert all the nests in the tree. I decided to climb and see if the owner was at home. Unfortunately, it was only when I had started to climb that I realized my mistake, for nearly every pigeon's nest in the tree contained eggs, and as I made my way slowly up the branches my movements created a sort of waterfall of pigeon eggs which bounced and broke against me, smearing my coat and trousers with yolk and bits of shell. I would not have minded this so much, but every single egg was well and truly addled, and by the time I had reached the top of the tree, hot and sweating, I smelt like a cross between a tannery and a sewage farm. To add insult to injury, I found that the occupant of the nest I had climbed up to was out, so I had gained nothing by my climb except a thick coating of egg and a scent that would have made a skunk envious. Laboriously I climbed down the tree again, looking forward to the moment when I would reach ground and could light a cigarette, to take the strong smell of rotten egg out of my nostrils. The ground under the tree was littered with broken eggs tastefully interspersed with the bodies of a few baby pigeons in a decomposed condition. I made my way out into the open as quickly as possible. With a sigh of relief, I sat down and reached into my pocket for my cigarettes. I drew them out dripping with egg-yolk. At some point during my climb, by some curious chance, an egg had fallen into my pocket and broken. My cigarettes were ruined. I had to walk two miles home without a smoke, breathing in a strong aroma of egg and looking as though I had rather unsuccessfully taken part in an omelette-making competition. I have never really liked pigeons since then.

Mammals, on the whole, are not such good builders as the birds, though, of course, a few of them are experts. The badger, for example, builds the most complicated burrow, which is sometimes added to by successive generations until the whole thing resembles an intricate underground system with passages, culs-de-sac, bedrooms, nurseries and feeding-quarters. The beaver, too is another master-builder, constructing his lodge half in and half out of the water: thick walls of mud and logs with an underground entrance, so that he can get in and out even when the surface of the lake is iced over. Beavers also build canals, so that when they have to fell a tree some distance inland for food or repair work on their dam, they can float it down the canal to the main body of water. Their dams are, of course, masterpieces – massive constructions of mud and logs, welded together, stretching sometimes many hundreds of yards. The slightest breach in these is frantically repaired by the beavers, for fear that the water might drain away and leave their lodge with its door no longer covered by water, an easy prey to any passing enemy. What with their home, their canals, and their dams, one has the impression that the beaver must be a remarkably intelligent and astute animal. Unfortunately, however, this is not the case. It appears that the desire to build a dam is an urge which no self-respecting beaver can repress even when there is no need for the construction, and when kept in a large cement pool they will solemnly and methodically run a dam across it to keep the water in.

But, of course, the real master-architects of the animal world are, without a doubt, the insects. You need only look at the beautiful mathematical precision with which a common-or-garden honeycomb is built. Insects seem capable of building the most astonishing homes from a vast array of materials – wood, paper, wax, mud, silk, and sand – and they differ just as widely in their design. In Greece, when I was a boy, I used to spend hours searching mossy banks for the nest of the trapdoor-spiders. These are one of the most beautiful and astonishing pieces of animal architecture in the world. The spider itself, with its legs spread out, would just about cover a two-shilling piece and looks as though it has been made out of highly polished chocolate. It has a squat fat body and rather short legs, and does not look at all the sort of creature you would associate with delicate construction work. Yet these rather clumsy-looking spiders sink a shaft into the earth of a bank about six inches deep and about the diameter of a shilling. This is carefully lined, so that when finished it is like a tube of silk. Then comes the most important part, the trapdoor. This is circular and with a neatly bevelled edge, so that it fits securely into the mouth of the tunnel. It is then fixed with a silken hinge, and the outside of it camouflaged with springs of moss or lichen; it is almost indistinguishable from the surrounding earth when closed. If the owner is not at home and you flip back the door, you will see on its silken underside a series of neat little black pinpricks. These are the handles, so to speak, in which the spider latches her claws to hold the door firmly shut against intruders. The only person, I think, who would not be amazed at the beauty of a trapdoor-spider's nest is the male trapdoor-spider himself, for once he has lifted the trapdoor and entered the silken shaft, it is for him both a tunnel of love and death. Once having gone down into the dark interior and mated with the female, he is promptly killed and eaten by her.

One of my first experiences with animal architects was when I was about ten years old. At that time I was extremely interested in freshwater biology and used to spend most of my spare time dredging about in ponds and streams, catching the minute fauna that lived there and keeping them in large jam jars in my bedroom. Among other things, I had one jam jar full of caddis larvae. These curious caterpillar-like creatures encase themselves in a sort of silken cocoon with one end open, and then decorate the outside of the cocoon with whatever materials they think will produce the best camouflage. The caddis I had were rather dull, for I had caught them in a very stagnant pool. They had merely decorated the outside of their cocoons with little bits of dead water-plant.

I had been told, however, that if you remove a caddis larva from its cocoon and place it in a jar of clean water, it would spin itself a new cocoon and decorate the outside with whatever materials you cared to supply. I was a bit sceptical about this, but decided to experiment. I took four of my caddis larvae and very carefully removed them, wriggling indignantly from their cocoons. Then I placed them in a jar of clean water and lined the bottom of the jar with a handful of tiny bleached sea-shells. To my astonishment and delight the creatures did exactly what my friend said they would do, and by the time the larvae had finished the new cocoons were like a filigree of sea-shells.

I was so enthusiastic about this that I gave the poor creatures a rather hectic time of it. Every now and then I would force them to manufacture new cocoons decorated with more and more improbable substances. The climax came with my discovery that by moving the larvae to a new jar with a new substance at the bottom when they were half-way through building operations, you could get them to build a parti-coloured cocoon. Some of the results I got were very odd. There was one, for example, who had half his cocoon magnificently arrayed in sea-shells and the other half in bits of charcoal. My greatest triumph, however, lay in forcing three of them to decorate their cocoons with fragments of blue glass, red brick and white sea-shells. Moreover, the materials were put on in stripes – rather uneven stripes, I grant you, but stripes nevertheless.

Since then I have had a lot of animals of which I have been proud, but

I never remember feeling quite the same sort of satisfaction as I did when I used to show off my red, white and blue caddis larvae to my friends. I think the poor creatures were really rather relieved when they could hatch out and fly away and forget about the problems of cocoon-building.

ANIMAL WARFARE

I remember once lying on a sun-drenched hillside in Greece – a hillside covered with twisted olive trees and myrtle bushes – and watching a protracted and bloody war being waged within inches of my feet. I was extremely lucky to be, as it were, war correspondent for this battle. It was the only one of its kind I have ever seen and I would not have missed it for the world.

The two armies involved were ants. The attacking force was a shining, fierce red, while the defending army was as black as coal. I might quite easily have missed this if one day I had not noticed what struck me as an extremely peculiar ants' nest. It contained two species of ants, one red and one black, living together on the most amicable terms. Never having seen two species of ants living in the same nest before, I took the trouble to check up on them, and discovered that the red ones, who were the true owners of the nest, were known by the resounding title of the blood-red slave-makers, and the black ones were in fact their slaves who had been captured and placed in their service while they were still eggs. After reading about the habits of the slave-makers, I kept a cautious eye on the nest in the hope of seeing them indulge in one of their slave raids. Several months passed and I began to think that either these slave-makers were too lazy or else they had enough slaves to keep them happy.

The slave-makers' fortress lay near the roots of an olive tree, and some thirty feet farther down the hillside was a nest of black ants. Passing this nest one morning, I noticed several of the slave-makers wandering about within a yard or so of it, and I stopped to watch. There were perhaps thirty or forty of them, spread over quite a large area. They did not appear to be foraging for food, as they were not moving with their normal brisk inquisitiveness. They kept wandering round in vague circles, occasionally climbing a grass blade and standing pensively on its tip, waving their antennae. Periodically, two of them would meet and stand there in what appeared to be animated conversation, their antennae twitching together. It was not until I had watched them for some time that I realized what they were doing. Their wanderings were not as aimless as they appeared, for they were quartering the ground very thoroughly like a pack of hunting-dogs, investigating every bit of the terrain over which their army would have to travel. The black ants seemed distinctly ill at ease. Occasionally one of them would meet one of the slave-makers and would turn tail and run back to the nest to join one of the many groups of his relatives who were gathered in little knots, apparently holding a council of war. This careful investigation of the ground by the scouts of the slave-makers' army continued for two days, and I had begun to think that they had decided the black ants' city was too difficult to attack. Then I arrived one morning to find that the war had started.

The scouts, accompanied by four or five small platoons, had now moved in closer to the black ants, and already several skirmishes were taking place within two or three feet of the nest. Black ants were hurling themselves on the red ones with almost hysterical fervour, while the red ones were advancing slowly but inexorably, now and then catching a black ant and with a swift, savage bite piercing it through the head or the thorax with their huge jaws.

Half-way up the hillside the main body of the slave-makers' army was marching down. In about an hour they had got within four or five feet of the black ants' city, and here, with a beautiful military precision which was quite amazing to watch, they split into three columns. While one column marched directly on the nest the other two spread out and proceeded to execute a flanking or pincer movement. It was fascinating to watch. I felt I was suspended in some miraculous way above the field of battle of some old military campaign – the battle of Waterloo or some similar historic battle. I could see at a glance the disposition of the attackers and the defenders; I could see the columns of reinforcements hurrying up through the jungle of grass; see the two outflanking columns of slave-makers moving nearer and nearer to the nest, while the black ants, unaware of their presence, were concentrating on fighting off the central column. It was quite obvious to me that unless the black ants very soon realized that they were being encircled, they had lost all hope of survival. I was torn between a desire to help the black ants in some way and a longing to leave things as they were and see how matters developed. I did pick up one of the black ants and place him near the encircling red-ant column, but he was set upon and killed rapidly, and I felt quite guilty.

Eventually, however, the black ants suddenly became aware of the fact that they were being neatly surrounded. Immediately they seemed to panic; numbers of them ran to and fro aimlessly, some of them in their fright running straight into the red invaders and being instantly killed.

Others, however, seemed to keep their heads, and they rushed down into the depths of the fortress and started on the work of evacuating the eggs, which they brought up and stacked on the side of the nest farthest away from the invaders. Other members of the community then seized the eggs and started to rush them away to safety. But they had left it too late.

The encircling columns of slave-makers, so orderly and neat, now suddenly burst their ranks and spread over the whole area, like a scuttling red tide. Everywhere there were knots of struggling ants. Black ones, clasping eggs in their jaws, were pursued by the slave-makers, cornered and then forced to give up the eggs. If they showed fight, they were immediately killed; the more cowardly, however, saved their lives by dropping the eggs they were carrying as soon as a slave-maker hove in sight. The whole area on and around the nest was littered with dead and dying ants of both species, while between the corpses the black ants ran futilely hither and thither, and the slave-makers gathered the eggs and started on the journey back to their fortress on the hill. At that point, very reluctantly, I had to leave the scene of battle, for it was getting too dark to see properly.

Early next morning I arrived at the scene again, to find the war was over. The black ants' city was deserted, except for the dead and injured ants littered all over it. Neither the black nor the red army were anywhere to be seen. I hurried up to the red ants' nest and was just in time to see the last of the army arrive there, carrying their spoils of war, the eggs, carefully in their jaws. At the entrance to the nest their black slaves greeted them excitedly, touching the eggs with their antennae and scuttling eagerly around their masters, obviously full of enthusiasm for the successful raid on their own relations that the slave-makers had achieved. There was something unpleasantly human about the whole thing.

It is perhaps unfair to describe animals as indulging in warfare, because for the most part they are far too sensible to engage in warfare as we know it. The exceptions are, of course, the ants, and the slave-makers in particular. But for most other creatures warfare consists of either defending themselves against an enemy, or attacking something for food.

After watching the slave-makers wage war I had the greatest admiration for their military strategy, but it did not make me like them very much. In fact, I was delighted to find that there existed what might be described as an underground movement bent on their destruction: the ant-lions. An adult ant-lion is very like a dragonfly, and looks fairly innocent. But in its childhood, as it were, it is a voracious monster that has evolved an extremely cunning way of trapping its prey, most of which consists of ants.

The larva is round-bodied, with a large head armed with great pincer-like jaws. Picking a spot where the soil is loose and sandy, it buries itself in the earth and makes a circular depression like the cone of a volcano. At the bottom of this, concealed by sand, the larva waits for its prey. Sooner or later an ant comes hurrying along in that preoccupied way so typical of ants, and blunders over the edge of the ant-lion's cone. It immediately realizes its mistake and tries to climb out again, but it finds this difficult, for the sand is soft and gives way under its weight. As it struggles futilely at the rim of this volcano it dislodges grains of sand which trickle down inside the cone and awake the deadly occupant that lurks there. Immediately the ant-lion springs into action. Using its great head and jaws like a steam-shovel, it shoots a rapid spray of sand grains at the ant, still struggling desperately to climb over the lip of the volcano. The earth sliding away from under its claws, knocked off its balance by this stream of sand and unable to regain it, the ant rolls down to the bottom of the cone where the sand parts like a curtain and it is enfolded lovingly in the great curved jaws of the ant-lion. Slowly, kicking and struggling, it disappears, as though it were being sucked down by quicksand, and within a few seconds the cone is empty, while below the innocent-looking sand the ant-lion is sucking the vital juices out of its victim.

Another creature that uses this sort of machine-gunning to bring down its prey is the archer-fish. This is a rather handsome creature found in the streams of Asia. It has evolved a most ingenious method of obtaining its prey, which consists of flies, butterflies, moths, and other insects. Swimming slowly along under the surface it waits until it sees an insect alight on a twig or leaf overhanging the water. Then the fish slows down and approaches cautiously. When it is within range it stops, takes aim, and then suddenly and startlingly spits a stream of tiny water droplets at its prey. These travel with deadly accuracy, and the startled insect is knocked off its perch and into the water below, and the next minute the fish swims up beneath it, there is a swirl of water and a gulp, and the insect has vanished for ever.

I once worked in a pet shop in London, and one day, with a consignment of other creatures, we received an archer-fish. I was delighted with it, and with the permission of the manager I wrote out a notice describing the fish's curious habits, arranged the aquarium carefully, put the fish inside and placed it in the window as the main display. It proved very popular, except that people wanted to see the archer-fish actually taking his prey, and this was not easy to manage. Eventually I had a brainwave. A few doors down from us was a fish shop, and I saw no reason why we should not benefit from some of their surplus bluebottles. So I suspended a bit of very smelly meat over the archer-fish's aquarium and left the door of the shop open. I did this without the knowledge of the manager. I wanted it to be a surprise for him.

It was certainly a surprise.

By the time he arrived, there must have been several thousand bluebottles in the shop. The archer-fish was having the time of his life, watched by myself inside the shop and fifty or sixty people on the pavement outside. The manager arrived neck and neck with a very unzoological policeman, who wanted to know the meaning of the obstruction outside. To my surprise the manager, instead of being delighted with my ingenious window display, tended to side with the policeman. The climax came when the manager, leaning over the aquarium to unfasten the bit of meat that hung above it, was hit accurately in the face by a stream of water which the fish had just released in the hope of hitting a particularly succulent bluebottle. The manager never referred to the incident again, but the next day the archer-fish disappeared, and it was the last time I was allowed to dress the window.

Of course, one of the favourite tricks in animal warfare is for some harmless creature to persuade a potential enemy that it is really a hideous, ferocious beast, best left alone. One of the most amusing examples of this I have seen was given to me by a sun bittern when I was collecting live animals in British Guiana. This slender bird, with a delicate, pointed beak and slow, stately movements, had been hand-reared by an Indian and was therefore perfectly tame. I used to let it wander freely round my camp during the day and lock it in a cage only at night. Sun bitterns are clad in lovely feathering that has all the hints of an autumn woodland, and sometimes when this bird stood unmoving against a background of dry leaves she seemed to disappear completely. As I say, she was a frail, dainty little bird who, one would have thought, had no defence of any sort against an enemy. But this was not the case.

Three large and belligerent hunting-dogs followed their master into camp one afternoon, and before long one of them spotted the sun bittern, standing lost in meditation on the edge of the clearing. He approached her, his ears pricked, growling softly. The other two quickly joined him, and the three of them bore down on the bird with a swaggering air. The bird let them get within about four feet of her before deigning to notice them. Then she turned her head, gave them a withering stare and turned round to face them. The dogs paused, not quite sure what to do about a bird that did not run squawking at their approach. They moved closer. Suddenly the bittern ducked her head and spread her wings, so that the dogs were presented with a fan of feathers. In the centre of each wing was a beautiful marking, not noticeable when the wings were closed, which looked exactly like the two eyes of an enormous owl glaring at you. The whole transformation was done so slickly, from a slim meek little bird to something that resembled an infuriated eagle owl at bay, that the dogs were taken completely by surprise. They stopped their advance, took one look at the shivering wings and then turned tail and fled. The sun bittern shuffled her wings back into place, preened a few of her breast feathers that had become disarranged and fell to meditating again. It was obvious that dogs did not trouble her in the slightest.

Some of the most ingenious methods of defence in the animal world are displayed by insects. They are masters of the art of disguise, of setting traps, and other methods of defence and attack. But, certainly, one of the most extraordinary is the bombardier beetle.

I was once the proud owner of a genuine wild black rat which I had caught when he was a half-grown youngster. He was an extremely handsome beast with his shining ebony fur and gleaming black eyes. He divided his time equally between cleaning himself and eating. His great passion was for insects of any shape or size: butterflies, praying mantis, stick-insects, cockroaches, they all went the same way as soon as they were put into his cage. Not even the largest praying mantis stood a chance against him, though they would occasionally manage to dig their hooked arms into his nose and draw a bead of blood before he scrunched them up. But one day I found an insect which got the better of him. It was a large, blackish beetle which had been sitting reflecting under a stone that I had inquisitively turned over; and, thinking it would make a nice titbit for my rat, I put it in a matchbox in my pocket. When I arrived home I pulled the rat out of his sleeping-box, opened the matchbox and shook the large succulent beetle onto the floor of his cage. Now the rat had two methods of dealing with insects, which varied according to their kind. If they were as fast-moving and as belligerent as a mantis, he would rush in and bite as quickly as possible in order to destroy it, but with anything harmless and slow, like a beetle, he would pick it up in his paws and sit scrunching it up as though it were a piece of toast.

Seeing this great fat delicacy wandering rather aimlessly around on the floor of his cage, he trotted forward, rapidly seized it with his little pink paws and then sat back on his haunches with the air of a gourmet about to sample the first truffle of the season. His whiskers twitched in anticipation as he lifted the beetle to his mouth, and then a curious thing happened. He uttered the most prodigious sniff, dropped the beetle and leapt backwards as though he had been stung, and sat rubbing his paws hastily over his nose and face. At first I thought he had merely been taken with a sneezing fit just as he was about to eat the beetle. Having wiped his face, he again approached it, slightly more cautiously this time, picked it up and lifted it to his mouth. Then he uttered a strangled snort, dropped it as though it were red-hot and sat wiping his face indignantly. The second experience had obviously been enough for him, for he refused to go near the beetle after that; in fact he seemed positively scared of it. Every time it ambled round to the corner of the cage where he was sitting, he would back away hurriedly. I put the beetle back in the matchbox and took it inside to identify it and it was only then that I discovered that I had offered my unfortunate rat a bombardier beetle. Apparently the beetle, when attacked, squirts out a liquid which, on reaching the air, explodes with a tiny crack and forms a sort of pungent and unpleasant gas, sufficiently horrible to make any creature who has experienced it leave the bombardier beetle severely alone in future.

I felt rather sorry for my black rat. It was, I felt, an unfortunate experience to pick up what amounted to a particularly delicious dinner, only to have it suddenly turn into a gas attack in your paws. It gave him a complex about beetles, too, because for days afterwards he would dash into his sleeping-box at the sight of one, even a fat and harmless dung-beetle. However, he was a young rat, and I suppose he had to learn at some time or another that one cannot judge by appearances in this life.

ANIMAL INVENTORS

I once travelled back from Africa on a ship with an Irish captain who did not like animals. This was unfortunate, because most of my luggage consisted of about two hundred-odd cages of assorted wild life, which were stacked on the forward well deck. The captain (more out of devilment than anything else, I think) never missed a chance of trying to provoke me into an argument by disparaging animals in general and my animals in particular. But fortunately I managed to avoid getting myself involved. To begin with, one should never argue with the captain of a ship, and to argue with a captain who was also an Irishman was simply asking for trouble. However, when the voyage was drawing to an end, I felt the captain needed a lesson and I was determined to teach him one if I could.

One evening when we were nearing the English Channel, the wind and rain had driven us all into the smoking-room, where we sat and listened to someone on the radio giving a talk on radar, which in those days was still sufficiently new to be of interest to the general public. The captain listened to the talk with a gleam in his eye, and when it had finished he turned to me.

'So much for your animals,' he said, 'they couldn't produce anything like that, in spite of the fact that, according to you, they're supposed to be so clever.'

By this simple statement the captain had played right into my hands, and I prepared to make him suffer.

'What will you bet,' I enquired, 'that I can't describe at least two great scientific inventions and prove to you that the principle was being used in the animal world long before man ever thought of it?'

'Make it four inventions instead of two and I'll bet you a bottle of whisky,' said the captain, obviously feeling he was onto a good thing. I agreed to this.

'Well,' said the captain smugly, 'off you go.'

'You'll have to give me a minute to think,' I protested.

'Ha,' said the captain triumphantly, 'you're stuck already.'

'Oh, no,' I explained, 'it's just that there are so many examples I'm not sure which to choose.'

The captain gave me a dirty look.

'Why not try radar, then?' he enquired sarcastically.

'Well, I could,' I said, 'but I really felt it was too easy. However, since you choose it, I suppose I'd better.'

It was fortunate for me that the captain was no naturalist; otherwise he would never have suggested radar. It was a gift, from my point of view, because I simply described the humble bat.

Many people must have been visited by a bat in their drawing-room or bedroom at one time or another, and if they have not been too scared of it, they will have been fascinated by its swift, skilful flight and the rapid twists and turns with which it avoids all obstacles, including objects like shoes and towels that are sometimes hurled at it. Now, despite the old saying, bats are not blind. They have perfectly good eyes, but these are so tiny that they are not easily detected in the thick fur. Their eyes, however, are certainly not good enough for them to perform some of the extraordinary flying stunts in which they indulge. It was an Italian naturalist called Spallanzani, in the eighteenth century, who first started to investigate the flight of bats, and by the unnecessarily cruel method of blinding several bats he found that they could still fly about unhampered, avoiding obstacles as though they were uninjured. But how they managed to do this he could not guess.

It was not until fairly recently that this problem was solved, at least partially. The discovery of radar, the sending out of sound-waves and judging the obstacles ahead by the returning echo, made some investigators wonder if this was not the system employed by bats. A series of experiments was conducted, and some fascinating things were discovered. First of all, some bats were blindfolded with tiny pieces of wax over their eyes, and as usual they had no difficulty in flying to and fro without hitting anything. Then it was found that if they were blindfolded and their ears were covered they were no longer able to avoid collisions, and, in fact, did not seem at all keen on flying in the first place. If only one ear was covered they could fly with only moderate success, and would frequently hit objects. This showed that bats could get information about the obstacles ahead by means of sound-waves reflected from them. Then the investigators covered the noses and mouths of their bats, but left the ears uncovered, and again the bats were unable to fly without collision. This proved that the nose, ears, and mouth all played some part in the bat's radar system. Eventually, by the use of extremely delicate instruments, the facts were discovered. As the bat flies along, it emits a continuous succession of supersonic squeaks, far too high for the human ear to pick up. They give out, in fact, about thirty squeaks a second. The echoes from these squeaks, bouncing off the obstacles ahead, return to the bat's ears and, in some species, to the curious fleshy ridges round the creature's nose, and the bat can thus tell what lies ahead, and how far away it is. It is, in fact, in every detail the principle of radar. But one thing rather puzzled the investigators: when you are transmitting sound-waves on radar, you must shut off your receiver when you are actually sending out the sound, so that you receive only the echo. Otherwise the receiver would pick up both the sound transmitted and the echo back, and the result would be a confused jumble. This might be possible on electrical apparatus, but they could not imagine how the bats managed to do it. It was then discovered that there was a tiny muscle in the bat's ear that did the job. Just at the moment the bat squeaks, this muscle contracts and puts the ear out of action. The squeak over, the muscle relaxes and the ear is ready to receive the echo.

But the amazing thing about this is not that bats have this private radar system – for after a while very little surprises one in Nature – but that they should have had it so long before man did. Fossil bats have been found in early Eocene rocks, and they differed very little from their modern relatives. It is possible, therefore, that bats have been employing radar for something like fifty million years. Man has possessed the secret for about twenty.

It was quite obvious that my first example had made the captain think. He did not seem quite so sure of winning the bet. I said that my next choice would be electricity, and this apparently cheered him up a bit. He laughed in a disbelieving way, and said I would have a job to persuade him that animals had electric lights. I pointed out that I had said nothing about electric lights, but merely electricity, and there were several creatures that employed it. There is, for example, the electric-ray or torpedo-fish, a curious creature that looks rather like a frying-pan run over by a steam-roller. These fish are excessively well camouflaged: not only does their colouring imitate the sandy bottom but they have also the annoying habit of half-burying themselves in the sand, which renders them really invisible. I remember once seeing the effect of this fish's electric organs, which are large and situated on its back. I was in Greece at the time, and was watching a young peasant boy fishing in the shallow waters of a sandy bay. He was wading up to his knees in the clear waters, holding in his hand a three-pronged spear such as the fishermen used for night-fishing. As he made his way round the bay, he was having quite a successful time: he had speared several large fish and a young octopus which had been concealed in a small group of rocks. As he came opposite where I was sitting a curious and rather startling thing happened. One minute he was walking slowly forward, peering down intently into the water, his trident at the ready; the next minute he had straightened up as stiffly as a guardsman and projected himself out of the water like a rocket, uttering a yell that could have been heard half a mile away. He fell back into the water with a splash and immediately uttered another and louder scream and leapt up again. This time he fell back into the water and seemed unable to regain his feet, for he struggled out onto the sand, half crawling, half dragging himself. When I got down to where he lay, I found him white and shaking, panting as though he had just run half a mile. How much of this was due to shock and how much to the actual effect of the electricity I could not tell, but at any rate I never again went bathing in that particular bay.

Probably the most famous electricity-producing creature is the electric-eel which, strangely enough, is not an eel at all but a species of fish that looks like an eel. These long, black creatures live in the streams and rivers of South America and can grow to eight feet in length and the thickness of a man's thigh. No doubt a lot of stories about them are grossly exaggerated, but it is possible for a big one to shock a horse fording a river strongly enough to knock down the animal.

When I was collecting animals in British Guiana I very much wanted to catch some electric-eels to bring back to this country. At one place where we were camped the river was full of them, but they lived in deep caves hollowed out in the rocky shores. Most of these caves communicated with the air by means of round pot-holes that had been worn by the flood waters, and in the cave beneath each pot-hole lived an electric-eel. If you made your way to a pot-hole and stamped heavily with your shoes it would annoy the eel into replying with a strange purring grunt, as though a large pig were entombed beneath your feet.

Try as I would I did not manage to catch one of these eels. Then one day my partner and I, accompanied by two Indians, went for a trip to a village a few miles away, where the inhabitants were great fishermen. We found several animals and birds in the village which we purchased from them, including a tame tree-porcupine. Then, to my delight, someone appeared with an electric-eel in a rather insecure fish basket. Having bargained for and bought these creatures, including the eel, we piled them into the canoe and set out for home. The porcupine sat in the bow, apparently very interested in the scenery, and in front of him lay the eel in its basket. We were half-way home when the eel escaped.

We were first made aware of this by the porcupine. He was, I think, under the impression that the eel was a snake, for he galloped down from the bows and endeavoured to climb onto my head. Struggling to evade the porcupine's prickly embrace, I suddenly saw the eel wriggling determinedly towards me, and indulged in a feat which I would not have believed possible. I leapt into the air from a sitting position, clasping the porcupine to my bosom, and landed again when the eel had passed, without upsetting the canoe. I had a very vivid mental picture of what had happened to the young peasant who had trodden on the torpedo-fish, and I had no intention of indulging in a similar experience with an electric-eel. Luckily none of us received a shock from the eel, for while we were trying to juggle it back into its basket it wriggled over the side of the canoe and fell into the river. I cannot say any of us were really sorry to see it go.

I remember once feeding an electric-eel that lived in a large tank in a zoo, and it was quite fascinating to watch his method of dealing with his prey. He was about five feet long and could cope adequately with a fish of about eight or ten inches in length. These had to be fed to him alive, and as their death was instantaneous, I had no qualms about this. The eel seemed to know when it was feeding-time and he would be patrolling his tank with the monotonous regularity of a sentry outside Buckingham Palace. As soon as a fish was dropped into his tank he would freeze instantly and apparently watch it as it swam closer and closer. When it was within range, which was about a foot or so, he would suddenly appear to quiver all over as if a dynamo had started within his long dark length. The fish would be, as it were, frozen in its tracks; it was dead before you realized that anything was happening, and then very slowly it would tilt over and start floating belly uppermost. The eel would move a little closer, open his mouth and suck violently, and, as though he were an elongated vacuum-cleaner, the fish would disappear into him.

Having dispensed quite successfully, I thought, with electricity, I now turned my attention to another field: medicine. Anaesthetics, I said, would be my next example, and the captain looked if anything even more sceptical than before.

The hunting-wasp is the Harley Street specialist of the insect world, and he performs an operation which would give a skilled surgeon pause. There are many different species of hunting-wasp, but most of them have similar habits. For the reception of her young the female has to build a nursery out of clay. This is neatly divided into long cells about the circumference of a cigarette and about half its length. In these the wasp intends to lay her eggs. However, she has another duty to perform before she can seal them up, for her eggs will hatch into grubs, and they will then require food until such time as they are ready to undergo the last stage of their metamorphosis into the perfect wasp. The hunting-wasp could stock her nursery with dead food, but by the time the eggs had hatched this food would have gone bad, so she is forced to evolve another method. Her favourite prey is the spider. Flying like some fierce hawk, she descends upon her unsuspecting victim and proceeds to sting it deeply and skilfully. The effect of this sting is extraordinary, for the spider is completely paralysed. The hunting-wasp then seizes it and carries it off to her nursery where it is carefully tucked away in one of the cells and an egg laid on it. If the spiders are small, there may be anything up to seven or eight in a cell. Having satisfied herself that the food supply is adequate for her youngsters, the wasp then seals up the cells and flies off. Inside this grisly nursery the spiders lie in an unmoving row, in some cases for as much as seven weeks. To all intents and purposes the spiders are dead, even when you handle them, and not even under a magnifying glass can you detect the faintest sign of life. Thus they wait, so to speak, in cold storage until the eggs hatch out and the tiny grubs of the hunting-wasp start browsing on their paralysed bodies.

I think even the captain was a little shaken by the idea of being completely paralysed while something comsumed you bit by bit, so I hastily switched to something a shade more pleasant. It was, in fact, the most delightful little creature, and a most ingenious one – the water-spider. Only recently in his history has man been able to live under water for any length of time, and one of his first steps in this direction was the diving-bell. Thousands of years before this the water-spider had evolved his own method of penetrating this new world beneath the surface of the water. To begin with, he can quite happily swim below the surface of the water, wearing his equivalent of the aqualung in the shape of an air bubble which he traps beneath his stomach and between his legs, so that he may breathe under water. This alone is extraordinary, but the water-spider goes even further: he builds his home beneath the surface of the water, a web shaped like an inverted cup, firmly anchored to the water-weeds. He then proceeds to make several journeys to the surface, bringing with him air bubbles which he pushes into this dome-shaped web until it is full of them, and in this he can live and breathe as easily as if he were on land. In the breeding-season he picks out the house of a likely-looking female and builds himself a cottage next door, and then, presumably being of a romantic turn of mind, he builds a sort of secret passage linking his house with that of his lady-love. Then he breaks down her wall, so that the air bubbles in each house intermix, and here in this strange underwater dwelling he courts the female, mates with her, and lives with her until the eggs are laid and hatched, and until their children, each carrying their little globule of air from their parents' home, swim out to start life on their own.

Even the captain seemed amused and intrigued by my story of the water-spider, and he was bound to admit, albeit reluctantly, that I had won my bet.

I suppose it must have been about a year later I was talking to a lady who had travelled on the same ship with the same captain.

'Wasn't he a delightful man?' she asked me. I agreed politely.

'He must have enjoyed having you on board,' she went on, 'because he was so keen on animals, you know. One night he kept us all spellbound for *at least* an hour, telling us about all these scientific discoveries – you know, things like radar – and how animals have been employing them for years and years before man discovered them. Really it was fascinating. I told him he ought to write it up into a talk and broadcast it on the B.B.C.'

VANISHING ANIMALS

Some time ago I was watching what must be the strangest group of refugees in this country, strange because they did not come here for the usual reasons, driven by either religious or political persecution from their own country. They came here quite by chance, and in doing so they were saved from extermination. They are the last of their kind, for in their country of origin their relatives were long ago hunted down, killed and eaten. They were, in fact, a herd of Père David deer.

Their existence was first discovered by a French missionary, one

Father David, during the course of his work in China in the early 1800s. In those days China was as little known, zoologically speaking, as the great forests of Africa, and so Father David, who was a keen naturalist, spent his spare time collecting specimens of the flora and fauna to send back to the museum in Paris. In 1865 his work took him to Peking, and while he was there he heard a rumour that there was a strange herd of deer in the Imperial Hunting Park, just south of the city. This park had been for centuries a sort of combined hunting- and pleasure-ground for the Emperors of China, a great tract of land completely surrounded by a high wall forty-five miles long. It was strictly guarded by Tartar soldiers, and no one was allowed to enter or approach it. The French missionary was intrigued by the stories he heard about these peculiar deer, and he was determined that, guards or no guards, he was going to look inside the walled park and try to see the animals for himself. One day he got his opportunity and was soon lying up on top of the wall, looking down into the forbidden park and watching the various game animals feeding among the trees below him. Among them was a large herd of deer, and Father David realized that he was looking at an animal he had never seen before, and one which was, very probably, new to science.

Father David soon found out that the deer were strictly protected, and for anyone caught harming or killing them the sentence was death. He knew that any official request he might put forward for a specimen would be politely refused by the Chinese authorities, so he had to use other, less legal methods to get what he wanted. He discovered that the Tartar guards occasionally improved their rather sparse rations by the addition of a little venison; they were well aware what the penalty for their poaching would be if they were caught, and so, in spite of the missionary's pleadings, they refused to sell him the skins and antlers of the deer they killed, or indeed anything that might be evidence of their crime. However, Father David did not give up hope, and after a considerable time he was successful. He met some guards who were either braver or perhaps poorer than the rest, and they obtained for him two deer skins, which he triumphantly shipped off to Paris. As he had expected, the deer turned out to be an entirely new species, and so it was named, in honour of its discoverer, the Père David deer – Father David's deer.

Naturally, when zoos in Europe heard about this new kind of deer they wanted specimens for exhibition, and after protracted negotiations the Chinese authorities rather reluctantly allowed a few of the animals to be sent to the Continent. Although no one realized it at the time, it was this action that was to save the animals. In 1895, thirty years after the Père David deer first became known to the world, there were great floods around Peking; the Hun-Ho river overflowed its banks and caused havoc in the countryside, destroying the crops and bringing the population to near starvation. The waters also undermined the great wall round the Imperial Hunting Park. Parts of it collapsed, and through these gaps the herd of Père David deer escaped into the surrounding countryside, where they were quickly killed and eaten by the hungry peasants. So the deer perished in China, and the only ones left were the handful of live specimens in the various zoos in Europe.

Shortly before this disaster overtook the deer in China, a small herd of them had arrived in England. The present Duke of Bedford's father had, on his estate at Woburn in Bedfordshire, a wonderful collection of rare animals, and he had been most anxious to try to establish a herd of this new Chinese deer there. He bought as many specimens as he could from the Continental zoos, eighteen in all, and released them in his park. To the deer this must have seemed like home from home, for they settled down wonderfully, and soon started to breed. Today, the herd that started with eighteen now numbers over a hundred and fifty animals, the only herd of Père David deer in the world.

When I was working at Whipsnade Zoo four newly born Père David deer were sent over from Woburn for us to hand-rear. They were delightful little things, with long gangling limbs over which they had no control and strange slanted eyes that gave them a distinctly Oriental appearance. To begin with, of course, they did not know what a feeding-bottle was for, and we had to hold them firmly between our knees and force them to drink. But they very soon got the hang of it, and within a few days we had to open the stable door with extreme caution if we did not want to be knocked flying by an avalanche of deer, pushing and shoving in an effort to get at the bottle first.

They had to be fed once during the night, at midnight, and again at dawn, and so we worked out a system of night duties, one week on, one week off, between four keepers. I must say that I rather enjoyed the night duties. To pick one's way through the moonlit park towards the stable where the baby deer were kept, you had to pass several of the cages and paddocks, and the occupants were always on the move. The bears, looking twice as big in the half-light, would be snorting to each other as they shambled heavily through the riot of brambles in their cage, and they could be persuaded to leave their quest for snails and other delicacies if one had a bribe of sugar-lumps. They would come and squat upright in the moonlight, like a row of shaggy, heavy-breathing Buddhas, their great paws resting on their knees. They would throw back their heads and catch the flying lumps of sugar and eat them with much scrunching and smacking of lips. Then, seeing that you had no more in your pockets, they would sigh in a long-suffering manner and shamble off into the brambles again.

At one point the path led past the wolf wood, two acres or so of pines, dark and mysterious, with the moonlight silvering the trunks and laying dark shadows along the ground through which the wolf pack danced on swift, silent feet, like a strange black tide, swirling and twisting among the trunks. As a rule they made no sound, but occasionally you would hear them panting gently, or the sudden snap of jaws and a snarl when one wolf barged against another.

Then you would reach the stable and light the lantern. The baby deer would hear you and start moving restlessly in their straw beds, bleating tremulously. As you opened the door they rushed forward, wobbling on their unsteady legs, sucking frantically at your fingers, the edge of your coat, and butting you suddenly in the legs with their heads, so that you were almost knocked down. Then came the exquisite moment when the teat was pushed into their mouths and they sucked frantically at the warm milk, their eyes staring, bubbles gathering like a moustache at the corners of their mouths. There is always a certain pleasure to be gained from bottle-feeding a baby animal, if only from its wholehearted enthusiasm and concentration on the job. But in the case of these deer there was something else as well. In the flickering light of the lantern, while the deer sucked and slobbered over the bottles, occasionally ducking their heads and butting at an imaginary udder with their heads, I was very conscious of the fact that they were the last of their kind.

At Whipsnade I had to look after another group of animals which belonged to a species now extinct in the wild state, and they were some of the most charming and comic animals I have ever had anything to do with. They were a small herd of white-tailed gnus.

The white-tailed gnu is a weird creature to look at: if you can imagine an animal with the body and legs of a finely built pony, a squat blunt face with very wide-spaced nostrils, a heavy mane of white hair on its thick neck, and a long white sweeping plume of a tail. The buffalo horns curve outward and upwards over the eyes, and the animal peers at you from under them with a perpetually indignant and suspicious expression. If the gnu behaved normally, this appearance would not be so noticeable, but the animal does not behave normally. Anything but, in fact. Its actions can only be described, very inadequately, as a cross between bebop and ballet, with a bit of yoga thrown in.

In the mornings, when I went to feed them, it always took me twice as long as it should have done because the gnus would start performing for me, and the sight was so ludicrous that I would lose all sense of time. They would prance and twist and buck, gallop, rear and pirouette, and while they did so they would throw their slim legs out at extraordinary and completely un-anatomical angles, and swish and curve their long tails as a circus ringmaster uses his whip. In the middle of the wild dance they would suddenly stop dead and glare at me, uttering loud, indignant belching snorts at my laughter. I watched them dancing their swift, wild dance across the paddock and they reminded me, in their antics and attitudes, of some strange heraldic creature from an ancient coat of arms, miraculously brought to life, prancing and posturing on a field of green turf.

It is difficult to imagine how anyone had the heart to kill these agile and amusing antelopes. However, the fact remains that the early settlers in South Africa found in the white-tailed gnu a valuable source of food, and so the great herds of high-spirited creatures were slaughtered unmercifully. The antelope contributed to its own downfall in an unusual way. They are incorrigibly curious creatures, and so when they saw the ox-drawn wagons of the early settlers moving across the veldt they simply had to go and investigate. They would dance and gallop round the wagons in circles, snorting and kicking their heels, and then suddenly stopping to stare. Naturally, with these habits of running away and then stopping to stare before they were out of range, they were used by enterprising 'sportsmen' for rifle practice. So they were killed, and their numbers decreased so rapidly that it is amazing that they did not become extinct. Today there are under a thousand of these charming animals left alive, and these are split up into small herds on various estates in South Africa. If they were to become extinct, South Africa would have lost one of the most amusing and talented of her native fauna, an antelope whose actions could enliven any landscape, however dull.

Unfortunately, the Père David deer and the white-tailed gnu are not the only creatures in the world that are nearly extinct. The list of creatures that have vanished altogether, and others that have almost vanished, is a long and melancholy one. As man has spread across the earth he has wrought the most terrible havoc among the wild life by shooting, trapping, cutting and burning the forest, and by the callous and stupid introduction of enemies where there were no enemies before.

Take the dodo, for example, the great ponderous waddling pigeon, the size of a goose, that inhabited the island of Mauritius. Secure in its island home, this bird had lost the power of flight since there were no enemies to fly from, and, since there were no enemies, it nested on the ground in complete safety. But, as well as losing the power of flight, it seems to have lost the power of recognizing an enemy when it saw one, for it was apparently an extremely tame and confiding creature. Then man discovered the dodos' paradise in about 1507, and with him came his evil familiars: dogs, cats, pigs, rats and goats. The dodo surveyed these new arrivals with an air of innocent interest. Then the slaughter began. The goats ate the undergrowth which provided the dodo with cover; dogs and cats hunted and harried the old birds; while pigs grunted their way round the island, eating the eggs and young and the rats followed behind to finish the feast. By 1681 the fat, ungainly and harmless pigeon was extinct – as dead as the dodo.

All over the world the wild fauna has been whittled down steadily and remorselessly, and many lovely and interesting animals have been so reduced in numbers that, without protection and help, they can never re-establish themselves. If they cannot find sanctuary where they can live and breed undisturbed, their numbers will dwindle until they join the dodo, the quagga, and the great auk on the long list of extinct creatures.

Of course, in the last decade or so much has been done for the protection of wild life: sanctuaries and reserves have been started, and the reintroduction of a species into areas where it had become extinct is taking place. In Canada, for instance, beavers are now reintroduced into certain areas by means of aeroplane. The animal is put in a special box attached to a parachute, and when the plane flies over the area it drops the cage and its beaver passenger out. The cage floats down on the end of the parachute, and when it hits the ground it opens automatically and the beaver then makes its way to the nearest stream or lake.

But although much is being done, there is still a very great deal to do. Unfortunately, the majority of useful work in animal preservation has been done mainly for animals which are of some economic importance to man, and there are many obscure species of no economic importance which, although they are protected on paper, as it were, are in actual fact being allowed to die out because nobody, except a few interested zoologists, considers them important enough to spend money on.

As mankind increases year by year, and as he spreads farther over the globe burning and destroying, it is some small comfort to know that there are certain private individuals and some institutions who consider that the work of trying to save and give sanctuary to these harried animals is of some importance. It is important work for many reasons, but perhaps the best of them is this: man, for all his genius, cannot create a species, nor can he recreate one he has destroyed. There would be a dreadful outcry if anyone suggested obliterating, say, the Tower of London, and quite rightly so; yet a unique and wonderful species of animal which has taken hundreds of thousands of years to develop to the stage we see today, can be snuffed out like a candle without more than a handful of people raising a finger or a voice in protest. So, until we consider animal life to be worthy of the consideration and reverence we bestow upon old books and pictures and historic monuments, there will always be the animal refugee living a precarious life on the edge of extermination, dependent for existence on the charity of a few human beings.

PART THREE

ANIMALS IN PARTICULAR

Keeping wild animals as pets, whether on an expedition or in your own home, can be a tedious, irritating, and frustrating business, but it can also give you a great deal of pleasure. Many people have asked me why I like animals, and I have always found it a difficult question to answer. You might just as well ask me why I like eating. But, apart from the obvious interest and pleasure that animals give me, there is another aspect as well. I think that their chief charm lies in the fact that they have all the basic qualities of a human being but with none of the hypocrisy which is now apparently such an essential in the world of man. With an animal you do know more or less where you are: if it does not like you it tells you so in no uncertain manner; if it likes you, again it leaves you in no doubt. But an animal who likes you is sometimes a mixed blessing. Recently I had a pied crow from West Africa who, after six months' deliberation, during which time he ignored me, suddenly decided that I was the only person in the world for him. If I went near the cage he would crouch on the floor trembling in ecstasy, or bring me an offering (a bit of newspaper or a feather) and hold it out for me to take, all the while talking hoarsely to himself in a series of hiccuping cries and ejaculations. This was all right, but as soon as I let him out of his cage he would fly onto my head and perch there, first digging his claws firmly into my scalp, then decorating the back of my jacket with a nice moist dropping and finally proceeding to give me a series of love pecks on the head. As his beak was three inches long and extremely sharp, this was, to say the least, painful.

Of course, you have to know where to draw the line with animals. You can let pet-keeping develop into eccentricity if you are not careful. I drew the line last Christmas. For a present I decided to buy my wife a North American flying-squirrel, a creature which I had always wanted to possess myself, and which I was sure she would like. The animal duly arrived, and we were both captivated by it. As it seemed extremely nervous, we thought it would be a good idea to keep it in our bedroom for a week or two, so that we could talk to it at night when it came out, and let it grow used to us. This plan would have worked quite well but for one thing. The squirrel cunningly gnawed its way out of the cage and took up residence behind the wardrobe. At first this did not seem too bad. We could sit in bed at night and watch it doing acrobatics on the wardrobe, scuttling up and down the dressing-table, carrying off the nuts and apple we had left there for it. Then came New Year's Eve when we had been invited to a party for which I had to don my dinner-jacket. All was well until I opened a drawer in my dressing-table, when I discovered the answer to the question that had puzzled us for some time: where did the flying-squirrel store all the nuts, apple, bread and other bits of food? My brand-new cummerbund, which I had never even worn, looked like a piece of delicate Madeira lacework. The bits that had been chewed out of it had been very economically saved and used to build little nests, one on the front of each of my dress shirts. In these nests had been collected seventy-two hazel nuts, five walnuts, fourteen pieces of bread, six mealworms, fifty-two bits of apple and twenty grapes. The grapes and the apple had, of course, disintegrated somewhat with the passage of time and had left most interesting Picasso designs in juice across the front of my shirts.

I had to go to the party in a suit. The squirrel is now in Paignton Zoo.

The other day my wife said that she thought a baby otter would make a delightful pet, but I changed the subject hurriedly.

ANIMAL PARENTS

I have the greatest respect for animal parents. When I was young I tried my hand at rearing a number of different creatures, and since then, on my animal-collecting trips for zoos to various parts of the world, I have had to mother quite a number of baby animals, and I have always found it a most nerve-racking task.

The first real attempt I made at being a foster-mother was to four baby hedgehogs. The female hedgehog is a very good mother. She constructs an underground nursery for the reception of her young; a circular chamber about a foot below ground-level, lined with a thick layer of dry leaves. Here she gives birth to her babies, which are blind and helpless. They are covered with a thick coating of spikes, but these are white and soft, as though made of rubber. They gradually harden and turn brown when the babies are a few weeks old. When they are old enough to leave the nursery the mother leads them out and shows them how to hunt for food; they walk in line, rather like a school crocodile, the tail of one held in the mouth of the baby behind. The baby at the head of the column holds tight to mother's tail with grim determination, and they wend their way through the twilit hedgerows like a strange prickly centipede.

To a mother hedgehog the rearing of her babies seems to present no problems. But when I was suddenly presented with four blind, white, rubbery-spiked babies to rear, I was not so sure. We were living in Greece at the time, and the nest, which was about the size of a football and made of oak leaves, had been dug up by a peasant working in his fields. The first job was to feed the babies, for the ordinary baby's feeding-bottle only took a teat far too large for their tiny mouths. Luckily the young daughter of a friend of mine had a doll's feeding-bottle, and after much bribery I got her to part with it. After a time the hedgehogs took to this and thrived on a diet of diluted cow's milk.

I kept them at first in a shallow cardboard box where I had put the nest. But in record time the original nest was so unhygienic that I found myself having to change the leaves ten or twelve times a day. I began to wonder if the mother hedgehog spent her day rushing to and fro with piles of fresh leaves to keep her nest clean, and, if she did, how on earth she found time to satisfy the appetites of her babies. Mine were always ready for food at any hour of the day or night. You had only to touch the box and a chorus of shrill screams arose from four little pointed faces poking out the leaves, each head decorated with a crew-cut of white spikes; and the little black noses would whiffle desperately from side to side in an effort to locate the bottle.

Most baby animals know when they have had enough, but in my experience this does not apply to baby hedgehogs. Like four survivors from a raft, they flung themselves onto the bottle and sucked and sucked and sucked as though they had not had a decent meal in weeks. If I had allowed it they would have drunk twice as much as was good for them. As it was, I think I tended to overfeed them, for their tiny legs could not support the weight of their fat bodies, and they would advance across the carpet with a curious swimming motion, their tummies dragging on the ground. However, they progressed very well: their legs grew stronger, their eyes opened, and they would even make daring excursions as much as six inches away from their box.

I was very proud of my prickly family, and looked forward to the day when I would be able to take them for walks in the evening and find them delicious titbits like snails or wild strawberries. Unfortunately this dream was never realized. It so happened that I had to leave home for a day, to return the following morning. It was impossible for me to take the babies with me, so I had to leave them in charge of my sister. Before I left, I emphasized the greediness of the hedgehogs and told her that on no account were they to have more than one bottle of milk each, however much they squeaked for it.

I should have known my sister better.

When I returned the following day and enquired how my hedgehogs were, she gave me a reproachful look. I had, she said, been slowly starving the poor little things to death. With a dreadful sense of foreboding, I asked her how much she had been giving them at each meal. Four bottles each, she replied, and you should just see how lovely and fat they are getting. There was no denying they were fat. Their little tummies were so bloated their tiny feet could not even touch the ground. They looked like weird, prickly footballs to which someone by mistake had attached four legs and a nose. I did the best I could, but within twenty-four hours all four of them had died of acute enteritis. No one, of course, was more sorry than my sister, but I think she could tell by the frigid way I accepted her apologies that it was the last time she would be left in charge of any of my foster-children.

Not all animals are as good as the hedgehog at looking after their babies. Some, in fact, treat the whole business with a rather casual and modern attitude. One such is the kangaroo. Baby kangaroos are born in a very unfinished condition. They are actually embryos, for a big red kangaroo squatting on its haunches may measure five feet high and yet give birth to a baby only about half an inch long. This blind and naked blob of life has to find its way up over the mother's belly and into her pouch. In its primitive condition you would think this would be hard enough, but the whole thing is made doubly difficult by the fact that as yet the baby kangaroo can use only its front legs; the hind legs are neatly crossed over its tail. During this time the mother just squats there and gives her baby no help whatever, though occasionally she has been seen to lick a kind of trail through the fur, which may act as some sort of guide. Thus the tiny, premature offspring is forced to crawl through a jungle of fur until, as much by chance as good management, it reaches the pouch, climbs inside and clamps itself onto the teat. This is a feat that makes the ascent of Everest pale into insignificance.

I have never had the privilege of trying to hand-rear a baby kangaroo, but I have had some experience with a young wallaby, which is closely related to the species and looks just like a miniature kangaroo. I was working at Whipsnade Zoo as a keeper. The wallabies there are allowed to run free in the park, and one female, carrying a well-formed youngster, was chased by a group of young lads. In her fright she did what all the kangaroo family does in moments of stress: she tossed her youngster out of her pouch. I found it some time afterwards, lying in the long grass, twitching convulsively and making faint sucking squeaks with its mouth. It was, quite frankly, the most unprepossessing baby animal I had ever seen. About a foot long, it was blind, hairless and a bright sugar-pink. It seemed to possess no control over any part of its body except its immense hind feet, which it kicked vigorously at intervals. It had been badly bruised by its fall and I had grave doubts as to whether it would live. None the less I took it back to my lodgings and, after some argument with the landlady, kept it in my bedroom.

It fed eagerly from a bottle, but the chief difficulty lay in keeping it warm enough. I wrapped it in flannel and surrounded it with hot-water bottles, but these kept growing cold, and I was afraid it would catch a chill. The obvious thing to do was to carry it close to my body, so I put it inside my shirt. It was then that I realized for the first time what a mother wallaby must suffer. Apart from the nuzzling and sucking that went on, at regular intervals the baby would lash out its hind feet, well armed with claws, and kick me accurately in the pit of the stomach. After a few hours I began to feel as though I had been in the ring with Primo Carnera for a practice bout. It was obvious I would have to think of something else, or develop stomach ulcers. I tried putting him round the back of my shirt, but he would very soon scramble his way round to the front with his long claws in a series of convulsive kicks. Sleeping with him at night was purgatory, for apart from the all-in wrestling in which he indulged, he would sometimes kick so strongly that he shot out of bed altogether, and I was constantly forced to lean out of bed and pick him up from the floor. Unfortunately he died in two days, obviously from some sort of internal haemorrhage. I am afraid I viewed his demise with mixed feelings, although it was a pity to be deprived of the opportunity of mothering such an unusual baby.

If the kangaroo is rather dilatory about her child, the pigmy marmoset is a paragon of virtue, or rather the male is. About the size of a large mouse, clad in neat brindled green fur, and with a tiny face and bright hazel eyes, the pigmy marmoset looks like something out of a fairy tale, a small furry gnome or perhaps a kelpie. As soon as the courtship is over and the female gives birth, her diminutive spouse turns into the ideal husband. The babies, generally twins, he takes over from the moment they are born and carries them slung on his hips like a couple of saddle-bags. He keeps them clean by constant grooming, hugs them to him at night to keep them warm, and only hands them over to his rather disinterested wife at feeding-time. But he is so anxious to get them back that you have the impression he would feed them himself if only he could. The pigmy marmoset is definitely a husband worth having.

Strangely enough, monkeys are generally the stupidest babies, and it takes them a long time to learn to drink out of a bottle. Having successfully induced them to do this, you have to go through the whole tedious performance again, when they are a little bit older, in an attempt to teach them to drink out of a saucer. They always seem to feel that the only way of drinking out of a saucer is to duck the face beneath the surface of the milk and stay there until you either burst for want of air or drown in your own drink.

One of the most charming baby monkeys I have ever had was a little moustached guenon. His back and tail were moss green and his belly and whiskers a beautiful shade of buttercup yellow. Across his upper lip spread a large banana-shaped area of white, like the magnificent moustaches of some retired brigadier. Like all baby monkeys, his head seemed too big for his body, and he had long gangling limbs. He fitted very comfortably into a teacup. When I first had him he refused to drink out of a bottle, plainly convinced that it was some sort of fiendish torture I had invented, but eventually, when he got the hang of it, he would go quite mad when he saw the bottle arrive, fasten his mouth onto the teat, clasp the bottle passionately in his arms and roll on his back. As the bottle was at least three times his size, he made one think of a desperate survivor clinging onto a large white airship.

When he learnt, after the normal grampus-like splutterings, to drink out of a saucer, the situation became fraught with difficulty. He would be placed on a table and then his saucer of milk produced. As soon as he saw it coming he would utter a piercing scream and start trembling all over, as if he were suffering with ague or St Vitus dance, but it was really a form of excited rage: excitement at the sight of the milk, rage that it was never put on the table quickly enough for him. He screamed and trembled to such an extent that he bounced up in the air like a grass-hopper. If you were unwise enough to put the saucer down without hanging onto his tail, he would utter one final shrill scream of triumph and dive headfirst into the centre of it, and when you had mopped the resulting tidal wave of milk from your face, you would find him sitting indignantly in the middle of an empty saucer, chattering with rage because there was nothing for him to drink.

One of the main problems when you are rearing baby animals is to keep them warm enough at night, and this, strangely enough, applies even in the tropics where the temperature drops considerably after dark. In the wild state, of course, the babies cling to the dense fur of the mother and obtain warmth and shelter in that way. Hot-water bottles, as a substitute, I have found of very little use. They grow cold so quickly and you have to get up several times during the night to refill them, an exhausting process when you have a lot of baby animals to look after, as well as a whole collection of adult ones. So in most cases the simplest way is to take the babies into bed with you. You soon learn to sleep in one position – half-waking up in the night, should you wish to move, so that you avoid crushing them as you turn over.

I have at one time or another shared my bed with a great variety of young creatures, and sometimes several different species at once. On one occasion my narrow camp-bed contained three mongooses, two baby monkeys, a squirrel and a young chimpanzee. There was just enough room left over for me. You might think that after taking all this trouble a little gratitude would come your way, but in many cases you get the opposite. One of my most impressive scars was inflicted by a young mongoose because I was five minutes late with his bottle. When people ask me about it now, I am forced to pretend it was given me by a charging jaguar. Nobody would believe me if I told them it was really a baby mongoose under the bedclothes.

THE BANDITS

My first introduction to the extraordinary little animals known as kusimanses took place at the London Zoo. I had gone into the Rodent House to examine at close range some rather lovely squirrels from West Africa. I was just about to set out on my first animal-collecting expedition, and I felt that the more familiar I was with the creatures I was likely to meet in the great rain-forest, the easier my job would be.

After watching the squirrels for a time, I walked round the house peering into the other cages. On one of them hung a rather impressive label which informed me that the cage contained a creature known as a Kusimanse (*Crossarchus obscurus*) and that it came from West Africa. All I could see in the cage was a pile of straw that heaved gently and rhythmically, while a faint sound of snoring was wafted out to me. As I felt that this animal was one I was sure to meet, I felt justified in waking it up and forcing it to appear.

Every zoo has a rule I always observe, and many others should observe it too: not to disturb a sleeping animal by poking it or throwing peanuts. They have precious little privacy as it is. However, I ignored the rule on this occasion and rattled my thumbnail to and fro along the bars. I did not really think this would have any effect. But as I did so a sort of explosion took place in the depths of the straw, and the next moment a long, rubbery, tip-tilted nose appeared, to be followed by a rather rat-like face with small neat ears and bright inquisitive eyes. This little face appraised me for a minute; then, noticing the lump of sugar which I held tactfully near the bars, the animal uttered a faint, spinsterish squeak and struggled madly to release itself from the cocoon of straw wound round it.

When only the head had been visible, I had the impression it was only a small creature, about the size of the average ferret, but when it eventually broke loose from its covering and waddled into view, I was astonished at its relatively large body: it was, in fact, so fat as to be almost circular. Yet it shuffled over to the bars on its short legs and fell on the lump of sugar I offered as though that was the first piece of decent food it had received in years.

It was, I decided, a species of mongoose, but its tip-tilted, whiffling nose and the glittering, almost fanatical eyes made it look totally unlike any mongoose I had ever seen. I was convinced now that its shape was due not to Nature but to overeating. It had very short legs and fine, rather slender paws, and when it trotted about the cage these legs moved so fast that they were little more than a blur beneath the bulky body. Each time I fed it a morsel of food it gave the same faint, breathless squeak: as much as to reproach me for tempting it away from its diet.

I was so captivated by this little animal that before I realized what I was doing I had fed it all the lump-sugar in my pocket. As soon as it knew that no more titbits were forthcoming, it uttered a long-suffering sigh and trotted away to dive into the straw. Within a couple of seconds it was sound asleep once more. I decided there and then that if kusimanses were to be obtained in the area I was visiting, I would strain every nerve to find one.

Three months later I was deep in the heart of the Cameroon rain-forests and here I found I had ample opportunity for getting to know the kusimanse. Indeed, they were about the commonest members of the mongoose family, and I often saw them when I was sitting concealed in the forest waiting for some completely different animal to make its appearance.

The first one I saw appeared suddenly out of the undergrowth on the banks of a small stream. He kept me amused for a long time with a display of his crab-catching methods: he waded into the shallow water and with the aid of his long, turned-up nose (presumably holding his breath when he did so) he turned over all the rocks he could find until he unearthed one of the large, black, freshwater crabs. Without a second's hesitation he grabbed it in his mouth and, with a quick flick of his head, tossed it onto the bank. He then chased after it, squeaking with delight and danced round it, snapping away until at last it was dead. When an exceptionally large crab succeeded in giving him a nip on the end of his

retroussé nose, I am afraid my stifled amusement caused the kusimanse
to depart hastily into the forest.

On another occasion I watched one of these little beasts using
precisely the same methods to catch frogs, but this time without much
success. I felt he must be young and inexperienced in the art of frog-
catching. After much laborious hunting and snuffling, he would catch a
frog and hurl it shorewards; but, long before he had waddled out to the
bank after it, the frog would have recovered itself and leapt back into the
water, and the kusimanse would be forced to start all over again.

One morning a native hunter walked into my camp carrying a small
palm-leaf basket, and peering into it I saw three of the strangest little
animals imaginable. They were about the size of newborn kittens, with
tiny legs and somewhat moth-eaten tails. They were covered with bright
gingery-red fur which stood up in spikes and tufts all over their bodies,
making them look almost like some weird species of hedgehog. As I gazed
down at them, trying to identify them, they lifted their little faces and
peered up at me. The moment I saw the long, pink, rubbery noses I
knew they were kusimanses, and very young ones at that, for their eyes
were only just open and they had no teeth. I was very pleased to obtain
these babies, but after I had paid the hunter and set to work on the task of
trying to teach them to feed, I began to wonder if I had not got more
than I bargained for. Among the numerous feeding-bottles I had
brought with me I could not find a teat small enough to fit their mouths,
so I was forced to try the old trick of wrapping some cotton-wool round
the end of a matchstick, dipping it in milk and letting them suck it. At
first they took the view that I was some sort of monster endeavouring to
choke them. They struggled and squeaked, and every time I pushed the
cotton-wool into their mouths they frantically spat it out again.
Fortunately it was not long before they discovered that the cotton-wool
contained milk, and then they were no more trouble, except that they
were liable to suck so hard in their enthusiasm that the cotton-wool
would part company with the end of the matchstick and disappear down
their throats.

At first I kept them in a small basket by my bed. This was the most
convenient spot, for I had to get up in the middle of the night to feed
them. For the first week or so they really behaved very well, spending
most of the day sprawled on their bed of dried leaves, their stomachs
bulging and their paws twitching. Only at meal-times would they grow
excited, scrambling round and round inside the basket, uttering loud
squeaks and treading heavily on one another.

It was not long before the baby kusimanses developed their front teeth
(which gave them a firmer and more disastrous grip on the cotton-

wool), and as their legs got stronger they became more and more eager to see the world that lay outside their basket. They had the first feed of the day when I drank my morning tea; and I would lift them out of their basket and put them on my bed so that they could have a walk round. I had, however, to call an abrupt halt to this habit, for one morning, while I was quietly sipping my tea, one of the baby kusimanses discovered my bare foot sticking out from under the bedclothes and decided that if he bit my toe hard enough it might produce milk. He laid hold with his needle-sharp teeth, and his brothers, thinking they were missing a feed, instantly joined him. When I had locked them up in their basket again and finished mopping tea off myself and the bed, I decided these morning romps would have to cease. They were too painful.

This was merely the first indication of the trouble in store for me. Very soon they had become such a nuisance that I was forced to christen them the Bandits. They grew fast, and as soon as their teeth had come through they started to eat egg and a little raw meat every day, as well as their milk. Their appetites seemed insatiable, and their lives turned into one long quest for food. They appeared to think that everything was edible unless proved otherwise. One of the things of which they made a light snack was the lid of their basket. Having demolished this they hauled themselves out and went on a tour of inspection round the camp. Unfortunately, and with unerring accuracy, they made their way to the one place where they could do the maximum damage in the minimum time: the place where the food and medical supplies were stored. Before I discovered them they had broken a dozen eggs and, to judge by the state of them, rolled in the contents. They had fought with a couple of bunches of bananas and apparently won, for the bananas looked distinctly the worse for wear. Having slaughtered the fruit, they had moved on and upset two bottles of vitamin product. Then, to their delight, they had found two large packets of boracic powder. These they had burst open and scattered far and wide, while large quantities of the white powder had stuck to their egg-soaked fur. By the time I found them they were on the point of having a quick drink from a highly pungent and poisonous bucket of disinfectant, and I grabbed them only just in time. Each of them looked like some weird Christmas cake decoration, in a coat stiff with boracic and egg yolk. It took me three quarters of an hour to clean them up. Then I put them in a larger and stronger basket and hoped that this would settle them.

It took them two days to break out of *this* basket.

This time they had decided to pay a visit to all the other animals I had. They must have had a fine time round the cages, for there were always some scraps of food lying about.

Now at that time I had a large and very beautiful monkey, called Colly, in my collection. Colly was a colobus, perhaps one of the most handsome of African monkeys. Their fur is coal black and snow white, hanging in long silky strands round their bodies like a shawl. They have a very long plume-like tail, also black and white. Colly was a somewhat vain monkey and spent a lot of her time grooming her lovely coat and posing in various parts of the cage. On this particular afternoon she had decided to enjoy a siesta in the bottom of her box, while waiting for me to bring her some fruit. She lay there like a sunbather on a beach, her eyes closed, her hands folded neatly on her chest. Unfortunately, however, she had pushed her tail through the bars so that it lay on the ground outside like a feathery black-and-white scarf that someone had dropped. Just as Colly was drifting off into a deep sleep, the Bandits appeared on the scene.

The Bandits, as I pointed out, believed that everything in the world, no matter how curious it looked, might turn out to be edible. In their opinion it was always worth sampling everything, just in case. When he saw Colly's tail lying on the ground ahead, apparently not belonging to anyone, the eldest Bandit decided it must be a tasty morsel of something or other that Providence had placed in his path. So he rushed forward and sank his sharp little teeth into it. His two brothers, feeling that there was plenty of this meal for everyone, joined him immediately. Thus was Colly woken out of a deep and refreshing sleep by three sets of extremely sharp little teeth fastening themselves almost simultaneously in her tail. She gave a wild scream of fright and scrambled towards the top of her cage. But the Bandits were not going to be deprived of this tasty morsel without a struggle, and they hung on grimly. The higher Colly climbed in her cage, the higher she lifted the Bandits off the ground, and when eventually I got there in response to her yells, I found the Bandits, like some miniature trapeze-artists, hanging by their teeth three feet off the ground. It took me five minutes to make them let go, and then I managed it only by blowing cigarette-smoke in their faces and making them sneeze. By the time I had got them safely locked up again, poor Colly was a nervous wreck.

I decided the Bandits must have a proper cage if I did not want the rest of my animals driven hysterical by their attentions. I built them a very nice one, with every modern convenience. It had a large and spacious bedroom at one end, and an open playground and dining-room at the other. There were two doors, one to admit my hand to their bedroom, the other to put their food into their dining-room. The trouble lay in feeding them. As soon as they saw me approach with a plate they would cluster round the doorway, screaming excitedly, and the moment the door was opened they would shoot out, knock the plate from my hand and fall to the ground with it, a tangled mass of kusimanses, raw meat, raw egg-and milk. Quite often when I went to pick them up they would bite me, not vindictively but simply because they would mistake my fingers for something edible. Yes, feeding the Bandits was not only a wasteful process but an extremely painful one as well. By the time I got them safely back to England they had bitten me twice as frequently as any animal I have ever kept. So it was with a real feeling of relief that I handed them over to a zoo.

The next day I went round to see how they were settling down. I found them in a huge cage, pattering about and looking, I felt, rather lost and bewildered by all the new sights and sounds. Poor little things, I thought, they have had the wind taken out of their sails. They looked so subdued and forlorn. I began to feel quite sorry to have parted with them. I stuck my finger through the wire and waggled it, calling to them. I thought it might comfort them to talk to someone they knew. I should have known better: the Bandits shot across the cage in a grim-faced bunch and fastened onto my finger like bulldogs. With a yelp of pain I at last managed to get my finger away, and as I left them, mopping the blood from my hand, I decided that perhaps, after all, I was not *so* sorry to see the back of them. Life without the Bandits might be considerably less exciting – but it would not hurt nearly so much.

WILHELMINA

Most people, when they learn for the first time that I collect wild animals for zoos, ask the same series of questions in the same order. First they ask if it is dangerous, to which the answer is no, it is not, providing you do not make any silly mistakes. Then they ask how I catch the animals – a more difficult question to answer, for there are many hundreds of ways of capturing wild animals: sometimes you have no set method, but have to improvise something on the spur of the moment. Their third question is, invariably: don't you become attached to your animals and find it difficult to part with them at the end of an expedition? The answer is, of course, that you do, and sometimes parting with a creature you have kept for eight months can be a heartbreaking process.

Occasionally you even find yourself getting attached to the strangest of beasts, some weird creature you would never in the normal way have thought you could like. One such beast as this, I remember, was Wilhelmina.

Wilhelmina was a whip-scorpion, and if anyone had told me that the day would come when I would feel even the remotest trace of affection for a whip-scorpion I would never have believed them. Of all the creatures on the face of this earth the whip-scorpion is one of the least prepossessing. To those who do not adore spiders (and I am one of those people) the whip-scorpion is a form of living nightmare. It resembles a spider with a body the size of a walnut that has been run over by a steam-roller and flattened to a wafer-thin flake. To this flake are attached what appear to be an immense number of long, fine and crooked legs which spread out to the size of a soup-plate. To cap it all, on the front (if such a creature can be said to have a front), are two enormously long slender legs like whips, about twelve inches long in a robust specimen. It possesses the ability to skim about at incredible speed and with apparently no effort – up, down or sideways – and to squeeze its revolting body into a crack that would scarcely accommodate a piece of tissue-paper.

That is a whip-scorpion, and to anyone who distrusts spiders it is the personification of the devil. Fortunately they are harmless, unless you happen to have a weak heart.

I made my first acquaintance with Wilhelmina's family when I was on a collecting trip to the tropical forest of West Africa. For many different reasons, hunting in these forests is always difficult. To begin with, the trees are enormous, some as much as a hundred and fifty feet high, with trunks as fat as a factory chimney. Their head foliage is thick, luxuriant and twined with creepers and the branches are decorated with various parasitic plants like a curious hanging garden. All this may be eighty or a hundred feet above the forest floor, and the only way to reach it is to climb a trunk as smooth as a plank which has not a single branch for the first seventy feet of its length. This, the top layer of the forest, is by far the most thickly populated, for in the comparative safety of the tree-tops live a host of creatures which rarely, if ever, descend to groundlevel. Setting traps in the forest canopy is a difficult and tedious operation. It may take a whole morning to find a way up a tree, climb it and set the trap in a suitable position. Then, just as you have safely regained the forest floor, your trap goes off with a triumphant clang, and the whole laborious process has to be endured once more. Thus, although trap-setting in the tree-tops is a painful necessity, you are always on the look-out for some slightly easier method of obtaining the animals you want. Probably one of the most successful and exciting of these methods is to smoke out the giant trees.

Some of the forest trees, although apparently sound and solid, are actually hollow for part or all of their length. These are the trees to look for, though they are not so easy to find. A day of searching in the forest might end with the discovery of six of them, perhaps one of which will yield good results when finally smoked out.

Smoking out a hollow tree is quite an art. To begin with, you must, if necessary, enlarge the opening at the base of the trunk and lay a small fire of dry twigs. Then two Africans are sent up the tree with nets to cover all the holes and cracks at the upper end of the trunk, and then station themselves at convenient points to catch any animals that emerge. When all is ready, you start the fire, and as soon as it is crackling you lay on top of the flames a large bundle of fresh green leaves. Immediately the flames die away and in their place rises a column of thick and pungent smoke. The great hollow interior of the tree acts like a gigantic chimney, and the smoke is whisked up inside. You never realize, until you light the fire, quite how many holes and cracks there are in the trunk of the tree. As you watch, you see a tiny tendril of smoke appear magically on the bark perhaps twenty feet from the ground, coiling out of an almost invisible hole; a short pause and ten feet higher three more little holes puff smoke like miniature cannon-mouths. Thus, guided by the tiny streamers of smoke appearing at intervals along the trunk, you can watch the progress of the smoking. If the tree is a good one, you have only time to watch the smoke get half-way up, for it is then that the animals start to break cover and you become very busy indeed.

When one of these hollow trees is inhabited, it is really like a block of flats. In the ground-floor apartments, for example, you find things like the giant land-snails, each the size of an apple, and they come gliding out of the base of the tree with all the speed a snail is capable of mustering, even in an emergency. They may be followed by other creatures who prefer the lower apartments or else are unable to climb: the big forest toads, for example, whose backs are cleverly marked out to resemble a dead leaf, and whose cheeks and sides are a beautiful mahogany red. They come waddling out from among the tree-tops with the most ludicrously indignant expressions on their faces, and on reaching the open air suddenly squat down and stare about them in a pathetic and helpless sort of way.

Having evicted all the ground-floor tenants, you then have to wait a short time before the occupants higher up have a chance to make their way down to the opening. Almost invariably giant millipedes are among the first to appear – charming creatures that look like brown sausages, with a fringe of legs along the underside of their bodies. They are quite harmless and rather imbecile creatures for which I have a very soft spot. One of their most ridiculous antics, when placed on a table, is to set off walking, all their legs working furiously, and on coming to the edge they never seem to notice it and continue to walk out into space until the weight of their body bends them over. Then, half on and half off the table, they pause, consider, and eventually decide that something is wrong. And so, starting with the extreme hind pair of legs, they go into reverse and get themselves onto the table again – only to crawl to the other side and repeat the performance.

Immediately after the appearance of the giant millipedes all the other top-floor tenants of the tree break cover together, some making for the top of the tree, others for the bottom. Perhaps there are squirrels with black ears, green bodies and tails of the most beautiful flame colour; giant grey dormice who gallop out of the tree, trailing their bushy tails behind them like puffs of smoke; perhaps a pair of bush-babies, with their great innocent eyes and their slender attenuated and trembly hands, like those of very old men. And then, of course, there are the bats: great fat brown bats with curious flower-like decorations on the skin of their noses and large transparent ears; others bright ginger, with black ears twisted down over their heads and pig-like snouts. And as this pageant of wild life appears the whip-scorpions are all over the place, skimming up and down the tree with a speed and silence that is unnerving and uncanny, squeezing their revolting bodies into the thinnest crack as you make a swipe at them with the net, only to reappear suddenly ten feet lower down the tree, skimming towards you apparently with the intention of disappearing into your shirt. You step back hurriedly and the creature vanishes: only the tips of a pair of antennae, wiggling from the depths of a crevice in the bark that would hardly accommodate a visiting-card, tell you of its whereabouts. Of the many creatures in the West African forest the whip-scorpion has been responsible for more shocks to my system than any other. The day a particularly large and leggy specimen ran over my bare arm, as I leant against a tree, will always be one of my most vivid memories. It took at least a year off my life.

But to return to Wilhelmina. She was a well-brought-up little whip-scorpion, one of a family of ten, and I started my intimate acquaintance with her when I captured her mother. All this happened quite by chance.

I had for many days been smoking out trees in the forest in search of an elusive and rare little animal known as the pigmy scaly-tail. These little mammals, which look like mice with long feathery tails, have a curious membrane of skin stretched from ankle to wrist, with the aid of which they glide around the forest with the ease of swallows. The scaly-tails live in colonies in hollow trees, but the difficulty lay in finding a tree that contained a colony. When, after much fruitless hunting, I did discover a group of these prizes, and moreover actually managed to capture some, I felt considerably elated. I even started to take a benign interest in the numerous whip-scorpions that were scuttling about the tree. Then suddenly I noticed one which looked so extraordinary, and was behaving in such a peculiar manner, that my attention was at once arrested. To begin with, this whip-scorpion seemed to be wearing a green fur-coat that almost completely covered her chocolate body. Secondly, it was working its way slowly and carefully down the tree with none of the sudden fits and starts common to the normal whip-scorpion.

Wondering if the green fur-coat and the slow walk were symptoms of extreme age in the whip-scorpion world I moved closer to examine the creature. To my astonishment I found that the fur-coat was composed of baby whip-scorpions, each not much larger than my thumbnail, which were obviously fairly recent additions to the family. They were, in extraordinary contrast to their dark-coloured mother, a bright and bilious green, the sort of green that confectioners are fond of using in cake decorations. The mother's slow and stately progress was due to her concern lest one of her babies lose its grip and drop off. I realized, rather ruefully, that I had never given the private life of the whip-scorpion much thought, and it had certainly never occurred to me that the female would be sufficiently maternal to carry her babies on her back. Overcome with remorse at my thoughtlessness, I decided that here was an ideal chance for me to catch up on my studies of these creatures. So I captured the female very carefully – to avoid dropping any of her progeny – and carried her back to camp.

I placed the mother and children in a large roomy box with plenty of cover in the way of bark and leaves. Every morning I had to look under these, rather gingerly I admit, to see if she was all right. At first, the moment I lifted the bark under which she was hiding, she would rush out and scuttle up the side of the box, a distressing habit which always made me jump and slam the lid down. I was very much afraid that one day I might do this and trap her legs or antennae, but fortunately after the first three days or so she settled down, and would even let me renew the leaves and bark in her box without taking any notice.

I had the female whip-scorpion and her babies for two months, and during that time the babies ceased to ride on their mother's back. They scattered and took up residence in various parts of the box, grew steadily and lost their green colouring in favour of brown. Whenever they grew too big for their skins they would split them down the back and step out of them, like spiders. Each time they did so they would emerge a little larger and a little browner. I discovered that while the mother would tackle anything from a small grasshopper to a large beetle, the babies were fussy and demanded small spiders, slugs and other easily digestible fare. They all appeared to be thriving, and I began to feel rather proud of them. Then one day I returned to camp after a few hours' hunting in the forest to find that tragedy had struck.

A tame Patas monkey I kept tied up outside the tent had eaten through his rope and been on a tour of investigation. Before anyone had noticed it he had eaten a bunch of bananas. three mangos and four hard-boiled eggs, he had broken two bottles of disinfectant, and rounded the whole thing off by knocking my whip-scorpion box onto the floor. It promptly broke open and scattered the family on the ground, and the Patas monkey, a creature of depraved habits, had set to work and eaten them. When I got back he was safely tied up again, and suffering from an acute attack of hiccups.

I picked up my whip-scorpion nursery and peered mournfully into it, cursing myself for having left it in such an accessible place, and cursing the monkey for having such an appetite. But then, to my surprise and delight, I found, squatting in solitary state on a piece of bark, one of the baby whip-scorpions, the sole survivor of the massacre. Tenderly I moved it to a smaller and more burglar-proof cage, showered it with slugs and other delicacies and christened it, for no reason at all, Wilhelmina.

During the time I had Wilhelmina's mother, and Wilhelmina herself, I learnt quite a lot about whip-scorpions. I discovered that though quite willing to hunt by day if hungry, they were at their most lively during the night. During the day Wilhelmina was always a little dull-witted, but in the evening she woke up and, if I may use the expression, blossomed. She would stalk to and fro in her box, her pincers at the ready, her long antennae-like legs lashing out like whips ahead of her, seeking the best route. Although these tremendously elongated legs are supposed to be merely feelers, I got the impression that they could do more than this. I have seen them wave in the direction of an insect, pause and twitch, whereupon Wilhelmina would brace herself, almost as if she had smelt or heard her prey with the aid of her long legs. Sometimes she would stalk her food like this; at other times she would simply lie in wait until the unfortunate insect walked almost into her arms, and the powerful pincers would gather it lovingly into her mouth.

As she grew older I gave her bigger and bigger things to eat, and I found her courage extraordinary. She was rather like a pugnacious terrier who, the larger the opponent, the better she likes the fight. I was so fascinated by her skill and bravery in tackling insects as big or bigger than herself that one day, rather unwisely, I put a very large locust in with her. Without a moment's hesitation, she flew at him and grasped his bulky body in her pincers. To my alarm, however, the locust gave a hearty kick with his powerful hind legs and both he and Wilhelmina soared upwards and hit the wire-gauze roof of the cage with a resounding thump, then crashed back to the floor again. This rough treatment did not deter Wilhelmina at all, and she continued to hug the locust while he leapt wildly around the cage, thumping against the roof, until eventually he was exhausted. Then she settled down and made short work of him. But after this I was always careful to give her the smaller insects, for I had visions of a leg or one of her whips being broken off in such a rough contest.

By now I had become very fond and not a little proud of Wilhelmina. She was, as far as I knew, the only whip-scorpion to have been kept in captivity. What is more, she had become very tame. I had only to rap on the side of her box with my fingers and she would appear from under her piece of bark and wave her whips at me. Then, if I put my hand inside, she would climb onto my palm and sit there quietly while I fed her with slugs, creatures for which she still retained a passion.

When the time drew near for me to transport my large collection of animals back to England, I began to grow rather worried over Wilhelmina. It was a two-week voyage, and I could not take enough insect food for that length of time. I decided therefore to try making her eat raw meat. It took me a long time to achieve it, but once I had learnt the art of waggling the bit of meat seductively enough I found that Wilhelmina would grab it, and on this unlikely diet she seemed to thrive. On the journey down to the coast by lorry Wilhelmina behaved like a veteran traveller, sitting in her box and sucking a large chunk of raw meat almost throughout the trip. For the first day on board ship the strange surroundings made her a little sulky, but after that the sea air seemed to do her good and she became positively skittish. This was her undoing.

One evening when I went to feed her, she scuttled up as far as my elbow before I knew what was happening, dropped onto a hatch-cover and was just about to squeeze her way through a crack on a tour of investigation when I recovered from my astonishment and managed to grab her. For the next few days I fed her very cautiously, and she seemed to have quietened down and regained her former self-possession.

Then one evening she waggled her whips at me so plaintively that I lifted her out of her cage on the palm of my hand and started to feed her on the few remaining slugs I had brought for her in a tin. She ate two slugs, sitting quietly and decorously on my hand, and then suddenly she jumped. She could not have chosen a worse time, for as she was in mid-air a puff of wind swept round the bulkhead and whisked her away. I had a brief glimpse of her whips waving wildly, and then she was over the rail and gone, into the vast heaving landscape of the sea. I rushed to the rail and peered over, but it was impossible to spot so small a creature in the waves and froth below. Hurriedly I threw her box over, in the vain hope that she might find it and use it as a raft. A ridiculous hope, I know, but I did not like to think of her drowning without making some attempt to save her. I could have kicked myself for my stupidity in lifting her out of her box; I never thought I would have been so affected by the loss of such a creature. I had grown very fond of her; she in her turn had seemed to trust me. It was a tragic way for the relationship to end. But there was one slight consolation: after my association with Wilhelmina I shall never again look at a whip-scorpion with quite the same distaste.

ADOPTING AN ANTEATER

Making a collection of two hundred birds, mammals and reptiles is rather like having two hundred delicate babies to look after. It needs a lot of hard work and patience. You have to make sure their diet suits them, that their cages are big enough, that they get neither too hot in the tropics nor too cold when you get near England. You have to de-worm, de-tick and de-flea them; you have to keep their cages and feeding-pots spotlessly clean.

But, above all, you have to make sure that your animals are *happy*. However well looked after, a wild animal will not live in captivity unless it is happy. I am talking, of course, of the adult, wild-caught creature. But occasionally you get a baby wild animal whose mother has perhaps met with an accident, and who has been found wandering in the forest. When you capture one of these, you must be prepared for a good deal of hard work and worry, and above all you must be ready to give the animal the affection and confidence it requires; for after a day or two you will have become the parent, and the baby will trust you and depend on you completely.

This can sometimes make life rather difficult. There have been periods when I have played the adopted parent to as many as six baby animals at once, and this is no joke. Quite apart from anything else, imagine rising at three o'clock in the morning, stumbling about, half-asleep, in an effort to prepare six different bottles of milk, trying to keep your eyes open enough to put the right amount of vitamin drops and sugar in, knowing all the time that you will have to be up again in three hours to repeat the performance.

Some time ago my wife and I were on a collecting trip in Paraguay, that country shaped like a boot-box which lies almost in the exact centre of South America. Here, in a remote part of Chaco, we assembled a lovely collection of animals. Many things quite unconnected with animals happen on a collecting trip, things that frustrate your plans or irritate you in other ways. But politics, mercifully, had never before been among them. On this occasion, however, the Paraguayans decided to have a revolution, and as a direct result we had to release nearly the whole of our collection and escape to Argentina in a tiny four-seater plane.

Just before our retreat, an Indian had wandered into our camp carrying a sack from which had come the most extraordinary noises. It sounded like a cross between a cello in pain and a donkey with laryngitis. Opening the sack, the Indian tipped out one of the most delightful baby animals I had ever seen. She was a young giant anteater, and she could not have been more than a week old. She was about the size of a corgie, with black, ash-grey and white fur, a long slender snout and a pair of tiny, rather bleary eyes. The Indian said he had found her wandering about in the forest, honking forlornly. He thought her mother might have been killed by a jaguar.

The arrival of this baby put me in a predicament. I knew that we would be leaving soon and that the plane was so tiny that most of our equipment would have to be left behind to make room for the five or six creatures we were determined to take with us. To accept, at that stage, a baby anteater who weighed a considerable amount and who would have to be fussed over and bottle-fed, would be lunatic. Quite apart from anything else, no one as far as I knew, had ever tried to rear a baby anteater on a bottle. The whole thing was obviously out of the question. Just as I had made up my mind the baby, still blaring pathetically, suddenly discovered my leg, and with a honk of joy shinned up it, settled herself in my lap and went to sleep. Silently I paid the Indian the price he demanded, and thus became a father to one of the most charming children I have ever met.

The first difficulty cropped up almost at once. We had a baby's feeding-bottle, but we had exhausted our supply of teats. Luckily a frantic house-to-house search of the little village where we were living resulted in the discovery of one teat, of extreme age and unhygienic appearance. After one or two false starts the baby took to the bottle far better than I had dared hope, though feeding her was a painful performance.

Young anteaters, at that age, cling to their mother's back, and, since we had, so to speak, become her parents, she insisted on climbing onto one or the other of us nearly the whole time. Her claws were about three inches long, and she had a prodigious grip with them. During meals she clasped your leg affectionately with three paws, while with her remaining paw held your finger and squeezed it hard at intervals, for she was convinced that this would increase the flow of milk from the bottle. At the end of each feed you felt as though you had been mauled by a grizzly bear, while your fingers had been jammed in a door.

For the first days I carried her about with me to give her confidence. She liked to lie across the back of my neck, her long nose hanging down one side of me and her long tail down the other, like a fur collar. Every time I moved she would tighten her grip in a panic, and this was painful. After the fourth shirt had been ruined I decided that she would have to cling to something else, so I filled a sack full of straw and introduced her to that. She accepted it without any fuss, and so between meals she would lie in her cage, clutching this substitute happily. We had already christened her 'Sarah', and now that she developed this habit of sack-clutching we gave her a surname, and so she became known as 'Sarah Huggersack'.

Sarah was a model baby. Between feeds she lay quietly on her sack, occasionally yawning and showing a sticky, pinky-grey tongue about twelve inches long. When feeding-time came round she would suck the teat on her bottle so vigorously that it had soon changed from red to pale pink, the hole at the end of it had become about the size of a matchstick, and the whole thing drooped dismally from the neck of the bottle.

When we had to leave Paraguay in our extremely unsafe-looking four-seater plane, Sarah slept peacefully throughout the flight, lying on my wife's lap and snoring gently, occasionally blowing a few bubbles of sticky saliva out of her nose.

On arriving in Buenos Aires our first thought was to give Sarah a treat. We would buy her a nice new shiny teat. We went to endless trouble selecting one exactly the right size, shape and colour, put it on the bottle and presented it to Sarah. She was scandalized. She honked wildly at the mere thought of a new teat, and sent the bottle flying with a well-directed clout from her paw. Nor did she calm down and start to feed until we had replaced the old withered teat on the bottle. She clung to it ever after; months after her arrival in England she still refused to be parted from it.

In Buenos Aires we housed our animals in an empty house on the outskirts of the city. From the centre, where we stayed, it took us half an hour in a taxi to reach it, and this journey we had to do twice and sometimes three times a day. We soon found that having a baby anteater made our social life difficult in the extreme. Have you ever tried to explain to a hostess that you must suddenly leave in the middle of dinner because you have to give a bottle to an anteater? In the end our friends gave up in despair. They used to telephone and ascertain the times of Sarah's feeds before inviting us.

By this time Sarah had become much more grown up and independent. After her evening feed she would go for a walk round the room by herself. This was a great advance, for up till then she had screamed blue murder if you moved more than a foot or so away from her. After her tour of inspection she liked to have a game. This consisted in walking past us, her nose in the air, her tail trailing temptingly. You were then supposed to grab the end of her tail and pull, whereupon she would swing round on three legs and give you a gentle clout with her paw. When this had been repeated twenty or thirty times she felt satisfied, and then you had to lay her on her back and tickle her tummy for ten minutes or so while she closed her eyes and blew bubbles of ecstasy at you. After this she would go to bed without any fuss. But try to put her to bed without giving her a game and she would kick and struggle and honk, and generally behave in a thoroughly spoilt manner.

When we eventually got on board ship, Sarah was not at all sure that she approved of sea-voyages. To begin with, the ship smelt queer; then there was a strong wind which nearly blew her over every time she went for a walk on deck; and lastly, which she hated most of all, the deck would not keep still. First it tilted one way, then it tilted another, and Sarah would go staggering about, honking plaintively, banging her nose on bulkheads and hatch-covers. When the weather improved, however, she seemed to enjoy the trip. Sometimes in the afternoon, when I had time, I would take her up to the promenade deck and we would sit in a deckchair and sunbathe. She even paid a visit to the bridge, by special request of the captain. I thought it was because he had fallen for her charm and personality but he confessed that it was because (having seen her only from a distance) he wanted to make sure which end of her was the front.

I must say we felt very proud of Sarah when we arrived in London Docks and she posed for the Press photographers with all the unselfconscious ease of a born celebrity. She even went so far as to lick one of the reporters – a great honour. I hastily tried to point this out to him, while helping to remove a large patch of sticky saliva from his coat. It was not everyone she would lick, I told him. His expression told me that he did not appreciate the point.

Sarah went straight from the docks to a zoo in Devonshire, and we hated to see her go. However, we were kept informed about her progress and she seemed to be doing well. She had formed a deep attachment to her keeper.

Some weeks later I was giving a lecture at the Festival Hall, and the organizer thought it would be rather a good idea if I introduced some animal on the stage at the end of my talk. I immediately thought of

Sarah. Both the zoo authorities and the Festival Hall Management were willing, but, as it was now winter, I insisted that Sarah must have a dressing-room to wait in.

I met Sarah and her keeper at Paddington Station. Sarah was in a huge crate, for she had grown as big as a red setter, and she created quite a sensation on the platform. As soon as she heard my voice she flung herself at the bars of her cage and protruded twelve inches of sticky tongue in a moist and affectionate greeting. People standing near the cage leapt back hurriedly, thinking some curious form of snake was escaping and it took a lot of persuasion before we could find a porter brave enough to wheel the cage on a truck.

When we reached the Festival Hall we found that the rehearsal of a symphony concert had just come to an end. We wheeled Sarah's big box down long corridors to the dressing-room, and just as we reached the door it was flung open and Sir Thomas Beecham strode out, smoking a large cigar. We wheeled Sarah into the dressing-room he had just vacated.

While I was on the stage, my wife kept Sarah occupied by running round and round the dressing-room with her, to the consternation and horror of one of the porters, who, hearing the noise, was convinced that Sarah had broken out of her cage and was attacking my wife. Eventually, however, the great moment arrived and amid tumultuous applause Sarah was carried onto the stage. She was very short-sighted, as all anteaters are, so to her the audience was non-existent. She looked round vaguely to see where the noise was coming from, but decided that it was not really worth worrying about. While I extolled her virtues, she wandered about the stage, oblivious, occasionally snuffling loudly in a corner, and repeatedly approaching the microphone and giving it a quick lick, which left it in a very sticky condition for the next performer. Just as I was telling the audience how well-behaved she was, she discovered the table in the middle of the stage, and with an immense sigh of satisfaction proceeded to scratch her bottom against one of the legs. She was a great success.

After the show, Sarah held court for a few select guests in her dressing-room, and became so skittish that she even galloped up and down outside in the corridor. Then we bundled her up warmly and put her on the night train for Devon with her keeper.

Apparently, on reaching the zoo again, Sarah was thoroughly spoilt. Her short spell as a celebrity had gone to her head. For three days she refused to be left alone, stamping about her cage and honking wildly, and refusing all food unless she was fed by hand.

A few months later I wanted Sarah to make an appearance on a television show I was doing, and so once again she tasted the glamour and glitter of show business. She behaved with the utmost decorum during rehearsals, except that she was dying to investigate the camera closely, and had to be restrained by force. When the show was over she resisted going back to her cage, and it took the united efforts of myself, my wife, Sarah's keeper and the studio manager to get her back into the box – for Sarah was then quite grown up, measuring six feet from nose to tail, standing three feet at the shoulder and with forearms as thick as my thigh.

We did not see Sarah again until quite recently, when we paid her a visit at her zoo. It had been six months since she had last seen us, and quite frankly I thought she would have forgotten us. Anteater fan though I am, I would be the first to admit that they are not creatures who are overburdened with brains, and six months is a long time. But the moment we called to her she came bounding out of her sleeping den and rushed to the wire to lick us. We even went into the cage and played with her, a sure sign that she really did recognize us, for no one else except her keeper dared enter.

Eventually we said goodbye to her, rather sadly, and left her sitting in the straw blowing bubbles after us. As my wife said: 'It was rather as though we were leaving our child at boarding school.' We are certainly her adopted parents, as far as Sarah is concerned.

Yesterday we had some good news. We heard that Sarah has got a mate. He is as yet too young to be put in with her, but soon he should be big enough. Who knows, by this time next year we may be grandparents to a fine bouncing baby anteater!

PORTRAIT OF PAVLO

It is a curious thing, but when you keep animals as pets you tend to look upon them so much as miniature human beings that you generally manage to impress some of your own characteristics onto them. This anthropomorphic attitude is awfully difficult to avoid. If you possess a golden hamster and are always watching the way he sits up and eats a nut, his little pink paws trembling with excitement, his pouches bulging as he saves in his cheeks what cannot be eaten immediately, you might one day come to the conclusion that he looks exactly like your own Uncle Amos sitting, full of port and nuts, in his favourite club. From that moment the damage is done. The hamster continues to behave like a hamster, but you regard him only as a miniature Uncle Amos, clad in a ginger fur-coat, for ever sitting in his club, his cheeks bulging with food. There are very few animals who have characters strong and distinct enough to overcome this treatment, who display such powerful personalities that you are forced to treat them as individuals and not as miniature human beings. Of the many hundreds of animals I have collected for zoos in this country, and of the many I have kept as pets, I can remember at the most about a dozen creatures who had this strength of personality that not only made them completely different from others of their kind, but enabled them to resist all attempts on my part to turn them into something they were not.

One of the smallest of these animals was Pavlo, a black-eared marmoset, and his story really started one evening when, on a collecting trip in British Guiana, I sat quietly in the bushes near a clearing, watching a hole in a bank which I had good reason to believe contained an animal of some description. The sun was setting and the sky was a glorious salmon pink, and outlined against it were the massive trees of the forest, their branches so entwined with creepers that each tree looked as though it had been caught in a giant spider's web. There is nothing quite so soothing as a tropical forest at this time of day. I sat there absorbing sights and colours, my mind in the blank and receptive state that the Buddhists tell us is the first step towards Nirvana. Suddenly my trance was shattered by a shrill and prolonged squeak of such intensity that it felt as though someone had driven a needle into my ear. Peering above me cautiously, I tried to see where the sound had come from: it seemed the wrong sort of note for a tree-frog or an insect, and far too sharp and tuneless to be a bird. There, on a great branch about thirty feet above me, I saw the source of the noise: a diminutive marmoset was trotting along a wide branch as if it were an arterial road, picking his way in and out of the forest of orchids and other parasitic plants that grew in clumps from the bark. As I watched, he stopped, sat up on his hind legs and uttered another of his piercing cries; this time he was answered from some distance away, and within a moment or two other marmosets had joined him. Trilling and squeaking to each other, they moved among the orchids, searching diligently, occasionally uttering shrill squeaks of joy as they unearthed a cockroach or a beetle among the leaves. One of them pursued something through an orchid plant for a long time, parting the leaves and peering between them with an intense expression on his tiny face. Every time he made a grab the leaves got in the way and the insect managed to escape round the other side of the plant. Eventually, more by good luck than skill, he dived his small hands in amongst the leaves and, with a twitter of triumph, emerged with a fat cockroach clutched firmly between his fingers. The insect was a large one and its wriggling was strenuous, so, presumably in case he dropped it, he stuffed the whole thing into his mouth. He sat there munching happily, and when he had swallowed the last morsel, he carefully examined both the palms and backs of his paws to make sure there was none left.

I was so entranced by this glimpse into the private life of the marmoset that it was not until the little party had moved off into the now-gloomy forest that I realized I had an acute crick in my neck and that one of my legs had gone to sleep.

A considerable time later my attention was once again drawn to marmosets. I went down to an animal dealer's shop in London, to enquire about something quite different, and the first thing I saw on entering the shop was a cage full of marmosets, a pathetic, scruffy group of ten, crouched in a dirty cage on a perch so small that they were continually having to jostle and squabble for a place to sit. Most of them were adults, but there was one youngster who seemed to be getting rather a rough time of it. He was thin and unkempt, so small that whenever there was a reshuffling of positions on the perch he was always the one to get knocked off. As I watched this pathetic, shivering little group, I remembered the little family party I had seen in Guiana, grubbing happily for their dinner among the orchids, and I felt that I could not leave the shop without rescuing at least one of the tiny animals. So within five minutes I had paid the price of liberation, and the smallest occupant of the cage was dragged out, screaming with alarm, and bundled into a cardboard box.

When I got him home I christened him Pavlo and introduced him to the family, who viewed him with suspicion. However, as soon as Pavlo had settled down he set about the task of winning their confidence, and in a very short time he had all of us under his minute thumb. In spite of his size (he fitted comfortably into a large teacup), he had a terrific personality, a Napoleonic air about him which was difficult to resist. His head was only the size of a large walnut, but it soon became apparent that it contained a brain of considerable power and intelligence. At first we kept him in a large cage in the drawing-room, where he would have plenty of company, but he was so obviously miserable when confined that we started letting him out for an hour or two every day. This was our undoing. Very soon Pavlo had convinced us that the cage was unnecessary, so it was consigned to the rubbish-heap, and he had the run of the house all day and every day. He became accepted as a diminutive member of the family, and he treated the house as though he owned it and we were his guests.

At first sight Pavlo resembled a curious kind of squirrel, until you noticed his very human face and his bright, shrewd, brown eyes. His fur was soft, and presented a brindled appearance because the individual hairs were banded with orange, black and grey, in that order; his tail, however, was ringed with black and white. The fur on his head and neck was chocolate brown, and hung round his shoulders and chest in a tattered fringe. His large ears were hidden by long ear-tufts of the same chocolate colour. Across his forehead, above his eyes and the aristocratic bridge of his tiny nose, was a broad white patch.

Everyone who saw him, and who had any knowledge of animals, assured me that I would not keep him long: marmosets, they said, coming from the warm tropical forests of South America, never lived more than a year in this climate. It seemed that their cheerful prophecies were right when, after six months, Pavlo developed a form of paralysis and from the waist downwards lost all power of movement. We fought hard to save his life while those who had predicted this trouble said he ought to be destroyed. But he seemed in no pain, so we persevered. Four times a day we massaged his tiny legs, his back and tail with warm cod-liver oil, and he had more cod-liver oil in his special diet, which included such delicacies as grapes and pears. He lay pathetically on a cushion, wrapped in cotton-wool for warmth, while the family took it in turn to minister to his wants. Sunshine was what he needed most, and plenty of it, but the English climate provided precious little. So the neighbours were treated to the sight of us carrying our Lilliputian invalid round the garden, carefully placing his cushion in every patch of sunlight that appeared. This went on for a month, and at the end of it Pavlo could move his feet slightly and twitch his tail; two weeks later he was hobbling round the house, almost his old self again. We were delighted, even though the house did reek of cod-liver oil for months afterwards.

Instead of making him more delicate, his illness seemed to make him tougher, and at times he appeared almost indestructible. We never pampered him, and the only concession we made was to give him a hot-water bottle in his bed during the winter. He liked this so much that he would refuse to go to bed without it, even in midsummer. His bedroom was a drawer in a tallboy in my mother's room, and his bed consisted of an old dressing-gown and a piece of fur-coat. Putting Pavlo to bed was quite a ritual: first the dressing-gown had to be spread in the drawer and the bottle wrapped in it so that he did not burn himself. Then the piece of fur-coat had to be made into a sort of furry cave, into which Pavlo would crawl, curl up into a ball and close his eyes blissfully. At first we used to push the drawer closed, except for a crack to allow for air, as this prevented Pavlo from getting up too early in the morning. But he very soon learned that by pushing his head into the crack he could widen it and escape.

About six in the morning he would wake up to find that his bottle had gone cold, so he would sally forth in search of alternative warmth. He would scuttle across the floor and up the leg of my mother's bed, landing on the eiderdown. Then he would make his way up the bed, uttering squeaks of welcome, and burrow under the pillow where he would stay, cosy and warm, until it was time for her to get up. When she eventually got out of bed and left him, Pavlo would be furious, and would stand on the pillow chattering and screaming with rage. When he saw, however, that she had no intention of getting back to bed to keep him warm, he would scuttle down the passage to my room and crawl in with me. Here he would remain, stretched luxuriously on my chest, until it was time for me to get up, and then he would stand on my pillow and abuse me, screwing his tiny face up into a ferocious and most human scowl. Having told me what he thought of me, he would dash off and get into bed with my brother, and when he was turned out of there would go and join my sister for a quick nap before breakfast. This migration from bed to bed was a regular morning performance.

Downstairs he had plenty of heating at his disposal. There was a tall standard-lamp in the drawing-room which belonged to him: in the winter he would crawl inside the shade and sit next to the bulb, basking in the heat. He also had a stool and a cushion by the fire, but he preferred the lamp, and so it had to be kept on all day for his benefit, and our electricity bill went up by leaps and bounds. In the first warm days of spring Pavlo would venture out into the garden, where his favourite haunt was the fence; he would sit in the sun, or potter up and down catching spiders and other delicacies for himself. Half-way along this fence was a sort of rustic arbour made out of poles thickly overgrown with creepers, and it was into this net of creepers that Pavlo would dash if danger threatened. For many years he carried on a feud with the big white cat from next door, for this beast was obviously under the impression that Pavlo was a strange type of rat which it was her duty to kill. She would spend many painful hours stalking him, but since she was as inconspicuous as a snowball against the green leaves she never managed to catch Pavlo unawares. He would wait until she was quite close, her yellow eye glaring, her tongue flicking her lips, and then he would trot off along the fence and dive in among the creepers. Sitting there in safety, he would scream and chitter like an urchin from between the flowers, while the frustrated cat prowled about trying to find a hole among the creepers big enough for her portly body to squeeze through.

Growing by the fence, between the house and Pavlo's creeper-covered hide-out, were two young fig trees, and round the base of their trunks we had dug deep trenches which we kept full of water during the hot weather. Pavlo was pottering along the fence one day, chattering to himself and catching spiders, when he looked up and discovered that his arch-enemy the cat, huge and white, was sitting on the fence between him and his creeper-covered arbour. His only chance of escape was to go back along the fence and into the house, so Pavlo turned and bolted, squeaking for help as he ran. The fat white cat was not such an expert tight-rope walker as Pavlo, so her progress along the fence top was slow, but even so she was catching up on him. She was uncomfortably close behind him when he reached the fig trees, and he became so nervous that he missed his footing and with a frantic scream of fright fell off the fence and straight into the water-filled trench below. He rose to the surface, spluttering and screaming, and splashing around in circles, while the cat watched him in amazement: she had obviously never seen an aquatic marmoset before. Luckily, before she had recovered from her astonishment and hooked him out of the water, I arrived on the scene and she fled. I rescued Pavlo, gibbering with rage, and he spent the rest of the afternoon in front of the fire, wrapped in a piece of blanket, muttering darkly to himself. This episode had a bad effect on his nerves, and for a whole week he refused to go out on the fence, and if he caught so much as a glimpse of the white cat he would scream until someone put him on their shoulder and comforted him.

Pavlo lived with us for eight years, and it was rather like having a leprechaun in the house: you never knew what was going to happen next. He did not adapt himself to our ways, we had to adapt ourselves to his. He insisted, for example, on having his meals with us, and his meals had to be the same as ours. He ate on the windowsill out of a saucer. For breakfast he would have porridge or cornflakes, with warm milk and sugar; at lunch he had green vegetables, potatoes and a spoonful of whatever pudding was going. At tea-time he had to be kept off the table by force, or he would dive into the jam pot with shrill squeaks of delight; he was under the impression that the jam was put on the table for his benefit, and would get most annoyed if you differed with him on this point. We had to be ready to put him to bed at six o'clock sharp, and if we were late he would stalk furiously up and down outside his drawer, his fur standing on end with rage. We had to learn not to slam doors shut without first looking to see if Pavlo was sitting on top, because, for some reason, he liked to sit on doors and meditate. But our worst crime, according to him, was when we went out and left him for an afternoon. When we returned he would leave us in no doubt as to his feelings on the subject; we would be in disgrace; he would turn his back on us in disgust when we tried to talk to him; he would go and sit in a corner and glower at us, his little face screwed up into a scowl. After half an hour or so he would, very reluctantly, forgive us and with regal condescension accept a lump of sugar and some warm milk before retiring to bed. Pavlo's moods were must human, for he would scowl and mutter at you when he felt bad-tempered, and, very probably, try to give you a nip. When he was feeling affectionate, however, he would approach you with a loving expression on his face, poking his tongue out and in very rapidly, and smacking his lips, climb onto your shoulder and give your ear a series of passionate nibbles.

His method of getting about the house was a source of astonishment to everyone, for he hated running on the ground and would never descend to the floor if he could avoid it. In his native forest he would have made his way through the trees from branch to branch and from creeper to creeper, but there were no such refinements in a suburban house. So Pavlo used the picture-rails as his highways, and he would scuttle along them at incredible speeds, hanging on with one hand and one foot, humping himself along like a hairy caterpillar, until he was able to drop onto the windowsill. He could shin up the smooth edge of a door more quickly and easily than we could walk up a flight of stairs. Sometimes he would cadge a lift from the dog, leaping onto his back and clinging there like a miniature Old Man of the Sea. The dog, who had been taught that Pavlo's person was sacred, would give us mute and appealing looks until we removed the monkey from his back. He disliked Pavlo for two reasons: firstly, he did not see why such a rat-like object should be allowed the run of the house, and secondly, Pavlo used to go out of his way to be annoying. He would hang down from the arm of a chair when the dog passed and pull his eyebrows or whiskers and then leap back out of range. Or else he would wait until the dog was asleep and then make a swift attack on his unprotected tail. Occasionally, however, there would be a sort of armed truce, and the dog would lie in front of the fire while Pavlo, perched on his ribs would diligently comb his shaggy coat.

When Pavlo died, he staged his deathbed scene in the best Victorian traditions. He had been unwell for a couple of days, and had spent his time on the windowsill of my sister's room, lying in the sun on his bit of fur-coat. One morning he started to squeak frantically to my sister, who became alarmed and shouted out to the rest of us that she thought he was dying. The whole family at once dropped whatever they were doing and fled upstairs. We gathered round the windowsill and watched Pavlo carefully, but there seemed to be nothing very much the matter with him. He accepted a drink of milk and then lay back on his fur-coat and surveyed us all with bright eyes. We had just decided that it was a false alarm when he suddenly went limp. In a panic we forced open his clenched jaws and poured a little milk down his throat. Slowly he regained consciousness, lying limp in my cupped hands. He looked at us for a moment and then, summoning up his last remaining strength, poked his tongue out at us and smacked his lips in a last gesture of affection. Then he fell back and died quite quietly.

The house and garden seemed very empty without his minute strutting figure and fiery personality. No longer did the sight of a spider evoke cries of: 'Where's Pavlo?' No longer were we woken up at six in the morning, feeling his cold feet on our faces. He had become one of the family in a way that no other pet had ever done, and we mourned his death. Even the white cat next door seemed moody and depressed, for without Pavlo in it our garden seemed to have lost its savour for her.

PART FOUR

THE HUMAN ANIMAL

When you travel round the world collecting animals you also, of necessity, collect human beings. I am much more intolerant of a human being's shortcomings than I am of an animal's, but in this respect I have been lucky, for most of the people I have come across in my travels have been charming. In most cases, of course, the fact that you are an animal-collector helps, since people always seem delighted to meet someone with such an unusual occupation, and they go out of their way to assist you.

One of the loveliest and most sophisticated women I know has helped me cram a couple of swans into a taxi-cab boot in the middle of Buenos Aires, and anyone who has ever tried to carry livestock in a Buenos Aires taxi will know what a feat that must have been. A millionaire has let me stack cages of livestock on the front porch of his elegant town house, and even when an armadillo escaped and went through the main flower-bed like a bulldozer, he remained unruffled and calm. The madame of the local brothel once acted as our housekeeper (getting all her girls to do the housework when not otherwise employed), and she once even assaulted the local chief of police on our behalf. A man in Africa – notorious for his dislike of strangers and animals – let us stay for six weeks in his house and fill it with a weird variety of frogs, snakes, squirrels and mongooses. I have had the captain of a ship come down into the hold at eleven at night, take off his coat, roll up his sleeves and set to work helping me clean out cages and chop up food for the animals. I know an artist who, having travelled thousands of miles to paint a series of pictures of various Indian tribes, got involved in my affairs and spent his whole time catching animals and none on painting. By that time, of course, he could not paint anyway, as I had commandeered all his canvas to make snake-boxes. There was the little cockney P.W.D. man who, not having met me previously, offered to drive me a hundred-odd miles, over atrocious African roads, in his brand-new Austin in order that I might follow up the rumour of a baby gorilla. All *he* got out of the trip was a hangover and a broken spring.

At times I have met such interesting and peculiar people I have been tempted to give up animals and take up anthropology. Then I have come across the unpleasant human animal. The District Officer who drawled, 'We chaps are here to help you chaps . . . ,' and then proceeded to be as obstructive and unpleasant as possible. The Overseer in Paraguay who, because he disliked me, did not tell me for two weeks that some local Indians had captured a rare and beautiful animal which I wanted, and were waiting for me to collect it. By the time I received the animal it was too weak to stand and died of pneumonia within forty-eight hours. The sailor who was mentally unbalanced and who, in a fit of sadistic humour, overturned a row of our cages one night, including one in which a pair of extremely rare squirrels had just had a baby. The baby died.

Fortunately these types of human are rare, and the pleasant ones I have met have more than compensated for them. But even so, I think I will stick to animals.

MACTOOTLE

When people discover my job for the first time, they always ask me for details of the many adventures they assume I have had in what they will persist in calling the 'jungle'.

I returned to England after my first West African trip and described with enthusiasm the hundreds of square miles of rain-forest I had lived and worked in for eight months. I said that in this forest I had spent many happy days, and during all this time I never had one experience that could with any justification be called 'hair-raising', but when I told people this they decided that I was either exceptionally modest or a charlatan.

On my way out to West Africa for the second time, I met on board ship a young Irishman called MacTootle who was going out to a job on a banana plantation in the Cameroons. He confessed to me that he had never before left England and he was quite convinced that Africa was the most dangerous place imaginable. His chief fear seemed to be that the entire snake population of the Continent was going to be assembled on the docks to meet him. In order to relieve his mind, I told him that in all the months I had spent in the forest I had seen precisely five snakes, and these had run away so fast that I had been unable to capture them. He asked me if it was a dangerous job to catch a snake, and I replied, quite truthfully, that the majority of snakes were extremely easy to capture, if you kept your head and knew your snake and its habits. All this soothed MacTootle considerably, and when he landed he swore that, before I returned to England, he would obtain some rare specimens for me; I thanked him and promptly forgot all about it.

Five months later I was ready to leave for England with a collection of about two hundred creatures, ranging from grasshoppers to chimpanzees. Very late on the night the ship was due to sail, a small van drew up with screeching brakes outside my camp and my young Irishman alighted, together with several friends of his. He explained with great glee that he had got me the specimens he had promised. Apparently he had discovered a large hole or pit, somewhere on the plantation he was working on, which had presumably been dug to act as a drainage sump. This pit, he said, was full of snakes, and they were all mine – providing I went and got them.

He was so delighted at the thought of all those specimens he had found for me that I had not the heart to point out that crawling about in a pit full of snakes at twelve o'clock at night was not my idea of a pleasurable occupation, enthusiastic naturalist though I was. Furthermore, he had obviously been boasting about my powers to his friends, and he had brought them all along to see my snake-catching methods. So, with considerable reluctance, I said I would go and catch reptiles; I have rarely regretted a decision more.

I collected a large canvas snake-bag, and a stick with a Y-shaped fork of brass at one end; then I squeezed into the van with my excited audience and we drove off. At half-past twelve we reached my friend's bungalow, and stopped there for a drink before walking through the plantation to the pit.

'You'll be wanting some rope, will you not?' asked MacTootle.

'Rope?' I said. 'What for?'

'Why, to lower yourself into the hole, of course,' he said cheerfully. I began to feel an unpleasant sensation in the pit of my stomach. I asked for a description of the pit. It was apparently some twenty-five feet long, four feet wide and twelve feet deep. Everyone assured me that I could not get down there without a rope. While my friend went off to look for one which I hoped very much he would not find, I had another quick drink and wondered how I could have been foolish enough to get myself mixed up in this fantastic snake-hunt. Snakes in trees, on the ground or in shallow ditches were fairly easy to manage, but an unspecified number of them at the bottom of a pit so deep that you had to be lowered into it on the end of a rope did not sound at all inviting. I thought that I had an opportunity of backing out gracefully when the question of lighting arose and it was discovered that none of us had a torch. My friend, who had now returned with the rope, was quite determined that nothing was going to interfere with his plans: he solved the lighting question by tying a big paraffin pressure-lamp onto the end of a length of cord, and informed the company that he personally would lower it into the pit for me. I thanked him in what I hoped was a steady voice.

'That's all right,' he said, 'I'm determined you'll have your fun. This lamp's much better than a torch, and you'll need all the light you can get, for there's any number of the little devils down there.'

We then had to wait a while for the arrival of my friend's brother and sister-in-law: he had asked them to come along, he explained, because they would probably never get another chance to see anyone capturing snakes, and he did not want them to miss it.

Eventually eight of us wended our way through the banana plantation and seven of us were laughing and chattering excitedly at the thought of the treat in store. It suddenly occurred to me that I was wearing the most inadequate clothing for snake-hunting: thin tropical trousers and a pair of plimsoll shoes. Even the most puny reptiles would have no difficulty in penetrating to my skin with one bite. However, before I could explain this we arrived at the edge of the pit, and in the lamplight it looked to me like nothing more nor less than an extremely large grave. My friend's description of it had been accurate enough, but what he had failed to tell me was that the sides of the pit consisted of dry, crumbling earth, honeycombed with cracks and holes that offered plenty of hiding-places for any number of snakes. While I crouched down on the edge of the pit, the lamp was solemnly lowered into the depths so that I might spy out the land and try to identify the snakes. Up to that moment I had cheered myself with the thought that, after all, the snakes might turn out to be a harmless variety, but when the light reached the bottom this hope was shattered, for I saw that the pit was simply crawling with young Gaboon vipers, one of the most deadly snakes in the world.

During the daytime these snakes are very sluggish and it is quite a simple job to capture them, but at night, when they wake up and hunt for their food, they can be unpleasantly quick. These young ones in the pit were each about two feet long and a couple of inches in diameter, and they were all, as far as I could judge, very much awake. They wriggled round and round the pit with great rapidity, and kept lifting their heavy, arrow-shaped heads and contemplating the lamp, flicking their tongues out and in in a most suggestive manner.

I counted eight Gaboon vipers in the pit, but their coloration matched the leaf-mould so beautifully that I could not be sure I was not counting some of them twice. Just at that moment my friend trod heavily on the edge of the pit, and a large lump of earth fell among the reptiles, who all looked up and hissed loudly. Everyone backed away hastily, and I thought it a very suitable opportunity to explain the point about my clothing. My friend, with typical Irish generosity, offered to lend me his trousers, which were of stout twill, and the strong pair of shoes he was wearing. Now the last of my excuses was gone and I had not the nerve to protest further. We went discreetly behind a bush and exchanged trousers and shoes. My friend was built on more generous lines than I, and the clothes were not exactly a snug fit; however, as he rightly pointed out, the bit of trouser-leg I had to turn up at the bottom would act as additional protection for my ankles.

Drearily I approached the pit. My audience was clustered round, twittering in delicious anticipation. I tied the rope round my waist with what I very soon discovered to be a slip-knot, and crawled to the edge. My descent had not got the airy grace of a pantomime fairy: the sides of the pit were so crumbly that every time I tried to gain a foothold I dislodged large quantities of earth, and as this fell among the snakes it was greeted with peevish hisses. I had to dangle in mid-air, being gently lowered by my companions, while the slip-knot grasped me ever tighter round the waist. Eventually I looked down and I saw that my feet were about a yard from the ground. I shouted to my friends to stop lowering me, as I wanted to examine the ground I was to land on and make sure there were no snakes lying there. After a careful inspection I could not see any reptiles directly under me, so I shouted 'Lower away' in what I sincerely hoped was an intrepid tone of voice. As I started on my descent again, two things happened at once: firstly one of my borrowed shoes fell off and, secondly, the lamp, which none of us had remembered to pump up, died away to a faint glow of light, rather like a plump cigar-end. At that precise moment I touched ground with my bare foot, and I cannot remember ever having been so frightened, before or since.

I stood motionless, sweating with great freedom, while the lamp was hastily hauled up to the surface, pumped up, and lowered down again. I have never been so glad to see a humble pressure-lamp. Now the pit was once more flooded with lamplight I began to feel a little braver. I retrieved my shoe and put it on, and this made me feel even better. I grasped my stick in a moist hand and approached the nearest snake. I pinned it to the ground with the forked end of the stick, picked it up and put it in the bag. This part of the procedure gave me no qualms, for it was simple enough and not dangerous provided you exercised a certain care. The idea is to pin the reptile across the head with the fork and then get a good firm grip on its neck before picking it up. What worried me was the fact that while my attention was occupied with one snake, all the others were wriggling round frantically, and I had to keep a cautious eye open in case one got behind me and I stepped back on it. They were beautifully marked with an intricate pattern of brown, silver, pink, and cream blotches, and when they remained still this coloration made them extremely hard to see; they just melted into the background. As soon as I pinned one to the ground, it would start to hiss like a kettle, and all the others would hiss in sympathy – a most unpleasant sound.

There was one nasty moment when I bent down to pick up one of the reptiles and heard a loud hissing apparently coming from somewhere horribly close to my ear. I straightened up and found myself staring into a pair of angry silver-coloured eyes approximately a foot away. After considerable juggling I managed to get this snake down onto the ground and pin him beneath my stick. On the whole, the reptiles were just as scared of me as I was of them, and they did their best to get out of my way. It was only when I had them cornered that they fought and struck viciously at the stick, but bounced off the brass fork with a reassuring ping. However, one of them must have been more experienced, for he ignored the brass fork and bit instead at the wood. He got a good grip and hung on like a bulldog; he would not let go even when I lifted him clear of the ground. Eventually I had to shake the stick really hard, and the snake sailed through the air, hit the side of the pit and fell to the ground hissing furiously. When I approached him with the stick again, he refused to bite and I had no difficulty in picking him up.

I was down in the pit for about half an hour, and during that time I caught twelve Gaboon vipers; I was not sure, even then, that I had captured all of them, but I felt it would be tempting fate to stay down there any longer. My companions hauled me out, hot, dirty and streaming with sweat, clutching in one hand a bag full of loudly hissing snakes.

'There, now,' said my friend triumphantly, while I was recovering my breath, 'I told you I'd get you some specimens, did I not?'

I just nodded; by that time I was beyond speech. I sat on the ground, smoking a much-needed cigarette and trying to steady my trembling hands. Now that the danger was over I began to realize for the first time how extremely stupid I had been to go into the pit in the first place, and how exceptionally lucky I was to have come out of it alive. I made a mental note that in future, if anyone asked me if animal-collecting was a dangerous occupation, I would reply that it was only as dangerous as your own stupidity allowed it to be. When I had recovered slightly, I looked about and discovered that one of my audience was missing.

'Where's your brother got to?' I asked my friend.

'Oh him,' said MacTootle with fine scorn, 'he couldn't watch any more – he said it made him feel sick. He's waiting over there for us. You'll have to excuse him – he couldn't take it. Sure, and it required some guts to watch you down there with all them wretched reptiles.'

SEBASTIAN

Not long ago I spent some months in Argentina, and it was while there that I first met Sebastian. He was a gaucho, the South American equivalent of the North American cowboy. Like the cowboy, the gaucho is becoming rare nowadays, for most of the farms or estancias in Argentina are increasingly mechanized.

My reasons for being in Argentina were twofold: firstly, I wanted to capture live specimens of the wild animal life to bring back for zoos in this country, and, secondly, I wanted to film these same animals in their natural haunts. A friend of mine owned a large estancia about seventy miles from Buenos Aires in an area noted for its wildlife, and when he invited me down there to spend a fortnight I accepted the invitation with alacrity. Unfortunately, when the time arrived my friend had some business to attend to, and all he could do was to take me down to the estancia and introduce me to the place before rushing back to the city.

He met me at the little country station, and as we jogged down the dusty road in the buggy he told me that he had got everything arranged for me.

'I'll put you in charge of Sebastian,' he said, 'so you should be all right.'

'Who's Sebastian?' I asked.

'Oh, just one of our gauchos,' said my friend vaguely. 'What he doesn't know about the animal life of this district isn't worth knowing. He'll be acting host in my absence, so just ask him for anything you want.'

After we had lunched on the veranda of the house, my friend suggested I should meet Sebastian, so we saddled horses and rode out across the acres of golden grass shimmering in the sun, and through the thickets of giant thistles, each plant as high as a man on horseback. In half an hour or so we came to a small wood of eucalyptus trees, and in the middle of it was a long, low, whitewashed house. A large and elderly dog, lying in the sun-drenched dust, lifted his head and gave a half-hearted bark before going back to sleep again. We dismounted and tied up the horses.

'Sebastian built this house himself,' said my friend. 'He's probably round the back having a siesta.'

We went round the house, and there, slung between two slender eucalyptus trees, was an enormous hammock, and in it lay Sebastian. My first impression was of a dwarf. I discovered later that he measured about five feet two inches, but lying there in that vast expanse of hammock he looked very tiny indeed. His immensely long and powerful arms dangled over the sides and they were burnt to a rich mahogany brown, with a faint mist of white hair on them. I couldn't see his face, for it was covered by a black hat that rose and fell rhythmically, while from underneath it came the most prolonged and fearsome snores I have ever heard. My friend seized one of Sebastian's dangling hands and tugged at it vigorously, at the same time bending down and shouting in the sleeping man's ear as loudly as he could: 'Sebastian – Sebastian! Wake up, you have visitors.' This noisy greeting had no effect whatever; Sebastian continued to snore under his hat. My friend looked at me and shrugged.

'He's always like this when he's asleep,' he explained. 'Here, catch hold of his other arm and let's get him out of the hammock.'

I took the other arm and we hauled him into a sitting position. The black hat rolled off and disclosed a round, brown chubby face, neatly divided into three by a great curved moustache, stained golden with nicotine, and a pair of snow-white eyebrows that curved up onto his forehead like the horns of a goat. My friend caught hold of his shoulders and shook him, repeating his name loudly, and suddenly a pair of wicked black eyes opened under the white brows and Sebastian glared at us sleepily. As soon as he recognized my friend he uttered a roar of anguish and struggled to his feet: 'Señor!' he bellowed, 'How nice to see you ... Ah, pardon me señor, that I'm sleeping like a pig in its sty when you arrive ... excuse me, please. I wasn't expecting you so early, otherwise I would have been prepared to welcome you properly.'

He wrung my hand as my friend introduced me, and then, turning towards the house, he uttered a full-throated roar: 'Maria – Maria –!' In response to this nerve-shattering cry an attractive young woman of about thirty appeared, whom Sebastian introduced, with obvious pride, as his wife. Then he clasped my shoulder in one of his powerful hands and gazed earnestly into my face.

'Would you prefer coffee or maté, señor?' he asked innocently. Luckily my friend had warned me that Sebastian based his first impressions of people on whether they asked for coffee or maté, the Argentine green herb-tea, for in his opinion coffee was a disgusting drink, a liquid fit only to be consumed by city people and other depraved members of the human race. So I said I would have some maté. Sebastian turned and glared at his wife.

'Well?' he demanded. 'Didn't you hear the señor say he would take maté? Are the guests to stand here dying of thirst while you gape at them like an owl in the sun?'

'The water is boiling,' she replied placidly, 'and they needn't stand, if you ask them to sit down.'

'Don't answer me back, woman,' roared Sebastian, his moustache bristling.

'You must excuse him, señor,' said Maria, smiling at her husband affectionately, 'he always gets excited when we have visitors.'

Sebastian's face turned a deep brick-red.

'Excited?' he shouted indignantly. '*Excited?* Who's excited? I'm as calm as a dead horse . . . please be seated, señors . . . excited indeed . . . you must excuse my wife, señor, she has a talent for exaggeration that would have earned her a wonderful political career if she had been born a man.'

We sat down under the trees, and Sebastian lighted a small and pungent cigar while he continued to grumble good-naturedly about his wife's shortcomings.

'I should never have married again,' he confided. 'The trouble is that my wives never outlive me. Four times I've been married now and as I laid each woman to rest I said to myself: Sebastian, never again. Then, suddenly . . . puff! . . . I'm married again. My spirit is willing to remain single but my flesh is weak, and the trouble is that I have more flesh than spirit.' He glanced down at his magnificent paunch with a rueful air, and then looked up and gave us a wide and disarming grin that displayed a great expanse of gum in which were planted two withered teeth. 'I suppose I shall always be weak, señor . . . but then a man without a wife is like a cow without an udder.'

Maria brought the maté, and the little pot was handed round the circle, while we each in turn took sips from the slender silver maté pipe, and my friend explained to Sebastian exactly why I had come to the estancia. The gaucho was very enthusiastic, and when we told him that he might be required to take part in some of the film shots he stroked his moustache and shot a sly glance at his wife.

'D'you hear that, eh?' he enquired. 'I shall be appearing in the cinema. Better watch that tongue of yours, my girl, for when the women in England see me on the screen they'll be flocking out here to try to get me.'

'I see no reason why they should,' returned his wife. 'I expect they have good-for-nothings there, same as everywhere else.' Sebastian contented himself with giving her a withering look, and then he turned to me.

'Don't worry, señor,' he said, 'I will do everything to help you in your work. I will do everything you want.' He was as good as his word: that evening my friend left for Buenos Aires, and for the next two weeks Sebastian rarely left my side. His energy was prodigious, and his personality so fiery that he soon had complete control of my affairs. I simply told him just what I wanted and he did it for me, and the more extraordinary and difficult my requests the more he seemed to delight in accomplishing them for me. He could get more work out of the peons, or hired men, on the estancia than anyone I met, and, strangely enough, he did not get it by pleading or cajoling them but by insulting and ridiculing them, using a wealth of glittering similes that, instead of angering the men, convulsed them with laughter and made them work all the harder.

'Look at you,' he would roar scathingly, 'just look at you all ... moving with all the speed of snails in bird-lime ... it's a wonder to me that your horses don't take fright when you gallop, because even I can hear your eyeballs rattling in your empty skulls ... you've not enough brain among the lot of you to make a rich soup for a bedbug ...' And the peons would gurgle with mirth and redouble their efforts. Apart from considering him a humorist, of course, the men knew very well that he would not ask them to do anything he could not do himself. But then there was hardly a thing that he did not know how to do, and among the peons an impossible task was always described as 'something even Sebastian couldn't do'. Mounted on his great black horse, his scarlet-and-blue poncho draped round his shoulders in vivid folds, Sebastian cut an impressive figure. On this horse he would gallop about the estancia, his lasso whistling as he showed me the various methods of roping a steer. There are about six different ways of doing this, and Sebastian could perform them all with equal facility. The faster his horse travelled, the rougher the ground, the greater accuracy he seemed to obtain with his throws, until you had the impression that the steer had some sort of magnetic attraction for the rope and that it was impossible for him to miss.

If Sebastian was a master with a rope, he was a genius with his whip, a short-handled affair with a long slender thong, a deadly weapon which he was never without. I have seen him, at full gallop, pull this whip from his belt and neatly take the head off a thistle plant as he passed. Flicking cigarettes out of people's mouths was child's play to him. I was told that in the previous year a stranger to the district had cast doubts on Sebastian's abilities with a whip, and Sebastian had replied by stripping the man's shirt from his back, without once touching the skin beneath. Sebastian preferred his whip as a weapon – and he could use it like an elongated arm – yet he was very skilful with both knife and hatchet. With the latter weapon he could split a matchbox in two at about ten places. No, Sebastian was definitely not the sort of man to get the wrong side of.

A lot of the hunting I did with Sebastian took place at night, when the nocturnal creatures came out of their burrows. Armed with torches, we would leave the estancia shortly after dark, never returning much before midnight or two in the morning, and generally bringing with us two or three specimens of one sort or another. On these hunts we were assisted by Sebastian's favourite dog, a mongrel of great age whose teeth had long since been worn down level with his gums. This animal was the perfect hunting-dog, for even when he caught a specimen it was impossible for him to hurt it with his toothless gums. Once he had chased and brought to bay some specimen, he would stand guard over it, giving one short yap every minute or so to guide us to the spot.

It was during one of these night hunts that I had a display of Sebastian's great strength. The dog had put up an armadillo, and after it had been chased for several hundred yards the creature took refuge down a hole. There were three of us that night: Sebastian, myself, and a peon. In chasing the armadillo the peon and I had far outstripped Sebastian, whose figure did not encourage running. The peon and I reached the hole just in time to see the rear end of the armadillo disappearing down it, so we flung ourselves onto the grass and while I got a grip on its tail the peon grasped its hind legs. The armadillo dug his long front claws into the sides of the hole, and though we tugged and pulled he was as immovable as though he were embedded in cement. Then the beast gave a sudden jerk and the peon lost his grip. The armadillo wriggled farther inside the hole, and I could feel his tail slipping through my fingers. Just at that moment Sebastian arrived on the scene, panting for breath. He pushed me out of the way, seized the armadillo's tail, braced his feet on either side of the hole and pulled. There was a shower of earth, and the armadillo came out of the hole like a cork out of a bottle. With one sharp tug Sebastian had accomplished what two of us had failed to do.

One of the creatures I wanted to film on the estancia was the rhea, the South American ostrich, which, like its African cousin, can run like a racehorse. I wanted to film the rheas being hunted in the old style, by men on horseback armed with boleadoras. These weapons consist of three wooden balls, about the size of cricket balls, each attached to the other by a fairly long string; they are whirled round the head and thrown so that they tangle themselves round the bird's legs and bring it to the ground. Sebastian arranged the whole hunts for me, and we spent my last day filming it. As most of the peons were to appear in these scenes, they all turned up that morning in their best clothes, each obviously trying to outdo the other by the brilliance of his costume. Sebastian surveyed them sourly from the back of his horse:

'Look at them, señor,' he said, contemptuously spitting. 'All done up and as shining as partridge eggs, and as excited as dogs on a bowling green, just because they think they're going to get their silly faces on the cinema screen ... they make me sick.'

But I noticed that he carefully combed his moustache before the filming started. We were at it all day in the boiling sun, and by evening, when the last scenes had been shot, we all felt in need of a rest – all of us, that is, except Sebastian, who seemed as fresh as when he started. As we made our way home, he told me that he had organized a farewell party for me that night, and everyone on the estancia was to be present. There would be plenty of wine and singing and dancing, and his eyes gleamed as he told me about it. I had not the heart to explain that I was dead tired and would much rather go to bed, so I accepted the invitation.

The festivities took place in the great smoke-filled kitchen with half a dozen flickering oil-lamps to light it. The band consisted of three guitars which were played with great verve. I need hardly say that the life and soul of the party was Sebastian. He drank more wine than everyone else, and yet remained sober; he played solos on the guitar; he sang a great variety of songs ranging from the vulgar to the pathetic; he consumed vast quantities of food. But, above all, he danced; danced the wild gaucho dances with their complicated steps and kicks and leaps, danced until the beams above vibrated with his steps and his spurs struck fire from the stone flags.

My friend, who had driven down from Buenos Aires to pick me up, arrived in the middle of the party and joined us. We sat in the corner, drinking a glass of wine together and watching Sebastian dance, while the peons clapped and roared applause.

'What incredible energy he's got,' I remarked. 'He's been working harder than anyone else today, and now he's danced us all off our feet.'

'That's what a life on the pampa does for you!' replied my friend. 'But, seriously, I think he's quite amazing for his age, don't you?'

'Why?' I asked casually, 'how old is he?'

My friend looked at me in surprise:

'Don't you know?' he asked. 'In about two months' time Sebastian will be ninety-five.'

THE END